A Writer's Diary

A
Writer's
Diary

ABRIDGED EDITION

Fyodor Dostoevsky

Edited and with an introduction by
Gary Saul Morson

Translated and annotated by
Kenneth Lantz

NORTHWESTERN UNIVERSITY PRESS

EVANSTON, ILLINOIS

Northwestern University Press
www.nupress.northwestern.edu

Printed in the United States of America

10   9   8   7   6   5   4   3   2   1

Library of Congress Cataloging-in-Publication Data

Dostoyevsky, Fyodor, 1821–1881.
   [Dnevnik pisatelia. English. Selections]
   A writer's diary / Fyodor Dostoevsky ; edited and with an introduction by Gary Saul
Morson ; translated and annotated by Kenneth Lantz. — Abridged ed.
   p. cm.
   Includes bibliographical references.
   ISBN 978-0-8101-2521-6 (pbk. : alk. paper)
   I. Morson, Gary Saul, 1948– II. Lantz, K. A. III. Title.
PG3326.A16M67 2009
891.78307—dc22

                        2008048250

Contents

1880

1881

from *Chapter Two*

Kenneth Lantz

The eminent Soviet scholar Dmitry Likhachev, in an article significantly entitled "'Stylistic Negligence' in Dostoevsky," remarked that
"Dostoevsky flaunts before the reader the rawness of his style and the
seemingly improvised nature of his narrative; at the same time he does
not conceal his quest for general and maximum accuracy, despite the
deliberate and even shocking inaccuracy in specific details. He lays bare
the structures of his works and his behind-the-scenes techniques."[1]
Likhachev is speaking of Dostoevsky the novelist, but the observation
holds true for Dostoevsky's writing generally. His prose is not elegant:
it is often convoluted, frequently repetitious, and is full of qualifications
such as "perhaps," "rather," "somewhat," "as if," "partly," "a certain,"
"some sort of," "evidently." Certain favorite phrases—"the main thing,"
"the most important thing," "above all," "on the contrary," and, of course,
"suddenly"—recur with dismaying regularity. Some of these traits may
derive from the tradition of nineteenth-century Russian journalistic
writing: all journalists wrote with the censor looking over their shoulders, so circumlocutions and qualifications were safer than simple and
unambiguous statements. And the weight of an article was, I suspect,
often equated with its length. But it would be quite wrong to dismiss
Dostoevsky's expository prose as merely a product of a journalistic
milieu; it is powerful and distinctive, a deliberately chosen vehicle to
convey his sense of life, as Likhachev argues.

Another discerning critic, P. M. Bitsilli, has noted that Dostoevsky's
style reveals his "awareness of the impossibility of finding any compre-
hensive formula to express all the complexity and inner contradictions of
this or that element of reality."[2] The truth, in other words, is elusive and
incredibly complex; Dostoevsky does not capture it, but circles around
it and approximates it. He himself often commented on the difficulty of

transferring his own insights into words. "We all know," he wrote, "that
entire trains of thought can sometimes pass through our heads in an
instant, like sensations of some sort, without being translated into human
language, never mind into literary language."[3] "Your idea, even though
it may be a bad one, is always more profound when it is within you, but
when you put it into words it is more ridiculous and less honest. . . ."[4] At
the same time, he was wary of making himself too clear: in July 1876, he
complained that his June *Diary,* which contained a fairly unambiguous
statement of his views on Russia's mission, had been a mistake:

> In my writings I had never yet permitted myself to bring *certain* of
> my convictions to their conclusion, to say *the very last* word. . . . Set
> forth any paradox you please, but do not bring it to a conclusion,
> and you'll have something witty and subtle and *comme il faut,* but
> bring some very speculative statement to a conclusion . . . directly
> and not merely by suggestion, and no one will believe you, precisely
> because of your naiveté, precisely because you have brought it to its
> conclusion and said your final word. On the other hand, however, if
> many of the most famous wits—Voltaire, for instance—had, instead
> of gibes, hints, innuendos and insinuations, suddenly resolved to
> state everything they believed in and revealed all their innermost
> reality, their essence—then, believe me, they would never have
> gained a tenth of the effect they did. Even more: people would only
> have laughed at them. Indeed, people in general somehow do not
> like the last word in anything, the "expressed" thought; they say
> that "the thought expressed is a lie."[5]

I have tried, therefore, to respect Dostoevsky's text, to preserve the
oddities, the complexities, the ambiguities, and even the "suddenlys."
Although they may be grammatically and logically superfluous, they
convey the contradictions and complexities of his view of life and of
his own personality. If one hopes to understand or, more accurately, to
experience that personality (and I think that Dostoevsky's personality
is revealed more fully in the *Diary* than in his novels and stories), the
rawness and rough edges of his prose must be preserved. This also means
attempting to preserve his long and torturous sentences. Russian can,
without any violation of stylistic norms, create "run-on" sentences, and

many of Dostoevsky's fall into this category. English is not so tolerant, so I have often resorted to stringing his clauses together with semicolons. I have also retained Dostoevsky's paragraphing, even though this means that the reader must confront some formidably long blocks of prose.

As he makes clear in the very first article of the *Diary*, Dostoevsky is *speaking* to his readers; he encourages a dialogue, not only by replying to letters and to critics of his *Diary*, but by anticipating a reply or a reaction or providing one himself. The ellipses, circumlocutions, and hesitations in his prose create an effect that is often closer to the spoken rather than the written language. The emotional tone of his dialogues shifts from solemn prophecy to whimsical playfulness, from bitter sarcasm to petty pique, from heartfelt compassion to sputtering outrage. But all the while he is concerned to engage his reader and pass on his meaning: hence the "most important thing," "the main thing," the repetitions, and the italics (both literal and figurative).

A few terms Dostoevsky uses present particular problems. The word *narod* is perhaps adequately rendered by "people," but the Russian word has many connotations that are lacking in English; for Dostoevsky, the Russian people—the long-suffering, unlettered, unwashed, often brutish and drunken peasants little more than a decade removed from virtual slavery—were the repository of the great "Russian idea" that was destined to redeem the world. If only to remind the English-speaking reader of the reverential connotations of the word as used by Dostoevsky, I have capitalized it throughout the translation. Other peoples not endowed with qualities Dostoevsky found in the Russian peasants must be content here with a small *p. Obosoblenie* is another concept that recurs throughout the *Diary*. The dictionary meanings of "isolation" or "setting apart" are not quite adequate, since Dostoevsky had in mind the fragmentation of Russian society, the alienation and separateness, which he saw as the product of the loss of common beliefs and the resulting fraying of the social fabric. I have translated this word as "dissociation."[6] *Kosnost'* is used less often, but again the dictionary meanings of "stagnation" or "inertness" do not convey the full sense of the word as he uses it, which is often to suggest the brute facts of life, that which refuses to change; it belongs, I think, in the same category as the Underground Man's "laws of nature," or Meier's wall in *The Idiot*. For example, in his "Notebook" of 1863–64 Dostoevsky remarked, "The doctrine of the materialists is universal *kosnost'* and the mechanism of things—death, in other words."[7] In most contexts I have translated the word as "immutability." Finally, Dostoevsky usually chooses the word *zhid*—in contemporary Russian a pejorative for "Jew"—over the standard *evrei*. Although *zhid* was acceptable in pre-nineteenth-century standard Russian (as are its cognates in contemporary Polish and Ukrainian), by the mid-nineteenth century it was certainly offensive; although it was perhaps not quite so strong as "Yid" or "Kike" in modern English, I have used the former to translate it.[8]

Some of the work on this translation was completed while I was on a research leave sponsored by the Centre for Russian and East European Studies of the University of Toronto; I gratefully acknowledge the Centre's support. I am also indebted to the University of Toronto for a grant-in-aid of this project.

Notes

1. D. S. Likhachev, "'Nebrezhenie slovom' u Dostoevskogo," *Izbrannye raboty* (Leningrad: Khudozhestvennaia literatura, 1987), 3:273.
2. P. M. Bitsilli, "K voprosu o vnutrennei forme romana Dostoevskogo," Sofia Universitet. Istorikofilologicheski fakultet. *Godishnik* 42 (1945–46): 6.
3. F. M. Dostoevsky, *Polnoe sobranie sochinenii* (Leningrad: Nauka, 1972–88), 5:12.
4. Quoted in L. P. Grossman, *Seminarii po Dostoevskomu: materialy, bibliografiia i kommentarii* (Moscow and Petrograd, 1922), p. 71.
5. Letter to Vsevolod Solovev, July 16, 1876, in *Polnoe sobranie sochinenii*, vol. 29, bk. 2, pp. 101–2. The last line of the letter is a quotation from F. I. Tiutchev's poem "Silentium."
6. I am indebted to Gary Saul Morson for this suggestion.
7. *Literaturnoe nasledstvo* 83: *Neizdannyi Dostoevskii: zapisnye knizhki i tetradi, 1860–1881* (Leningrad: Nauka, 1971), p. 175.
8. Dostoevsky's use of the word *zhid,* and his anti-Semitism generally, are discussed in detail by David Goldstein, *Dostoevsky and the Jews* (Austin and London: University of Texas Press, 1981).

Editor's Introduction: The Process and Composition of *A Writer's Diary*

Gary Saul Morson

Reality strives toward fragmentation.
—Dostoevsky

Reality is transfigured, passing through art.
—Dostoevsky

Part One: What Is *A Writer's Diary* and How Should It Be Read?

A Writer's Diary, Dostoevsky's oddest and longest work, has fascinated me for over three decades. I keep changing my mind about it.

With the confidence of a beginner, I devoted my doctoral dissertation to defining and solving the *Diary*'s puzzles. Immersed in intellectual history as well as literary theory, I then saw the work as a literary apocalypse. I supposed that its combination of journalism and fiction, and its focus on the places where one shades into the other, reflect the sense that reality itself is in the process of transition. By the time I wrote my first book, I had decided that the *Diary*'s heterogeneity of genres needed to be treated in terms of a more general theory of genres and their combination. I came to view the *Diary* as one of a group of works, for which I coined the term *meta-utopias,* that create an inconclusive dialogue between utopian and anti-utopian thought. Two antithetical genres together shape its odd form and shifting perspectives. But before too long, I decided that this approach, too, left out too much.[1]

When Kenneth Lantz offered Northwestern University Press the first good English translation of the *Diary,* I again rethought the work's strangeness and produced a lengthy "introductory study" with yet another account of the book's oddities.[2] At this point I was writing my book on time, *Narrative and Freedom,* and so I focused on the strangeness of the

Diary's periodical form.[3] After all, I reasoned, there is a great difference
between a work that appears *in* a periodical (like the novels of Dickens,
Trollope, Tolstoy, and Dostoevsky) and a work that *is* a periodical.
Dostoevsky stressed this difference in the work's title—*A Writer's Diary:
A Monthly Publication*—as well as in numerous formal markers in the text.
I now conjectured that the *Diary* took this form because it concerned the
very nature of temporality. Its puzzles seemed designed to illustrate the
many paradoxes of open and closed time.

I decided as well that one reason the *Diary* sometimes seems so formless is that, in fact, it sometimes *is* formless. (I still think so.) In some
issues, Dostoevsky departed from the work's initial design. He did so in
large part because that design arose from a specific sense of human experience that Dostoevsky sacrificed to adopt the very opposite.

In the first few monthly issues of the *Diary,* the original design is
apparent, and if that were all one read, the work would appear more
successful than it does in its entirety. As the *Diary* progresses, however,
the design is repeatedly lost and partially resumed. The result must be
deemed a fascinating muddle.

In short, I realized that one reason I had found it so difficult to see
how the parts of this work cohere is that only some of them do cohere as
Dostoevsky originally intended. Since that intention is itself highly idiosyncratic, it is hardly surprising that most readers have not been able to
see *A Writer's Diary* as anything but an anthology and not as a work in
its own right.

I will doubtless change my mind again, but I still believe all these
approaches have merit, even if none of them is sufficient.

Anomaly and Russianness

Although *A Writer's Diary* resembles, and has usually been taken as, a
mere collection, external evidence confirms that Dostoevsky intended the
work to be a "new genre." Here I can only state that Dostoevsky thought
of this new literary form as early as 1865; that his idea of it drew on his
earlier writing and continued to evolve; that in 1873, the opportunity to
publish a partial and preliminary version of his plan occurred; and that
with the January 1876 issue he was at last able to realize his design for

the work as a monthly periodical for which he served as editor, publisher, and sole contributor. At one point he was able to state, probably with his usual febrile exaggeration, that "the *Diary* has at last evolved to the point where even the slightest change in its form is impossible."[4]

Nevertheless, Dostoevsky's notebooks and letters show him experimenting with and agonizing over the *Diary*'s form in much the way that he struggled with the novels that gave him the most trouble, most notably, *The Idiot.* He confides that "I have not yet succeeded in clarifying to myself the form of the *Diary*" (*Pis'ma,* 3:206). If Dostoevsky at some moments thought he had perfected his new literary genre, at others he despaired that he had ruined it. Both reactions testify that he did not view the *Diary* as a mere grab bag.

For a Russian writer, creating a new form was hardly unique. Claims to the unprecedented were almost routine. Dostoevsky was doubtless aware of the essay Tolstoy published while *War and Peace* was being serialized. Responding to critics who could not comprehend the work's many formal oddities, Tolstoy characterized his "book"—he refused to call it a "novel"—as defying all genres. "What is *War and Peace?*" he asked, and answered by saying what it is not:

> It is not a novel, still less a *poema,* still less a historical chronicle. *War and Peace* is what the author wished to express and was able to express in that form in which it is expressed. Such a statement of the author's disregard for the conventional forms of an artistic prose work might seem presumptuous if it were not deliberate and if there were no precedents for it. But the history of Russian literature since the time of Pushkin not only affords many examples of such a departure from European form, but does not offer so much as one example to the contrary. From Gogol's *Dead Souls* to Dostoevsky's *Dead House,* in the recent period of Russian literature there is not a single work, at all rising above mediocrity, that quite fits the form of a novel, a poem, or a story.[5]

Tolstoy was neither the first nor the last to identify the Russianness of Russian literature with formal anomaly. The critic Vissarion Belinsky had already maintained that, just as Russian history is utterly unlike that of European countries, so

the same applies to the history of Russian literature. . . . It has been
in existence for a mere hundred and seven years, yet it already
possesses several works whose only interest for foreigners is that
they strike them as being unlike the works of their own literature,
hence, as being original, independent, i.e., nationally Russian.[6]

Belinsky's argument rapidly became a cliché. The idea, as he and
others developed it, was that Russia had "entered History" late with the
reforms of Peter the Great. At that point the cultural forms that Europe
had developed over centuries were imposed on Russia overnight. In the
space of a few decades, the nobility adopted European manners, women
came out of seclusion, men shaved their beards, and both sexes adopted
European dress. The nobility became literate, society abandoned the old
Russian calendar that dated from the Creation, and the monarchy west-
ernized the army and the government, along with many similar reforms.
By the end of the eighteenth century, the upper nobility spoke French
as a first language and the empire was governed from St. Petersburg, a
planned city built on European models as a window to the West.

The result was a sense of the radical arbitrariness of cultural norms:
customs and values evidently could be otherwise because they had just
been so. Manners, political institutions, literary forms, and, for that matter,
all moral norms easily seemed to be nothing more than mere conventions, alterable at will. Those who thought this way sought opportunities
to defy conventions, play with them, invert them, or seek ways of doing
away with them altogether. "The will to destroy is also a creative will," as
the Russian anarchist Mikhail Bakunin famously stated.[7] And once the
traditions of anarchism, nihilism, and extremism became established, it
became a point of national pride to extend them. However talented he or
she might be, a Russian writer who excelled in conventional "European"
forms—a writer like Turgenev—risked the charge of being somehow
un-Russian.

In *A Writer's Diary,* Dostoevsky refers to "the Russian aspect" of
European ideas, by which he means the tendency of Russian intellectuals
to draw conclusions from those ideas that their European formulators
never suspected but which in Russia seem quite natural. Push all notions
to their extreme, beyond all reason and common sense, and then try to put
these extremities into practice as soon as possible: that is the tendency of

the Russian intelligentsia! A Russian, Dostoevsky observes in the *Diary,* is someone who can read Darwin on the struggle for survival and promptly become a pickpocket. It is hardly surprising that Dostoevsky foresaw—so far as I know, he was the only one in the nineteenth century to do so—that the twentieth century would not be a time of increasing enlightenment and liberalism but the century giving rise to what we have come to call totalitarianism. And totalitarianism, for all its successes elsewhere, was created first in Russia by members of the Russian intelligentsia who had seized power.

In Russia, literature itself was felt to be a foreign product. Because European secular genres entered Russia only in the eighteenth century, tragedy, lyric, and narrative fiction seemed new and in need of domestication. They resembled the many Gallic words and syntactic forms redefining the Russian literary language. Moreover, because all these foreign genres entered Russia at the same time, literary history was telescoped: in terms of their impact on Russian culture, Virgil, Dante, Rabelais, and Milton were all equally recent. For this reason, too, nothing had deep roots; it seemed that everything could be, and for true Russians should be, redefined.

Victor Shklovsky, the best-known member of the Russian Formalist school of criticism, saw Formalism itself as the product of the Russian obsession with literary anomaly. In Shklovsky's view, to judge *War and Peace* according to the norms of European poetics would be like judging General Kutuzov (the book's military hero) according to the norms of European military strategy. *War and Peace* combines fiction with nonfictional essays much as Gogol's *Arabesques* does: and Shklovsky insists that *Arabesques* is no mere anthology but an experimental new form. He regarded Herzen's combination of essay and fictional dialogues, *From the Other Shore,* as a typical (because atypical) Russian product. Shklovsky referred to the "Herzenification" of Russian literature and saw his own metaliterary novel-with-essays, *Zoo, or Letters Not About Love, or The Third Eloise*—as yet another Herzenified work.[8]

Writing his description of Russian literature, Shklovsky almost certainly had *A Writer's Diary* in mind. Not only is it the most extreme example of such anomaly, but it cites Herzen as a model and combines heterogeneous genres in the way Shklovsky recommends. But in the Soviet period, Dostoevsky's politically unacceptable book was unmentionable.

Absent Structure and Closure

Even by Russian standards, *A Writer's Diary* is decidedly strange, strange enough that it has proven hard to regard it as a literary work at all. Intermittently, to be sure, a few critics have recognized the *Diary* as a whole, but even then, the nature of that whole has remained elusive.[9] Why?

Let me briefly outline a few of the *Diary*'s puzzles. Three in particular strike the reader: its form as a periodical, its heterogeneity of genres, and its at times odd, as well as varied, content.

As I have already mentioned, the *Diary* does not just appear in a periodical but is a periodical. The author is also the editor and publisher, and all three roles are essential to the work, as they would not be if it resembled a serialized novel. Beginning in January 1876, when Dostoevsky at last had the chance to publish the *Diary* as he wished, he added a subtitle and the work became *A Writer's Diary: A Monthly Publication.* Because the periodical form is essential to the *Diary*'s identity, each issue was denominated by the month (or occasionally two months) it covered. Subscribers would receive an issue for "February 1876" or for "May and June 1877." The author (or editor) promised in advance that at the end of each year, a book would be formed from the separate monthly issues in a way that preserved the periodical form. Readers would still be able to see exactly when specific installments appeared as well as the dividing lines between them. Monthly issues would maintain their relative integrity.

So important was the *Diary*'s periodical form to its purpose that when Dostoevsky decided, after the suspension of the *Diary*, to publish a single issue containing his speech on Pushkin and an account of the reaction to it, he chose to call it the "August 1880" issue even though there was no other installment that year. When the *Diary* resumed in 1881, Dostoevsky continued the periodical form with the January 1881 issue; unfortunately, he died shortly thereafter.

Works published in a periodical are of course also reissued in book form, as *Bleak House* and *Crime and Punishment* were. But in such cases, authors do not include in the text an indication of when a given part originally appeared. Indeed, they typically strive to amend the text so as to erase the signs of periodical publication. If one wants to know where the breaks between installments originally were, one has to look in footnotes or other external sources. That is not the case with the *Diary* in book form. The designation of month and year appears as the title of each section. We know both the originally serialized novels and the *Diary* in book form, but the status and meaning of "book" differ.

A moment's reflection suggests that periodical form poses structural problems. For one thing, it precludes the possibility of closure, a point at which all loose ends are tied up and the complete pattern is fulfilled. After all, time has no natural stopping point. Until the apocalypse, when there will be time no longer, time goes on. To propose a work the length of *Remembrance of Things Past* is to promise a very long work, but to propose publishing an issue each month is to promise not a *very* long but an *indefinitely* long publication. The *Diary* can stop, and given human mortality, it must; but in principle it cannot end, if by an ending we mean the point at which a structure is completed and the design of the whole is visible. In principle, as well as in fact, the *Diary* can have no more closure than time itself.

At the end of a well-made novel or play, any continuation would be gratuitous, and from a very early age as critics, we are all trained to see that, unless a work is flawed, every detail has a place in an overall structure. But structure of this sort is impossible when a work can never be completed. There will always be details not yet accounted for. Lacking structure and closure, such a work must achieve its integrity some other way.

How then are we to determine the place of particular articles, stories, or reported events in the work as a whole?

Present

The periodical form Dostoevsky chose presents another challenge to reading the Diary as a literary work. As the author repeatedly reminds us, and as readers were well aware, the *Diary* was designed to respond to *whatever* happened in the real world between issues. Or more specifically, the diarist bound himself to consider anything of significance pertaining to Russia's spiritual development. By definition, therefore, the *Diary* would be shaped by incidents that the author could not foresee

and would contain elements that in principle *could not* have been part
of any initial plan. The design of the *Diary* not only tolerated but even
demanded discrepant and unanticipatable elements. Unavoidably, these
elements either do not cohere, or cohere only by accident, with earlier
ones. Surprising events took place and were bound to take place.

In the *Diary*, therefore, the author places himself on the same level as
his readers insofar as he, no more than they, can foresee what later installments of the work will contain. That is evidently not the case with *Bleak
House*. In Dickens's novel, earlier events are presented *so as* to prepare for
later ones. They are there in part because of what is to come; causation
is both backward and forward, which is why the author, like an oracle,
knows more than the readers. Suspense belongs to them, not to him. But
in the *Diary* causation works only forward. The author, too, experiences
suspense, and readers are meant to perceive him as experiencing it along
with them.[10]

Let me clarify. To be sure, authors of well-planned novels, like *Bleak
House* or *Middlemarch,* are often surprised during the process of creation.
They commonly testify: characters did what they wanted to do, not what
the author planned for them. While composing, the author was surprised,
and such surprises may constitute part of the pleasure of creation. But
they are not part of the design of the work itself, nor are they supposed to
be visible to the reader. After surprise comes reintegration and adjustment
so that what once surprised the author is now prepared for. It contributes
to the structure of the now revised whole. Acts of discovery belong to the
history of the work's creation, not to its final text.

Sometimes, of course, periodical publication makes it impossible to
revise earlier portions of the work to fit with a serendipitous discovery
made during the work's composition. When *Martin Chuzzlewit* did not
prove popular, Dickens changed its design midstream and took his hero
off to America, and the change in design shows. But for that very reason, it
marks a flaw. Changing design was not itself part of some larger design.

But in the *Diary* it is. The *Diary* was composed *so that* the author
would be surprised and so that he would not know what was coming next.
Deliberately, readers would witness the slips and recoveries, the lapses
and inspirations of the author's creative mind dealing with a world that
keeps changing in unpredictable ways. They would watch him struggle
with what he had not expected and could not retroactively rewrite earlier

parts to prepare for. Sometimes the author would stumble, sometimes succeed brilliantly, and both would be visible to the reader.

In this way, the drama of creation would be part of the work's interest. Even its occasional lapses would contribute to its overall effect because they would make the successes all the more evidently spontaneous and anything but guaranteed. We value all the more what could not have been preplanned and must have been generated on the spot. We are there when creation is not already over but is still *present*.

Literature as Heuristic

The *Diary* may be called *literature as heuristic*. Instead of an overall structure, the work exhibits a consistent set of *procedures* and tools. The idea is that readers will witness the author deploying these tools so as to make literature out of whatever life throws in our way. Dostoevsky was a great admirer of Pushkin's story "The Egyptian Nights," in which an improvisatore undertakes to compose a poem on any topic that a member of his audience might suggest, and actually manages to do so. Like Pushkin's improvisatore, Dostoevsky must work under considerable time pressure, and in fact, he sometimes fails, thus leading to his missing the deadline for a monthly issue and publishing instead a double issue the following month. Sometimes we also watch how the procedures for making art out of recalcitrant material themselves evolve bit by bit from issue to issue, a kind of second-order creation in response to experience.

A Special Composite

The January 1876 issue, the first to appear in the form Dostoevsky had envisaged, filters a few themes—especially children—through a variety of literary genres, each with its own set of values, favorite material, narrative voice, and predominant tone. It is as if each genre served as a set of eyes and as if the complexity of the world demanded many sets to represent it with even minimal adequacy.

In a letter written while he was preparing this issue, Dostoevsky explained:

In issue No. 1 there will be, first of all, the very littlest *preface,* then something or other about children—about children in general, about children with fathers, especially about children without fathers, about children at Christmas parties, without Christmas parties, about child criminals. . . . Of course, these will not be strict studies or accounts, but only some hot words and indications. Then about *what has been heard or read*—anything and everything that strikes me each month. Without doubt, *A Writer's Diary* will resemble a feuilleton, with the difference that a monthly feuilleton naturally cannot resemble a weekly feuilleton. Here the account will be not so much about events or news as about what from an event remains most constantly, most connected with the general, whole idea. Finally, I do not at all want to bind myself with the task of rendering an account. I am not a chronicler: this, on the contrary, will be a perfect *diary* in the full sense of the word, that is, an account of what has most interested me personally—here there will even be caprice. (*Pis'ma,* 3:201–2)

"The general, whole idea" should appear indirectly through its treatment from a variety of angles and genres. The author's efforts at shaping would themselves be apparent. We would sense him present *at* the events, not structuring them afterwards: that is why this periodical is also a *diary.* A diary is written day by day, as events unfold. As in a diary, there would be surprise and, at times, even caprice.

With such an approach, it is clear why the feuilleton was to set the *Diary*'s predominant tone. The feuilleton was a genre, halfway between the literary and the journalistic, that was quite well known in Russia at the time and that Dostoevsky was known to have perfected. Having begun as a mere journalistic miscellany listing disconnected bits of information in a single sheet (thus the term *feuilleton,* or sheet), this sort of work eventually became interesting in its own right. As often happens in literary history, the constraints of a purely practical form proved fascinating enough to inspire creativity even without the practical function. By much the same dynamic, authors in antiquity came to supply possible last words for people still alive or to compose epitaphs that would never be carved; and more recent authors have written closet dramas never to be staged.

In the case of the feuilleton, authors learned to make mere lists of recent events interesting by linking them as the haphazard observations of a particular kind of dreamy narrator. This dreamer wandered from place and place and from topic to topic, and so, in addition to the information from the list, the reader encounters digressions, random encounters, and self-absorbed ruminations. Metaliterary humor alternates with nostalgia and quixotic sentiment.

Dostoevsky discerned that the feuilleton lent itself to combining not only discrete events but also different genres, among which the feuilleton itself might be included. That insight was key to shaping the *Diary*. In observing that a monthly feuilleton was bound to differ from a weekly one, Dostoevsky evidently meant to indicate that he would extend the feuilleton's principle of whimsical heterogeneity to a longer form and thus arrive at each issue of the *Diary*. Each monthly installment was to consist of a *composite* of diverse genres placed in a feuilletonistic frame. The feuilleton proper would not only appear as one genre among many but would also set the overall tone of their combination.

Chapter Titles and Annoying Readers

Dostoevsky realized this plan in the first few monthly issues of the *Diary*, and it is for this reason that they may be regarded as its most successful.

The January 1876 issue exemplifies the design. A dreamy, typically feuilletonistic narrator wanders from article to article as he offers diverse material, mostly, as we have seen, about children. We get sociological sketches about child beggars and an account of a Christmas party from which (it later turns out) a freezing boy is turned away while the narrator dreams about paradise or utopia. This utopian dream answers, and is answered by, an anti-utopian sketch about the "cleverness of devils" and the motivations of belief. The author also offers some autobiographical comments as well as a good deal of whimsical self-referential material, including a digressive opening article, "In Place of a Foreword. On the Great and Small Bear, on Great Goethe's Prayer, and Generally on Bad Habits." This foreword that is not a foreword efficiently introduces the work while professing incapacity to do so. Dostoevsky had done much the same thing when, in 1873, the *Diary* appeared in a preliminary form as a column in another publication. (He was to use the technique for the foreword to *The Brothers Karamazov* as well.)

The non-foreword's lengthy and whimsical title, the first of many similar ones, follows the logic of the feuilleton: apparently discrepant elements are whimsically presented as if they cohered when they are in fact unified only as the dreamy author's reflections. Such titles might as well be addressed to the author himself, as a set of reminders of where his thoughts have gone. To readers, they seem like so many riddles that, far from introducing topics to be covered in the article, are comprehensible only *after* it has been read. Deciphering such titles becomes a game that the reader is frequently invited to play. Since phrases in the titles often relate to an article's content in unexpected ways, the game becomes a recurrent source of wit.

Of the *Diary*'s many kinds of self-referential play, such chapter titles are probably the most striking:

> The Christmas Party at the Artists' Club. Children Who Think and Children Who Are Helped Along. A "Gluttonous Boy." "Oui" Girls. Jostling Raw Youths. A Moscow Captain in a Hurry. (January 1876)

> The Russian Society for the Protection of Animals. The Government Courier. Demon-Vodka. The Itch for Debauch and Vorobev. From the End or from the Beginning? (January 1876)

> The First Root. Instead of an Authoritative Financial Tone I Lapse into Old Words. The Broad Ocean. The Longing for Truth and the Necessity for Serenity, So Useful in Financial Matters. (January 1881)

The example from 1881 is the issue's fourth chapter title, and the first three also promise to talk about "finances" only (as the subsequent parts of the title indicate) to omit doing so. Impatient with the first broken promise to talk about finances, readers instantly respond to the title of the second article, "Can We Expect European Finances in Russia?" and so that article begins:

"So what about finances? Where's your article on finances?" I'll
be asked. But, again, what sort of economist am I? What kind of
expert on financial matters? In fact, I don't think I even have the
nerve to write about finances. So why, then, did I embark on such a
venture and start writing such an article? I did so precisely because
I'm sure that once I've begun to talk about finances I'll change the
subject to something else entirely and the result will be an article
not about finances but something altogether different. That's the
only thing that encourages me. (*Diary*, 1/81, 1.2)

Such interruptions from imagined readers constitute an important
element of the *Diary*. Sometimes Dostoevsky includes replies from
genuine readers; at other times (like this), he imagines the objections,
vituperation, or smirks of his opponents; at still others, it is hard to tell
whether the replies are fabricated or not.

The *Diary* presents one of its most famous short stories, "Bobok,"
as a contribution by an insane reader, whom the diarist calls simply "a
certain person" ("That person is not I, but someone else entirely"). This
"certain person," who suffers, as so many Dostoevsky characters do, from
the psychology of *ressentiment*, invades Dostoevsky's editorial office and
forces him to print not only this story but also his "letter."[11] A vituperative
diatribe against vituperative diatribes, this letter begins with such nastiness
that Dostoevsky simply snips it off, and so the contribution—now entitled
"A Half-Letter from 'A Certain Person'"—begins in mid-sentence.

The "Announcement" and the Joints

A short story sets the predominant tone of the January 1881 issue and,
if we are to judge from the first few monthly installments, a fictional or
quasi-fictional narrative was to serve as the pivot for each. In January
1876, "The Boy at Christ's Christmas Party," a tale about an urchin who
freezes to death on Christmas but whose soul then rises to a heavenly
Christmas festival, echoes the issue's concern with the suffering of children. In the February issue "The Peasant Marey" and in the March issue
"A Hundred-Year-Old Woman" play a similar pivotal role.

Despite, or because of, their centrality, Dostoevsky whimsically presents these stories as if they were violations of his contract with the reader. That "contract" appears as the "Announcement"—published just before the *Diary*'s first issue—describing the work and soliciting subscriptions. So essential is this "Announcement" to the *Diary,* and so important are the references to it, that it must be considered a part of the work, as in the present translation.

In the passage to which Dostoevsky refers, the "Announcement" promises:

> It will be a diary in the literal sense of the word, an account of impressions actually experienced each month, an account of what was seen, heard, and read. Of course, some stories and tales may be included, but preeminently it will be about actual events.

This promise would seem to leave ample room for fiction—or anything else, for that matter—but the conclusion of "The Boy at Christ's Christmas Party" "apologizes" for its ostensibly illegitimate presence:

> So why did I make up a story like that, so little in keeping with the usual spirit of a sober-minded diary, and a writer's diary at that? All the more since I promised stories preeminently about actual events! But that's just the point: I keep imagining that all this could really have happened—I mean the things that happened in the cellar and behind the woodpile [where the boy froze]; as for Christ's Christmas party—well, I really don't know what to say: could that have happened? That's just why I'm a novelist—to invent things.

This story also begins oddly. In a sense, it seems not to begin at all, but to proceed directly from the previous article, a sketch about child beggars:

> A wild creature such as this sometimes knows nothing at all—neither where he lives, nor what nation he comes from; whether God exists, or the tsar. There are even stories told about them that are hard to believe, yet they are facts.
>
> Article 2. The Boy at Christ's Christmas Party

> But I am a novelist and one "story," it seems, I made up myself.
> Why do I say "it seems" when I know very well that I made it up?
> Yet I keep imagining that it really happened somewhere, sometime,
> and happened precisely on Christmas Eve in *a certain* huge city
> during a terrible cold spell.

Here we get one of the *Diary*'s recurrent elements, its dramatization of the "joints" where nonfiction turns into fiction (or back again). In such passages, the *Diary*'s strange poetics (or as I prefer to say, its prosaics) of transition becomes the center of our attention. "Reality is transfigured, *passing through art*," Dostoevsky once wrote; these joints seem designed to dramatize the process of "passing through."[12] In the February 1876 issue, the joint occurs at the beginning of "The Peasant Marey" and in the March issue at the end of "A Hundred-Year-Old Woman," which shades into the next article with another reference to the "contract" in the "Announcement."

Reading Horizontally and Vertically

Sometimes this process of "passing through" occurs across issues. The author (let us say) reads an article about a crime or suicide in the local press and comments on both the incident and the way it is reported. He may indicate why, with his sense of psychology, he senses something important missing in the received accounts. In subsequent issues, he returns to the theme, and imagines what might have—or must have?—really happened. If later news reports—say, of the trial—add information, he integrates that information into his half-real, half-imagined portrait.

Based on this portrait, he sometimes goes on to provide a sketch for a short story. At last, a story may appear. This is pretty much the process by which we get "The Dream of a Ridiculous Man" and "The Meek One." These stories interest readers all the more because they have witnessed the process by which real events are deepened and transformed into psychologically realist fiction. They read the story not just "horizontally," in terms of its plot, but also "vertically," as the culmination of a creative process they have witnessed. "The Dream" is the last event in the story of its own composition.

The Creative Process and the Openness of Time

In some cases, we do go only part way toward a finished short story. Recognizing that many outcomes are possible, we sense the creative process as one of *open time*. For Shelley, by contrast, the time of creativity is closed, and there is essentially no process at all: "The future is contained within the present, as the plant within the seed" and the work is given whole to the poet.[13] It is somehow already there to be discovered: "Milton conceived the *Paradise Lost* as a whole before he executed it in portions. We have his own authority also for the Muse having 'dictated' to him the 'unpremeditated song'" (Shelley, 511).

For Shelley and similar theorists, the process of composition can produce nothing of value not already contained in the initial inspiration, for "when composition begins, inspiration is already on the decline" (Shelley, 511). The *Writer's Diary* illustrates quite the opposite view, that the creative process is genuinely *processual* in the sense that what happens at each moment truly matters. More than one successful outcome is possible, just as all of us could lead more lives than one. At each moment, the artist can make more than one good choice; nothing is already given. Freedom is real, and multiple potential futures lead from each moment. Inviting us into the author's workshop, the *Diary* allows us to sense the throb of creative presentness.

In fact, Dostoevsky often had the experience of making more than one work out of the same material. In the *Diary*, we see the same meditations—on crime, on suicide, on "dissociation"—leading to different sketches and stories.

The *Diary* therefore represents the creative process as Dostoevsky actually experienced it, as anything but inevitable. It is a supreme example of why life itself is not product—not something already given and merely lived out—but truly processual in the sense that each present moment makes a real difference in selecting among many possible paths that *could* proceed from it. The openness of time—the indeterminist view according to which each moment is not entirely specified in advance but dependent in part on human choice or sheer contingency—is in fact one of the *Diary*'s key themes.

The *Diary* illustrates, as it argues for, the openness of time.

Semifictions

Some of the *Diary*'s most memorable entries appear as stories somehow caught in the act of their own making. I like to call these emerging works *semifictions*. They may take several forms.

Sometimes, like the "Plan for a Satirical Novel of Contemporary Life," a semifiction appears as an outline for a story that *might* be, but is not yet, written. Instead of a narration, we are given a possible narration, and so the "Plan for a Satirical Novel" sketches its ending only hypothetically: "One could invent some very natural and contemporary finale for him; for example, how kicked out of the service, he is hired for a hundred rubles to take part in a fictitious marriage; after the ceremony, he goes one way and she another, to her flour dealer" (*Diary*, 5–6/77, 1.3)

Of course, one way to tell a story is to pretend one is not doing so. Hypothetical narration could be either genuine or a mere device. After all, Dostoevsky's most famous narrative—"The Grand Inquisitor"—is narrated in precisely this way, as Ivan Karamazov's outline for a story he might someday write. When he needs to express the ineffable, Ivan remarks: "That might be one of the finest passages in the poem. I mean, why they recognized him."[14]

Some semifictions seem to work both ways: they are complete stories, but the author also leaves himself the option of taking them a step further. Leaving himself two options in this way is characteristic of Dostoevsky. For example, some critics take the narrator of *The Brothers Karamazov* at his word when he claims that the novel we know is only the first part of a two-volume work; and in fact there is external evidence to support this view. Other critics, pointing to Dostoevsky's tendency to write complete works in the form of fragments and to the way *Karamazov* functions as a whole, regard the suggestion of a second volume as a mere device. But it could easily be both: the novel works as complete, but also allows the author to continue should he decide to. It is a structure with a loophole.

Transition

Other semifictions begin with the report of a real event and then imagine what its continuation might be. Someone (it was in fact Dostoevsky's wife)

meets a hundred-year-old woman slowly making her way to her grandchildren, and describes the scene to Dostoevsky. He decides to guess what
might have happened when the old woman arrived. Characteristically, we
get the joint, the moment of transition from the factual to the imagined:

> I had listened to the story that morning—indeed, it wasn't even
> a story but only some sort of impression of a meeting with a
> hundred-year-old woman (and in fact how often do you meet a
> hundred-year-old woman, let alone one so full of inner life?)—and
> had forgotten it entirely, but then, late at night, I was reading an
> article and when I set the magazine aside I suddenly recalled that
> old woman, and for some reason I at once sketched in an ending to
> the story of how she reached her own folks to have dinner: there
> emerged another, perhaps quite plausible scene. (*Diary*, 3/76, 1.2)

Transition itself seems to be a key theme of this story, and its most dramatic
moment takes place when the old woman dies in mid-sentence and mid-
action, with the exact moment of her passing impossible to determine.

The boundary between what is "quite plausible" in the sense of
appropriately imagined and in the sense of what the author has accurately guessed is a thin one. Sometimes Dostoevsky begins by offering
a purely hypothetical continuation of an event but then declares that, in
fact, he has guessed how things must have actually happened. He may
even check, and report back in subsequent issues, as he does with the
Kornilova case.

The end of "A Hundred-Year-Old Woman," like that of "The Boy
at Christ's Christmas Party," also dwells on its own passage back to
nonfiction.

> Well, still, this is just an inconsequential little scene without a
> story. True enough, one sets out to recount something with a bit
> of interest in it from the things heard in the course of a month, but
> when you sit down to write it turns out to be quite impossible to
> retell or is irrelevant, or it's simply a case of "not telling everything
> you know," and so in the end you're left with only little things such
> as this with no story to them. . . .

Article 3. Dissociation

But still, I'm supposed to be writing about "the things I have seen, heard, and read." And at least it's a good thing that I didn't limit myself with a promise to write about *everything* I have "seen, heard, and read." And I keep hearing things that are stranger and stranger. How can I convey them when they all go off on their separate ways and simply refuse to arrange themselves into one neat bundle! Indeed, I keep thinking that we have begun the epoch of universal "dissociation." (*Diary*, 2/76, 1.2–3)

The story concludes by denying it is a story, just an inconsequential scene. And like some other pieces, it ends, in the process of meditation, on an ellipsis. . . . Beginning on a conjunction, the next entry proceeds directly from this narrative, as if the title separating the two might itself be an arbitrary transitional marking.

Composition of Decomposition

Once in the story, and twice in the following article, the author alludes to or quotes the promise in the "Announcement" to speak about what he has "seen, heard, and read" in the course of the month. Regretting that the story of the hundred-year-old woman has proved inadequate, he fears the fact to be described in the article—the current spiritual state of Russia—is so strange as to appear still less credible than fiction itself. And so, Dostoevsky confides, it is a good thing I did not promise to write about *everything* I have seen or heard because then I would have to tell something I cannot tell; and then he tells it.

Dostoevsky reports that society is, like this very passage, in a moment of transition between the ordinary and the fantastic. People do not know what to believe because reality stands on the threshold of a new kind of world, an epoch of "dissociation." "Dissociation"—Kenneth Lantz was kind enough to use my version of this odd word—turns into one of the *Diary*'s key and frequently repeated themes. The word itself recurs in the *Diary*, sometimes when least expected.

"Dissociation" is simultaneously a psychological, a spiritual, and a sociological characteristic of the new epoch. It is, roughly, the state of mind of individuals, most sensitive to the spirit of the times, who sense their utter separateness from others and the world's spiritual atomization. A character in Dostoevsky's novel *The Idiot* asks whether it is possible to describe in an image that which has no image, and in the *Diary* Dostoevsky struggles with the need to represent utter fragmentation without imposing an order that is utterly untrue to what it represents.

How does one coherently describe a state of affairs that is itself incoherent? Of course, that is just what the peculiar form of the *Diary* is designed to do. An icon of chaos, a composition of decomposition, the *Diary* offers a picture of the perhaps futile struggle to paint one.

Poetics and Prosaics

Beginning with the February 1876 issue, Dostoevsky includes reports on crimes and trials. One may see these reports as preparation for the lengthy description of Dmitri's trial in *The Brothers Karamazov*, but they are also amazingly interesting in their own right. I imagine that Dostoevsky, with his unprecedented psychological insight, was the greatest crime reporter who ever lived. These articles from the *Diary* constitute an essential, if often overlooked, part of his literary legacy.

As it happens, his reports on one case—that of Kairova in the May 1876 issue—also offer a key to the *Diary*'s own inner logic. Once we grasp this logic, we can see the work's similarity to several other great works that we may think of as "processual literature."

The logic of processual works differs from that assumed by almost all schools of criticism currently practiced. For the purposes of this introduction, I shall call that processual logic *prosaics*, to distinguish it from works governed by the logic with which we are familiar, that of poetics. Structure demands poetics, process requires prosaics.[15] If the tools of poetics are applied to processual works, those works will necessarily be misunderstood.

An understanding of prosaics would necessarily change our understanding of literature as such. For what we now usually take for granted as true of all successful literary works is in fact true of only some—probably most, but not all. What we have deemed universal is simply one possibility, albeit the most common.

Once we recognize that other possibilities exist, we can no longer just presume that the usual poetics governs any particular work. Rather, we must examine whether it, or an alternative, applies. As Bakhtin liked to say, we leave a Ptolemaic world, in which there is only one possibility (the way the earth is the only center of the universe), and enter a Galilean one, where there are many possibilities for art (the way the earth is but one of several planets).

To be sure, critical schools assuming poetics may differ profoundly from each other. But however varied the Formalist, structuralist, new critical, new historicist, psychoanalytic, deconstructionist, and other approaches may be, they all tacitly posit that an overall structure of some sort governs any successful work. The source of that structure may alter, along with its nature and the appropriate tools for detecting and analyzing it. It may or may not include the experience of the reader. But there must be some principle explaining the work as a whole and the place of each detail. Nothing is just there, or the work is flawed. We can understand why, even though critical practice changes, a common exercise given to students is to explain the relevance of some apparently irrelevant detail according to a school's particular tenets. And criticism continues to discover new grounds for proving such relevance. Such an exercise and such criticism would make no sense without the presumption of an overarching structure, a unified intention or plan that is in principle graspable at a moment.

Closure, Suspense, and Rereading

In presuming structure, poetics ensures closure, the moment when, in principle, all loose ends are tied up and the pattern of the whole becomes visible. As we have seen, successful works do not just stop; they end. Again, different schools detect different kinds of closure, but share the assumption that if closure is missing, the work is either flawed or incomplete. Indeed, when dealing with great writers whom they are reluctant to accuse of failure, critics typically take lack of closure as a sign of incompleteness.

When structure is presumed, the creative process becomes irrelevant to critical analysis except insofar as it is represented (or misrepresented) in the structure itself. To be sure, we know that the finished intention or design probably did not arise without false starts or proceed without detours and rejected developments. We may even be able to consult earlier versions where parts do not yet fit and closure remains unachieved. But if the work is successful, *at some point* the creative process is over and what we read is its end point, the design that at last adequately governs the whole. For poetics, creative struggles remain in the notebooks and are not properly a part of the work itself. Once the design is discovered, the work proceeds from *a single governing intention*—whether conscious or unconscious, individual or social, visible or concealed does not matter— that is in principle locatable at a moment.

This design ensures that, when we have finished reading the work, we sense that it *could not* have developed in any other way. Once we see the pattern and discover how everything fits, we recognize that everything tends to the ending we have. To be sure, the characters may experience suspense, and insofar as we identify with them as we read, so may we. But when the work is complete and we can see the work whole, we recognize that, for the pattern to be fulfilled, what did happen had to happen. Suspense is ultimately illusory. In a sense, such works are properly read only when *re*read.[16]

Intention, Surprise, Product

Poetics presumes and best explains a work offered as a finished and (in principle) perfect *product*. The successful literary work created according to the poetics of product resembles the world created by a perfect God, whose providential design makes everything meaningful. But that meaningfulness is apparent only where the whole is visible, from outside time or the work. Characters in a work or people in the real world do not have access to this view from outside. But God does, and in a literary work so does the author and the reader who has completed the work.

Crucially for this kind of thinking, the creator cannot be affected by events *in* the represented world. Everything must proceed from a single intentional moment; there can be no surprises after that. If God could be surprised by what people do, He would be less than omniscient; and an author surprised by what his characters do would not yet have completed the process of revision. He may revise many times, but if the work is to be successful, he will at last arrive at a design that proceeds from a single moment.

It is just that conception of intentionality that Dostoevsky wished to challenge, both in life and in literature. To be sure, some real actions and literary works proceed from such an intentionality, but it is a mistake to assume that all acts and works necessarily do. However commonsensical it may be, this assumption belies the complexity of things. It misconceives the relation of decision to action as it often actually happens.

Dostoevsky chose to attack the received view as it appears in the assumptions of the criminal code, but once we grasp his point, we can easily see how it applies to literature, and to the *Diary* itself, as well.

Processual Intentionality

In *An Essay Concerning Human Understanding,* John Locke paraphrases the commonsense view. It is obvious, he contends, that our actions necessarily derive from a prior complete intention. Of course, we may change our intentions, and we may "hold our wills undetermined until we have examined" the relevant circumstances. But if we are to act at all, then *at some point* we must arrive at an intention. Once we have, then, if no external obstacles intervene, "what follows after that, follows in a chain of consequences, linked to one another, all depending on the last determination of the will."[17] The literary analogy of the "last determination of the will" would be the final plan of the work, as distinguished from all the trials and explorations of the creative process.

In his articles on the Kairova case and elsewhere, Dostoevsky argues that this scenario does not always obtain. To be sure, it accurately describes a case in which someone carefully plans a crime in advance—the way Raskolnikov in *Crime and Punishment thinks* he has and the way Pyotr Stepanovich in *The Possessed* actually does. But some intentions are not like that. There may be no moment corresponding to Locke's "last determination" or criminal law's idea of a premeditated decision.

In such cases, the intention is never complete or wholly present; there is no single moment of decision we can locate, no instant when the design was completely formed or its result envisaged. Instead, such intentions may be *genuinely processual* and always incomplete. The action or literary work that results from them will be misunderstood if traced to a Lockean, rather than to a processual, intention.

Consider the Kairova case as the *Diary* presents it. Having an affair with a married man, Kairova discovered that her lover was betraying her by sleeping with his wife. What is more, Kairova learned, the couple was asleep in Kairova's own bed. She entered the room and attacked the wife, Velikanova, with a razor. The couple awoke and prevented her from continuing. The jury at her trial was asked to determine her prior intention: had she intended to kill Velikanova and would she have done so if not prevented?

Dostoevsky argues that this question cannot be answered because it presumes a prior intention when it is entirely possible that such an intention, one way or the other, did not exist. Most likely, he argues, there was never a moment when Kairova intended either to kill or not to kill Velikanova. Instead, her intention might well have been *processual.*

If it was processual, then at no single point was the "determination of her will" complete. At every moment, Kairova's *evolving* intentionality allowed for many possible actions at the next moment. The actions she took did not follow from a prior intention but were part of the *process* by which her incomplete intention was developing.

Dostoevsky then advances a striking conclusion: if the identical situation could be repeated with no external obstacles, each time the result might be different. Repeat it once, and Kairova, instead of doing what she did, might have passed the razor over her rival's throat, shuddered, and run away. Repeat it again, and she might have turned the razor on herself. Yet again, and she might have flown into a frenzy "when she felt the first spurts of hot blood and not only murdered Velikanova but even begun to abuse the body, cutting off the head, the nose, and the lips; and only later, suddenly, when someone took that head away from her, realized what she had done" (*Diary,* 5/76, 1.3). All these possibilities and more would be consistent with a single processual intention as it was evolving.

Dostoevsky insists: it is not that Kairova was unconscious of what she was doing. On the contrary, she was intensely conscious at every moment.

But she did not know what she would do at the next moment and had no overall plan for the whole action. That action developed according to internal and external contingencies as they arose.

It is quite likely that many crimes happen this way. So fond was Dostoevsky of this idea that he used it again in *Karamazov*. Murderously angry with his father, Dmitri picks up a pestle and goes to the old reprobate's house. At Dmitri's trial, the prosecutor claims this action proves prior intent, but in fact it is simply one action in an evolving intentionality that might or might not have led to Dmitri's murdering his father. One would be missing Dostoevsky's point if one concluded (as most critics have) that in refraining from murdering his father, Dmitri was *changing* his intention. On the contrary, he never had a complete intention and the same state of mind could have led to a different outcome.

Neither with Dmitri nor Kairova does the lack of a completed intention indicate innocence. On the contrary, the murderously angry state of mind is itself culpable. It *could,* and often does, lead to violence. In the *Diary,* Dostoevsky contends not that Kairova is innocent of any crime but only that she was not guilty of the charge as worded. Given that wording, the jury was right to acquit her; but had the charge been more carefully phrased, it might well have been right to convict her.

The crucial point with this kind of processual intentionality is that it takes place in and presumes *open time.* At every moment there are more possibilities than actualities, which is why, if the situation could be repeated, *something else* might have happened. For the determinist, there is no "something else"; what did happen, had to happen, and the number of possibilities and actualities is always the same. Dostoevsky's psychology is also a philosophy. They both pertain to time.

With Dmitri and Kairova, nothing is inevitable. Kairova's many possible actions "all could have happened and could have been done by this very same woman and sprung from the very same soul, in the very same mood and under the very same circumstances" (*Diary,* 5/76, 1.3). If identical circumstances can lead to different outcomes, then, by definition, determinism and all other forms of closed time are false. If moments have many possible outcomes, then what happens depends on *presentness* and cannot, even in principle, be foreseen in advance—even by God or by Laplace's demon, who knows all the laws of nature and the position of every particle in the universe.

Processual Literature

Could there be a literary work composed in this way, in which each moment could deliberately have more than one outcome, unforeseeable by the author? Is it possible that a work could be governed by an intention that is, like Kairova's or Dmitri Karamazov's, essentially processual? If so, then no prior intention would dictate, or be meant to dictate, a single structure of the whole. Even upon completing the work, readers would experience no sense of inevitability. Rather, they would sense that, whatever did happen, something else might have happened, and that whatever the author made from his material, he might have made something else. The work would be sensed, and would really be, one of many possible works that the same author might have written in identical circumstances.

A Writer's Diary in fact unfolds according to just such a processual intentionality. Its design consists in not having a design of the usual sort; it lies not in the perfection of a finished product but in the integrity of a process. Inasmuch as that process involves responding to whatever might happen between issues, its openness to accident is no accident.

I would guess that Dostoevsky stumbled upon his appreciation of processuality while he was writing *The Idiot.* That work really was written from installment to installment with the author having not the faintest idea of the whole. At first under pressure of necessity, he wrote, as his characters lived, in the present, improvising from what had already happened and drawn to no predetermined conclusion. As he confessed when sending off the novel's beginning, "I took a chance as at roulette. Maybe it will develop under my pen!"[18]

At some point—I suspect when he was writing part 3 of this four-part work—Dostoevsky realized that processual creation could dramatize what was turning out to be the novel's central theme: that life itself should be conceived as a process. It would take us too far afield to explore this theme, or how it relates to *The Idiot* in detail, but we may observe that in the novel's most famous passage, Ippolit Terentiev, himself a minor character who surprised the author by taking over the work, remarks:

> Oh, you may be sure that Columbus was happy not when he had
> discovered America, but while he was discovering it. Take my word

for it, the highest moment of his happiness was just three days
before the discovery of the New World, when the mutinous crew
were on the point of returning to Europe in despair. It wasn't the
New World that mattered, even if it had fallen to pieces.

Columbus died almost without seeing it; and not really knowing
what he had discovered. It's life that matters, nothing but life—the
everlasting and perpetual process, not the discovery at all.[19]

The temporality of a processual work takes place not when it has been
written but while it is being written, and not when we have read it but
while we are reading it.

Suspense is not an illusion dissipated when we view the processual work from the author's point of view, because the author is himself
surprised by events, and readers are supposed to sense that surprise. The
author knows no more than do his characters what the future may hold.
For that matter, whatever it does hold, it might have held something else,
because any set of events could have more than one outcome. We sense
The Idiot as one of many possible *Idiots*.

When a work is processual, author and reader are simultaneous with,
not after, the characters, and it is reading, not rereading, that is closer to
the work's design.

With *A Writer's Diary* as with all other works of processual literature,
closure is in principle precluded. The work is essentially accompanied by
a sense of *something else*. For the same reason, there can be no foreshadowing, because no plan of the whole dictates what is going to happen.
There is always a might have been and a might be. Or as Ippolit says,
"there is always something left over" (*Idiot*, 375).

"The Extraordinary Cleverness of Devils"

From its beginning in the January 1876 issue, the monthly *Diary* alerts
us to its theme of processuality. In what is arguably the *Diary*'s most
profound piece of semifiction—the article wryly entitled "Spiritualism.
Something About Devils. The Extraordinary Cleverness of Devils, If Only
These Are Devils"—Dostoevsky pursues a number of themes that recur

in subsequent articles on spiritualism (what we today call "channeling"). He discusses the nature of fundamental beliefs and their imperviousness to evidence; and he demonstrates how supposedly skeptical materialists often make the very same logical or psychological errors in justifying their beliefs as the spiritualists do in justifying theirs. But the entry's key point concerns processuality.

Dostoevsky purports to respond to the anti-spiritualist argument that there cannot be spirits or devils because if there were, they would shower humanity with inventions that would prove their existence. Turning life into paradise, these inventions would make ingratitude, let alone disbelief, impossible. If the devils do not prove their existence in this way, the argument goes, then either they do not exist or they are awfully stupid.

Not at all, Dostoevsky replies, it is just their refusal to create paradise that shows just how extraordinarily clever the devils are (if they exist). For what would happen if they did give us all that "our Russian socialists" might desire? Oh, of course, for a generation or so, people would be ecstatic, but then they would realize that in taking away striving, the devils had taken away life itself. As a finished product, life is pointless; meaning must lie in process. People would realize

> that they had no more life left, that they had no freedom of spirit, no will, no personality, that someone had stolen all this from them. . . . And humanity would begin to decay; people would . . . bite their tongues in torment, seeing that their lives had been taken away for the sake of bread, for "stones turned into bread." People would realize that there is no happiness in inactivity, that the mind which does not labor will wither, that it is not possible to love one's neighbor without sacrificing something to him of one's own labor . . . and that *happiness lies not in happiness but only in the attempt to achieve it.* (*Diary*, 1/76, 3.2)

And realizing this, people would banish the devils, along with all utopian dreams, forever. Foreseeing this result, the devils confine themselves to trivial tricks. It is their very refusal to create utopia, therefore, that refutes the charge of stupidity!

Life is process and so is *A Writer's Diary.*

Development Itself

A Writer's Diary is interesting in part because it allows us to understand processual works in general. These works include Dostoevsky's *The Idiot* and perhaps *The Possessed;* Tolstoy's *War and Peace,* Sterne's *Tristram Shandy,* Byron's *Don Juan,* and Pushkin's *Eugene Onegin,* to name but a few. The *defining* characteristic of processual works is that they are created and governed by processual intentionality. They reflect, and are designed to reflect, not a single will but a succession of changing wills.

Some creations, such as buildings that take generations to construct, are likely to reflect a succession of wills. It is hardly surprising that the design of works made by different people at different times might alter. Folklore often reflects a similar process, which may be rendered invisible by editors who assume an aesthetics of product. Despite pious attempts to treat the Hebrew Bible as governed by a single will (the interpretive principle that there is no earlier and later in the Bible), it may also be read as a process.

In the case of works created by many hands over long periods of time, processuality *turns out* to be the creation's guiding principle. But in the case of processual works written by a single author, like *A Writer's Diary, War and Peace,* or *Tristram Shandy,* processuality is part of the work's design from the outset.

In composing *War and Peace,* Tolstoy chose processual creation as a way to illustrate his key theme of uncertainty and contingency. As its wisest characters learn, a story that looks too neat, and in which we sense events unfolding according to an advance plan, is necessarily false to life as it really is. Reality in all its messiness and openness is best represented by a processual work, in which there is no overall plan and the author does not know what will happen.

In a draft preface to *War and Peace,* Tolstoy explained:

> In printing the beginning of my proposed work, I promise neither a continuation nor a conclusion for it. . . . This proposed work can least of all be called a novel—with a plot that has growing complexity and a happy or unhappy denouement, with which interest in the narration ceases.[20]

In fact, Tolstoy published the first sections of his narrative under the title *The Year 1805* and changed it to *War and Peace* only when he decided to follow the characters into 1806 (and after).

Tolstoy explains to his readers that he hoped, but probably would not manage, to guide his characters all the way through 1856. If he had done so, the *War and Peace* we have would have been a small portion of the book! But it hardly matters where he stops, for he means the work to have no closure, no "denouement."

Tolstoy also explains that in setting out he has no idea how the story will proceed (except, of course, for the novel's historical events): "I do not foresee the outcome of these characters' relationships in a single one of these epochs" (Jubilee edition, 13:55). At each point, he promises, the present moment will display an integrity unencumbered by any preconceived future, and the events of each period will explore some, though not all, possibilities suggested by earlier events and current contingencies. Readers will sense that the events described could have happened, but not that they had to happen.

Not knowing how long the work would turn out to be, readers would also be unable to assess likely outcomes by proximity to the ending. Tolstoy adds that serial publication is thus not a mere fact of publication, but essential to its design. Properly speaking, *War and Peace* is not a very long work, but a work of *indeterminate* length. Of course, for later readers, these aspects of Tolstoy's book have to be reconstructed. That is perhaps why Dostoevsky, who knew *War and Peace* well, insisted that when a book was made of the *Diary*'s separate issues, the monthly dating must be retained.

Created by a succession of wills and an intentionality in the process of development, *War and Peace* was bound to have, and does have, numerous loose ends. Foreshadowing was out of the question, and anyone who tries to read incidents as signs of events to come is bound to be disappointed. Far from crafting installments as preparations for future installments, Tolstoy explains in one draft preface, "I strove only so that each part of the work would have an independent interest." Tolstoy then wrote, and struck out, the following remarkable words: "which would consist not in the development of events, but in development [itself]" (Jubilee edition, 13:55).

Some Characteristics of Processual Works

Development itself is what processual works are peculiarly well adapted to describe. Let me suggest a few characteristics of processual works in general:

(a) As a result of having no overall plan, they lack foreshadowing and display loose ends. Events can only proceed from earlier events, not from later ones or from their contribution to the entire structure. Unlike works of product, but like life itself, there is only forward, never backward, causation.

(b) Their unity consists in the integrity of a process.

(c) In contrast to works created according to a singular plan, the author resembles his characters in his ignorance of future events. Suspense is real for him, as well as for them.

(d) There neither is, nor can be closure. There may be relative closure at the end of particular installments, but the whole can have no closure because there is no whole. There is only the amount the author has written so far, and he could always write more. The work stops, but does not end. Instead of closure, it displays what might be called aperture, the possibility of its perpetual continuation.

(e) Such works are typically published in parts, the better to display that they are not the product of a preconceived plan.

(f) They are often shaped by events that take place in the real world *between* installments. Sometimes—both *The Idiot* and *Anna Karenina* come to mind—characters respond to newsworthy events in the real world that had not taken place when the first installments were published. Those events evidently could not have been part of an initial design and therefore *must* reflect an evolving intentionality. Or the work's later installments may be shaped by the response of readers to earlier ones, and so the readers come to participate in creating the work, as happens with *Tristram Shandy*. Or, if the work is published over several years, the author's aging or ongoing life, whose events he could not have foreseen, may become part of it, as happens with *Don Juan* or *Eugene Onegin*. *A Writer's Diary* uses all these ways of signaling its evolving intentionality.

This list is only partial. "Development itself" may be developed in many ways.

Composite Works

A Writer's Diary challenges traditional poetics in yet another way. It belongs not only to the class of processual works, but also to another class that violates the assumptions of poetics and challenges the usual types of criticism. The Galilean universe, it seems, has yet another planet.

I call this other peculiar class *composite works*. As I shall use the term, a work is composite when it invites dismemberment into separate parts. It may properly be read either as a whole or for parts that may be treated as wholes. Excerptible sections may mean something different, depending on which way they are read.

Sometimes composite works are shaped by what has been called an "encyclopedic" impulse: like Burton's *Anatomy of Melancholy* or the works of Rabelais, they aspire to unlimited capacity. But some do not aim at great size or compass at all.

Some composite works are also processual; the two classes overlap. The *Diary* belongs to both.

Separability

Composite works challenge a tenet of critical interpretation we have all been taught is universal, but which is not. Supposedly, it is always a mistake to extract a section of a work and read it apart from the whole. When a long work contains an embedded short one, the way novels and epics often encompass stories, the story can properly be understood only in relation to the structure in which it participates.

To put the point another way, the part does not "mean directly" and is necessarily distorted when read as if it did. Irony, for example, is often lost through anthologization. If someone were to offer (as some have) a reading of "Rebellion" or "The Grand Inquisitor" without reference to their place in *The Brothers Karamazov*, critics from virtually all schools would easily discredit the reading as the result of a naïve methodological error.

And yet, this aesthetic of wholes is not the only possible one. Scholars have noted that medieval and Renaissance literature often reflected an aesthetic of parts. Such an aesthetic lies behind commonplace books, so common in the Renaissance, in which discrete quotations or longer sections of works appeared outside their original context. Parts could stand on their own and readers were taught what Rebecca Bushnell has called a "disintegrative approach" to reading.

A sixteenth-century humanist who read this way "addressed the parts in great detail but was little concerned with seeing them as a whole. The point of reading a book was not to provide an 'anatomy' or understanding of its argument or structure; rather the end was a harvesting or mining of the book for its functional parts."[21] As readers read this way, writers wrote for them accordingly, and vice versa. Erasmus was only one scholar who described different ways of composing commonplace books or (to use a word we still have) "treasuries" of specific jewels. Jewels, it must not be forgotten, are valuable on their own, not only as parts of a larger ornament containing them.

"Harvesting" served as a common metaphor for such reading. One harvests the best parts and discards the rest, as one separates wheat from chaff. Erasmus uses another metaphor common at the time: the good reader "flies about like a diligent bee through the whole garden of authors, where he would fall on every little flower, collecting a bit of nectar from each to carry to his hive."[22] Bushnell also cites the aesthetic of the garden at that time, which ranged between extremes. At one extreme, gardens might reflect a sense of an organic whole resembling a living body that cannot be dismembered and still remain alive. At the other, they might be composed to display a series of separate visual experiences designed to draw the visitor's eye to the best parts more than to any design of a whole.

We have generally lost this aesthetic of separability in theory but not entirely in practice. W. H. Auden and Louis Kronenberger are not the only modern writers to compose a commonplace book, readable, as theirs are, both as a whole and as a collection of parts. Perhaps guiltily, even critics devoted to poetics analyze specific poems from a cycle of poems or stories from a cycle of stories. Evidently, not all wholes are equally demanding: it is perhaps theory alone that would prompt one to state (and then tacitly forget) that one cannot read one of the *Canterbury Tales* or a story from *The Decameron* on its own. Encyclopedic works, like Burton's *Anatomy,* the books of Rabelais, or Sterne's *Tristram*

Shandy, almost seem to demand reading as both wholes and collections of parts. Even the supremely classical Pope explicitly invites readers to both kinds of reading. In the preface to his *Essay on Man,* he explains that he has designed the poem precisely to encourage the common practice of extracting memorable parts. Indeed, that is why he has written his essay in rhyme: "The principles, maxims, or precepts so written, both strike the reader more strongly at first, and are more easily retained by him afterwards."[23]

The *Essay on Man* is both a whole and a collection of parts, and demands both readings. To insist on either reading as the only proper one is to reduce the work and mistake its design. The requirement of such double reading defines the class of composite works.

The Continuum of Separability

I believe that works lie on a continuum of separability. At one extreme we find those governed by an aesthetic of the whole, as envisaged by traditional poetics. When this aesthetic governs, to extract is to deform. At the other extreme, we discover mere anthologies: no one, I think, regards it as improper to extract from *Bartlett's Familiar Quotations* or, to take a work from an earlier era, Erasmus's *Adages.* In between lie works in which the sense of the whole may be stronger or weaker and the propriety of extraction correspondingly weaker or stronger.

At or near the center of the continuum lie works that equally invite, or even demand, both kinds of reading. That is more or less where Pope situates the *Essay on Man.*

Anthony Trollope's six Palliser novels and six Barchester novels each clearly lie *somewhere* between the extremes of the continuum because, in each case, the particular novels can be read either as parts of the series or as entirely separate from it. *Barchester Towers* is the second novel of the Barchester series, but one does not have to have read the first, *The Warden,* to comprehend it. The second Palliser novel, *Phineas Finn,* narrates a complete story but is also interesting as the first of several intriguing stories about its eponymous hero.

I remember first reading *Barchester Towers* and the first Palliser novel, *Can You Forgive Her?* separately, and subsequently reading each as part of its series. I experienced the sense of a different work. When *Can You Forgive Her?* is read outside the series, Lady Glencora functions as a sort of foil to the main heroine, Alice Vavasor; as part of the series, she is herself the main heroine, and Alice becomes a foil to her. Each of the other novels in both series also makes sense, but a different sense, read on its own or as a part of the whole.

But how strong is the sense of each series? Which reading seems more important? Some stories in cycles almost demand knowledge of the others, whereas others seem most impressive on their own. For my purposes here, it is important not to answer this question in any particular case, but to clarify that such a question may be legitimate and that more than one answer may be possible. One author's series of novels may barely tolerate separable reading, while another's may owe little to a recognition that there is a series at all. There may be ample room for critics to argue.

The Diary as Separable, Multiply Separable, and Hierarchically Separable

I believe that the *Diary* was designed to lie somewhere near the middle of the continuum of separability. It asks or demands reading *both* as an anthology and as an integral work.

The *Diary*'s heterogeneity of genres makes excerpting easy, and yet the dramatized "joints" between entries may remind us to read the parts in context as well. As we have seen, "The Dream of a Ridiculous Man" and "The Meek One" can each be doubly read—both as a complete story and as the end point of the drama of its creation.

"The Meek One" has so often been interpreted as a complete work that one needs no proof to show the possibility of doing so; but it is also apparent that its themes and vocabulary echo, affect, and are affected by other passages in the *Diary*. Read in the context of the whole, for instance, the very title seems to allude to Jesus's promise that the meek shall inherit the earth. Arguments in support of or opposed to the utopian interpretation of "The Dream of a Ridiculous Man" either insist that it be read in the context of the *Diary* or as a distinct work. Some treat the rest of the *Diary* as an intrinsic part of this story and some as external evidence.

When excerpted, the narrator of "The Peasant Marey" appears to be part of a first-person fiction, but in context, and in many readings, the narrative is offered as factual autobiography. Such doubleness is characteristic of the semifictions, and of some articles, as well. Each story, semifiction, or journalistic account of "dissociation" allows us to understand that concept more deeply, and yet these entries may also be read as complete in themselves.

We may sometimes speak not only of excerptability but also of *multiple* excerptability. It is often possible to extract *different* separate works depending on where one draws the boundaries. The narrator of "Bobok" makes another appearance, and so we may ask whether these are two separate works or parts of a single portrait of a character? "The Boy at Christ's Christmas Party" not only functions both as the pivot of the January 1876 issue and as a commonly anthologized story but has also been anthologized in two ways, either with or without the article that leads into it.

Sometimes we may speak of a hierarchy of excerptability. Not only does the *Diary* itself lie along the continuum of separability, but so do some of its parts. One could easily read the particular articles on the Kornilova case separately; or as part of the *Diary*; or, somewhere in between, as parts of an ongoing but recognizable story. Dostoevsky's insistence that the monthly form be preserved when annual volumes were published also suggests such a hierarchy of separability. Particular entries may stand on their own, or as part of a monthly issue, or as part of the *Diary* as a whole.

The Diary Loses Its Way

Unfortunately, as we continue to read the *Diary*, the integrity of particular issues becomes less visible or seems to disappear altogether. Some issues also seem to lose the heterogeneity of genres that was essential to the original plan, along with the feuilletonistic narrator who was supposed to set the overall tone. That tone is replaced by the quite different voice of a hectoring prophet pronouncing absurd and obnoxious judgments on world affairs. What gave shape to the *Diary*, a shape discernible in the first few issues, is lost, partly recovered, and lost again.

In short, readers have failed to perceive the *Diary* as the integral work that Dostoevsky intended not only because of the inherent strangeness of its conception but also because the author intermittently abandoned that conception. What led him to do so?

I believe the answer is that his philosophy of time, so integral to this processual work, temporarily changed. Although it is hard to credit, it is really true that Dostoevsky—the very same author who insists on the unknowability of people and events—came to believe that he himself had discovered the formula of history. According to that formula, the millennium of Christian belief was literally imminent. I can never read these passages without wondering whether one of Dostoevsky's characters, like the mad narrator of "Bobok," had not at last succeeded in taking over the work.

The Principle of Simultaneity

Critics of great writers often adopt the role of apologists, and so it is not surprising that this aspect of Dostoevsky's thought usually goes unmentioned. Even when it is mentioned, it is rarely given much attention. Nevertheless, Dostoevsky clearly endorses what he calls "The Utopian Conception of History" (*Diary*, title of 6/76, 2.5). In this article and elsewhere, Dostoevsky (not a fictional narrator) insists that, having defined history's plot, he can predict the future. The *Diary* contains several such predictions.

According to Dostoevsky, "Three Ideas" (*Diary*, title of 1/77, 1.1) govern world history: Catholicism, Protestantism, and Orthodoxy. Each of these ideas represents a timeless principle and therefore existed long before those religions themselves. The Catholic idea, for instance, developed from the pagan Roman idea and has given birth to the atheist socialist idea, but all three are versions of the same thing. As it happens, we are living at the critical moment when these three ideas are reaching their ultimate form and entering into their final conflict.

In Dostoevsky's view, Catholicism is now in its ultimate death throes, as Bismarck perceives; it will clash with Protestantism and this final conflict will raise—no, already has raised—the apparently quite different

Eastern Question (the status of the Balkan Slavs under Turkish rule). That question seems distinct to most commentators only because they judge events superficially.

Why should all the timeless questions of world history come to their climax at once? Why should the ultimate conceptions of human life, as embodied in the three ideas, all reach their final formulation at the same time? Evidently, Dostoevsky explains, a *principle of simultaneity* (or synchronism) operates. Such "simultaneity" demonstrates that a guiding hand or underlying story is at work, as in a novel reaching its "denouement." History is well plotted and is bringing discrete causal lines together to achieve a satisfying closure. To be sure, Dostoevsky describes this underlying story differently in different issues, but he maintains for a considerable time his faith that *some* such plot is leading history to its rapid end.

Metternich and Don Quixote

Dostoevsky proclaims that because of the Eastern Question, Russian (the only true) Christianity will suddenly be spiritually (and militarily) renewed. Then everyone will at last appreciate that the Eastern Question is not really about the control of "the seas and the straits, access and egress, by any means," as some wily Austrian diplomat might suppose. No, "it is much deeper, more fundamental, more elemental, more necessary, more essential, more primary" (*Diary*, 5–6/77, 2.2). In truth, it is "a worldwide, universal question with an extraordinary significance, even though this preordination may occur before eyes that . . . are incapable until the last minute of seeing the obvious and comprehending the meaning of what has been preordained." Finally—"and you may call this the most hypothetical and fantastic of my predictions, I'll admit that beforehand"—Russia will win the war and history, as we have known it, will be over. "Now again someone is knocking; someone, a new man, with a new word, wants to open the door and come in. . . . But who will come in? That's the question. Will it be an entirely new man, or will it once more be someone like all of us, the old homunculi?" (*Diary*, 9/77, 2.5). For Dostoevsky, the answer to that question is clear:

> What is awaiting the world, not only in the remaining quarter of this century, but even (who can tell?) in the current year, perhaps? Europe is restless, of this there is no doubt. But is this restlessness only temporary, a thing of the moment? Certainly not: it is evident that the time is at hand for the fulfillment of something eternal, something millenarian, something that has been in preparation in the world since the very beginning of its civilization. (*Diary*, 1/77, 1.1)

At times, Dostoevsky imagines what some paltry Metternich would say in reply: "Heavens, what a mocking smile would appear on the face of some Austrian or Englishman if he had the opportunity to read of these *daydreams* I have just written down" (*Diary*, 6/76, 2.4). Earlier in the *Diary*, an evidently sane author encounters madmen; now it is the author himself who appears, and knows he appears, hysterical, if not insane.

If his skeptical opponents resemble Metternich, then, Dostoevsky is proud to say, he resembles Don Quixote. But at the end of the world, when the laws of history change, Don Quixote is the realist. Consider: those who assumed, just before the French Revolution, that tomorrow would resemble today as today resembled yesterday, turned out to be the fools. So it always is before an upheaval (*Diary*, 2/77, 1.4).

To be sure, no argument will ever convince the skeptics, but they will be answered by actual events. "If not we, then our children will see how England ends. Now, for everyone in the world 'the time is at hand.' And it's about time, too" (*Diary*, 4/77, 1/3). "The time is at hand" is, of course, a citation from Revelation and it announces the end of the world.

In the rare cases when critics mention these ravings (as Dostoevsky himself calls them), they cite "The Utopian Conception of History" in the June 1876 issue. In that article's culminating passage, he insists that Russian foreign policy is entirely selfless. To think otherwise is to demonstrate that one cannot even seriously conceive of unselfishness and is therefore to convict oneself. In fact, Russia's goal is

> a true exaltation of the truth of Christ, which has been preserved in the East, a true, new exaltation of the cross of Christ and the ultimate word of Orthodoxy, at whose head Russia has long been standing. It will be a temptation for all the mighty of this world who have been triumphant until now and who have always regarded all

such "expectations" with scorn and derision and who do not even
comprehend that one can seriously believe in human brotherhood,
in the universal reconciliation of nations, in a union founded on
principles of universal service to humanity and regeneration of
people through the true principles of Christ. And if believing in
this "new word," which Russia at the head of a united Orthodoxy
can utter to the world—if believing in this is a "utopia" worthy only
of derision, then you may number me among these Utopians, and
leave the ridicule to me. (*Diary*, 6/76, 2.4)

I quote these passages at length to make clear that they are offered
perfectly seriously.

The Idea of the Jews

When Dostoevsky adheres to his conception of history as guided by *three*
ideas, then the main enemy of his ideals turns out to be "the worldwide
Catholic conspiracy" (*Diary*, 11/77, 3.2 and elsewhere), as represented
by the pope and his treasonous Polish allies. Often enough, however,
Dostoevsky thinks not of three but of *two* ideas. Sometimes he imagines
that the true Christianity of Russia struggles against conservative adher-
ence to old ways. He is thinking of those who, like Dostoevsky himself
in his novels and in other issues of the *Diary*, defend tradition and
argue that reforms can be accomplished only bit by bit. At other times,
he adopts a more sinister position: he sees Christianity opposed by
"Yiddism," the Jewish idea of rational calculation and capitalism. Even
when they are not Jews and would laugh at the very notion of a Yiddish
idea, these capitalists see the world only in "Yiddish" terms, that is, as
a matter of money and profits. They consequently reject any idealistic
war as harmful to business. Whether its editors know it or not, the *Stock
Exchange Gazette* belongs—"objectively," as the Marxists would say—to
the Jewish conspiracy. History is a Manichean battle between love and
commercialism, idealism and skepticism.

In fact, Jews turn out to embody both conservatism and commercialism. Thus, the reason that England opposes Russian expansion in
the Balkans is that its leader is Disraeli, who, as "a Spanish Yid," follows

Yiddish principles designed to achieve Jewish world conquest. Just as in apocalyptic theology the Antichrist will temporarily triumph, so will the Jews:

> Their reign, their complete reign, is drawing nigh! Coming soon is the complete triumph of ideas before which feelings of love for humanity, the longing for truth, Christian feelings, the feelings of nationhood and even of national pride of Europe's peoples must give way. What lies ahead, on the contrary, is materialism, a blind, carnivorous lust for *personal* material security. (*Diary*, 3/77, 2/3)

Jewish individualism, like Jewish materialism, contradicts the Christian concern for universal brotherhood.

If Jews should ever rule over Russians, Dostoevsky contends, they will enslave them, or even "massacre them altogether, exterminate them completely, as they did more than once with alien peoples in times of old in their ancient history" (*Diary*, 3/77, 2.2). Passages like these belong to the great tradition (great in terms of influence at home and abroad) of Russian anti-Semitic thought. That tradition—alas, one of the least attractive features of Russian intellectual history—led eventually to the most influential of all anti-Semitic documents, the infamous (and originally Russian) forgery, *The Protocols of the Elders of Zion*. The *Protocols* also purports to discover and document the universal Jewish conspiracy to enslave the world. Dostoevsky does not draw the conclusion that those whom the Jews would enslave or exterminate would be justified in expelling or exterminating the Jews first. But it is clear that such thinking easily could lead to such a conclusion and, from the Third Reich to the Soviet Union and some Middle Eastern countries, has done so for fanatics of diverse sorts. Anti-Semitism would seem to be the only thing that Russia has been able continually to export without creating a shortage at home.

The Changes

Such thinking contradicts the very ideas on which the *Diary* was initially based. As Dostoevsky planned the work, it was to explore the immense complexity of current life, in which the author would try, somehow, to discover a guiding thread. He would, at best, find one temporarily, and then, losing sight of it, search some more. But as a prophet, Dostoevsky grasps not only the present but also the future. No searching is needed.

The *Diary*'s form reflects the sense that reality is hopelessly fragmented and that events "all go off on their separate ways and simply refuse to arrange themselves into a bundle" (*Diary, 3/76*, 1.3). Against all odds, the author fights a desperate battle for such "arrangement" and readers experience a special suspense in watching him struggle. But when he believes he has discerned history's plot, Dostoevsky instead demands of his readers conversion to the final truth.

Initially, the work's heterogeneity of genres derived from the author's conviction that no single way of looking at things could ever be sufficient. But as a utopian prophet, Dostoevsky has no need of multiple viewpoints. The *Diary* then loses much or all of its heterogeneity. A single, repetitive voice predominates, and we alternate between shock and boredom. As originally planned, the *Diary*'s periodical form illustrated the openness of time and the sense that whatever does happen, something else might have. It is the radical intellectuals, seeing only a "linearity" of history, who grossly oversimplify. But Dostoevsky comes to see history in just such a linear fashion, with a future that is both inevitable and visible.

The *Diary*'s initial attention to the minute, apparently trivial events of everyday life, like the visit of an old woman to her grandchildren, grows from the work's idea that what matters is not great events but ordinary, prosaic ones. What makes the world a better place is not grand plans, but what Dostoevsky in the January 1876 issue calls "microscopic efforts" (*Diary, 1/76*, 2.3). "From the End or From the Beginning?" Dostoevsky asks in the title of one article in this issue, and the question turns out to mean: do we begin by imposing an abstract utopian plan (from the end) or by taking small steps to help our neighbors and improve ourselves (from the beginning)? Dostoevsky makes clear, here and elsewhere, that he favors the prosaic approach "from the beginning." He argues: no one has or will find any grand "formula" for society, and even if they did, it still would do no good if people as individuals did not improve their "human image."

In becoming a utopian himself, Dostoevsky could hardly have altered more. He seems, like Shatov in *The Possessed*, to have been "crushed" by an idea. And yet, even after he embraces his "utopian understanding," Dostoevsky still returns now and then to the opposite, prosaic, anti-utopian approach. It is as if he did not know which vision to endorse, all the more so because both could be directed against the self-satisfied liberal materialists whose opinions, voices, or comments in other journals play such a large role in the *Diary*'s polemics.

The changes that accompany his utopian "soothsayings," as he calls them, reduce the *Diary* to a shell of its former self. Issues continue to be named by month and to contain a hierarchy of chapters and articles; but the very purpose of that hierarchy is lost. Whole issues—say, October 1877—seem essentially uniform in genre, tone, and vision. To be sure, Dostoevsky is inconsistent in his new consistency, and the original design, or something like it, sometimes reemerges. But since that design was already quite complex, and after the first few issues, pursued only erratically, it is hardly surprising that most readers have entirely lost or overlooked any sense of the immensely interesting and challenging experiment the *Diary* was originally intended to be.

Part Two: What This Abridgment Contains and Why

In preparing the present one-volume abridgment, I have kept in mind the many reasons that may lead readers to use it. Selections that do not suit one reader's interests may satisfy another's. Articles on the Eastern Question may try the patience of those looking for Dostoevsky's best fiction, but engage the interest of intellectual historians.

Some omissions were easy because it is hard to imagine that they could interest anyone. Particularly in the articles on foreign policy, Dostoevsky tends to repeat himself frequently. In such cases, shortening may actually improve the work. Other omissions proved more difficult because I had to choose between sections of interest to different readers. As a result, most but not all of the crime reporting is retained; the same is true of the material usually treated as a source for *The Brothers Karamazov*.

I suppose that most readers today will be primarily interested in Dostoevsky the artist. In his day, he was almost as well known for his journalism as for his fiction, but that is no longer the case. The present volume allows readers to encounter Dostoevsky's stories both on their own and in their larger context within the *Diary*. It can readily serve as an anthology for undergraduate courses. After all, Dostoevsky was at the height of his powers during these years, and no one interested in him will want to overlook the *Diary*'s fiction. "The Meek One" is arguably the best short story he ever wrote.

I have therefore kept the *Diary*'s four short stories, "Bobok," "The Boy at Christ's Christmas Party," "The Meek One," and "The Dream of a Ridiculous Man." Along with these works, I have preserved other passages of the *Diary* that apparently contributed to their creation or echoed them later on. At times, it almost seems as if the character or narrator of a story had been a reader of the *Diary*, and as if his words seem in turn to provoke responses in subsequent issues.

Contrary to some anthologizers, I include the nonfictional preface to "The Meek One," in which the author explains why this supreme piece of realism is subtitled "a fantastic story." The reader can judge whether to take this preface as merely helpful in grasping the story or, like the preface to *Karamazov*, as an intrinsic part of it. "The Meek One" evidently grows out of the account of a real suicide with an icon, which is in turn part of the *Diary*'s ongoing meditation on suicides of various kinds. The suicide articles also shape "The Dream of a Ridiculous Man," in which the hero attempts to take his own life, but then discovers—or, as some critics argue, insanely imagines he discovers—life's utopian possibilities. Whether one reads this story as utopia or as anti-utopia, one will find the relevant articles from the *Diary* included.

Both stories, and much else, in the *Diary* develop Dostoevsky's ideas about "Dissociation"—the title of an article in the March 1876 issue— that figure prominently, and at times unexpectedly, in the *Diary*. I have included some passages because they develop this key concept.

The author of "Bobok" also contributes a "Half-Letter," which I include. His particular kind of spiritual materialism—his view of the other world in material terms—recurs in the entries on spiritualism, the most important of which are also here. The magnificent semifictional article in the January 1876 issue on "The Extraordinary Cleverness of Devils, If Only These Are Devils" looks back to "Bobok" and forward to the devil chapter in *Karamazov*. Much of the humor of that chapter, like that of the article, derives from the devil's mixture of supernaturalism and materialism. In his attempt to keep up with fashionable opinion, the devil adopts agnosticism and so doubts the existence of beings like himself. Descartes notwithstanding, he suspects he is not, and although he has seen God, he wonders whether Descartes' demon is deceiving him. With the condescension of an intellectual liberal, the devil professes a yearning for the simple faith that he can never have.

The paradoxes present in the *Diary*'s articles on spiritualism multiply in *The Brothers Karamazov*. And as it happens, this devil, who has read much of the great literature about devils, may also have been reading those very articles:

> Look at the spiritualists, for instance. . . . I am very fond of them.
> . . . only fancy, they imagine they are serving the cause of religion,
> because the devils show them their horns from the other world.
> That, they say, is a material proof, so to speak, of the existence of
> another world. The other world, and material proofs, what next!
> (*Karamazov*, 725)

Semifictions

For reasons I have mentioned, "The Peasant Marey," which has been taken as a short story and as a piece of autobiography, seems to invite both readings. And as we have seen, some of the *Diary*'s semifictions invite readings both as sketches and as complete works. Readers may decide which way to take "A Hundred-Year-Old Woman," "The Sentence," "Plan for a Satirical Novel of Contemporary Life," and other semifictions.

Like the "certain person" of "Bobok," two other evidently fictional characters, whom Dostoevsky presents as acquaintances, contribute extended "paradoxical" arguments. The "paradoxicalist" appears a few times, and the "witty bureaucrat," whom we encounter in the last issue, seems to have been designed to play a similar role. I have included these pieces as well.

And yet, once one understands the logic of the work's semifictional discourse, it is hard to say whether I have included *all* semifictions. The fact is that Dostoevsky frequently breaks into a narrative describing what might have happened. Some of these hypotheticals are rather brief, and others go on for a few pages but less than a whole entry. In "Environment," for instance, Dostoevsky refutes the liberal view that crime is merely a response to poor social conditions by picturing a specific act of criminal cruelty: "Have you seen how a peasant beats his wife? I have," he begins. After describing an imagined but realistic beating, Dostoevsky also anticipates the response of his readers. Should we call this part of the article a semifiction? The decision is evidently arbitrary.

Dostoevsky's vision and aesthetics lead by their nature to semifictional moments, which are, I think, the *Diary*'s defining ones. In the journalism, the diarist alternates between the real and the possible, between what did happen and what might have happened. He does so in part to show the complexity of things and in part to illustrate that the real includes not only actualized possibilities but also some unactualized ones.

The openness of time means that each of us could have been, and could still be, different. Semifictions become a way to dramatize the difference that could be, a way to "sideshadow" the actual. They encourage us to realize our best possibilities.

The Diary's Overall Design

I have taken some effort to exhibit Dostoevsky's intentions to make of a heterogeneous periodical an idiosyncratic literary work of a new type. For this reason, I have kept the complete issue for January 1876, which Dostoevsky carefully planned with his overall idea for the work in mind. With much the same purpose, I have also preserved several "joints" between pieces of different genres—for example, between "The Peasant Marey" and the article that precedes it and between "A Hundred-Year-Old Woman" and the article that follows it. These echo the first dramatized joint, the transition leading to "The Boy at Christ's Christmas Party."

The *Diary* makes metaliterature out of its own self-referential pieces and chapter titles, and so I have retained some of these. Even during his moments of apocalyptic frenzy, some chapter titles follow a similar pattern, but without the playfulness. We get, so to speak, the form of a joke without the humor.

Autobiography

Biographers and historians often focus on the *Diary*'s autobiographical passages. In addition to "The Peasant Marey," the *Diary* contains some of the best-known anecdotes about Dostoevsky's remarkable life. We learn of his psychology as a young revolutionary. Dostoevsky refutes from his own experience naïve accounts, whether offered as defense or criticism, of radicals and terrorists. The author explains how he, like many decent young radicals, could have wound up committing some bloody or foul crime while considering himself noble for doing so. Indeed, one of the diarist's recurrent themes is how good people can wind up performing horrendous acts.

Dostoevsky also describes or alludes to his state of mind as he faced mock execution for his revolutionary activity, as he suffered in his Siberian imprisonment, and as he rediscovered faith. In one remarkable passage, we learn of the happiest moment of his life, when, having written his first work of fiction, he was immediately discovered as a great artist. We also get his impressions of other significant writers he has known.

Poles and Jews, Pushkin and Tolstoy

I have tried to keep a representative sample of the *Diary*'s journalistic genres. Although I have eliminated or contracted several of the foreign policy pieces, enough remain to indicate the kind of thinking that took possession of Dostoevsky. I have always thought—I realize how naïve this will sound to many—that critics should be neither defense attorneys nor prosecutors because their prime loyalty should be to the truth. I have therefore included the passages where Dostoevsky seems to verge on madness (his prediction of the imminent end of the world, his account of history as a disembodied conflict of personified abstractions, and his notion of "simultaneity" or similar claims about history's inner plot).

For the same reason, I have kept those morally awful places where Dostoevsky speaks of the universal Catholic conspiracy, of Poles as treacherous agents of the pope, and, I think worst of all, the terrible sections on the Jews. Here is a place where Dostoevsky himself came to illustrate the *Diary*'s argument that decent people can be led to awful actions they consider noble. As both a commentator on and unwitting exemplar of this insight, he helps explain why the twentieth century has been, as he predicted, the bloodiest in human history. We need to learn from Dostoevsky in both roles, if we are to avoid a repetition.

I have kept only some of the work's literary criticism and commentary on great authors, but I think the most important pieces are here. I have of course included his famous Pushkin speech, along with his reply to a response to it, and most of his amazing comments on *Anna Karenina*. He praises Tolstoy's novel as sufficient to justify the existence of the Russian people; criticizes Levin and the author for their views on human suffering at a distance; and expresses sheer wonder at Tolstoy's capacity to describe true Christian forgiveness in a psychologically convincing way as no one—and here we need to hear, not even Dostoevsky himself—ever did or could. I have retained some comments on art and artistic vision even when they occur in articles primarily about other topics.

"Environment"

Dostoevsky's essay on "Environment" is arguably one of the best in Russian literature. Here it is worth explaining that by "environment," Dostoevsky does not mean nature. Rather, he means the idea that social conditions, rather than individual people, are responsible for human actions. It is therefore shortsighted to hold people responsible for crimes, which represent protests against the social conditions that truly caused them. (Even in my own childhood, the term *environmentalist* still meant a person who considered "society" responsible for all evil.)

Most critics have recognized that for Dostoevsky this view, in denying human freedom, destroys people's "human image" as well. It turns them into so many fleshy automatons and can therefore easily lead to either a suicidal sense of meaninglessness or mass murder in the name of some ideal. It is worth taking Dostoevsky seriously on this point.

But critics often overlook a still subtler argument in this article. The doctrine of the environment itself becomes part of the environment. That is, it is bound to occur not only to sociologists or judges contemplating a crime after it has been committed, but also to people considering whether to commit a crime. Unlike physical objects, people can know and respond to the laws purporting to describe them.

If people accept that sociological (or other) laws fully explain everything they do, then for them the very idea of crime, in the sense of an action that not only risks punishment but is also morally wrong, disappears. (The discussion of church courts and state courts in book 2 of *Karamazov* develops this theme.) How could such a belief, if widespread, not make crime more common? We can grasp the logic behind Dostoevsky's prediction that liberal societies, despite their growing prosperity and extension of rights, will witness an increase in crime. The reason for this unexpected outcome is that improvements that reduce crime will be overwhelmed by the growing acceptance of the doctrine of the "environment."

Aphorisms

Because of his rambling style, Dostoevsky has not developed a reputation for pithy sayings. He has few entries in Bartlett's or similar collections.

One can easily think of reasons for such nonquotability. A style in which alien voices interrupt the author favors dialogicity but not concision. The sense of the unspeakable complexity of things leads to qualifications on qualifications. And although writing in process may create a special kind of suspense—how will the author end this scene or complete this thought?—it does not usually lead to a sense of polish.

Nevertheless, in his novels and his journalism, Dostoevsky does offer a surprisingly large number of quotable lines overlooked by anthologizers. Students of Russian literature cite, more or less accurately, a few famous lines: "Beauty will save the world," "Compassion is the chief and perhaps only law of all human existence," "If there is no God, all is permitted," "Twice two equals five can also be a charming little thing," and some others. In discussions of totalitarianism one often encounters two famous comments from *The Possessed:* Shigalev's avowal that "starting with unlimited freedom, I arrive at unlimited despotism," and Pyotr Stepanovich's declaration that in the quest for equality "Cicero will have his tongue cut out, Copernicus will have his eyes put out, Shakespeare will be stoned. . . . Only the necessary is necessary."

Quotable phrases are also more common than one might suppose. Dmitri Karamazov famously refers to "the beauty of Sodom." *The Gambler* describes the emotion that leads people to fawn on their superiors with no hope of personal gain as "disinterested obsequiousness." And in *The Possessed* a bureaucrat's enjoyment of the power to make one wait is described as "administrative ecstasy."

Pyotr Stepanovich, Dmitri Karamazov, and many of Dostoevsky's narrators are ramblers, but it is perhaps for this very reason they feel the need to sum up their thought with an epigram. In *A Writer's Diary* such conclusions help define the essential rhythm of a work that searches for form and expression before our eyes.

Controlled, finished epigrams or phrases, when expression has at last been attained, come as a surprise. Like the *Diary*'s stories, they can often be read either for themselves or as the end point of the process leading to them.

A few examples will have to do:

> Some ideas exist that are unexpressed and unconscious but that simply are strongly felt; many such ideas are fused, as it were, with the human heart.—*Diary*, 73.3

> aggrieved aroma—73.8

> microscopic efforts [as the most effective]—1/76, 2.3

> Happiness lies not in happiness but only in the attempt to achieve it.—1/76, 3.2

> If the world came to an end and people were asked somewhere *there*: "Well, did you understand anything from your life on earth and draw any conclusion from it?" a person could silently hand over *Don Quixote:* "Here is my conclusion about life; can you condemn me for it?"—3/76, 2.1

> There is a primordial law of nature stating that, where mystical notions are concerned, even strictly mathematical proofs carry

no weight whatsoever . . . Faith and mathematical proof are two irreconcilable things.—3/76, 2.3

Suicides lately have become so common that people don't even talk about them any more. The Russian land seems to have lost the capacity to hold people on it.—5/76, 2.2

Here in Russia an idea falls on a person like a huge boulder and half crushes him; there he is, squirming under it, unable to get free.—5/76, 2.2

We can never exhaust a whole phenomenon and never reach its end, or its beginning. We know only the daily flow of the things we see, and this only on the surface; but the ends and the beginnings are things that, for human beings, still lie in the realm of the fantastic.—10/76, 1.3

The Noblest of Men, but I Don't Believe It Myself—11/76, 1.3 (chapter title in "The Meek One")

The Meek One Rebels—11/76, 1.5 (chapter title in "The Meek One")

Hurrah for the electric speed of human thought!—11/76, 1.6

Immutability [or: Inertia]! Oh, nature! People are alone on earth. . . . Everything is dead, and everywhere there are corpses. There are only people alone, and around them is silence—that is the earth!—11/76, 2.4

In a family dying of starvation the father or mother, toward the end when the sufferings of the children have become unbearable, will begin to hate those same children whom they had previously loved so much, precisely because their suffering has become *unbearable*. . . . I maintain that the awareness of one's own utter inability to assist or bring any aid or relief at all to suffering humanity, coupled with one's complete conviction of the existence of that suffering, can even *transform the love of humanity in your heart to hatred for humanity.*—12/76, 1.3

In Russia Darwin is quickly transformed into a pickpocket.—2/77, 1.3

. . . toadyism to someone else's ideas, for people are terribly in love with all things they are given ready-made.—2/77, 1.3

I swear, we would sooner believe in a miracle and an impossibility than in reality, than in the truth *we did not wish to see.* And so it always happens on earth; in this is the whole history of humanity.—5-6/77, 1.1

It is clear and intelligible to the point of obviousness that evil lies deeper in human beings than our socialist-physicians suppose; that no social structure will eliminate evil; that the human soul will remain as it always has been; that abnormality and sin arise from that soul itself; and, finally, that the laws of the human soul are still so little known, so obscure to science, so undefined, and so mysterious, that there are not and cannot be either physicians or *final* judges.—7-8/77, 2.3

It would be absurd to suppose that nature has endowed us [Russians] only with literary talents.—7-8/77, 2.3

The Fascination of the Diary

The *Diary* fascinates as a digressive work that focuses, as a whole of separable parts, and as a process that is its own product. It both is a work and illustrates the process of making a work. We watch the author struggling to use his artistic methods to shape whatever contingencies that ongoing reality presents. He sometimes succeeds brilliantly, sometimes succeeds only partially, and sometimes fails, but even these failures dramatize genuine searching with no guarantee of success. Such failures make the successes all the more dramatic, much as rambles set the stage for epigrams. As part of the design, they are not really failures at all.

The *Diary*'s genuine failures occur when it departs from its design altogether. Heterogeneity, uncertain processuality, and the search for meaning in prosaic, "microscopic" circumstances give way to the hectoring of a self-proclaimed seer.

To be sure, these passages have a kind of morbid fascination of their own, especially when, as in this abridgment, they do not occur too often. But I am most drawn to the book Dostoevsky originally intended. My hope is that readers will come to appreciate the *Diary* for the innovative work it sometimes succeeds in becoming; for the many stories, semifictions, and autobiographical narratives that show Dostoevsky's genius at its height; and for the articles on crime, psychology, and art that offer illuminating insights.

Notes

In the text of this introduction, references to parts of *A Writer's Diary* are given as follows. For the 1873 *Diary,* reference is to year and article; for example, 73.6 is "Bobok." For the monthly *Diary* (1876 and after), reference is to month/year, chapter.article. For example, 1/76, 2.1 is "A Boy at Christ's Christmas Party"; and 5–6/77, 1.3 is the "Plan for a Satirical Novel of Contemporary Life."

1. My dissertation was Dostoevsky's *"Diary of a Writer": Threshold Art* (Ph.D. diss., Yale, 1974), and my first book was *The Boundaries of Genre: Dostoevsky's "Diary of a Writer" and the Traditions of Literary Utopia* (Austin: University of Texas Press, 1981; reprinted, Evanston, Ill.: Northwestern University Press, 1988).

2. Gary Saul Morson, "Introductory Study: Dostoevsky's Great Experiment," in Fyodor Dostoevsky, *A Writer's Diary: Volume 1, 1873–1876,* trans. and anno. Kenneth Lantz (Evanston, Ill.: Northwestern University Press, 1994), 1–117. Henceforth cited in text and notes as "IS."

3. Gary Saul Morson, *Narrative and Freedom: The Shadows of Time* (New Haven, Conn.: Yale University Press, 1994).

4. For a more detailed account of the origin and refinement of the idea for *A Writer's Diary,* see chapter 1 of *The Boundaries of Genre.* This letter, to Dostoevsky's friend Stefan Yanovsky, appears in the four-volume edition of Dostoevsky's letters edited by A. S. Dolinin (Moscow and Leningrad: Gosizdat, 1929–58), 3:284. Henceforth this edition is cited in text as *Pis'ma.* This and other quotations about the diary's form are discussed in *Boundaries of Genre,* 32–33.

5. Lev Tolstoi, "Neskol'ko slov po povody knigi 'Voina i mir'" [Some words about the book *War and Peace*], in L. N. Tolstoi, *Polnoe sobranie sochinenii* [Complete works], 90 vols., ed. V. G. Chertkov, et al. (Moscow: Khudozhestvennaia literatura, 1929–58), 16:7. Henceforth cited in text and notes as the Jubilee edition. The article first appeared in *Russkii arkhiv* [Russian archive] in 1868.

6. V. G. Belinsky, *Selected Philosophical Works* (Moscow: Foreign Languages, 1956), 373, 386–87.

7. Mikhail Bakunin, *Selected Writings*, ed. Arthur Lehning, trans. Steven Cox and Olive Stevens (New York: Grove, 1974), 58.

8. For more on Shklovsky's views, see Morson, "IS," 3–4.

9. For a list of such studies of the *Diary*, see Morson, *Boundaries of Genre*, 189, note 5.

10. I discuss "backward causation" in more detail in *Narrative and Freedom*.

11. On *ressentiment* and its relation to Dostoevsky, see the classic study by Michael André Bernstein, *Bitter Carnival: "Ressentiment" and the Abject Hero* (Princeton, N.J.: Princeton University Press, 1992).

12. From "Otvet 'Russomu vestniku'" [Answer to the *Russian Herald*], in F. M. Dostoevskii, *Polnoe sobranie sochinenii v tridtsati tomakh* [Complete Works in Thirty Volumes] (Leningrad: Nauka, 1972–90), 19:134.

13. Percy Bysshe Shelley, "A Defense of Poetry," in *Critical Theory Since Plato*, ed. Hazard Adams (New York: Harcourt Brace, 1971), 499. Henceforth cited in text as Shelley.

14. Fyodor Dostoevsky, *The Brothers Karamazov*, trans. Constance Garnett (New York: Modern Library, 1966), 276. Henceforth cited in text as *Karamazov*.

15. Elsewhere I have used the term *prosaics*, my own coinage, in a quite different sense. The two senses should not be confused.

16. For the experienced reader, indeed, even a first reading takes the form of an anticipated rereading, which is why in novels, but not in life, we can presume that apparently chance events will turn out to have a meaning. If the hero gives a pie to a convict in chapter 1, that incident will turn out to matter. Good artists bake marvelous pies.

17. John Locke, *An Essay Concerning Human Understanding*, ed. A. C. Fraser (New York: Dover, 1959), 1:349.

18. As cited in Joseph Frank, *Dostoevsky: The Miraculous Years, 1865–1871* (Princeton, N.J.: Princeton University Press, 1995), 271. I discuss *The Idiot* and its creation in detail in "Tempics and *The Idiot*," in *Celebrating Creativity: Essays in Honour of Jostein Bortnes*, ed. Knut Grimstad and Ingun Lunde (Bergen: University of Bergen, 1997). *Tempics* was the term I then used for the prosaics of process.

19. Fyodor Dostoyevsky, *The Idiot*, trans. Constance Garnett (New York: Modern Library, 1935), 375. Henceforth cited in text as *Idiot*.

20. Tolstoi, Jubilee edition, 13:54.

21. Rebecca W. Bushnell, *A Culture of Teaching: Early Modern Humanism in Theory and Practice* (Ithaca, N.Y.: Cornell University Press, 1996), 129.

22. Cited (from Erasmus's *De Copia*) in Bushnell, *Culture of Teaching*, 135–36.

23. Alexander Pope, *Selected Poetry and Prose,* ed. William K. Wimsatt, Jr. (New York: Holt, Rinehart, 1965), 128.

A Note on the Abridged Text

Dostoevsky often uses ellipses for rhetorical reasons. Unless otherwise noted, ellipses indicate ellipses in the original. Editorial ellipses, indicating that part of an article has been omitted to create the abridgment, are bracketed [...].

A WRITER'S DIARY

1873

Article 1. Introduction

On the twentieth of December I learned that everything had been settled and that I was the editor of *The Citizen*. This extraordinary event—extraordinary for me at least (I don't wish to offend anyone)—came about in a rather simple fashion, however. On the twentieth of December I had just read in the *Moscow News* the account of the wedding of the Chinese emperor; it left a strong impression on me. This magnificent and, apparently, extremely complex event also came about in a remarkably simple fashion: every last detail of the affair had been provided for and decreed a thousand years ago in nearly two hundred volumes of ceremonial. Comparing the enormity of the events in China with my own appointment as editor, I felt a sudden sense of ingratitude to our Russian practices, despite the ease with which my appointment had been confirmed. And I thought that we, that is, Prince Meshchersky and I, would have found it incomparably more advantageous to publish *The Citizen* in China. Everything is so clear over there. . . . On the appointed day we both would have presented ourselves at China's Main Administration for Press Affairs. After kowtowing and licking the floor, we would rise, raise our index fingers, and respectfully bow our heads. The Plenipotentiary-in-Chief for Press Affairs would, of course, pretend to take no more notice of us than he would of an errant fly. But the Third Assistant to the Third Secretary would rise, holding the warrant of my appointment as editor, and would pronounce in an impressive but gentle voice the admonition prescribed by the ceremonial. It would be so clear and so comprehensible that we both would be immensely pleased to hear it. Were I in China and were I stupid and honest enough, when taking on the editorship and acknowledging my own limited abilities, to experience fear and pangs of conscience, someone would at once prove to me that I was doubly stupid to entertain such feelings and that from that very moment I would have no need of intelligence at all, assuming I had had any in the first place; on the contrary, it would be far better if I had none at all. And without a doubt, this would be a most pleasant thing to hear. Concluding with the fine words: "Go thou, Editor; henceforth thou mayest eat rice and drink tea with thy conscience newly set at rest," the Third Assistant to the Third Secretary would hand me a beautiful warrant printed in gold letters on red silk. Prince Meshchersky would pass over a substantial bribe, and the two of us would go home and immediately put out such a magnificent edition of *The Citizen* as we could never publish here. In China we would put out an excellent publication.

I suspect, however, that in China Prince Meshchersky would certainly have tricked me by inviting me to be editor; he would have done it mainly so that I could stand in for him at the Main Administration of Press Affairs whenever he was summoned to have his heels beaten with bamboo sticks. But I would outsmart him: I would at once stop publication of *Bismarck* and would myself commence writing articles so excellent that I would be summoned to the bamboo sticks only after every other issue. I would learn to write, however.

I would be an excellent writer in China; here, that sort of thing is much more difficult. There, everything has been anticipated and planned for a thousand years ahead, while here everything is topsy-turvy for a thousand years. There I would have no choice but to write clearly, so that I'm not sure who would read me. Here, if you want people to read you it's better to write so that no one understands. Only in the *Moscow News* do they write column-and-a-half editorials and—to my astonishment—they are written clearly, even if they are the products of a well-known pen. In *The Voice* such editorials go on for eight, ten, twelve, and even thirteen columns. And so you see how many columns you must use up in order to win respect.

In Russia, talking to other people is a science; at first glance, at least, it seems just the same as in China. Here, as there, there are a few very simplified and purely scientific techniques. Formerly, for instance, the words "I don't understand a thing" meant only that the person who uttered them was ignorant; now they bring great honor. One need only say, proudly and with a frank air, "I don't understand religion; I don't understand anything about Russia; I don't understand anything about art," and immediately you place yourself above the crowd. And it's especially good if you really don't understand anything.

But this simplified technique proves nothing. In essence, each one of us in Russia, without thinking much about it, suspects that everyone else

is ignorant and never asks, conversely, "What if I'm the one who's ignorant, in fact?" It's a situation that ought to please us all, and yet no one is
pleased and everyone gets angry. Indeed, sober thought in our time is all
but impossible: it costs too much. It is true that people buy ready-made
ideas. They are sold everywhere, and even given away; but the ones that
come free of charge prove to be even more expensive, and people are
already beginning to realize that. The result is benefit to none and the
same old disorder.

We are, if you like, the same as China, but without her sense of order.
We are barely beginning the process that is already coming to an end in
China. No doubt we will reach that same end, but when? In order to get a
thousand volumes of ceremonial so as at last to win the right not to think
deeply about anything, we must experience at least another thousand
years of sober thought. And there you have it—no one wants to hasten
this term because no one wants to think.

Something else that is true: if no one wants to think, then, it would
seem, so much the easier for the Russian writer. Indeed, it really is easier;
and woe to the writer and publisher who in our time begins to think
soberly. It's even worse for one who decides to study and to understand
things on his own, and still worse for one who makes a sincere declaration of his intention. And if he declares that he has already managed to
understand a tiny smidgen and wants to express his ideas, then everyone
quickly drops him. The only thing he can do is to seek out some suitable
individual, or even hire one, and simply talk to him and to him alone.
Perhaps he could publish a magazine for that one individual. It's a loathsome situation, because it amounts to talking to yourself and publishing a
magazine only for your own amusement. I strongly suspect that for a long
time yet *The Citizen* will have to talk to itself and appear only for its own
amusement. Remember that medical science considers talking to oneself
a sign of predisposition to insanity. *The Citizen* certainly must speak to
citizens, and that is precisely its whole dilemma!

And so this is the sort of publication with which I have become
involved. My situation is as uncertain as it can be. But I shall talk to myself
and for my own amusement, in the form of this diary, whatever may come
of it. What shall I talk about? About everything that strikes me and sets
me to thinking. If I should find a reader and, God forbid, an opponent, I
realize that one must be able to carry on a conversation and know whom

to address and how to address him. I shall try to master this skill because among us, that is to say, in literature, it is the most difficult one of all. Besides, there are different kinds of opponents: one cannot strike up a conversation with every one. I'll tell you a story I heard the other day. They say it is an ancient fable, perhaps even of Indian origin, and that's a very comforting thought.

Once upon a time the pig got into a quarrel with the lion and challenged him to a duel. When the pig came home he thought the matter over and lost his nerve. The whole herd assembled to consider the matter and announced their decision as follows: "Now then, brother pig, there is a wallow not far from here; go and have a good roll in it and then proceed to the duel. You'll see what happens."

The pig did just that. The lion arrived, took a sniff, wrinkled up his nose, and walked away. And for a long time thereafter the pig boasted that the lion had turned tail and fled the field of battle.

That's the fable. Of course we don't have any lions here—we don't have the climate for them and they're too grand a thing for us in any case. But in place of the lion put an honest person, such as each of us is obliged to be, and the moral comes out the same.

Apropos of that, I'll tell you another little story.

Once when speaking with the late Herzen I paid him many compliments on his book *From the Other Shore.* To my great pleasure, Mikhail Petrovich Pogodin heaped praise on this same book in his excellent and most curious article about his meeting abroad with Herzen. The book is written in the form of a dialogue between Herzen and his opponent.

"What I especially like," I remarked in passing, "is that your opponent is also very clever. You must agree that in many instances he backs you right to the wall."

"Why that's the essence of the whole piece," laughed Herzen. "I'll tell you a story. Once when I was in St. Petersburg, Belinsky dragged me off to his place and sat me down to listen to him read an article, 'A Conversation Between Mr. A and Mr. B,' that he had written in some heat. (You can find it in his *Collected Works.*) In this article, Mr. A., who is Belinsky himself, of course, is made out to be very clever, while his opponent, Mr. B., is rather shallow. When Belinsky had finished reading, he asked me with feverish anticipation:

"'Well, what do you think?'"

" 'Oh, it's fine, very fine, and it's obvious that you are very clever. But whatever made you waste your time talking to a fool like that?'

"Belinsky threw himself on the sofa, buried his face in a pillow, and shouted, laughing for all he was worth:

" 'Oh, you've got me there, you really have!' "

Article 3. Environment

I think that all jurors the whole world over, and our jurors in particular, must share a feeling of power (they have other feelings as well, of course); more precisely, they have a feeling of autocratic power. This can be an ~~ugly feeling, at least when it dominates their other feelings.~~ Even though it may not be obvious, even though it may be suppressed by a mass of other, nobler emotions, this sense of autocratic power must be a strong presence in the heart of every juror, even when he is most acutely aware of his civic duty. I suppose that this is somehow a product of the laws of nature themselves. And so, I recall how terribly curious I was, in one respect at least, when our new (just) courts were instituted. In my flights of fancy I saw trials where almost all the jurors might be peasants who only yesterday were serfs. The prosecutor and the defense lawyers would address them, trying to curry favor and divine their mood, while our good peasants would sit and keep their mouths shut: "So that's how things are these days. If I feel like lettin' the fella off, I'll do it; and if not, it's Siberia for him."

And yet the surprising thing now is that they do not convict the accused but acquit them consistently. Of course, this is also an exercise, almost even an abuse of power, but in one direction, toward an extreme, a sentimental one, perhaps—one can't tell. But it is a general, almost preconceived tendency, just as if everyone had conspired. There can be no doubt how widespread this "tendency" is. And the problem is that the mania for acquittal regardless of the circumstances has developed not only among peasants, yesterday's insulted and humiliated, but has seized all Russian jurors, even those from the uppermost classes such as noblemen and university professors. The universality of this tendency in itself presents a most curious topic for reflection and leads one to diverse and sometimes even strange surmises.

Not long ago one of our most influential newspapers briefly set forth, in a very modest and well-intentioned little article, the following hypothesis: perhaps our jurors, as people who suddenly, without rhyme or reason, sense the magnitude of the power that has been conferred upon them (simply out of the blue, as it were), and who for centuries have been oppressed and downtrodden—perhaps they are inclined to take any opportunity to spite authorities such as the prosecutor, just for the fun of it or, so to say, for the sake of contrast with the past. Not a bad hypothesis and also not without a certain playful spirit of its own; but, of course, it can't explain everything.

"We just feel sorry to wreck the life of another person; after all, he's a human being too. Russians are compassionate people"—such is the conclusion reached by others, as I've sometimes heard it expressed.

However, I have always thought that in England, for instance, the people are also compassionate; and even if they do not have the same softheartedness as we Russians, then at least they have a sense of humanity; they have an awareness and a keen sense of Christian duty to their neighbor, a sense which, perhaps, taken to a high degree, to a firm and independent conviction, may be even stronger than ours, when you take into account the level of education over there and their long tradition of independent thought. Over there, such power didn't just tumble down on them out of the blue, after all. Indeed, they themselves invented the very system of trial by jury; they borrowed it from no one, but affirmed it through centuries; they took it from life and didn't merely receive it as a gift.

Yet over there the juror understands from the very moment he takes his place in the courtroom that he is not only a sensitive individual with a tender heart but is first of all a citizen. He even thinks (correctly or not) that fulfilling his civic duty stands even higher than any private victory of the heart. Not very long ago there was a clamor throughout the kingdom when a jury acquitted one notorious thief. The hubbub all over the country proved that if sentences just like ours are possible over there, then all the same they happen rarely, as exceptions, and they quickly rouse public indignation. An English juror understands above all that in his hands rests the banner of all England; that he has already ceased to be a private individual and is obliged to represent the opinion of his country. The capacity to be a citizen is just that capacity to elevate oneself to the level of the opinion of the entire country. Oh, yes, there are "compassionate" verdicts there, and the influence of the "corrupting environment" (our favorite doctrine now, it seems) is taken into consideration. But this is done only up to a certain limit, as far as is tolerated by the common sense of the country and the level of its informed and Christian morality (and that level, it seems, is quite high). Nonetheless, very often the English juror grudgingly pronounces the guilty verdict, understanding first of all that his duty consists primarily in using that verdict to bear witness to all his fellow citizens that in old England (for which any one of them is prepared to shed his blood) vice is still called vice and villainy is still called villainy, and that the moral foundations of the country endure—firm, unchanged, standing as they stood before.

"Suppose we do assume," I hear a voice saying, "that your firm foundations (Christian ones, that is) endure and that in truth one must be a citizen above all, must hold up the banner, etc., etc., as you said. I won't challenge that for the time being. But where do you think we'll find such a citizen in Russia? Just consider our situation only a few years ago! Civic rights (and what rights!) have tumbled down on our citizen as if from a mountain. They've crushed him, and they're still only a burden to him, a real burden!"

"Of course, there's truth in what you say," I answer the voice, a bit despondent, "but still, the Russian People. . . ."

"The Russian People? Please!" says another voice. "We've just heard that the boon of citizenship has tumbled down from the mountain and crushed the People. Perhaps they not only feel that they've received so much power as a gift, but even sense that it was wasted on them because they got it for nothing and aren't yet worthy of it. Please note that this certainly doesn't mean that they really aren't worthy of the gift, and that it was *unnecessary* or *premature* to give it; quite the contrary: the People themselves, in their humble conscience, acknowledge that they are unworthy, and the People's humble, yet lofty, awareness of their own unworthiness is precisely the guarantee that they are worthy. And meanwhile the People, in their humility, are troubled. Who has peered into the innermost secret places of their hearts? Is there anyone among us who can claim truly to know the Russian People? No, it's not simply a matter here of compassion and softheartedness, as you, sir, said so scoffingly. It's that this power itself is frightful! We have been frightened by this dreadful power over human fate, over the fates of our brethren, and until we mature into our citizenship, we will show mercy. We show mercy out of fear. We sit as jurors and think, perhaps: 'Are we any better than the accused? We have money and are free from want, but were we to be in his position we might do even worse than he did—so we show mercy.' So maybe it's a good thing, this heartfelt mercy. Maybe it's a pledge of some sublime form of Christianity of the future which the world has not yet known!'"

"That's a partly Slavophile voice," I think to myself. It's truly a comforting thought, but the conjecture about the People's humility before the power they have received gratis and that has been bestowed upon them, still "unworthy" of it, is, of course, somewhat neater than the suggestion that they want to "tease the prosecutor a bit," although even the latter still appeals to me because of its realism (accepting it, of course, more as an individual case, which indeed is what its author intended). But still . . . this is what troubles me most of all: how is it that our People suddenly began to be so afraid of a little suffering? "It's a painful thing," they say, "to convict a man." And what of it? So take your pain away with you. The truth stands higher than your pain.

In fact, if we consider that we ourselves are sometimes even worse than the criminal, we thereby also acknowledge that we are half to blame for his crime. If he has transgressed the law which the nation prescribed for him, then we ourselves are to blame that he now stands before us. If we were better, then he, too, would be better and would not now be standing here before us. . . .

"And so now we ought to acquit him?"

No, quite the contrary: now is precisely the time we must tell the truth and call evil evil; in return, we must ourselves take on half the burden of the sentence. We will enter the courtroom with the thought that we, too, are guilty. This pain of the heart, which everyone so fears now and which we will take with us when we leave the court, will be punishment for us. If this pain is genuine and severe, then it will purge us and make us better. And when we have made ourselves better, we will also improve the environment and make it better. And this is the only way it can be made better. But to flee from our own pity and acquit everyone so as not to suffer ourselves—why, that's too easy. Doing that, we slowly and surely come to the conclusion that there are no crimes at all, and "the environment is to blame" for everything. We inevitably reach the point where we consider crime even a duty, a noble protest against the environment. "Since society is organized in such a vile fashion, one can't get along in it without protest and without crimes." "Since society is organized in such a vile fashion, one can only break out of it with a knife in hand." So runs the doctrine of the environment, as opposed to Christianity which, fully recognizing the pressure of the environment and having proclaimed mercy for the sinner, still places a moral duty on the individual to struggle with the environment and marks the line where the environment ends and duty begins.

In making the individual responsible, Christianity thereby acknowledges his freedom. In making the individual dependent on every flaw in the social structure, however, the doctrine of the environment reduces him to an absolute nonentity, exempts him totally from every personal moral duty and from all independence, reduces him to the lowest form of slavery imaginable. If that's so, then if a man wants some tobacco and has no money, he can kill another to get some tobacco. And why not? An educated man, who suffers more keenly than an uneducated one from unsatisfied needs, requires money to satisfy them. So why shouldn't he kill an uneducated man if he has no other way of getting money? Haven't you listened to the voices of the defense lawyers: "Of course," they say, "the law has been violated; of course he committed a crime in killing this uneducated man. But, gentlemen of the jury, take into consideration that...." And so on. Why such views have almost been expressed already, and not only "almost." ...

"But you, however," says someone's sarcastic voice, "you seem to be charging the People with subscribing to the latest theory of the environment; but how on earth did they get that theory? Sometimes these jurors sitting there are all peasants, and every one of them considers it a mortal sin to eat meat during the fasts. You should have just accused them squarely of harboring social tendencies."

"Of course, you're right—what do they care about 'environment,' the peasants as a whole, that is?" I think to myself. "But still, these ideas float about in the air; there is something pervasive about an idea...."

"Listen to that, now!" laughs the sarcastic voice.

"But what if our People are particularly inclined toward this theory of the environment, by their very nature, or by their Slavic inclinations, if you like? What if they are the best raw material in Europe for those who preach such a doctrine?"

The sarcastic voice guffaws even louder, but it's a bit forced.

No, this is still only a trick someone is pulling on the People, not a "philosophy of the environment." There's a mistake here, a fraud, and a very seductive fraud.

One can explain this fraud, using an example at least, as follows:

Let's grant that the People do call criminals "unfortunates" and give them pennies and bread. What do they mean by doing that, and what have they meant over the course of perhaps some centuries? Is it Christian truth or the truth of the "environment"? Here is precisely where we find the stumbling block and the place where the lever is concealed which the propagator of "the environment" could seize upon to effect.

Some ideas exist that are unexpressed and unconscious but that simply are strongly felt; many such ideas are fused, as it were, with the human heart. They are present in the People generally, and in humanity taken as a whole. Only while these ideas lie unconscious in peasant life and are simply felt strongly and truly can the People live a vigorous "living life." The whole energy of the life of the People consists in the striving to bring these hidden ideas to light. The more obstinately the People cling to them, the less capable they are of betraying their instincts, the less inclined they are to yield to diverse and erroneous explanations of these ideas—the stronger, more steadfast, and happier they are. Among such ideas concealed within the Russian People—the ideas of the Russian People—is the notion of calling a crime a misfortune and the criminal an unfortunate.

This notion is purely Russian. It has not been observed among any European people. In the West it's proclaimed only by some philosophers and thinkers. But our People proclaimed it long before their philosophers and thinkers. It does not follow, however, that the People would never be led astray at least temporarily or superficially by some thinker's false interpretation of this idea. The ultimate interpretation and the last word will remain, undoubtedly, always the People's, but *in the short term* this might not be the case.

To put it briefly, when they use the word "unfortunate," the People are saying to the "unfortunate" more or less as follows: "You have sinned and are suffering, but we, too, are sinners. Had we been in your place we might have done even worse. Were we better than we are, perhaps you might not be in prison. With the retribution for your crime you have also taken on the burden for all our lawlessness. Pray for us, and we pray for you. But for now, unfortunate ones, accept these alms of ours; we give them that you might know we remember you and have not broken our ties with you as a brother."

You must agree that there is nothing easier than to apply the doctrine of "environment" to such a view: "Society is vile, and therefore we too are vile; but we are rich, we are secure, and it is only by chance that we escaped encountering the things you did. And had we encountered them, we would have acted as you did. Who is to blame? The environment is to blame. And so there is only a faulty social structure, but there is no crime whatsoever."

And the trick I spoke of earlier is the sophistry used to draw such conclusions.

No, the People do not deny there is crime, and they know that the criminal is guilty. The People know that they also share the guilt in every crime. But by accusing themselves, they prove that they do not believe in "environment"; they believe, on the contrary, that the environment depends completely on them, on their unceasing repentance and quest for self-perfection. Energy, work, and struggle—these are the means through which the environment is improved. Only by work and struggle do we attain independence and a sense of our own dignity. "Let us become better, and the environment will be better." This is what the Russian People sense so strongly but do not express in their concealed idea of the criminal as an unfortunate.

Now imagine if the criminal himself, hearing from the People that he is an "unfortunate," should consider himself only an unfortunate and not a criminal. In that case the People will renounce such a false interpretation and call it a betrayal of the People's truth and faith.

I could offer some examples of this, but let us set them aside for the moment and say the following.

The criminal and the person planning to commit a crime are two different people, but they belong to the same category. What if the criminal, consciously preparing to commit a crime, says to himself: "There is no crime!" Will the People still call him an "unfortunate"?

Perhaps they would; in fact they certainly would. The People are compassionate, and there is no one more unfortunate than one who has even ceased to consider himself a criminal: he is an animal, a beast. And what of it if he does not even understand that he is an animal and has crippled his own conscience? He is only doubly unfortunate. Doubly unfortunate, but also doubly a criminal. The People will feel compassion for him but will not renounce their own truth. Never have the People, in calling a criminal an "unfortunate," ceased to regard him as a criminal! And there could be no greater misfortune for us than if the People agreed with the criminal and replied to him: "No, you are not guilty, for there is no 'crime'"!

Such is our faith—our common faith, I should like to say; it is the faith of all who have hopes and expectations. I should like to add two more things.

I was in prison and saw criminals, hardened criminals. I repeat: it was a hard school. Not one of them ceased to regard himself as a criminal. In appearance they were a terrible and a cruel lot. Only the stupid ones or newcomers would "put on a show," however, and the others made fun of them. For the most part they were a gloomy, pensive lot. No one discussed his own crimes. I never heard a protest of any kind. Even speaking aloud of one's crimes was not done. From time to time we would hear a defiant or bragging voice, and all the prisoners, as one man, would cut the upstart short. Talking about *that* was simply not acceptable. Yet I believe that perhaps not one of them escaped the long inner suffering that cleansed and strengthened him. I saw them lonely and pensive; I saw them in church praying before confession; I listened to their single, unexpected words and exclamations; I remember their faces. Oh, believe me, in his heart not one of them considered himself justified!

I would not like my words to be taken as harsh. Still, I will risk speaking my mind and say plainly: with strict punishment, prison, and hard labor you would have saved perhaps half of them. You would have eased their burden, not increased it. Purification through suffering is easier—easier, I say, than the lot you assign to many of them by wholesale acquittals in court. You only plant cynicism in their hearts; you leave them with a seductive question and with contempt for you yourselves. You don't believe it? They have contempt for you and your courts and for the justice system of the whole country! Into their hearts you pour disbelief in the People's truth, in God's truth; you leave them confused. . . . The criminal walks out of the court thinking: "So that's how it is now; they've gone soft. They've gotten clever, it seems. Maybe they're afraid. So I can do the same thing again. It's clear enough: I was in such a hard pinch, I couldn't help stealing."

And do you really think that when you let them all off as innocent or with a recommendation for mercy you are giving them the chance to reform? He'll reform, all right! Why should he worry? "It looks like I didn't do anything wrong at all"—this is what he thinks *in the final analysis*. You yourselves put that notion in his head. The main thing is that faith in the law and in the People's truth is being shaken.

Not long ago I spent several years living abroad. When I left Russia the new courts were only in their infancy. How eagerly I would read in our newspapers there everything concerning the Russian courts. With real sorrow I also observed Russians living abroad and their children, who did not know their native language or who were forgetting it. It was clear to me that half of them, by the very nature of things, would eventually become expatriates. I always found it painful to think about that: so much vitality, so many of the best, perhaps, of our people, while we in Russia are so in need of good people! But sometimes as I left the reading room, by God, gentlemen, I became reconciled to the temporary emigration and émigrés in spite of myself. My heart ached. I would read in the newspaper of a wife who murdered her husband and who was acquitted. The crime is obvious and proven; she herself confesses. "Not guilty." A young man breaks open a strongbox and steals the money. "I was in love," he says, "very much in love, and I needed money to buy things for my mistress." "Not guilty." It would not be so terrible if these cases could be justified by compassion or pity; but truly I could not understand the reasons for the acquittal and I was bewildered. I came away with a troubled feeling, almost as if I had been personally insulted. In these bitter moments I would sometimes imagine Russia as a kind of quagmire or swamp on which someone had contrived to build a palace. The surface of the soil looks firm and smooth, but in reality it is like the surface of some sort of jellied green-pea aspic, and once you step on it you slip down to the very abyss. I reproached myself for my faintheartedness; I was encouraged by the thought that, being far away, I might be mistaken and that I myself was the kind of temporary émigré I spoke of; that I could not see things at first hand nor hear clearly. . . .

And now I have been home again for a long while.

"But come now—do they really feel pity?" That's the question! Don't laugh because I put so much stress on it. At least pity provides some sort of explanation; at least it leads you out of the darkness, and without it we comprehend nothing and see only gloomy blackness inhabited by some madman.

A peasant beats his wife, inflicts injuries on her for many years, abuses her worse than his dog. In despair to the point of suicide and scarcely in her right mind, she goes to the village court. They send her away with an indifferent mumble: "Learn to live together." Can this be pity? These are the dull words of a drunkard who has just come to after a long spree, a man who is scarcely aware that you are standing in front of him, who stupidly and listlessly waves you away so you won't bother him; a man whose tongue doesn't work properly, who has nothing in his head but alcohol fumes and folly.

The woman's story, by the way, is well known and happened only recently. We read about it in all the newspapers and, perhaps, we still remember it. Plainly and simply, the wife who suffered from her husband's beatings hanged herself; the husband was tried and found deserving of mercy. But for a long time thereafter I fancied I could see all the circumstances of the case; I see them even now.

I kept imagining his figure: he was tall, the reports said, very thick-set, powerful, fair-haired. I would add another touch: thinning hair. His body is white and bloated; his movements slow and solemn; his gaze is steady. He speaks little and rarely and drops his words like precious pearls, cherishing them above all else. Witnesses testified that he had a cruel nature: he would catch a chicken and hang it by its feet, head down, just for his own pleasure. This amused him—a most characteristic trait! For a number of years he had beaten his wife with anything that was at hand—ropes or sticks. He would take up a floorboard, thrust her feet into the gap, press the board down, and beat and beat her. I think he himself did not know why he was beating her; he just did it, probably from the same motives for which he hung the chicken. He sometimes also starved her, giving her no bread for three days. He would place the bread on a shelf, summon her, and say: "Don't you dare touch that bread. That's *my* bread." And that's another remarkably characteristic trait! She and her ten-year-old child would go off begging to the neighbors: if they were given bread they would eat; if not, they went hungry. When he asked her to work she did everything with never a hesitation or a murmur, intimidated, until finally she became a virtual madwoman. I can imagine what she looked like: she must have been a very small woman, thin as a rail. It sometimes happens that very large, heavyset men with white, bloated bodies marry very small, skinny women (they are even inclined to choose such, I've noticed), and it is so strange to watch them standing or walking together. It seems to me that if she had become pregnant by him in her final days it would have been an even more characteristic and essential finishing touch; otherwise the picture is somehow incomplete. Have you seen how a peasant beats his wife? I have. He begins with a rope or a strap. Peasant life is without aesthetic pleasures such as music, theaters, and magazines; it is natural that this void be filled with something. Once he has bound his wife or thrust her feet into an opening in the floorboards, our peasant would begin, probably methodically, indifferently, even sleepily; his blows are measured; he doesn't listen to her cries and her pleading; or rather, he does listen, and listens with delight—otherwise what satisfaction would there be in beating her? Do you know, gentlemen, people are born in various circumstances: can you not conceive that this woman, in other circumstances, might have been some Juliet or Beatrice from Shakespeare, or Gretchen from *Faust*? I'm not saying that she was—it would be absurd to claim that—but yet there could be the embryo of something very noble in her soul, something no worse, perhaps, than what could be found in a woman of noble birth: a loving, even lofty, heart; a character filled with a most original beauty. The very fact that she hesitated so long in taking her own life shows something so quiet, meek, patient, and affectionate about her. And so this same Beatrice or Gretchen is beaten and whipped like a dog! The blows rain down faster and faster, harder and harder—countless blows. He begins to grow heated and finds it to his taste. At last he grows wild, and his wildness pleases him. The animal cries of his victim intoxicate him like liquor: "I'll wash your feet and drink the water," cries Beatrice in an inhuman voice. But finally she grows quiet; she stops shrieking and only groans wildly, her breath catching constantly; and now the blows come ever faster and ever more furiously. . . . Suddenly he throws down the strap; like a madman he seizes a stick or a branch, anything he can find, and shatters it with three final, terrible blows across her back—enough! He steps away, sits down at the table, heaves a sigh, and sets to drinking his kvass. A small girl, their daughter (and they did have a daughter!) trembles on the stove in the corner, trying to hide: she has heard her mother crying. He walks out of the hut. Toward dawn the mother would revive and get up, groaning and crying with every movement, and set off to milk the cow, fetch water, go to work.

And as he leaves he tells her in his slow, methodical, and serious voice: "Don't you dare eat that bread. That's *my* bread."

Toward the end he also liked hanging her by her feet as well, the same way he had hung the chicken. Probably he would hang her, step aside, and sit down to have his porridge. When he had finished his meal he would suddenly seize the strap again and set to work on the hanging woman.... The little girl, all atremble and huddled on the stove, would steal a wild glance at her mother hanging by her heels and try to hide again.

The mother hanged herself on a May morning, a bright spring day, probably. She had been seen the night before, beaten and completely crazed. Before her death she had also made a trip to the village court, and there it was that they mumbled to her, "Learn to live together."

When the rope tightened around the mother's neck and she was making her last strangled cries, the little girl called out from the corner: "Mamma, why are you choking?" Then she cautiously approached her, called out to the hanging woman, gazed wildly at her. In the course of the morning she came out of her corner to look at the mother again, until the father finally returned.

And now we see him before the court—solemn, puffy-faced, closely following the proceedings. He denies everything. "We never spoke a sharp word to each other," he says, dropping a few of his words like precious pearls. The jury leaves, and after a "brief deliberation" they bring in the verdict: "Guilty, but with *recommendation for clemency.*"

Note that the girl testified against her father. She told everything and, they say, wrung tears from the spectators. Had it not been for the "clemency" of the jury he would have been exiled to Siberia. But with "clemency" he need spend only eight months in prison and then come home and ask that his daughter, who testified against him on behalf of her mother, be returned to him. Once again he will have someone to hang by the heels.

"A recommendation for clemency!" And this verdict was given in full cognizance of the facts. They knew what awaited the child. Clemency to whom, and for what? You feel as if you are in some sort of whirlwind that's caught you up and twists and turns you around.

Wait a moment, I'll tell you one more story.

Once, before the new courts were established (not long before, however), I read of this particular little incident in our newspapers: a mother was holding in her arms her baby of a year or fourteen months. Children of that age are teething; they are ailing and cry and suffer a good deal. It seems the mother lost patience with the baby; perhaps she was very busy, and here she had to carry this child and listen to its heart-rending cries. She got angry. But can such a small child be beaten for something like this? It's a pity to strike it, and what can it understand anyway? It's so helpless and can't do a thing for itself. And even if you do beat it, it won't stop crying. Its little tears will just keep pouring out and it will put its arms around you; or else it will start to kiss you and just go on crying. So she didn't beat the child. A samovar full of boiling water stood in the room. She put the child's little hand right under the tap and opened it. She held the child's hand under the boiling water for a good ten seconds.

That's a fact; I read it. But now imagine if this happened today and the woman was brought to trial. The jury goes out and, "after a brief deliberation," brings in the verdict: "Recommendation for clemency."

Well, imagine: I invite mothers, at least, to imagine it. And the defense lawyer, no doubt, would probably start twisting the facts:

"Gentlemen of the jury, this is not what one could call a humane act, but you must consider the case as a whole; you must take into account the circumstances, the environment. This woman is poor; she is the only person working in the household; she puts up with a lot. She had not even the means to hire a nurse for her child. It is only natural that at a moment when, filled with anger caused by the corroding environment, so to say, gentlemen, it is only natural that she should have put the child's hand under the samovar tap . . . , and so. . . . "

Oh, of course I fully appreciate the value of the legal profession; it is an elevated calling and a universally respected one. But one cannot help sometimes looking at it from a particular point of view—a frivolous one, I agree—but involuntary nonetheless: what an unbearable job it must be at times, one thinks. The lawyer dodges, twists himself around like a snake, lies against his own conscience, against his own convictions, against all morality, against all humanity! No, truly, he earns his money.

"Come, come!" exclaims suddenly the sarcastic voice we heard before. "Why this is all nonsense, nothing but a product of your imagination. A jury never brought in such a verdict. No lawyer ever contorted the facts like that. You made it all up."

But the wife, hung by her heels like a chicken; the "This is *my* bread, don't you dare eat it"; the girl trembling on the stove, listening for half an hour to her mother's cries; and "Mamma, why are you choking?"—isn't that just the same as the hand under the boiling water? Why it's *almost* the same!

"Backwardness, ignorance, the environment—have some pity," the peasant's lawyer insisted. Yet millions of them do exist and not all hang their wives by their heels! There ought to be some limit here. . . . On the other hand, take an educated person: suppose he hangs his wife by her heels? Enough contortions, gentlemen of the bar. Enough of your "environment."

Article 6. Bobok

On this occasion I shall include "The Notes of a Certain Person." That person is not I, but someone else entirely. I think no further foreword is needed.

NOTES OF A CERTAIN PERSON

The other day Semyon Ardalonovich up and said to me, "Ivan Ivanych, tell me, for Heaven's sake, will there ever be a day when you'll be sober?"

That's a strange thing to ask. I'm not offended; I'm a timid fellow. But just the same, they made me out to be a madman. An artist once happened to paint my portrait. "You're a literary man, after all," he says. So I let him have his way, and he put the portrait on exhibit. And now I read: "Go and look at this sickly face that seems to border on insanity."

My face may well be like that, but do they have to say it right in print? Everything that appears in print should be noble; we need some ideals, but this. . . .

He could at least have said it indirectly—that's the whole point of style. But no, he won't say it indirectly. Humor and elegance of style are disappearing nowadays, and abuse is taken for witticism. But I don't take offense: I'm not some distinguished man of letters who'll go off his head over a thing like that. I wrote a story, but they wouldn't publish it. I wrote an article, but it was rejected. I've taken a lot of articles around to various publishers, but they always turn me down: "There's no salt in it," they say.

"What sort of salt do you want, then?" I ask, with sarcasm in my voice. "Attic?"

He doesn't even understand. Mostly I do translations from the French for booksellers. I also write advertisements for shopkeepers: "A rare item! The finest tea from our own plantations. . . ." I made a pile of money writing a eulogy for His Excellency the late Piotr Matveevich. I put together *The Art of Appealing to the Ladies* on commission from a bookseller. I've put out about six of these little books in my lifetime. I want to do a collection of Voltaire's bon mots, but I fear that people here may find them a bit too tame. What's Voltaire nowadays? These days we need an oak cudgel, not a Voltaire! We ought to be knocking one another's teeth out! Well, that's my entire literary output. From time to time I'll send letters to the editor, fully signed, but for which I'm not paid. I'm always giving advice and admonitions, criticizing things and pointing out the way. Last week I sent my fortieth letter in two years to the same newspaper; they've set me back four rubles in postage stamps alone. I have a nasty disposition, that's what it is.

I don't think the artist painted me on account of my literary work; it probably was on account of the two symmetrical warts on my forehead: that's a phenomenon of nature, he says. They don't have any ideas, you see, so now they go on about these phenomena. But what a job he did on my warts in the portrait—they're as good as life! That's what they call realism.

As far as madness is concerned, we've had a lot of people reckoned among the insane in the past year. And it's done in such a fine literary style: "Given such an original talent . . . and then, at the very end, we see that . . . however, it should have long been apparent. . . ." It's done very slyly—in fact from the point of view of pure art one might even admire it. But yet these "lunatics" come back even more clever than they were before. That's just how it is: we can drive people mad, but we've never yet made anyone more clever.

I think the cleverest of all is the one who calls himself a fool at least once a month. Now that's something we never hear of these days! There was a time when a fool realized that he was a fool once a year at the very least, but now it never happens. Everything's so muddled now that you can't tell a fool from a clever man. They've done that on purpose.

I recall the witty saying of the Spaniards, some two hundred and fifty years ago, at the time the French built their first madhouse: "They have locked up all their fools in a special building to make people think that they themselves are wise." Just so: you can't prove your own intelligence by shutting someone else up in a madhouse. "Mr. K. has gone mad, so now we are wise." No, that's not how it works.

But damn it, why have I started carrying on about my own intelligence? All I do is grumble. Even my maid is fed up with it. A friend of

mine dropped in yesterday. "Your style is changing," he says. "It's like
mincemeat. You chop things finer and finer. You put something in parentheses with other parentheses inside and then insert something else in
brackets, and start chopping it some more. . . ."

He's right. Something queer is happening to me. My character is
changing, and my head aches. I'm beginning to see and hear some strange
things. Not voices, exactly, but it's as if someone right beside me is saying:
"Bobok, bobok, bobok!"

What is this bobok? I must find some distraction.

I was walking around looking for some distraction when I came upon
a funeral. It was a distant relative of mine. He was a Collegiate Councilor,
however. A widow, five daughters, none of them married. Think what it
must cost in shoes alone! The deceased earned a regular salary, but now
there's only a miserable little pension. They'll have to tighten their belts.
They always received me coldly. And I wouldn't have gone now, had it
not been such a special occasion. I joined the others in the procession to
the cemetery; they kept apart from me and looked down their noses. My
uniform coat really is rather shabby. It must be twenty-five years since I've
been to a cemetery. What a place it is!

First of all, there's the smell. About fifteen corpses had arrived. Funeral
palls of various prices. There were even two catafalques: one for a general
and one for a lady. A lot of mournful faces, a lot of faces pretending
to mourn, and a lot of obviously happy faces as well. The clergy have
nothing to complain about: it's an income for them. But the smell, the
smell! I wouldn't want to be a clergyman here.

I took a cautious look at the faces of the corpses, unsure of my own
impressionability. Some of them have soft expressions, others unpleasant
ones. On the whole their smiles aren't nice, and some of them are particularly not nice. I don't like them; I'll have dreams about them.

During the service I went out of the church to get some air. It was
overcast but dry. Cold, too; but it's October, after all. I took a walk round
the graves. They have various categories. The third category costs thirty
rubles; it's decent and not too expensive. The first two categories mean
burial inside the church or in the entry; they make you pay through the
nose for those. This time they buried six, including the general and the
lady, in the third category.

I took a look in these wretched graves, and it was dreadful: water, and what water! It was quite green and . . . but why go on about it? The grave-digger was constantly bailing it out with a bucket. While the service was still going on I went out the gate to stroll around a bit. There's an alms-house there, and a restaurant a little farther along. Not a bad little place; you can get a bite to eat and everything. Quite a few of the mourners had come in here as well. I could see a lot of good cheer and genuine liveli-ness. I had a snack and a drink.

Then I lent a hand in carrying a coffin to the grave. Why is it these corpses get so heavy when they're in the coffin? I've heard it's some sort of inertia, that the body can't manage itself any more, it seems . . . or some such nonsense. It goes against common sense and the laws of mechanics. I don't like it when people with only a general education butt in to try to solve specialized problems, but it's done all the time in Russia. Civilians love to make judgments on military matters—even on things only a field marshal should decide, while people trained as engineers more often talk of philosophy and political economy.

I didn't go to the Litany afterward. I'm a proud man, and if they are going to receive me only because of special circumstances, then why bother trudging off to their dinners, even if they are funeral dinners? I just don't understand why I stayed at the cemetery. I sat down on a tombstone and fell into an appropriate reverie.

I began thinking about the Moscow Exhibition and ended thinking about astonishment; I mean astonishment in general, as a topic. This is what I concluded about "astonishment."

It's ridiculous, of course, to be astonished at everything, while being astonished at nothing is much more attractive and for some reason is considered good form. But, practically speaking, it's hardly like that. I think it's far more ridiculous to be astonished at nothing than to be aston-ished at everything. Besides, to be astonished at nothing is almost the same as to respect nothing. And a stupid man isn't even capable of respect.

"Above all I want to feel respect. I *long* to feel respect," an acquain-tance of mine told me just the other day.

He longs to feel respect! My God, I thought, what would happen to you if you ventured to say that in print!

At this point my mind began to wander. I don't like reading inscrip-tions on gravestones; you always see the same thing. On the stone next to

me lay a half-eaten sandwich: stupid and inappropriate. I threw it on the
ground, since it wasn't bread, only a sandwich. However, I think it's not a
sin to throw bread crumbs on the ground; it's only a sin when it's on the
floor. I must check it in Suvorin's *Almanac*.

I imagine I must have sat there for a long time, perhaps too long; I
mean to say that I even lay down on a long stone carved like a marble
coffin. And how was it that suddenly I began hearing various things?
At first I didn't pay any attention and tried to ignore the voices. But the
conversation went on. I could hear some muffled sounds, as if the mouths
were covered with pillows; and yet they were audible and seemed quite
near. I came to life, sat up, and began listening carefully.

"That's simply not possible, Your Excellency. You declared in hearts,
sir; I'm your partner, and now, suddenly, you have seven in diamonds. We
should have agreed about the diamonds beforehand, sir."

"What, then, are we to play entirely by memory? What charm is there
in that?"

"It's absolutely impossible, Your Excellency, without stipulations
of some sort. We must have a dummy, and we must have one hand not
turned up."

"Well, you won't find any dummy here."

What presumption! Both strange and surprising. One voice was
very weighty and authoritative, the other sounded soft and saccharine; I
wouldn't have believed it, had I not heard it myself. I didn't think I could
be at the Litany. But how can they be playing preference here, and who is
this general? The sounds were coming from the grave; that was certain.
I bent down and read the inscription on the headstone: "Here lies the
body of Major-General Pervoedov . . . Chevalier of this order and that."
Hmm. "Passed away in August of this year . . . fifty-seven . . . Rest, beloved
ashes, until the joyous morn."

Well, damn it, he really was a general! On the other little grave, where
the obsequious voice came from, there was still no monument, only a
stone slab; a newcomer, no doubt. A Court Councilor, by the sound of
his voice.

"Oh-ho-ho!" said a new voice, about thirty feet away from the general's place and coming from a fresh grave. This was a rough, masculine
voice, but softened by a sanctimonious touch.

"Oh-ho-ho!"

"Oh, he's hiccuping again!" suddenly came the fussy and haughty voice of an irritated lady, apparently one from high society. "What a punishment to lie next to this shopkeeper!"

"I wasn't hiccuping at all; I've had nothing to eat in any case; it's just my nature. Anyhow, madam, it's your own fussiness about things here that keep you from settling down."

"Then why did you have to lie next to me?"

"It was my wife and little ones who put me here; it wasn't my wish. The mystery of death! I wouldn't have lain next to you for anything, not for gold of any color. I'm here because of my means—it's a matter of price, ma'am. Because that's something we can always manage, to pay for a third-class grave."

"You must have piled up a good bit with your overcharging."

"How can we overcharge you when you haven't paid a thing on your account since January? You've a tidy little bill in the shop."

"That's ridiculous. In my opinion it is utterly ridiculous to try to collect debts here! Go up above. Ask my niece; she inherited it all."

"There's not much chance of asking anywhere, or going anywhere now. We've both come to the end of our days, and we are equal in sin before God's judgment."

"Equal in sin," the deceased lady mimicked scornfully. "Don't you dare say another word to me!"

"Oh-ho-ho!"

"Still, the shopkeeper is doing as the lady says, Your Excellency."

"And why should he not do as she says?"

"As we all know, Your Excellency, because of the new order down here."

"What new order do you mean?"

"Well, you see, Your Excellency, we have, so to say, died."

"Ah, yes! But still, the order. . . ."

Well, I was obliged to them; they certainly cheered me up! If that is the state of affairs down there, what can we expect of the upper floor? But the things that were going on down there! I went on listening, however, but it was with real irritation.

"No, I wish I could have lived a bit longer! No . . . you know . . . I wish I could have lived a bit longer!" said a new voice, coming from somewhere in the space between the general and the irritated lady.

"Listen to that, Your Excellency, our neighbor is at it again. He doesn't say a word for three days, and suddenly: 'I wish I could have lived a bit longer; no, I wish I could have lived!' And he says it with such appetite, he-he-he!"

"And without thinking of what he's saying."

"It gets the better of him, Your Excellency, and he falls asleep, fast asleep. He's been here since April, you know, and all of a sudden: 'I wish I could have lived!'"

"It is a bit dull, though," remarked His Excellency.

"It does get dull, Your Excellency. Shall we tease Avdotia Ignatevna again, he-he-he?"

"No, please, spare me that. I cannot abide that twittering busybody."

"And I cannot abide either one of you," replied the woman with disgust. "You are both extremely boring and have no capacity for discussing elevated matters. You needn't put on airs, Your Excellency; I know a little story about how a servant swept you out from under the bed of a married lady one morning."

"Wretched woman!" muttered the General.

"Avdotia Ignatevna, ma'am," the shopkeeper muttered again suddenly, "tell me, dear lady, and don't bear me a grudge: are these my forty days of torment, or is it something else . . . ?"

"Oh, he's on about that again. I just knew it, because I can smell the stench of him, and that means he's tossing and turning!"

"I'm not tossing and turning, ma'am, and I don't have any stench because my body is still whole and sound. But you, my lady, have already begun to turn bad, because the stench is truly unbearable, even for a place like this. It's only out of politeness that I haven't mentioned it."

"Oh, you are a nasty creature to insult me so. He reeks to high heaven, but he talks about me."

"Oh-ho-ho-ho! If only my forty-day memorial would come. I can hear the tearful voices up there, the wailing of my wife and the quiet weeping of my children!"

"Much they have to weep about: they'll stuff themselves full of rice porridge and go home. Oh, I wish someone would wake up!"

"Avdotia Ignatevna," the unctuous official spoke up. "Just wait a wee while and the newcomers will begin to talk."

"Are there any young people among them?"

"There are, Avdotia Ignatevna. There are even some young men."

"Isn't that just what we need!"

"Well, haven't they begun yet?" the general inquired.

"The ones from the other day haven't even come to yet, Your Excellency. I'm sure you are aware that sometimes they don't say a word for a week. It's good that they brought a lot of them all at once yesterday, the day before, and again today. Aside from them, almost everyone for twenty-five yards around is from last year."

"Yes, it should be interesting."

"Just today, Your Excellency, they buried the Actual Privy Councilor Tarasevich. I recognized the voices. I know his nephew who helped lower the coffin."

"Hmm, where is he, then?"

"Only about five paces from you, Your Excellency, on your left. Almost at your very feet. . . . You ought to make his acquaintance, Your Excellency."

"Hmm, perhaps not. . . . I don't think I should make the first move."

"He'll take the initiative himself, Your Excellency. He'll even be flattered. Let me look after things, Your Excellency, and I. . . ."

"Ah, ah . . . oh, what's happening to me?" groaned the thin, frightened voice of a newcomer.

"A newcomer, Your Excellency, a newcomer, thank God, and how quickly! Sometimes they don't say a word for a week."

"A young man, it seems!" squealed Avdotia Ignatevna.

"I . . . I . . . I had complications, and so suddenly!" the young man babbled again. "Schultz told me just last night: 'You have complications,' he said, and I was dead by morning. Ah, ah!"

"There's nothing to be done, young man," said the General kindly, evidently delighted by the presence of someone new. "You must stop grieving! Welcome to our Vale of Jehoshaphat, as it might be called. We are good people, and you'll get to know us and like us. Major-General Vasily Vasilievich Pervoedov, at your service."

"Oh, no, no! I won't accept this! I'm being treated by Schultz; I developed complications, you see; first I had chest pains and a cough, and then I caught a cold; chest congestion and influenza . . . and then suddenly, quite unexpectedly . . . that's the main thing, it was quite unexpected."

"You say it was your chest first," the official joined in gently, as if wishing to raise the spirits of the newcomer.

"Yes, my chest, with a lot of phlegm; then suddenly, no more phlegm, just my chest. I couldn't breathe . . . and, you know. . . .

"I know, I know. But with chest problems you should have gone to Ekk right away, not to Schultz."

"I kept intending to go to Botkin, you know . . . and suddenly. . . ."

"Well, Botkin will skin you," remarked the General.

"Botkin doesn't skin you, not at all. I've heard he's got such a fine manner and he can tell you everything beforehand."

"His Excellency was remarking about Botkin's fees," the official corrected.

"What do you mean? He only charges three rubles, and he gives you such an examination, and a prescription. . . . And I certainly wanted to consult him, because I was told that. . . . So, gentlemen, what should I do: go to Ekk or to Botkin?"

"What? To whom?" The General's corpse shook with friendly laughter. The official's falsetto joined in.

"My dear boy, my dear, delightful boy, how I love you!" squealed Avdotya Ignatevna with delight. "How I wish they would put someone like you next to me!"

No, I cannot put up with this! Is this what corpses are like today? But I must listen to more of this and not jump to any conclusions. This whining newcomer—I remember seeing him in his coffin not long ago and he looked like a frightened chicken, an absolutely repulsive expression on his face! But let's hear what comes next.

But next there developed such a row that I couldn't even keep it all in my memory, since very many of them woke up all at once. An official, a State Councilor, awoke and immediately, without a moment's hesitation, began taking up with the General a proposal for a new subcommittee in the Ministry of —— Affairs and for the probable transfer of various functionaries connected with this subcommittee; and the General was utterly carried away by this discussion. I confess that I myself learned many a new thing and was amazed at the ways one can glean news of officialdom in this capital city of ours. Then a certain engineer awoke; but he went on mumbling utter nonsense for a long time, so that our friends paid him no heed and simply let him work it out of his system. At last the prominent lady who had been buried under the catafalque that morning began to display signs of sepulchral animation. Lebeziatnikov (for the name of the obsequious Court Councilor whom I so despised and who was located near General Pervoedov was in fact Lebeziatnikov) began fussing and expressing his astonishment that they were awakening so quickly this time. I confess that I was amazed as well. However, some of those who were waking up had been buried two days earlier, such as a certain very young girl of about sixteen who could, however, only giggle in a most vile and rapacious manner.

"Your Excellency, the Privy Councilor Tarasevich is awakening!" Lebeziatnikov announced suddenly and hastily.

"Eh? What?" mumbled the newly awakened Privy Councilor in a fussy, lisping voice. There was something capriciously imperious in the sound of that voice. I listened with curiosity, since I had heard some things about this Tarasevich of late, things that were highly suggestive and alarming.

"It is I, Your Excellency, for the moment it is only I, sir."

"What is your problem? How may I help you?"

"I wish only to inquire about Your Excellency's health. At first, everyone here, being unaccustomed to the place, feels somewhat cramped. . . . General Pervoedov would like to have the honor of making Your Excellency's acquaintance and hopes. . . ."

"Never heard of him."

"Surely, Your Excellency—General Pervoedov, Vasily Vasilievich. . . ."

"Are you General Pervoedov?"

"Indeed not, Your Excellency, I am only Court Councilor Lebeziatnikov at your service, sir; but General Pervoedov. . . ."

"Nonsense! I must ask you to leave me in peace."

"Let him be," said General Pervoedov with dignity, at last putting an end to the vile overzealousness of his sepulchral minion.

"He hasn't quite awakened yet, Your Excellency, and you must keep that in mind. It's only that he's unaccustomed to things here; once he wakes up fully he'll receive you properly. . . ."

"Let him be," repeated the General.

"Vasily Vasilievich! Hallo, Your Excellency!" came the sudden exclamation of a new voice, loud and excited, from the vicinity of Avdotia

Ignatevna. This was an impertinent, aristocratic voice with a fashionably weary tone and impudent intonation. "I've been listening to you all for the past two hours; I've been here for three days now. Do you remember me, Vasily Vasilievich? Klinevich: we met at the Volokonskys' where you—I can't imagine why—were also received."

"What? Count Piotr Petrovich? Have you really . . . at such tender years. . . ? I am truly sorry!"

"And I am sorry as well, yet what does it matter? I want to get all that I can from this place. And I'm not a count but a baron, only a baron. We're merely some mangy little family of barons who originated in the servants' quarters; how we came to be barons I don't know, nor do I care. I'm only a good-for-nothing from the pseudo-upper class and consider myself a charming rascal. My father is a general of some sort, and my mother was once received *en haut lieu*. Sieffel the Yid and I passed off fifty thousand rubles'-worth of false banknotes last year, but I informed on him, and Julie Charpentier de Lusignan went off to Bordeaux with all the money. And just imagine—I was already quite properly engaged to Miss Shchevalevsky, who's three months short of being sixteen and still at school. She was bringing ninety thousand with her. Avdotia Ignatevna, do you remember how you seduced me fifteen years ago when I was fourteen and still in the Corps of Pages?"

"Ah, it's you, wretch. Well, God sent you, at least, otherwise there would be no one here. . . ."

"You were wrong when you thought it was your neighbor, the merchant, who was smelling bad. . . . I just kept quiet and laughed. That was me; they had to bury me in a sealed coffin."

"What a vile creature you are! Still, I'm glad; you will simply not believe, Klinevich, what lack of life and wit there is here."

"Yes, indeed, and I have some original ideas to try out. Your Excellency—not you, Pervoedov—the other Excellency, Mister Tarasevich, Privy Councilor! Answer me! It's Klinevich, who took you to see Mlle. Furie last Lent. Do you hear me?"

"I hear you, Klinevich. I'm very pleased, and you have my assurance that. . . ."

"I don't have any assurance of anything, and don't give a hang. I would only like to give you a big kiss, you dear old fellow, but I can't, thank God. Do you know, gentlemen, what this *grand-père* cooked up? He died

three or four days ago and—can you imagine?—he left a deficit of some
four hundred thousand in government funds. The sum was supposed to
support widows and orphans, but it seems for some reason he was the sole
administrator and so his accounts hadn't been audited for eight years. I
can imagine what long faces they're all wearing up there and how they'll
remember him. The very thought makes one's mouth water, doesn't it!
All last year I was amazed at how a seventy-year-old fellow like him, with
gout and rheumatism, could have such stores of energy for dissipation;
but now we have the answer! It was those widows and orphans: the very
thought of them must have warmed his blood! I've known about it for a
long time, and I was the only one who knew; Charpentier told me, and
when I found out I at once leaned on him, the blessed man, in friendly
fashion: 'Let's have twenty-five thousand, unless you'd like your accounts
audited tomorrow.' But he could only scrape up thirteen thousand, and
so, it seems, he died just in time. *Grand-père,* hey, do you hear me?"

"*Cher* Klinevich, I am fully in agreement with you, and you need not
. . . enter into such details. Life contains so much suffering, so many
torments, and so little retribution. . . . I wanted some peace at last and,
as far as I can see, I have hopes of deriving something from this place as
well. . . ."

"I'll wager he's already sniffed out Katish Berestova!"

"Who? . . . Which Katish?" came the trembling, rapacious voice of
the old man.

"Ah, which Katish indeed? She's here, not more than five paces from
me, on the left, and ten paces from you. This is her fifth day here, and if
you had known, *grand-père,* what a wicked little creature she is . . . a good
home, a good education, and a monster to the tips of her fingers! I didn't
show her to anyone up there; I was the only one who knew. . . . Katish,
say something!"

"Hee-hee-hee!" responded a cracked, girlish voice; but in that voice
one felt something like the prick of a needle. "Hee-hee-hee!"

"And is she a nice little blo-onde?" babbled the *grand-père,* drawing
out the last word.

"Hee-hee-hee!"

"For a long time now . . . a long time," babbled the old fellow, trying to
catch his breath, "I've loved to dream about a nice little blonde . . . about
fifteen . . . in circumstances just like these. . . ."

"Monster!" exclaimed Avdotia Ignatevna.

"Enough!" Klinevich announced flatly. "I see that I have excellent material to work with. We shall at once set to arranging things here in a better fashion. The main thing is that we pass our remaining time here happily. But how much time have we? Hey, you, the official of some sort—Lebeziatnikov, was it, that someone called you?"

"Lebeziatnikov, Semyon Evseeich, Court Councilor, at your service, and absolutely delighted to be so."

"I couldn't give a damn if you're delighted, but you seem to know everything about this place. Tell me, first (and I've been amazed at it since yesterday), how is it that we can speak here? We've died, after all, and yet we're speaking; we seem to be able to move, and yet we shouldn't be able to speak and move. What sort of hocus-pocus is this?"

"If you please, baron, Platon Nikolaevich could explain it better than I."

"Who is this Platon Nikolaevich? Just answer my question!"

"Platon Nikolaevich, our local homegrown philosopher, natural scientist, and Master of Arts. He's published several little books of philosophy, but for the past three months he's gone right off to sleep so that there's no way we can rouse him now. Once a week he mutters a few irrelevant words."

"Get to the point!"

"He explains it all by a very simple fact, namely, that up above, while we were still alive, we were wrong in thinking that death up there was really death. Here the body more or less comes to life again; the remnants of life are concentrated, but only in the consciousness. This is—I don't quite know how to put it—a continuation of life as if by inertia. In his view, everything is concentrated somewhere in the consciousness and continues for two or three months . . . sometimes even for half a year. . . . We have one person here, for instance, whose body has almost entirely decomposed, but every six weeks or so he will still suddenly mumble one word—meaningless of course—about a bean or something: 'Bobok, bobok.' So that means there is still a faint spark of life glowing in him. . . ."

"Quite silly. But how is it that I have no sense of smell, and yet I can smell the stench?"

"That's . . . he-he! Well, at this point our philosopher got completely lost in a fog. He remarked specifically about the sense of smell, that the

stench here was a moral one, so to say—he-he! Apparently the stench is
from the soul, so that after two or three months it can reach a new awareness . . . this being, so to say, the final concession of mercy. . . . Yet it seems
to me, baron, that these are all mystical ravings, quite understandable in
his circumstances. . . ."

"That's enough; I'm sure the rest is all nonsense. The main thing is
that we have two or three months of life and then, finally, bobok. I propose
to you that we spend these two months as pleasantly as possible and to do
so, that we arrange things on an entirely new basis. Ladies and gentlemen!
I propose that we abandon all sense of shame!"

"Oh, indeed, let us abandon all sense of shame!" came the sound of
many voices; strangely enough, there were entirely new voices among
them, meaning that they belonged to people who had only just awakened. The bass voice of the engineer, who had now completely awakened,
rumbled among them with special eagerness. The girl Katish burst into
a fit of joyous giggles.

"Oh, how I long to lose my sense of shame!" exclaimed Avdotia
Ignatevna rapturously.

"Do you hear that? If even Avdotia Ignatevna wants to abandon her
sense of shame. . . ."

"No, no, Klinevich. I used to feel shame; I was still ashamed up there,
but here I have a terrible urge to be ashamed of nothing!"

"As I understand it, Klinevich," growled the engineer's bass voice,
"you want to organize our life here, so to say, on new and rational
principles."

"I really don't give a damn about that. We should wait for Kudeiarov
for that; they brought him in yesterday. Once he wakes up he'll explain
it all to you. What a personality he is—a giant among men! I think they'll
be hauling in another one of your natural scientists tomorrow, and probably an officer and, if I'm not mistaken, a certain newspaper columnist
in three or four days and his editor, too, I think. But never mind them!
We're getting a nice little group together and everything will take shape
of itself. But meanwhile, I don't want any lying. That's the only demand
I make, because it's the most important thing. It's impossible to live on
earth without lying, for life and lies are synonymous; but down here, just
for fun, let's not lie. The grave means something after all, damn it! We'll
each tell our stories to the others and be ashamed of nothing. I'll tell you

about myself first of all. I'm a carnivore in essence, you see. Up there, all such things were held together with rotten ropes. Down with ropes! Let's live these two months in the most shameless truth! Let us bare our bodies and our souls!"

"Let us bare ourselves!" cried all the voices.

"I'm terribly, terribly eager to bare myself," squealed Avdotia Ignatevna.

"Ah . . . ha . . . I can see that we are going to have a very fine time here. I don't want to go see Ekk!"

"No, I wish I could live a bit longer, just a bit longer, you know!"

"Hee-hee-hee!" giggled Katish.

"The main thing is that no one can stop us, and even though Pervoedov may get angry, as I can see, he still can't touch me. *Grand-père,* do you agree?"

"I agree, absolutely and with the greatest pleasure, but on condition that Katish begin her autobiography first."

"I protest; I protest with every ounce of my strength!" said General Pervoedov forcefully.

"Your Excellency!" babbled the wretched Lebeziatnikov in a flurry of excitement, lowering his voice to coax the General. "Your Excellency, it would be much better for us if we agreed. That girl is right here, you know . . . and finally, there are all those other things. . . ."

"To be sure, there is the girl, but. . . ."

"It would be better, Your Excellency, it truly would be better! Let's at least give it a try; let's at least have an example. . . ."

"Even in the grave they don't give you any peace!"

"In the first place, General, you play cards in the grave, and in the second place, we don't give a damn about you," intoned Klinevich with measured emphasis.

"My dear sir, I must ask you not to forget yourself."

"What? You can't get your hands on me, and I can tease you from here just as I used to tease Julie's lapdog. In any case, ladies and gentlemen, what sort of a general is he down here? He was a general up there, but down here he's not even small potatoes!"

"No, I'm not small potatoes . . . even here I'm. . . ."

"Down here you'll rot in your coffin, and six brass buttons will be all that's left."

"Bravo, Klinevich!" howled several voices.

"I served my emperor. . . . I have a sword. . . ."

"Your sword is fit only for killing mice, and besides, you've never drawn it from its scabbard."

"All the same, I was a part of the whole."

"There was no shortage of parts of the whole."

"Bravo, Klinevich, bravo, ha-ha-ha!"

"I don't understand what significance the sword has," announced the engineer.

"We shall flee from the Prussians like mice, and they'll smash us to smithereens!" cried a new voice from far away, literally choking with delight.

"A sword, my dear sir, signifies honor!" the General tried to shout, but only I heard him. Thereupon began a long and furious uproar with riotous shouting and racket; only Avdotia Ignatevna's squeals, impatient to the point of hysteria, could be recognized.

"Quickly, quickly! Oh, when are we going to give up our sense of shame?"

"Oh-ho-ho! In truth my soul is going through its torment!" came the voice of the shopkeeper, and. . . .

And at this point I suddenly sneezed. It happened unexpectedly and unintentionally, but the effect was striking: everything fell silent as the grave and vanished like a dream. A real sepulchral silence ensued. I do not think that they were shamed by my presence: they had resolved to be ashamed of nothing, after all! I waited about five minutes and heard not a word and not a sound. I cannot suppose, either, that they feared I would denounce them to the police, for what could the police do in this case? I cannot help but conclude that they still had some sort of secret, unknown to mortal men, which they carefully concealed from every mortal.

"Well, dear friends," I thought, "I'll come and visit you again." And with this I left the cemetery.

No, I cannot accept this, in truth, I cannot! Bobok does not trouble me (that's what it turned out to be, this bobok)!

Debauchery in a place like that, debauchery of one's final hopes, debauchery among sagging, decomposing bodies, debauchery that does not even spare the final moments of consciousness! These moments are

given to them as a gift and. . . . And the main thing—in a place like that!
No, this I cannot accept. . . .

I shall visit other "categories" in the graveyard and listen everywhere.
That's just what has to be done—to listen everywhere, not just at one end
of the cemetery, so as to form an understanding. Perhaps I'll stumble on
something to give comfort as well.

But I'll certainly come back to these people. They did promise to tell
their autobiographies and various other little stories. Foo! No, I won't go,
certainly not; it's a matter of conscience!

I'll bring this to *The Citizen.* One of the editors there has also had his
portrait exhibited. Perhaps he'll print this.

Article 8. A Half-Letter from "A Certain Person"

I am printing below a letter, or more precisely a half-letter, from "a certain person" to the editor of *The Citizen;* it was quite impossible to print the whole letter. This is still that same "person," the very one who has already once distinguished himself in *The Citizen* on the subject of graves. I must confess that I am printing this simply in order to be rid of him. The editor's office has received literally stacks of his articles. In the first place, this person appears as my resolute defender against my supposed literary enemies. On my behalf he has already written three "anticriticisms," two "notes," three "marginal notes," one article "apropos," and finally "an admonition on behavior." In this latter polemical composition of his he purports to admonish my "enemies" but in fact attacks me, and even does it in a tone whose energy and fury I have never encountered, even among my "enemies." And he wants me to print it all! I made it very plain to him that, in the first place, I have no "enemies" and that he is only imagining the whole thing; and, in the second place, he is too late, for all that journalistic racket we heard after the appearance of the first issue of *The Citizen* this year—all the fury unprecedented in literature, the intolerance and the simple-minded methods of attack—stopped two or three weeks ago just as suddenly and inexplicably as it began. Finally, if I were to take it into my head to answer anyone, I could manage to do it myself, without his help.

He got angry, quarreled with me, and left. I was relieved. He is not a well man. . . . In the article that he already published here, he revealed a few features of his biography: he is a man in distress who "distresses" himself every day. But what frightens me most is the excessive force of the "civic energy" of this contributor. Imagine that from the very beginning he made it plain that he expected no honorarium whatsoever but was writing simply out of his "civic duty." He even confessed, with a proud but self-damaging frankness, that he was not writing to defend me at all but only wanted to use the opportunity to expound his own ideas, since not a single periodical would accept his articles. Plainly and simply, he was cherishing the fond hope of creating his own little corner for himself in our journal from which—even without pay—he would have the opportunity to expound his ideas on a regular basis. What sort of ideas does he have? He writes about everything; he expresses opinions about everything with bitterness, with rage, with venom, and with "a tear of tenderness." "Venom for ninety percent and a tear of tenderness for one percent," he himself declares in one of his manuscripts. If a new magazine or newspaper should begin publication, he is there at once: he imparts his wisdom and offers his admonitions. It's absolutely true that he sent off as many as forty letters full of advice to one newspaper: advice on publishing, on how to behave, on what to write about, and on what to pay attention to. In the course of two and a half months some twenty-eight of his letters have accumulated in our editor's office. He always writes over his full signature so that he is known everywhere; he spends his last kopecks on postage stamps and even encloses return postage in his letters, supposing that he will at last achieve his end and manage to begin correspondence on civic matters with various editors. What amazes me most is that even after twenty-eight letters I am completely unable to discover what his views are and exactly what he is aiming at. It's all a great muddle. . . . Along with crude methods, red-nosed cynicism, and the "aggrieved aroma" of a frenzied style and worn-out boots, there are flashes of a certain covert longing for tenderness, for some ideal; there is faith in beauty, *Sehnsucht* for something lost, and the result of it all is something quite revolting. I'm quite fed up with him. True, he's open about his rudeness and expects no payment for his efforts, so in that sense he is an honorable person; but I've had enough of him and his honor! No more than three days after our quarrel he appeared again with his "final attempt," and brought this "Letter of a Certain Person." What could I do but take it? And now I'd better print it.

It's quite impossible to publish the first half of the letter. Here he writes only of personalities and abuses beyond all limits almost all the Petersburg and Moscow press. Not one of the periodicals he reproaches ever reached the level of shameless mockery of his abuse. And yet his own main point is to abuse them solely for the vulgarity and sneering tone of their polemics. I simply took a scissors, cut off the first half of his letter, and returned it to him. The concluding part of his letter I am printing only because it contains what one might call a general topic: here he exhorts some imaginary columnist, and his exhortation is general enough to be applicable to columnists of all periods and all nations. The style is very elevated, and the force of the style is equaled only by the simple-mindedness of the ideas expressed. When he addresses his exhortation to the columnist he uses the "thou" form, as in the classical odes. The author was very firm in his wish that I should not begin his half-letter after a full stop but insisted that it begin right in the middle of a sentence, just where I had cut it off with the scissors, as if to say, "Let them see how they mutilated me!" He also insisted on the title: I wanted to print "A Letter from 'A Certain Person,'" but he absolutely insisted that it be entitled "A Half-Letter from 'A Certain Person.'"

And so, here is this half-letter:

A HALF-LETTER FROM "A CERTAIN PERSON"

. . . and does the word "swine" truly contain such magical and alluring meaning that you at once take it to apply inevitably to yourself? I have observed for a long time that in Russian literature this little word has always had a certain special and even mystical meaning, as it were. Dear old Krylov himself realized that and used the word "swine" with particular fondness in his fables. The literary man who reads this word, even when he is completely alone, will shudder forthwith and at once commence to thinking: "Could that be me? Does that refer to me?" Granted, it is a powerful little word, but why must you always assume that it refers to yourself and yourself alone? There are others besides you. Or perhaps you have your own private reasons for thinking this? For how else can I explain your suspicious cast of mind?*

---

*This is certainly an exaggeration, but it does contain a measure of truth. There is a hint here specifically at the fact that in the first issue of *The Citizen* I had the misfortune to cite an ancient Indian fable about the duel of the lion and the pig; in doing so, however, I carefully eliminated even the possibility of supposing that I was immodestly using the word "lion" to refer to myself. And what happened? In fact, many people expressed extreme and hasty suspicions about it. It was a regular phenomenon: a letter to the editor arrived from a subscriber in a remote border region of Russia; the subscriber brazenly and recklessly accused the editors of referring to their subscribers as "swine"—an assumption so absurd that even certain Petersburg columnists did not venture to make use of it when casting their aspersions . . . and of course that is the measure of everything. *The Editor.* [Dostoevsky's note]

The second thing I wish to point out to you, my columnist friend, is that you lack restraint in preparing your columns. The pages you write are so crammed with generals, wealthy stock-holders, and princes who need you and your witty words that on reading you I have to conclude that their excessive number suggests rather that you do not know even one of them. At one point you are present at an important meeting and utter some bon mot, carelessly and haughtily, but in doing so you cast a ray of light on the proceed-ings, and the meeting at once takes a turn for the better. At another point you ridicule a certain wealthy prince to his face, in exchange for which he promptly invites you to dinner; but you pass him by and proudly, yet in proper liberal fashion, decline the invitation. And then, in an intimate salon conversation you jokingly reveal the whole secret inner workings of Russia to a visiting foreign lord: in trepidation and delight he at once telegraphs London, and on the following day Victoria's whole cabinet is turned out. And again, while taking your stroll from two to four on the Nevsky, you propose the solution to a thorny problem of state to three retired cabinet ministers who are, nonetheless, running after you; you encounter a captain of the Guards who has lost everything at cards and toss him a loan of two hundred rubles; you go with him to Finfina to express your noble (supposedly) indignation. . . . In short, you are here, you are there, you are everywhere: you move through all society; people are always plucking at your sleeve; you gobble up truffles and sample bonbons, drive here and there in cabs, are on intimate terms with the waiters at Palkin's—in a word, without you nothing can happen. A position as lofty as yours at last begins to seem suspi-cious. The unassuming reader in the provinces may indeed take you for one who has been passed over for some honor, or at least for a retired minister who wants to regain his office by means of a free, but opposition, press. But the experienced reader in either of the capitals knows otherwise: for he knows that you are no more than a pen-pusher hired by a publisher determined to make a profit; you have been hired, and you are obliged to defend the interests of your employer. It is he (and no other) who sets you against any person he chooses.

And so all your anger and passion and barking is nothing more than the work of a hireling who attacks in whatever direction his employer's hand points. If you would at least stand up for yourself! But it is quite the contrary: what surprises me most about you is that you really do grow heated and take things to heart as if they really meant something to you; you abuse a rival columnist supposedly over some cherished idea or matter of principle which is truly precious to you. Meanwhile you know very well that you have no ideas of your own, never mind principles. Or have you, perhaps, after so many years of excitement and savoring the stench of your success, at last imagined that you have an idea or are capable of having principles? If such is the case, then how can you count on my respect?

There was a time when you were an honest and decent young man. . . . Oh, recall Pushkin's verse—a translation from the Persian, if I am not mistaken: a venerable old man speaks to a youth who is avid to go off to battle:

> I fear amidst war's strident clamor
> Thou canst but lose and ne'er reclaim
> Thy modesty, thy timid manner,
> Thy tender charm, thy sense of shame.

Alas, you have lost all these things, lost them long ago, and lost them forever! Just look at how you have quarreled with your columnist-enemy and try to comprehend the depths to which you both have sunk in your abuses! For neither of you is as despicable as you paint each other. Remember that in their early years children fight with one another largely because they have still not learned how to express their ideas intelligently. And you—a child with gray hair— from a lack of ideas use all the words you know to abuse someone else. A bad method! It is precisely your lack of convictions and genuine learning that leads you to try to pry into your rival's private life. You are avid to learn of his failings; you exaggerate them and expose them to salutary publicity. Neither do you spare his wife and children. You both pretend the other is dead and you write one another lampoons in the form of obituaries. Tell me, who will ever believe you in the end? As I read your column, spattered with your saliva and ink, I cannot help but be led to think that you are not right, that there must be some special, secret meaning to your article, that you and your rival must have come to blows at a dacha somewhere and neither of you can forget the incident. I cannot help but find in favor of your rival, and the effect of your case is ruined. Is that really what you were setting out to do?

How childishly clumsy you are! Having heaped abuse on your rival, you end your column as follows: "I can see you now, Mr. N.N.: after you have read these lines you rush about your room in a fury; you tear your hair; you shout at your wife who has come running into the room in alarm; you drive your children away; grinding your teeth, you pound the wall with your fist in impotent rage...."

Oh, my friend, you are only a naive but overwrought victim of your own fictitious fury affected for your employer's benefit! My columnist friend! Tell me: when I read in your column the lines that supposedly describe your rival, do you not realize that I see this is you—you yourself, and not your rival—who is rushing about the room tearing your hair; that it is you who beats your servant who rushes in, frightened (that is, if you have a servant and if he has not lost his primitive innocence since February 19th); it is you who, with shrieking and gnashing of teeth, flings yourself against the wall and beats it with your fists until they are bloody! For who will believe that you can send such lines to your rival unless you have first pounded the wall until your own fists were bloody? In such a manner you betray yourself.

Come to your senses; show some compunction. And when you show some compunction, you will also acquire some ability to write a column. That is the benefit you can derive from this.

Let me give you an allegory. Out of the blue you suddenly put up posters announcing that next Thursday or Friday (imagine the day on which you write your column) in Berg's Theater or in some facility specially set up for the purpose, you will display yourself naked, right down to the last detail. I believe that you will find willing spectators; such spectacles are particularly attractive to today's society. I believe that a crowd will assemble—even a large crowd. But will they come to show their respect for you? And if not, then what have you accomplished?

Consider, now, if you are able: are your columns not doing this very same thing? Do you not come out on the very same day every week, naked to the last detail, and display yourself to the public? And for what, and for whom do you do this?

The most amusing thing here is that all your readers know the secret behind your war; they know, yet they don't wish to know and pass by you indifferently, while you both rush about in fury and think that everyone is following your doings. Oh, simpleminded man! The public knows all too well that the owner of a newspaper in the capital, seeing another newspaper established on the same lines as his own, pats the pocket where he keeps his wallet and says to himself: "This wretched new paper may do me out of a couple of thousand subscribers. I'll hire myself a shaggy great mongrel and set him on my rival." That mongrel is you!

The owner is pleased with you; he strokes his whiskers and, after breakfast, thinks with a smile, "Yes, indeed, I've hounded him, and no mistake!"

Do you recall Turgenev's Antropka? This is truly a brilliant piece by a favorite writer. Antropka is a little urchin in a village—or, more correctly, he is the brother of another village urchin (whose name, let's say, is Nefed)—who has disappeared from the hut one dark summer night on account of some misdeed. The strict father has sent the older boy to bring his miscreant little brother home. And so, on the bank of a ravine we hear the shrill cries:

"Antropka! Antropka!"

For a long time the guilty little scamp does not reply, but at last, "as if from another world," a quavering, meek little voice is heard from the other side of the ravine:

"Wha-a-t?"

"Daddy wants to be-e-at you!" says the older brother, with malicious, eager joy.

The voice "from another world" is not heard again, of course. But in the dark night the strained, tormented, malicious cries still continue:

"Antropka-a! Antropka-a-a!"

This brilliant little picture of crying out to Antropka and—most important—its impotent but angry distress is heard again, not only among village urchins but also among adults who have attained hoary venerability, members of today's society who, however, have been upset by the reforms. And isn't there a thing or two in our capital that reminds you of these Antropkas? For do you not see something of Antropka in the relationship between these two owners of city newspapers? Have not you and your rival both been sent out by your masters to find Antropkas? And the Antropkas— aren't these the new subscribers who you assume might believe in your innocence? You both know that all your rage, all your strained efforts will be in vain and that Antropka will not answer, that you will not manage to steal away a single subscriber from the other, that each of you will have enough subscribers in any case. But you have both become so wrapped up in this game of yours and enjoy this impotent journalistic laceration so much that you cannot restrain yourselves! And so every week, on the established days, there come the furious, strained cries: "Antropka-a! Antropka-a!" And we listen to them.

I'll permit myself one more allegory.

Imagine that you have been invited into proper society (for I suppose that you too move in proper social circles). You are one of the invited guests at an evening party for the name day of a State Councilor (one as high in rank as that). The host has already informed the guests that you are a very witty man. You enter politely, well dressed; you pay your respects to the hostess and compliment her graciously. You sense with pleasure that people are looking at you, and you prepare to distinguish yourself. And suddenly—oh, horrors!—in the corner of the room you notice your literary rival who has arrived before you; until now you never even suspected he knew your hosts. Your expression has changed, but the host, assuming this is due to a passing indisposition, naively hurries to introduce you to your literary enemy. You both mutter something and at once turn your backs on one another. The host is embarrassed but takes courage, supposing that this is no more than a new literary fashion of which he is unaware, being always caught up in official business. In the meantime, card games are arranged and the hostess, with her usual graciousness, invites you to play whist. To get away from your rival you happily choose a card. A new horror: it turns out that you are to share his table. You cannot refuse since as partners you have two congenial and agreeable society ladies. They both quickly take their seats, while various relatives and friends gather around, all eager to listen to two literary men, all staring fixedly at your mouths, ready to seize upon your first words. Your rival turns to one of the ladies and calmly says, "You have the opportunity to make a good deal, madam." Everyone smiles and exchanges glances: his witty remark has gone over well, and your heart contracts with envy. The lady deals the cards. You pick up your cards and find deuces, threes, sixes; the highest card is a jack. You grind your teeth while your rival smiles. He has a good hand and proudly declares a slam. Your eyes grow dim. You seize a heavy bronze candlestick, a family heirloom and the pride of the host (the hostess keeps it locked in a cupboard all year, exhibiting it only on name days). You seize this candlestick and fling it violently at your rival's head. Screams and confusion! Everyone jumps to his feet, but you two have already leapt at each other, mouths foaming with rage, and are pulling at each other's hair.* Judging by the lack of patience and self-restraint exhibited in your writing, I am justi-fied in concluding that you have a similar lack of patience in private society. Your partner, the young lady who was expecting such witty conversation from you, screams and takes refuge under the wing of her husband, an important lieutenant-colonel of engineers. He, pointing at the two of you twisting each other's hair, tells her, "I warned you what to expect from contemporary literature, my dear!" But the two of you have already been dragged down the stairs and kicked out onto the street. The host, whose name day is being cele-brated, feels responsible and apologizes to his guests, suggesting they forget about Russian literature and continue with whist. You have deprived yourself of a social evening, some pleasant yet inno-cent moments with a Petersburg lady, and a supper. But neither of you is concerned about that: each of you takes a cab and rushes away through the malodorous Petersburg streets, each to his own

*The editor finds this picture somewhat exaggerated. [Dostoevesky's note]

apartment to sit right down and compose a column. You urge your driver on, with a fleeting moment of envy of his innocence; but you are already mulling over your article. You arrive, seize your pen, and relate exactly, down to the last detail, what happened to you at the home of the Councilor!

You denounce your host; you denounce his wife and the refreshments; you inveigh against the custom of celebrating name days; you criticize the engineer lieutenant-colonel and the lady, your partner; and at last you come to your rival. And now you set it all down to the last detail in your well-known, usual, current fashion of revealing all inside information. You tell of how he beat you and how you beat him; you vow that you will beat him again in the future and that he has promised to beat you. You want to append to your article the handful of his hair that you have torn out. But it's already morning. . . . You rush around the room, waiting for the editorial offices to open. You arrive at the editor's office, and suddenly he, with a calm air, announces that on the previous night he has made up with his rival publisher, who has closed down his newspaper, transferring the subscribers to him, your employer; the two of them have celebrated their peace with a bottle of champagne at Dussault's. Then he thanks you for your services and announces that he no longer needs you. Now tell me what a spot you are in!

What I like least of all are the last days of the pre-Lenten carnival, when the common people are drinking themselves into the last stages of ugliness. The dull, ugly faces of besotted figures in torn coats crowd around the taverns. Two of them stop on the street: one claims he is a general, while the other shouts, "Liar!" The first curses in rage, while the second again shouts, "Liar!" The first works himself up still more furiously, while the second goes on with his "Liar!" And so it continues for perhaps two hundred times! It is beauty that they both find in this impotent and endless repetition of the same words, wallowing, as it were, in the enjoyment of the impotence of their own degradation.

When I read your columns I cannot help but imagine a kind of endless, drunken, senseless carnival that has gone on in our literature for much too long already. For aren't you two doing the same thing as these two mindless drunkards in peasant coats standing on the street corner? Does your rival not claim in each of his columns that he is a general, and do you not reply to him, like the peasant on the corner, "Liar!"? And it all goes on a countless number of times without even the least suspicion that the whole thing has at last made us sick to death. I imagine you both just as if you were on the last day of Carnival (the day of forgiveness!), deprived of your senses by intoxication; I picture you both on the street in front of the offices of your respective editors, wallowing in the dirty brown snow of our capital, thrashing about and shouting hoarsely at each other with all your might: "Help! Police! He-e-elp!"

But I say nothing and hurry past. . . .

A Silent Observer.

N.B. "Silent Observer" is the pseudonym of "A Certain Person"; I neglected to mention this before.

Article 9, extract. Apropos of the Exhibition

[. . .] I have a great fear when "tendency" takes hold of a young artist, especially at the beginning of his career; and what do you think causes me the most concern? Precisely that the purpose of this tendency will not be achieved. There is a certain dear critic whom I have been reading recently and whose name I don't wish to mention here. Will he believe that any work of art without a preconceived tendency, a work created exclusively out of the demands of art and even on an entirely noncontroversial subject which doesn't contain the least hint of anything "tendentious"—will this critic believe that such a work contributes far more *for his purposes* than all the "songs about the shirt," for instance (not Hood's, but those of our own writers), even though superficially the work may appear to belong to the category called "satisfaction of idle curiosity"? If even scholars, apparently, have still not realized this, then what may sometimes happen in the hearts and minds of our young writers and artists? What a muddle of conceptions and preconceived notions they must have! To satisfy social demands, the young poet suppresses his own natural need to express himself in his own images, fearing that he will be censured for "idle curiosity"; he suppresses and obliterates the images that arise out of his own soul; he ignores them or leaves them undeveloped, while extracting from himself with painful tremors the images that satisfy common, official, liberal, and social opinion. What a terribly simple and naive mistake, what a serious mistake this is! One of the most serious mistakes is that the denunciation of vice (or what liberal opinion accepts as vice) and the arousal of feelings of hatred and vengeance is considered the only possible way to achieve the purpose! But even with such a narrow approach as this, a powerful talent could still wriggle free and not suffocate at the very beginning of his career; he need only keep in mind the golden rule that a word spoken may be silver, but one unspoken is gold. There are so many significant talents who promised so much but who were so badly corroded by "tendency" that it essentially put them into uniform. I have read the two latest poems by Nekrasov, and this honorable poet of ours is now certainly wearing a uniform. Yet even in these poems there are some good things that hint at Mr. Nekrasov's former talent. But what is to be done? His subject is also "wearing a uniform"; his technique, his ideas, his vocabulary, his verisimilitude are uniformed . . . yes, even verisimilitude itself has donned a uniform. Does our esteemed poet know, for instance, that no woman, not even one overflowing with the finest of civic sentiments and who has gone to such efforts in order to see her unfortunate husband by traveling four thousand miles in a cart "and coming to know its delights"; who has, as you tell us, fallen "from the lofty heights of the Altai" (which, by the way, is quite impossible)—do you know, sir, that this woman would never kiss the chains of her beloved husband first of all? She would first kiss him, and only then, if seized by such a powerful and noble upsurge of civic feeling, would she kiss his chains; and any woman certainly would act that way. Of course, this is only a minor observation, and it would not be worth mentioning since the poem itself was written for no particular reason except, maybe, to toss off something for January 1st. Mr. Nekrasov, however, still has a solid reputation in literature, one that is established and almost complete, and has produced many excellent verses. He is a poet of suffering, and has almost earned this appellation. But I can't help feeling sorry for the new poets: not a single one of them has a talent strong enough to keep him from submitting to "uniformed" ideas at the beginning of his career and thus saving himself from literary consumption and death. What is to be done? A uniform is a pretty thing, after all, with its embroidery and glitter. . . . And what an advantage to wear one! These days, especially advantageous.

No sooner had I read in the newspapers of Mr. Repin's barge-haulers than I got frightened. Even the subject itself is terrible: we have accepted somehow that barge-haulers are the best means of representing the well-known social notion of the unpaid debt of the upper classes to the People. I came expecting to see these barge-haulers all lined up in uniforms with the usual labels stuck to their foreheads. And what happened? To my delight, all my fears turned out to be vain: they are barge-haulers, real barge-haulers and nothing more. Not a single one of them shouts from the painting to the viewer: "Look how unfortunate I am and how indebted you are to the People!" And in that alone we can credit the artist with a great service. They are marvelous, familiar figures: the two foremost haulers are almost laughing; at any rate they are certainly not crying, and

aren't thinking at all about their social status. A little soldier is slyly trying
to conceal the fact that he wants to fill his pipe. The little boy has put
on a serious face; he is shouting, even arguing. He is a wonderful figure,
almost the best in the picture and equal in conception to that of the very
last hauler, a wretched, drooping little peasant who is trudging along on
his own and whose face isn't even visible. One simply can't imagine that
any notion of the politicoeconomic and social debts of the higher classes
to the People could ever penetrate the poor, drooping head of this little
peasant, oppressed by perpetual grief . . . and—and do you know, my
dear critic, that the very humble innocence of thought of this peasant
achieves your purpose far more readily than you think?—precisely your
tendentious, liberal purpose! More than one spectator will walk away
with pain in his heart and with love (and with what love!) for this poor
little peasant, or for this boy, or for this sly scoundrel, the soldier! Why,
you can't help but love them, these defenseless creatures; you can't walk
away without loving them. You can't help but think that you are indebted,
truly indebted to the People. . . . You will be dreaming of this whole group
of barge-haulers afterward; you will still recall them fifteen years later!
And had they not been so natural, so innocent, and so simple, they would
not have produced such an impression and would not have composed
such a picture. Why, it's almost complete! Anyway, all these uniform
collars are disgusting, no matter how much gold embroidery they have!
Still, what need is there to go on about this? One can't recount a painting;
they're far too difficult to convey in words. I will say only that the figures
are Gogolian. That is a large thing to say, but I am not claiming that Mr.
Repin is a Gogol in his own medium. Our genre painting still has not
reached the level of Gogol and Dickens.

One can see, though, that even Mr. Repin overdoes it a bit: this is
noticeable specifically in the costumes, and there only in two figures. It's
quite impossible for rags like that even to exist. That shirt, for instance,
must have accidentally fallen into a bowl where meat was being chopped
for cutlets. To be sure, barge-haulers are not noted for wearing finery. We
all know where such people come from: at home at winter's end, at least
according to a number of reports, they subsist on bark and in the spring
go off to find a boss who'll hire them to haul barges, some of them, at
least, only for the porridge they eat, with scarcely any formal contract.
There have been some cases where a barge-hauler died of eating porridge

on his first days on the job; he would fall upon it in his hunger, choke to death, and "burst." Doctors doing autopsies, it is said, found such people stuffed with porridge right up to their throats. So there are some subjects of this sort. But still, an unspoken word is golden, the more so that one couldn't even put on a shirt like that once it had been taken off: you'd never get into it again. However, in comparison with the merits and the independent conception of the painting, this minor exaggeration in costumes is insignificant.

It's a pity that I know nothing of Mr. Repin. It would be interesting to know if he is a young man. How I wish he were still a young man who is only beginning his artistic career. A few lines above I was quick to stipulate that he is still not a Gogol. Yes, Mr. Repin, it's a long, long trip to reach Gogol; don't let your well-earned success go to your head. Our genre painting has made a good start and we have talented people, but it lacks something to enable it to broaden and expand. Why, even Dickens is genre and nothing more, but Dickens created Pickwick, *Oliver Twist,* and the grandfather and grand-daughter in *The Old Curiosity Shop.* No, our genre painting is a long way from that; it is still at the stage of "Hunters" and "Nightingales." Dickens has a lot of "Hunters" and "Nightingales" on the periphery of his works. So far as I can tell from various indicators, it seems that at the present moment in our art our genre painting regards Pickwick and the grand-daughter even as something ideal, and as far as I could gather from conversations with certain of our major artists, they fear the ideal like some kind of unclean spirit. No doubt this is a noble fear, but it is a prejudicial and unjust one. Our artists need a bit more boldness, a bit more independence of thought, and, perhaps, a bit more education. And that's why I think our historical painting is not strong and is somehow languishing. Evidently our contemporary artists are afraid of historical subjects and have fastened upon genre as the sole true and legitimate outlet for any real talent. I think that an artist seems to sense that (in his conception) he will certainly have to "idealize" in historical painting, and thus, to lie. "One must portray reality as it is," they say, whereas reality such as this does not exist and never has on earth because the essence of things is inaccessible to man; he perceives nature as it is reflected in his ideas, after it has passed through his senses. Accordingly, more scope must be given to the idea, and the ideal should not be feared. A portraitist, for example, seats his subject to paint its portrait; he prepares; he studies the subject carefully. Why does he do that? Because he knows from experience that a person does not always look like himself, and therefore he seeks out "the principal idea of his physiognomy," that moment when the subject most resembles his self. The portraitist's gift consists in the ability to seek out and capture that moment. And so what is the artist doing here if not trusting first his own idea (the ideal) more than the reality before him? The ideal is also reality, after all, and just as legitimate as immediate reality. Many artists in Russia don't seem to realize that. Take Bronnikov's "Hymn of the Pythagoreans," for instance. Some genre painter (even one of our most talented) might even be surprised at how a contemporary artist could pick such subjects. And yet subjects such as these (almost fantastic ones) are just as real and just as essential to art and to humans as is immediate reality.

What is genre, in essence? Genre is the art of portraying contemporary, immediate reality that the artist has himself felt personally and has seen with his own eyes, in contrast with historical reality, for instance, which cannot be seen with one's own eyes and which is portrayed not in its immediate but in its completed aspect. (Let me make a *nota bene* here: I said "seen with his own eyes." But Dickens never saw Pickwick with his own eyes; he perceived him only in a variety of forms of reality that he had observed; he created a character and presented him as the result of his observations. Thus this character is every bit as real as one who really exists, even though Dickens took only an ideal of the reality.) But what happens here is a confusion of conceptions of reality. Historical reality in art, for instance, is naturally not that of immediate reality (genre) precisely because the former is completed and not current. Ask any psychologist you like and he will tell you that if you imagine some event of the past, especially of the distant past—one that is completed and historical (and to live without imagining the past is impossible)—then the event will *necessarily* be imagined in its completed aspect, i.e., with the addition of all its subsequent developments that had not yet occurred at the historical moment in which the artist is trying to depict a person or event. And thus the essence of a historical event cannot even be imagined by an artist exactly as it probably happened in reality. And so the artist is overcome by a kind of superstitious fear of the fact that he will perhaps have to "idealize" despite himself, which to his mind means to lie. So, to avoid this imaginary error, he tries (and there were cases of this) to combine both realities—the historical and the immediate; from this unnatural combination arises the worst kind of untruth. In my view this pernicious error can be seen in certain of Mr. Ge's paintings. For instance, he took his "Last Supper," which once created such a stir, and made a regular genre painting out of it. Look at it more carefully: this is an ordinary quarrel of some very ordinary people. There sits Christ—but is that Christ? It may be a very good young man, deeply hurt by his quarrel with Judas, who is standing there getting dressed to go off and denounce him, but this is not the Christ we know. His friends have crowded around the Teacher to comfort him; but we must ask the question: where are the eighteen centuries of Christianity that followed, and how are they connected with the event? How is it possible that from such an ordinary quarrel of such ordinary people gathered to have supper, such as Mr. Ge depicts, there could arise something so colossal?

Nothing at all is explained here; there is no historical truth here; there is not even any truth of genre here; everything here is false.

No matter from which point of view you judge, this event could not have happened this way: everything here is disproportionate and out of scale with the future. Titian, at least, would have given this Teacher a face like the one he gave him in his famous picture "Render unto Caesar"; then many things would have become clear at once. In Mr. Ge's picture some good people have simply gotten into a quarrel; the result is something false, a preconceived idea. And falsity is always a lie and not realism at all. Mr. Ge was trying for realism. [. . .]

Article 15, extract. Something about Lying

[...] "Innocuous things, old hat; we've heard it a thousand times," people will say again. That may well be, but here is something still more characteristic. There is a point on which any Russian person of the educated category, when appearing in society or in public, is terribly exacting and will not yield an inch. (At home or in his own mind it's another matter.) This point is intellect, the desire to appear more clever than he is and—this is remarkable—it is certainly not a desire to seem cleverer than everybody else or even cleverer than anyone in particular but only *not to be stupider than anyone else.* "Just admit," he says, "that I'm not stupider than anyone else and I'll admit that you're not stupider than anyone else." Once again we have something in the nature of mutual gratitude here. To take an example: as we know, the Russian will happily and eagerly defer to European authority without even permitting himself any analysis of the matter; he particularly does not like to analyze such instances. Oh, it's another matter should the authority of genius come down from his pedestal or simply go out of fashion: then no one is more severe to that authority than the Russian intelligentsia; there is no limit to its arrogance, contempt, and mockery. We stand in naive amazement later if we find out that in Europe they continue to respect the authority who has come down from his pedestal here and that they still pay him his full due. But that very same Russian, although he may have bowed before that fashionable genius without ever analyzing why, will still never ever admit that he is stupider than this genius before whom he has just bowed, no matter how ultra-European he may be. "Well, so there's a Goethe and a Liebig and a Bismarck, we'll say ... but still, I amount to something too"—this is how every Russian, even the most wretched, if it comes to that, pictures it. In fact, it's not a matter of "picturing," since there is scarcely any conscious thought here; it is more of a spasmodic reaction. It is a kind of continual sensation of idle, random, and quite unjustified self-esteem. In short, the Russian of the higher classes can never, under any circumstances, attain that highest, perhaps, degree of manifestation of human dignity which is to acknowledge oneself less intelligent than another when this truly is the case; I don't even know if there can be exceptions to this. I hope that people don't find my "paradox" too amusing. A rival of Liebig who, perhaps, never finished his high-school course, will naturally not try to argue that he is the better man when he's told that he is in the presence of Liebig himself. He'll hold his peace; but still, something will be urging him on to make a claim, even in Liebig's presence. . . . It's another matter if, let's say, he were to meet Liebig without knowing it in a railway car, say. And if the talk turned to chemistry and our gentleman managed to get into the conversation, then there's no doubt that he could keep up a most complete, learned argument, knowing no more about the subject than the single word "chemistry" itself. Liebig would be astonished, of course, but in the eyes of the other listeners our gentleman might emerge the victor. For in terms of boldness the learned language of the Russian knows scarcely any bounds. Here there arises a phenomenon that exists only in the soul of the Russian educated classes: in that soul, *as soon as it finds itself in public,* not only is there no doubt of its own intelligence but there is not even any doubt of its own complete erudition, if the matter comes to erudition. One might understand the matter of intelligence; but as concerns one's erudition, I should think that each person ought to have the most accurate information on the subject. [. . .]

Article 16. One of Today's Falsehoods

Some of our critics have noted that in my latest novel, *The Devils*, I used the story of the well-known Nechaev affair; but at the same time they stated that I did not include specific portraits in my novel, nor did I make a literal reproduction of the Nechaev story; they said that I took a phenomenon and attempted only to explain how it could arise in our society, and this in the sense of a social phenomenon, not in an anecdotal sense, and not merely as an account of a particular incident in Moscow. For my part, I may say that all of this is quite correct. In my novel I do not touch personally upon the notorious Nechaev or his victim, Ivanov. *My* Nechaev character is, of course, unlike the actual Nechaev. I wanted to pose the question and, as clearly as possible, provide an answer to it in the form of a novel: how is it possible in our changing and astonishing society of today to have not a Nechaev but *Nechaevs*, and how does it happen that these *Nechaevs* eventually acquire their own Nechaevists?

And so, recently—a month ago in fact—I read in *The Russian World* the following curious lines:

> ... we think that the Nechaev case ought to convince us that *students* in Russia do not get mixed up in such lunacy. An idiotic fanatic such as Nechaev could find proselytes only among the idle and underdeveloped and not among young people involved in studies.

And further:

> ... the more so that only recently the Minister of Education (in Kiev) stated that after an inspection of educational institutions in seven districts he could say that "*in recent years our young people regard their studies with incomparably greater seriousness and study much more, and much more diligently.*"

By themselves—judging entirely independently—these lines do not signify very much (I hope the author will pardon me for saying so). But they contain a distortion and an old, tiresome lie. The complete and basic idea here is that if Nechaevs occasionally do surface among us, then they absolutely must be idiots and fanatics; and if they also manage to find followers, then it absolutely must be *"only* among the idle and underdeveloped and *not* among young people involved in studies." I don't know just what the author of the little article in *The Russian World* meant to prove by this distortion: did he want to flatter our students? Or, to the contrary, did he, through this sly maneuver, try, by seeming to flatter them, to trick them a little—but with the most honest intentions, for their own good; I mean did he use for this end the well-known method that governesses and nurses apply to little children: "Look, children, how *those* bad creatures are shouting and fighting; they'll certainly be punished for their bad behavior. But you, now, are such dear, sweet, good children; you sit up straight while you're eating; you don't swing your feet under the table; and for that you'll certainly be given some sweets"? Or, finally, did the author simply want to "defend" our students from the government and use for this end a means which, perhaps, he considers extraordinarily sly and subtle?

Let me say frankly: although I posed all these questions, the personal aims of the author of the little article in *The Russian World* do not arouse the slightest interest in me. And so as to make my point absolutely clear, I will even add that the falsehood and tiresome old distortion in the idea expressed by *The Russian World* I am inclined to consider in the present instance as something accidental and unpremeditated: I mean that the author of the article himself believed his own words fully and accepted them for the truth with that elevated simplicity which in any other case would be most laudable and even touchingly disarming. But aside from the fact that a falsehood taken as truth always has a most dangerous appearance (even though it may appear in *The Russian World*)—aside from that, one can't help but be struck by the fact that never before has it appeared in such a stark, precise, and artless form as in this little article. Truly, there are some people who, if made to bow down and worship God, would break their foreheads. So it is from that point of view that it is interesting to trace the development of this falsehood and clarify it as well as possible, for we shall wait a long time before finding another example of such artless candor!

For longer than anyone can remember in our pseudoliberal times it has been the accepted rule of our newspaper press to "defend our young people": from whom? from what? The answers to those questions sometimes remain in a fog of uncertainty, and thus the matter takes on a most ridiculous and even comic aspect, especially when it involves attacks on other organs of the press in the sense that "we're more liberal than you are, you see; you are attacking young people and so you must be more reactionary." I'll note in parentheses that that same little article in *The Russian World* contains an accusation plainly directed at *The Citizen*: we are supposedly making a blanket accusation against students in Petersburg, Moscow, and Kharkov. Leaving aside the fact that the author of the article *knows full well* himself that we never made any such wholesale accusation, I would simply ask him to explain what he means by a wholesale accusation against young people. I don't understand this at all! It means, of course, to dislike for some reason all young people as a whole, and not even young people so much as young people of a certain age! What kind of muddled thinking is this? Who can put any stock in such an accusation? It's clear that both the accusation and the defense have been made off the cuff, as it were, without even taking much thought. It's worth pondering this: "I've demonstrated that I am liberal, that I praise our young people and take to task those who don't praise them—that's enough to keep our subscribers happy, and the matter's done with, thank goodness!" Indeed, "the matter's done with," for only the bitterest enemy of our young people could undertake to defend them *in this way* and to come up with such an astounding distortion (accidentally—I am now more than ever convinced) as did the naive author of the little article in *The Russian World*.

The whole importance of this matter lies in the fact that this technique is not the invention of *The Russian World* alone but one common to many organs of our pseudoliberal press, and there, perhaps, it is used in not so naive a fashion. Its essence, *in the first place,* is in wholesale praise of our young people, in everything and in every instance, and in crude attacks on all those who may on occasion permit themselves to take a critical attitude even toward youth. The technique is based on the absurd assumption that young people are still so immature and so fond of flattery that they will not understand and will accept everything at face value. And, in truth, things have reached the stage where very many of our young people (I firmly believe not all of them, by any means) really have come to like this crude praise, demand flattery, and are prepared to accuse without discrimination all those who do not indulge them in everything and at every step, particularly in some situations. The damage done by this is still only temporary, however; with age and experience the views of our young people will change as well. But there is also another side to the falsehood, which involves direct and material damage.

This second aspect of the technique of "defending our young people from society and from the government" consists in the simple *denial of the fact,* a denial that is sometimes crude and brazen: "There is no fact," they say. "There never was and there never could have been; he who says there was is therefore slandering our youth and is therefore the enemy of our youth!"

That is the technique. I repeat, the bitterest enemy of our young people could not have invented anything more prejudicial to their direct interests. This I certainly wish to prove.

By denying the fact at all costs one can achieve amazing results.

Well, gentlemen, what are you going to prove and how are you helping the matter when you begin asserting (and why—God only knows) that young people who are "led astray"—those, that is, who can be led astray (even by Nechaev)—must absolutely consist only of "the idle and under-developed," those who do not study at all; in short, that they must be loafers with the very worst tendencies? In such a fashion, by isolating the case and by removing it from the sphere of those who do study and reducing it only to "the idle and underdeveloped," you thus indict in advance these unfortunate people and disavow them once and for all: "You yourselves are to blame; you're rowdy and lazy and haven't learned to sit quietly at the table." By isolating the case and depriving it of the right to be examined in the context of the whole (and it is precisely here that the only possible defense of these unfortunate "lost sheep" lies), you thus not only sign the final sentence against them, as it were, but even deprive them of compassion itself, for you flatly assert that their very errors were caused only by their despicable qualities and that these youths, even without committing any crime, must arouse contempt and disgust.

On the other hand, what would happen if we suddenly found that those involved in some *case* or other were by no means underdeveloped rowdies who swing their feet under the table, were by no means only idlers but, on the contrary, were diligent, ardent young people who were in fact studying and who possessed good hearts but who had only been set off on a wrong tendency? (Please understand this phrase "set off on a tendency": wherever in Europe could you now find more uncertain shifting among all sorts of tendencies than in Russia today?) And so, according to your theory of "idlers and underdeveloped people," these new "unfortunates" appear as thrice guilty: "They were given the proper means; they finished their education; they worked hard—they have no justification! They are three times less deserving of compassion than idle, underdeveloped people!" That is the result that comes directly from your theory.

Please, gentlemen (I am speaking in general and not only to the writer from *The Russian World*), on the basis of your "denial of the fact" you assert that the Nechaevs absolutely must be idiots, "idiotic fanatics." Is that really so? Is that just? In the present instance I set Nechaev aside and say "Nechaevs," in the plural. Yes, among the Nechaevs there can be creatures who are very shadowy, very dismal and misshapen, with a thirst for intrigue and power of most complex origins, with a passionate and pathologically premature urge to express their personalities, but why must they be "idiots"? On the contrary, even the genuine monsters among them may be very well developed, extremely clever, and even educated people. Or do you think that knowledge, a course of training, a few facts picked up in school (or even in university) form the soul of a youth so thoroughly that with the receipt of his diploma he at once acquires an unfailing talisman that once and for all enables him to recognize the truth and avoid temptations, passions, and vices? And so, by your way of thinking, all these youths who complete their studies at once become something like a multitude of little popes with the power of infallibility.

And why do you suppose that the Nechaevs must absolutely be fanatics? Very often they are simply scoundrels. "I am a scoundrel, not a socialist," says one Nechaev. True, he says that in my novel *The Devils,* but I assure you that he could have said it in real life. These scoundrels are very crafty and have thoroughly studied the magnanimous aspect

of the human soul—and most often the soul of youth—so as to be able
to play on it as on a musical instrument. And do you really think that
the proselytes whom some such Nechaev could gather in Russia must
absolutely consist only of loafers? I don't believe that; not all of them
would be. I myself am an old "Nechaevist"; I also stood on the scaffold
condemned to death, and I assure you that I stood in the company of
educated people. Almost that whole company had graduated from the
highest institutions of learning. Some of them, later on, *when everything
had passed,* distinguished themselves by making remarkable contribu-
tions to specialized fields. No, gentlemen, the Nechaevists do not always
come only from idlers who have never studied anything.

I know that you will doubtless reply that I wasn't a Nechaevist at all
but only one of the Petrashevsky Circle (although I think that name is
incorrect, since a far greater number—compared with those who were
standing on the scaffold but who were members of the circle the same as
we—remained absolutely untouched and undisturbed. True, they never
even knew Petrashevsky, but this long-past story was not at all about
Petrashevsky in any case. That is all I wanted to note).

But let that be; I was a member of the Petrashevsky Circle, then. How
do you know that the members of that circle could not have become
Nechaevists, i.e., set off on Nechaev's path, *in the event that things had
taken such a turn?* Of course, one couldn't even have imagined that at
the time: how could things have ever *taken such a turn?* Times then
were completely different. But let me say one thing about myself alone:
a *Nechaev* I probably could never have become, but a *Nechaevist*—well,
of that I can't be sure; perhaps I could have become one . . . in the days
of my youth.

I spoke of myself just now in order to have the right to speak about
others. Nonetheless, I will go on talking only about myself, and if I do
mention others then it is in general, impersonally, and in a completely
abstract sense. The *case* of the Petrashevsky Circle is such an old one and
belongs to such ancient history that probably no harm will come from my
recalling it now, the more so that I do it in such an elusive and abstract
way.

There was not a single "monster" or "scoundrel" among the
Petrashevsky Circle (whether we speak of those who stood on the scaffold or those who remained untouched—it's all the same). I think that no

one can refute this statement. That there were educated people among
us—that, too, as I have already noted, is not likely to be disputed. But
there were not many among us who could resist that well-known cycle
of ideas and concepts that had then taken such a firm hold on young
society. We were infected with the ideas of the then theoretical socialism.
Political socialism did not exist in Europe at that time, and the European
ringleaders of the socialists even rejected it.

It was in vain that Louis Blanc had his face slapped and his hair
pulled (as if deliberately, he had hair that was very thick and black) by his
colleague-members of the National Assembly, the deputies of the right,
from whose hands Arago (the astronomer and member of the government,
now deceased) tore him on that unhappy morning in May of 1848 when
a mob of impatient and hungry workers broke into the Chamber. Poor
Louis Blanc, who had been a member of the Provisional Government
for a time, had certainly not incited them: he had only given a lecture in
the Luxembourg Palace, on the "right to work," to these wretched and
hungry people who had been deprived of their livelihood as a result of the
revolution and the republic. It is true that since he was still a member of
the government his lectures in that sense were extremely indiscreet and,
of course, absurd. Considérant's journal, just like Proudhon's articles
and pamphlets, tried to spread among these hungry, destitute workers
a complete loathing for the right of hereditary private property, among
other things. There is no doubt that from all this (i.e., from the impatience
of hungry people inflamed by theories of future bliss) there later arose
political socialism, whose essence, despite all the goals it proclaims, still
consists only in the desire for the universal robbery of all the property-
owning classes by the have-nots, and then "let things happen as they
will." (For as yet they have not properly decided anything about the kind
of society that will replace the current one; all they are certain of is that
the present has been a total failure—and to date that is the entire formula
of political socialism.) But in those days the matter was still seen in the
rosiest and most blissfully moral light. It is really true that at the time this
nascent socialism was being compared—even by some of its ringleaders—
with Christianity, and was taken as merely a correction and improvement
of the latter, in accordance with the spirit of the age and civilization. All
these new ideas of the time had tremendous appeal for us in Petersburg;
they seemed to be sacred and moral in the highest degree and, most of all,

they seemed to be universal—the future law of all humanity without exception. Even well before the Paris revolution of 1848 we were caught up by the fascinating power of these ideas. Even in 1846 Belinsky had initiated me into the whole *truth* of this coming "regenerated world" and into the whole *sanctity* of the future communistic society. All these convictions of the immorality of the very foundations (Christian ones) of contemporary society and of the immorality of religion and the family; of the immorality of the right to private property; of the elimination of nationalities in the name of the universal brotherhood of people and of contempt for one's fatherland as something that only slowed universal development, and so on and so forth—all these things were influences we were unable to resist and which, in fact, captured our hearts and minds in the name of something very noble. In any case, the whole topic seemed a majestic one that stood far above the level of the prevailing ideas of the day, and that was precisely what was so seductive. Those of us—that is, not only those of the Petrashevsky Circle alone but those in general who were then *infected* but who later on utterly rejected all these visionary ravings, all this gloom and horror being prepared for humanity supposedly to regenerate it and restore it to life—those of us at the time still did not know the causes of our illness and therefore were still unable to struggle against it. And so why, then, do you think that even murder à la Nechaev would have stopped us—not all of us, of course, but at least some of us—in those frenetic times, surrounded by doctrines that had captured our souls, in the midst of the devastating events in Europe at the time—events that we, neglecting our own country, followed with feverish anxiety?

There can be no doubt whatever that the murderer Nechaev portrayed the monstrous and repulsive murder of Ivanov in Moscow to his victims, the "Nechaevists," as a political matter, useful to the future "common and *great* cause." Otherwise one simply cannot comprehend how a few youths (whoever they might have been) could have agreed to such a dismal crime. Once again, in my novel *The Devils,* I attempted to depict those diverse and multifarious motives by which even the purest of hearts and the most innocent of people can be drawn into committing such a monstrous offense. And therein lies the real horror: that in Russia one can commit the foulest and most villainous act without being in the least a villain! And this happens not only in Russia but all over the world, and it has happened since time began, in times of transition when people's lives are being thoroughly unsettled, when there are doubts and denials, skepticism and uncertainty in fundamental social convictions. But this is more possible in Russia than anywhere else, particularly in our time, and this trait is the most unhealthy and melancholy one of our present age. The possibility of considering oneself—and sometimes even being, in fact—an honorable person while committing obvious and undeniable villainy—that is our whole affliction today!

What, in particular, are young people—in comparison with people of other ages—being defended from which makes you, the people who defend them, demand that almost as soon as they have done something and studied diligently they show a steadfastness and maturity of conviction which even their fathers did not possess and which today is less evident than ever? Our young people of the educated classes, raised in families where one most often encounters dissatisfaction, impatience, crude ignorance (despite the level of education of these classes), and where genuine education is almost everywhere replaced by an insolently negative attitude copied from others; where material concerns hold sway over every higher idea; where children are brought up without any grounding in their native soil, with no natural truth, with that disrespect or indifference toward their native land and that scornful contempt for the People which has become so common in recent times—is it here, from this wellspring, that our young people are to draw the truth and integrity of conviction to guide them on their first steps in life? This is where the source of the evil lies: in the tradition; in the legacy of ideas; in our national, age-old stifling in ourselves of any kind of independent thought; in the notion of the high status of a European, unfailingly with the proviso of disrespect to oneself as a Russian!

But probably you won't put any stock in these very general remarks of mine. "Education," you say; "hard work." "Lazy, underdeveloped people," you repeat. Keep in mind, gentlemen, that all these exalted European teachers of ours—our light and our hope—all these Mills and Darwins and Strausses sometimes have a very strange view of the moral obligations of a person of today. And yet these are not idlers who have learned nothing, and they are not rowdy children who swing their feet under the table. You'll laugh and ask me why I took it into my head to mention these names in particular. It's because when one speaks of our intelligent, ardent young students it's difficult even to imagine that they could escape these names as they take their first steps in life. Can a Russian youth remain indifferent to the influence of these leaders of progressive European thought and others like them, and in particular to the Russian aspect of their teachings? Please allow me this funny phrase "the Russian aspect of their teachings" because a Russian aspect of their teachings really does exist. It consists of those conclusions drawn from their teachings that take on the form of an invincible axiom, conclusions that are drawn only in Russia; in Europe, as people say, the possibility of these conclusions is not even suspected. People will tell me, perhaps, that these thinkers are certainly not propagating evil notions; that, for example, even if Strauss does hate Christ and has set himself the life's goal of mocking and despising Christianity, he nevertheless worships humanity as a whole and his teaching is as elevated and noble as can be. It's very possible that all this is true and that the goals of all today's leaders of progressive European thought are philanthropic and magnificent. But what I believe to be certain is this: if you were to give all these grand, contemporary teachers full scope to destroy the old society and build it anew, the result would be such obscurity, such chaos, something so crude, blind, and inhuman that the whole structure would collapse to the sound of humanity's curses before it could ever be completed. Once having rejected Christ, the human mind can go to amazing lengths. That's an axiom. Europe, or at least the highest representatives of her thought, rejects Christ; we, as we know, are obliged to copy Europe.

There are historical moments in the lives of people in which obvious, brazen villainy of the crudest sort can be considered no more than greatness of soul, no more than the noble courage of humanity tearing itself free from its chains. Do you really need examples of this? Are there not thousands of examples? Tens of thousands? Hundreds of thousands? ... It's a complicated and immense topic, of course, and it's very difficult to take it up in an article like this; but nevertheless, in the final analysis I think that my own proposition might also be considered: that even an honest and open-hearted boy, even one who does well in school, may, sometimes, become a Nechaevist . . . again, of course, assuming he happens to come across a Nechaev; that's a sine qua non. . . .

We of the Petrashevsky Circle stood on the scaffold and listened to our sentences without the least bit of repentance. Obviously, I cannot testify for all of us; but I think that I'm not mistaken in saying that at that moment, if not each one of us, then the great majority would have deemed it dishonorable to renounce our convictions. This is a matter from the distant past, and therefore, perhaps, one might also ask the question: could that stubbornness and lack of repentance not be merely the signs of a bad nature, signs of underdeveloped and rowdy children? No, we were not rowdy children and perhaps were not even bad young people. The sentence of death by firing squad that was read to us at first was certainly not pronounced as a joke; almost all the condemned were convinced that the sentence would be carried out and underwent at least ten dreadful, infinitely terrible minutes expecting to die. During these final moments, some of us (I know this for certain) instinctively withdrew into ourselves and, in examining our whole, still so young lives, did repent of certain of our meaner actions (those which lie lifelong in secret on the conscience of every person); but that deed for which we had been condemned, those ideas and those notions which possessed our spirits, we saw as not only requiring no repentance but even somehow as purifying us in a martyrdom for which we would be forgiven much! And so it continued for a long time. It was not the years of exile and not the sufferings which broke us. On the contrary: nothing broke us, and our convictions only supported our spirits by the awareness of a duty fulfilled. No, it was something else which changed our views, our convictions, and our hearts. (I permit myself, of course, to speak only of those of us whose change of conviction became known and who themselves testified to this in one way or another.) This "something else" was the direct contact with the People, the brotherly union with them in common misfortune, the awareness that we ourselves had become as they, equal to them, and even placed on the very lowest of their levels.

I repeat that this did not happen very quickly, but gradually and after a very long, long time. It was not pride and not vanity that stood in the way of confession. And yet I was, perhaps, one of those (I again am speaking only of myself) who found it easiest to return to the root of the People, to discover the Russian soul, to recognize the People's spirit. I came from a family that was Russian and pious. As far back as I can remember I recall my parents' love for me. In our family we knew the Gospels virtually from our earliest childhood. I was only ten years old when I already knew almost all the main episodes from Karamzin's Russian history, which our father read aloud to us in the evenings. Each visit to the Kremlin and the Moscow cathedrals was a solemn event for me. Others, perhaps, did not have the kinds of memories I had. I very often ponder the question and ask it now: what are the chief impressions that today's young people gain from their childhood? And if even I, who naturally could not haughtily pass by that new, fateful milieu into which misfortune thrust us and could not regard the spirit of the People as it manifested itself before me with only a superficial, haughty glance—if I, I am saying, found it so difficult to convince myself at last of the falsehood and injustice of almost all that we had previously regarded as light and truth, then what of the others, who were even more deeply alienated from the People, whose alienation was hereditary and acquired from their fathers and grandfathers?

It would be very difficult to tell the story of the rebirth of my convictions, the more so because it is not that interesting, perhaps; and somehow it is not appropriate for a feuilleton article. . . .

. . . .

Gentlemen who defend our young people: will you take into account that milieu and that society in which these young people grow up and ask yourselves: can there be anything in our time which is less protected from *certain influences?*

First of all, pose the question: if the very fathers of these young people are not better, not firmer, and not healthier in their convictions; if from their earliest childhood these children have encountered in their own families nothing but cynicism, haughty and indifferent (for the most part) negation; if the words "native land" have only been uttered before them with a mocking intonation and all those who brought them up regarded Russia's cause with scorn or indifference; if the noblest among their fathers and educators spoke only to them of "universally human" ideas; if even in childhood their nurses were dismissed because they read the Prayer to the Virgin Mary over their cradles—then tell me: what can one ask of these children, and is it humane when one is defending them—if any such defense is needed—to escape by a mere denial of the fact?

Not long ago I happened to find the following *entrefilet* in the newspapers: "*The Kama-Volga Gazette* reports that recently three *high-school students* in their third year at the Second Kazan High School *have been charged* with a crime connected with *their proposed flight to America.*"

(*St. Petersburg Gazette*, November 13). Twenty years ago the news of some third-year high-school students running off to America would have seemed utter nonsense to me. But the fact alone that *now* this doesn't seem like nonsense but something I can *understand*—in that alone I can see its justification!

Justification! Good Lord, can one use that word?

I know that these are not the first such students and that others have run off even before, and they did so because their elder brothers and fathers had run off. Do you remember Kel'siev's story of the poor officer who fled ~~on foot,~~ via Tornio and Stockholm, to Herzen in London, where the latter found work for him as a compositor in his printing shop? Do you remember Herzen's own story of that *cadet* who set off for the Philippine Islands, I think, to set up a commune and who had left Herzen 20,000 francs for future emigrants? And yet all that is already ancient history! Since then, old men, fathers, brothers, young women, and guards officers have run off to America to experience "free labor in a free country." . . . Probably the only ones who haven't tried it are seminary students. Can we blame little children such as these three high-school students if their poor heads were turned by the grand ideas of "free work in a free country" and the commune and the common-European man? Can we blame them if all this rubbish seems a religion to them, while emigration and betrayal of one's native land seems a virtue? And if we do blame them, then to what extent? That's the question.

In order to support his idea that *only* layabouts and idling defectives become involved in "such lunacy" in Russia, the author of the article in *The Russian World* cites the well-known and encouraging remarks of the Minister of Education, who said not long ago in Kiev that he had been convinced, after an inspection of educational institutions in seven districts, that "*in recent years our young people regard their studies with incomparably greater seriousness and study much more, and much more diligently.*"

These are encouraging words, of course, words in which, perhaps, lies our *only* hope. The educational reform carried out during the present reign contains almost *all* our future possibilities, and we know it. But the Minister of Education himself, if I recall, stated in that same speech that we have long to wait before we shall see the final results of the reform. We always believed that our young people were quite capable of taking a more serious attitude toward their studies. But meanwhile we are still blanketed by such a fog of false ideas; we and our young people are surrounded by so many mirages and prejudices, while our whole social life—the lives of the fathers and mothers of these young people—takes on a stranger and stranger aspect, so that one cannot help but look for any and all ways to lead us out of our confusion. One of those ways is for us to be less callous, not to be ashamed when someone calls us on occasion a citizen and . . . once in a while to tell the truth, even though, to your way of thinking, it may be insufficiently liberal.

1876

Announcement: Subscriptions to *A Writer's Diary* for 1876

In the coming year F. M. Dostoevsky's publication, *A Writer's Diary*, will appear monthly in separate issues.

Each issue will be composed of sixteen to twenty-four pages of small print in the format of our weekly newspapers. But this will not be a newspaper; all twelve issues (for January, February, March, etc.) will form a whole, a book written by a single pen. It will be a diary in the literal sense of the word, an account of impressions actually experienced each month, an account of what was seen, heard, and read. Of course, some stories and tales may be included, but preeminently it will be about actual events. Each issue will come out on the last day of the month and will be sold separately in all bookstores for twenty kopecks. But those wishing to subscribe to the whole year's edition will enjoy a discount and will pay only two rubles (not including delivery and mailing); the cost with mailing and home delivery will be two rubles, fifty kopecks.

Subscriptions from local subscribers in Petersburg are being accepted in A. F. Bazunov's bookstore, near the Kazan Bridge, house No. 30, and in M. P. Nadein's "Store for Out-of-Towners," 44 Nevsky Prospect. In Moscow: at the Central Bookstore, Nikolsky Street, Slavyansky Bazaar Building.

Those from outside the capitals are kindly requested to deal solely with the author, who may be reached at the following address: Fedor Mikhailovich Dostoevsky, Apt. 6, Strubinsky House, Greek Street, by the Greek church, St. Petersburg.

January

[COMPLETE ISSUE]

CHAPTER ONE

Article 1. In Place of a Foreword. On the Great and Small Bears, on Great Goethe's Prayer, and, Generally, on Bad Habits.

. . . At least Khlestakov, when he was spinning his lies to the Mayor, was still just a tiny bit apprehensive that they might grab him and throw him out of the drawing room. Our contemporary Khlestakovs are afraid of nothing and lie with complete composure.

Nowadays they all are completely composed. Composed and perhaps even happy. Scarcely anyone takes stock of himself; everyone acts "naturally," and sees this as complete happiness. Nowadays, just as before, vanity eats away at everyone, but yesterday's vanity would enter timidly, casting feverish glances about, looking intently at others' reactions: "Did I make the right sort of entrance? Did I say the right thing?" But nowadays when someone enters a room he is firmly convinced that everything belongs to him alone. And if it turns out not to be his alone, he doesn't even get angry but resolves the matter at once. Haven't you heard about notes like this: "Dear Papa, I am twenty-three years old and I still have accomplished nothing. I am certain that I will never amount to anything, so I have decided to end my life. . . ."

And he shoots himself. But here at least we can understand something: "What is there to live for if not for pride?" he says. But another fellow will take a look around and go off and shoot himself in silence, solely because he hasn't the money to acquire a mistress. And that is the act of a total swine.

The newspapers assure us that this happens because such people think too much. "He spends a long time thinking quietly, and suddenly he hits on just the thing he had been aiming for all along." My conviction is quite the contrary: he doesn't think at all; he simply isn't capable of formulating an idea; he is as benighted as a savage, and if he conceives a longing for something, it comes from deep within him and not from conscious thought. It's the behavior of an utter swine, and there is nothing liberal about it.

And there is not a moment of Hamlet's pondering "that dread of something after death. . . ."

And there is something terribly strange about this. Is such thoughtlessness really a part of the Russian character? I say thoughtlessness, not senselessness. Don't believe, then; but think, at least. Our suicide doesn't have even a shadow of a suspicion that he is called *I* and is an immortal being. It seems he hasn't even heard a thing about that. And yet he's by no means an atheist. Remember the atheists of times gone by: when they lost their faith in one thing, they at once began to believe passionately in something else. Remember the passionate faith of Diderot, Voltaire. . . . But among us they are a complete tabula rasa, and it's not a matter of Voltaire at all: our fellow just had no money to acquire a mistress, and nothing more.

When young Werther ends his life, he regrets, in the last lines he left, that he will never again see "the beautiful constellation, the Great Bear," and bids it farewell. Oh, how that little touch reveals Goethe, who was only then beginning his career! Why did young Werther feel so deeply about these constellations? Because every time he contemplated them he realized that he was no mere atom or nonentity before them, and that the whole infinitude of divine, mysterious wonders were by no means beyond his thought, nor beyond his consciousness, nor beyond the ideal of beauty that lay in his soul, and that, accordingly, they were equal to him and revealed his kinship with the infinity of being . . . and that for all the happiness of experiencing such a grand idea, an idea that revealed who he was, he was obliged only *to his image as a human being.*

"O Great Spirit, I thank Thee for the human image that Thou hast given me."

And that should have been great Goethe's prayer throughout his life. We, however, take the human image that has been given to us and smash it to pieces, quite simply and without any of these German tricks; and as for the Great Bear, or the Little Bear for that matter—well, no one would think of bidding them farewell; and if anyone did think of it, he wouldn't do it: that would be just too embarrassing.

"Now what are you on about?" an astonished reader asks.

"I just wanted to write a foreword, because you simply can't do without one altogether."

"If that's the case then you'd better make clear what your tendency is and what your convictions are. Explain: what sort of man are you, and how did you make so bold as to announce this *Writer's Diary?*"

But that's very difficult, and I can see that I'm not much of a hand at writing forewords. Writing a foreword is perhaps as difficult as writing a letter. As far as liberalism is concerned (instead of the word "tendency" I'll simply use the word "liberalism")—as far as liberalism is concerned, the well-known "Mr. X," in a recent feuilleton in which he commented on how the press greeted the new year of 1876, recalls in passing, and not without sarcasm, that everything went off rather liberally. I'm pleased that he was sarcastic. In truth, our liberalism lately has been transformed everywhere into either a trade or a bad habit. I mean, in itself it certainly would not be a bad habit, but among us it somehow turned out that way. It's strange, even: our liberalism, it seems, belongs to the category of quiescent liberalisms; quiescent and tranquil which, in my opinion, is not very nice, because quietism least of all, it seems, is compatible with liberalism. And yet, in spite of all this tranquility, there are undeniable signs appearing everywhere that very gradually the notions of what is liberal and what is not are disappearing altogether in our society; and in that respect people are becoming thoroughly confused; there are examples of even extreme cases of such confusion. In a word, our liberals, instead of becoming more free, have bound themselves up with liberalism as with ropes, and so I too, taking advantage of this interesting occasion, can pass over the details of my liberalism in silence. But in general I will say that I consider myself more liberal than anyone, if only because I have no wish whatsoever to become quiescent. Well, that's enough about that. As to the type of man I am, I would say the following about myself: "Je suis un homme heureux qui n'a pas l'air content," i.e., "I am a happy man who isn't satisfied with everything...."

With that I finish my foreword. I only wrote it for the sake of form, anyway.

Article 2. A Future Novel. Another "Accidental Family."

There was a Christmas tree and a children's party at the Artists' Club, and I went to have a look at the children. Even formerly I always watched children, but now I pay particular attention to them. For a long time now I have had the goal of writing a novel about children in Russia today, and about their fathers too, of course, in their mutual relationship of today. The "poem" or "idea" is ready and it was the first thing to be created, as should always be the case with a novelist. I will take fathers and children from every level of Russian society I can and follow the children from their earliest childhood.

A year and a half ago, when Nikolai Alekseevich Nekrasov asked me to write a novel for *Notes of the Fatherland,* I almost began my *Fathers and Sons;* but I held back, and thank God I did, for I was not ready. In the meantime I wrote only *A Raw Youth,* this first attempt at my idea. But here the child had already passed his childhood and appeared only as an unprepared person, timidly yet boldly wanting to take his first step in life as quickly as possible. I took a soul that was sinless yet already tainted by the awful possibility of vice, by a premature hatred for its own insignificance and "accidental" nature; tainted also by that breadth of character with which a still chaste soul already consciously allows vice to enter its thoughts, cherishes it and admires it in shameful yet bold and tempestuous dreams—and with all this, left solely to its own devices and its own understanding, yet also, to be sure, to God. All such are the miscarriages of society, the "accidental" members of "accidental" families.

We read in the newspapers not long ago of the murder of a woman named Perova and of the suicide of her murderer. She lived with him; he worked in a printer's shop but had lost his job; she rented an apartment and took in lodgers. Quarrels began. Perova asked him to leave her. The murderer was a man of thoroughly modern character. "If I can't have her then no one can." He gave her his word that he would leave her, then stabbed her barbarically at night, deliberately and with premeditation; then he cut his own throat. Perova left two children, boys of twelve and nine, whom she had borne illegitimately, but not by the murderer and even before she knew him. She loved them. They both witnessed the terrible scene on the evening of the murder when he tormented their mother with reproaches until she fell into a faint; they begged her not to go to his room, but she went.

The newspaper *Voice* appeals to the public to help the "unfortunate orphans," one of whom, the elder, attends High School No. 5; the other is still at home. Here is yet another "accidental family," yet other children with dark shadows cast over their young souls. This dismal picture will remain in their souls forever and might painfully undermine youthful pride from the very days when "all the impressions of existence were new to us." The result will be an inability to cope with life's problems, early pangs of vanity, a blush of false shame for their past, and a dull, sullen hatred for people; and this, perhaps, may last a lifetime. May the Lord bless the future of these innocent children, and may they never cease to love their poor mother without reproach and shame for their love. And we absolutely must help them. On that score our society will respond nobly and with sympathy. Surely they will not have to leave their school once they have begun it. And the elder, apparently, will not leave school and his future seems already arranged; but what of the younger? Surely we won't just collect some seventy or a hundred rubles and then forget about them? Thanks to *The Voice* for reminding us of these unfortunates.

Article 3. The Christmas Party at the Artists' Club.
Children Who Think and Children Who Are Helped Along.
A "Gluttonous Boy." "Oui" Girls. Jostling Raw Youths.
A Moscow Captain in a Hurry.

Of course I'm not going to describe in detail the Christmas party and the dancing at the Artists' Club: all that was done long ago at the proper time, and I read about it myself with much pleasure in other feuilletons. I will say only that prior to this affair I had not been to a single social event anywhere for far too long and had been leading a solitary life for a considerable time.

First the children, all in charming costumes, performed their dances. It's interesting to observe how the most complex concepts are implanted quite imperceptibly in a child and to realize that one who is still unable to connect two thoughts sometimes may have an excellent grasp of life's most profound matters. One German scholar suggested that when a child completes his first three years of life he has already acquired fully a third of the ideas and knowledge that he will take to his grave as an old man. There were even six-year-olds at the Artists' Club, but I am certain that they already fully understood the reasons they had come here, adorned in such fine costumes, while at home they went about bedraggled (and given the means of the middle class of society today, they certainly would be bedraggled). Besides that, they probably already understand that this is exactly how it must be, that this is by no means an exception but a normal law of nature. Of course, they can't express that in words, but they know it inwardly, even though it is a very complex notion.

The smallest children were my favorites; they were very charming and quite at ease. The older ones were at their ease too, but with a certain boldness. Of course, the most free and easy and cheerful were those who will be mediocre and untalented in the future. This is a general rule: medi-ocrities are always free and easy, whether as children or as adults. The more gifted and exceptional among children are always more restrained, and if they are spirited, then they are always disposed toward leading the others and taking charge. It's a pity, too, that everything is made so easy for children nowadays—not only all their studies and acquisition of knowledge, but even their games and toys. The child scarcely begins to lisp his first words and at once people begin to make things easy for him. Our whole system of pedagogy these days is concerned with making things easier. There are times when making things easy does nothing for development but, to the contrary, can even promote dullness. Two or three ideas, two or three impressions deeply experienced in childhood through one's own effort (through one's own suffering as well, if you like) will lead the child much more deeply into life than the easiest school, which quite often produces people who are neither this nor that, neither good nor bad, who are not even depraved in their depravity or virtuous in their virtue.

> What, have the oysters come? Oh, joy!
> And off he rushes, gluttonous boy,
> To swallow. . . .

Now this same "gluttonous boy" (Pushkin's only second-rate verse, because he wrote it quite without irony, and almost with praise) must be the result of something, mustn't he? He's a nasty fellow, and one we have no need of, and I am certain that an education made all too easy greatly facilitates the emergence of such a type; and we have more than enough of his sort already!

Girls, still, are easier to understand than boys. Why is it that girls, almost up to the age of their maturity (but no further) are always more developed or seem more developed than boys of the same age? You can gain a particular understanding of girls while watching them dance: in some you can quickly see a future "oui" girl who will never manage to get married despite all her wishes to do so. I call "oui" girls those who, until almost thirty years of age, answer only *oui* or *non*. On the other hand, there are some who, one can already see, will shortly get married, just as soon as they make up their minds to do so.

It is even more cynical, in my view, to dress a girl who is all but grown up in a child's outfit at a dance; it is truly wrong, in fact. Some such girls, in their short little dresses and bare legs, stayed on to dance with the grownups after the children's ball had ended at midnight and the parents had begun to dance.

Still, I found everything very much to my liking, and had I not been jostled about by the "raw youths," it all would have gone most satisfactorily. In fact, the adults were all elegantly polite, in keeping with the holiday, while the youths (not the children, but the raw youths—future young men, hordes of them, in all sorts of uniforms) jostled about intolerably with no apology, passing to and fro as if they had the right to behave this way. I must have been elbowed fifty times; perhaps they are taught to do that as a means of developing a free and easy manner. Nonetheless, having grown unaccustomed to social events, I was pleased with everything, in spite of the stifling heat in the room, the electric illumination, and the frenzied, imperious shouts of the master of ceremonies.

The other day I picked up a copy of the *Petersburg Gazette* and read a report from Moscow about the various disturbances over the holidays in the Noblemen's Club, in the Circle of Artists, in the theater, at the masquerade, and elsewhere. If one is to believe the correspondent (for when a correspondent reports on vice he may intentionally keep silent about virtue), our society has never been more prone to scandal than at present. It is strange indeed: why is it that, since childhood and all through my life, no sooner do I find myself in a large holiday gathering of Russians than I at once begin thinking that they are only making a pretense and suddenly will jump up and commence a first-rate row, just as they might in their own homes. It's an absurd and fantastical notion, and how ashamed I was of it and how I reproached myself for it, even as a child! It's a notion that won't stand up to the slightest analysis. Oh, of course the shopkeepers and captains the honest correspondent writes about (and I have complete faith in him) existed before and have always existed; they are perennial types; but still, they used to be more timid and hid their feelings, while now, every so often, such a fellow will pop up right on center stage, a fellow who is absolutely convinced he is asserting his new rights. Undeniably, in the last twenty years a terrific number of Russians suddenly imagined that, for some reason, they had become fully entitled to act disgracefully and that now it's a good thing and they will be praised for doing so and not thrown out. On the other hand, I also realize that it's remarkably pleasant (oh, for many, many people!) to stand up in the middle of a social gathering where everyone around—ladies, gentlemen, and even authorities—is so sweet-tongued, polite, and treating one another as equals, as if this were really in Europe somewhere—to stand up amid these Europeans and suddenly bellow out something in the purest national idiom, to fetch someone a cuff on the ear, to blurt out some obscenity to a young lady, and, in general, to commit some indecency right there in the middle of the hall: "There you are, that's what you get for two hundred years of Europeanism; but we're still here, just as we were; we haven't disappeared!" It's pleasant. Still, the savage will be wrong: he won't be acknowledged and will be thrown out. Who will throw him out? The police force? Certainly not—not the police force, but some other savages just like him! That's where the force is. Let me explain.

Do you know who probably most enjoys and appreciates this European and festive gathering of Russian society in European style? Why it's precisely the Skvoznik-Dmukhanovskys, the Chichikovs, and even, perhaps, the Derzhimordas; that is to say, those people who, at home and in their private lives are most completely "national." Oh, yes, they have their own social events and dances *there*, at home, but they have little appreciation or respect for them; what they appreciate is the Governor's ball, a ball with high society like the ones Khlestakov has told them about. But why? Precisely because they themselves are not like polite society. That's why our savage treasures European forms even though he knows very well that he, personally, will not change and will come home from the European ball just the same brawler he was before; but he's comforted by the thought that he's paid homage to virtue, even in the form of an ideal. Oh, he knows very well that all this is only a mirage; yet still, having attended the ball, he's assured himself that this mirage continues and is maintained through some invisible but extraordinary force; and that he himself didn't dare to come out to the middle of the hall bellowing something in the national idiom; and the thought that he had not been permitted to do so and will not be in the future he finds remarkably pleasant. You will not believe how much a barbarian can come to love Europe; such love enables him also to participate in a cult, as it were. Doubtless he often cannot even define the meaning of this cult. Khlestakov, for instance, maintained that the cult consisted of the hundred-ruble melons that were served at high-society balls. Perhaps Skvoznik-Dmukhanovsky, even now, keeps his faith in the watermelon, even though he eventually saw through Khlestakov and scorned him; yet he is happy to pay homage to virtue even in the form of the watermelon. This certainly isn't a matter of hypocrisy here but of the most genuine sincerity—a need, moreover. Hypocrisy works well here, for what is hypocrisy? Hypocrisy is that very tribute which vice is obliged to pay to virtue—an enormously comforting thought for one who wants to remain vicious in practice yet still not break his link, in his heart at least, with virtue. Oh, vice is terribly fond of paying tribute to virtue, and that's a very fine thing; we ought to be satisfied with that much for the time being, should we not? And so the captain, bellowing in the middle of the hall in Moscow, continues to be only an exception and a man in a hurry—well, for the time being at least. Even "for the time being" is a comfort in this shaky age of ours.

Thus the ball is something decidedly conservative, in the best sense of the word; and I'm definitely not joking when I say that.

Article 4. The Golden Age in Your Pocket

Still, I also found the ball rather wearisome; not wearisome, exactly, but somewhat annoying. The children's ball ended and the parents' began, and Lord, what a poor thing it was! Everyone in new clothes, and no one knowing how to wear them; everyone celebrating, and no one happy; everyone full of pride, and no one knowing how to make the most of himself; everyone envious, and everyone silent and aloof. They don't even know how to dance. Look at that very short officer twirling over there (you're certain to encounter such a very short, furiously twirling officer at any middle-class ball). The entire technique of his dancing consists only in the almost brutish way he twirls and jerks his lady about and in his capacity to go on twirling thirty or forty ladies in a row and taking pride in it; but is there anything graceful in that? After all, a dance is almost a declaration of love (think of the minuet), while this fellow looks just as if he's in a brawl. And one quite fantastic and utterly improbable thought occurred to me: "What if all these dear and respectable guests wanted, even for one brief moment, to become sincere and honest? How would this stuffy hall be transformed then? What if each of them suddenly learned the whole secret? What if each one of them suddenly learned how candid, honest, and sincere he really was? What if he knew how much heartfelt joy, purity, noble feelings, goodwill, and intellect—never mind intellect, but wit, most subtle and sociable—he had, and that each and every one of them shared these qualities? Yes, ladies and gentlemen, all that exists within every one of you, and no one, not a single one of you knows anything about it! Oh, dear guests, I swear that each lady and gentleman among you is cleverer than Voltaire, more sensitive than Rousseau, incomparably more alluring than Alcibiades or Don Juan, or any Lucretia, Juliet, or Beatrice! You don't believe that you are that beautiful? But I give you my solemn word that neither in Shakespeare nor in Schiller nor in Homer, nor in all of them put together, can you find anything so charming as now, this very minute, you can find here in this very ballroom. What is Shakespeare! Here you would see something of which our wise men have not dreamed. But your trouble is that you yourselves don't know how beautiful you are! Do you know that each of you, if you only wanted, could at once make everyone in this room happy and fascinate them all? And this power exists in every one of you, but it is so deeply hidden that you have long ceased to believe in it. Do you really think that the golden age exists only on porcelain teacups?

Don't frown at the words *golden age*, Your Excellency: I give you my word of honor that you won't be compelled to walk around in the costume of the golden age wearing only a fig leaf; you can keep your full general's uniform. I assure you that even people of general's rank can get into the golden age. You just have to try, Your Excellency, right now even; you're the senior rank, after all, and the initiative is yours. And you will see yourself what Piron's wit, so to speak, you could display, which would be a complete surprise to you. You're laughing; you don't believe it? I'm glad I made you laugh, and yet my whole outburst just now is not a paradox but the complete truth. . . . And your whole trouble is that you don't believe it.

Chapter Two

Article 1. The Boy with His Hand Out

Children are a strange lot; I dream of them and see them in my fancies. In the days before Christmas and on Christmas Eve itself I kept meeting on a certain street corner a little urchin who could have been no more than seven. In the terrible cold he was wearing clothes more fit for summer, but he did have some sort of old rag wrapped around his neck, which meant that someone had dressed him before sending him out. He was wandering "with hand out"; that's a technical term meaning to go begging, a term coined by such boys themselves. There are many like him; they hang about you, whining some well-rehearsed phrases. But this boy didn't whine; his speech was innocent and unpracticed and he looked trustingly into my eyes; obviously he was only beginning this profession. In answer to my questions he said that he had a sister who was out of work and ill. Perhaps that was true, but only later did I learn that there are hordes of these urchins: they are sent "with hands out" even in the most terrible cold, and if they collect nothing, they probably can expect a beating. Once a boy has collected a few kopecks, he returns with red, numbed hands to some cellar where a band of "dodgers" are drinking. These are people who, "quitting work at the factory on Saturday night, return to work no earlier than Wednesday evening." In the cellars their hungry and beaten wives drink with them; their hungry babies cry here too. Vodka, filth, and depravity, but vodka above all. With the kopecks he has collected in hand, the urchin is at once sent to a tavern and he brings back more vodka. Sometimes, for the fun of it, they pour half a bottle into his mouth and roar with laughter when, his breath catching, he falls to the floor scarcely conscious: ". . . and pitilessly he poured and poured/The horrid vodka into my mouth. . . ."

When he gets older he's quickly packed off to a factory somewhere, but he's forced once again to bring all that he earns back to the dodgers, and they drink it up. But even before they get factory jobs these children become fully fledged criminals. They roam about the city and know places in various cellars into which they can crawl to spend the night unnoticed. One boy slept several nights in succession in a basket in the quarters of a janitor who never even noticed him. It is only natural that they become thieves. Thievery becomes a passion even among eight-year-olds, who sometimes even have no awareness of the criminality of their actions. In the end they bear it all—the hunger, cold, beatings—only for one thing, for freedom. And they run away from the dodgers to take up a vagrant's life on their own. A wild creature such as this sometimes knows nothing at all—neither where he lives, nor what nation he comes from; whether God exists, or the tsar. There are even stories told about them that are hard to believe, yet they are facts.

Article 2. The Boy at Christ's Christmas Party

But I am a novelist and one "story," it seems, I made up myself. Why do I say "it seems" when I know very well that I made it up? Yet I keep imagining that it really happened somewhere, sometime, and happened precisely on Christmas Eve in *a certain* huge city during a terrible cold spell.

I dreamed there was a boy—still very small, about six or even younger—who awoke one morning in the damp and cold cellar where he lived. He was wearing a wretched wrapper of some sort and he was trembling. His breath escaped in a white cloud and, while he sat, bored, in the corner on a trunk, he would let this white vapor out of his mouth and amuse himself by watching it billow up. But he was very hungry. Several times that morning he had approached the bed on which his sick mother lay on a mattress as thin as a pancake, a bundle beneath her head to serve as a pillow. How did she come to be here? Probably she had come with her boy from another city and suddenly fell ill. The landlady of this wretched tenement had been picked up by the police two days ago; the other tenants had all gone off, it being the holiday season, leaving but one dodger who had been lying in a drunken stupor for the last twenty-four hours, having been unable even to wait for the holiday. In another corner of the room an old woman of eighty groaned with rheumatism. She had once worked somewhere as a children's nurse but now was dying alone, moaning, grumbling, and complaining at the boy so that he had become frightened of approaching her corner. In the entry way he managed to find some water to quench his thirst, but nowhere could he find a crust of bread; again and again he went to wake his mother. At last he grew frightened in the darkness; the evening was well advanced, but still no candle had been lit. When he felt his mother's face he was surprised that she made no movement and had become as cold as the wall. "And it's dreadful cold in here," he thought. He stood for a time, absently resting his hand on the dead woman's shoulder; then he breathed on his fingers to warm them, and suddenly his wandering fingers felt his cap that lay on the bed; quietly he groped his way out of the cellar. He would have gone even before but he was afraid of the big dog that howled all day long by the neighbor's door on the stairway above. But the dog was no longer there, and in a trice he was out on the street.

Heavens, what a city! He had never seen anything like it before. In the place he had come from there was such gloomy darkness at night, with only one lamppost for the whole street. The tiny wooden houses were closed in by shutters; as soon as it got dark you wouldn't see a soul on the street; everyone would lock themselves in their houses, only there would be huge packs of dogs—hundreds and thousands of dogs—howling and barking all night. Still, it was so nice and warm there, and there'd be something to eat; but here—Dear Lord, if only there was something to eat! And what a rattling and a thundering there was here, so much light, and so many people, horses, and carriages, and the cold—oh, the cold! Frozen vapor rolls from the overdriven horses and streams from their hot, panting muzzles; their horseshoes ring against the paving stones under the fluffy snow, and everyone's pushing each other, and, Oh Lord, I'm so hungry, even just a little bite of something, and all of a sudden my fingers are aching so. One of our guardians of the law passed by and averted his eyes so as not to notice the boy.

And here's another street—look how wide it is! I'll get run over here for sure. See how everyone's shouting and rushing and driving along, and the lights—just look at them! Now what can this be? What a big window, and in the room behind the glass there's a tree that stretches right up to the ceiling. It's a Christmas tree, with oh, so many lights on it, so many bits of gold paper and apples; and there's dolls and little toy horses all around it; children are running around the room, clean and dressed in nice clothes, laughing and playing, eating and drinking something. Look at that girl dancing with the boy, how fine she is! And you can even hear the music right through the glass. The little boy looks on in amazement and even laughs; but now his toes are aching and his fingers are quite red; he can't bend them any more, and it hurts when he tries to move them. The boy suddenly thought of how much his fingers hurt, and he burst into tears and ran off, and once more he sees a room through another window, and this one also has trees, but there are cakes on the tables, all sorts of cakes—almond ones, red ones, yellow ones; and four rich ladies are sitting there giving cakes to anyone who comes in. The door is always opening to let in all these fine people from the street. The boy crept up, quickly pushed open the door, and went in. Heavens, how they shouted at him and waved him away! One of the ladies rushed up to him and shoved a kopeck in his hand; then she opened the door to let him out on the street again. How frightened he was! And the kopeck rolled right out of his hand and bounced down the stairs: he couldn't bend his red fingers to hold on to it. The boy ran off as quickly as he could, but had no notion of where he was going. He felt like crying again, but he was afraid and just kept on running, breathing on his fingers. And his heart ached because suddenly he felt so lonely and so frightened, and then—Oh, Lord! What's happening now? There's a crowd of people standing around gaping at something: behind the glass in the window there are three puppets, little ones dressed up in red and green and looking just like they were alive! One of them's a little old man, sitting there like he's playing on a big violin, and the others are standing playing on tiny fiddles, wagging their heads in time to the music and looking at one another; their lips are moving and they're talking, really talking, only you can't hear them through the glass. At first the boy thought that they were alive, but when he finally realized that they were puppets he burst out laughing. He had never seen such puppets before and had no idea that such things existed! He still felt like crying, but it was so funny watching the puppets. Suddenly he felt someone grab him from behind: a big brute of a boy stood beside him and suddenly cracked him on the head, tore off his cap, and kicked at his legs. The boy fell down, and the people around him began shouting; he was struck with terror, jumped to his feet and ran off as fast as he could, wherever his legs would take him—through a gateway into a courtyard where he crouched down behind a pile of wood. "They won't find me here, and it's good and dark as well."

He sat there, cowering and unable to catch his breath from fear, and then, quite suddenly, he felt so good: his hands and feet at once stopped aching and he felt as warm and cozy as if he were next to the stove. Then a shudder passed over him: "Why I almost fell asleep!" How nice it would be to go to sleep here: "I'll sit here for a bit and then go back to have a look at those puppets," he thought, and grinned as he recalled them. "Just like they were alive! . . ." Then suddenly he heard his mother singing him a song as she bent over him. "Mamma, I'm going to sleep; oh, how nice it is to sleep here!"

Then a quiet voice whispered over him: "Come with me, son, to my Christmas party."

At first he thought that it was still his mamma, but no—it couldn't be. He couldn't see who had called him, but someone bent over him and hugged him in the darkness; he stretched out his hand . . . and suddenly— what a light there was! And what a Christmas tree! It was more than a tree—he had never seen anything like it! Where can he be? Everything sparkles and shines and there are dolls everywhere—but no, they are all girls and boys, only they are so radiant and they all fly around him, kissing him, picking him up and carrying him off; but he's flying himself; and he sees his mother looking at him and laughs joyously to her.

"Mamma! Mamma! How lovely it is here, mamma!" cries the boy; and he kisses the children again and wants at once to tell them about the puppets behind the glass. "Who are you, boys and girls?" he asks, laughing and feeling that he loves them all.

"This is Christ's Christmas party," they answer. "On this day Christ always has a Christmas party for those little children who have no Christmas tree of their own. . . ." And he learned that all these boys and girls were children just like him, but some had frozen to death in the baskets in which they had been abandoned on the doorsteps of Petersburg officials, others had perished in the keeping of indifferent nurses in orphans' homes, still others had died at the dried-up breasts of their mothers during the Samara famine, and yet others had suffocated from the fumes in third-class railway carriages. And now they are all here, all like angels, all with Christ; and He is in their midst, stretching out His hands to them, blessing them and their sinful mothers. . . . And the mothers of the children stand apart, weeping; each one recognizes her son or daughter; and the children fly to their mothers and wipe away their tears with their tiny hands, begging them not to weep because they are so happy here. . . .

Down below, the next morning, the porters found the tiny body of the runaway boy who had frozen to death behind the woodpile; they found his mother as well. . . . She had died even before him; they met in God's Heaven.

So why did I make up a story like that, so little in keeping with the usual spirit of a sober-minded diary, and a writer's diary at that? All the more since I promised stories preeminently about actual events! But that's just the point: I keep imagining that all this could really have happened—I mean the things that happened in the cellar and behind the woodpile; as for Christ's Christmas party—well, I really don't know what to say: could that have happened? That's just why I'm a novelist—to invent things.

Article 3. A Colony of Young Offenders. Dark Individuals. The Tranformation of Blemished Souls into Immaculate Ones. Measures Acknowledged as Most Expedient Thereto. Little and Bold Friends of Mankind.

On the third day of the holiday I saw all these "fallen" angels, a whole fifty of them altogether. Please don't think I'm joking when I call them that; there can be no doubt that these are children who have been "wronged." Wronged by whom? Who is to blame, and how, and for what? For the moment these are but idle questions for which I have no answer. We'd best get down to business.

I paid a visit to the colony for young offenders that's located beyond the Powder Works. I had been wanting to go there for a long time but hadn't managed; then, unexpectedly, I had some free time and found some good people who offered to show me everything. We set off on a mild, rather overcast day, and once past the Powder Works we drove right into a forest; in the forest is the colony. How lovely it is in winter in a snow-covered forest; how fresh, how pure the air, and how isolated it is here. Some thirteen hundred acres of forest have been donated to the colony, which consists entirely of a few attractive wooden houses set some distance apart from each other. The whole colony has been built with donated money; each house cost some three thousand rubles, and in each house lives a "family." A family is a group of twelve to seventeen boys, and each family has its tutor. The plan is to have up to seventy boys, judging from the size of the colony, but at present, for some reason, there are only about fifty. I must admit that the colony had been generously endowed, and the yearly expenses for each young offender are considerable. It's odd, too, that the sanitary conditions in the colony, as was recently reported in the newspapers, are not entirely satisfactory: there has been a good deal of illness of late, even though, it would seem, the air is fine and the children are well looked after. We stayed in the colony for several hours, from eleven in the morning right until twilight, but I came to see that one visit was not enough to take in everything and comprehend it all. The director invited me to come and spend two days with them; and that's a very tempting offer.

The director, P. A. R——sky, is known in the world of belles-lettres; his articles appear occasionally in *The European Messenger*. He greeted me most cordially and courteously. The office keeps a book in which visitors enter their names if they choose. I noticed many well-known names among those inscribed; this suggests that people know about the colony and take an interest in it. In spite of all his courtesy, the esteemed director is, it seems, a man of great reserve, even though he emphasized almost with delight the positive features of his colony while somewhat playing down all those things that were not so pleasant or not yet put right. I hasten to add that this reserve—or so it seemed to me—derives from his most ardent love for the colony and for the project he has taken on.

All four tutors (I think there are four—one for each family) are by no means old people; they are young, in fact, and receive some three hundred rubles a year in salary; almost all of them are seminary graduates. They live full-time with their pupils and even wear almost the same clothes—a kind of blouse with a belt. The dormitories were empty when we toured. It was a holiday, and the children were off playing somewhere; but it was all the more convenient to inspect the facilities. There is no luxury, nothing superfluous resulting from the excessive kindness or humane feelings of the donors and founders of the institution. Such a thing could happen very easily, and it would be a major error. The folding iron cots, for instance, are the simplest kind; the sheets are made from rather coarse linen; the blankets are also of the plainest variety, but are warm. The tutors get up early, and they and all the pupils tidy and clean the dormitories and wash the floors when necessary. I caught a certain scent near some of the beds, and learned something almost incredible:

some of the pupils (not many, but some eight or nine), not even the very young ones but those aged twelve or thirteen, simply wet their beds in their sleep. When I asked whether this was the result of some ailment, I was told that it was not; it happened simply because the children were uncivilized; when they are admitted they are in so savage a state that they cannot even comprehend that they can and must behave differently. But if that's the case, then where must they have been before? In what wretched slums must they have been raised, and what people must they have dealt with! There is scarcely a peasant family so impoverished that it would not teach a child how to behave in such a case and where even the smallest child would not know what to do. So what sort of people has such a young offender encountered? How bestially indifferent must they have been toward his very existence! Yet this is an actual fact, and I consider it of the greatest significance. Please don't laugh at my inflating this nasty little detail to such dimensions: it is much more serious that it might seem. It indicates that there truly are individuals so dark and dreadful that every trace of their humanity and civic duty has disappeared. When one realizes that, one can also understand what such a tiny, savage soul will become when forsaken and rejected by the human community this way. Yes, these children's souls have witnessed some gloomy scenes and they are accustomed to strong impressions that will remain with them for ever, of course, and will recur in terrible dreams for the rest of their lives. And so those who would reform and educate such children must struggle with these terrible impressions; they must eradicate them and implant new ones—an enormous task.

"You will not believe the savage state some of them are in when they come here," P.A. told me. "There are some who know nothing of them-selves or of their place in society. Such a boy has been wandering around the streets scarcely knowing what he is doing, and the only thing on earth he knows and can make any sense of is his freedom—the freedom to wander about, half dead from cold and hunger, but only to wander freely. There is one small boy here, no more than ten, and even now he is utterly unable to get along without stealing. He steals aimlessly, not for profit, but mechanically, simply to steal."

"So how do you hope to reform such children?"

"Through work, a completely different way of life, and through fair treatment. And finally there's the hope that in three years their old weaknesses and habits will be forgotten of their own accord, simply through the passage of time."

I inquired whether there were not yet other notorious and nasty adolescent habits among the boys. I would remind you, by the way, that the boys here ranged in age from ten to seventeen, even though only children under fourteen are supposed to be admitted for treatment.

"Oh, no; we give no chance for such nasty habits to exist," P.A. quickly replied. "The tutors are always with them and watch constantly for things like that."

But I found this difficult to believe. There are several boys in the colony who are from the division of young offenders, now abolished, that used to be located in the Lithuanian Castle. I visited that prison three years ago and saw these boys. Then I learned from absolutely reliable sources that perversion in the Castle was rampant, and that those vagabond children who were admitted but not yet infected with this perversion and who initially loathed it eventually submitted to it almost against their will because their fellows made fun of their chastity.

"And have you had many recidivists?" I inquired.

"Not so many; there were only eight among all those released from the colony." (Yet this is still a goodly number.)

I note that the pupils are released primarily as tradesmen, and that preliminary accommodation is found for them. Formerly the passports issued by the colony were a great handicap to them. But now the means have been found to issue them passports from which, at first glance at least, one cannot tell that the bearer is from the colony of young offenders.

"On the other hand," P.A. hastened to add, "there are some among those released who even now cannot forget about the colony, and whenever there's a holiday, they'll most certainly come to spend some time and visit us."

And so the surest means of reform, of transforming a soul that has been dishonored and defamed into one that is serene and honest, is work. The day in the dormitory begins with work, and then the pupils go to the workshops. In the metal working and carpentry shops I was shown the things they had crafted. These articles are good, considering everything, and will naturally improve greatly when things are better organized. They are sold for the pupils' benefit, and in such a manner each one accumulates something for the day of his release. The children are busy with

their work in the morning and afternoon but they do not tire; it seems
that work truly does produce a rather strong effect on them morally: they
strive to outdo one another and take pride in their success.

Another means for their spiritual development is, of course, the system
introduced in the colony whereby the boys mete out their own justice.
Each one guilty of an offense is tried by a court of the whole "family"
to which he belongs, and the boys either acquit him or sentence him to
punishment. The only punishment is being excluded from games. Those
who do not submit to the judgment of their fellows are punished by
total exclusion from the colony. For that they have their "Peter-and-Paul
Fortress," as the boys call it, a special, isolated hut equipped with cells
for those temporarily isolated. However, it seems that confinement in the
"Fortress" depends exclusively on the director. We visited this fortress; at
that time there were two boys confined in it. I note that this confinement
is carried out with great caution and solicitude and is imposed for something particularly serious and inveterate. Each of the two was kept in his
own small room under lock and key, but we did not get to see them.

This self-administered justice in essence is a good thing, of course, but
it smacks of something literary. There are many proud children—proud
in a good sense—who can be hurt by the "democratic" power of boys and
offenders like themselves, so that they may not even gain a proper understanding of this power. There may be personalities who are much more
talented and clever than the others in the "family," and they may be stung
by vanity and hatred of the majority decision; and the majority is almost
always mediocre. And do the boys who sit in judgment truly understand
what they are doing? On the contrary, isn't it likely that, as always and
inevitably happens among children in all schools, childish "parties"
will form among them, parties grouped around rival boys who are a bit
stronger and smarter than the others and who set the tone and lead the
others around as if on a string? They are still children, after all, and not
adults. Finally, will those who are convicted and who suffer punishment
subsequently regard their former judges in the same simple, brotherly
fashion as they did before? Doesn't this self-administered justice destroy
the sense of comradeship? Of course, this is a means of educating and
developing and is based on and was devised with the notion that these
previously delinquent children, by having the right of self-administered
justice, will accustom themselves to the law, to self-restraint, and to

justice, about which they had hitherto known nothing; that it will ultimately develop a sense of duty in them. These are all beautiful and subtle
ideas, but to some extent they can be said to cut both ways. As far as
punishment is concerned, of course, the most effective of restraints has
been chosen—the deprivation of one's freedom.

Let me insert here, by the way, one odd *nota bene*. The other day I
happened to hear a very surprising observation about corporal punishment, which has now been abolished in all our schools: "We've now
abolished corporal punishment everywhere in the school, and it's a fine
thing we did; but what were the repercussions of that? Just that now we
have many more cowards among our young people, as compared with
the past. They've begun to fear even the slightest physical pain, the least
suffering or deprivation, even any kind of insult, any sting to their vanity,
so much so that some of them, as we have seen, hang or shoot themselves
when faced with the slightest threat or some difficult lesson or examination." Several actual instances of this can in fact best be explained solely
by the cowardice of the young people when faced with something threatening or unpleasant; still, this is a strange point of view on the matter, and
the *observation* is original at least. I set it down for the record.

I saw all the boys at dinner. The dinner was very simple but nour-
ishing, abundant, and prepared excellently. We sampled it with pleasure
before the boys arrived; and yet the cost of food for each boy is only
fifteen kopecks a day. They serve soup or cabbage stew with beef, and
have porridge or potatoes for a second course. When they get up in the
morning they have tea and bread, and bread and kvass between dinner
and supper. The boys are well fed; they take turns serving at the table.
Once they had taken their places at the table they sang, extremely well,
the prayer "Thy Nativity, O Christ Our Lord." One of the tutors teaches
them to sing the prayers.

Here at dinner, when all the boys were gathered together, I was most
interested in studying their faces. Their faces were not too bold or brazen;
they were simply faces that would not be taken aback by anything. Scarcely
a single face could be described as dull (although I was told there were
dullards among them; former inmates of the foundling home were most
prominent in this category). On the contrary, there were even some very
intelligent faces. Some faces were ugly, but not physically so; all their
features were nearly handsome, but in some faces there was something

that would not reveal itself. There were not very many joyous faces, yet the pupils were very much at ease with their superiors and with anyone else, although not at ease in quite the same way as other children whose hearts are more open. And probably a great number of them wanted to slip away from the colony at once. Many of them, evidently, try not to let their secrets slip out inadvertently—that much can be seen from their faces.

The tutors treat the boys humanely and are courteous to the point of delicacy (although they know how to be strict when necessary); but I think this treatment in some cases does not touch the boys' hearts and of course does not touch their intellects. They address them using the formal *you,* even the smallest boys. This *you* sounded somewhat artificial to me, a little unnecessary. Perhaps the boys who come here see this only as a case of "the gentlemen having a bit of fun." In short, this *you* is perhaps a mistake, even a rather serious one. It seems to me that it puts a certain distance between the children and the tutor; there is something formal and bureaucratic in that *you,* and it is a bad thing if some boy takes it as an expression of contempt. After all, how can he, who has seen such outlandish sights and heard the most unnatural cursing, who has lived by unrestrained thievery—how can he believe that suddenly he merits such treatment from a gentleman? In a word, the familiar *thou* would, in my opinion, more closely reflect the real truth in this case; but as it stands, everyone seems to be playacting a little. It's much better, after all, if the children would finally realize that the tutors are not their instructors but their fathers, and that they themselves are only naughty children who must be reformed. However, this *you* perhaps may not spoil the boys, and when he later winces on hearing a *thou,* or even the curses that he inevitably will hear the very day of his release from the institution, then he will sigh for his colony even more tenderly.

Among the things that still need to be put right, particularly prominent is reading. I was told that the children like reading very much; that is, they like listening to someone read aloud on holidays or when they have spare time. There are, apparently, good readers among them. I heard only one of them, and he read well; they say that he loves to read aloud to the others and have them listen to him. But among them are also those who are barely literate and totally illiterate. And the things they read! In one of the families after dinner I saw a book by some sort of author lying on the table; and they read how a certain Vladimir conversed with some Olga on various profound and strange topics, and how later the inevitable environment "shattered their existence." I saw their "library"; it is a cupboard containing Turgenev, Ostrovsky, Lermontov, Pushkin, and so on; there are several useful travel stories, etc. The whole collection is haphazard and has also been donated. Once reading has been permitted, it can have a remarkable formative influence, of course; but I also know that if all Russia's educative forces, led by all the pedagogical councils, wanted to determine or stipulate what children in such circumstances ought to be given to read, then of course they would have to adjourn before they ever reached a conclusion; for this is a very difficult problem, and its final solution will not come from some meeting. On the other hand, our literature has absolutely no books which the People can understand. Neither Pushkin nor the *Sevastopol Tales* nor *Evenings on a Farm* nor the tale of Kalashnikov or Koltsov (particularly Koltsov) is at all understood by the People. Of course, these boys are not the People but are God only knows who—such human specimens as almost escape classification: to what category and type do they belong? But even if they did understand something, they still would be utterly incapable of appreciating it because all this wealth would drop on them out of the blue, as it were; their past lives have simply not prepared them for this. And what of the muckraking writers and satirists? Is this the sort of spiritual influence needed by these poor children who have seen so much filth already? Perhaps these little people have no wish at all to laugh at others. Perhaps these souls, obscured by darkness, would open themselves with joy and tenderness to the most naive, elementary, and artless impressions; to things utterly childish and simple, at which today's secondary-school student, of the same age as these delinquent children, would smile condescendingly and pull a face.

There is also a school, quite in its infancy, but there are plans to organize it better in the very near future. Drawing and painting are scarcely taught. There is no religious instruction at all: there is no priest. But they will have a priest of their own when their church is completed. This wooden church is now being built. The leaders of the colony and the builders are proud of it. Its architecture is truly not bad, but it is done in the somewhat official, markedly Russian style that has become boring. I note, by the way, that religious instruction in schools—whether for delinquents or for our other primary schools—must certainly be entrusted to no one other than a priest. But why could not even primary schoolteachers tell simple stories from the Bible? I won't dispute the fact that one can find truly bad people among the great multitude of village schoolteachers; but if one of them wants to teach atheism to a boy, he can do it without teaching church history; he need only tell him about the duck and "what it is covered with." On the other hand, what do we hear of our clergy? Oh, I certainly don't want to offend anyone, and I am sure that the school for delinquents will have the worthiest of priests to tend it; however, what have almost all our newspapers been writing about lately with particular zeal? They have printed the most unpleasant facts about clergy who were giving religious instruction in schools and who, by the dozens, quit the schools and refused to teach in them unless they were given extra pay. I don't dispute that "he who labors is worthy of his payment," but this eternal whining about extra pay grates on the ear and lacerates the heart. Our newspapers take the side of the whiners, as I do myself; yet I still dream of those ancient zealots and preachers of the Gospel who traveled barefoot and naked, enduring beatings and sufferings and preaching Christ without any additional pay. Oh, I'm not an idealist; I understand all too well that times are different now. But would it not be gratifying to hear that our spiritual educators had increased their goodwill by even an iota before increasing their salaries? I repeat: please don't be offended. Everyone knows very well that the spirit has not run dry in the hearts of our clergy and that there are ardent workers among them. And I am already convinced that just such a one will work in the colony. But it would be better if the boys were simply told stories from the Bible without any "official" moral; for the time being that would be enough for religious instruction. A series of pure, holy, beautiful pictures would work powerfully on these souls which thirst after beautiful impressions. . . .

Still, I said farewell to the colony with a cheerful heart. There may be things in need of fixing up, yet there are facts which indicate substantial progress toward achieving its goals. Let me tell you about two of them by way of conclusion. When I was in the colony one of the pupils, a lad of about fifteen, was confined in the "Fortress." Before coming here he had been held for some time in the prison of the Lithuanian Castle while the division of young offenders was still located there. He was sentenced to join the colony but tried to escape from it twice, I believe; he was caught both times, once outside the colony itself. At last he stated flatly that he would not submit to the rules of the institution, and for this he was put into solitary confinement. At Christmas his relatives brought him some presents, but he was not allowed to have them because he was being kept in confinement; a tutor confiscated them. The boy was terribly offended and much affected by this, and when the director visited him he began to complain bitterly, harshly accusing the tutor of confiscating the parcel of gifts for his own use; at the same time he spoke angrily and sarcastically about the colony and his fellow pupils, making accusations against all of them. "I sat down and had a serious talk with him," P.A. told me. "He maintained a gloomy silence the whole time. Two hours later he suddenly sent for me again, begging me to come and see him; and what do you think he did? He rushed to me, his eyes full of tears, utterly shaken and transformed; he began to repent and to reproach himself; he also told me things that had happened to him previously and that he had kept hidden from everyone; he told me his secret—that he had long been addicted to a most shameful habit from which he could not free himself, and that this tormented him. In short, it was a complete confession. I spent two hours with him," P.A. added. "We had a real talk; I advised him of certain methods to help him struggle with his habit, and so on."

When P.A. told me this he deliberately passed over the content of their conversation; but you will have to agree that it is a gift to be able to enter into the sick soul of a deeply embittered young offender who has never had any notion of the truth. I confess I would very much like to know all the details of that conversation. Here is another fact: every tutor in every family not only sees that the pupils tidy the dormitory and wash and clean it but also joins them in the work. They wash the floors on Saturdays; the tutor not only demonstrates how this is to be done but himself sets to washing the floor with the boys. This is a most thorough understanding of one's vocation and one's human dignity. Would you ever find such an attitude to one's work among bureaucrats, for example? And if, indeed, these people resolve to unite the colony's goals with their own private aims in life, then, of course, the matter will be "fixed up," even despite some theoretical errors, if such should occur initially.

A man who has seen a good deal of life said to me the other day: "Heroes—that's what you novelists are looking for. And when you can't find any heroes among us Russians, you start to grumble at the whole country. Let me tell you a little story: once upon a time, a good while ago now, during the reign of the late emperor, there lived a government official who served first in St. Petersburg and then in Kiev, I think, where he died. Now on the surface of it, that would seem to be his whole life's story. Yet, what do you think? This humble and quiet little fellow all his life suffered such inner torments over serfdom, over the fact that in Russia a man created in the likeness and image of God could be so slavishly dependent on a man such as himself, that he began to scrape and save out of his own meager salary, denying his wife and children almost the necessities of life; and when he managed to accumulate enough he would buy some serf's freedom from his landowner. Of course, it would take him ten years to free one man. In the course of his whole life he managed in this way to redeem about three or four people, and when he died he left nothing to his family. This all happened without publicity, quietly, unknown to everyone. What sort of hero can he be, of course! He's 'an idealist of the forties' and nothing more; perhaps even ridiculous and not very skillful, because he thought that he could struggle against all this evil with only his own petty, individual effort. Yet still, it seems that our Potugins ought to be a bit more charitable toward Russia and not throw mud at her for anything and everything."

I am setting down this little story here (it's not entirely relevant, I suppose) only because I have no reason to doubt its authenticity.

Yet these are the sort of people we need! I am terribly fond of this ridiculous type of petty official who seriously imagines that he, with his microscopic efforts and stubborn persistence, is capable of aiding the common cause without waiting for some widespread campaign and general initiative. That's the kind of little man who might be very useful in a colony of young offenders as well. . . . Oh, naturally, working under better-educated and higher supervisors. . . .

However, I spent only some few hours in the colony, and there was much that I might have conceived wrongly or missed or been mistaken about. In any case, I find that the means for making blemished souls over into immaculate ones are still insufficient.

CHAPTER THREE

Article 1. The Russian Society for the Protection of Animals. The Government Courier. Demon-Vodka. The Itch for Debauch and Vorobev. From the End or from the Beginning?

In no. 359 of *The Voice* I happened to read of the celebration of the tenth anniversary of the Russian Society for the Protection of Animals. What a kind and humane society this is! As far as I understand, its main idea is almost entirely conveyed in these words from the speech of the Society's president, Prince A. A. Suvorov: "In fact, the task of our new charitable institution seemed all the more difficult because the majority was unwilling to see in the protection of animals those same moral and material benefits for humans as derive from their kind and sensible treatment of domestic animals."

And in fact the Society is concerned not only about poor dogs and horses; man, too—Russian man—needs to humanize and "image himself"* and this is something which the Society for the Protection of Animals can undoubtedly promote. Once the peasant has learned to have pity for his animals, he will begin to have pity for his wife. And therefore, although I am very fond of animals, I am delighted that the worthy Society values people even more than animals—people who have become coarse, inhumane, semibarbaric, and who are seeking the light! Any means of enlightenment are precious, and one can only wish that the Society's idea in fact becomes one means of enlightenment. Our children are raised and grow up encountering many disgusting sights. They see a peasant who has grossly overloaded his cart lashing his wretched nag, who gives him his living, across the eyes as she struggles in the mud; or, something I myself saw not very long ago, for instance: a peasant was hauling calves to the slaughterhouse in a large cart in which he had loaded about ten of the

---

*To image oneself is an expression heard among the People; it means to give an image, to restore in man his human image. One who has been drinking for a long time is told, with reproach: "You ought to image yourself." I heard this from the convicts. [Dostoevsky's note]

creatures; he climbed into the cart with an air of utmost calm and sat down upon a calf. He found a soft seat there—just like a sofa with springs—but the calf, its tongue hanging out and its eyes bulging, may have drawn its last breath even before it reached the slaughterhouse. I am sure that this scene didn't trouble anyone on the street: "Doesn't matter—it's going to be slaughtered anyway." But scenes such as these undoubtedly brutalize and corrupt people, especially children. It's true that the worthy Society has already been attacked; I have heard people make fun of it more than once. I've heard mention, for example, of the time about five years ago when the Society laid charges against a cabman for mistreating his horse. He was fined fifteen rubles, I think. And that, of course, was a miscalculation, because after such a heavy fine many people truly did not know whom to pity: the cabman or his horse. Nowadays, it's true, the new law provides for a fine of not more than ten rubles. Then I heard about the Society's allegedly excessive concerns for putting to death by chloroform stray, and thus harmful, dogs who had lost their owners. People noted that at a time when people are starving in the provinces struck by famine, such tender concern for dogs might seem to grate on the ear. But objections such as these do not stand up to criticism. The aim of the Society is more enduring than the vicissitudes of day-to-day living. It is based on something splendid and true which sooner or later must take root and triumph. Nevertheless, looking at it from another point of view, it would be extremely desirous that the activities of the Society and the aforementioned "vicissitudes of day-to-day living" should enter into a mutual equilibrium, so to say; then, of course, it would be easier to chart that salvational and charitable course the Society should follow in order to achieve abundant and, above all, practical results that would truly achieve its purpose.... Perhaps I am not expressing myself clearly; I shall tell you a little story which really happened and hope that by its graphic account I can convey more clearly what I want to express.

This happened to me a long, long time ago—in my "prehistoric" period, as it were—in 1837 to be precise. It happened on the road from Moscow to St. Petersburg; I was then only fifteen years old. My elder brother and I and our late father were traveling to St. Petersburg where the two of us were to enroll in the Chief Engineering School. It was May, and it was very warm. We were traveling without changing horses, almost at a walking pace, and we would spend two or three hours at each posting station. I recall how weary we finally became of this journey, as it dragged on for almost a week. My brother and I were eager to enter a new life and were terribly prone to dreaming of the "beautiful and the sublime" (this phrase was still fresh then and was spoken without irony). And how many such beautiful phrases existed and circulated at that time! We believed passionately in something, and although we both knew very well every- thing that was required for the mathematics examination, we dreamed only of poetry and poets. My brother wrote verses—three a day—and even on the road I was continually composing in my mind a novel from Venetian life. Only two months earlier Pushkin had died, and my brother and I had agreed on the road that when we arrived in St. Petersburg we would at once stop off at the scene of his duel and seek out his former apartment to see the room in which he had yielded up his spirit. And so it was that once, before evening, we stopped at an inn by a posting station—I don't remember the village, but I think it was in Tver Province; the village was large and prosperous. Within half an hour we were to make ready to leave, but in the meantime I was looking out the window and saw the following.

Directly across the street from the inn was the station building. Suddenly a courier's troika came flying up to the station entrance and a government courier leapt out; he had on a full-dress coat with the little narrow flaps on the back that were worn then, and he wore a large tricor- nered hat with white, yellow, and, I think, green plumes (I forget this detail and could check it, but I seem to recall the flash of a green plume). The courier was a tall, extremely stout, and strong fellow with a purplish face. He ran into the station and, no doubt, knocked back a glass of vodka there. I recall that our driver said that such couriers always drink a glass of vodka at every station, since without it they couldn't stand up to "the punishment they have to take." In the meantime a new troika of fresh, spirited horses rolled up to the station and the coachman, a young lad of twenty or so, wearing a red shirt and carrying his coat on his arm, jumped onto the seat. The courier at once flew out of the inn, ran down the steps, and got into the carriage. Before the coachman could even start the horses, the courier stood up and, silently, without any word whatso- ever, raised his huge right fist and dealt a painful blow straight down on the back of the coachman's neck. The coachman jolted forward, raised his whip, and lashed the shaft horse with all his might. The horses started off with a rush, but this did nothing to appease the courier. He was not angry; he was acting according to his own plan, from something preconceived and tested through many years of experience; and the terrible fist was raised again, and again it struck the coachman's neck, and then again and again; and so it continued until the troika disappeared from sight. Naturally the coachman, who could barely hold on because of the blows, kept lashing the horses every second like one gone mad; and at last his blows made the horses fly off as if possessed. Our coachman explained to me that all government couriers travel in almost the same fashion and that this particular one was universally known for it; once he had had his vodka and jumped into the carriage, he would always begin by beating, "always in that same way," for no reason whatsoever; he would beat in a measured manner, raising and lowering his fist, and "he'll keep using his fists on the coachman like that for nearly a mile, and then he'll quit. And if he gets to feeling bored, he might take it up again in the middle of the trip; then again, maybe God will prevent it. But he'll always start up again when they're getting close to the station: he'll start about a mile away, and you'll see his fist going up and down, and that's how they'll drive up to the station, so's everybody in the village can marvel at it. Your neck aches for a month afterward." When the young lad comes back people laugh at him: "Didn't that courier whack you across the neck, though!" And the lad, perhaps, that very day will beat his young wife: "At least I'll take it out on you"; and perhaps also because she "looked on and saw it. . . ."

Doubtless it is cruel of the coachman to whip his horses that way: they come galloping into the next station worn out and barely able to breathe. But tell me, in truth, could any member of the Society for the Protection of Animals resolve to bring charges against that peasant for cruel and inhumane treatment of his horses?

This disgusting scene has stayed in my memory all my life. I could never forget the courier, and for a long time thereafter I couldn't help but explain many of the shameful and cruel things about the Russian People in too one-sided a manner. You realize that I am talking about something that happened long ago. This little scene was like an emblem, so to say; something that very graphically demonstrated the link between a cause and its effect. Every blow that rained down on the animal was the direct result of every blow that fell on the man. At the end of the 1840s, in the era of my most selfless and passionate dreams, I suddenly had a notion that if I should ever found a philanthropic society I would certainly have this courier's troika engraved on the society's seal as an emblem and an admonition.

Oh, there's no doubt that times now are not what they were forty years ago, and couriers do not beat the People; but the People beat one another, having retained flogging in their courts. The point is not that, but in the causes that bring effects after them. The courier is gone, but on the other hand there is "demon-vodka." In what way can demon-vodka resemble the courier? It can do so very easily in the way it coarsens and brutalizes a man, makes him callous, and turns him away from clear thinking, desensitizes him to the power of goodness. A drunkard doesn't care about kindness to animals; a drunkard will abandon his wife and children. A drunken man came to the wife he had abandoned and whom, along with her children, he had not supported for many months; he demanded vodka and set to beating her to force her to give him still more vodka; the unfortunate woman, compelled to virtual forced labor (just recall what women's work is and what value we place on it now) and not knowing how to feed her children, seized a knife and stabbed him. This happened recently, and she will be brought to trial. But there is little point in telling you about her because there are hundreds and thousands of such cases— just open a newspaper. But the chief similarity between demon-vodka and the courier is certainly that it, just as fatally and irresistibly, towers over the human will.

The worthy Society for the Protection of Animals comprises 750 members; people who can be influential. Suppose it wanted to help reduce drunkenness among the People even a little and stop the poisoning of a whole generation by liquor! The strength of the People is fading away; the source of our future wealth is drying up; their intellect is becoming impoverished and their development retarded. And what will the children of today's People carry away in their minds and hearts when they grow up in the abominations of their fathers? A fire broke out in a village; there was a church in the village, but the tavernkeeper came out and shouted that if the villagers abandoned the church and saved his tavern, he would stand them a barrel of vodka. The church burned down, but the tavern was saved. These instances are still trivial compared with the countless horrors yet to come. If the worthy Society wished to assist, even in a small way, in eradicating these prime causes, it would, in so doing, both improve its own status and further its excellent campaign of education. Otherwise, how can they compel people to be compassionate when things are arranged precisely with the aim of destroying every trace of humanity in humans? And is it only liquor that incites and depraves the People in our remarkable times? It is as if the very atmosphere contains some sort of intoxicant, a kind of itch for depravity. An unprecedented distortion of ideas has begun among the People, along with a general worship of materialism. In this instance what I mean by materialism is the People's adoration of money and the power of the bag of gold. The notion has suddenly burst forth among the People that a bag of gold now is every-thing, that it holds every sort of power, and that everything their fathers have told them and taught them hitherto is all nonsense. It would be a great misfortune if this way of thinking should become firmly established among the People, and yet, how else are they to think? For example, the recent railway disaster in which over a hundred army recruits were killed on the Odessa line—do you really believe that such power will not have a corrupting effect on the People? The People see and marvel at such might—"They do whatever they like"—and they begin to doubt in spite of themselves: "So that's where the real power is; and that's where it has always been. Just get rich and you can have it all; you can do anything you like." There can be no notion more corrupting than this one. And it is in the very air and gradually is permeating everything. The People have no defense against this idea; they have no education, and there is no means whatsoever of exposing them to other opposing ideas. Over the whole of Russia there now stretch nearly twenty thousand versts of railways, and throughout this system even the most minor official stands as one who spreads these ideas; he appears to have total power over you and your fate, over your family, and over your honor should you happen to fall into his clutches on the railway. Not long ago one stationmaster, on his own authority and by his own hand, dragged a lady out of the railway carriage in which she was traveling and delivered her to some gentleman who had complained to this stationmaster that she was his wife and was running away from him—and this without any judicial process and without any doubt that he had the right to do it. It is clear that this stationmaster, if he was in possession of his faculties, still must have become crazed by the notion of his own authority. All these incidents and examples burst in on the People in a continual process of temptation; they see them every

day and they draw the inevitable conclusions. In the past I was ready
to condemn Mr. Suvorin for his incident with Mr. Golubev. I thought
then that an innocent man should not be dragged into disrepute in such a
fashion and have all the stirrings of his soul described in the bargain. But
now I have changed my view somewhat even on this incident. What business is it of mine that Mr. Golubev is not guilty! Mr. Golubev may be as
pure as the driven snow, but still Vorobev is guilty. Who is this Vorobev?
I have no idea; and I am certain that he does not even exist, but it is that
same Vorobev who charges furiously over all the railway lines, who arbi-
trarily sets fares, who forcibly ejects passengers from railway carriages,
who destroys trains, who allows goods to rot at stations for months
on end, who brazenly inflicts damage on entire towns, provinces, the
whole country, and who only shouts in a wild voice, "Clear the way, I'm
coming!" But the chief thing this pernicious upstart is to be blamed for is
that he has placed himself above the People as a seductive and fatal idea.
However, why do I attack Vorobev? Is he the only such corrupting idea? I
repeat: this new materialism and skepticism seems to be wafting through
the air; we have begun to worship gratuitous gain, pleasure without labor;
all sorts of deceit and villainy are committed in cold blood; people are
murdered for the sake of a ruble in their pocket. I know very well that the
past also had its share of terrible things, but certainly things are ten times
worse now. What is most important is that this notion is circulating as if
it were a doctrine or a faith. Two or three weeks ago in St. Petersburg a
young lad, a cabbie who was scarcely of age, was driving an old couple at
night; when he noticed that the man had passed out from drink, he drew
his *penknife* and began stabbing the old woman. He was captured, and
the poor fool confessed at once: "I don't know how it happened and how
the knife got into my hands." And, in truth, he really did not know. This
is specifically a matter of the environment. He was caught up and drawn
in—as if into a machine—by today's itch for debauchery, by the popular
tendency of today: gratuitous gain. Why not give it a try, even with only
a penknife?

"No, we're not interested in the protection of animals these days;
that's only a scheme the gentlemen have thought up." I have heard that
very same statement, but I totally reject it. Not being a member of the
Society myself, I am still ready to serve it and, I think, already am serving
it. I don't know whether I expressed with even partial clarity my wish for

that "equilibrium of the activities of the Society with the vicissitudes of day-to-day living" which I wrote of above; but understanding the humane and humanizing purpose of the Society, I am still deeply devoted to it. I could never understand the notion that only one-tenth of people should get higher education while the other nine-tenths of people should serve only as their material and means while themselves remaining in darkness. I do not wish to think and live in any other way than with the belief that all our ninety million Russians (or however many will subsequently be born) will all someday be educated, humanized, and happy. I am fully convinced that universal education can harm none of us. I even believe that the kingdom of thought and light is possible to achieve here, in our Russia, even sooner, perhaps, than anywhere else, for even now no one here will stand up for the idea that we must bestialize one group of people for the welfare of another group that represents civilization, such as is the case all over Europe. It is here, after all, that serfdom was voluntarily abolished by the upper classes with the will of the tsar at their head! And therefore, once more, I give a most warmhearted welcome to the Society for the Protection of Animals; I wanted only to express the thought that it would be a good thing if we were to begin taking action not always from the end but, partly at least, from the beginning.

Article 2. Spiritualism. Something about Devils. The Extraordinary Cleverness of Devils, If Only These Are Devils.

And now, however, I've covered a whole sheet with writing and there is no more room. And I had wanted to talk a bit about the war, about our border regions; I wanted to say something about literature, about the Decembrists, and about at least fifteen other topics. I see that I must write more succinctly and compress things—something to keep in mind in the days ahead. A word, by the way, about the Decembrists before I forget: in announcing the recent death of one of them, our journals stated that he apparently was one of the very last of the Decembrists; this is not quite accurate. Among the surviving Decembrists are Ivan Aleksandrovich Annenkov, the one whose original story was told in such distorted fashion by the late Alexandre Dumas-père in his well-known novel *Les Mémoires d'un maitre d'armes.* Matvei Ivanovich Muravev-Apostol, the brother of the one who was executed, is alive, as are Svistunov and Nazimov. Perhaps there are yet other survivors.

In a word, there is much I shall have to put off until the February issue. But I would like to conclude the present January diary with something a bit more cheery. There is one very amusing and, most important, fashionable topic, and that is devils and spiritualism. In fact, something amazing is going on: people write and tell me, for instance, that a young man sits in an armchair, tucks up his feet, and the chair begins to dance around the room—and this is in St. Petersburg, the capital! Now why was it that no one ever did this before—dancing around the room while sitting in a chair with his legs tucked up? Instead, everyone just went on working and meekly earning their ranks. People insist that there's a lady somewhere in the provinces who has a house with so many devils in it that even Uncle Eddy's cabin doesn't have half as many. And don't we have devils of our own! Gogol writes to Moscow from the next world and states positively that devils exist. I read the letter, and the style is his. He urges us not to summon them up, not to turn tables, and not to have anything to do with them: "Do not tease the devils, do not hob-nob with them; it is a sin to tease devils. . . . If nervous insomnia begins to torment you by night, do not grow angry, but pray: this is the work of devils. Make the sign of the cross over your nightshirt and say a prayer." The voices of clergymen are raised advising even scientists to have nothing to do with "witchery" nor to study it scientifically. When even clergymen have spoken out, it means the thing has grown beyond a joke. But the whole problem is: are these really devils? Now this is a question the Committee of Inquiry into Spiritualism recently formed in St. Petersburg ought to resolve! Because if they finally do establish that these things are not the work of devils but of some sort of electricity or other, some new manifestation of universal energy, then total disillusionment would set in at once: "What a marvel," people would say, "and how boring!" They would all drop spiritualism, forget about it at once, and go back to their own business as before. But in order to investigate the question of whether these are devils at work at least one member of the committee must be able and have the opportunity to admit the existence of devils, even as a hypothesis. But it is hardly likely that even one member of the committee can be found who believes in devils, despite the fact that a terrific number of people who do not believe in God still believe in the Devil, readily and happily. And therefore the question is beyond the committee's competence. My whole problem is that I simply cannot believe in devils myself, and so it is a great pity that I have developed a very clear and astonishing theory of spiritualism, but one wholly founded on the existence of devils; without them my whole theory collapses of itself. And it is this theory that I, in concluding, wish to pass on to the reader. The fact is that I am defending devils: this time they are being unfairly attacked and treated as fools. Don't worry, they know what they are doing; that is just what I want to prove.

In the first place, people write that spirits are stupid (by spirits I mean devils, the Unclean Power, for other than devils, what spirits can be at work here?); that when they are summoned up and questioned (through table-turning), they only give silly answers, know no grammar, and have never communicated a new idea or passed on a single new discovery. Thinking that way is a grave mistake. What would happen, for instance, if the devils at once showed their power and overwhelmed humans with their discoveries? What if they suddenly revealed the electric telegraph (i.e., assuming it had not already been invented) or passed on various secrets to people: "Dig in such-and-such a place and you'll find a treasure or find deposits of coal" (firewood, incidentally, is such a price these days). Still, all these things are just trifles! Of course, you understand that human science is still in its infancy and has not done much more than begin its work; about all it has accomplished is to get itself firmly on its feet. And now, suppose, suddenly a whole shower of revelations commences, of the order, say, that the sun stands still while the earth revolves around it (because there are probably many discoveries of that magnitude, things which our wise men have not dreamt of, that still await discovery). Suddenly all this knowledge would simply tumble down on humanity and, the main thing, it would come quite gratuitously, as a gift. What would happen to people then, I ask? Oh, of course, everyone would be in raptures at first. People would embrace one another in ecstasy; they would rush off to study these revelations (and that would take time); they would suddenly feel themselves overcome by happiness and up to their necks in material blessings; perhaps they would walk or fly through the air, covering immense distances ten times faster than they now do by railway; they would extract fabulous harvests from the earth, create new organisms through chemistry; and there would be beef enough to supply three pounds per person, just as our Russian socialists dream—in short, eat, drink, and be merry. "And now," all the lovers of humanity would cry, "now that human needs are taken care of, now we will reveal our true potential! There are no more material deprivations, no more corrupting environment, once the source of all flaws; now humans will become beautiful and righteous! There is no more ceaseless labor to try to feed oneself, and now everyone will occupy himself with sublime, profound thoughts and with universal concerns. Now, only now, has life in the higher sense begun!" And what clever and good people, perhaps, would give voice to such words, and the novelty of it all might attract still others until, at last, they would raise their voices in a common hymn: "Who can be likened unto this beast? Praise be to him who has brought fire down from the heavens!"

But such rapturous outpourings would scarcely be enough for even one generation! People would suddenly see that they had no more life left, that they had no freedom of spirit, no will, no personality, that someone had stolen all this from them; they would see that their human image had disappeared and that the brutish image of a slave had emerged, the image of an animal, with the single difference that a beast does not realize that it is a beast, but a human would realize that he had become a beast. And humanity would begin to decay; people would be covered in sores and begin to bite their tongues in torment, seeing that their lives had been taken away for the sake of bread, for "stones turned into bread." People would realize that there is no happiness in inactivity, that the mind which does not labor will wither, that it is not possible to love one's neighbor without sacrificing something to him of one's own labor, that it is vile to live at the expense of another, and that *happiness lies not in happiness but only in the attempt to achieve it*. People would be overcome by boredom and sickness of heart: everything has been done and there is nothing more to do; everything has become known and there is nothing more to discover. There would be crowds of people seeking to end their lives, but not as they do now, in some obscure corner; masses of people would gather, seizing one another's hands, and suddenly destroy themselves by the thousands through some new method that they discovered along with all their other discoveries. And then, perhaps, those who remained would cry out to God: "Thou art right, O Lord: man does not live by bread alone!" Then they would rise up against the devils and abandon witchery. . . . Oh, never would God send down such torments on humanity! And the kingdom of the devils would collapse! No, the devils won't make such a grave political error. They are sophisticated politicians and move toward their goal by a most subtle and logical route (I repeat: that is, if devils indeed do exist!).

The fundamental principle of their kingdom is discord; that is, they want to found it on discord. Why do they specifically need discord here? Why, it's obvious: just remember that discord itself is a dreadful force; discord, after a long period of strife, drives people to folly; it dulls and distorts their reason and their feelings. In discord he who gives offense, once he realizes what he has done, does not go to be reconciled with the one he has offended, but says: "I offended him, and so I must take revenge on him." But the main thing is that the devils have the most thorough knowledge of the history of the human race and particularly remember all those things on which discord has been based. They know, for instance, that if in Europe sects exist that have broken away from Catholicism and continue up to now as religions, then this is only because blood was spilled because of them at one time. Should Catholicism, for example, come to an end, then all the Protestant sects would inevitably collapse as well: what would be left for them to protest against? Even now they are almost inclined to move into some sort of "humanism," or even simply to atheism, and people have remarked on that for some time now. And if these sects still continue to cling to life as religions, then it is because they still continue to protest. They protested even last year, and what a protest it was!—they took on the pope himself.

Oh, of course in the final analysis the influence of the devils will prevail and they will crush humanity like a fly with their "stones turned into bread." That is their principal goal, but they will undertake to fulfill it only after having first ensured that their future kingdom will be safe from human rebellion and so guarantee its longevity. But how can humans be subdued? Of course: *divide et impera* (divide the enemy and you will conquer him). And for this they need discord. On the other hand, people will get tired of the stones turned into bread, and so something must be found for them to do so they won't get bored. And isn't discord a fine occupation for human beings!

Now please observe how the devils introduce discord among us and, so to say, from the very first step begin spiritualism with discord. Our frenzied age makes this so much easier. Just look at how many believers in spiritualism among us have already been offended. People shout and laugh at them for believing in table-turning, as if they had done or planned to do something dishonest; but still they carry on investigating the question despite the discord. How can they stop investigating it in any case? The devils start their work in a very roundabout way: they arouse curiosity but confuse people instead of explaining; they make people uncertain and openly laugh in their faces. An intelligent person, worthy of all respect, stands with a puzzled frown on his face and painfully seeks an answer: "Whatever can this be?" At last he is ready to give up and abandon his quest, but the laughter of the crowd grows louder, and the matter develops to the point where the believer has to continue despite himself, out of his own sense of pride.

Before us, armed with all the weapons science has to offer, sits the Committee to Investigate Spiritualism. The public waits in anticipation, but what happens? The devils have no intention of offering any resistance; to the contrary, in a most disgraceful manner they decide they will "pass." Seances are unsuccessful; deceit and trickery are exposed. Malicious laughter rings out from all sides; the committee retires with scornful glances; believers in spiritualism are thoroughly put to shame; a desire for revenge creeps into the hearts of both sides. Now, it would seem, the devils are gone for good, but no! No sooner have the scientists and sober-minded people turned away than the devils at once perform some even more supernatural trick for the erstwhile believers, and once again they are convinced, now even more firmly than before. More temptation, more discord! Last summer in Paris a certain photographer was brought to trial for various spiritualistic frauds; he would summon up the dead and take their photographs; he was overwhelmed with orders. But they picked him up, and he made a complete confession in court; he even brought in the lady who had been helping him by representing the spirits he summoned up. And what do you think—were those whom the photographer deceived convinced? Not in the least. One of them, apparently, said: "Three of my children have died, and I have no photos of them; but the photographer took their pictures, which all resemble my children, and I could recognize each one. What do I care if he's confessed to fraud? He has his reasons for doing that, but I'm holding a fact in my hand, so leave me alone." This was in the newspapers. I don't know whether I reported all the details correctly, but the essence is accurate.

Now imagine if such a thing happened here. No sooner would the learned committee, its work finished and the wretched fraud exposed, turn its back than the devils would seize one of its most obdurate members— even, say, Mr. Mendeleev himself, who has exposed spiritualism in his public lectures—and catch him up at once in their nets, just as they caught Crookes and Olcott in their time. They would take him aside and lift him into the air for five minutes, materialize before him various dead people he had known, and do it all in such a manner that he could no longer have any doubts. And what would happen then, tell me? As a true scientist he would have to accept actual fact—he, who has been giving lectures! What a picture, what a shame, what an uproar, what shouts and cries of indignation! Of course this is only a joke, and I am sure that nothing of this sort will happen to Mr. Mendeleev, although in England and in America it seems that the devils have acted precisely according to this plan. And what if the devils, having prepared the ground and planted sufficient discord, suddenly want to broaden the sphere of their activities and turn to something genuine and serious? They're an unpredictable lot with a strong sense of irony and could do something of that sort. For instance, what if they suddenly burst into the midst of the People, along with literacy, say? And our People are so defenseless, so given to igno- rance and debauchery, and there are so few who can guide them in this sense, it seems! The People might put their faith in these new phenomena with a passion (they believe in Ivan Filippovich, after all). Then how their spiritual development would be delayed! What damage might be done, and for what a period of time! What an idolatrous worship of materi- alism, and what discord; discord a hundred, a thousand times worse than before; and this is exactly what the devils need. And discord certainly will ensue, especially if spiritualism manages to provoke restrictions and persecution (and persecution would inevitably follow from the rest of the People who do not believe in spiritualism). Then it would spread in an instant, like burning kerosene, and set everything ablaze. Mystical ideas love persecution; they are created by it. Every such persecuted idea is like that petroleum which the arsonists poured over the floors and walls of the Tuileries before the fire and which, in turn, could only feed the blaze in the building that was under guard. Oh, the devils know the force of a forbidden faith and they, perhaps, have already been waiting many centu- ries for mankind to trip over a turning table! Of course, they are governed by some sort of enormous unclean spirit of awesome power, more clever than the Mephistopheles whom Goethe made famous, as Yakov Polonsky tells us.

I have been most definitely joking and having fun from the first word to the last; but this is what I would like to express in conclusion: if we regard spiritualism as something that bears within it some sort of new religion (and almost all, even the most sober-minded among the spiritualists, are inclined to share even a little of that view), then something of what I have said above might be taken seriously. And therefore, may God grant speedy success to free study of the question from both sides. This alone will help to eradicate quickly the nasty spirit that is spreading about, and will, perhaps, enrich science by some new discovery. But to shout at one another, to heap scorn on one another and ostracize one another for spiritualism, means, in my view, only to strengthen and disseminate the idea of spiritualism in its worst sense. This is the beginning of intolerance and persecution. That's just what the devils want!

Article 3. A Word Apropos of My Biography

The other day someone showed me a copy of my biography included in *The Russian Encyclopedic Dictionary* (Second Year, Volume 5, Book 2, 1875), published by Professor I. N. Berezin of St. Petersburg University and complied by Mr. V. Z. It is hard to imagine so many mistakes being made on one half-page. I was born not in 1818 but in 1822. My late brother, Mikhail Mikhailovich, the publisher of the journals *Time* and *Epoch,* was my elder brother, not younger than I by four years. After my term of hard labor, to which I was exiled in 1849 as a *state criminal* (Mr. V. Z. mentions not a word about the nature of my crime, saying only that "he was involved in the Petrashevsky affair," i.e., in God knows what sort of affair, since no one is obliged to know and remember the Petrashevsky affair, while the *Encyclopedic Dictionary* is intended for general reference; people might think that I was exiled for robbery). After my term of hard labor, by the will of the late emperor, I directly entered the army as a private soldier and after three years of service was promoted to officer's rank. I was never deported ("settled") to Siberia, as Mr. V. Z. says.

The order of my literary works is mixed up: tales that belong to the very first period of my literary activity are attributed in the biography to the latest period. There are many such mistakes, and I am not listing them all so as not to weary the reader; but I will point them all out if challenged. There are, however, outright fabrications. Mr. V. Z. states that I was the editor of the newspaper *The Russian World;* to that I declare that I was never the editor of *The Russian World;* furthermore, not a single line of mine has ever appeared in that worthy publication. I don't deny that Mr. V. Z. (Mr. Vladimir Zotov?) can have his own point of view and consider it utterly trivial, in a biographical account of a writer, to indicate accurately when he was born, what interesting experiences he has had, where, when, and in what order he published his works, which works can be his earlier and which his later, which periodicals he published, which ones he edited, and which ones he merely worked for. Just the same, one would wish for a little more good sense, only for the sake of accuracy. Otherwise, readers may think that all the articles in Mr. Berezin's dictionary have been put together in such a sloppy fashion.

Article 4. A Turkish Proverb

Just in passing, I will insert here a Turkish proverb (a real one—I haven't made it up): If you set off to a certain goal and keep stopping along the way to throw stones at every dog that barks at you, you will never reach your destination.

As far as possible, I'll follow the advice of that wise proverb in my *Diary,* although I wouldn't want to tie myself down with promises beforehand.

February

from Chapter One

Article 2. On Love of the People. An Essential Contract with the People.

I wrote, for instance, in the January issue of the *Diary* that our People are coarse and ignorant, devoted to darkness and depravity, "barbarians, awaiting the light." Meanwhile, I've only just read in *Fraternal Aid* (an anthology published by the Slavic Committee in aid of the Slavs fighting for their freedom)—in an article by the late and unforgettable Konstantin Aksakov, a man dear to every Russian—that the Russian people have long been enlightened and "educated." What can I say? Was I troubled by my apparent disagreement with the opinion of Konstantin Aksakov? Not in the least; I completely share that view, and have had warm sympathy for it for a long time. So how can I reconcile such a contradiction? But the point is just that it can be very easily reconciled, I think; but to my astonishment others think that these two notions are irreconcilable. One must know how to segregate the beauty in the Russian peasant from the layers of barbarity that have accumulated over it. Through the circumstances of nearly the whole of Russian history, our People have been so dedicated to depravity, and so corrupt, led astray, and continually tormented, that it is a wonder they have survived preserving their human image at all, never mind preserving its beauty. But, indeed, they have also preserved the beauty of their image. He who is a true friend of humanity, whose heart has even once throbbed for the sufferings of the People—he will understand and overlook all the impenetrable deposits of filth that weigh down our People and will be able to find diamonds in this filth. I repeat: judge the Russian People not by the abominations they so frequently commit, but by those great and sacred things for which, even in their abominations, they constantly yearn. Yet not all of the People are villains; there are true saints, and what saints they are: they are radiant and illuminate the way for us all! I have a kind of blind conviction that there is no such scoundrel and villain among the Russian People who would not recognize that he is low and vile; but there are others who can commit some vile act and even exalt themselves for it, raising their villainy into a

127

principle and maintaining that in it lies *l'Ordre* and the light of civilization; such unhappy people end by believing that sincerely, blindly, even
honestly. No, do not judge our People by what they are, but by what they
would like to become. Their ideals are powerful and sacred; it is these
ideals that have preserved our People through centuries of torment; these
ideals have fused with the People's soul since time immemorial and have
conferred upon it the blessings of frankness, honor, sincerity, and a broad
mind, receptive to everything; and all this is combined in a most attractive, harmonious fashion. And if, along with this, there is so much filth,
then the Russian himself grieves over it all the more and believes that it
is all only extrinsic and temporary, a delusion of the Devil, and that the
darkness will end and one day the eternal light will shine forth. I will
not remind you of the People's historical ideals, of their saints—Sergei,
Theodosius of Pechersk, even Tikhon of Zadonsk. Incidentally, are there
many of us who know about Tikhon of Zadonsk? Why is it that we know
absolutely nothing of this and take an oath never to read anything? Are
we short of time? Believe me, gentlemen, you would be astonished at the
beautiful things you would learn. But I'll turn, rather, to our literature:
everything in it of true beauty has been taken from the People, beginning with the meek and simple type, Belkin, created by Pushkin. Why,
everything we have comes from Pushkin. His turning to the People at
such an early stage of his career was so unprecedented and astonishing; it
provided a point of view which, in those days, was so astonishingly novel
that it can only be explained, if not by a miracle, then by the remarkable
magnitude of his genius, which, I might add, even now we are incapable
of appreciating. I will not mention the purely national types that have
appeared in our time, but think of *Oblomov,* think of Turgenev's *Nest of
Gentlefolk.* In the latter, of course, it's not the People, yet everything that
is lasting and beautiful in Turgenev's and Goncharov's characters comes
from the fact that through them the writers came into contact with the
People; this contact with the People gave them exceptional powers. They
borrowed the People's simplicity, purity, meekness, breadth of outlook,
and lack of malice, as opposed to all that was twisted, false, extrinsic,
and slavishly borrowed. Don't be astonished that I have suddenly
begun to speak about Russian literature. The service our literature has
performed is that almost all of its best representatives paid homage to the
People's truth and acknowledged the People's ideals as truly beautiful

even before our intelligentsia did (note that). However, literature often had little choice but to accept these ideas as exemplary. It is true, I think, that artistic feeling rather than goodwill was at work here. But enough of literature for the moment; I took up the topic only apropos of the People in any case.

The question of the People and our view of them, our present understanding of them, is our most important question, a question on which our whole future rests; one might even say it is the most practical question at the moment. However, the People are still a theory for all of us and still stand before us as a riddle. All of us who love the People look at them as if at a theory and, it seems, not one of us loves them as they really are but only as each of us imagines them to be. And even if the Russian people eventually were to turn out to be not as we imagined them, then we all, despite our love for them, would likely renounce them at once with no regrets. I am speaking about all of us, including even the Slavophiles, who, perhaps, would be the first to renounce them. As for me, I won't hide my convictions because I specifically want to define more clearly the further tendency my *Diary* will take and so avoid misunderstandings, so that each one of you might know beforehand whether it is worth extending a literary hand to me or not. This is what I think: we are hardly so good and so beautiful that we could set ourselves up as an ideal for the People and demand that they become absolutely like us. Don't be surprised at hearing the question posed from such an absurd angle. In fact, we have never posed the question any other way: "Who is better, we or the People? Are the People to follow us, or are we to follow them?" This is what everyone is saying now, everyone who has even the tiniest thought in his head and some concern in his heart for the common cause. And so I reply frankly: it is we who ought to bow down before the People and wait for everything from them, both ideas and the form of those ideas; we must bow down before the People's truth and acknowledge it as the truth, even in the terrible event that some of it comes from the *Lives of the Saints.* To put it briefly: we must bow down like prodigal children who have been away from home for two hundred years but who, however, have returned still Russians (and in that, incidentally, is our great merit). But, on the other hand, we should bow down on only one condition, and that is a sine qua non: the People must accept much of what we bring with us. We cannot utterly annihilate ourselves before them and their truth, whatever that truth might be. Let that which is ours remain with us; we will not give it up for anything on earth, even, at the very worst, for the joy of unity with the People. If such does not happen, then let us both perish on our separate ways. Yet certainly it will happen; I am completely convinced that this *something* which we brought with us truly exists—it is not a mirage but has an image and a form and a weight. Nonetheless, I repeat once more: there is much ahead of us that is an enigma, so much that even the expectation is frightening. People predict, for example, that civilization will ruin the People: events supposedly will take such a course that, along with salvation and light, so much untruth and deceit will enter in; there will be so much tumult and such filthy habits will develop that only in generations to come—in two hundred years, if you like—will the good seeds sprout, while something dreadful awaits our children and us, perhaps. Is that how you see it, gentlemen? Are the People consigned to pass through yet a new phase of depravity and falsehood such as we passed through when inoculated with civilization? (I think no one will disagree that we began our civilization directly with depravity.) I would like to hear something more reassuring on this account. I am very much inclined to believe that our People are such an enormity that all such new, muddy torrents, should they burst forth from somewhere and overflow, will simply dissipate by themselves. And on this, give me your hand; let's work together, each through his own "microscopic" actions, so that the cause may advance more directly and with fewer mistakes. It is true that we ourselves have no ideas how to do anything in this area; we only "love our country," will not agree on the means, and will quarrel many times yet; still, if we've already agreed that we are good people, then, whatever may happen, things will finally work themselves out in the end. That's my credo. I repeat: we have here a two-hundred-year period of being unaccustomed to any work and nothing more than that. And through being unused to work we have ended our "period of culture" by everywhere ceasing to understand one another. Of course, I am speaking only of serious and sincere people—it's only they who fail to understand one another; opportunists are a different matter: they have always understood one another. . . .

Article 3. The Peasant Marey

But reading all these *professions de foi* is a bore, I think, and so I'll tell you a story; actually, it's not even a story, but only a reminiscence of something that happened long ago and that, for some reason, I would very much like to recount here and now, as a conclusion to our treatise on the People. At the time I was only nine years old. . . . But no, I'd best begin with the time I was twenty-nine.

It was the second day of Easter Week. The air was warm, the sky was blue, the sun was high, warm, and bright, but there was only gloom in my heart. I was wandering behind the prison barracks, examining and counting off the pales in the sturdy prison stockade, but I had lost even the desire to count, although such was my habit. It was the second day of "marking the holiday" within the prison compound; the prisoners were not taken out to work; many were drunk; there were shouts of abuse, and quarrels were constantly breaking out in all corners. Disgraceful, hideous songs; card games in little nooks under the bunks; a few convicts, already beaten half to death by sentence of their comrades for their particular rowdiness, lay on bunks covered with sheepskin coats until such time as they might come to their senses; knives had already been drawn a few times—all this, in two days of holiday, had worn me out to the point of illness. Indeed, I never could endure the drunken carousals of peasants without being disgusted, and here, in this place, particularly. During these days even the prison staff did not look in; they made no searches, nor did they check for alcohol, for they realized that once a year they had to allow even these outcasts to have a spree; otherwise it might be even worse. At last, anger welled up in my heart. I ran across the Pole M——cki, a political prisoner; he gave me a gloomy look, his eyes glittering and his lips trembling: "Je hais ces brigands!" he muttered, gritting his teeth, and passed me by. I returned to the barrack despite the fact that a quarter-hour before I had fled it half-demented when six healthy peasants had thrown themselves, as one man, on the drunken Tatar Gazin and had begun beating him to make him settle down; they beat him senselessly with such blows as might have killed a camel; but they knew that it was not easy to kill this Hercules and so they didn't hold back. And now when I returned to the barracks I noticed Gazin lying senseless on a bunk in the corner showing scarcely any signs of life; he was lying under a sheepskin coat, and everyone passed him by in silence: although they firmly hoped he would revive the next morning, still, "with a beating like that, God forbid, you could finish a man off." I made my way to my bunk opposite a window with an iron grating and lay down on my back, my hands behind my head, and closed my eyes. I liked to lie like that: a sleeping man was left alone, while at the same time one could daydream and think. But dreams did not come to me; my heart beat restlessly, and M——cki's words kept echoing in my ears: "Je hais ces brigands!" However, why describe my feelings? Even now at night I sometimes dream of that time, and none of my dreams are more agonizing. Perhaps you will also notice that until today I have scarcely ever spoken in print of my prison life; I wrote *Notes from the House of the Dead* fifteen years ago using an invented narrator, a criminal who supposedly had murdered his wife. (I might add, by the way, that many people supposed and are even now quite firmly convinced that I was sent to hard labor for the murder of my wife.)

Little by little I lost myself in reverie and imperceptibly sank into memories of the past. All through my four years in prison I continually thought of all my past days, and I think I relived the whole of my former life in my memories. These memories arose in my mind of themselves; rarely did I summon them up consciously. They would begin from a certain point, some little thing that was often barely perceptible, and then bit by bit they would grow into a finished picture, some strong and complete impression. I would analyze these impressions, adding new touches to things experienced long ago; and the main thing was that I would refine them, continually refine them, and in this consisted my entire entertainment. This time, for some reason, I suddenly recalled a moment of no apparent significance from my early childhood when I was only nine years old, a moment that I thought I had completely forgotten; but at that time I was particularly fond of memories of my very early childhood. I recalled one August at our home in the country: the day was clear and dry, but a bit chilly and windy; summer was on the wane, and soon I would have to go back to Moscow to spend the whole winter in boredom over my French lessons; and I was so sorry to have to leave the country. I passed by the granaries, made my way down into the gully, and climbed up into the Dell—that was what we called a thick patch of bushes that stretched from the far side of the gully to a grove of trees. And so I make my way deeper into the bushes and can hear that some thirty paces away a solitary peasant is plowing in the clearing. I know he's plowing up the steep side of a hill and his horse finds it heavy going; from time to time I hear his shout, "Gee-up!" I know almost all our peasants, but don't recognize the one who's plowing; and what difference does it make, anyway, since I'm quite absorbed in my own business. I also have an occupation: I'm breaking off a switch of walnut to lash frogs; walnut switches are so lovely and quite without flaws, so much better than birch ones. I'm also busy with bugs and beetles, collecting them; some are very pretty; I love the small, nimble, red-and-yellow lizards with the little black spots as well, but I'm afraid of snakes. I come across snakes far less often than lizards, however. There aren't many mushrooms here; you have to go into the birch wood for mushrooms, and that's what I have in mind. I liked nothing better than the forest with its mushrooms and wild berries, its insects, and its birds, hedgehogs, and squirrels, and with its damp aroma of rotting leaves that I loved so. And even now, as I write this, I can catch the fragrance from our stand of birches in the country: these impressions stay with you all your life. Suddenly, amid the deep silence, I clearly and distinctly heard a shout: "There's a wolf!" I screamed, and, beside myself with terror, crying at the top of my voice, I ran out into the field, straight at the plowing peasant.

It was our peasant Marey. I don't know if there is such a name, but everyone called him Marey. He was a man of about fifty, heavy-set, rather tall, with heavy streaks of gray in his bushy, dark-brown beard. I knew him but had scarcely ever had occasion to speak to him before. He even stopped his little filly when he heard my cry, and when I rushed up to him and seized his plow with one hand and his sleeve with the other, he saw how terrified I was.

"It's a wolf!" I cried, completely out of breath.

Instinctively he jerked his head to look around, for an instant almost believing me.

"Where's the wolf?"

"I heard a shout. . . . Someone just shouted, 'Wolf' " . . . I babbled.

"What do you mean, lad? There's no wolf; you're just hearing things. Take a look. What would a wolf be doing here," he murmured, reassuring me. But I was all a-tremble and clung to his coat even more tightly; I suppose I was very pale as well. He looked at me with an uneasy smile, evidently concerned and alarmed for me.

"Why you took a real fright, you did!" he said, wagging his head. "Never mind, now, my dear. What a fine lad you are!"

He stretched out his hand and suddenly stroked my cheek.

"Never mind, now, there's nothing to be afraid of. Christ be with you. Cross yourself, lad." But I couldn't cross myself; the corners of my mouth were trembling, and I think this particularly struck him. He quietly stretched out a thick, earth-soiled finger with a black nail and gently touched it to my trembling lips.

"Now, now," he smiled at me with a broad, almost maternal smile. "Lord, what a dreadful fuss. Dear, dear, dear!"

At last I realized that there was no wolf and that I must have imagined hearing the cry of "Wolf." Still, it had been such a clear and distinct shout; two or three times before, however, I had imagined such cries (not only about wolves), and I was aware of that. (Later, when childhood passed, these hallucinations did as well.)

"Well, I'll be off now," I said, making it seem like a question and looking at him shyly.

"Off with you, then, and I'll keep an eye on you as you go. Can't let the wolf get you!" he added, still giving me a maternal smile. "Well, Christ be with you, off you go." He made the sign of the cross over me, and crossed himself. I set off, looking over my shoulder almost every ten steps. Marey continued to stand with his little filly, looking after me and nodding every time I looked around. I confess I felt a little ashamed at taking such a fright. But I went on, still with a good deal of fear of the wolf, until I had gone up the slope of the gully to the first threshing barn; and here the fear vanished entirely, and suddenly our dog Volchok came dashing out to meet me. With Volchok I felt totally reassured, and I turned toward Marey for the last time; I could no longer make out his face clearly, but I felt that he was still smiling kindly at me and nodding. I waved to him, and he returned my wave and urged on his little filly.

"Gee-up," came his distant shout once more, and his little filly once more started drawing the wooden plow.

This memory came to me all at once—I don't know why—but with amazing clarity of detail. Suddenly I roused myself and sat on the bunk; I recall that a quiet smile of reminiscence still played on my face. I kept on recollecting for yet another minute.

I remembered that when I had come home from Marey I told no one about my "adventure." And what kind of adventure was it anyway? I forgot about Marey very quickly as well. On the rare occasions when I met him later, I never struck up a conversation with him, either about the wolf or anything else, and now, suddenly, twenty years later, in Siberia, I remembered that encounter so vividly, right down to the last detail. That means it had settled unnoticed in my heart, all by itself with no will of mine, and had suddenly come back to me at a time when it was needed; I recalled the tender, maternal smile of a poor serf, the way he crossed me and shook his head: "Well you did take a fright now, didn't you, lad!" And I especially remember his thick finger, soiled with dirt, that he touched quietly and with shy tenderness to my trembling lips. Of course, anyone would try to reassure a child, but here in this solitary encounter something quite different had happened, and had I been his very own son he could not have looked at me with a glance that radiated more pure love, and who had prompted him to do that? He was our own serf, and I was his master's little boy; no one would learn of his kindness to me and reward him for it. Was he, maybe, especially fond of small children? There are such people. Our encounter was solitary, in an open field, and only God, perhaps, looking down saw what deep and enlightened human feeling and what delicate, almost feminine tenderness could fill the heart of a coarse, bestially ignorant Russian serf who at the time did not expect or even dream of his freedom. Now tell me, is this not what Konstantin Aksakov had in mind when he spoke of the advanced level of development of our Russian People?

And so when I climbed down from my bunk and looked around, I remember I suddenly felt I could regard these unfortunates in an entirely different way and that suddenly, through some sort of miracle, the former hatred and anger in my heart had vanished. I went off, peering intently into the faces of those I met. This disgraced peasant, with shaven head and brands on his cheek, drunk and roaring out his hoarse, drunken song—why he might also be that very same Marey; I cannot peer into his heart, after all. That same evening I met M——cki once again. The unfortunate man! He had no recollections of any Mareys and no other view of these people but "Je hais ces brigands!" No, the Poles had to bear more than we did in those days!

March

from CHAPTER ONE

Article 2. A Hundred-Year-Old Woman

"I was really very late that morning," a lady told me the other day, "and it was almost noon when I left home; to make matters worse, there were so many things to be done. I had to stop in at two places on Nikolaevsky Street, one not far from the other. At the first place, going into an office, I met this really old woman near the gate, and she looked so old and bent as she walked along with her cane; but I just couldn't tell how old she was. She went as far as the gate and sat down on the porter's bench at the corner to rest. I walked past and only caught a glimpse of her.

"Ten minutes later I come out of the office; two doors down the street is the store where I ordered some shoes for Sonia last week, and since I was passing I went to pick them up; but I look and see that same old woman now sitting by that building, sitting on another bench and looking at me; I smiled at her, went into the store, and got the shoes. Well, three or four minutes passed, I went on along to the Nevsky, and—who do I see but my little old lady, now at another building, sitting by the gate again, but now she's not on a bench—she's managed to find a cosy spot on a projecting bit of the foundation, since there was no bench by this gate. I couldn't help but pause in front of her, wondering why it was that she stopped and sat down in front of every building.

" 'Are you tired, my good woman?' I asked.

" 'I do get tired, my dear; I'm always getting tired. It's a warm day, I'm thinking, and the sun's shining; so why don't I go and have dinner at my granddaughters'.'

" 'So you're on your way to have dinner?'

" 'Indeed I am, my dear.'

" 'But you'll scarcely make it at the pace you're going.'

" 'Oh, I'll make it. I'll go on a bit and then take a rest, and then get up and walk a bit more.'

"Looking at her I got terribly curious. She was a tiny little thing, neat but dressed in old clothes, a townswoman probably, with a cane and a pale, yellow face, colorless lips, and her skin stretched dryly over her bones like a mummy. But she sits there smiling, the sun shining right on her.

"'You must be pretty well on in years, Granny,' I ask, trying to make a little joke.

"'A hundred and four, my dear, one hundred and four years old, *that's all*' (she was joking now). . . . 'And where might you be going?'

"She looks at me, laughing, pleased, I imagine, to have someone to talk to; only it seemed odd to me that this hundred-year-old would be concerned to know where I was going.

"'Look at this, Granny,' said I, laughing as well. 'I picked up some shoes for my little girl in the store and I'm taking them home.'

"'What tiny wee shoes they are. She's a little one, your girl? Now that's good. And do you have other wee ones?'

"And again she's all smiles as she looks at me. Her eyes are dim with scarcely any life left in them, and yet they seem to radiate warmth.

"'Granny, please take five kopecks from me and buy yourself a roll,' and I give her the coin.

"'Now why should I need five kopecks? Never mind, I'll take it with thanks.'

"'There you are, Granny. Take it with my good wishes.'

"She took the coin. It was clear she'd not been reduced to begging, but she took the coin with such dignity, not at all like charity but as if from politeness or the goodness of her heart. And, who knows, maybe she was very pleased that someone should strike up a conversation with her, an old woman, and not only talk to her but even show some loving concern for her.

"'Well, good-bye, Granny,' I say. 'I hope you reach your granddaughters' without trouble.'

"'I'll manage it, my dear, don't worry. And you get back to your granddaughter,' the old woman said (in error), forgetting that I had a daughter, not a granddaughter, and thinking, evidently, that everyone had granddaughters. I went on and turned to look at her for the last time; I see that she's risen and is slowly, painfully tapping her cane as she makes her way down the street. Perhaps she'll stop to rest ten more times along the way before she reaches her granddaughters' place to have dinner. And where might that place be? Such a strange old woman."

I had listened to the story that morning—indeed, it wasn't even a story but only some sort of impression of a meeting with a hundred-year-old woman (and in fact how often do you meet a hundred-year-old woman, let alone one so full of inner life?)—and had forgotten it entirely, but then, late at night, I was reading an article in a magazine and when I set the magazine aside I suddenly recalled that old woman, and for some reason I at once sketched in an ending to the story of how she reached her own folks to have dinner: there emerged another, perhaps quite plausible little scene.

Her granddaughters, and perhaps her great-granddaughters (still, she calls them all granddaughters) are probably tradespeople of some sort, married women, of course, or else she would not be going to have dinner with them. They live in a basement and maybe they rent a barber's shop as well; they are poor people, of course, yet they eat well and observe the proprieties. It was probably past one o'clock when the old woman managed to get there. They weren't expecting her, yet they probably greeted her quite warmly.

"Well, and here's Maria Maximovna! Come in, come in, and welcome to you, servant of God!"

The old woman comes in, laughing a bit, while the little bell at the door goes on ringing sharply and shrilly for a long time. Her granddaughter is probably the barber's wife; he, the barber, is not yet an old man—about thirty-five, perhaps—and has the dignity of his trade, even though the trade may be a frivolous one; and of course he's wearing a frock coat as greasy as a pancake; that's caused by the pomade, I suppose, but I never saw a barber dressed any other way. And the collars on their coats always look as if they had been rolled in flour. Instantly three little children— a boy and two girls—run in to their great-grandmother. Such very aged women almost always have some very close kinship with children: they themselves become very much like children in their hearts, and sometimes exactly the same. The old woman sat down; someone else, perhaps a guest or someone on business—a man of forty or so and acquainted with the barber—was just getting ready to leave. In addition they have a nephew staying with them, the son of his sister, a lad of about seventeen who wants to find work in a printer's shop. The old woman crosses herself and sits down, looking at the guest.

"Oh, but I'm tired out! Now who's this you have here?"

"Do you mean me?" asks the guest, laughing. "Don't tell me you didn't recognize me, Maria Maximovna! Why, a couple of years ago you and I were planning to go out into the woods to look for mushrooms."

"Oh, now I know who you are. What a tease! I know who you are, only I just can't place your name, but I remember. Oh, I'm just worn out."

"Well now, Maria Maximovna, I've been wanting to ask you why it is that a venerable old lady like yourself just doesn't seem to grow at all?" the guest teases.

"Go on with you," laughs the grandmother, evidently pleased.

"I'm a good man, Maria Maximovna."

"And it's worthwhile to talk to a good man. Ah, Heavens, I can't seem to catch my breath. I see you've already had an overcoat made for little Seriozha."

She points at the nephew.

The nephew, a chubby, healthy little fellow, gives a broad smile and moves closer. He is wearing a new gray coat that still gives him a thrill to put on. He will only be able to wear it with equanimity in a week or so, but now he is constantly examining the cuffs and the lapels and checking himself in the mirror; he feels particularly proud of himself.

"Come on, now, turn around and show us," chatters the barber's wife. "Look at that, Granny, what a job we did; six rubles exactly. They were telling us over at Prokhorych's that it's not worth starting the job for less; you'd regret it afterward, they said; but there's no end of wear in this one. Just feel that material! Turn around now! Look at that lining—feel the strength of it! Turn around, you! And so the money goes, Granny. Our last kopeck's drained away."

"Oh, Heavens, everything's so dear these days there's just no way of making ends meet. You'd better not talk to me about things like that, it just upsets me," Maria Maximovna remarks fervently, still out of breath.

"Yes, enough of that," says the husband. "We ought to have a bite to eat. Maria Maximovna, I can see that you've really got yourself tired out."

"Oh, I certainly have, my dear. It's a warm day, and the sun's shining, so I think why not pay them a visit . . . what's the point of lying around? Ah! And I met a nice lady on the way, a young woman, who'd bought some shoes for her wee children. 'Now why are you so tired, Granny?' she asks me. 'Here's five kopecks for you, buy yourself a roll. . . .' And you know, I took the five kopecks. . . ."

"Come on, Granny, you'd better have a little rest before we do anything else. Why is it you're so short of breath today?" the husband says suddenly, with particular concern.

Everyone is looking at her; she has suddenly become very pale, and her lips have gone quite white. She also looks around at everyone, but her gaze seems somehow dull.

"So, I think . . . some gingerbread for the children . . . that five kopecks. . . ."

Once more she stops, trying to catch her breath. Everyone suddenly falls silent for about five seconds.

"What is it, Granny?" says the husband, bending over her.

But the grandmother gives no reply; there is silence for another five seconds. The old woman seems to grow even more pale and her face suddenly seems to shrink. Her eyes stop moving and the smile freezes on her lips; she looks straight ahead but apparently sees nothing.

"We ought to get a priest!" the guest says suddenly in a quiet voice behind them.

"Yes . . . but . . . I think it may be too late," murmurs the husband.

"Grandmother! Listen, Grandmother!" the barber's wife, suddenly alarmed, calls out to the old woman; but the grandmother is motionless, her head leaning to one side. Her right hand, which rests on the table, holds the five kopecks, while her left hand has remained on the shoulder of her eldest great-grandson Misha, a boy of about six. He stands stock still, staring at his great-grandmother with huge, astonished eyes.

"She has passed on!" says the husband, slowly and with dignity, stooping and crossing himself unobtrusively.

"She has indeed! I could just see her fading away," the guest says tenderly, with a catch in his voice. He is quite shaken and looks around at everybody.

"My Lord, such a thing! What are we to do now, Makarych? Should we have her taken away?" the wife says excitedly, deeply upset.

"What do you mean, away?" her husband solemnly replies. "We'll look after everything ourselves; she's part of your family, is she not? But we'll have to go off and report it."

"A hundred and four years, think of that!" says the guest, squirming in his chair and growing more and more moved. He even blushes furiously.

"Yes, these last years she even began forgetting life itself," remarks the husband even more solemnly and soberly as he looks for his cap and puts on his coat.

"And only a minute ago she was laughing and so cheerful! Look at the coin in her hand! 'Gingerbread,' she said. What a life we have!"

"Well, shall we go, then, Petr Stepanych?" the host interrupts, and they both leave. There is no mourning, of course, for a woman such as this. One hundred and four years old and "she passed on without pain or regrets." The barber's wife sends to the neighbor women for help. They rush over at once, almost pleased to hear the news, sighing and exclaiming. First of all, of course, the samovar is put on. The children crowd into a corner, looking at the dead grandmother with astonished faces. No matter how long Misha lives he will always remember the old woman and how she died, forgetting her hand on his shoulder. And when he dies not a single person on the whole earth will remember or will realize that once upon a time there was such an old woman who lived out her hundred and four years, how and why no one knows. Why remember anyway? It doesn't matter. Millions of people pass away like this: they live unnoticed and they die unnoticed. But maybe only at the very moment of the deaths of these hundred-year-old men and women there is something that seems touching and peaceful, something that seems even solemn and calming: even these days, a hundred years can have a strange effect on people. May God bless the lives and deaths of simple, good people!

Well, still, this is just an inconsequential little scene without a story. True enough, one sets out to recount something with a bit of interest in it from the things heard in the course of a month, but when you sit down to write it turns out to be quite impossible to retell or is irrelevant, or it's simply a case of "not telling everything you know," and so in the end you're left with only little things such as this with no story to them. . . .

Article 3. Dissociation

But still, I'm supposed to be writing about "the things I have seen, heard, and read." At least it's a good thing that I didn't limit myself with a promise to write about *everything* I have "seen, heard, and read." And I keep hearing things that are stranger and stranger. How can I convey

them, when they all go off on their separate ways and simply refuse to
arrange themselves into one neat bundle! Indeed, I keep thinking that
we have begun the epoch of universal "dissociation." All are dissociating
themselves, isolating themselves from everyone else, everyone wants to
invent something of his own, something new and unheard of. Everybody
sets aside all those things that used to be common to our thoughts and
feelings and begins with his own thoughts and feelings. Everybody wants
to begin from the beginning. The links that once united us are broken
without regret, and everyone acts on his own accord and finds his only
consolation in that. If he doesn't act, then he would like to. Granted, a
great many people don't undertake anything and never will, yet they
still have torn themselves away and stand apart, looking at the torn place
and waiting idly for something to happen. Everyone in Russia is waiting
for something to happen. Meanwhile, there is scarcely anything about
which we can agree morally; everything has been or is being broken up,
not even into clusters but into single fragments. And the main thing is
that sometimes this is done with the simplest and most satisfied manner.
Take, for instance, our contemporary man of letters—one of the "new
people," I mean. He begins his career and will have nothing to do with
anything that came before; what he has comes from himself, and he acts
by himself. He preaches new things and flatly sets as his ideal a new word
and a new man. He knows neither European literature nor his own; he
has read nothing, nor will he take up reading. Not only has he not read
Pushkin and Turgenev, he has scarcely even read his own people, that is
Belinsky and Dobroliubov. He depicts new heroes and new women, and
their whole novelty consists in the fact that they confidently take their
tenth step having forgotten about the nine preceding ones, and so they
suddenly find themselves in the most false situation one can conceive;
and they perish so that the reader may be edified and enticed. The false-
ness of the situation comprises the entire edification. There is very little
new in all this; to the contrary, there is an extraordinary lot of worn-out
old castoffs. But that's not the point at all; the point is that the author
is completely convinced that he has spoken his new word, that he is
acting independently, that he has dissociated himself; and, of course, this
pleases him a good deal. This little example, however, is old and trivial;
but the other day I heard a story about one of these "new words." There
was a certain "nihilist" who did his denying and his suffering and, after

getting into many scrapes and even spending time in prison, he suddenly found religious feeling in his heart. And what do you think he immediately did? He instantly "isolated and dissociated himself"; promptly and gingerly he steered clear of our Christian faith, disposed of all our legacy from the past, and quickly invented his own faith, also Christian, yet "his very own." He has a wife and children. He does not live with his wife, and his children are looked after by others. Recently he ran off to America, very likely to preach his new faith there. In a word, everyone is on his own, doing things his own way. Can they all only be trying to appear original or be pretending to be so? By no means. We are now living in a period that is more concerned with truth than reflection. Many, and perhaps very many, are truly sorrowing and suffering; they have indeed, and in the most serious fashion, broken all their former links and they are *compelled* to begin from the beginning, for no one gives them light. And our wise men and intellectual leaders only nod in agreement, some of them out of Judaical fear ("Why not let him go to America?" they say; "running off to America is something liberal, after all"), while others are simply making money off them. And so our fresh energies perish. You might say that these are still only two or three facts that don't mean anything; that, on the contrary, everything is undoubtedly more solidly integrated and united than before; that banks, societies, and associations are coming onto the scene. But can you really and truly hold up as an example this crowd of triumphant Jews and kikes that has thrown itself on Russia? Triumphant and full of enthusiasm, because nowadays there have appeared even kikes full of enthusiasm, both of the Hebraic and the Orthodox persuasions. Just think: our newspapers write that even they are isolating themselves and that, for instance, the foreign press will make even more fun of the congresses of representatives of our Russian land banks because of "the secret sessions of the first two congresses, asking, not without irony: in what manner and by what right have the Russian land-credit institutions the boldness to make a claim on the public's trust when their secret sessions, held behind carefully guarded Chinese walls, hide everything from the public, thereby making it obvious that something unsavory is being cooked up. . . ."

So it seems that even these gentlemen are isolating themselves, shutting themselves up, and devising something of their own to be done their way, not the way it is done in the rest of the world. The business about the

banks I slipped in as a joke, however: that's not my topic at the moment.
I'm speaking only about "dissociation." How can I better explain my
thought? By the way, I'll mention a few ideas about our corporations and
associations that come from a certain manuscript. It's not one of mine but
was sent to me and has never been published. The author addresses his
opponents in the provinces:

> You say that the artels, associations, corporations, cooperatives,
> trading companies and all these other associations are based on
> man's inborn sense of sociability. Defending the Russian artel,
> which has still been researched far too little to be spoken of posi-
> tively, we believe that all these associations, corporations, etc., are
> only unions of some against others, unions founded on the sense of
> self-preservation evoked by the struggle for survival. Our opinion is
> supported by the history of the origin of these unions, which were
> first formed by the poor and weak against the wealthy and strong.
> Subsequently, the latter began to employ the same weapon against
> their opponents. History indeed testifies that all these unions origi-
> nated out of fraternal enmity and were based not on the need for
> social intercourse, as you suppose, but on the feeling of fear for
> one's survival or on the wish for gain, profit, or benefit, even at the
> expense of one's neighbor. When we examine the structure of all
> these progeny of utilitarianism, we see that their main concern is to
> organize firm control of everyone over all and of all over everyone—
> to put it simply, wholesale espionage arising from the fear that
> one person may cheat another. All these associations, with their
> internal controls and their external activity that envies everything
> outside them, present a striking parallel with what is happening
> in the world of politics, where the mutual relations of nations are
> characterized by an armed peace, broken by occasional bloody
> clashes, while their internal life is one of endless factional strife.
> How can one speak of communion or love in such a case? Is that
> not why such institutions take root so poorly in Russia? We still
> live too expansively, so that we still have insufficient basis to take
> up arms against one another; we still have too much affection for
> and faith in one another, and these feelings hinder us from setting
> up the control and mutual espionage that is required when all of

these associations, cooperatives, trading, and other companies are established. With insufficient control they cannot work and inevitably go bankrupt.

So should we lament these defects of ours as compared with our better-educated Western neighbors? No: for we, at least, can perceive in these defects our wealth; we can see that the feeling of unity, without which human societies cannot exist, is still effective among us, even though it acts unconsciously on people and leads them not only to do great deeds, but also, very often, to do great wrong. Yet one in whom this feeling is not yet dead is capable of everything, provided that the feeling can be transformed from something unconscious and instinctual into a conscious force, one that would not toss him this way and that by the blind caprice of chance but would direct him toward the realization of rational aims. Without this feeling of unity and mutual love, of communion among people, nothing great is conceivable because society itself is inconceivable.

So the author, you see, perhaps is not entirely condemning these associations and corporations; he is simply stating that their *present* governing principle consists only in utilitarianism, and in espionage as well, and that this is certainly not a *unity of people.* This is all something youthful, fresh, theoretical, and impractical, yet in principle it is absolutely correct and is written not only with sincerity but with suffering and distress. Note the common trait: the whole issue in Russia now depends on the first step, on the practice, but everyone to the last man is shouting and worrying only about principles, so that the practice has, willy-nilly, fallen into the hands of the Israelites alone. The history of the manuscript from which I took the above excerpt is as follows. The worthy author (I don't know if he is a young man or one of those young old men) published one small item in a certain provincial publication, while next to it the editor printed his own note of qualification, which partly disagreed with the author. Then, when the author of the item wrote a whole article (not a very long one, however) to refute the editor's note, the latter refused to print it under the pretext that it was "more of a sermon than an article." Then the author wrote to me, forwarding the rejected article and asking that I read it, think about it, and express my opinion in my *Diary.* First, I thank him for his confidence

in my opinion; and second; I thank him for the article, because it has
given me a great deal of satisfaction: rarely have I read anything more
logical, and although I am unable to include the whole article, I used the
preceding excerpt with an intention I do not hide: the fact is that in its
author, who pleads for a genuine unity of humans, I also noted a certain
"dissociationist" flourish, specifically in those parts of the manuscript
which I will not venture to quote but which are so "dissociated" that one
rarely meets the like. And so it is not only the article but also the author
himself who bears out my thought of the "dissociation" of individuals
and the remarkable, virtually chemical decomposition of our society into
its constituent elements, a process that has begun suddenly in our time.

I might add, however, that if nowadays everybody is "on his own and
by himself," then there still is some link with what has gone before. Indeed,
this link absolutely must exist, even if all might seem to be uncoordinated
and full of mutual misunderstanding, and it is most interesting to follow
this link. To put it briefly (although the comparison is an old one), our
educated Russian society reminds me most of all of that ancient bundle
of twigs which is strong only so long as the twigs are bound together;
but as soon as the bonds are broken, the whole bundle flies apart into
many weak stalks that the first wind will carry off. And so it is just this
kind of bundle that has come apart and been scattered in our Russia.
Isn't it true that our government, all through the twenty-year period of
its reforms, never enjoyed the *full* support of its intelligentsia? On the
contrary, did not the vast majority of young, fresh, precious talents go off
on some tangent, toward a dissociation full of scorn and threats? And this
happened precisely because, instead of taking the first nine steps, they
immediately took the tenth one, forgetting that the tenth step without the
preceding nine will *in any case* certainly become only an illusory one,
even if it meant anything on its own. What is most painful is that only one
in a thousand of these "solitudinarians," perhaps, understands anything
about the meaning of this tenth step, while the others have only been
listening to common rumors and gossip. The result is a farce: the egg the
hen laid was sterile. Have you ever seen a forest fire during a hot summer?
What a pitiful, sad sight it is! How much valuable material perishes in
vain, how much energy, fire, and heat are used up for nothing and disappear without a trace, having accomplished no useful purpose.

from CHAPTER TWO

Article 1, extract. Don Carlos and Sir Watkin. More Signs of "The Beginning of the End."

I was most interested to read of the arrival of Don Carlos in England. People always say that real life is dull and monotonous; they turn to art and fantasy for diversion; they read novels. For me the opposite is true: what could be more fantastic and surprising than real life? What can be even more improbable than real life sometimes is? A novelist could never imagine possibilities such as real life offers every day by the thousand in the guise of the most ordinary things. There are times when no fantasizing could come up with the like. And what an advantage over the novel! Just try to *invent* an episode in a novel such as happened to, say, the lawyer Kupernik; concoct it yourself, and the following Sunday a critic in his column would prove to you clearly and beyond dispute that you are talking nonsense and that things like that never happen in real life and, most important, that they never can happen due to this reason and that reason. And, in the end, embarrassed, you would agree with him. But then someone gives you an issue of *The Voice* and suddenly you read in it the whole episode of our marksman—and what happens? At first you read in amazement—in terrible amazement, such that you cannot believe what you are reading; but as soon as you have read through to the final period, you put down the newspaper, and suddenly, not knowing why yourself, you say at once, "Yes, it all absolutely must have happened this way." And some people might even add, "I had a feeling something like that would happen." Why a newspaper produces such a different impression from a novel I don't know, but such is the privilege of real life.

Don Carlos makes his calm and majestic entry into England as a guest after all the blood and butchery "in the name of the King, the Faith, and the Madonna." Now here's a figure, here's another example of "dissociation!" Could anyone invent something like that? By the way, do you remember what happened to Count Chambord (Henry V) two years ago? He's another king, a legitimist, who was making his claim to the French throne at the same time that Don Carlos was making his claim in Spain.

They can consider each other relatives, being of the same lineage and the same ancestry, but what a difference between them! One is firmly bound up in his own convictions, a melancholy, elegant, humane figure. Count Chambord, at that fatal moment when he really could have become king (only for an instant, of course) was never tempted by anything; he never gave up his "white banner," and thereby proved that he was a true and magnanimous knight, almost a Don Quixote, an ancient knight with a vow of chastity and poverty, a figure worthy of bringing his ancient and royal lineage to a majestic end (majestic and just a touch absurd, for life does not exist without absurdity). He rejected power and the throne simply because he wanted to become the king of France not merely for himself but for the salvation of his country; and since in his view that salvation could not be reconciled with the concessions demanded of him (the concessions were quite within his means), he did not want to rule. How different from the recent Napoleon, a wily old fox and a proletarian, a man who promised everything, gave away everything, and cheated everyone just to attain power. I made a comparison between Count Chambord and Don Quixote just now, but this is the highest praise I know. It was Heine, wasn't it, who told of how, when reading *Don Quixote* as a child, he burst into tears on reaching the place where the hero was overcome by the wretched and commonsensical barber Samson Carrasco. There is nothing deeper and more powerful in the whole world than this piece of *fiction*. It is still the final and the greatest expression of human thought, the most bitter irony that a human is capable of expressing, and if the world came to an end and people were asked somewhere *there:* "Well, did you understand anything from your life on earth and draw any conclusion from it?" a person could silently hand over *Don Quixote:* "Here is my conclusion about life; can you condemn me for it?" I don't claim that the person would be right in saying that, but [. . .]

Article 3, extract. A Word or Two about the Report of the Scholarly Commission on Spiritualistic Phenomena

[. . .] Could the commission itself, composed of so many learned people, have seriously hoped in its very first effort to suppress such a silly idea? Alas, if the commission had produced even the most obvious and direct proofs of trickery, even if it had caught and exposed people in the act of producing fakeries, seizing them by the arms, as it were (which, of course, never happened)—even then, no one who is now an enthusiast for spiritualism would have believed it, nor would those who only want to take a mild interest in it, because there is a primordial law of nature stating that, where mystical notions are concerned, even strictly mathematical proofs carry no weight whatsoever. And here, in our nascent spiritualism, the mystical idea alone is foremost, believe me—and what can you do about that? Faith and mathematical proof are two irreconcilable things. There's no stopping someone who makes up his mind to believe. Besides, the proofs in this case are far from mathematical. [. . .]

April

from CHAPTER TWO

Article 2. A Paradoxicalist

By the way, a word or two about war and rumors of war. I know a man who is a paradoxicalist. I have known him for a long time. He is an obscure person with an odd character: he is a *dreamer.* I shall certainly talk about him in more detail sometime. But now I recall how once, some years ago, he got into an argument with me about war. He defended war in general and did so, perhaps, solely out of his love of paradox. I can tell you that he is a civilian and the most peaceable, affable person you could find on earth and here in Petersburg.

"It is an outrageous notion," he said, in passing, "that war is the scourge of mankind. On the contrary, it is a most useful thing. There is only one form of war that is hateful and truly pernicious: that is a civil, fratricidal war. It paralyzes and shatters the state; it always goes on too long; and it brutalizes the people for centuries on end. But a political, international war brings only benefit in every respect, and thus it is absolutely essential."

"Wait now—a nation goes against another nation, and people set out to kill one another—what is essential in that?"

"Everything is, and to the highest degree. But in the first place, it's a lie that people set forth to kill one another; this is never uppermost in their minds. On the contrary, they set out to sacrifice their own lives; that must be uppermost in their minds. And that is something altogether different. There is no idea more elevated than sacrificing one's own life while defending one's brothers and one's fatherland or even simply defending the interests of one's fatherland. Humanity cannot live without noble ideas, and I even suspect that humanity loves war precisely in order to be a part of some noble idea. It is a human need."

"But does humanity really love war?"

"Of course it does. Who is in low spirits in time of war? Quite the contrary: everyone is full of cheer, their spirits rise, and there is no mention of the usual apathy or boredom you hear of in peacetime. And then, when the war ends, how people love to reminisce about it, even if they were defeated! And don't believe those who, when they meet during time of war, shake their heads and say to each other: 'Such a calamity. We've come to this!' They're only being polite. In reality, everyone is in a festive mood. Do you know, there are some ideas one finds terribly difficult to admit having. People will call you a beast and a reactionary and condemn you; they fear these ideas. No one dares to praise war."

"But you're talking about noble ideas and about humanizing. Can't there be noble ideas without war? On the contrary, in peacetime there is even more scope for such ideas to flourish."

"No, it's quite the reverse. Nobility perishes during periods of prolonged peace, and in its place appear cynicism, indifference, boredom, and, most of all, an attitude of malicious mockery—and that almost as an idle pastime, not for any serious purpose. I can say positively that a prolonged peace hardens people's hearts. During such a prolonged peace the social balance always shifts to the side of all that is stupid and coarse in humanity, principally toward wealth and capital. Immediately after a war honor, philanthropy, and self-sacrifice are respected, valued, and highly regarded; but the longer the peace lasts, the more these beautiful, noble things grow pale, wither, and die off, while everyone is in the grip of wealth and the spirit of acquisition. In the end, the only thing left is hypocrisy—hypocrisy of honor, self-sacrifice, and duty; these things may continue to be respected despite all the cynicism, but only formally, in fine words. There will be no genuine honor, but the formulas will remain. When honor becomes a formula, it dies. A prolonged peace produces apathy, mean-spirited ideas, depravity, a dulling of the feelings. Pleasures do not grow refined but coarsen. Crude wealth cannot take delight in nobility but demands less elevated and more immediate pleasures, i.e., the most direct satisfaction of the urges of the flesh. Pleasures become carnivorous. Sensuality evokes lechery, and lechery is always cruel. You cannot deny all this, because you cannot deny the main fact: that the social balance during a prolonged peace in the end always shifts toward crude wealth."

"But science, the arts—can they truly flourish in wartime? And these are great and noble ideas."

"Ah, but this is where I catch you. Science and the arts flourish particularly in the immediate postwar period. War renews and refreshes them; it stimulates and strengthens thought and gives it some impetus. But a long peace, on the other hand, will stifle even science. There's no doubt that the pursuit of science demands a certain nobility, even self-denial. But can many of these scientists survive the pestilence of peace? False honor, self-love, and sensuality will catch them up as well. Just try to cope with a passion like envy, for example: it is crude and vulgar, but it also will find its way into the noblest heart of a scientist. He, too, will want to participate in the general prosperity and glamour. Compared to the triumph of wealth, what can the triumph of some scientific discovery mean, unless it is something as sensational as the discovery of the planet Neptune, for example? Now what do you think: will there be many left who are truly devoted to humble toil? On the contrary, there will be a desire for fame, and so charlatanism will invade science; there will be the pursuit of the sensational; and there will be utilitarianism above all, because there will be a desire for wealth as well. The same will be true of art: the same pursuit of the sensational, the ultrarefined. Simple, clear, noble, and healthy ideas will no longer be in fashion: something much meatier will be in demand; simulated passions will be in demand. Little by little the sense of measure and harmony will be lost; distorted feelings and passions will appear—the so-called ultrarefinement of the feelings which in essence is only their vulgarization. Art inevitably falls victim to this at the end of a prolonged peace. Had war never existed on this earth, art would have completely died. All the best ideas of art are provided by war and by struggle. Think of tragedy, look at statues: here is Corneille's *Horace;* here is the Apollo Belvedere overpowering a monster. . . ."

"And what about the Madonnas; what about Christianity?"

"Christianity itself recognizes the fact of war and prophesies that the sword shall not pass until the end of the world: this is quite remarkable and striking. Oh, there's no doubt that in the highest sense, in the moral sense, it rejects war and demands brotherly love. I myself shall be the first to rejoice when the swords are beaten into plowshares. But the question is: when is this going to happen? And is it worth beating the swords into plowshares at present? The peace of today is always and everywhere worse than war, so much worse that it even becomes immoral in the end to support the peace. It is nothing to value, nothing worth preserving; it is shameful and vulgar to preserve it. Wealth and vulgarity give birth to indolence, and indolence gives birth to slaves. In order to keep slaves in their servile state, one must take away their free will and their opportunity to better themselves. For can you not help but feel the need to have a slave, even though you may be the most humane sort of person? I note as well that during a period of peace cowardice and dishonesty take root. Man by nature is terribly inclined to cowardice and shameless acts, and he himself knows this very well. And that, perhaps, is why he is so fond of war: he senses a medicine in it. War fosters brotherly love and unites nations."

"How does it unite nations?"

"By forcing them to respect one another. War refreshes people. Love for one's fellow human beings develops best on the field of battle. It's a strange fact, indeed, that war does less to rouse people's anger than peace. In fact, something that could be considered a political outrage in time of peace, some treaty that demanded too much, some political pressure, some demand couched in arrogant language—of the sort that Europe made of us in 1863—all these things rouse people's anger much more than open warfare. Think back: did we hate the French and the English during the Crimean campaign? Not in the least; in fact we seemed to grow closer to them, almost as if they had become our kin. We were interested to hear their views on our courage in battle; we treated their prisoners with great kindness; during times of truce our soldiers and our officers left their forward positions and almost embraced the enemy; they even drank vodka together. Russia was delighted to read about this in the newspapers, yet it did not prevent us from putting up a magnificent fight. A spirit of chivalry was fostered. And I won't even bring up the material losses of war: everyone knows the law by which things seem to come to life with renewed vigor in the postwar period. The economic forces of the country are stimulated ten times more than before, just as if a storm cloud had poured down an abundant rain on the parched earth. Everyone at once lends a hand to those who have suffered during the war, while in peacetime whole provinces can die of hunger before we get around to doing anything or donating a few rubles."

"But don't the People suffer more than anyone else in wartime? Don't they suffer the ruination and bear burdens that are inevitable and incomparably greater than those borne by the upper levels of society?"

"Perhaps, but only temporarily. Yet they do gain much more than they lose. It is specifically for the People that war has the finest and the most sublime consequences. Say what you like: you may be the most humane person, yet you still consider yourself above the common folk. These days who measures soul against soul by a Christian standard? The standard is money, power, and strength, and the common folk as a mass know this very well. This isn't exactly envy; there is some oppressive feeling of moral inequality here that is extremely painful for the common person to live with. You can liberate them however you like and write any sort of laws you choose, but inequality cannot be ended in today's society. The only medicine is war. It is only a palliative, and it is instantaneous, but it brings comfort to the People. War raises the spirits of the People and their awareness of their own dignity. War makes everyone equal in time of battle and reconciles the master and the slave in the most sublime manifestation of human dignity—the sacrifice of life for the common cause, for everyone, and for the fatherland. Do you really think that the masses, even the most benighted masses of peasants and beggars, do not feel this urge for an *active* display of noble feelings? And how can the mass show its nobility and its human dignity in time of peace? We look at isolated noble acts among the common People, barely condescending to take notice of them, sometimes with a skeptical smile, sometimes simply not believing what we've seen. And when we do acknowledge the heroism of some isolated individual, we at once make a fuss as if it were something utterly unusual; the result is that our astonishment and our praise amount to contempt. All this disappears of its own accord in time of war and there ensues the complete equality of heroism. Blood that has been shed is an important thing. A noble exploit that is shared creates the most solid bond between unequal classes. The landowner and the peasant were closer to each other on the battlefield in 1812 than they were while living on some peaceful estate in the country. War gives the masses a reason to respect themselves, and therefore the People love war: they compose songs about it, and for many years thereafter they are eager to hear stories and legends about it. . . . Blood that has been shed is an important thing! Say what you like, but war *in our time* is necessary; without it the world would have collapsed or, at least, would have been transformed into some sort of slime, some squalid muck full of putrefaction. . . ."

I gave up the argument, of course. There is no point in arguing with dreamers. There is, however, one very strange fact: people are now beginning to argue and raise issues that, it would seem, were long ago resolved and consigned to the archives. These things are all being dug up once more. And what's most important is that this is happening everywhere.

Article 3, two extracts. Just a Bit More about Spiritualism

[. . .] Mr. Mendeleev, who is delivering his lecture in Solianoi Gorodok at the very moment I am writing these lines, probably looks at the matter differently and is lecturing with the noble intent of "crushing spiritualism." It's always pleasant to listen to lectures with such admirable tendencies; yet I think that whoever *wants* to put his faith in spiritualism will not be stopped by lectures or even by entire commissions, while those who do not believe, at least if they truly *do not want* to believe, will not be swayed by anything. That was precisely the conviction I took away from the February seance at A. N. Aksakov's; it was, at least, my first strong impression then. Up to that time I had *simply* rejected spiritualism, i.e., in essence I was perturbed only by the mystical sense of its doctrine. (I was never able *completely* to reject spiritualistic phenomena, with which I had had some acquaintance even before the seance with the medium, nor can I now—especially now—after having read the report of the Scholarly Commission on Spiritualism.) But after that remarkable seance I suddenly surmised—or rather, I suddenly discovered—not only that I do not believe in spiritualism but that I haven't the least *wish* to believe in it, so that there is no evidence that will *ever* cause me to change my views. That is what I took away from the seance and later came to understand. And, I confess, this impression was almost gratifying because I had been a little apprehensive on my way to the seance. I might add that this is not merely a personal matter: I think there is something that applies to us all in this observation of mine. I have a sense of some special law of human nature, common to all and pertaining specifically to faith and disbelief in general. I somehow came to understand then—specifically through experience, specifically through this seance—what power disbelief can uncover and develop within you at a given moment, absolutely despite your own will, although it may be in accordance with your secret desire. . . . The same thing is probably true of faith. That's what I wanted to talk about. [. . .]

P.S. I have just read the account of Mr. Mendeleev's second lecture on spiritualism. Mr. Mendeleev is already saying the commission's report has had a salutary influence on writers: "Suvorin no longer is such a believer in spiritualism as before; Boborykin, too, has evidently been cured, or at least is on the road to recovery. Finally, Dostoevsky in his *Diary* has made a recovery as well: in January he was inclined toward spiritualism, but in March he attacks it. It seems that the 'Report' has had something to do with this." So, it seems the esteemed Mr. Mendeleev thought that I was praising spiritualism in January. I wonder if that was because of the devils? [...]

May

from CHAPTER ONE

Article 1. From a Private Letter

People ask if I am planning to write about the Kairova case. I have already had several letters asking this question. One letter is especially characteristic and was not, apparently, written for publication; still, I'll venture to quote a few lines of it while preserving strict anonymity, of course. I hope that my worthy correspondent will not complain; I'm quoting him only because I am convinced of his complete sincerity, which I can fully respect.

> . . . It was with a feeling of the deepest repugnance that we read about the Kairova case. This case reveals, as in the focus of a lens, a picture of the carnal instincts which the leading personage of the case (Kairova) developed under the influence of her milieu: her mother, during pregnancy, abandoned herself to drink; her father was a drunkard; her brother lost his mind because of drink and shot himself; a cousin murdered his wife; her father's mother was insane. And this was the milieu that gave birth to a despotic person with unbridled carnal urges. Even those who prosecuted the case were baffled by her and had to ask themselves whether she was insane. Some of the experts positively denied this, while others admitted the possibility of insanity, not in her personally, but in her actions. Yet it is not insanity that one sees through this whole trial; it is a woman who has reached the extreme limits of rejection of everything sacred: for her there exists neither the family nor the rights of another woman—not only that woman's right to a husband but to her very life: all these things exist for herself and her carnal lusts alone.
>
> She was acquitted, perhaps, on grounds of insanity, and we must thank God for that! At least moral depravity was attributed not to intellectual progress but to the category of mental illnesses.
>
> However, in the "lower section of the courtroom, filled *exclusively with ladies,* applause broke out" (*Stock Exchange News*).

What was the applause for? Was it for the acquittal of an insane
woman, or was it for the triumph of an uncontrolled, passionate
nature, for the cynicism the woman personifies?

Ladies applaud! Wives and mothers applaud! They ought to
weep and not applaud the spectacle of such desecration of the feminine ideal. . . .

[N.B. I omit several very harsh lines here.]

Will you really pass over this case in silence?

Article 3. The Court and Mrs. Kairova

However, we've strayed far from the Kairova case. I wanted only to draw
my correspondent's attention to the fact that, although I agree with his
view on the "depraved instincts and despotic lack of restraint of her
urges," I still find the opinions of my worthy correspondent to be overly
harsh; there is not even any point to his harshness (for he all but admits
that the woman is insane); he also exaggerates unduly, the more so that
he finishes by acknowledging *the influence of the environment* almost to
the point of admitting the futility of struggling against it. As for me, I am
just happy that Kairova was released; I am only unhappy that she was
acquitted. I am happy she was released, even though I don't for a moment
believe she is insane, despite the views of some experts: accept this as
my personal opinion, which I will not force on anyone else. Besides, if
this poor woman is not insane, one feels even more pity for her. If she
is insane, then "she knew not what she did"; but if she is not, how will
she be able to go off bearing such a burden of torment! A murder, at least
when it is not committed by some "Jack of Hearts," is a difficult and a
complex thing. These several days of her indecision after the lawful wife
of Kairova's lover returned to him; her sense of insult that kept seething
away day after day; her resentment that grew stronger every hour (oh,
Kairova is the offender here—I still haven't lost my senses—but what
is all the more pitiable is that in her fall she could not even understand
that it was she who was the offender and kept seeing and feeling exactly
the opposite!); and finally, this last hour before the "deed," at night, on
the stairs, holding the razor that she had bought the day before—say
what you will, but this is all rather difficult to bear, especially for such

a disorderly and unstable soul as Kairova! The burden is too much for her; one seems to hear her groans as she is crushed by it. And then, ten months of tribulations, madhouses, experts. How they dragged her about here and there and everywhere, and all the while this wretched, heinous criminal, completely guilty, represents in essence something so lacking in seriousness, so careless, so totally uncomprehending and unaccomplished, trivial, licentious, incapable of self-control, and mediocre—and so she was to the very last moment of the verdict, so that it somehow was a relief when she was let off. It's a pity only that this could not have been done without acquitting her because—say what you like—it caused a scandal. I think that Mr. Utin, her attorney, should certainly have sensed an acquittal coming and so could have limited himself simply to setting forth the facts rather than starting in to sing praises to the crime, because he *almost sang praises to the crime,* after all. . . . That's just the point: we have no sense of measure in anything. In the West, Darwin's theory is a brilliant hypothesis; in Russia it has long become an axiom. In the West the notion that crime is very often only an illness makes a good deal of sense because people there *discriminate* carefully among crimes; but in Russia this same notion makes no sense at all because we do not discriminate at all, and everything, every sort of nasty villainy committed even by a Jack of Hearts we also accept almost as an illness and—alas!— people even see something liberal in this! Of course, I'm not talking about serious people (although do we have many serious people in that sense?). I'm talking about the man in the street, about the untalented mediocrities, on the one hand, and about the scoundrels who trade in liberalism on the other, and these latter people are ones who couldn't care a fig for anything, so long as it is or seems to be liberal. As far as the attorney Utin is concerned, he "sang praises to crime" probably imagining that as an attorney he could do nothing else—and this is just how undeniably clever people get carried away and achieve results that aren't clever at all. Had the jurors been in different circumstances, i.e., had they had the opportunity of pronouncing a different verdict, then I think they probably would have taken exception to Mr. Utin's exaggerations, so that he would have weakened his client's case. But the fact was that they literally were unable to bring in a different verdict. Some newspapers commended them for it, while others, I've heard, censure them. I think there is no place here either for praise or for blame: they simply brought in the verdict they did

because they were utterly unable to bring in any other. Judge for yourselves; this is what we read in the newspaper account:

> In accordance with the request of the prosecution, the following
> question was put by the court: "Did Kairova, *having premedi-*
> *tated her act,* inflict on Alexandra Velikanova, *with intent to take*
> *her life,* several wounds with a razor on her neck, head and chest,
> *but was prevented from the ultimate consummation of her intent* of
> murdering Velikanova by Velikanova herself and her husband?"
> The jury answered this question in the negative.

Let us pause here. This is the answer to the first question. But really,
can one give an answer to a question posed *that way*? Who, and whose
conscience, will undertake to answer such a question in the affirmative?
(It's true that it's equally impossible to answer in the negative, but we are
discussing only the jury's affirmative decision.) One can only give an affirmative answer to a question posed that way if one has supernatural, divine
omniscience. Indeed, even Kairova herself might have no idea of whether
she would slash her rival to death or not, and yet the jury was asked positively: "Would she have murdered her had they not stopped her?" When
she bought the razor the day before, she might well have known why she
bought it but still might not have known whether she would attack her
with it, never mind whether she would slash her to death. Most likely she
hadn't the slightest idea of this even when sitting on the steps with the
razor in her hand, while just behind her, on her own bed, lay her lover
and her rival. No one, no one in the world could have had the slightest
idea of this. Moreover, even though it may seem absurd, I can state that
even when she had begun slashing her rival she might *still not have known*
whether she wanted to kill her or not and whether *this was her purpose* in
slashing her. Note, please, that I certainly am not arguing here that she was
acting unconsciously; I don't even admit the slightest element of insanity.
To the contrary: it is very likely that at the moment when she was slashing
her rival *she knew what she was doing,* but whether she consciously,
having made it her purpose, wanted to take her rival's life—of this she
may well have not had the least idea. For Heaven's sake, don't think this
is absurd: she could be slashing with the razor, in anger and hatred, with
not the slightest thought of the consequences. Judging by the character

of this disorderly and tormented woman, it likely happened exactly that way. And note that the whole fate of this unfortunate woman hung on the jury's answer (an affirmative one, say) to the question of whether she would have gone through with the murder and, most important, whether she attacked her rival with the deliberate intent to kill her. She would be ruined, condemned to forced labor. How can a jury take such a burden on their conscience? And so they answered in the negative because they had no alternative answer to give. You might say that Kairova's crime was not something premeditated, not a rational or bookish one, but simply "women's business," very uncomplicated, very simple; her rival was lying on Kairova's own bed as well. But is it that way and that simple? What if she had passed the razor across Velikanova's throat once and then cried out, shuddered, and ran off as fast as she could? How do you know that this might not have happened? And if it had happened, it's very likely that the affair would never have come to court. But now you've been pinned to the wall and are being forced to make a definite answer: "Would she have murdered Velikanova or not?" And of course this is done so that your answer will determine whether or not she is exiled. And the slightest variation in your answer corresponds to whole years of imprisonment or forced labor! And what if she made one slash and then took fright and turned the razor on herself and, indeed, perhaps even killed herself right there? And what, finally, if she not only had not taken fright but had flown into a frenzy when she felt the first spurts of hot blood and not only murdered Velikanova but even begun to abuse the body, cutting off the head, the nose, the lips; and only later, suddenly, when someone took that head away from her, had realized what she had done? I am asking this because it all could have happened and could have been done by this very same woman and sprung from the very same soul, in the very same mood and under the very same circumstances; I say this because I somehow sense that I am not mistaken. And so how could one answer such a tricky question from the court? This isn't a family conversation around the tea table, after all: someone's fate is being decided here. Posing questions in this way runs the strong risk of getting no answer at all.

Yet you may respond that if such were the case, we would never be able to charge or try anyone for murder or attempted murder so long as the crime was not brought to completion or the victim survived. No, I think that there is no cause for alarm here because there are very obvious cases of murder where, though the crime was never completed (even because of the criminal's own will), it is still quite evident that they were undertaken solely *with the intent to murder* and could have had no other purpose. But I repeat the most important thing: for this we have the conscience of the jury, and that is something great and important; that is the good service rendered by the new courts, and that conscience truly will prompt the jury to a new decision. If a person feels within himself, at such an important moment, the resolve to answer firmly, "Yes, guilty," then in all likelihood he will not be mistaken about the criminal's guilt. At least mistakes have happened so rarely as to be anecdotal. Only one thing is desirable: that the conscience of the jury be truly enlightened, truly firm, and strengthened by a civic sense of duty; that it should avoid being diverted toward one side or the other, i.e., toward harshness or pernicious sentimentality. It's also true that this second hope, i.e, the avoidance of sentimentality, is rather difficult to achieve. Everyone is capable of senti-mentality; it's such an easy thing and requires no effort; sentimentality is so profitable these days; sentimentality with the right tendency will make even an ass look like a refined man. . . .

The second question posed to the jury—"Did she inflict these wounds with *the same intent,* in a state of frenzy and passion?"—could likewise be answered only negatively, i.e., "No, she did not"; for here again the phrase "with the same intent" signifies "with the premeditated inten-tion of taking Velikanova's life." It became especially difficult to answer this because "frenzy and passion" in the vast majority of cases exclude "premeditated intention." And so this second question of the court seems even to contain an element of the absurd.

However in the court's *third* question—"Did Kairova act in a clearly established state of mental derangement?"—there is a rather larger element of the absurd, for the first two questions and the third are mutu-ally exclusive. If the jury had answered the first two questions in the negative, or even if they had simply left them unanswered, it would then have been unclear what was being asked and even what the word "act" meant, i.e., what sort of act are they asking about and how do they define it? The jury had no room at all to modify their answer because of their duty to answer only yes or no and nothing in between.

Finally, the *fourth* question of the court—"If she was not acting under the influence of mental derangement, is she guilty of the aforesaid crime?"—was naturally also left unanswered by the jury in view of the fact that it only repeated the first two questions.

So it was that the court *let Kairova off.* The jury's answer, "No, she did not inflict . . ." also contains an absurdity, of course, for it is repudiated by the very fact that wounds were inflicted, a fact which no one disputes and which is obvious to all. But the jury found it difficult to give any other answer because of the way the question was put. But at least one could not say that in letting Kairova off, or at least in "pardoning" her, the court vindicated the defendant; but Mr. Utin certainly does justify the act of this criminal, and he almost finds it right and good. This is hard to believe, but this is what happened.

Article 5, extract. The Defense Attorney and Velikanova

[. . .] Can you really say, as you did, Mr. Utin, that Velikanova lost nothing in this case because only a few days after the incident she appeared on the stage and then performed all winter long, while Kairova was incarcerated for ten months? We have no less pity for your poor client than you do, but you must agree that Mrs. Velikanova has endured more than a little. Never mind what she lost as a wife and a self-respecting woman (the latter is something I have no right to take away from her); but just imagine, Mr. Utin—you, the subtle jurist who so clearly revealed himself as a humane person in his speech—just imagine how much she must have endured that terrible night! She endured several minutes (far too many minutes) of *mortal fear*. Do you know what *mortal fear* is? One who has not had a close confrontation with death has difficulty in understanding it. She was awakened at night by the razor of the woman who wanted to murder her as the razor passed across her throat; she saw the infuriated face bending over her; she fought off her attacker, while Kairova continued slashing at her; naturally, she must have been convinced in these first savage, impossible moments that she had been fatally slashed and that death was inevitable. That's unbearable, after all; it's a delirious nightmare, but a nightmare while awake and so a hundred times more painful. It's almost the same as a death sentence being read to one tied to the stake for execution while they pull the hood over his head. . . . Merciful Heavens, Mr. Utin—you regard even torment like that as insignificant! Can it be that not one of the jurors smiled when he listened to that? And what of the fact that Mrs. Velikanova was performing onstage two weeks later? Does that make the horror that she had to endure two weeks earlier any less, or does it lessen the guilt of your client? We had a case not long ago of a stepmother who threw her six-year-old stepdaughter out of a fourth-floor window, but the child got up quite unharmed. Does that in any way alter the cruelty of the crime, and did this little girl truly not suffer at all? By the way, I can't help but imagine how a defense attorney would defend this stepmother: he could cite her hopeless situation, the fact that she was recently married against her will or by mistake to a widower. We would have pictures of the impoverished lives of impoverished people, their endless labor. She, a simple, innocent woman who, like an inexperienced girl (especially given our manner of child rearing!), married thinking that there were only joys awaiting her thereafter; but instead of joys she has the washing of dirty linen, cooking, bathing the child—"Gentlemen of the jury, it is only natural that she should conceive a hatred for this child"—(who knows, we might even find such a "defense attorney" who would begin to blacken the child's character and seek out some nasty, hateful qualities in this six-year-old!)—"in a moment of despair, in a passing fit of madness, scarcely knowing what she was doing, she seizes the girl and. ...Gentlemen of the jury, who among you would not do the same? Which one of you would not have thrown the girl out the window?" [...]

from CHAPTER TWO

Article 2. One Inappropriate Thought

I said "independence" just now. But do we love independence?—that's
the question. And what do we mean by independence? Could we find
two people who would understand it in the same way—in fact, I'm not
sure if we have even one such idea in which anyone seriously believes.
Our average, unexceptional person, rich or poor, doesn't like to think
about anything and so, without paying much mind to it, simply indulges
in a little vice while he has the strength and the interest. People who are
better than the average "dissociate" themselves in little groups and give
the appearance of believing in something; yet it seems they force themselves to do it and do so only as an amusement. There are also particular
people who have seized upon the formula "The worse, the better," and
are working out its implications. There are, finally, paradoxicalists, who
are occasionally very honest but on the whole rather untalented; these,
especially if they are honest, most often end by suicide. And, in truth,
suicides lately have become so common that people don't even talk about
them any more. The Russian land seems to have lost the capacity to hold
people on it. And how many truly honest people—and honest women in
particular—there are among them! Our women are beginning to make
their presence felt and, perhaps, will save a great deal; I'll say more about
that later. Women are perhaps our great hope and will serve the whole
of Russia in her fateful moment. But this is the problem: we have a lot
of honest people, a terrific lot of them; I mean to say that they are good
rather than honest, but none of them knows the meaning of honesty and
hasn't the least shred of belief in any expression of honesty; they even
reject its clearest expressions from the past, and that is the case almost
everywhere and with everyone. Should that surprise us? But the so-called
living force, the vital sense of existence, without which no society can
live and no land endure, is vanishing away, God knows where. So why
was it that in this building I set to thinking about suicides, looking at
this nursery and at these infants? Now that really is an inappropriate
thought.

We have many inappropriate thoughts, and it is they that crush us. Here in Russia an idea falls on a person like a huge boulder and half crushes him; there he is, squirming under it, unable to get free. Some people accept living crushed, while others do not, and they kill themselves. Extremely characteristic is the long letter, published in *New Times*, of a girl who committed suicide. She was twenty-five, and her name was Pisareva. She was the daughter of landowners who had once been prosperous; but she came to Petersburg and paid her dues to progress by becoming a midwife. She got through the course, passed the examination, and found a position as a zemstvo midwife. She herself states that she was never in need and was able to earn a rather good living. But she got *tired*, very tired, so tired that she wanted to rest. "Where better to rest than in the grave?" She had really become terribly tired! This poor girl's whole letter simply exudes fatigue. The letter is even cranky and impatient: just leave me alone, I'm tired. "Don't forget to have them pull off my new blouse and stockings; I have some old ones on my night table. Have them dress me in those." She doesn't write *take off* but *pull off,* and it's all like that—in terrible impatience. All these sharp words come from being impatient, and the impatience from fatigue; she even uses some abusive language: "Did you really think that I would come home? Why the hell would I go there?" Or: "Now, Lipareva, forgive me and may Petrova forgive me as well" (it was in her apartment the girl took poison) "especially Petrova. I'm doing a filthy, swinish thing. . . ." She evidently loves her family, but she writes: "Don't let Lizanka know, or else she'll tell her sister and they'll come here and start sniveling. I don't want anyone sniveling over me, but a family never fails to do that when one of them dies." *Snivel,* she writes, and not *weep*—all that obviously comes from impatient fatigue: hurry up and get it over with as quickly you can, and let me rest! There is a terrible, agonizing amount of disgusted and cynical unbelief in her: she has no faith in Lipareva or Petrova, whom she loves so. This is how the letter begins: "Don't lose your heads, don't start moaning. Get a grip on yourselves and read this to the end. And then decide what's the best thing to do. Don't frighten Petrova. Maybe nothing will come of it but a good laugh. My residence permit is on top of the trunk."

Only a good laugh! The thought that they would laugh at her, at her wretched body—and who else but Lipareva and Petrova! And that thought flashed through her mind at such a moment! That's dreadful!

It is truly strange how concerned she is with the arrangements for disposing of that little sum of money she left: "This bit of money must not be taken by my relatives; this bit is to go to Petrova; the twenty-five rubles that the Chechetkins gave me for my trip should be returned to them." This importance she attributes to money is, perhaps, the last echo of the main prejudice of her life—"that these stones be made bread." In sum, one sees here the conviction that guided her whole life, i.e., "if everyone were provided for, everyone would be happy; there would be no poor people and no crimes. There would be no crimes whatsoever. Crime is a pathological condition resulting from poverty and from an unhappy environment," etc., etc. This is the entire petty, well-worn, and very typical, self-enclosed catechism of convictions to which such people so faithfully devote themselves in life (despite the fact that they so quickly grow bored with their convictions, as well as their lives). For them, such convictions take the place of everything: a living life, the link with the earth, belief in truth—simply everything. Evidently, having lost all belief in the truth and all faith in duty, the tedium of life tired her. In short, there was a complete loss of any higher ideal of existence.

And the poor girl died. I'm not going to snivel over you, you poor thing, but let me at least have pity for you; allow me that, please. Let me wish that your soul be resurrected into a life where you will not be bored. You people who are kind and good and honest (and you have all of these qualities!)—where are you going, and why has the dark, solitary grave become so attractive to you? Just look: there is a bright spring sun in the sky, the buds are forming on the trees, and you have grown tired before you have lived. How can your mothers, who raised you and who looked at you so fondly when you were still tiny children, help but *snivel* over you? Think how much hope is invested in a tiny child! I've just been seeing how these "outcast" children in the Foundling Home want so much to live; how they declare their right to live! You were also such an infant and you wanted to live; and your mother remembers that; and when she now compares your dead face with that laughter and joy she saw and remembers on your tiny infant's face, how can she help but break out "sniveling," and how can you reproach her for doing so? Just now I was shown a little girl, Dunia; she was born with a crippled leg, or rather with no leg at all; instead of a leg she had something that looked like a cord dangling down. She is only a year and a half old, healthy, and very pretty; everyone cuddles her, and she nods and smiles to everyone and babbles to anyone who comes near. She still is not aware of the problem with her leg; she doesn't know that she is a freak and a cripple. But is she also destined to develop a hatred for life? "We'll make her an artificial leg and give her a crutch, and when she learns to walk she won't notice the difference," said a doctor as he cuddled her. May God grant she doesn't *notice the difference.* No, to grow tired, to come to hate life and thus to hate everyone—oh, no, that cannot be. This pitiful, monstrous, prematurely born generation squirming under the boulders that have fallen on them will disappear; a new and great idea will start to shine like the sun; erratic minds will grow firm, and everyone will say, "Life is good; it is we who have been bad." I'm not accusing anyone when I say that we have been bad. I see that peasant woman over there, that rough wet-nurse who is only "hired milk," suddenly kiss a child, one of those very "outcast" children! I never thought that the wet-nurses here would kiss these children; why, to see this alone would have made the trip here worthwhile! And she kissed the child and didn't notice that I was watching her. Do you think they are paid to love these children? They are hired to feed the children, but they're not required to kiss them. Children who are raised by Finnish women in villages have it worse, so I'm told, but some of the women become so attached to their nurslings that they are in tears when they have to return them to the home; and then come especially from far away to look at them, bringing them little presents from the village and "sniveling over them." No, this isn't a matter of money: "the family, after all, always wants to snivel," as Pisareva concluded in her suicide note, and so these women come to snivel and bring their poor presents from the village. These are not merely hired breasts, taking the place of the breasts of the mother, this is *motherhood;* this is that "living life" of which Pisareva had grown so tired. But is it true that the Russian land no longer holds Russian people on it? Why, then, do we see right at hand a life that is in the full flower of health?

And of course there are many babies here also born of that interesting sort of mother who will sit on the steps of a dacha, honing a razor for her rival. In conclusion I will say: these razors may be nice things in their way, but I was very sorry that I came here, to this building, at a time when I was following the trial of Mrs. Kairova. I know nothing at all of Mrs. Kairova's life story and I certainly cannot, nor have I the right, to connect her in any way to this building. But this whole romance of hers and this whole eloquent analysis of her passions at the trial somehow lost any power they had for me and destroyed any of my sympathy for her once I left this building. I admit this quite frankly, because perhaps that was the reason I wrote so unsympathetically about Mrs. Kairova's "case."

Article 3, extract. A Democratic Spirit, for Certain. Women.

[...] And in conclusion I want to add one more word about the Russian woman. I have already said that she contains one of our great hopes, one of the pledges of our renewal. The renaissance of the Russian woman in the last twenty years is undeniable. The upsurge in her strivings has been lofty, frank, and fearless. This upsurge has inspired respect from the very first; it has at least caused people to think, despite several superfluous irregularities that have turned up in this movement. Now, however, one can already make an accounting and not fear to reach a conclusion. The Russian woman has chastely ignored obstacles and mockery. She has firmly declared her wish to participate in the common cause and has applied herself to it not only disinterestedly but even self-denyingly. The Russian man, in these last decades, has become terribly prone to the vices of acquisition, cynicism, and materialism; woman has remained much more purely devoted than he to the idea and to serving the idea. In her eagerness for higher education she has displayed seriousness and patience and showed an example of the greatest courage. *A Writer's Diary* has given me the means to see the Russian woman at closer hand; I have received some remarkable letters; they ask me, who knows so little, "What is to be done?" I value these questions, and by being frank I try to compensate for my lack of knowledge in answers. I regret that there is so much that I cannot and have not the right to say here. I see, however, some flaws as well in today's woman, and the principal flaw is her extraordinary dependence on certain specifically masculine notions, her capacity to accept these as given and to believe in them without question. I am speaking by no means of all women; but this flaw also testifies to the good qualities of her heart: she values above all spontaneity of feeling and a living word, but principally and above all she values sincerity; and having put her faith in sincerity, sometimes sincerity that is not genuine, she is carried away by certain opinions, and sometimes carried away too far. In the future, higher education could do a great deal to help this. By permitting, sincerely and completely, higher education for women along with all the rights that this bestows, Russia would once more take an enormous and original step ahead of all Europe in the great cause of the regeneration of humanity. God grant that the Russian woman might also grow less tired and become less disillusioned than the tired Miss Pisareva, for example. Let her, rather, assuage her own grief like Shchapov's wife, through self-sacrifice and love. But both Mrs. Shchapova and Miss Pisareva are painful and memorable phenomena— the former because of her high level of feminine energy that reaped such a poor reward, the latter as a poor, tired, withdrawing, succumbing, and vanquished woman. . . .

June

from CHAPTER TWO

Article 1, extract. My Paradox

Again a tussle with Europe (oh, it's not a war yet: they say that we—Russia, that is—are still a long way from war). Again the endless Eastern Question is in the news; and again in Europe they are looking mistrustfully at Russia. . . . Yet why should we go running to seek Europe's trust? Did Europe ever trust the Russians? Can she ever trust us and stop seeing us as her enemy? Oh, of course this view will change *someday;* someday Europe will better be able to make us out and realize what we are like; and it is certainly worth discussing this *someday;* but meanwhile a somewhat irrelevant question or side issue has occurred to me and I have recently been busy trying to solve it. No one may agree with me, yet I think that I am right—in part, maybe, but right.

I said that Europe doesn't like Russians. No one, I think, will dispute the fact that they don't like us. They accuse us, among other things, of being terrible liberals: we Russians, almost to a man, are seen as not only liberals but revolutionaries; we are supposedly always inclined, almost lovingly, to join forces with the destructive elements of Europe rather than the conserving ones. Many Europeans look at us mockingly and haughtily for this—they are hateful: they cannot understand why we should be the ones to take the negative side *in someone else's affair;* they positively deny us the right of being negative as Europeans on the grounds that they do not recognize us as a part of "civilization." They see us rather as barbarians, reeling around Europe gloating that we have found something somewhere to destroy—to destroy purely for the sake of destruction, for the mere pleasure of watching it fall to pieces, just as if we were a horde of savages, a band of Huns, ready to fall upon ancient Rome and destroy its sacred shrines without the least notion of the value of the things we are demolishing. That the majority of Russians have really proclaimed themselves liberals in Europe is true, and it is even a strange fact. Has anyone ever asked himself why this is so? Why was it that in the course of our century, virtually nine-tenths of the Russians who acquired their culture in Europe always associated themselves with the stratum of Europeans who were liberal, with the left—i.e., always with the side that rejected its own culture and its own civilization? (I mean to a greater or a lesser degree, of course: what Thiers rejects in civilization and what the Paris Commune of 1871 rejected are very different things.) And like these European liberals, Russians in Europe are liberals "to a greater or lesser degree" and in many different shades; but nonetheless, I repeat, they are more inclined than the Europeans to join directly with the extreme left at once rather than to begin by dwelling among the lesser ranks of liberalism. In short, you'll find far fewer Thierses than you will Communards among the Russians. And note that these are not some crowd of ragamuffins—not all of them, at least—but people with a very solid, civilized look about them, some of them almost like cabinet ministers. But Europeans do not trust appearances: "Grattez le russe et vous verrez le tartare," they say (scratch a Russian and you'll find a Tatar). That may be true, but this is what occurred to me: do the majority of Russians, in their dealings with Europe, join the extreme left because they are Tatars and have the savage's love of destruction, or are they, perhaps, moved by other reasons? That is the question, and you'll agree that it is a rather interesting one. The time of our tussles with Europe is coming to an end; the role of the window cut through to Europe is over, and something else is beginning, or ought to begin at least, and everyone who has the least capacity to think now realizes this. In short, we are more and more beginning to feel that we ought to be ready for something, for some new and far more original encounter with Europe than we have had hitherto. Whether that encounter will be over the Eastern Question or over something else no one can tell! And so it is that all such questions, analyses, and even surmises and paradoxes can be of interest simply through the fact that they can teach us something. And isn't it a curious thing that it is precisely those Russians who are most given to considering themselves Europeans, and whom we call "Westernizers," who exult and take pride in this appellation and who still taunt the other half of the Russians with the names "kvasnik" and "zipunnik"? Is it not curious, I say, that these very people are the quickest to join the extreme left—those who deny civilization and who would destroy it—and that this surprises absolutely no one in Russia, and that the question has never even been posed? Now isn't that truly a curious thing?

I'll tell you frankly that I have framed an answer to this question, but I don't intend to try to prove my idea. I shall merely explain it briefly in an effort to bring forth the facts. In any case, it cannot be proven, because there are some things which are incapable of proof.

This is what I think: does not this fact (i.e., the fact that even our most ardent Westernizers side with the extreme left—those who in essence reject Europe) reveal the protesting Russian soul which always, from the very time of Peter the Great, found many, all too many, aspects of European culture hateful and always alien? That is what I think. Oh, of course this protest was almost always an unconscious one; but what truly matters here is that the Russian instinct has not died: the Russian soul, albeit unconsciously, has protested precisely in the name of its Russianness, in the name of its downtrodden and Russian principle. People will say, of course, that if this really were so there would be no cause for rejoicing: "the one who rejects, be he Hun, barbarian, or Tatar, has rejected not in the name of something higher but because he himself was so lowly that even over two centuries he could not manage to make out the lofty heights of Europe."

People will certainly say that. I agree that this is a legitimate question, but I do not intend to answer it; I will only say, without providing any substantiation, that I utterly and totally reject this Tatar hypothesis. Oh, of course, who now among all us Russians, especially when this is all in the past (because this period certainly has ended)—who, among all us Russians can argue against the things that Peter did, against the window he cut through to Europe? Who can rise up against him with visions of the ancient Muscovy of the tsars? This is not the point at all, and this is not why I began my discussion; the point is that, no matter how many fine and useful things we saw through Peter's window, there still were so many bad and harmful things there that always troubled the Russian instinct. That instinct never ceased to protest (although it lost its way so badly that in most cases it did not realize what it was doing), and it protested not because of its Tatar essence but, perhaps, precisely because it had preserved something within itself that was higher and better than anything it saw through the window. . . . (Well, of course it didn't protest against everything: we received a great many fine things from Europe and we don't want to be ungrateful; still, our instinct was right in protesting against at least half of the things.)

I repeat that all this happened in a most original fashion: it was precisely our most ardent Westernizers, precisely those who struggled for reform, who at the same time were rejecting Europe and joining the ranks of the extreme left. . . . And the result: in so doing they defined themselves as the most fervent Russians of all, the champions of old Russia and the Russian spirit. And, of course, if anyone had tried to point that out to them at the time, they would either have burst out laughing or been struck with horror. There is no doubt that they were unaware of any higher purpose to their protest. On the contrary, all the while, for two whole centuries, they denied their own high-mindedness, and not merely their high-mindedness but their very self-respect (there were, after all, some such ardent souls!), and to a degree that amazed even Europe; yet it turns out that they were the very ones who proved to be genuine Russians. It is this theory of mine that I call my paradox. [. . .]

Article 4. The Utopian Conception of History

The whole century and a half that followed Peter's reforms was nothing more than a period of living in contact with all the human civilizations and of making their history and their ideals our own. We studied and learned to love the French, the Germans, and all the rest as if they were our brothers, despite the fact that they never loved us and had made up their minds that they never would. But that was the essence of our reform and of everything that Peter did: in the course of a century and a half we derived from it a *broadening* of our outlook that perhaps has no precedent in any other nation in either the ancient or the modern world. Pre-Petrine Russia was active and strong, although she developed slowly in a political sense. She worked out her own form of unity and set about consolidating her border regions. She understood implicitly that she bore within her a precious thing—Orthodoxy—that no longer existed anywhere else and that she was charged with preserving the truth of Christ, the real truth, the genuine image of Christ which had been obscured in all the other religions and in all the other nations. The best Russians of the time believed that this precious gift, this truth—eternal, inherent in Russia, and given to her to preserve—could somehow relieve their consciences of the obligation to acquire any other form of enlightenment. Moreover, Moscow came to believe that any closer contact with Europe could even have a harmful, corrupting influence on the Russian mind and on the Russian *idea;* that it could distort Orthodoxy itself and lead Russia on to the road to perdition, "in the manner of all other nations." So it was that ancient Russia, isolated within herself, was *prepared to be unjust:* unjust to humanity in her decision passively to keep her treasure, her Orthodoxy, to herself and to isolate herself from Europe—from humanity, that is—in the manner of certain religious sectarians who will not eat from the same dish as you and consider it a sacred duty for each to keep his own cup and spoon. This is a fair comparison, because prior to Peter we had evolved almost this very sort of political and spiritual relationship to Europe. With Peter's reforms came an enormous broadening of our outlook and this, I repeat, constitutes Peter's whole great achievement. This also constitutes that same precious gift of which I have already spoken in one of the preceding issues of my *Diary.* It is a precious gift which we, the higher cultured level of Russia, are bringing to the People after our century-and-a-half absence from Russia and which the People, once we ourselves have acknowledged their truth, should accept from us as a sine qua non, "without which it will be impossible to unite the People and the cultured classes and everything will come to ruin." What is this "broadening of outlook," what does it consist of, and what does it signify? It is not a matter of enlightenment in the strict sense of the word, and it is not science; neither is it a betrayal of the moral principles of the Russian People in the name of European civilization. No, it is specifically something characteristic of the Russian People alone, for a reform such as Peter's has never taken place anywhere else. It is really and truly our almost brotherly love for other nations, which derived from our century and a half of contact with them; it is our need to serve humanity in every way, even if sometimes at the expense of our own best and major immediate interests; it is our reconciliation with their civilizations, our comprehension and our *excusing* of their ideals when these ideals were not in harmony with our own; it is our acquired capacity to discover the truth contained in each of the civilizations of Europe or, more correctly, in each of the personalities of Europe, despite the fact that they contain much with which we cannot agree. It is, finally, our need to be just above all and to seek only the truth. In short, it perhaps is the beginning, the first step toward that active application of our gift, our Orthodoxy, to the universal service of humanity for which it was intended and which, in fact, constitutes its very essence. So it was that from Peter's reform there came a broadening of our *former* idea, the Russian Muscovite idea; there came an expanded and strengthened conception of that idea: through the reform we became aware of our universal mission, our personality, and our role in humanity, and we could not help but become aware that this mission and this role were unlike those of other nations, for among them each individual nationality lives only for itself and in itself, while we, now that the time has come, will begin directly by becoming the servant of all for the sake of universal reconciliation. And there is no shame in this whatsoever; to the contrary, it is what makes us great, because it all leads to the ultimate unifying of humanity. He who would be first in the Kingdom of God must become the servant of all. This is how I understand Russia's destiny *in its ideal form*. The first step of our new policy appeared of itself after Peter's reform: this first step had to consist in the uniting of all of Slavdom, so to say, under the wing of Russia. And this process of unification is not for seizing territory, nor for committing violence, nor for crushing the other Slavic personalities beneath the Russian colossus; it is for restoring them and placing them in their proper relationship to Europe and to humanity; it is for giving them, at last, the opportunity for relief and rest after their innumerable and centuries-long sufferings; it is for renewing their spirits and, once they have found new strength, for enabling them to contribute their own mite to the treasury of the human spirit so that they can utter their own word to civilization. Oh, of course you may laugh at all these "daydreams" about Russia's destiny, but still, tell me: is this not precisely the basis on which all Russians want the Slavs to be resurrected, precisely for their complete personal freedom and for the restoration of their spirit? But it is certainly not so that Russia may acquire them politically and use them to enhance her own political might (although Europe suspects the latter). This is so, is it not? And accordingly, this lends weight to at least some of my "daydreams," does it not? It follows that for this same purpose Constantinople must, sooner or later, be ours. . . .

Heavens, what a mocking smile would appear on the face of some Austrian or Englishman if he had the opportunity to read all these *daydreams* I have just written down and if he were to read as far as such a *positive* conclusion: "Constantinople, the Golden Horn, the most critical political area in the world—is this not a seizure of territory?"

Yes, I answer, the Golden Horn and Constantinople—all that will be ours, but not for the sake of merely annexing territory and not for the sake of violence. And in the first place it will happen of its own accord precisely because the time has come, and if the time has not yet arrived just now, then it is truly at hand, as all the signs indicate. This is a natural result; this is something decreed by Nature herself, as it were. If this has not happened before, it is simply because the time was not yet ripe. People in Europe believe in some sort of "Testament of Peter the Great." This is no more than a forged document concocted by the Poles. But had Peter then hit upon the notion of seizing Constantinople rather than founding Petersburg, then it seems to me that he would have abandoned the idea after some thought, even if he had had sufficient strength to crush the Sultan, precisely because the matter was still inopportune and might even have led to Russia's ruination.

If in Finnish Petersburg we couldn't avoid the influence of neighboring Germans (who, despite their usefulness, paralyzed Russian development before its true path had been clearly revealed), then how, in the huge and distinctive city of Constantinople with its remnants of a mighty and ancient civilization—how could we have avoided the influence of the Greeks, a nation far more subtle than the coarse Germans, a nation with whom we have much more in common than the Germans, who are utterly unlike us? The throne would have at once been surrounded by throngs of courtiers; they would have become educated and learned sooner than the Russians; they would have enchanted Peter himself, not to mention his immediate successors, exploiting his weak point by demonstrating their knowledge and skill in seamanship. In short, they would have gained political power in Russia; they would have at once dragged her off on some new Asiatic road, into another sort of seclusion, and of course the Russia of that time would not have survived it. The development of Russia's strength and her sense of nationhood would have been halted in their course. The mighty Great Russian would have remained in isolation in his gloomy and snowy North, serving as no more than raw material for the renewal of Tsargrad, and ultimately, perhaps, the Russian would have found it unnecessary even to follow Constantinople. The South of Russia would have fallen entirely into the clutches of the Greeks. Orthodoxy itself might even have divided into two entirely separate worlds: one in a renewed Tsargrad, the other in old Russia. . . . In short, the matter would have been most untimely. Now, however, things are quite different.

Now Russia has already spent time in Europe and is herself educated. The principal thing is that she has become aware of all her power and has in truth become powerful; she also has become aware of where her real strength lies. Now she understands that Tsargrad can certainly not be ours as Russia's capital, but two centuries ago, had Peter seized Tsargrad, he could not have done other than transfer his capital there, and this would have been a fatal move since Tsargrad is not in Russia and *could not* have become Russia. Had Peter been able to resist making this error, then his immediate successors would not have been able to resist. And if Tsargrad can now be ours not as Russia's capital, then neither can it be ours as the capital of Slavdom as a whole, as some people imagine. Slavdom as a whole, without Russia, would exhaust itself there in struggling with the Greeks, even if it could manage to create some sort of political unity from its various entities. But to leave Constantinople as a legacy to the Greeks alone is now utterly impossible: we must not give them such a critical point on the globe; this would be altogether too generous a gift to them. But the whole of Slavdom with Russia at its head—oh, of course, that is a different matter entirely. Whether it is a proper matter is another question. Would this not look like a Russian political annexation of the Slavs, something we surely have no need of? And so in the name of what, in the name of what *moral* right could Russia make a claim on Constantinople? What lofty purpose could we use as a basis to demand it from Europe? On just this lofty purpose: as leader of Orthodoxy, as its protector and guardian, a role set out for Russia since Ivan III, who placed as an emblem the double-headed eagle of Tsargrad above the ancient coat of arms of Russia, but a role revealed clearly only after Peter the Great, when Russia realized that she had the power to fulfill this mission and in fact became the actual and sole guardian both of Orthodoxy and of the nations who profess it. This is the reason and the *right* to ancient Tsargrad, one that would be clear and inoffensive even to the Slavs who guard their independence most jealously, or even to the Greeks themselves. This would be the means to reveal the essence of the political relationships that must inevitably ensue in Russia toward all the other Orthodox nationalities, Slavic and Greek alike: Russia is their protector and even, perhaps, their leader, but not their ruler; she is their mother, but not their mistress.

And if she should become their sovereign at some time, then it would be only because they would have proclaimed her so, allowing themselves to keep all those things by which they would define their own independence and individuality. And so, sometime, even the non-Orthodox European Slavs might join such a union, for they themselves would see that such a unity under Russia's protection means only the consolidation of the independent individuality of each, while without this immense unifying force they, perhaps, would again exhaust themselves in mutual strife and discord, even if they should one day achieve political independence from the Moslems and the Europeans to whom they now belong.

"What's the point of playing with words?" people will say. "What is this 'Orthodoxy'? Where can one find here any such idea, any such right to unify the nations? And is this not a purely political union like all the others, even though it may be based on the broadest foundations, like those of the United American States or perhaps broader still?" That is a question which may be put, and I will answer it. No, it will not be like that, and this is not playing with words; there *truly* will be something special and unprecedented here; it will be not merely a political union, and certainly not a matter of political annexation and violence (the only way in which Europe can conceive of something like this). And it will not be done merely in the name of some merchants' wheeling and dealing, personal gain, and all those eternal, unchanging, and idolized vices cloaked in an official Christianity in which no one aside from the *mob* can truly believe. No, it will be a true exaltation of the truth of Christ, which has been preserved in the East, a true, new exaltation of the cross of Christ and the ultimate word of Orthodoxy, at whose head Russia has long been standing. It will be a temptation for all the mighty of this world who have been triumphant until now and who have always regarded all such "expectations" with scorn and derision and who do not even comprehend that one can seriously believe in human brotherhood, in the universal reconciliation of nations, in a union founded on principles of universal service to humanity and regeneration of people through the true principles of Christ. And if believing in this "new word," which Russia at the head of a united Orthodoxy can utter to the world—if believing in this is a "utopia" worthy only of derision, then you may number me among these Utopians, and leave the ridicule to me.

"But," people may still object, "it is utopian indeed to imagine that Russia will ever be *permitted* to stand at the head of the Slavs and enter Constantinople. You can dream about it, but these are still only dreams!"

Is that really so? Russia is powerful, and perhaps much more powerful than she herself may suppose. Aside from that, have we not seen, even in recent decades, mighty empires rise to power in Europe, one of which has disappeared like dust and ashes, swept away in a day by the winds of God, while in its place arose a new empire whose might, it seemed, had never been equaled on earth? Who could have predicted this? If such revolutionary changes are possible, and if they happen in our time and before our very eyes, then can the human mind predict without error the outcome of the Eastern Question? What real basis is there to despair of the resurrection and the unity of the Slavs? Who can know the ways of the Lord?

Article 5, extract. About Women Again

[. . .] I was about to conclude my *Diary* and was already checking the proofs when a young girl unexpectedly called on me. I had met her in the winter after I had begun publishing my *Diary*. She wants to take a rather difficult examination and is energetically preparing for it; she'll pass it, of course. She's from a wealthy family and doesn't lack means, but is very concerned about her education. She would come to ask my advice on what to read and what to pay particular attention to. She has been visiting me about once a month, staying no more than ten minutes; she would speak only of her own affairs, but briefly, modestly, almost shyly, showing remarkable trust in me. Yet I could also see she had a very resolute nature, and it seems I was not mistaken. This time she came to me and said directly: "People are needed to tend the sick in Serbia. I have decided to postpone my examination for the time being so I can go look after the wounded. What do you think?"

And she looked at me almost timidly, yet her look told me clearly that she had already made her decision and that it was an absolutely firm one. She wanted some parting words of approval from me, however. I cannot convey all the details of our conversation lest I might in some small way violate her anonymity; I am passing on only its general content.

I suddenly felt very sorry for her—she is so young. It would have been quite pointless to frighten her with the difficulties, the war, the typhus in the field hospitals; this would mean only pouring oil on the flames. Here was a pure case of longing for sacrifice, for some noble feat, for some good deed; most significant and most precious was her total lack of conceit and self-infatuation; she wanted only to "look after the wounded" and to be of help.

"But do you know anything about treating wounded soldiers?"

"No, but I've been collecting information and have been to the Committee. Those who enlist are given two weeks to prepare, and of course I'll manage."

And she will, of course; here the word is equal to the deed.

"Listen," I told her, "I don't want to frighten you or dissuade you, but consider my words well and try to weigh them in your conscience. You have grown up in surroundings quite different from those you'll encounter there; you've seen only good society and have met people only in that calm state of mind where they remain within the bounds of etiquette. But the same people at war, in crowded conditions, in hardship and labor, may change utterly. Suppose you spend a whole night tending the sick; you've worn yourself out and are so exhausted that you can barely stand, when a doctor—a very good man at heart, perhaps, but tired and overstrained after just amputating a number of arms and legs—turns to you in irritation and says: 'All you do is make a mess of things; you can't do anything! If you've taken on this job, then do it properly!' and so on. Won't you find that hard to bear? Yet you certainly have to expect that sort of thing, and what I'm suggesting is only a tiny part of what's ahead of you. Real life often surprises us. And finally, are you certain that, even with all your resolve, you'll be able to cope with looking after the wounded? Might you not faint at the sight of some death, some wound or operation? This happens despite one's will, unconsciously. . . ."

"If I'm told that I'm doing things wrong and not working properly, then I'll certainly understand that this doctor is himself irritable and tired; it's enough to know in my own heart that I'm not to blame and have done everything properly."

"But you're still so young; how can you be certain what you'll do?"

"What makes you think I'm young? *I'm already eighteen;* I'm not so young at all. . . ."

In short, it was impossible to dissuade her: she was ready to go off the very next day, in any case, regretting only that I did not approve of what she was doing.

"Well, God be with you," I said. "Go on; but come back just as soon as the thing is finished."

"Of course. I have to take my examination. But you'll never believe how happy you've made me."

She went away radiant and, of course, she will be *there* in a week.

At the beginning of this *Diary*, in the article about George Sand, I wrote a few words about the young female characters I had found particularly appealing in the stories of her earliest period. Well, this girl was just like one of them. She had just the same sort of direct, honest, but inexperienced young feminine character, along with that proud chastity which is unafraid and which cannot be stained even by contact with vice. This girl felt the need for sacrifice, for undertaking a task that seemed to be asked of her specifically; she had the conviction that she must first begin herself, with no excuses, to do all those fine things that we expect and demand from others. This is a conviction which is genuine and moral to the highest degree, but which, alas, is most often characteristic only of youthful purity and innocence. But the main thing, I repeat, is that here there is only a cause and not the slightest element of vanity, conceit, or infatuation with one's own heroism, something that we very often see among today's young people, even among mere adolescents.

After she had left I could not help but think once more about the need for higher education for women in Russia, a need that is most urgent at this moment in particular, in view of the serious pressure among today's women to be active, to be educated, and to participate in the common cause. I think that the fathers and mothers of these daughters ought themselves to insist on it for their own sake, if they love their children. In fact, it is only higher learning that is serious, attractive, and powerful enough to settle what is almost an agitation that has begun among our women. Only science can provide answers to their questions, strengthen their intellects, and take their heterogeneous thoughts under its wing, as it were. As far as this girl was concerned, though I had pity for her youth (and even though I was unable to stop her in any case), I rather think that this journey might even be of some value to her in a sense: this is not the world of books or abstract convictions after all; it is an immense experience that awaits her, an experience that perhaps God Himself, in His immeasurable goodness, fated for her in order to save her. Here a lesson in the living life is being prepared for her; before her stands the possibility of expanding her ideas and her views; she will have something to remember all her life, something precious and beautiful in which she participated, something that will compel her to value life and not weary of it before she has lived, as did the unfortunate suicide Pisareva of whom I spoke in my last, May, *Diary*.

July and August

from CHAPTER ONE

Article 1, two extracts. Going Abroad. Something about Russians in Railway Carriages.

I haven't chatted with the reader for two months now. Once I had brought out the June issue (marking six months of my publication), I immediately boarded a train and set off for Ems—oh, not to have a rest but for the reasons people usually go to Ems. And of course all this is extremely personal and private; but the fact is that I sometimes write my *Diary* not only for the public but for myself (that's probably why it occasionally contains some rough spots and surprising ideas—I mean ideas quite familiar to me and which I've been inwardly elaborating for a long time but which seem to the reader to have sprung up unexpectedly and unconnected to what has preceded them); and so how can I fail to include my trip abroad as well? [...]

It is a long trip from Petersburg to Berlin—almost two days—and so I took along two pamphlets and a few newspapers just in case. And I truly meant "just in case," because I have always been afraid of being left in a crowd of strange Russians of our educated class, wherever it may be—in a railway carriage, a steamship, or in any kind of public gathering. I admit this is a weakness and blame it, above all, on my own suspicious nature. When I am abroad among foreigners I always feel more at ease: there, when some foreigner wants to get somewhere he heads straight to his destination, but our Russian goes on looking around the whole time, thinking, "What will people say about me?" He may look decisive and unshakeable, but in actual fact there is no one more uncertain and lacking in self-confidence. If a Russian stranger begins a conversation with you, it is always in an extremely confidential and friendly manner; but from the first word he utters you can see his deep mistrust and even his underlying suspicious irritation, which will burst out in the form of some biting or even downright rude remark the moment he finds something not to his liking, and this despite all his "good upbringing." What's significant is that this can happen for the very slightest of reasons. Every one of these people seems to want to avenge himself on someone else for

his own insignificance, yet he may not be an insignificant person at all—
sometimes just the reverse. There is no person who will say oftener than
a Russian: "What do I care what people say about me?" or "I don't worry
a bit about public opinion." And there is no person who is more afraid
than a Russian (again, I mean a civilized Russian), who has more fear
and trepidation of public opinion and of what people will say or think
of him. This comes precisely from his deep-seated lack of self-respect,
which, of course, is concealed behind his boundless egotism and vanity.
These two opposing factors are always present in *almost* every educated
Russian, and he is also the first to find them intolerable, so that each
one of them bears his own "hell" in his soul, as it were. It is especially
awkward to meet a Russian stranger abroad somewhere, face to face (shut
up with him in a railway car, for instance), so that there is no possibility
of running away should something disastrous happen. And yet, it would
seem, "it's so nice to meet a fellow countryman on foreign shores." And
the conversation almost always begins with that very phrase. Once he's
found out that you're a Russian, your fellow countryman will be certain to
begin: "So you're a Russian? How nice to meet a fellow countryman on
foreign shores. I'm here as well. . . ." And then at once come some candid
remarks in a most cordial and, so to say, brotherly manner appropriate to
two compatriots who have embraced each other on some foreign shore.
But don't be misled by the manner: although your compatriot may be
smiling, he already has his suspicions of you, and that's obvious from
his eyes, from the little lisp he has when he speaks, and from the careful
way he stresses his words. He's sizing you up; he's certainly afraid of you
already; he already wants to tell you some lies. And, indeed, he can't help
but regard you suspiciously and tell lies simply because you are also a
Russian and he, willy-nilly, is measuring himself against you; and also,
perhaps, because you really deserve such treatment. It's worth noting as
well that a Russian stranger abroad (more often when abroad, and indeed
almost always when abroad) will always, or at least frequently, hasten to
put in after the first three sentences he utters that he has only just met
so-and-so or has only just heard something from so-and-so, i.e., from
some prominent or famous Russian personage. But he brings up this
person in the nicest and most familiar manner, as if he were one of his
friends and one of yours as well: "You know him, of course. The poor
fellow has been making pilgrimages from one local medical luminary to

another. They send him off to watering places, and the fellow is absolutely
worn out. You know him, do you not?" If you reply that you don't know
him at all, the stranger will at once find something personally offensive in
this circumstance: "Surely you didn't think that I wanted to boast of my
acquaintance with a prominent person?" You can already read that question in his eyes, and yet that may be precisely what he wanted to imply. And
if you reply that you do know the person, he will take even more offense;
but just why that is I truly don't know. In short, insincerity and animosity
grow on both sides; the conversation suddenly breaks off, and you fall
silent. Your compatriot suddenly turns away from you. He is prepared to
go on chatting the whole while with some German baker sitting opposite,
as long as he doesn't speak to you, and he does this specifically so that you
will notice it. Having begun in such a friendly fashion, he now will have
nothing more to do with you and rudely ignores you altogether. When
night comes he stretches out on the cushions if there is room enough,
almost putting his feet on you or perhaps even deliberately putting his
feet on you; and when the journey is over he leaves the carriage without
even nodding good-bye. "Why did he take such offense?" you think to
yourself, saddened and greatly confused. Best of all is an encounter with
a Russian general. The Russian general abroad is most concerned with
ensuring that none of the Russians he meets ventures to address him in a
manner inappropriate to his rank, trying to take advantage by assuming
that "we're abroad, and so we're all equal." And so, for instance, when he's
traveling he sinks into a stern, marmorial silence from the very beginning.
So much the better: he doesn't disturb anyone. By the way, a Russian
general setting off for foreign parts is sometimes very fond of putting on
a civilian suit he's ordered from the best tailor in Petersburg. And when
he arrives at the spa, where there are always so many pretty ladies from all
over Europe, he is very fond of making a show. When the season is over
he takes particular pleasure in being photographed in civilian clothes so
that he can give out pictures to his friends in Petersburg or use one to
gladden the heart of a devoted subordinate. But in any case, keeping a
book or a newspaper on a journey is a great help, particularly to ward off
Russians: it tells them, "I'm reading; leave me alone."

from CHAPTER FOUR

Article 1. What Effects the Cure When Taking the Waters: The Water or the *Bon Ton?*

I do not intend to describe Ems; besides, there are already some very detailed descriptions of Ems in Russian, such as Doctor Hirschorn's little book *Ems and Its Healing Springs,* published in St. Petersburg. You can get all the information you need there, beginning with medical facts about the springs right down to the tiniest details of life in the hotels, hygiene, walks, the town itself, and even the people who come here. As for me, I'm incapable of describing these things, and if I were compelled to do so, now that I have returned home, I would recall first of all the bright sun, the truly picturesque gorge of the Taunus in which Ems is situated, the immense and well-dressed crowd of people from all over the world, and my own deep, deep sense of isolation in that crowd. And yet, despite the isolation, I even love such a crowd, but in a special way, of course. I even found an acquaintance among that crowd, a Russian, that very same *paradoxicalist* who once, some time ago, defended war in an argument with me and found in war all the truth and justice that one cannot find in contemporary society (see the April issue of my *Diary*). I have already said that he is most humble and civilian in appearance. Everyone knows that we Russians or, to be more precise, we who live in Petersburg, have arranged our lives so that we visit and do business sometimes with God knows what sorts of people, and although we do not forget our friends (can a resident of Petersburg ever forget anyone or anything?), we can go quite calmly for years on end without ever seeing them. My friend was also taking the waters in Ems. He is about forty-five years old, or perhaps younger.

"You're right, you know," he told me. "You develop a certain fondness for this crowd here and can't even tell why. In fact, one likes a crowd anywhere—a fashionable crowd, of course, the cream of society. You needn't hobnob with anyone from this society, but on the whole there's still nothing on earth that's better."

"Oh, come now. . . ."

"I'm not going to argue with you, not at all," he agreed hastily. "When a better society comes into being and people consent to live more sensibly, we'll have no regard at all for today's society and won't even give it a thought; it will only be a couple of words in the history of the world. But now—today—can you conceive of anything better to take its place?"

"Can we really conceive of nothing better than this idle crowd of well-off people, people who, if they weren't now jostling one another at the mineral springs, probably would have no idea of what to do with themselves and how to waste another day? There are some fine individual personalities, that's true; you can still find them even in this crowd. But as a whole—as a whole, this crowd doesn't deserve particular praise, let alone particular attention! . . ."

"You're speaking like a confirmed misanthrope or simply following the fashion. You say: 'They wouldn't know what to do with themselves and how to waste their day!' Believe me, every one of them has his things to do, even things on which he's wasted his whole life, not just one day. Each one of them can't be blamed because he's unable to make a paradise of his life and suffers in consequence. I enjoy watching all these suffering people laugh."

"Aren't they laughing out of politeness?"

"They're laughing because of the habit that crushes them all and compels them to participate in playing at paradise, if you want to call it that. They don't believe in paradise; they have to force themselves to play the game, but they still play it and so find diversion. The habit has already become too ingrained. There are some here who have taken this habit as a very serious thing, and so much the better for them, of course: they are already living in a real paradise. If you love them all (and you ought to), then you ought to rejoice that they have the opportunity to rest and forget themselves, if only in a mirage."

"But you're making fun of them. And why should I love them?"

"Why, they are humanity, and there is no other; how can you not love humanity? Over the past decade it's been impossible not to love humanity. There is one Russian lady here who is a great lover of humanity. And I'm not making fun at all. To put an end to this topic, I'll conclude by telling you frankly that every society of *bon ton*—this one, this fashionable crowd—has a number of positive qualities. For example: every fashionable society is good in that, even though it may look like a caricature, it is in closer touch with nature than any other society, even agricultural ones, which mostly all still live in a quite unnatural fashion. Now I'm not talking about factories, armies, schools, universities: all those are the ultimate in unnaturalness. The people here are the freest of all because they are the richest of all, and therefore they can at least live as they choose. Oh, of course they are in touch with nature only insofar as decorum and *bon ton* permit. To open oneself, to dissolve oneself, to reveal oneself totally to nature, to this golden ray of sun, for example, that shines down from the blue sky on us sinners without discriminating between those who are worthy of it and those who are not—that would doubtless be indecorous, at least in the degree which the two of us or some poet might want at this moment; the little steel lock of *bon ton* is set over every heart and every mind, as it was before. Still, one cannot but agree that *bon ton* has taken just a tiny step on the road to contact with nature, not only in our century but even in our generation. I have observed this and I can conclude that the further we go into our century, the more we realize and agree that contact with nature is the very latest word in progress of every sort, be it science, reason, common sense, good taste, or exquisite manners. Go into that crowd and lose yourself in it: you see joy and good cheer on their faces. They all speak to one another in a gentle manner; they are unusually polite, kind, and unusually cheerful. Just think, the entire happiness of that young man with a rose in his buttonhole lies in raising the spirits of that stout lady of fifty. In fact, what is it that compels him to try so hard to please her? Can he really want her to be happy and cheerful? Of course not; and he probably has some particular and very private reasons for making such efforts, reasons that are none of our business. But the most important thing is this: it is probably only *bon ton* that can compel him to do this, without any special, private reasons, and that is an extremely important fact; it shows the degree to which *bon ton* in our age can overcome even the wild nature of some young fellow. Poetry produces Byrons, and they produce the Corsairs, the Childe Harolds, the Laras; but just look how little time has gone by since they appeared, and already all these characters have been cast aside by *bon ton*, recognized as the very worst kind of society. And that's even more true of our own Pechorin or the Captive of the Caucasus: they have turned out to be altogether *mauvais ton;* they're only Petersburg officials who had a brief moment of social success. And why have they been cast aside? Because

these characters truly are evil, impatient, and quite openly concerned
only with themselves, so that they disrupt the harmony of *bon ton*, which,
above all, has to maintain the appearance that each is living for everyone
else and everyone for each. Look at them over there, bringing flowers.
There are bouquets for the ladies and single roses for the buttonholes of
the gentlemen; and just look at how beautifully tended those roses are,
how well chosen, sprayed with water! No young maid of the fields will
ever choose or cut anything more elegant for the young lad she loves.
But these roses are brought here for sale at five and ten German groschen
apiece, and the maid of the fields has had nothing to do with them at all.
The golden age is still to come, while now we have the age of enterprise.
But what concern is it of yours? Does it matter at all? They are beautiful and finely dressed, and the scene looks truly like paradise. Does it
make any difference whether it is 'real paradise' or 'just like paradise'?
Now think about what is happening here: what good taste we see; what
a fine idea this is! What is better suited to taking the waters, that is, to a
hope of regaining one's health, than flowers? Flowers are hopes. How
much taste there is in that notion. Remember the verses: 'And why take
ye thought for raiment? Consider the lilies of the field, how they grow . . .
and Solomon in all his glory was not arrayed like one of these. Wherefore
. . . shall God not more clothe you?' I don't remember it exactly, but what
wonderful words! All the poetry of life is there, all the truth of nature. But
until the truth of nature is made manifest and people in their simplicity
and joy of heart adorn one another with the flowers of genuine human
love—all this can be bought and sold for five groschen without any love.
And again I say: does it make any difference to you? I think it's even better
this way because, in truth, there are some kinds of love that make you take
to your heels, for they demand too much nobility; but here you pull out
five groschen and you're done with it. And still, in reality, we have something very like the golden age; and if you're a man with imagination, then
you're satisfied. No, the wealth of the present day ought to be encouraged, even though at other people's expense. It provides luxury and *bon
ton*, things the rest of humanity can never give me. I can look at a beautiful
picture here that brings me joy, and joy always costs money. Gladness
and joy have always been the most expensive things; yet I, a poor man,
paying nothing, can also participate in the general joy, at least vicariously.
Look: the band is playing, people are laughing, the ladies are dressed like

no one ever dressed in the days of Solomon—and although this is all a mirage, you and I are still happy. Finally—and quite honestly—aren't I a decent man? (I am speaking only about myself.) But thanks to the mineral waters, here am I rubbing shoulders with the very *crème de la crème*. And what an appetite you'll have now to go and drink your wretched German coffee! That's what I call the positive aspect of good society."

"Well, you're just making fun; and what you say isn't even new."

"I *am* making fun, but tell me: has your appetite improved since you came here to take the waters?"

"Of course it has, remarkably."

"That means the positive aspect of *bon ton* is so powerful that it acts even on your stomach."

"Oh, come now. That's the effect of the mineral water, not the *bon ton*."

"And of the *bon ton* as well, unquestionably. And so we still do not know what has the most effect at the mineral springs: the waters or the *bon ton*. Even the local doctors are not sure which factor should be given more weight. And on the whole it's difficult to express the immense step medicine has taken in our age: it now can even produce ideas, while in the past it had only drugs."

Article 4. The Land and Children

"The land is everything," my paradoxicalist continued. "I make no distinction between the land and children, and this point will emerge of itself from what I say. However, I am not going to develop the point for you: you will realize it if you think about it carefully. The point is that it all comes from a mistake in our management of the land. It may even be that all the rest, and all of humanity's other misfortunes as well, perhaps, come from that same mistake. Millions of paupers have no land, particularly in France, where there is little enough land to begin with; and so they have no place where they can give birth to children and are compelled to give birth in some cellar, and not to children but Gavroches, half of whom cannot name their own fathers, and the other half, perhaps, their own mothers. That's one side of the problem, and on the other side—the higher side if you like—there is also the error in land use; but it's quite different. It's an error of the opposite extreme that may even stem from the time of Clovis, the conqueror of the Gauls. The people on this side all have too much land; they have seized far more than they need and keep too strong a hold on it, giving up nothing. And so in both cases you have abnormality. Something must happen to change this; I know only that everyone should have land, and that children ought to be born on the land and not on the street. I truly don't know how this will be set right, but I know that at present there is nowhere there to give birth to children. I think that it's fine to work in a factory: a factory is also a legitimate business, and it is always set up alongside land that is already being worked: that's the way it's done. But every factory worker should know that he has his own Garden somewhere, with golden sun and vineyards, a place of his own or, rather, a communal Garden; and he should know that living there is his wife—a fine woman, not one from the street—who loves him and waits for him; and along with his wife are his children, who play at horsies and who all know their own father. *Que diable,* every decent and healthy little child is born with his own 'horsie,' and every decent father ought to know that, if he wants to be happy. This is where he'll bring the money he's earned; he won't drink it up in the tavern with some female of the species he's found on the street. In the worst cases (in France, for instance, where there is so little land), the Garden may not feed him and his family, so that he won't be able to manage without the factory; but he should know, at least, that his children will grow up there with the land, the trees, the quail they catch; they will go to school, and the school will be in a field; and he himself, when he has ended his working life, will still go there to take his rest and at last to die. And yet, who knows? Perhaps the Garden will be able to feed him; in any case, there's no cause to fear the factories—perhaps the factory will be built in the middle of the Garden. In short, I'm not sure how all this will happen, but it will happen; there will be a Garden. Mark my words: though it be a hundred years from now, remember that I explained it to you in Ems, in the middle of an artificial garden among artificial people. Humanity will be renewed in the Garden, and the Garden will restore it—that is the formula. Do you see how it happened? First there were castles and around them only mud huts; the barons lived in the castles and the vassals in the huts. Then the bourgeoisie began to arise in walled cities, slowly, microscopically. Meanwhile the castles came to an end and the capital cities of kings arose, large cities with royal palaces and halls for the courtiers; and so it was until our age. In our age came the terrible revolution, and the bourgeoisie prevailed. With it appeared the terrible cities, which no one had even dreamt of. Humanity had never seen cities of the sort that appeared in the nineteenth century. These are cities with crystal palaces, international expositions, international hotels, banks, budgets, polluted rivers, railway platforms, and all that goes with them. Around them stand factories and mills. And now we await the third phase: the bourgeoisie will depart the scene and Regenerated Humanity will come to the fore. This new humanity will divide the land into communes and will begin to live in the Garden. 'It will be regenerated in the Garden, and the Garden will restore it.' And so it proceeds, from castles to cities to the Garden. If you want to hear all of my idea, then I think that children—I mean real children, I mean children of human beings—should be born on the land and not on the street. One may live on the street later, but a nation—in its vast majority—should be born and *arise* on the land, on the native soil in which its grain and its trees grow. But now the entire proletariat of Europe is a creature of the street. But in the Garden the little children will be springing directly up from the earth, like Adams, and not going to work at the factories at the age of nine when they still want to play; they won't be breaking their backs over some lathe, deadening their minds before some common machine to which the bourgeois says his prayers; they will not exhaust and ruin their imaginations before endless rows of gas lamps, and ruin their morals through the depravity of the factory, which is such as was never seen in Sodom. And these are boys and girls of ten. That's terrible enough here; but it's happening in Russia, where there is so much land and where factories are still only a joke, but wretched little towns exist wherever there are three petty bureaucrats. And yet if there is any place where I can see the seed or the idea of the future, it is in Russia. Why is that? It's because we have had and still preserve among the People one principle: that the land for them is *everything,* and that they derive everything from the land; this is still what the huge majority of them believe. But the main thing is that this principle is the normal law of humanity. There is something sacramental in the land, in one's native soil. If you want humanity to be reborn into something better, if you want to make human beings out of creatures that are almost beasts, then give them land and you will achieve your aim. At least in Russia the land and the commune exist—in a most wretched state, I agree; but still they are an immense seed for the future idea, and that is my point. I think that order arises in the land and from the land, and this happens everywhere, throughout humanity. The whole order in every country, be it political, civil, or whatever, is always linked with the soil and with the character of agriculture in that country. The character in which agriculture has developed has determined the way everything else developed. If there is anywhere in Russia now where maximum disorder prevails, it is in the area of land tenure, in the relationship between landowner and worker and among landowners themselves; it is in the very way the land is worked. And until all that is set right, do not expect anything else to be set right. I do not assign blame to anyone or anything: this is a matter of world history, and we realize it. I think that we have still paid very cheaply to end serfdom, thanks to the *consent* of the whole country. And it is on this consent that I stake everything else. This consent is, after all, one more principle of the People, another one of those same principles which the Potugins still deny. Well, all these railways of ours, all our new banks and associations and credit institutions—all these things, in my opinion, are still only dust and ashes; as far as the railways are concerned, I recognize only the strategic ones. All these things should have come about only after the land question had been properly settled; then they would have appeared naturally, but now it is only a matter of a game on the stock exchange, the stirrings of the Jew. You're laughing; you don't agree. Well, so be it. But just lately I was reading the memoirs of a certain Russian landowner written in the middle of this century; as far back as the 1820s he wanted to set his peasants free. That was a rare novelty in those days. By the way, when he went to the country, he set up a school and began teaching the peasant children choral church music. When a neighboring landowner called on him and heard the choir, he said: 'That's a clever thing you've thought up; train them well and you'll surely find a buyer for the whole choir. People like that sort of thing and will pay good money for a choir.' So at a time when one could still sell choirs of young children 'for export' away from their mothers and fathers, freeing peasants was still cause for bafflement and amazement in our Russian land. And so he began telling the peasants about this new and curious thing; they heard him out and were amazed and frightened; they spent a long time talking it over among themselves, and then they came to him: 'Well, and what

about the land?' 'The land is mine; you can have the huts and your farm
buildings, but you will work the land for me each year and we'll share the
harvest equally.' The peasants scratched their heads: 'No, it's better the
old way; we belong to you, and the land belongs to us.' Of course this
surprised the landowner: these, he thought, are a savage people, on such
a lowly moral plane that they don't even want their own freedom—
freedom, this first blessing of a human being, and so on. Subsequently
this saying or, rather, formula—'We are yours, but the land is ours'—
became known to everyone and no longer caused any surprise. However,
the most important thing is this: where could such an 'unnatural and
utterly unique' notion of world history have come from, at least if one
compares it to Europe? And bear in mind that it was just at this time that
the war was raging most furiously among all our learned compatriots on
the question: 'Do our People, in fact, have any principles that might be
worthy of the attention of our educated classes?' No, indeed, sir: this
means that the Russian from the very beginning could never imagine
himself without land. But what is most surprising here is that even after
serfdom the People kept the essence of that same formula, and the overwhelming majority of them still cannot conceive of themselves without
land. Since they didn't want to accept freedom without land, it means
that the land came first for them; it was the basis for everything else. The
land is everything, and everything else derives from it—freedom, life,
honor, family, children, order, the church—in short, everything that has
any value. It's because of that same formula that the People have maintained such a thing as the commune. And what is the commune?
Sometimes a much heavier burden than serfdom! Everyone has his
opinion about communal land tenure; everyone knows what a hindrance
it is to economic progress alone. But at the same time, does it not contain
the seed of something new and better, a future ideal that awaits us all? No
one knows how it will come to pass, but we alone have it in embryo, and
it will only happen among us because it will be realized not through war
and rebellion but, once more, through a grand and universal consent. It
will be through consent because even now great sacrifices are being made
for it. And so children will be born in the Garden and they will be set
right; no longer will ten-year-old girls drink cheap vodka in taverns with
factory hands. It's a hard thing for children to grow up in our age, sir! I
intended, after all, to talk to you only about children, and that's why I

took up your time. Little children are the future, you see, and one only loves the future. Who worries about the present? Not I, of course, and probably not you either. And that's why one loves children more than anything else."

Article 5, extract. An Odd Summer for Russia

The other day I told this peculiar fellow of mine: "You keep talking about children, but just now in the *Kursaal* I read in the Russian papers (and I might say that all the Russians here are crowding around the newspapers now) a story about a Bulgarian mother. Entire districts have been massacred over there in Bulgaria. An old woman who survived in one village was found wandering through the ashes of her home, out of her mind. When they began questioning her, she did not reply in ordinary words but at once put her right hand to her cheek and began to sing. She sang improvised verses of how she once had had a home and family, a husband, children—six of them—and how her eldest children had children of their own, her little grandchildren. But cruel people came and by the wall they burned her old man to death, butchered her fine children, raped a young girl, and carried off another one, a beauty; they tore out the bellies of the infants with their sabers; then they set fire to the house and threw them all into the raging flames; and she had seen it all and heard the shrieks of the children."

"Yes, I also read it," replied my peculiar friend. "It's truly remarkable. And in verse, that's the main thing. But in Russia, although our critics have sometimes had praise for poetry, they are generally inclined to the view that poetry is created more as a form of indulgence. It's interesting to be able to follow a spontaneous epic in its elemental conception. It's really a question of art."

"Stop it; you're not being serious. However, I've noticed that you're not overly fond of discussing the Eastern Question."

"No, I've also made a donation to the cause. But since you mention it, there is something about the Eastern Question that I don't care for."

"What, specifically?"

"Well, the great outpouring of love, for instance."

"Come now; I'm sure. . . ."

"I know; I know; you needn't finish; and you're quite right. Besides, I sent in my contribution at the very beginning. You see, the Eastern Question up to now has been only a question of love, so to say, and it came from the Slavophiles. In fact, a lot of people have done very well from this outpouring of love, especially last winter with the Herzegovinians; there were even some careers made on it. Mind you, I'm not making accusations; besides, an outpouring of love in itself is an excellent thing, but a jaded old nag can be ridden to death, after all. That's just what I've been afraid of ever since spring, and so I was skeptical. Later in the summer I was still concerned that this whole feeling of brotherhood might somehow wear off. But now—now I'm not afraid any more; Russian blood has been shed, and shed blood is an important thing, a unifying thing!" [...]

September

from CHAPTER TWO

Article 3, extract. Continuation of the Preceding

[. . .] Aside from that, I venture to observe—only in general, however—that seeking out "categories" for good deeds is a dangerous thing. If I help a Slav as a fellow believer, for example, then this is not a category at all; it is only a designation of his historical situation at the given moment: "He is a fellow believer and so a Christian, and for that he is being oppressed and tormented." But if I say that I am helping him because of the "noble cause of freedom," in so doing I am exhibiting, as it were, the reasons for my help. And if one is to look for reasons for help, then the Montenegrins, for instance, and the Herzegovinians, who have displayed a nobler quest for freedom than the others, turn out to be more worthy of help than the rest. The Serbs are then somewhat less worthy, while the Bulgarians did not rise up for their freedom at all except in the beginning, in some insignificant little groups at a few places in the mountains. They could only howl when the tormenters would take little children and, in the presence of their fathers and mothers, would cut a child's finger off every five minutes to prolong the agony; but they did not defend themselves; they could only wail in agony, as if demented, and kiss the feet of the torturers so that they would stop the torture and give them back their poor little children. Well, perhaps we shouldn't give these people much help because all they did was suffer; they did not elevate themselves to the noble cause of freedom, "this first blessing of man." But let's suppose that you do not think in such a base way; still you must admit that once you introduce reasons and "motives" for love of your fellow man, you almost always arrive at rather similar opinions and conclusions. The best thing of all is to help simply because another person is unfortunate. [. . .]

October

CHAPTER ONE

Article 1. A Case That Is Not as Simple as It Seems

On October 15 the court reached its decision on the case of the step-mother who, some six months ago, in May, you may recall, threw her little six-year-old stepdaughter from a fourth-story window; the little girl, through some miracle, survived in good health. The stepmother, a peasant woman of twenty named Ekaterina Kornilova, was married to a widower who, she testified, regularly quarreled with her; he did not allow her to visit her relatives or allow relatives to visit her; he criticized her by comparing her to his late wife, claiming that the latter was a better house-keeper, and so on. In short, he "drove her to the point where she could no longer love him," and to get even with him she conceived the notion of throwing the daughter of his former wife out the window; this, in fact, she did. In sum, it would seem—apart from the miraculous survival of the child—to be a rather simple and clear-cut story. The court regarded the case from this same "clear-cut" point of view and itself, in the simplest fashion, sentenced Ekaterina Kornilova, "being more than seventeen and less than twenty years of age when she committed the crime, to be exiled to hard labor for a term of two years and eight months and on completion of this sentence to be exiled permanently to Siberia."

However, despite all its simplicity and clarity, there remains something in this case that seems not entirely clarified. The defendant (a rather pretty young woman) went to trial in the late stages of pregnancy, so that a midwife had been summoned to the courtroom for any eventuality. Back in May, when the crime was committed (and when, accordingly, the accused was in her fourth month of pregnancy), I wrote in my May *Diary* (briefly and just in passing, however, while looking at the predictable and bureau-cratic ways of our legal profession) the following words: "And what is truly shocking . . . is that the act of this monster-stepmother is *truly bizarre;* perhaps it really should be given a detailed and deep analysis that might even serve to lighten the case against this criminal woman." That is what I wrote then. Now please look at the facts. In the first place, the defendant herself admitted her guilt, and did so immediately after committing the crime; she reported it herself. Right at the police station she told of how, on the night before the crime, she had decided to kill her stepdaughter, whom she had come to hate out of resentment of her husband; but her husband's presence that evening prevented her from doing anything. The next day, however, when he had gone to work, she opened the window and moved all the flowerpots to one side of the windowsill; then she told the girl to climb onto the sill and look down through the open window. The girl did this, perhaps even eagerly; goodness knows what she expected to see below the window. When she had climbed up and knelt, looking out and clinging to the sides of the window, the stepmother lifted the girl's legs from behind and sent her tumbling out into space. After looking down on the fallen child, the woman (as she recounts it herself) closed the window, got dressed, locked the room, and went off to the police station to report what had happened. Those are the facts, and it would seem that nothing could be more straightforward; and yet, how fantastic, is it not? Our juries are still frequently accused of bringing in some truly fantastic acquittals. Sometimes even the moral feelings of people utterly unconnected with the case have been aroused. We realized that one could have mercy on the criminal, but that good could not be called evil in such an important and great matter as criminal justice; and yet there were acquittals of almost this kind, i.e., evil was *almost* acknowledged as good, or at least it almost reached that point. Either there was pseudosentimentality or a lack of understanding of the very principle of justice, a misunderstanding of the fact that in court the first thing, the very first principle, is to define and specify, as far as possible, what is evil, and to proclaim it publicly as evil. And only then come the issues of easing the criminal's lot, concern for his rehabilitation, and so on. The latter are different problems, very profound and immense, but totally distinct from the business of the court; they belong to other areas of social life entirely, areas which, we must admit, have still not been properly defined and not even formulated in Russia, so that we perhaps have not yet pronounced our first word in these areas of our public life. And, in the meantime, our courts confuse both these *different ideas;* the results, Heaven knows, are bizarre. Crime seems not to be acknowledged as crime at all; to the contrary: it seems that a public proclamation is made—and by the court, indeed—that there is no crime and that crime, don't you see, is only an illness caused by the abnormal state of society, a notion that *in some* specific instances and *in some* certain categories is dazzling in its truth, but which is absolutely mistaken when applied as a whole and in general; for here there is a certain line that cannot be crossed without altogether depriving people of their human image, without removing their very selfhood and life and reducing them to the level of a tiny bit of fluff whose fate hangs on the first breath of wind. In short, this amounts to announcing that some new kind of science has just discovered some new kind of human nature. However, this new science does not yet exist and has not yet even begun. And so all these compassionate verdicts by juries—verdicts in cases where a crime clearly proved and supported by the criminal's full confession, was sometimes flatly denied: "He's not guilty; he didn't do it; he committed no murder"—all these compassionate verdicts (aside from some rare instances when they were really appropriate and correct) have caused astonishment among the People and aroused mockery and perplexity in society. And so now, just having read of the verdict on the fate of the peasant woman Kornilova (two years and eight months at hard labor), the thought suddenly occurred to me: "This is a time when they should have let her off; this time they should have said: 'There was no crime; she committed no murder; she did not throw the girl out the window.'" I will not, however, develop my ideas on the basis of abstractions or emotions. It *simply* seems to me that in this case there was a most legitimate legal ground for acquitting the accused: this is the fact that she was pregnant.

Everyone knows that a pregnant woman (particularly when she is carrying her first child) is very often subject to certain strange influences and impressions that take a strange and fantastic hold on her psyche. These influences sometimes—in rare instances, however—assume extraordinary, abnormal, almost bizarre forms. But despite the fact that they happen rarely (I mean the truly extraordinary manifestations), in the present case the fact that they do happen, or even that they can happen, is more than enough for those who must decide the fate of a human being. Doctor Nikitin, who examined the woman (after the crime), stated that in his opinion Kornilova committed her crime *consciously,* although her angry state of mind and the possibility of a fit of passion could be taken into account. But in the first place, what could the word *consciously* mean here? People rarely do anything unconsciously, apart from those who are insane or delirious or suffering from delirium. Even medicine surely recognizes that someone can commit an act quite consciously but yet not be fully responsible for committing it. Take insane people, for instance: the majority of their insane acts are committed quite consciously, and those who commit them remember doing so. Moreover, they can give an account of what they have done, defend their actions, argue with you about them, and sometimes argue so logically that you may well be at a loss for an answer. I'm not a doctor, of course, but I can remember being told as a child about a certain Moscow lady who, whenever she was pregnant and during specific periods of her pregnancy, would acquire an unusual and irresistible passion for stealing things. She would steal things and money from friends she visited, from her own visitors, and even from the shops and stores where she made her purchases. Afterward, her family would return the stolen things to their owners. Yet she was a lady who was well-educated, from respectable society, and by no means poor; after these few days of strange passion had passed, the thought of stealing would never enter her head. At that time everyone, including medical people, realized that this was only a temporary affect of her pregnancy. Still, of course, she stole consciously and with full awareness of what she was doing. She was completely conscious but simply was unable to resist this impulse when it came upon her. I must suppose that even now medical science can say little with certainty about such cases—I mean about their psychological aspect: which laws produce such crises, manias, and influences in the human psyche; what causes such fits of madness in a sane person; what precisely does consciousness mean here and what role does it play? There seems no doubt of the possibility of these influences and extraordinary manias during pregnancy, and that is sufficient. . . . And what, I repeat, of the fact that these very extraordinary influences occur so rarely? For the conscience of one sitting in judgment in such cases it is enough to consider that they still may occur. Suppose, though, that people argue as follows: she did not go off to steal things like that lady or think up something very unusual to do; on the contrary, she did precisely the thing that was *relevant to the case*, i.e., she simply took revenge on her hated husband by trying to murder his daughter by his former wife, whose example the husband was always citing. Well, say what you like, but even though this may be comprehensible, it is still *not simple;* it may be logical, but you must agree that, had she not been pregnant, perhaps this logical thing would never have happened. It might have happened like this, for instance: left alone with her stepdaughter, abused by her husband and angry at him, she might have thought to herself in her fury, "What if I throw this wretched little girl out the window just to spite him?" She might have thought it, *but she would not have done it.* She would have sinned in mind but not in deed. But now, pregnant, *she carried it out.* The logic is the same in both cases, but the difference is immense.

At least if the jury had acquitted the defendant they would have had something on which to base their verdict: "Although such pathological affects occur but rarely, they do occur. What if there was an affect of pregnancy in this case as well?" That is something to consider. At least in this case everyone would have understood the grounds for mercy and no doubts would have been aroused. And what of the possibility of an error? Surely an error on the side of mercy is better than an error on the side of punishment, the more so as there is no way of verifying anything in this case. The woman is the first to consider herself guilty; she confessed immediately after committing the crime, and she confessed again in court six months later. So she will go to Siberia, perhaps, in conscience and in the depths of her soul considering herself guilty; so she will die, perhaps, repenting in her final hour and considering herself a murderer. And never will it occur to her, nor to anyone else on earth, that there is a pathological affect that can arise during pregnancy and that it, perhaps, was the cause of it all, and that, had she not been pregnant, nothing would have happened. . . . No, of two errors here, it is better to choose the error of mercy. One would sleep better afterward. . . . And yet, what am I saying? A busy man cannot be thinking of sleep; a busy man has a hundred such cases, and he sleeps soundly when he crawls into bed, exhausted. It's the idle man who encounters one or two such cases a year who has a lot of time to think. He's the one who might have such thoughts, from lack of anything better to do. In short, idleness is the mother of all vices.

By the way, there was a midwife present in court, and just imagine: when they convicted the woman, they convicted along with her an infant not yet born. Don't you find that strange? But let's suppose that's not entirely true: still, you must agree that it seems very close to the truth, and indeed, the whole truth. In fact, here he is, condemned to Siberia before he's even born, along with his mother who has to look after him. If he goes with his mother, he loses his father; if the outcome of the case should be such that his father keeps him (I don't know whether the father can do

that now), then the child loses his mother. . . . In short, in the first place
the child loses his family even before he's born, and in the second place,
when he eventually grows up, he'll learn everything about his mother and
he'll. . . . However, who knows what he'll do? It's best to take a *simplified*
view of the case. Looking at it from such a point of view, all the phantas-
magoria disappear. So it should be in life. I even think that all such things
that seem so unusual are in actuality arranged in a most ordinary fashion,
prosaic to the point of indecency. Just look, in fact: this Kornilov is now
a widower again; he's also free once more, since his marriage has been
annulled by his wife's exile to Siberia; his wife, or non-wife, will shortly
bear him a son (because they will surely allow her to bear the child before
she sets off), and while she is recuperating in the prison hospital or
wherever they place her, Kornilov—and I'll stake a bet on this—will visit
her in a most prosaic manner and—who knows—perhaps he will bring
along this same little girl who flew out the window. And they will get
together and talk about the simplest, most everyday things—about some
wretched canvas cloth, about warm shoes or felt boots for the journey.
Who knows, they may strike up a very close relationship now that they
have been divorced, whereas formerly they used to quarrel. And they may
never utter a word of reproach to one another but only sigh over their fate
with compassion for one another. And that same little girl who flew out
the window, I repeat, will likely run errands every day from her father to
her "sweet mummy," taking her fancy loaves of bread: "Here, Mummy,"
she'll say, "Daddy's sent you some tea and sugar as well, and tomorrow
he'll come himself." The most tragic thing may be that when they bid one
another farewell at the railway station they will break into wailing, just
at the last minute, between the second and the third bell. The little girl
will also begin to wail, her mouth gaping, as she looks at them; and each,
one after the other, will probably fall down at the other's feet. "Forgive
me, Katerina Prokofievna, my dearest," he'll say. "Don't think badly of
me." And she will say to him: "And you forgive me, Vasily Ivanovich
(or whatever his name is), my dear; I'm guilty before you, and there's
much to blame me for. . . ." And now the infant, still being nursed—he
will certainly be there as well—will raise his voice, whether she takes him
along or leaves him with his father. In short, with our People the result
will never be an epic poem, will it? They are the most prosaic people in
the world, so that one is almost ashamed of them in that respect. Now

just compare this with how it would happen in Europe: what passions, what vengeance, and what dignity there would be! Just try to describe this case in a story, event by event, beginning with a young wife of a widower, going on to throwing the girl out the window, up to the minute when she looked out to see whether the child had been hurt and at once went off to the police; then to the moment when she sat in court with the midwife, and right to those last words of farewell and bows and . . . and imagine, I almost wrote, "And of course nothing would come of it," yet it might well turn out better than any of our poems and novels with heroes "with deep insight and lives torn asunder." Do you know, I simply don't understand why our novelists have to go off looking for material; here would be a subject for them. Why not just describe the whole truth, step by step? And yet, it seems, I forgot the old rule: what matters is not the subject but the eye. If there is an eye, a subject will be found; if there is no eye, if you are blind, you won't find anything in any subject. Oh, the eye is an important thing; what one eye sees as an epic poem, another sees as only a heap of. . . .

Is it really not possible now to reduce this sentence on Kornilova somehow? Is there no way this could be done? Truly, there might be an error here. . . . I just keep thinking that there was an error!

Article 2, extract. A Few Remarks about Simplicity and Simplification

Now, another topic. Now I would like to state something about simplicity in general. I recall a little thing that happened to me a long time ago. Some thirteen years ago, during what to some people was the height of our "time of troubles" and to others was most "straight and direct," one winter evening I dropped into a library on Meshchansky Street (as it was then called), not far from my home. I had decided to write a critical article and I needed to make some excerpts from a Thackeray novel. In the library I was served by a certain young lady (she was then a young lady). I asked for the novel; she listened with a stern expression.

"We don't keep such rubbish," she said before I had even finished, with inexpressible scorn, which, God knows, I didn't deserve.

Of course, I wasn't surprised and realized what was the matter. Many things of the sort happened at that time, and they seemed to happen in a rush of rapture. An idea dropped onto the street and took on a most common, street-corner appearance. Pushkin was given a terrible going-over at that time, while "boots" were praised to the skies. Nevertheless, I still attempted to talk it over with the girl.

"Do you really consider Thackeray to be rubbish?" I asked, assuming a most humble air.

"You ought to be ashamed for asking. The olden days are past; now there is rational demand. . . ."

With that I departed, leaving the young lady remarkably pleased with the lesson she had given me. But I was powerfully struck by the simplicity of her view, and it was just at that time that I began to ponder *simplicity* in general and our Russian haste for generalization in particular. Our capacity for being satisfied with the simple, small, and insignificant is striking, to say the least. People may object that this incident was trivial and insignificant; that the young lady was an uninformed and, more important, uneducated fool; that it was not worth recalling the incident; and that it was all too easy for the young lady to imagine that until she arrived the whole of Russia had been populated only by fools, but that now, suddenly, a lot of wise people had materialized and that she was one of them. I know all that myself; I also know that this young lady was straining her abilities in saying what she did—that is, about the "rational demand" and about Thackeray—and even then she had to use someone else's words—one could tell that from her face. But still this incident has stayed in my mind until now as a metaphor, as a kind of fable, almost even as an emblem. Think carefully about today's common opinions, about today's "rational demand," about today's flat judgments—not only upon Thackeray but upon the whole Russian People: what *simplicity* there is at times! What a straight-line approach; what quick satisfaction with the petty and insignificant as means of expression; what a general rush to set one's mind at rest as quickly as possible, to pronounce judgment so as not to have to trouble oneself any longer. Believe me, this tendency will remain with us for a long time. Just look: everyone now believes in the sincerity and actuality of the People's movement of this year, and yet even this belief does not satisfy; something even more simple is demanded. One of the members of a certain committee related in my presence that he had received rather a lot of letters with questions such as the following: "Why are the Slavs so important now? Why are we helping the Slavs as Slavs? If the Scandinavians were in a similar position, would we be helping them as we are the Slavs?" In short, why this category "Slavs" (recall the concerns over the rubric "common faith" in *The European Messenger* that I spoke about in the last issue of my *Diary*). It would seem at first glance that this is not a case of simplicity at all, and not an urge for simplification; to the contrary, one can sense disquiet in these questions. But the simplicity in this case consists precisely in the effort to achieve *nihil* and a *tabula rasa* and so, in a way, to set one's mind at rest. For what is simpler and more restful than a zero? Note as well that in these questions one can catch the sound of "rational demand" and "you ought to be ashamed of yourself." [. . .]

Article 3. Two Suicides

Not long ago I happened to be speaking to one of our writers (a great artist) about the comical aspects of life and the difficulty of defining a thing and giving it its proper name. Just prior to that I had remarked to him that I, who have known *Woe from Wit* for almost forty years, had only this year properly understood one of the most vivid characters of this comedy, Molchalin, and had come to this sudden understanding of him only when he (the writer with whom I was speaking) had portrayed him in one of his satirical sketches. (I shall have something to say about Molchalin some time in the future; he's an important topic.)

"But do you know," the writer said to me suddenly, apparently deeply struck by his long-held idea, "do you know, whatever you write or portray, whatever you set down in a work of art, you can never match real life. It doesn't matter what you depict—it will always come out weaker than real life. You might think you've found the most comical aspect of some certain thing in life and captured its most grotesque aspect—but not at all! Real life will at once present you with something of this same sort that you never even suspected and that goes far beyond anything your own observation and imagination were able to create! . . ."

I had known this ever since 1846, when I began writing, and perhaps even earlier, and this fact has struck me more than once and has caused me no small bewilderment: what is the use of art when we can see it so lacking in power? In truth, if you investigate some fact of real life—even one that at first glance is not so vivid—you'll find in it, if you have the capacity and the vision, a depth that you won't find even in Shakespeare. But here, you see, is the whole point: *whose vision and whose capacity?* Not only to create and to write a work of literature, but merely even to pick out the fact requires something of the artist. For some observers all the facts of life pass by in the most touchingly simple manner and are so plain that it's not worthwhile to think about them or even to look at them. Those same facts of life will sometimes perplex another observer to the extent that he (and this happens not infrequently) is at last incapable of simplifying and making a general conclusion about them, of drawing them out into a straight line and so setting his mind at rest. He resorts to simplification of another sort and *very simply* plants a bullet in his head so as to quench at one stroke his tormented mind and all its questions. These are only the two extremes, but between them lies the entire range of the human intellect. But of course we can never exhaust a whole phenomenon and never reach its end, or its beginning. We know only the daily flow of the things we see, and this only on the surface; but the ends and the beginnings are things that, for human beings, still lie in the realm of the fantastic.

By the way, one of my respected readers wrote last summer to tell me of a strange and unexplained suicide, and I have been wanting to talk about it. Everything about this suicide, both its external and its internal aspects, is a riddle. I, of course, following the dictates of human nature, have tried to come up with some solution to this riddle so as to be able "to pause and rest my mind." The victim is a young girl of no more than twenty-three or twenty-four, the daughter of one very well-known Russian émigré; she was born abroad, Russian by origin but scarcely Russian at all by education. The newspapers made some vague mention of her at the time, but the details of the case are very curious: "She soaked a piece of cotton wool in chloroform, bound this to her face and lay down on the bed. . . ." And so she died. She wrote the following note before her death:

> Je m'en vais entreprendre un long voyage. Si cela ne réussit pas
> qu'on se rassemble pour fêter ma résurrection avec du Cliquot. *Si
> cela réussit,* je prie qu'on ne me laisse enterrer que tout à fait morte,

puisqu'il est très désagréable de se réveiller dans un cercueil sous terre. *Ce n'est pas chic!*

Which, translated, is:

I am setting off on a long journey. If the suicide should not succeed, then let everyone gather to celebrate my resurrection with glasses of Cliquot. *If I do succeed,* I ask only that you not bury me until you have determined that I am completely dead, because it is most unpleasant to awaken in a coffin underground. *That would not be* chic *at all!*

In this nasty, vulgar *chic* I think I hear a challenge—indignation, perhaps, or anger—but about what? Persons who are simply vulgar end their lives by suicide only for material, obvious, external reasons; but it is apparent from the tone of this note that she could not have such reasons. What could she be angry about? About the simplicity of the things she saw around her? About the lack of any meaningful content in life? Was she one of those very well-known judges and negators of life who are angry at the "stupidity" of man's presence on earth, at the senseless unintentionality of his appearance here, at the tyranny of brute causality with which they cannot reconcile themselves? Here we have a soul of one who has rebelled against the "linearity" of things, of one who could not tolerate this linearity, which was passed on to her from childhood in her father's house. The most hideous thing of all is that she died, of course, without any apparent doubt. Most probably, there was no conscious doubt in her soul, no "questions." It is most likely of all that she believed everything she had been taught since childhood, without question. And so she simply died from "chilly gloom and tedium," in animal, so to say, and unaccountable suffering; it was as if she could not get enough air and she began to suffocate. Her soul instinctively could not tolerate linearity and instinctively demanded something more complex. . . .

About a month ago all the Petersburg newspapers carried several short lines in fine print concerning a suicide in the city. A poor young girl, a seamstress, threw herself out of a fourth-floor window "because she was absolutely unable to find enough work to make a living." These accounts

added that she leapt and fell to the ground *holding an icon in her hands.*
This icon in the hands is a strange and unprecedented feature in suicides!
This, now, is a meek and a humble suicide. Here, apparently, there was
no grumbling or reproach: it was simply a matter of being unable to live
any longer—"God did not wish it"—and so she died having said her
prayers. There are some things which, no matter how simple they seem
on the surface, one still goes on thinking about for a long time; they recur
in one's dreams, and it even seems as if one is somehow to blame for
them. This meek soul who destroyed herself torments one's mind despite
oneself. It was this latter death that reminded me of the suicide of the
émigré's daughter I had heard about last summer. But how different these
two creatures are—just as if they had come from two different planets!
And how different the two deaths are! And which, I ask, of these two
souls bore more torment on this earth—if such an idle question is proper
and permissible?

Article 4. The Sentence

By the way, here are the thoughts of one person—a materialist, of course—
who committed suicide *out of boredom.*

> . . . In fact, what right did this Nature have to bring me into the
> world as a result of some eternal law of hers? I was created with
> consciousness, and I was *conscious* of this Nature: what right did
> she have to produce me, a conscious being, without my willing it?
> A conscious being, and thus a suffering one; but I do not want to
> suffer, for why would I have agreed to that? Nature, through my
> consciousness, proclaims to me some sort of harmony of the whole.
> From this message human consciousness has created religions.
> Nature tells me—even though I know full well that I cannot partici-
> pate in the "harmony of the whole" and never will be able to and
> haven't the least idea what this means in any case—that I still ought
> to submit to this message, to humble myself, to accept suffering in
> view of the harmony of the whole and agree to live. However, if I
> am to make a conscious choice, then naturally I would prefer to
> be happy only during the moment while *I* exist; but as regards the

whole and its harmony, once *I* have been annihilated, I haven't the least concern if this whole with its harmony remains after I am gone or is annihilated at the same instant as I am. And why should I have to worry so whether it is preserved after I am gone? That is the question. It would have been better had I been created like all animals, that is, as a living being, but without a rational conception of myself. My consciousness is certainly not a harmony but just the opposite, a disharmony, because I am unhappy with it. Just look at those who are happy on earth, look at the sort of people who *consent* to go on living. It is precisely those people who are like animals and who are most closely akin to those species because of the limited development of their consciousness. They willingly consent to live, but on condition that they live like animals; that is, they eat, drink, sleep, build their nests, and raise their offspring. To eat, drink, and sleep in human fashion means to grow rich and to steal; building a nest above all means to steal. You may object, perhaps, that one can arrange one's life and build one's nest on a rational foundation, on scientifically proven social principles and not by stealing, as was the case heretofore. Granted; but I ask you: what for? What is the point of arranging one's life and expending so much effort to arrange social life correctly, rationally, and in a morally righteous manner? No one, of course, can give me an answer to that. All that anyone could reply is: "In order to derive pleasure." Indeed, if I were a flower or a cow I would derive some pleasure. But continually posing questions to myself, as I do now, I cannot be happy, even with the supreme and *direct* happiness of love for my neighbor and the love of humanity for me, since I know that tomorrow it will all be annihilated. I, and all this happiness, and all the love, and all of humanity will be transformed into nothing, into the original chaos. And under such a condition I simply cannot accept any happiness—not from my refusal to agree to accept it, not from stubbornness based on some principle, but simply because I will not and cannot be happy under the condition of the nothingness that threatens tomorrow. This is a feeling, a direct feeling, and I cannot overcome it. Well, suppose I were to die but humanity were to remain eternal in my place; then, perhaps, I might still find some comfort in it. But our planet, after all, is not eternal, and humanity's allotted span is just such a moment as has been allotted to me. And no matter how rationally, joyously, righteously, and blessedly humanity might organize itself on earth, it will all be equated tomorrow to that same empty zero. Though there may be some reason why this is essential, in accordance with some almighty, eternal, and dead laws of Nature, believe me, this idea shows the most profound disrespect to humanity; it is profoundly insulting to me, and all the more unbearable because there is no one here who is to blame.

And finally, even if one were to admit the possibility of this fairy tale of a human society at long last organized on earth on rational and scientific bases; if one were to believe in this, to believe in the future happiness of people at long last, then the mere thought that some implacable laws of Nature made it essential to torment the human race for a thousand years before allowing it to attain that happiness—that thought alone is unbearably loathsome. Now add the fact that this very same Nature, which has permitted humanity at last to attain happiness, tomorrow will find it necessary for some reason to reduce it all to zero, despite the suffering with which humanity has paid for this happiness; and, more important, that Nature does all this without concealing anything from me and my consciousness as she hid things from the cow. In such a case one cannot help but come to the very amusing yet unbearably sad thought: "What if the human race has been placed on the earth as some sort of brazen experiment, simply in order to find out whether such creatures are going to survive here or not?" The sad part of this thought lies mainly in the fact that once again no one is to blame; no one conducted the experiment; there is no one we can curse; it all happened simply due to the dead laws of Nature, which I absolutely cannot comprehend and with which my consciousness is utterly unable to agree. *Ergo:*

Whereas Nature replies through my consciousness to my questions about happiness only by telling me that I can be happy in no other way than through harmony with the whole, which I do not understand and, evidently, never will be capable of understanding;

And whereas Nature not only refuses to recognize my right to receive an account from her and indeed refuses to answer me at all, and not because she does not want to answer, but because she cannot answer;

And whereas I have become convinced that Nature, in order to answer my questions, has assigned to me (unconsciously) *my own self* and she answers me through my own consciousness (because I am saying all this to myself);

And whereas, finally, under such circumstances I must assume simultaneously the roles of plaintiff and defendant, accused and judge, and find this comedy utterly absurd on Nature's part and even humiliating on my part;

Therefore, in my incontrovertible capacity as plaintiff and defendant, judge and accused, I condemn this Nature, which has so brazenly and unceremoniously inflicted this suffering, to annihilation along with me. . . . Since I am unable to destroy Nature, I am destroying only myself, solely out of the weariness of enduring a tyranny in which there is no guilty party.

N. N.

November

[COMPLETE ISSUE]

THE MEEK ONE: A FANTASTIC STORY

CHAPTER ONE

Author's Foreword

I apologize to my readers for providing, in place of my *Diary* in its usual form, merely a story this time. However, I truly have been working on this story for the better part of a month. In any case, I beg the indulgence of my readers.

Now, a few words about the story itself. I called it "fantastic," even though I consider it to be realistic to the highest degree. But it truly does contain something fantastic, which is the form of the story itself, and it is this which I find necessary to explain beforehand.

The fact is, this is neither a story nor a memoir. Imagine a husband whose wife only a few hours earlier has killed herself by jumping out a window; her body now lies on the table before him. He is in a state of bewilderment and still has not managed to collect his thoughts. He paces through the apartment, trying to make sense of what has happened, to "focus his thoughts." He is, as well, an out-and-out hypochondriac, the sort who talks to himself. And so he is talking to himself, telling the story, and trying to *make it clear* to himself. Despite the apparent coherence of his speech, he contradicts himself several times, both logically and emotionally. At times he justifies himself and blames her, then he launches into explanations of things which have little to do with the case: we see here the crudity of his thoughts and spirit, and we see deep feeling as well. Little by little he really does *make it clear* and "focus his thoughts." The series of memories he has evoked irresistibly leads him at last to *truth;* and truth irresistibly elevates his mind and his spirit. By the end, even the tone of the story changes as compared with its confused beginning. The truth is revealed quite clearly and distinctly to the unhappy man—at least as far as he is concerned.

That is the subject. Of course, the process of the narrative goes on for a few hours, with breaks and interludes and in a confused and inconsistent form: at one point he talks to himself; then he seems to be addressing an invisible listener, a judge of some sort. But so it always happens in real life. If a stenographer had been able to eavesdrop and write down everything he said, it would be somewhat rougher and less finished than I have it here; still, it seems to me that the psychological structure would perhaps be just the same. And so it is this assumption of a stenographer recording everything (and whose account I simply polished) that I call the fantastic element of my story. Yet something quite similar to this has already been employed more than once in art: Victor Hugo, for example, in his master-piece *The Last Day of a Man Condemned to Death*, employed virtually this same device, and even though he did not depict any stenographer, he allowed an even greater breach of verisimilitude when he presumed that a man condemned to execution could (and would have time to) keep a diary, not only on his last day, but even in his last hour and literally in his last moment of life. But had he not allowed this fantastical element, the work itself—among the most real and most truthful of all his writings—would not have existed.

Article 1. Who Was I and Who Was She?

. . . So as long as she's still here everything's all right: every minute I go up to have a look at her; but they'll take her away tomorrow, and how will I ever stay here by myself? She's on the table in the anteroom now, they put two card tables together, but tomorrow there'll be a coffin, a white one—white *gros de Naples*. That's not the point, though. . . . I just keep walking, trying to find some explanation for this. It's been six hours now, and I still can't focus my thoughts. The fact is that I just keep on walking, back and forth, back and forth. . . . This is how it happened. I'll just tell it in order. (Order!) Gentlemen, I'm certainly not a literary man, and you'll see that for yourselves; but never mind: I'll tell you what happened as I understand it myself. That's what I find so horrible: I understand it all!

If you really want to know—I mean, if I'm going to start from the very beginning—then it was she who just started coming to me then to pawn some things in order to pay for an advertisement in *The Voice:* "So-and-so, a governess, willing to travel, give lessons in private homes, etc., etc." That was at the very beginning, and I, of course, didn't see her as any different from the others. She came like all the rest, and so on. And then I did begin to see something different about her. She was so delicate and blonde, a little taller than average; she was always a little awkward with me, as if she were embarrassed (I suppose she was the same with all strangers, and of course to her I was no different from anyone else, I mean if you take me as a man and not as a pawnbroker). As soon as she got her money she would turn around and leave at once. And never a word. The others would argue, plead, try to haggle. Not this one, she'd just take what I offered. . . . Wait now, I think I'm getting confused. . . . Yes. What struck me first were the things she brought: cheap silver-plated earrings, a trashy little locket—twenty kopecks was all she'd get. And she herself knew they were worth next to nothing, but I could tell by her face that to her they were treasures. And sure enough, as I learned later, these were the only things she had left from mommy and daddy. Only once I allowed myself a little smirk at her things. You see, I never allow myself to do anything like that. I maintain a gentlemanly tone with my clients: keep it short, keep it polite, and be strict. "Strict, strict, strict." But one day, to my surprise, she actually brought in the remnants (I mean, literally) of an old hare-skin jacket. I couldn't help myself and made a joke of sorts about it. Heavens, how she flushed! She had big, blue, wistful eyes, but there was fire in them then! She didn't say a word, though. Just took up her "remnants" and left. It was then that I *particularly* noticed her for the first time and thought something of this sort about her—I mean something quite particular. Oh yes, and I also recall an impression. What I mean is the main impression, the synthesis of everything: she seemed terribly young, so young she might have been fourteen. Whereas in actual fact she was only a few months short of sixteen. But that's not what I meant; that certainly wasn't the synthesis. She came back again the next day. I found out later that she had gone to Dobronravov's and to Moser's with this jacket, but neither of them takes anything but gold, so they wouldn't even talk to her. I, on the other hand, had once taken a cameo from her (a cheap little thing), but later, when I had thought about it for a while, I was surprised. You see, I don't accept anything but gold and silver either, yet I allowed her to pawn a cameo. And that was my second thought about her at the time; that I remember.

This time—I mean after she had come from Moser's—she brought an amber cigar-holder. It wasn't much of a thing, amateurish workmanship, and again, worthless to me because I only accept gold. Since this was right after her little *rebellion* of the previous day, I was strict with her. With me, being strict means being curt. However, as I was handing her the two rubles, I couldn't resist and said, as if somewhat irritated: "You know I'm only doing this *for you;* Moser wouldn't take a thing like this." I particularly stressed the words "for you," and did so deliberately, to give them *a certain implication.* I was angry. She flushed again when she heard the "for you," but she didn't say a word, didn't throw down the money; she took it. Well, that's what poverty is! How she flushed, though! I realized that I had stung her. And when she had gone I suddenly asked myself: "Is this victory over her really worth two rubles? Hee-hee-hee!" I recall that I asked myself that very question twice: "Is it worth it? Is it worth it?" And with a laugh I answered the question in the affirmative. I had tremendous fun at the time. But it wasn't a bad feeling on my part: I had something in mind; there was a purpose to what I was doing. I wanted to test her, because certain ideas about her suddenly began floating around in my mind. This was my third *particular* thought about her.

. . . Well, it all began from that time. Of course, I immediately tried to find out everything about her indirectly, and I waited with particular impatience for her to come again. You see, I had a feeling she would come soon. When she did come, I began a friendly conversation, was as polite as could be. I've not been badly brought up, after all, and have good manners. Hmm. It was just then that I realized she was kind and meek. Kind, meek people don't resist for long, and though they don't open themselves very easily, they still just don't know how to duck out of a conversation: they may not give you much of an answer, but they do answer, and the further you go, the more you get out of them. Only you mustn't let up if there's something you want. Of course, she didn't explain anything at that time. It was only later that I found out about *The Voice* and all the rest. At that time she was using her last resources on advertisements, and of course these were a bit presumptuous, at least at first: "Governess, willing to travel. Submit offers by return mail." But later: "Willing to accept any work: teach, serve as companion, manage household, nurse an invalid lady; have sewing skills" and so on—you know what it is! Of course, all these latter things were added to the advertisements bit by bit, while at last, when she had reached the point of despair, they would read: "Willing to work without salary, for board alone." No, she couldn't find a position! I decided then to give her a final test: I suddenly picked up the latest issue of *The Voice* and showed her an ad: "Young lady, orphaned, seeks position as governess to young children, preferably with elderly widower. Can provide comforts in the home."

"There, you see, this girl's placed her ad this morning, and by evening she'll surely have found a position. That's how to write an ad!"

She flushed again, and again her eyes flashed; she turned and walked out at once. I was very pleased. However, at that time I was already certain of everything and wasn't the least bit concerned: no one else was going to take her cigar-holders. But she had used up even her cigar-holders. And so it was that she came in two days later, so pale and upset—I realized that something must have happened at home, and something really had happened. I'll explain in a minute what it was, but now I only want to recall how I managed to show her a bit of style and raise myself in her esteem. Suddenly this plan popped into my head. The fact was that she had brought this icon (she had at last made up her mind to bring it). . . . Oh, but listen to me! It had already begun then, and I'm getting things mixed up. . . . The point is that now I want to bring it all back in my mind, every little thing about it, every tiny detail. I just want to focus my thoughts and I can't, and all these tiny details. . . .

It was an image of the Virgin Mary. The Virgin with the Infant Jesus—an ancient, family household icon in a silver, gilded frame, worth, maybe, six rubles. I could see that the icon meant a lot to her, and she was pawning it all, frame included.

"Wouldn't it be better to remove the frame and take back the icon?" I said. "It's an icon, after all, and somehow it seems not quite the thing to do. . . ."

"Is it against the rules to take an icon?"

"No, it's not against the rules, but still, you yourself, perhaps. . . ."

"Well, take off the frame."

"I'll tell you what," I said, after a little thought, "We'll keep it in the frame; I'll put it over there in the icon case with my others, under the lamp" (ever since I opened my pawnshop I've kept an icon lamp burning), "and I'll just give you ten rubles for it."

"I don't need ten. Just give me five, and I'll certainly redeem it."

"You don't want ten? The icon's worth that much," I added, noticing that her eyes again were flashing. She said nothing. I brought her the five rubles.

"Don't despise me," I said. "I've been in a similar bind myself, and even worse. And if you see me now, working at a profession like this . . . it's just the result of all that I've been through. . . ."

"You're taking revenge on society? Is that it?" she interrupted suddenly, with a rather sarcastic smile which, however, contained a good deal of innocence (I mean her sarcasm was general and not directed at me personally, because at that time she did not see me as any different from the others, so she said it almost without malice). "Aha!"—I thought to myself. "That tells me something about you! You're showing your character. One of the new generation."

"You see," I remarked, half in jest, half mysteriously, " 'I am a part of that whole that wills forever evil but does forever good. . . .'"

She cast a quick glance at me, showing great interest (and also a good deal of childish curiosity).

"Wait. . . . What does that mean? Where does it come from? I've heard it somewhere. . . ."

"You needn't rack your brain; Mephistopheles introduces himself to Faust with those words. Have you read *Faust*?"

"Not . . . not very carefully."

"In other words, you haven't read it at all. You must read it. But I can see that sarcastic smile again. Please, don't assume I have so little taste as to embellish my role as a pawnbroker by passing myself off as Mephistopheles. A pawnbroker is a pawnbroker, and so he shall remain. We all know that."

"You are a strange sort of person. . . . I didn't mean to imply anything of the kind. . . ."

She meant to say, "I never expected you to be a man of education," but she didn't say it, although I knew that she thought it. I had pleased her immensely.

"You see," I remarked, "one can do good in any field of endeavor. I'm not speaking of myself, of course. Quite possibly I do nothing but evil, but. . . ."

"Of course one can do good in any place in life," she said, casting a swift and penetrating glance at me. "In any place, to be sure," she added suddenly.

Oh, I recall it; I recall all those moments! And I want also to add that when young people, those dear young people, want to say something very clever and profound they suddenly, with excessive sincerity and naiveté, put on a face that says: "There! Now I'm telling you something very clever and profound." And they do it not from vanity, as people like myself might. But you can see that they themselves put great store in all that; they believe in it and respect it, and think that you have the same respect as they do. Oh, the candor of youth! That is how they conquer. And in her it was so charming!

I remember it, I've forgotten nothing! When she left I at once made my decision. That same day I went off on my final investigation and learned the remaining facts about her, right down to the most intimate details of her current life. I had learned her earlier history from Lukeria, who was then their servant and whom I had bribed several days before. These details were so terrible that I simply cannot understand how she was able to laugh, as she had just now, and to take any interest in the words of Mephistopheles when she herself had to face such horrors. But such is youth! That was just how I thought of her then, proudly and joyfully, because here I could also see the signs of a great soul. It was as if she were saying: "Even on the very edge of perdition, the great words of Goethe shine out for me." Young people always have some greatness of soul—to a tiny degree, at least and perhaps in the wrong direction. I am speaking of her, I mean, of her alone. And the main thing was that I regarded her then as *my own* and had no doubt about my power over her. Do you know, that is a terribly voluptuous thought—when one no longer has any doubts.

But what's wrong with me? If I go on this way, when will I ever focus my thoughts? I must get on with it! Lord, this isn't the point at all!

Article 2. A Proposal of Marriage

"The intimate details" I discovered about her I can explain in a few words: her father and mother had died some time ago, three years before I met her, and she had been left in the charge of some aunts whose way of life was rather improper; in fact, "improper" is not a strong enough word to describe them. One aunt was a widow with a large family—six little children, all close in age; the other aunt, a spinster, was a nasty old piece of work. They were both nasty, in fact. Her father had been a minor civil servant, a copying clerk who had only personal, but not hereditary, nobility. In short, the whole situation suited me to a tee. I appeared as if from another, higher world: I was still a retired junior captain from a renowned regiment, a nobleman by birth, of independent means, and so on, and as far as the pawnshop was concerned, the aunts could only look upon that with respect. She had been enslaved to the aunts for three years, but still had managed to qualify at some sort of examination; she had managed to qualify, snatching moments from her merciless daily labor, and that signified something of her striving for what was sublime and noble! And why did I want to marry her? However, let's forget about me for the moment; that will come later. . . . As if that mattered, in any case! She gave lessons to her aunt's children, sewed their underclothes, and, in the end, not only washed clothes but, with her weak chest, scrubbed floors as well. To put it plainly, they even beat her and reproached her for every crust of bread. It ended by their planning to sell her. Foo! I'm omitting the sordid details. Later she told me the whole story. A fat shop-keeper in the neighborhood had watched the whole thing for a year (he was not simply a shopkeeper, in fact, but owned two grocery stores). He had already driven two wives to their graves with his beatings, and now he was looking for a third. His eye fell on her. "She's a quiet one," he thinks, "raised in poverty, and I'll marry her for the sake of my motherless children." He had children, to be sure. He started courting her and nego-tiating with the aunts. On top of everything else, he was a man of fifty; she was horrified. It was at this point that she started coming to me to get money for the advertisements in *The Voice.* At last she began pleading with the aunts to give her just a tiny bit of time to think the matter over. They allowed her a little time, but only a little, and kept nagging at her: "We don't know where our next meal is coming from ourselves, never mind having an extra mouth to feed." I already knew all about this, and during the day that followed our morning encounter I made my decision. The shopkeeper called on her in the evening, bringing a pound of sweets worth half a ruble from his store. She was sitting with him, while I called Lukeria from the kitchen and told her to go back and whisper that I was at the gate with something urgent to tell her. I was pleased with myself. On the whole, I was terribly pleased that whole day.

Right there at the gate, with Lukeria standing by, I explained to her (and she was still amazed at my sending for her) that I would be happy and honored if. . . . In the second place, so that she shouldn't be surprised

at the way I proposed to her right on the street, I told her, "I'm a straightforward man, and I know the circumstances of your case." And I wasn't
lying when I said I was straightforward. Well, to hell with it; it doesn't
matter. I spoke not only politely, that is, showing myself as a man with
good manners, but also with originality, and that was the most important
thing. Well, and what of it? Is it a sin to admit that? I want to judge myself
and I am judging myself. I'm supposed to speak both *pro* and *contra*, and
that's what I'm doing. Even afterward I would recall those moments with
pleasure, as silly as it might have been. I told her plainly then, without
any embarrassment, that in the first place I was not particularly talented
or particularly clever, and, perhaps, not even particularly kind. I said I
was a rather cheap egotist (I remember that expression; I made it up on
the way to her house and was pleased with it) and that it was very likely
that I had many other disagreeable qualities as well. All this was spoken
with a particular kind of pride—you know how it is done. I had enough
taste, of course, not to launch into listing all my virtues after having so
nobly declared my shortcomings to her. I didn't say, "On the other hand,
I am such-and-such." I could see that she was still terribly frightened,
but I didn't tone down anything; in fact, seeing that she was frightened,
I deliberately laid it on: I told her plainly that she would have enough
food to eat, but there would be no fine dresses, theater, or balls. These
might come at some future time when my goal had been achieved. I was
quite carried away with this severe tone of mine. I added—doing my best
to make it seem like a passing thought—that if I had taken up such an
occupation (meaning the pawnshop), it was only because I had a certain
goal, that there was one particular circumstance. . . . But I had the right
to speak that way, after all: I really did have such a goal, and there really
was such a circumstance. Wait a moment, ladies and gentlemen: I was
the first to hate that pawnshop, and I hated it all my life. But you see, in
essence (and even though it's ridiculous to talk to oneself in mysterious
phrases), I was "taking my revenge on society," I really and truly was! So
her little joke that morning about my "taking revenge" was unfair. You
see, if I had told her directly: "Yes, I'm taking my revenge on society," she
would have laughed as she did in the morning and it really would have
turned out to seem amusing. But by making an indirect hint and slipping
in a mysterious phrase, I was able to capture her imagination. Besides,
at that time I wasn't afraid of anything: I knew that the fat shopkeeper

was more repulsive to her than I in any case, and that I, standing by her gate, would appear as her liberator. That I certainly did understand. Oh, human beings understand nasty tricks very well! But was that a nasty trick? How can one pass judgment on a man in a case like this? Did I not love her already, even then?

Wait a moment: of course, I didn't say a single word to her then about my doing her a good deed. On the contrary, quite on the contrary: "It is *I*," I said, "who is the beneficiary here, and not you." So I even expressed this in words, unable to restrain myself, and perhaps it came out stupidly, because I noticed a wrinkle pass over her brow. But on the whole I won a decisive victory. Wait now, if I'm going to recall this whole sordid thing, then I'll recall it down to the last bit of nastiness: I stood there and a thought stirred in my mind: "You are tall, well-built, well-mannered, and finally—speaking without any boasting—you're not bad-looking either." That was what was running through my mind. I scarcely need to tell you that she said yes right there by the gate. But . . . but I ought to tell you as well that she stood there by the gate and thought for a long time before she said, "Yes." She thought so long and hard that I was about to ask her, "Well, what is your answer?" And indeed, I couldn't restrain myself and asked, with a little flourish but very politely, "Well, what is your answer, Miss?"

"Wait a moment, let me think."

And her little face was so serious, so serious that even then I might have read it! But I was mortified. "Can she really be choosing between me and the shopkeeper?" I thought. Oh, but I still didn't understand it then. I didn't understand anything then, not a thing. I didn't understand until today! I remember Lukeria running out after me as I was leaving, stopping me on the road and saying, all in a rush: "God will reward you, sir, for taking our dear miss! Only don't tell her that; she's such a proud one."

A proud one, indeed! "I like those proud ones," I thought. Proud women are especially beautiful when . . . well, when you have no more doubts about your power over them, isn't it so? Oh, you mean, clumsy man! Oh, how pleased I was! You know, when she was standing there by the gate, deep in thought about whether to answer yes, I was amazed, you know, that she could even be thinking such a thing as this: "If there's misery in store both here and there, then wouldn't it be better just to choose the worse—the fat shopkeeper—straightaway? Then he can beat me to death in a drunken fit." Eh! So what do you think, could she have had such a thought?

But even now I don't understand; I don't understand a thing! I just said that she might have had such a thought: to choose the worse of two evils, meaning the shopkeeper. But who was the worse for her then: the shopkeeper or I? A shopkeeper or a pawnbroker who quotes Goethe? That's still a question! What question? And you don't understand even that: the answer is lying on the table, and you're talking about a "question"! Well, to hell with me! I'm not the issue here at all. . . . And what do I care now, anyway, whether I'm the issue or not? That's something I certainly can't solve. I'd better go to bed. My head aches. . . .

Article 3. The Noblest of Men, but I Don't Believe It Myself

I couldn't get to sleep. Anyhow, how could I sleep with this throbbing in my head? I want to come to terms with all this, all this filth. Oh, the filth! Oh, the filth I rescued her from then! Why, she must have understood that and appreciated what I did! There were other ideas I savored as well. For example: I'm forty-one, and she's only sixteen. That was alluring, that feeling of inequality; a thing like that is delectable, very delectable.

I wanted to arrange our wedding *à l'anglaise,* meaning just the two of us with only two witnesses, one of whom would be Lukeria, and then straight off to the train, to Moscow, say (it happened that I had some business to do there), to a hotel for a couple of weeks. She was very much against that and wouldn't hear of it, and I had to go pay my respects to the aunts as her nearest relatives from whom I was taking her. I gave in, and the aunts were paid appropriate respect. I even presented the creatures with a hundred rubles each and promised them still more—not saying anything to her, of course, so as not to grieve her with sordid dealings like this. The aunts at once became as cordial as could be. There was also an argument about her trousseau: she had—almost literally—nothing, but she didn't want anything. However, I managed to show her that it simply wouldn't do to have nothing at all, and so it was I who collected her trousseau, for if I hadn't, then who would have? But never mind about me; that's not important. I did manage to pass on some of my ideas to her then, so that at least she knew. Perhaps I was even hasty. What mattered was that, right from the very start, despite some attempt at restraint, she rushed to meet me with love, she would greet me with delight when I visited her in the evening, she would babble on (that charming, innocent babble of hers) about her childhood, her earliest years, her parents' home, her father and mother. But I at once threw cold water on all this rapture of hers. That was just my plan, you see. When she was elated, I would respond with silence—a benevolent silence, of course . . . but still she would quickly see that we were two very different people and that I was an enigma. And my main point was to keep working at that enigma! Maybe it was just for the sake of solving an enigma that I did this whole stupid thing! Strictness, in the first place. It was strictness when I brought her into my house. In short, while I went on with my daily round, quite satisfied, I created a whole system. Oh, it happened without any effort and just sprang up on its own. And it couldn't have happened any other way: the course of events compelled me to create this system—why on earth should I slander myself! It was a genuine system. Wait a moment, now, and listen: if you are going to judge a man, then you have to know the facts of his case. . . . So listen.

I'm not sure how to begin this, because it's very difficult. When you begin to justify yourself—that's when it becomes difficult. You see, young people generally are scornful of money, for instance. So I at once set to work on the issue of money. I stressed the money question. And I stressed it so much that she began more and more to keep silent. She would open her big eyes, listen to me, look at me, and not say a word. Young people are noble, you see—the best young people, I mean; they are noble and impulsive, but have little tolerance; just as soon as something doesn't go quite their way, they show their contempt. But I wanted her to have a broad, tolerant outlook; I wanted to instill this breadth right into her heart, to make it a part of her. Don't you see what I had in mind? Let me take a trivial example: how could I explain my pawnshop to a person like her, for instance? Of course, I didn't start to talk of it immediately, or else it would have seemed as if I were apologizing for keeping a pawnshop; but I acted with pride, and barely said a word of it. I am an expert at speaking while barely saying a word; I've been speaking without saying a word all my life, and have endured whole inner tragedies without saying a word. Oh, of course I myself was unhappy! Everyone had cast me off, cast me

off and forgotten me, and not a single soul knows it! And suddenly this
sixteen-year-old got hold of a few details about me from some contempt-
ible people and thought she knew everything; but the real secret still lay
in the bosom of this man alone! I just kept silent, and especially with her I
kept silent, right until yesterday. Why did I do that? Because I'm a proud
man. I wanted her to find out herself, with no help from me, and this time
not from tales told by scoundrels. No, she should come to a conclusion
herself about this man and discover what he is! When I took her into
my home I wanted complete respect. I wanted her to stand before me
in ardent homage because of my sufferings, and I deserved that. Oh, I
was always proud; I always wanted all or nothing! And that's just why
I'm not content with halfway measures where happiness is concerned; I
wanted it all. That's just why I had to act as I did then, as if to say to her:
"You draw your own conclusion and appreciate my worth!" Because you
have to agree that if I began explaining things to her myself and dropping hints, ingratiating myself and asking her to respect me, it would be
no better than begging for charity. . . . But yet . . . yet why am I talking
about this!

Stupid, stupid, stupid, and stupid again! Frankly and mercilessly
(and I stress the fact that it was merciless), I explained to her then, in a
few words, that "the nobility of youth is very charming but isn't worth a
penny. And why not? Because it is acquired cheaply and is not obtained
through experience. It's all 'the first impressions of existence.' But let's
have a look at you when you have to earn your daily bread! Cheap nobility
is always easy; even sacrificing your life—even that is cheap, because it's
just a matter of a stirring of the blood and an excess of energy, a passionate
longing for beauty! No, take on some noble deed that is difficult, unobtru-
sive, unsung, one with no glamour, but which involves criticism, a great
deal of sacrifice, and not a drop of glory, one where you, the radiant youth,
are held up as a scoundrel by everyone when you are more honorable
than any of them. Well, now, try taking on a deed like that! No, ma'am,
you'll turn it down! And I—I have done nothing but bear the weight
of such a deed my whole life long." At first she would argue. And how
she argued! But then she began to keep quiet, and at last she wouldn't
say a word; only she would open her eyes as wide as could be while she
listened, such big, big eyes, full of attention. And . . . and apart from that
I suddenly noticed a smile, a skeptical, silent, unpleasant smile. And so it

was with this smile that I brought her into my house. It's true, of course, that she had nowhere else to go. . . .

Article 4. Plans and More Plans

Which one of us first began it? Neither of us. It began by itself right from the very start. I said that I was going to be strict when I brought her into the house, but from the first step I softened. Even before we married I explained to her that she would take charge of accepting the articles for pawn and paying out the money, and she didn't say a word at the time (I draw your attention to that). Moreover, she set about the job even with some enthusiasm. Of course, the apartment and the furniture all remained as they had been. It's a two-room apartment: the large anteroom has the pawnshop and is divided by a counter; the other room, also large, is our parlor and serves as a bedroom as well. I only have a little furniture; even her aunts had better. The icon case and lamp are in the anteroom with the pawnshop; the other room has my bookcase, with a few books in it, and a chest the key for which I keep; and then there's the bed, a couple of tables, and some chairs. Before we married I told her that I set aside a ruble a day and no more for our subsistence—I mean for food for me, her, and Lukeria (whom I'd managed to lure away). "I need thirty thousand in three years," I told her, "and there's no other way to raise it." She didn't object, but I raised our subsistence allowance by thirty kopecks. The same with the theater. I had told my fiancée that there wouldn't be any theater, but all the same I decided that once a month I would take her to a play, and do it in proper fashion, too, with orchestra seats. We went together, three times, and saw *The Pursuit of Happiness* and *The Singing Birds,* I think. (Oh, to hell with it; what difference does it make!) We went in silence, and we came back in silence. Why was it that we started by keeping silent right from the very beginning? Why? We didn't quarrel at first, you see, but still we kept silent. I remember how she would always steal furtive glances at me; as soon as I noticed that, I kept an even more determined silence. True enough, it was I who insisted on the silence, not she. Once or twice she had fits of affection when she rushed to embrace me; but since these outbursts of hers were unhealthy and hysterical, while

I needed happiness that was solid, with respect from her, I reacted coldly. And I was right: the day after every outburst we would have a quarrel.

They weren't really quarrels, I mean, but there was silence, and it took on a more and more insolent manner on her part. "Rebellion and independence"—that's what she had in mind, only she didn't know how to manage it. Yes, that gentle face of hers grew more and more insolent. Believe it or not, she began to find me obnoxious; I could tell that. And it was obvious enough that she was having fits of temper. Now tell me, how could she, coming from such squalor and poverty—after scrubbing floors, in fact—how could she suddenly start fuming because we lived poorly! But you see, ladies and gentlemen, it was not poverty, it was frugality, and in the things that mattered—even luxury: in our linen, for instance, or in cleanliness. I had always imagined before that a wife finds cleanliness attractive in her husband. However, it wasn't poverty that bothered her, it was my supposed stinginess in housekeeping: "He has a goal," she would probably say to herself, "and is showing off his strong character." She herself suddenly refused to go to the theater. And that mocking look of hers became more and more obvious . . . while I made my silence more and more intense.

Should I have tried to justify myself? The pawnshop caused the most trouble. Let me explain: I knew that a female, and especially a girl of sixteen, could do nothing other than submit completely to her husband. Women have no originality: why, that's an axiom, and even now, even now I consider that an axiom! What does it prove that she's lying out there in the anteroom: truth is truth, and even John Stuart Mill himself can do nothing about it! But a loving woman—oh, a loving woman will worship even the flaws, even the vices of her beloved. He himself can't find such ways to excuse his vices as she can. This is noble, but it's not original. It is lack of originality, and only that, that has been the ruin of women. And so, I repeat: what if you do point to that table out there? Is it something original that's lying on the table? Oh-h-h!

Listen to me: I was confident she loved me then. Why, she used to rush over to embrace me. So she loved me, or rather she wanted to love me. Yes, that's how it was: she wanted to love me; she was trying to love me. And the main thing was that I didn't have any vices that she'd have to try to excuse. "Pawnbroker," you say; everybody says it. And what if I am a pawnbroker? It means there must be reasons for the noblest of men to become pawnbrokers. You see, ladies and gentlemen, there are certain ideas . . . I mean, there are some ideas which, when you try to put them into words, sound very silly. They simply make one ashamed. Why is that? No reason at all. Because we are all worthless, and none of us can bear the truth. That's the only reason I can think of. I said "the noblest of men" just now. That may sound ridiculous, yet that's just how it was. It's the truth; it's the truest truth of all! Yes, at the time I *had the right* to try to secure my future and to open this pawnshop: "You have rejected me (you people, I mean); you have cast me out with your scornful silence. You answered my passionate longing to love you with an insult I will feel all my life. So now I am quite justified in walling myself off from you, collecting my thirty thousand rubles, and living the rest of my life somewhere in the Crimea, on the Southern Shore, amid mountains and vineyards, on my own estate, purchased with that thirty thousand. What matters most is to live faraway from all of you, bearing no malice, but with an ideal in my soul, with the woman I love next to me, with a family, if God blesses me with one, spending my days helping the neighboring settlers." It's all very well, of course, to say this to myself now, but what could have been stupider than to try painting her a picture of all that back then? That explains my proud silence; that explains why we sat without exchanging a word. Because what could she have understood? Sixteen years old, barely into her youth! Could she have accepted my justifications? Could she have understood my sufferings? She has a simple, "straight-line" way of thinking; she knows little of life, is full of young, cheap convictions, suffers from the blindness of "the beautiful soul"; and above all, there's the pawnshop—that was enough! (But was I some criminal in the pawnshop? Didn't she see how I acted? Did I ever charge more than my due?) Oh, what a dreadful thing is truth in the world! This charming girl, this meek one, this heavenly creature—she was a tyrant, an insufferable tyrant over my soul, a tormenter! I am defaming myself unless I say that! You think I didn't love her? Who can say that I didn't love her? Don't you see the irony here, the wicked irony of fate and nature? We are damned; human life in general (and mine, in particular) is damned! Of course, I understand now that I made some mistake! Something went wrong back then. Everything was clear; my plan was as clear as the air: "Severe, proud, needing no one's moral consolation, suffering in silence."

That is how it was; I didn't lie, really I didn't! "One day she will see for herself that it was a matter of my nobility"—only she wasn't able to see it then—"and when she eventually realizes it, she will have ten times more esteem for me and will fall to her knees, her hands folded in ardent prayer." That was the plan. But at this point I forgot something; or there was something I didn't take into consideration. There was something I couldn't manage to do properly. But, never mind, that's enough. Whose forgiveness is there to ask now? What's done is done. Take courage, man, and be proud! It's not your fault! . . .

And so, I'll tell the truth; I'm not afraid to face the truth head on: it was *her* fault, *her* fault! . . .

Article 5. The Meek One Rebels

The quarrels started because she suddenly took it into her head to loan money on her own terms and to appraise articles at higher than their real value. Twice she even presumed to quarrel with me on the topic. I wouldn't agree to what she was doing. It was at this point that the captain's widow turned up.

An old widow came in with a locket, a gift of her late husband, the captain, and a keepsake, of course. I gave her thirty rubles for it. She started whining and pleading for us not to sell the thing, and of course I said we wouldn't. Well, to cut the story short, she suddenly turned up five days later to exchange the locket for a bracelet that wasn't worth even eight rubles; I refused her, of course. I suppose she must have been able to read something in my wife's eyes; anyway, she came again when I wasn't there, and my wife exchanged the bracelet for the locket.

When I found out that same day what had happened, I spoke mildly but firmly and reasonably to her. She was sitting on the bed, looking at the floor, flicking her right toe against the carpet (a gesture of hers); a nasty smile played on her lips. Then, without raising my voice at all, I stated calmly that the money was *mine,* that I had the right to regard life through *my* eyes, and that when I brought her into my house I had hidden nothing from her.

Suddenly she jumped to her feet, all a-tremble, and—can you believe it?—suddenly started stamping her feet at me. She was a wild beast; she was having a fit; she was a wild beast having a fit. I was numb with amazement: I had never expected antics like this. But I kept my head and didn't even make a move; once more, in the same calm voice as before, I told her plainly that henceforth I would let her have no more part in my business affairs. She laughed in my face and walked out of the apartment.

The fact is, she did not have the right to walk out of the apartment. Nowhere without me: such was the agreement made before we married. She came back toward evening; I didn't say a word.

The next day she went out in the morning, and did the same the day after that. I closed up the shop and went off to see her aunts. I had had no dealings with them since the wedding: I would not have them call on me or call on them. But it turned out that she had not been visiting them. They listened to my story with interest and then laughed in my face: "That's just what you deserve." Yet I had expected them to laugh. Right then I offered the younger aunt, the old maid, a hundred-ruble bribe, giving her twenty-five in advance. Two days later she came to see me, saying: "There's an officer, a Lieutenant Efimovich, one of your army friends, who's involved in the affair." I was astonished. This Efimovich had done me more harm than anyone in the regiment, and about a month before, being the shameless creature he is, he had come into the pawnshop twice, pretending he wanted to pawn something, and I recall he began laughing with my wife. I approached him right then and told him that in view of our former relations he should not dare to call on me again, but I hadn't the least notion of anything like this; I simply thought he was being impudent. And now, suddenly, the aunt tells me that she already has a rendezvous arranged with him and the whole affair is being managed by a former acquaintance of the aunts, a certain Julia Samsonovna, and a colonel's wife to boot. "She's the one your wife visits now," the aunt tells me.

Let me summarize this episode. The whole affair cost me nearly three hundred rubles, but within two days I had arranged things so that I could stand in an adjoining room behind a door and listen to my wife's first rendezvous alone with Efimovich. In anticipation of this, I had a brief but—for me—very significant encounter with her on the eve of the event.

She had returned home toward evening and sat on the bed looking mockingly at me, tapping her little foot against the rug. Looking at her, the thought suddenly flew into my head that for this whole past month or, rather, for the previous two weeks, she had absolutely not been herself; one could even say that she had become the antithesis of herself: here was a violent, aggressive creature—I couldn't call her shameless, but she was agitated and looking to cause a commotion. She was deliberately seeking out ways to cause a commotion. Her gentle spirit held her back, however. When a woman like that begins to revolt, even if she may have stepped over the limit, you can still always tell that she is only forcing herself, pushing herself further, and that she herself cannot overcome her own sense of morality and shame. And that is the reason such women sometimes go to such lengths that you can scarcely believe your eyes. The woman used to debauchery will, on the contrary, always tone things down; such a one will do something far worse, but will do it with an air of decorum and respectability that attempts to claim superiority over you.

"Tell me, is it true they kicked you out of the regiment because you were afraid to fight a duel?" she asked me suddenly, right out of the blue, her eyes flashing.

"It's true. By decision of the officers I was asked to leave the regiment, though I had sent in my resignation even before that."

"They kicked you out as a coward?"

"Yes, the verdict was that I was a coward. But I refused the duel not as a coward but because I didn't want to submit to their tyrannical decree and challenge a man who, in my view, had caused me no offense. You must realize," I couldn't resist adding, "that standing up to that sort of tyranny and accepting all the consequences meant showing far more courage than fighting in any duel."

I couldn't resist; I said it as if to justify myself. But this was all she needed, this new humiliation for me. She laughed spitefully.

"And is it true that for three years afterward you wandered the streets of Petersburg like a tramp, begging for small change and spending the nights under billiard tables?"

"I even used to sleep in the Haymarket, at the Viazemsky house. Yes, that's true. After leaving the regiment there were a good many shameful things in my life, and much degradation. But it wasn't moral degradation, because I was the first to despise my own actions even then. It was only a degradation of my will and my mind, and it was caused only by despair at my situation. But that's all past. . . ."

"Oh, and now you are an important figure—a financier!"

That was a dig at the pawnshop. But by then I had managed to gain my self-restraint. I could see that she was eager to hear some humiliating explanations and—I didn't provide any. At that point a customer rang and I went to the anteroom to look after him. An hour later, when she had suddenly dressed to go out, she stopped in front of me and said, "Still, you didn't tell me anything about that before the wedding?"

I did not reply, and she left.

And so, on the next day, I stood behind the door in this room listening to my fate being decided. I had a revolver in my pocket. She was sitting at the table, nicely dressed, and Efimovich was preening himself in front of her. And what do you think? What happened (and it's to my credit that I say this) was exactly the thing I had supposed and anticipated would happen, although I was not conscious of supposing and anticipating it. I don't know if that makes sense to you.

This is what happened. I listened for a whole hour, and for a whole hour I was present at a duel between the noblest and most elevated of women and a depraved, dull creature of society with a groveling soul. And how, I thought in utter amazement, how could this naive, this meek, this reticent girl possibly know all this? The wittiest author of a high-society comedy could not have created this scene of ridicule, naive laughter, and the saintly scorn of virtue for vice. And what brilliance there was in her words and little turns of phrase; how witty were her quick replies; what truth there was in her condemnations! And, at the same time, how much almost girlish naiveté. She laughed in his face at his declarations of love, at his gestures, at his propositions. Having arrived with the notion of storming the fortress head on and not anticipating any resistance, he suddenly was disarmed. At first I was prepared to believe that she was simply playing the flirt: "the coquetry of a creature who, though depraved, is witty, and so works to increase her own value." But no: truth radiated like the sun, and there was no possibility of doubt. She, with her lack of experience, might have decided to arrange this rendezvous out of hatred for me, a hatred that was both insincere and impetuous, but when it came to the crux of the matter her eyes were opened at once. It was simply a matter of a woman who was trying desperately to injure me in any way she could but who, once she had resolved to do such a dirty deed, was unable to bear the messy consequences. And could Efimovich, or any of those other society creatures, seduce a woman like her—she, pure and sinless, with her ideals? On the contrary: he only made her laugh. The whole truth rose up from her soul, and her anger brought the sarcasm from her heart. I repeat: this buffoon at last fell into a complete daze and sat frowning, scarcely answering her, so that I even began to fear that he might go so far as to insult her out of a mean wish for revenge. Again I repeat: it is to my credit that I listened to this whole scene with scarcely any surprise. It was as if I were encountering only things I already knew. It was as if I had gone there to have that encounter. I had come believing nothing, with no accusation against her—although I had taken a revolver in my pocket: that's the truth! And could I have imagined her in any other way? Why was it I loved her? Why was it I cherished her? Why was it I had married her? Oh, of course I was all too convinced of how much she hated me then, but I was also convinced of how pure she was. I put a sudden end to the scene when I opened the door. Efimovich leapt up; I took her hand and invited her to leave with me. Efimovich recovered and suddenly burst into a loud peal of laughter.

"Oh, there's nothing I can say against sacred conjugal rights! Take her away! And do you know," he shouted as I left, "even though a real gentleman wouldn't stoop to fight a duel with you, out of respect for your lady, I'm at your service . . . that's if you dare, of course. . . ."

"Do you hear that!" said I, stopping her for a moment on the threshold.

And then not a single word all the way home. I led her by the hand, and she offered no resistance. On the contrary: she seemed terribly shocked. But that lasted only until we reached the apartment. When we arrived she sat down on a chair and fixed her gaze on me. She was extraordinarily pale; even though her lips at once assumed their mocking expression, she looked at me with a solemn and stern challenge, and I think for the first few moments she seriously believed that I was going to shoot her. But I silently drew the revolver from my pocket and laid it on the table. She looked at me and at the revolver. (Note this: she was already familiar with this revolver. I had acquired it when I opened the pawnshop and had kept it loaded ever since. When I opened the shop, I decided not to keep huge dogs or a muscular manservant as Moser does, for example. The cook lets in my customers. But those who practice our trade cannot deprive themselves of the means of self-defense—one never knows what might happen. And so I kept a loaded revolver. During her first days in my house, she took a great interest in this revolver and had a lot of questions about it. I explained its mechanism and how it works and once even persuaded her to fire at a target. Keep all that in mind.) Paying no heed to her frightened glance, I lay down on the bed, half undressed. I felt quite exhausted; it was around eleven o'clock. She went on sitting in the same spot, not stirring, for nearly an hour more and then put out the light and lay down, also dressed, on the sofa by the wall. This was the first time she did not lie down beside me. Bear that in mind as well. . . .

Article 6. A Dreadful Recollection

Now, this dreadful recollection. . . .

I woke up the next morning about eight o'clock, I think, and the room was already quite light. I awakened at once, my mind fully clear, and opened my eyes. She was standing by the table, holding the revolver. She didn't notice that I was awake and was looking at her. And suddenly I saw her begin to move toward me, still holding the revolver. I quickly closed my eyes and pretended to be sound asleep.

She came up to the bed and stood over me. I could hear everything; even though a deathly silence had fallen on the room, I could hear that silence. Then a shudder passed through me and, unable to resist, I suddenly—I couldn't help it—I had to open my eyes. She was staring right into my face, holding the pistol to my temple. Our eyes met. But we looked at each other for no more than a moment. With an effort I closed my eyes again and at the same time resolved with all the strength I could muster that I would not move another muscle and would not open my eyes no matter what fate awaited me.

In actual fact it happens that a soundly sleeping person can suddenly open his eyes, and even raise his head for a second and look around the room; then, a moment later, he can lay his head on the pillow once more and fall asleep without remembering a thing. When I, having met her gaze and having felt the pistol at my temple, suddenly closed my eyes again and did not stir, as if I were sound asleep, she certainly might have assumed that I really was sleeping and had seen nothing, the more so that it would be quite improbable for one who had seen what I had to close his eyes again at *such* a moment.

Yes, quite improbable. But still, she might have guessed the truth as well: that thought also flashed in my mind at that same moment. Oh, what a whirlwind of thoughts and sensations rushed through my mind in less than an instant. Hurrah for the electricity of human thought! If that were the case (I felt)—if she had guessed the truth and knew I was not sleeping—then I had already crushed her by my readiness to accept death, and her hand might be trembling in hesitation at this moment. The resolve she had shown earlier might have been shattered by this amazing new realization. I've heard that people standing on a great height seem to be drawn downward, into the abyss, by their own accord. I think that many suicides and murders have been committed simply because the person had already taken the pistol into his hand. There's an abyss here as well, a forty-five-degree slope that you cannot help but slip down; there is an irresistible call for you to pull the trigger. But the awareness that I had seen it all, that I knew it all, and was silently awaiting death at her hand—that might keep her from sliding down the slope.

The silence continued, and suddenly I felt the cold touch of iron at the hair on my temple. You might ask: was I firmly convinced I would survive? I will answer, as before God: I counted on nothing, except perhaps one chance in a hundred. Why, then, could I accept death? But let me ask you: what was my life worth now, after the creature I loved had pointed a revolver at me? Besides, I knew with all the strength of my being that a struggle was going on between us at that very moment, a terrible duel of life and death, a duel fought by that very same coward of yesterday, the man whose comrades had thrown him out of his regiment for cowardice. I knew it, and she knew it—as long as she had guessed the truth that I was not asleep.

Perhaps this didn't happen, perhaps I didn't think anything of the sort at the time; yet it all must have happened—without my thinking anything, perhaps—because I have done nothing but think of it every hour of my life ever since.

But now you ask: why didn't I save her from this criminal act? Oh, I have asked myself that same question a thousand times since, every time when, a chill gripping my spine, I recall that second. But I was in such a state of black despair at the time: I myself was perishing, truly perishing, so how could I save anyone else? And what makes you think I even wanted to save anyone? Who knows what I was feeling at the time?

Still, my mind was seething with activity; seconds passed; the silence was deadly; she continued to stand over me, and suddenly I shuddered with hope! I opened my eyes at once. She was no longer in the room. I rose from the bed: I had conquered, and she had been vanquished forever!

I went out to get myself some tea. The samovar was always set up in our other room, and she was always the one to pour the tea. I took a seat at the table without saying a word and accepted a glass of tea from her. Five minutes later I glanced at her. She was dreadfully pale, even paler than yesterday, and she was looking at me. And suddenly—suddenly, noticing that I was looking at her, her pale lips broke into a pale smile; her eyes posed a timid question. "So, she still doesn't know for sure and is asking herself: does he know, or doesn't he? Did he see, or didn't he?" Indifferently, I looked away. After I had tea I closed the shop, went to the market, and bought an iron bedstead and a screen. On returning home, I had the bed set up in the anteroom with the screen around it. This was a bed for her, but I said not a word to her about it. She needed no words to understand. This bed told her that I "had seen it all and knew it all," and that there could be no more doubts. I left the revolver on the table for the night, as always. That night she lay down in silence on this new bed: the marriage was dissolved, she was "vanquished, but not forgiven." During the night she became delirious, and by morning had developed a high fever. She was in bed for six weeks.

Chapter Two

Article 1. A Dream of Pride

Lukeria has just announced that she will not go on living here and will leave as soon as the mistress has been buried. I spent five minutes on my knees in prayer. I wanted to pray for an hour, but I kept thinking and thinking, and all my thoughts were painful. My head aches—so how can I pray? It would only be a sin! It's strange as well that I don't feel sleepy: when there is an immense grief—one that can scarcely be borne—one always wants to sleep, at least after the first paroxysms. I've heard that those condemned to death sleep exceptionally soundly on the last night. And so it should be; this is nature's way; otherwise they wouldn't have the strength. . . . I lay down on the sofa, but I couldn't fall asleep. . . .

. . . We looked after her day and night for the six weeks of her illness— I, Lukeria, and a trained nurse whom I hired from the hospital. I didn't begrudge the money and even wanted to spend it on her. I called in Dr. Schroeder and paid him ten rubles per visit. When she regained consciousness I spent less time around her. Still, why bother to describe all this? When she was completely on her feet again, she quietly and without a word sat herself down in my room at a special table which I had also bought for her at that time. . . . Yes, it's true: we said not a word to one another. Well, actually, we did begin speaking later on, but only about quite ordinary things. I made a point, of course, of not letting myself talk too much, but I could see very well that she, too, was happy not to say more than she had to. It seemed to me that this was absolutely natural on her part: "She's too distraught, and feels too crushed," I thought, "and naturally I have to give her time to forget and to come to terms." And so it was that we went on in silence, although privately I was constantly preparing myself for the future. I assumed that she was doing the same thing, and I found it awfully intriguing to speculate on just what was going on in her mind.

One more thing: no one knows, of course, how much I suffered while grieving over her during her illness. But I suffered in silence and stifled my groans even from Lukeria. I couldn't imagine, I couldn't even suppose, that she might die before learning everything. But when she was out of danger and her health began to return, I recall that I quickly recovered my composure. Besides, I had decided to *put off our future* as far as possible and keep things in their present form for the time being. Yes, something very odd and peculiar happened to me then—I don't know how else to describe it. I was triumphant, and the very awareness of that turned out to be quite sufficient for me. And so the whole winter passed this way. Oh, I was satisfied as I had never been before, and for the whole winter.

You see, there had been one terrible external event in my life which up to this point—that is, until the catastrophe with my wife—had oppressed me every day and every hour: this was my loss of reputation and my leaving the regiment. To put it briefly, there had been a tyrannical injustice committed against me. It is true that my fellow officers did not like me because I was not an easy person to get along with and, perhaps, because there was an element of the ridiculous about me, although it often happens that something which you revere and regard as sublime and sacred will at the same time be cause for the amusement of your whole crowd of friends. Oh, even in school people never liked me. No one anywhere ever liked me. Even Lukeria isn't able to like me. That same incident in the regiment, while a consequence of the general dislike for me, still was largely a matter of chance. I mention this because there is nothing more offensive and painful than to be ruined by a matter of chance, by something that might or might not have happened, by an unlucky conglomeration of circumstances that might have simply passed over like a cloud. For an intelligent creature this is humiliating. The incident happened as follows.

Once, in the theater, I went to the bar during the intermission. The hussar A——v came in suddenly and, in the presence of all the officers and general public who were standing there, began loudly telling two of his fellow hussars that Captain Bezumtsev of our regiment had only just caused a disgraceful row in the corridor and that "he was drunk, by the look of it." This conversation did not go any further, and it was a mistake in any case, since Captain Bezumtsev was not drunk and, strictly speaking, the row wasn't really a row. The hussars began speaking of something else, and there the matter ended. But the next day the story had reached our regiment and talk at once began to the effect that I had been the only officer of our regiment present in the bar, and that when the hussar

A——v had made such an impertinent remark about Captain Bezumtsev,
I had not gone up and rebuked him. But what would have been the point
of that? If he had a grudge against Bezumtsev, then it was their personal
affair; why should I get involved? Meanwhile, our officers began insisting
that it was not a personal affair but concerned the regiment as a whole;
and since I was the only officer of our regiment present, in failing to act I
had proved to all the other officers and civilians in the bar that our regiment could have officers who were not particularly fussy about their own
honor and the honor of their regiment. I could not agree with such a view.
They let me know that I could correct the matter even now—although
belatedly—by asking for a formal explanation from A——v. I did not want
to do this, and in my exasperation I gave them a haughty refusal. Then I
resigned at once. That's the whole story. I left the regiment proudly, yet
crushed in spirit. My will and my mind had suffered a very severe blow.
At the same time, as it happened, my sister's husband in Moscow had
squandered our modest legacy, including my own tiny share in it, so I
was left on the street without a penny. I could have taken some civilian
job, but I didn't: after wearing a brilliant uniform I couldn't accept work
for some railway. And so: if it's to be shame, let it be shame; if disgrace,
then disgrace; if degradation, then degradation—the worse, the better.
That is what I chose. Thereafter, three years of gloomy memories, and
even the Viazemsky house. A year and a half ago a wealthy old woman,
my godmother, died in Moscow, and to my surprise she left me (among
her other bequests) three thousand rubles. I thought things over for a
time and then chose my fate. I decided on a pawnshop, offering apologies
to no one: money, then a cozy home and, at last, a new life far removed
from my old memories—that was my plan. Nevertheless, my gloomy
past and my once honorable reputation, now destroyed forever, haunted
me every hour and every minute. But then I married. Whether that was
chance or not I don't know. But when I brought her into my house I
thought that I was bringing in a friend, and I was so much in need of a
friend. But I saw clearly that I had to train my friend, that I had to add
the final touches to her, even conquer her. And could I have explained
it all at once to this sixteen-year-old with her prejudices? For example,
how could I, without the chance assistance of the terrible catastrophe
with the revolver, have convinced her that I was not a coward and that
my regiment had unjustly accused me of cowardice? But the catastrophe

came along at the right moment. When I held up against the revolver, I
avenged myself on all my gloomy past. And even though no one knew
about it, *she* knew, and that meant everything to me, because she herself
meant everything to me—all my hope for the future of my dreams! She
was the only human being whom I was developing for myself, and I
had no need of any other. And now she had discovered it all; she had
discovered, at least, that she had been unjust in rushing off to ally herself
with my enemies. I was delighted by this thought. I could no longer be
a scoundrel in her eyes, merely an odd sort of fellow. But after everything that had happened, even this thought was not entirely displeasing
to me. Oddness is not a vice; on the contrary, women sometimes find it
attractive. In short, then, I was deliberately putting off the denouement:
what had already happened was, for the moment, more than enough to
ensure my peace of mind and contained abundant images and material
for me to dream about. That's the trouble, you see: I am a dreamer. I
had enough raw material for myself, and as for her, I thought that she
could *wait*.

And so the whole winter passed in a kind of expectation of something.
I loved to steal glances at her as she sat at her little table. She would work
at her sewing, and sometimes in the evening would read books she took
from my shelf. The selection of books on my shelf also should have testified on my behalf. She scarcely went out at all. Just before dusk every day,
after dinner, I would take her out for a walk for the sake of some exercise,
but not in complete silence as before. I tried to keep up the appearance
that we were not keeping silent but talking cordially; but as I said, neither
of us spoke too much. I did this deliberately; as for her, I thought it was
essential to "give her some time." It's odd, of course, that it was almost the
end of winter before it occurred to me that while I loved to steal glances
at her, never once through the winter did I catch her looking at me! I
thought this was simply a matter of her shyness. Besides, she had a look
of such submissive timidity, such weakness after her illness. No, better
wait and "suddenly she will approach you herself. . . ."

I was absolutely delighted by this thought. I'll add one thing more:
sometimes, as if deliberately, I would work myself up and in fact push my
emotions and my mind to the point where I actually seemed to feel as if
she had offended me. And so it continued for some time. But my hatred
never managed to ripen and take root in my inner being. And I myself felt

that this was really only a game of some sort. And even then, although I had dissolved the marriage when I bought the cot and the screen, I never ever regarded her as a guilty party. That was not because I judged her offense lightly, but because I had the sense to forgive her completely, from the very first day, even before I bought the cot. In short, it was an oddity on my part, for I am a morally strict person. To the contrary: I could see that she was so vanquished, so humbled, so crushed, that there were times when I was in an agony of pity for her, even while sometimes being absolutely pleased with the notion of her humiliation. The idea of this inequality between us appealed to me. . . .

That winter I deliberately did several good deeds. I forgave two loans; I loaned money to one poor woman without a pawn. And I said nothing to my wife about it, and did not do it in order for her to find out; but the old woman herself came to thank me, almost on her knees. And so the deed became known. I think that my wife truly was pleased to learn about the old woman.

But spring was coming on. It was already the middle of April, the storm windows had been taken down and the sun began to bring bright patches of light into our silent rooms. But a shroud hung before me and blinded my reason. That terrible, fateful shroud! How did it happen that it all suddenly fell away from my eyes and that suddenly my sight was restored and I understood it all! Was it a matter of chance, or had the appointed day simply arrived, or was it a ray of sunlight that kindled the thought and the surmise in my benumbed mind? No, it was not a thought and not a surmise; it was a little vein that suddenly began to throb, a little vein that had all but atrophied but which twitched and came to life, bringing new feeling to my benumbed soul and exposing my diabolical pride. At the time it seemed as though I leapt from my chair. And it happened suddenly, when I least expected it. It happened before evening, about five o'clock, after dinner. . . .

Article 2. Suddenly the Shroud Fell Away

A word or two first. As long as a month before I had noticed a peculiar sort of melancholy in her. It wasn't just her silence, it was real melancholy. That also I noticed suddenly. She was sitting at her work, her head bent over her sewing, and she didn't notice that I was looking at her. And it suddenly struck me right then how thin and gaunt she had become; her face was pale, her lips white. All this, together with her melancholy, gave me a great shock. Even before this I had heard her little dry cough, especially at nights. I got up at once to call Doctor Schroeder, saying nothing to her.

Schroeder came the next day. She was quite surprised and looked first at Schroeder, then at me.

"But I'm quite well," she said, smiling uncertainly.

Schroeder did not give her a very careful examination (the haughty manner of these medical men sometimes doesn't permit them to be careful) and told me only, in the next room, that this was a result of her illness and that when spring came it would not be a bad idea to go to the seaside or, if that were impossible, simply to move to a country place. In short, he didn't tell me anything except that she was sickly or something of the sort. When Schroeder left she said once more, looking at me with terrible seriousness, "I am quite, quite well."

But having said that she blushed at once, evidently from shame. Evidently it was shame. Oh, now I understand: she felt ashamed that I, who was still *her husband,* was looking after her just as if I still were her real husband. But at that time I did not understand and assumed she blushed out of modesty. (The shroud!)

And so it was, a month after this, some time after four o'clock on a bright, sunny day in April, I was sitting in the shop checking my accounts. Suddenly I heard her, sitting in our room and working at her table, begin ever so softly . . . to sing. This new event surprised me enormously, and even now I do not understand it. Previously I had scarcely ever heard her sing—oh, perhaps in the very first days after I brought her home, when we still could rollick about, target shooting with the pistol. Then her voice was still quite strong and clear, although not always true, but very pleasant and sound. But now her little song was so weak. I don't mean to say it was mournful (it was an old love song of some sort); but it was as if something in her voice had cracked and broken, as if her little voice could not cope any more, as if the song itself were ill. She was singing in a low voice which rose and then suddenly broke off—such a poor little voice, and it broke off so pitifully. She cleared her throat and once more began to sing ever so quietly. . . .

You may laugh at my getting upset, but no one will ever understand why I was so moved! No, I still wasn't sorry for her; this was something quite different. At first, at least in the first moments, I felt suddenly perplexed and greatly surprised, strangely and terribly, painfully and almost spitefully surprised: "She's singing, and in my presence! *Has she forgotten about me or what?*"

Completely shocked, I remained at my place for a time; then I suddenly rose, took my hat, and went out, scarcely knowing what I was doing. At least I didn't know where I was going and why. Lukeria came to help me with my overcoat.

"She's singing?" I couldn't help but ask Lukeria. She did not understand and looked at me, still uncomprehending; however, it's no surprise that she failed to understand me.

"Is that the first time she's been singing?"

"No, she sometimes sings when you're not home," Lukeria answered.

I recall it all. I went down the stairs, onto the street, and set off with no notion of where I was going. I reached the corner and stared off into the distance. People passed and jostled me, but I didn't feel anything. I hailed a cab and told the driver to take me to the Police Bridge—Lord knows why. Then, suddenly, I gave him twenty kopecks and dismissed him.

"That's for your trouble," I said, laughing senselessly; in my heart, however, a sort of ecstasy suddenly welled up.

I turned toward home, increasing my pace. The poor, cracked, broken note began to ring in my soul once more. I could scarcely catch my breath. The shroud was falling from my eyes! If she could start singing in my presence, it meant she had forgotten about me—that was clear and that was dreadful. My heart could sense that. But rapture radiated in my soul and overcame the dread.

Oh, the irony of fate! You see, there had been nothing and could not have been anything in my soul that whole winter apart from this rapturous feeling. But where had I been all winter? Was I aware of what was happening in my soul? I ran up the stairs in a great rush; I don't recall if I had any apprehension when I entered the room. I remember only that the whole floor seemed to undulate beneath my feet and I moved as if floating down a river. I came into the room; she was sitting in her usual place sewing, her head bent over her work, but wasn't singing any more. She cast a passing, uncurious glance at me; in fact, it was not a glance but merely an instinctive and indifferent gesture, the kind directed at anyone who enters a room.

I made straight for her and took a chair close beside her, like one scarcely in his right mind. She glanced quickly at me, as if taking fright; I took her hand and don't recall what I said to her—or rather, what I tried to say to her, because I couldn't even speak properly. My voice had broken and would not obey me. And in any case, I didn't know what to say; I was gasping for breath.

"Let's talk . . . you know . . . say something to me!" I babbled something stupid. How could I collect my thoughts? She shuddered and drew back in great fear, staring at my face. But suddenly I could see *stern amazement* in her eyes. Amazement, yes, and it was *stern*. She looked at me wide-eyed. This sternness, this stern amazement was like a blow that shattered my skull. "So is it still love you want? Is it love?" This was what her amazed expression seemed to be asking me, although she still didn't say a word. But I could read everything, absolutely everything. I felt a tremor pass through my whole being and I simply collapsed at her feet. Yes, I fell down at her feet. She leapt up quickly, but with extraordinary strength I grasped both her hands to hold her back.

And I understood the full depth of my despair, I understood it completely! But—can you believe it?—my soul was so overflowing with rapture that I thought I would die. I kissed her feet in happiness, in ecstasy. Yes, in immeasurable, boundless happiness—and this with complete awareness of the hopelessness of my despair! I wept, I tried to say something but could not. Her frightened and amazed expression suddenly changed to one of concern, to a look of profound questioning, and she gazed at me strangely, even wildly; there was something she wanted to understand at once and she smiled. She felt terribly ashamed that I was kissing her feet and pulled them away, but I at once began kissing the spot on the floor where her feet had been. She noticed that and laughed with embarrassment (you know how people laugh with embarrassment). She was about to go into hysterics, I could see; her hands were trembling. But I wasn't thinking about that and kept mumbling that I loved her, that I would not get up: "Let me kiss the hem of your dress . . . let me worship you this way for the rest of my life. . . ." I don't know—I don't remember, but suddenly she broke into shudders and sobs; a terrible fit of hysterics began. I had frightened her.

I carried her over to the bed. When her fit had passed, she sat up on the edge of the bed, and with a terribly distraught air she seized my hands and begged me to calm down: "Enough! Don't torment yourself, calm down!" And she began to cry again. I didn't leave her the whole evening. I kept telling her that I would take her to Boulogne to bathe in the sea—right away, this moment, in two weeks; that her poor voice was so weak, as I had heard the other day; that I would close the shop, sell it to Dobronravov; that everything would begin anew. Above all, Boulogne, Boulogne! She listened, growing more frightened all the while. But the most important thing for me was not that, it was my urge—which grew ever stronger—to lie down again at her feet, to kiss them, to kiss the ground on which her feet stood, to worship her. "There is nothing, nothing more that I ask of you," I kept repeating. "Don't say anything, don't pay any attention to me, just let me sit in the corner and look at you. Turn me into your thing, your lapdog. . . ." She wept.

"And I thought you would just let me go on like that." This burst forth from her involuntarily, so much so that perhaps she wasn't even aware of saying it. And meanwhile—oh, this was the most important thing, the most fateful thing she said, the thing I understood best during that whole evening, and it was like a knife slashing my heart! It made everything clear to me, everything! But as long as she was by my side, as long as I could look at her, hope was overpowering and I was terribly happy. Oh, I exhausted her terribly that evening and I knew it, but I kept thinking that I would at once be able to remake everything anew. At last, much later in the evening, she became completely exhausted; I persuaded her to go to sleep, and she at once fell into a sound sleep. I expected that she might become delirious, and she was delirious, but only very slightly. I kept getting up during the night and tiptoeing quietly in my slippers to have a look at her. I wrung my hands over her, looking at that frail creature on that poor little bed, that iron cot I had bought her for three rubles. I got down on my knees but did not dare kiss her feet while she slept (without her permission!). I knelt to pray to God, but jumped up again. Lukeria kept coming out of the kitchen to keep an eye on me. I went out and told her to go to bed and that tomorrow "something altogether different" would begin.

And I believed that, blindly, madly, terribly. Oh, I was drowning in ecstasy! I could barely wait for the next day. The main thing was that I couldn't believe any disaster would happen, despite all the symptoms.

My good sense had still not entirely returned to me, despite the shroud that had fallen; it did not return for a very long time—oh, not until today, not until this very day!! But then how could my good sense have returned to me then: she was still alive, after all; she was right before me, and I before her. "She'll wake up tomorrow and I'll tell her all this, and she will see everything." That was how I thought at the time—simply and clearly—and that was why I was in ecstasy! The main thing was this trip to Boulogne. For some reason I kept thinking that Boulogne was everything, that something conclusive would happen in Boulogne. "To Boulogne, to Boulogne! . . ." And with that insane thought I awaited the morning.

Article 3. I Understand All Too Well

Why this was only a few days ago, five days, just five days ago, last Tuesday! No, no, if there had been only a little more time, if only she had waited just a little and—and I would have cleared away all the fog that surrounded us! But she did calm down, didn't she? The next day she listened to me with a smile, despite her confused state of mind. . . . The main thing was that this whole time, all five days, she was in a state of confusion or shame. And she was afraid, too, very much afraid. I won't dispute it; I won't contradict you like some madman: she was frightened, but why shouldn't she be, after all? We had been like strangers to one another for such a long time, you see; we had grown so far apart from one another, and then suddenly all this. . . . But I paid no attention to her fear; our new life was shining before my eyes! . . . It's true, absolutely true, that I made a mistake. And perhaps there were even many mistakes. Just as soon as we woke the next day I made a mistake, right that same morning (this was on Wednesday): I suddenly made her my friend. I was in far too great a rush, of course, but I absolutely needed to confess—much more than confess, in fact! I didn't even hide the things that I had been hiding from myself my whole life. I declared frankly that all winter long I had thought of nothing but the certainty of her love for me. I explained to her that my pawnshop had only been the perversion of my mind and my will, my personal idea of both punishing and exalting myself. I explained that in the theater bar I truly had been a coward—it was a matter of my character and my overly self-conscious nature: I had been taken aback by the circumstances, by the bar itself; taken aback by the thought that if I did step forward I might make a fool of myself. It wasn't the duel that made me fearful, it was the possibility of making a fool of myself. . . . And later I didn't want to admit it and tormented everyone, and tormented her because of it; in fact, that was the reason I married her—to torment her for my past. I spoke for the most part as if in a delirious fever. She took my hands and begged me to stop: "You are exaggerating . . . you're tormenting yourself." And the tears began again, and again she was on the verge of hysterics! She kept pleading with me to say no more about it and to stop dredging up my past.

I paid no heed to her pleas, or scarcely any heed: Spring! Boulogne! The sun over there, our new sun—that was all I could talk about! I closed the pawnshop and transferred my business to Dobronravov. I suddenly suggested to her that we should give it all away to the poor, apart from the original three thousand which I had inherited from my godmother. That we would use to go to Boulogne, and then return and begin a new life of honest labor. And so it was decided, because she didn't say a word . . . she only smiled. And I think that she smiled more as a matter of tact, so as not to hurt my feelings. I could see, after all, that I was putting a great burden on her, don't think that I was so stupid and such an egotist that I didn't see that. I could see it all, right down to the last detail; I saw it and knew it better than anyone: all my despair stood out for all to see!

I told her everything about me and about her. And about Lukeria. I told her that I had wept. . . . Oh, of course I would talk on other subjects. I was also trying hard not to remind her of certain things. And she even showed some enthusiasm once or twice, I remember that! Why do you say that I looked and saw nothing? And if only *this* had not happened, then everything would have been restored to life again. Why, she was telling me just the other day, when we began talking about reading and what she had read that winter; she laughed when she recalled that scene between Gil Blas and the archbishop of Granada. And how she laughed: sweet, childish laughter, just as she used to, before we were married. (A moment! A moment!) How delighted I was! I was much struck, however, by her mention of the archbishop: so she had found enough happiness and peace of mind to be able to laugh at this masterpiece as she sat there in the winter. That meant she must have begun to recover her stability; she must have begun to believe that I would not leave her *like that.* "I

thought you would just let me go on *like that.*" That's what she told me
that Tuesday! Oh, this was how a ten-year-old girl would think! And yet
she believed, she truly did, that everything in fact would remain *like that:*
she sitting at her table and I at mine, and so we would both go on until we
were sixty. And suddenly I come up to her, the husband; and the husband
needs love! Oh, what misunderstanding, what blindness on my part!

It was also a mistake for me to look at her with such rapture on my
face: I should have kept a grip on myself so my rapture wouldn't frighten
her. And in fact I did keep a grip on myself. I didn't kiss her feet any
more. Never once did I let it show that . . . well, that I was her husband.
Oh, that never entered my mind; I only wanted to worship her! But, you
see, I couldn't keep altogether silent; I had to say something! I suddenly
told her how much I enjoyed her conversation and that I considered her
vastly, incomparably more educated than I, and better developed mentally.
She blushed terribly and said, embarrassed, that I was exaggerating. And
here, like a fool, I couldn't restrain myself and told her of the ecstasy I had
felt that time when I stood outside the door listening to her duel—a duel
of innocence with that creature—and how I delighted in her intelligence,
her brilliant wit, both coupled with her childish naiveté. Her whole body
seemed to shudder and she mumbled something about my exaggeration;
but suddenly her whole face clouded over and she covered it with her
hands and burst into sobs. . . . And here again I couldn't restrain myself:
once more I knelt before her; once more I began kissing her feet; and
once more it ended in her having a fit, as she had on Tuesday. That was
yesterday evening, and the next morning. . . .

The next morning?! Madman, why that was this morning, just a little
while ago!

Listen and try to comprehend: when we sat together by the samovar a
few hours ago (this was after her fit of yesterday), she surprised me by her
air of calm. That's how she was! But I spent the whole night trembling
with terror over what had happened that day. But suddenly she came up
to me, stood before me, folding her hands (only hours ago!), and began to
tell me that she was the guilty party and she knew it, that her crime had
tormented her all winter and was tormenting her even now . . . that she
cherished my magnanimity. . . . "I will be your faithful wife; I will respect
you. . . ." At this point I jumped up and, like a madman, I embraced her! I
kissed her; I kissed her face and her lips, and I kissed her like a husband

for the first time after a long separation. And why did I ever leave her? Only for two hours . . . our passports for abroad. . . . Oh, God! Just five minutes, if only I had come back just five minutes earlier! . . . And here was this crowd of people at our gate, people staring at me. . . . Oh, Lord!

Lukeria says—(oh, now I'll never let Lukeria go; she knows everything. She was here all winter; she'll be able to tell me)—she says that after I left the house, and only some twenty minutes before I came back, she suddenly went to the mistress in our room to ask something—I don't remember what—and noticed that her icon (that same icon of the Virgin Mary) had been removed from the icon case and was standing before her on the table; the mistress, it seemed, had just been praying before it.

"What is it, ma'am?"

"It's nothing, Lukeria, you may go. . . . Wait, Lukeria."

She came up to Lukeria and kissed her.

"Are you happy, ma'am?" Lukeria asked.

"Yes, Lukeria."

"The master should have come to ask your forgiveness a long time ago, ma'am. Thanks be to God you've made it up."

"That's fine, Lukeria," she said. "You may go now."

And she smiled, but oddly somehow. It was such an odd smile that ten minutes later Lukeria came in again to have a look at her: "She was standing by the wall, right near the window, her arm against the wall and her head against her arm, just standing there, thinking. And she was so deep in thought that she didn't even notice me standing there watching her from the other room. I could see she had a kind of smile on her face, standing there, thinking and smiling. I looked at her, turned and went out on tiptoe, wondering about her. But suddenly I heard the window open. Right away I went in to tell her that it was still cool outside and she might catch a cold if she wasn't careful. And I saw that she'd climbed up on the windowsill and was standing upright in the open window, her back to me, holding the icon. My heart just sank inside me, and I shouted 'Ma'am, ma'am!' She heard me and made a move as if to turn toward me, but didn't. She took a step, pressed the icon to her bosom, and leapt out the window!"

I remember only that when I came through the gate she was still warm. The worst thing was that they were all staring at me. They shouted at first, and then suddenly they all fell silent and made way before me, and ... and she was lying there with the icon. I have a vague memory of coming up to her, silently, and looking for a long time. They all surrounded me and were saying something to me. Lukeria was there, but I didn't see her. She tells me she spoke to me. I only remember some fellow shouting to me that "there wasn't but a cupful of blood came out of her mouth, you could hold it in your hand!" And he showed me the blood there on the paving stone. I think I touched the blood and smeared the end of my finger with it; I recall looking at my finger while he kept on: "You could hold it in your hand!"

"What do you mean, in your hand?" I yelled at the top of my voice (so people say) and raised my arms to attack him....

Oh, savage, how savage! A misunderstanding! It's unbelievable! Impossible!

Article 4. I Was Only Five Minutes Late

And isn't it so? Can you believe this? Can you really say it was possible? For what, why did this woman die?

Oh, believe me, I understand; but why she died is still a question. She was frightened by my love, asked herself the solemn question whether to accept it or not, found the question too much for her to bear, and thought it better to die. I know—there's no point racking my brain about it: she had made too many promises and got frightened that she wouldn't be able to keep them; that much is clear. There are some facts about the case that are absolutely terrible.

Because why did she die? The question remains. The question keeps pounding in my brain. I would have left her *like that* if she had wanted to be left *like that*. She didn't believe it, that was the thing! But no, wait, I'm not telling the truth; it wasn't that way at all. It was simply because with me there had to be honesty: if she was going to love me, then she had to love me completely, not as she would have loved that shopkeeper. And since she was too chaste and too pure to compromise on the kind of love that would have satisfied the shopkeeper, she didn't want to deceive me. She didn't want to deceive me with a half-love or a quarter-love that masked itself as complete love. People like her are just too honest, that's the thing! And I wanted to instill some breadth of feeling into her then, you remember? A strange idea.

I'm awfully curious: did she respect me? I wonder, did she despise me or not? I don't think she did despise me. It's awfully queer: why didn't it even once, all winter long, enter my head that she despised me? I was as convinced as could be of the contrary, right until that moment when she looked at me with *stern amazement.* And it was specifically *stern.* At that point I realized at once that she despised me. I realized it unalterably and forever! Ah, let her despise me, even for the rest of her life, but let her go on living! Only hours ago she was still walking about, talking. I simply can't understand how she could have jumped out of the window! And how was I to have suspected it even five minutes before? I've called Lukeria in. I will never let Lukeria go now. Never!

Oh, we still could have come to terms. It was just that we had grown so terribly alienated from one another over the winter. But couldn't we have made that up? Why, oh why couldn't we have come together and begun a new life? I'm a noble, generous person, and so is she: and there's a point in common! Just a few more words, no more than a couple of days, and she would have understood everything.

What hurts me most is that the whole thing was a matter of chance—simple, barbaric, blind chance! That's what hurts! Five minutes, just five short minutes late! Had I arrived five minutes earlier, the moment would have passed over like a cloud and the notion would never have entered her head again. And the result would have been her understanding everything. And now the empty rooms again, and I'm alone again. There's the pendulum ticking; what does it care? It has pity for no one. I have no one now—that's the calamity.

I just keep pacing and pacing the floor. I know, I know—don't tell me: you think it's ridiculous for me to be complaining about a matter of chance and "five minutes." But it's obvious, surely. Just think of this one thing: she didn't even leave a note saying, "Don't blame anyone for my death," as all the others do. Couldn't she have realized that even Lukeria might get into some trouble: "You were alone with her," they could say, "and you pushed her out." They might have dragged Lukeria off to jail if it hadn't been for the four people looking out of the windows of the building in the courtyard. They saw her standing with the icon in her hands and saw her throw herself out. But the fact that there were people standing there looking on is also a matter of chance, you see. No, the whole thing was just a moment, only one unaccountable moment. An impulse, a passing fancy! And what of the fact that she prayed before the icon? That doesn't mean she was saying her prayers just before dying. The moment lasted no more than ten minutes, perhaps; the decision was made just while she was standing by the wall, her head resting against her arm, and smiling. The thought flew into her head, made her dizzy and—and she couldn't resist it.

Say what you like, but this is a clear case of misunderstanding. She could have gone on living with me. And what if anemia were the cause? Simply a case of anemia, of exhaustion of her vital energy? She was worn out from that winter, that's all. . . .

I was too late!!!

How slender she looks in her coffin, and how sharp her little nose has become! Her eyelashes lie straight as arrows. And when she fell she didn't break anything, she wasn't disfigured! There was only this little bit of blood, "you could hold it in your hand." Not more than a spoonful. It was internal concussion. Here's a queer idea: what if I didn't have to bury her? Because if they take her away, then . . . oh, no, it's hardly possible that they can take her away! Oh, of course I know that they should take her away; I'm not a madman and I'm not raving. On the contrary, my mind was never so clear. But how can it be? No one in the house again, these two rooms again, alone with my pawned goods again. I'm raving! Now I'm raving! I tormented her till she couldn't take it any more. That's it!

What do I care for your laws now? What do I care for your customs and your manners, your life, your state, your religion? Let your judge judge me, let them bring me to court, to your public court, and I will say that I don't acknowledge any of it. The judge will shout, "Be silent, sir!" And I will shout in reply: "What force do you have that can compel me now to obey? Why did this blind, immutable force destroy what was dearest to me? Why do I need your laws now? I will withdraw from your world." Oh, what do I care!

She cannot see! She's dead; she cannot hear! You don't know what a paradise I would have created for you. I had a paradise in my soul and I would have planted it all around you! So what if you wouldn't have loved me—what would that matter? Everything would have been *like that,* everything would have remained *like that.* You would only have talked to me as to a friend, and we would have been happy and laughed joyously as we looked into each other's eyes. And so we would have lived. And if you had come to love another, well so be it! You would have walked with him, laughing, and I would have watched you from the other side of the street. . . . I don't care what would have happened, if only she would open her eyes just once! Just for a moment, only one moment, if she would look at me just as she did a little while ago when she stood before me and vowed to be my faithful wife! Oh, in one glance she would understand everything!

Immutability! Oh, nature! People are alone on earth, that's the calamity! "Is there a man alive on the field?" cries the hero of the Russian epic. I cry the same, though not a hero, and no one responds. They say the sun gives life to the universe. The sun will rise and—look at it, is it not a corpse? Everything is dead, and everywhere there are corpses. There are only people alone, and around them is silence—that is the earth! "Love one another." Who said that? Whose commandment is that? The pendulum ticks, unfeelingly, disgustingly. It's two o'clock in the morning. Her little shoes stand by her cot, just as if they were waiting for her. . . . No, in all seriousness, when they take her away tomorrow, what will become of me?

December

CHAPTER ONE

Article 1, extract. More About a Case That Is Not as Simple as It Seems

[...] When I had finished that article and put out the issue of my *Diary*, still in the grip of my own speculations, I decided to try my very best to have a meeting with Kornilova while she was still in prison. I confess that I was very curious to test whether there was any truth in what I had written about Kornilova and speculated about her later. And, indeed, one very fortunate circumstance arose that soon allowed me to visit her and get to know her. And I myself was amazed: imagine, at least three-quarters of my speculations proved to be true. I had discerned what had happened nearly as well as if I had been present myself. Her husband really had visited her, and was continuing to do so; they both really do weep and grieve over one another; they say their farewells and forgive one another. "My little girl would have come," Mrs. Kornilova told me, "but she is in a kind of school now where the children are not allowed out." I regret that I cannot pass on everything that I learned about the life of this devastated family; there are some features of the case that are most curious, in their own way, of course. Oh, naturally I was mistaken in some things; but not in the essentials. For example, although the husband is a peasant, he wears German clothes; he is a good deal younger than I had supposed. He works as a "ladler," dealing with the dyes used for bank notes in the Government Printing Office, and he earns a rather substantial monthly salary for a peasant; thus he is considerably better off than I had supposed. She is a seamstress and works at sewing even now, in prison, where she gets orders and also earns good money. In short, it's not at all a matter of "coarse cloth and felt boots for her journey, tea, and sugar"; the tone of their conversations is rather higher than that. She had given birth a few days before my first visit, not to a son but a daughter, and so on. These are minor differences from my imaginings, but in the main and in the essence there was no mistake at all. [...]

Article 2. A Belated Moral

That October issue of my *Diary* caused me problems of a sort in other ways as well. It contains a short article, "The Sentence," which left me in a certain amount of doubt. This "Sentence" is the confession of a suicide, his last words written to justify himself and, perhaps, to provide a *moral lesson* before he put the gun to his head. Several of my friends, whose opinions I most value, praised my little article but also confirmed my doubts. They praised it for truly discovering what might be called the formula for suicides of this sort, a formula that clearly expresses their essence. But they too were skeptical: would the intent of the article be understood by each and every reader? Might it not, on the contrary, produce just the opposite impression on some? Moreover, might not some of them—those very ones who had already begun to have visions of a revolver or a noose—even be seduced on reading it and have their unfortunate intentions confirmed even more deeply? In short, my friends expressed those very same doubts which had begun to creep into my own mind. As a result, they concluded that the article should have been followed by a clear and simple explanation from the author of his intent in writing it, and even that a clear moral should be added.

I agreed with that. Indeed, I myself, even while writing the article, felt that a moral was essential, yet somehow I felt embarrassed to add one. I felt ashamed to assume that even the most naive of readers would be so simple-minded as to miss the *inner sense* of the article, its intent and its moral. Its intent was so clear to me that I could not help but assume that it was equally clear to everyone. It seems that I was mistaken.

Some years ago one writer observed, quite justly, that it used to be considered shameful for a person to admit he did not understand certain things because it gave direct evidence of his dullness and ignorance, of the stunted development of his mind and heart and the weakness of his mental faculties. But now, by contrast, the phrase "I don't understand it" is very often uttered almost proudly or at least with an air of importance. As far as his listeners are concerned, this phrase at once seems to place the man on a pedestal; what is even more absurd is that he shares his listeners' feelings and isn't the least bit ashamed at the cheapness of the pedestal he has mounted. Nowadays the words "I don't understand a thing about

Raphael" or "I made a point of reading the whole of Shakespeare and I confess that I found absolutely nothing special in him"—these words nowadays might be taken not only as a sign of profound intellect but even as something valorous, almost a great moral accomplishment. And is it only Shakespeare or Raphael who is subjected to such judgment and skepticism these days?

That comment which I paraphrased here regarding people who take pride in their ignorance is quite true. Indeed, the pride of the ignorant has become excessive. Dull or poorly educated people aren't the least bit ashamed of their unfortunate qualities; on the contrary, things seem to have reached the stage where these same qualities even add some life to their characters. I have also often noticed that a strong tendency toward specialization and dissociation has developed in literature and in personal life, and that the polymath is becoming extinct. People who argue with their opponents to the point of frothing at the mouth haven't read a line their opponents have written for decades: "My convictions are different," they say, "and I do not intend to read nonsense like that." It's truly a case of a kopeck's-worth of ammunition and a ruble's-worth of ambition. Such extremes of one-sidedness and seclusion, dissociation and intolerance, have appeared only in our own time, meaning the last twenty years in particular. Along with these things many people display a bold audacity: those having scarcely any learning laugh at those who know and understand ten times as much, and even laugh in their faces. But worst of all is the fact that the more time passes, the more firmly entrenched this "straight-line" approach to things becomes. One can see, for example, a noticeable weakening of the feeling for language, for metaphor and allegory. One can also see that people (generally speaking) have begun to lose their sense of humor, and this itself, according to one German thinker, is one of the surest signs of the intellectual and moral decline of an epoch. What we have, rather, are gloomy dullards with wrinkled brows and narrow minds who can only move in one way, in a single direction along a single straight line. Do you imagine that I'm talking only about our young generation and about our liberals? I assure you that I have our elders and our conservatives in mind as well. As if in imitation of the young generation (who are now gray-haired, however), some twenty years ago there had already appeared strange, straight-line conservatives, irritated little old men, who understood absolutely nothing about current affairs or about the "new people" or the younger generation. Their "straight-linedness," if you can call it that, was sometimes even more severe, harsh, and obtuse than the straight-linedness of the new people. Oh, it's quite possible that all this came from an excess of good intentions and from noble feelings that had been offended by the follies of the time. But still, these people are sometimes more blind than even the latest straight-line individuals. However, I think that in denouncing straight-linedness I have strayed too far from my topic.

As soon as my article appeared I was overwhelmed by inquiries—by letter and in person—about what I meant in my "Sentence." "What are you trying to say here?" people asked; "Aren't you justifying suicide?" Others, so it seemed to me, had found something to be happy about. And so the other day a certain author, a Mr. N. P., sent me his little article, written in a politely abusive style, which he published in Moscow in the weekly *Recreation*. I don't subscribe to *Recreation* and don't believe that it was the editor who sent me this particular issue, so I attribute its receipt to the kindness of the author himself. He condemns and ridicules my article:

> I received the October issue of *A Writer's Diary*, read it, and fell to thinking. There are many good things in this issue, but many *strange* things as well. I will set forth my perplexity in the most concise manner I can. What was the point, for instance, of printing in this issue the "reflections" of one who killed himself out of boredom? I truly do not understand the point of this. These "reflections"—if one can so call the ravings of this semilunatic— have been known for a long time, in somewhat paraphrased form of course, *by all those whose business it is to know such things,* and thus their appearance *in our time,* in the diary of a writer such as F. M. Dostoevsky, serves only as an absurd and pitiful anachronism. Our age is one of *cast-iron conceptions,* an age of positive opinions, an age whose banner bears the motto: "To live by all means! . . ." In everything and everywhere, of course, there are exceptions; there are suicides *with* and *without* deliberation, but no one nowadays pays any attention to such cheap heroics. Heroism of that sort is

only too ridiculous! There was a time when suicide, especially suicide *with deliberation,* was elevated to the level of the greatest "awareness" (but awareness of *what?*) and heroism (again, heroism of what kind?), but that *rotten* time has passed and has passed irretrievably. Thank heaven for that; there is nothing to be regretted in its loss.

Any suicide who dies with deliberation of the sort that was printed in Mr. Dostoevsky's diary deserves no sympathy at all. Such a person is no more than a coarse egotist and attention-seeker and a most harmful member of human society. He is even unable to complete his ridiculous deed without having people talk about it. Even here he is unable to sustain his role and his affectations; he has to write his "reflections," though he could die very well with no reflection at all. . . . Oh, the Falstaffs of life! These knights mounted on stilts! . . .

I felt very depressed after reading this. Good Lord, do I have many readers like this? Did Mr. N. P., who states that my suicide doesn't deserve any compassion, seriously believe that I described his case in order to win him sympathy? Naturally, the single opinion of Mr. N. P. would not have been so important. But the fact is that in the present instance Mr. N. P. surely represents a type, a whole collection of people like himself, a type which is even somewhat similar to that brazen type I was speaking about just now, brazen and single-minded, a type holding those same "cast-iron conceptions" of which Mr. N. P. himself spoke in the excerpt I quoted from his article. The notion that there might be a whole collection of people like that truly scares me. Of course, I may be taking this too much to heart. Yet I'll tell you frankly: despite my sensitivity, I still would not consider writing a reply to this "collection" of people. This is certainly not because I am scornful of them—why not have a little chat with people, after all?—but simply because there is little space in this issue. And so, if I am replying now and sacrificing space, then I am, so to say, answering my own doubts and replying to myself, as it were. I can see that I have to add a moral to my October article, and do so without delay; I must explain its purpose and spell it out in plain words. At least my conscience will be at rest, that's the point.

Article 3. Unsubstantiated Statements

My article "The Sentence" concerns the fundamental and the loftiest idea of human existence: the necessity and the inevitability of the conviction that the human soul is immortal. Underlying this confession of a man who is going to die "by logical suicide" is the necessity of the immediate conclusion, here and now, that without faith in one's soul and its immortality, human existence is unnatural, unthinkable, and unbearable. And it certainly seemed to me that I had clearly expressed the formula of the logical suicide, that I had found the formula. Faith in immortality does not exist for him; he explains that at the very beginning. Little by little the thought of his own aimless existence and his hatred for the unresponsiveness of the stagnant life around him leads to the inevitable conviction of the utter absurdity of human existence on earth. It becomes as clear as day to him that only those people can *consent* to live who are akin to the lower animals and who most closely resemble them through their weakly developed consciousness and their strongly developed and purely carnal needs. They consent to live precisely as animals do, that is, in order to "eat, drink, sleep, build their nests, and raise their young." Oh, yes, eating, sleeping, despoiling the earth, sitting on a soft chair—these things will long attract people to the earth, but cannot attract the higher types of people. Meanwhile, it is the higher types who rule over the earth and who have always ruled; and always the result has been that millions of people follow them when the times demand it. What is the most sublime of words and the most sublime of thoughts? This word, this thought (without which humanity cannot live) is very often first spoken by poor, unknown, and insignificant people who are very often oppressed and who die in oppression and obscurity. But the thought and the word they utter does not die and never disappears without leaving a mark; it can never disappear once it has been uttered—and that is a remarkable thing in human history. In the next generation, or two or three decades later, the thought of a genius already envelops everything and everyone and captures their imaginations—and it turns out that it is not the millions of people who are triumphant, and not the material powers that seem to be so awesome and unshakeable; it is not money, not the sword, not physical might, but the thought that was imperceptible at first—often the thought of one who seemed to be the least among men. Mr. N. P. writes that the appearance of such a confession in my *Diary* "serves" (serves whom and what?) "as an absurd and wretched anachronism," for now we have "an age of cast-iron convictions, an age of positive opinions, an age that holds up a banner with the slogan 'To live by all means!' . . ." (Indeed! That's probably just why suicide has become so prevalent among our educated class.) I can assure the respected Mr. N. P. and all those like him that when the time comes, all this "cast iron" will be swept away like down before some idea, no matter how insignificant that idea may at first seem to these gentlemen of "cast-iron convictions." For me personally, however, one of the most dreadful portents for our future, and even for our very near future, lies in the very fact that, in my view, in an all-too-large portion of educated Russians, by some particular, strange . . . well, let me call it predestination—there has taken root more and more, and with remarkable progressive rapidity, an absolute lack of faith in one's soul and its immortality. And this lack of faith takes root not only through a conviction (we still have very few convictions about anything); it does so through some strange, universal indifference to this most sublime idea of human existence, an indifference at times even derisive. God only knows what laws caused it to become established among us. It is an indifference not only to this idea alone but toward everything that is vital and expresses the truth of life, toward everything that generates and nourishes life, gives it health, and does away with corruption and putrefaction. In our time this indifference is even almost a Russian peculiarity, at least in comparison with other European nations. It has long since permeated the educated Russian family and has all but destroyed it. Neither a person nor a nation can exist without some higher idea. And there is *only one* higher idea on earth, and it is the idea of the immortality of the human soul, for all other "higher" ideas of life by which humans might live *derive from that idea alone.* Others may dispute this point with me (about the unity of the source of all higher things on earth, I mean), but I am not going to get into an argument just yet and simply set forth my idea in unsubstantiated form. It cannot be explained all at once, and it will be better to do it little by little. There will be time to do this in the future.

The man I told you about who committed suicide is indeed a passionate exponent of his idea—that is, the necessity of suicide—and not an indifferent or "cast-iron" sort of person. He is truly tormented and suffering, and I think I conveyed that clearly enough. It is all too clear to him that he cannot go on living, and he is utterly convinced that he is correct and cannot be refuted. He cannot escape confronting the highest and most fundamental questions: "What is the point of living when he is already aware that it is disgusting, abnormal, and inadequate for a human to live like an animal? And what is there to keep him living on earth in such a case?" He can find no answers to these questions and he knows it, for although he has realized that there exists, as he expresses it, "a harmony of the whole," still, he says, "I don't understand it and I never will be able to understand it. That I will never be able to share in that harmony is the necessary and inevitable conclusion." And it was this sort of clear-cut conclusion that led him to his end. So what was the trouble here? Where did he make his mistake? The trouble was entirely in his loss of faith in immortality.

But he himself is avidly seeking (at least he was seeking, while he lived, and his quest caused him real pain) some reconciliation; he tried to find it in "love for humanity." "If not I, then at least humanity as a whole may be happy and someday attain harmony. This notion might have kept me living on earth," he says. And of course this is a noble thought, the noble thought of a martyr. But the inescapable conviction that the life of humanity as a whole is essentially only such a moment as his own life, and that on the day after this "harmony" is achieved (if one can believe that this dream can be achieved), humanity will be transformed into just such a *nonentity* as he through the force of the immutable laws of nature, and this after all the sufferings borne in realizing this dream—this thought fills him with utter indignation precisely because of his love for humanity. He feels insulted on behalf of all of humanity and, by virtue of the law of reflection of ideas, even his original love for humanity is destroyed. In just the same fashion, it more than once has been noted how, in a family dying of starvation the father or mother, toward the end when the sufferings of the children have become unbearable, will begin to hate those same children whom they had previously loved so much, precisely because their suffering has become *unbearable*. Moreover, I maintain that the awareness of one's own utter inability to assist or bring any aid or relief at all to suffering humanity, coupled with one's complete conviction of the existence of that suffering, can even *transform the love for humanity in your heart to hatred for humanity*. Those gentlemen of cast-iron convictions will not believe this, of course, and won't even understand it: for them,

love for humanity and its happiness are such cheap things; everything
has been so conveniently arranged, and has been given and set down
for so long, that it is not worth even thinking about. But I intend to give
them a good laugh: I declare (again, without substantiation, at least *for
the moment*) that love for humanity is even entirely unthinkable, incomprehensible, and *utterly impossible without faith in the immortality of
the human soul to go along with it.* Those who deprived humanity of
its faith in its own immortality want to replace that faith, in the sense of
the highest purpose of existence, by "love for humanity." Those people,
I say, are raising their hands against themselves; for in place of love for
humanity they plant in the heart of one who has lost his faith the seed of
hatred for humanity. Let all those wise men of cast-iron convictions shrug
their shoulders at this statement of mine. But this thought is wiser than
their wisdom, and I believe without a doubt that it will someday become
an axiom for humanity. Once more, though, I am setting forth this idea as
well without substantiation—for the moment, at least.

I even affirm and venture to declare that love for humanity *in general* is,
as an idea, one of the most difficult ideas for the human mind to comprehend. Precisely as an idea. Feeling alone can justify it. But such a feeling
is possible only with the conviction of the immortality of the human soul
to accompany it. (Again, an unsubstantiated assertion.)

The result, clearly, is that when the idea of immortality is lost, suicide
becomes an absolute and inescapable necessity for any person who
has even developed slightly above the animal level. On the other hand,
immortality, promising eternal life, binds people all the more firmly to
earth. This, it would seem, is a contradiction: if there is so much life—that
is, if there is an eternal one apart from the earthly—then why place such a
value on this earthly life? But it turns out to be just the contrary: for only
with faith in his immortality does a person comprehend his whole wise
purpose on earth. Without the conviction of his immortality, the links
between the person and the earth are broken; they grow more fragile,
they decay, and the loss of a higher meaning in life (experienced at least
in the form of unconscious anguish) surely brings suicide in its wake.
Working back from this point, I derive the moral to my October article:
"If the conviction of immortality is so essential for human existence, then
it follows that it is the normal state of humanity; and if that is the case,
then the very immortality of the human soul *exists with certainty.*" In

short, the idea of immortality is life itself, life in the full sense; it is its final
formula and humanity's principal source of truth and understanding.
That was the purpose of my article, and I supposed that it could not help
but be clear to everyone who read it.

Article 5, extract. On Suicide and Arrogance

[...] And, in conclusion, something quite comical. In that same October
issue I informed my readers about the suicide of the daughter of an
emigrant: "She soaked a piece of cotton wool in chloroform, bound this
to her face, and lay down on the bed. And so she died. Before her death
she wrote a note: 'I am setting off on a long journey. If the suicide should
not succeed, then let everyone gather to celebrate my resurrection with
glasses of Cliquot. If I do succeed, I ask that you not bury me until you
have determined that I am completely dead, because it is most unpleasant
to awaken in a coffin underground. That would not be *chic* at all!'"
    Mr. N.P. mounted his high horse after reading of this "frivolous"
suicide and decided that her act "merits no attention at all." He was
angry at me for my "exceedingly naive" question about which of the two
suicides suffered more on earth. But then there was an absurd note. He
unexpectedly added: "I daresay that a person who wants to *greet* her
return to life with a glass of champagne in her hand" (where else?) "could
not have *suffered* very much in this life if she chooses to enter it again with
such ceremony and without altering her way of life one bit, in fact, not
even considering any alterations...."
    What a funny thing to say! What beguiled him most of all was the
champagne: "Anyone who drinks champagne cannot possibly suffer."
But you see, if she had loved champagne so much, then she would have
gone on living in order to drink it; but as it was, she wrote about the
champagne just before her death—before the serious fact of death—
knowing full well that she would certainly die. She could not have had
much faith in her chances of recovery, and recovery, in any case, did not
hold any attraction for her since it only meant a recovery for another
attempt at suicide. So the champagne is of no real consequence here;
she had no intention of drinking it. Does that really require explanation? She mentioned the champagne simply out of the desire to make an

outlandish and cynical statement when dying. She settled on champagne because she could find no picture more vile and obscene than sipping champagne at her "resurrection from the dead." She had to write this obscenity as an insult to everything she was leaving on earth, to curse the earth and her earthly life, to spit on it and so make that spitting her final statement to those friends she was leaving behind. What was the cause of such malice in this seventeen-year-old girl? (N.B.: She was seventeen, and not twenty, as I wrote in my article. Several people who knew more about the case corrected me afterward.) And at whom was the malice directed? No one had offended her; she was not wanting for anything; she died, apparently, also for no reason whatsoever. But it was precisely that note, precisely the fact that at such a moment she was so *concerned* to make such an obscene and outlandish statement that (obviously) leads one to the thought that her life had been immeasurably purer than this grotesque obscenity would suggest, and that the malice, the boundless bitterness of this gesture testifies, rather, to the great suffering and pain she had borne and her despair at the final moment of her life. Had her death been caused by some apathetic boredom that she herself could not recognize, she would not have made this grotesque statement. One must take a more compassionate attitude toward such a spiritual condition as hers. Obviously she was suffering, and certainly she died from spiritual yearning, having undergone great inner torment. What was it that caused her so much torment in her seventeen years? But here we raise the terrible question of our age. I have suggested that she died from heartache (much too precocious a heartache) and from a sense of the pointlessness of life, solely the result of the warped theory of child-rearing in her parents' home, a theory with a mistaken concept of the higher meaning and purposes of life, a theory that deliberately destroyed in her soul any faith in its immortality. Let this be only my suggestion; but surely she did not die only in order to leave this mean little note behind her so as to astonish people, as Mr. N.P. supposes. "No man shall hate his flesh." Destroying one's self is a serious thing, despite any *chic* that may be involved, and an epidemic of self-destruction spreading among the educated classes is an extremely serious thing which warrants constant observation and examination. A year and a half ago one highly talented and competent member of our judicial system showed me a bundle of letters and notes he had collected that were written by suicides, in their own hand, immediately before they had taken their lives, i.e., five minutes before death. I can recall two lines written by a fifteen-year-old girl; I also recall a note scribbled in pencil, written in a moving carriage in which the man shot himself before reaching his destination. I think that if Mr. N.P. had even glanced through this most interesting bundle of letters, then even in his soul, perhaps, there might have been a certain change and his peaceful heart would have become troubled. But I don't know for certain. In any case, one must look at these facts with greater compassion, and certainly not with such arrogance. We ourselves, perhaps, are to blame for these facts, and there is no cast iron that will later save us from the disastrous consequences of our complacency and arrogance when, in the fullness of time, we suffer the consequences.

But that's enough. My reply has been made, not to Mr. N.P. alone, but to many Messrs. N.P.

from CHAPTER TWO

Article 1. A Story from the Lives of Children

Let me tell you about this so that I won't forget it.

On the outskirts of Petersburg—in fact, even beyond the outskirts—there live a mother and her twelve-year-old daughter. The family is not well-off, but the mother has a job and earns her own living. The daughter attends school in Petersburg and always travels by public coach, which makes several scheduled trips a day between the Gostiny Dvor and the place where they live.

And so, recently, a couple of months ago, just at the time when winter so quickly and unexpectedly set in with a week of calm, bright days and a few degrees of frost and it first became possible to travel by sled, the mother looked at her daughter one evening and said: "Sasha, I don't see you studying your lessons. I haven't seen you do anything for some days now. Do you know your lessons?"

"Oh, Mama, don't worry; everything's done. I've even prepared a whole week ahead."

"Well, then, I suppose it's all right."

Sasha went off to school the next day; sometime after five o'clock the conductor of the coach on which Sasha was to return home jumped off as he was passing their house and handed Mama a note from her which read as follows: "Dear Mama, I have been a very bad girl all week. I got three zeros and I've been lying to you all the time. I'm ashamed to come home, and I'm never coming back again. Good-bye, dear Mama, forgive me. Your Sasha."

You can well imagine how the mother felt. She naturally wanted to drop everything at once, rush off to the city, and somehow try to find her Sasha. But where should she look? How could she ever find her? A close friend of the family happened to be there; he was deeply concerned about the matter and volunteered to go at once to Petersburg to make inquiries at the school and then to check at all the homes of her acquaintances; if need be, he would search all night long. The main consideration that led the mother to put her trust in the deep concern of this kind man and stay at home herself was that, should Sasha think better of her decision and come back, she might leave again if she did not find her mother there. They decided that if Sasha were not found by morning, they would notify the police at dawn. The mother spent some very difficult hours at home, which you can well understand without my description.

"And so," the mother relates, "about ten o'clock I suddenly heard the familiar, hurried little steps in the snow outside and then on the stairs. The door opened, and there was Sasha."

"Mama, dear Mama, I'm so glad I came back to you!"

She clasped her little hands together, then hid her face behind them and sat down on the bed. She was so tired and worn out. Well then, of course, came the first cries and the first questions. The mother proceeded very cautiously, still afraid to reproach her daughter.

"Oh, Mama, after I told you those lies yesterday about my lessons I made up my mind: I wasn't going to go to school anymore and I wasn't going to come back home; because once I stopped going to school, how could I lie to you every day and tell you that I was?"

"But what on earth were you going to do? If you weren't at school and you weren't living here, then where would you go?"

"I thought I'd live on the street. As soon as it was day, I'd just keep walking around the streets. I've got a warm coat, and if I got cold I could stop in at the Arcade. I could buy a roll for my dinner every day, and I'd manage to find something to drink—there's snow on the ground now. One roll would be enough. I've got fifteen kopecks, and a roll costs three, so that's five days."

"And then?"

"And then I don't know what. I hadn't thought about it."

"And at night? Where were you planning to spend your nights?"

"Oh, I've thought about that. When it got dark and late I was going to go to the railway, way past the station where there aren't any people around, but there're an awful lot of railway cars. I'd crawl into one of those cars that looked like it wouldn't be moved anywhere and spend the night. And I did go there. I walked a long way, well past the station, and there wasn't a soul around. Off to one side I saw some cars, but not at all like the ones everyone rides in. There, I thought, I'll crawl into one of those and nobody will see me. I was just starting to get in, and suddenly a watchman shouted at me: 'Where do you think you're going? Those cars are for hauling dead people.'

"As soon as I heard that I jumped down; but I could see he was already getting close."

" 'What do you think you're doing here?' "

"I just ran away from him as fast as I could go. He shouted something, but I just ran off. I went along, scared out of my wits. I came back to the street and I'm walking around when suddenly I see a building, a big stone house that's being built—it's only just bare bricks, no glass in the windows and no doors—they're boarded up—and there's a fence around it. Well, I think, if I can somehow get into that house, no one will see me there 'cause it's dark. I went down a little alleyway and found a spot where the boards were open enough for me to squeeze through. So I squeezed through and came right into a pit, still full of earth; I felt my way along the wall to a corner where there were some boards and bricks. Well, I thought, I can spend the night here on these boards. And so I lay down. But all of I sudden I hear voices speaking ever so quietly. I raised my head and right in the corner I hear people talking in low voices and I see someone's eyes that seem to be staring right at me. I was scared out of my wits and right away I ran out through that same door and onto the street again. I can hear them calling after me. I managed to slip away. And here I had thought that there was no one in the house!

"When I got back on the street again I suddenly felt so tired. So very, very tired. I walk around the streets, there're people about; what time it is I don't know. I came out on Nevsky Prospect and I'm walking by the Gostiny Dvor, crying my eyes out. 'Now,' I think, 'if only some nice person would come along and take pity on a poor little girl who has nowhere to spend the night. I'd tell him everything, and he'd say: "Come and stay with us for the night." ' I keep thinking about that as I walk along, and suddenly I look up and see our coach standing there, ready to start off for its last trip here. And I thought it had surely left a long time ago. 'Ah,' I think, I'll go back to Mama!' I got on the coach, and now I'm so glad that I came back, Mama. I'll never lie to you again, and I'll study hard! Oh, Mama, Mama!"

"And so I asked her," the mother went on, "Sasha, did you really think up this whole plan yourself—about not going to school and living on the streets?"

"Well, Mama, you see, quite a while ago I made friends with a girl my age, only she's at a different school. But can you believe she hardly ever goes to school—she just tells them at home every day that she goes. She told me that she's bored in school, but it's lots of fun on the street. 'Once I leave the house,' she says, 'I just keep walking around. I haven't showed up at school for two weeks now. I look in the windows of the shops; I go to the Arcade, I eat a roll. And when evening comes, I go home.' When I heard that I thought: 'That's what I'd like to do.' And school started to seem so dull. But I didn't have the least notion of actually doing it until yesterday. And yesterday, after I lied to you, I made up my mind. . . .'"

This story is true. Now, of course, the mother has taken some precautions. When the story was told to me I thought that it might fit very well into my *Diary*. I was given permission to publish it, without revealing the real names of the participants, of course. Naturally I will at once hear objections: "This is only one isolated case, and it happened simply because the girl was very stupid." I know for certain that the girl is not at all stupid. I also know that in these young souls, already past early childhood but still far from attaining even the first stage of maturity, there sometimes arise amazing, fantastic notions, dreams, and intentions. This age (twelve or thirteen years) is an unusually interesting one, even more so in a girl than in a boy. Speaking of boys, by the way: do you recall an item that appeared in the newspapers some four years ago about three very young high-school students who decided to run off to America? They were caught quite a distance away from their city and had a pistol in their possession. On the whole, even formerly—a generation or two ago—the heads of these young folks were just as full of dreams and fantastic plans as are the heads of today's youth. But today's young people are somehow more decisive and much less prone to doubt and reflection. Young people of past days might think up some project (running off to Venice, say, after reading all about the city in the tales of Hoffmann and George Sand—I knew one such person), but they never went on to carry it out. At most they might tell a friend about it after making him take an oath of secrecy; but today's young people think up plans and then carry them out. In the past, however, young people felt bound by a sense of duty and an awareness of their responsibility to their fathers and mothers and to certain beliefs and principles. But nowadays this sense of obligation has undoubtedly grown weaker. They have fewer restraints on them, both outer and inner. That, perhaps, is why their minds work in a more one-sided manner; and of course there are reasons for all this.

The main thing is that these are not isolated instances caused by stupidity. I repeat: this remarkably interesting age of twelve or thirteen years truly needs special study by our educational experts, who are so much involved with pedagogy, and by parents, who are now so much involved with matters of "business" and nonbusiness. And how easily all this can happen—the most terrible thing, I mean—and to whom? To our very own children! Just think of the place in this mother's story when the girl "*suddenly felt tired,* was walking along and crying, dreaming of meeting some kind man who would feel sorry for a poor girl with nowhere to spend the night and invite her to come home with him." Just imagine how easily this wish of hers, which reveals her childish innocence and immaturity, might have been fulfilled, given the fact that everywhere on our streets and in our wealthiest homes there are swarms of "kind men" of just that sort! And what, then, the next morning? Either a hole in the ice, or *the shame of confessing,* and after the shame of confessing would develop the capacity to *come to terms with this memory*—keeping everything to oneself but now pondering over it from a different point of view, to keep thinking and thinking about it, but with all sorts of new imaginings. And all this would happen little by little and of its own accord; and then at last, perhaps, would come the desire to repeat the experience, and then all the rest. And this at the age of twelve! And everything kept well concealed. Concealed in the full meaning of the word! What about this other girl who spent her time looking in the shops and visiting the Arcade instead of going to school and who taught our Sasha to do the same? I have often heard things of this sort about boys who found school boring and *vagrancy* fun. (N.B.: Vagrancy is a habit, an unhealthy one, and, in part, our national one; it is one of the things that distinguishes us from Europe. It is a habit which then is transformed into an unhealthy obsession, and it very often originates in childhood. I will certainly say something later about this national obsession of ours.) And so now, it seems, it is possible to have *vagrant* girls as well. And such a girl, let's say, is still completely *innocent;* but even if she is as innocent as the very first creature in the Garden of Eden, she still can't avoid "the knowledge of Good and Evil," even if only a bit of it, even if only in her imagination and in her dreams. The street, after all, is such a quick and ready school. And the main thing, which I repeat again and again: this is such a curious age, an age that, on the one hand, still completely preserves the most childish, touching innocence and immaturity but, on the other hand, has already acquired an avidly quick capacity for the perception of and rapid familiarization with such ideas and conceptions of which, in the view of so many parents and pedagogues, this age supposedly hasn't the haziest idea. It is this division, it is this joining together of these two so dissimilar halves of the young person, which presents such a danger and such a critical point in the lives of these young creatures.

1877

January

from CHAPTER ONE

Article 1. Three Ideas

I shall begin my new year on the same topic with which I ended last year. The final sentence in my December *Diary* said that "almost all our Russian disunities and dissociations have been founded merely on misunderstandings, the crudest sort of misunderstandings, which contain nothing of real substance and nothing that cannot be surmounted." Again I repeat: all our disputes and disunity have arisen only from errors and diverse attitudes of mind but not of heart; and it is this formula that expresses all the essence of our disunity. We may take some consolation in this fact. Errors and quandaries of the mind vanish more quickly and completely than do errors of the heart; their cure is to be found not so much in debate and logical explanation as in the overpowering logic of events of a real, living life, events that very often bear the correct and necessary conclusion within and that indicate the proper path to take; and if this does not happen at once, at the actual moment, then it does happen within a very short time, sometimes even before a new generation appears. The same cannot be said for errors of the heart. Errors of the heart are something terribly significant: they represent the contaminated spirit, sometimes even of the nation as a whole, that very often bears with it a degree of blindness that cannot be cured by facts of any kind, no matter how clearly they might indicate the proper path to take. Quite to the contrary: blindness of this sort modifies the facts to suit its purposes and adjusts them to suit its contaminated spirit; it sometimes even happens that the whole nation deliberately chooses to perish, aware of its blindness but *not wishing* to be cured of it. I hope people will not scoff because I take errors of the mind too lightly and see them as easily corrected. There would be far more cause to scoff at someone—never mind me—who assumed the role of the corrector in this case, firmly and calmly assured that his words could sway or reverse the convictions held by a society at a given moment. I am aware of all that. Nonetheless, one needn't be ashamed of one's convictions, and at the present time one mustn't be ashamed of them; he who has a word to say should say it without fear that he will not be heeded, without fear even that he will be laughed at and that he will produce no impression on the minds of his contemporaries. In that sense *A Writer's Diary* will never stray from its path, will never yield to the spirit of the age or to the force of dominant and prevailing influences so long as it considers them to be unjust, will not fall in line with them or flatter them or try to manipulate them. After publishing for a whole year, we think a statement like that can be made. After all, we fully and quite clearly realized even last year that much of what we wrote with passion and conviction did us only real harm and that, rather, we would have gained far more had we sung with equal passion in unison with others.

We repeat: we think that at present *each one* must say his piece as frankly and as directly as possible, without feeling any shame for naively laying bare certain of his ideas. Indeed, events that are, perhaps, extraordinary and enormous are awaiting us—all Russia, that is. "Some great events may suddenly come to pass and catch our intelligentsia by surprise; then, might it not be too late?" as I said when I closed my December *Diary*. In saying that I had in mind not only political events to come in this "near future," although they, too, cannot help but capture the attention of even the most inferior and "Yiddifying" minds that take no thought for anything beyond their own affairs. Indeed, what is awaiting the world, not only in the remaining quarter of this century, but even (who can tell?) in the current year, perhaps? Europe is restless, of this there is no doubt. But is this restlessness only temporary, a thing of the moment? Certainly not: it is evident that the time is at hand for the fulfillment of something eternal, something millenarian, something that has been in preparation in the world since the very beginning of its civilization. Three ideas rise up before the world and, it seems, are already in their final stage of formulation.

On one side, at the edge of Europe, there is the Catholic idea— condemned and waiting in great torment and perplexity: is it to be or not to be? Is it still to live or has its end come? I am speaking not about the Catholic religion alone but about the entire *Catholic idea,* about the fate of the nations which have formed themselves under this idea over the course of a millennium and which have been entirely permeated with it. In that sense, for instance, France over the ages has seemed to be the most complete incarnation of the Catholic idea; she is the head of this idea, which she inherited from the Romans, of course, and which is in their spirit. This France who, though she has now lost her religion *almost entirely* (Jesuits and atheists are all one and the same thing there), who has closed her churches more than once and who on one occasion subjected God himself to a vote in the Assembly; this France, who developed from the ideas of 1789 her own particular French socialism—i.e., the pacification and organization of human society without Christ and outside of Christ, as Catholicism tried but was unable to organize it in Christ; this same France—in her revolutionary Convention, in her atheists, in her socialists, and in her communards of today—is and continues to be in the highest degree a Catholic nation wholly and entirely, completely contaminated by the spirit and the letter of Catholicism, proclaiming through the mouths of its confirmed atheists: *Liberté, Egalité, Fraternité—ou la mort,* i.e., exactly as the pope himself would have proclaimed had he been compelled to proclaim and formulate a Catholic *liberté, égalité, fraternité* in his style and in his spirit—the actual style and spirit of a pope of the Middle Ages. Today's French socialism itself appears to be a passionate and fateful protest against the Catholic idea by all the people and nations who have been tormented and oppressed by it and who wish, whatever the cost, to go on living without Catholicism and its gods. The protest itself, which to all intents and purposes began at the end of the last century (but in essence much earlier), is nothing other than the truest and direct continuation of the Catholic idea, its most complete and final fulfillment, its fateful consequence elaborated over the course of centuries. For French socialism is nothing other than the *compulsory* union of humanity, an idea that derived from ancient Rome and that was subsequently preserved completely in Catholicism. Thus socialism's idea of the liberation of the human spirit from Catholicism has become incarnated here in the very most restricted of Catholic forms, borrowed from the very core of its spirit, from its letter, from its materialism, from its despotism, from its morality.

On the other side rises up the old Protestantism, protesting for nineteen centuries now against Rome and her idea, against the ancient pagan idea and the renewed Catholic one; against Rome's universal idea of possessing man both morally and materially all the world over, against Rome's civilization; protesting since the time of Arminius and the Teutoburger Wald. This is the German, believing blindly that the renewal of humanity is to be found only in him and not in Catholic civilization.

Through his entire history he dreamed only of and longed only for his
unification so he could proclaim his own proud idea, an idea that had
been powerfully formulated and that had had a unifying effect even in
the heresy of Luther; while now, five years after the defeat of France—the
foremost, principal, and most Christian Catholic nation—the German is
confident in his complete triumph and in the fact that no one can stand
in his place at the head of the world and its renewal. He believes in this
proudly and unwaveringly; he believes that there is nothing else in the
world that is higher than the Germanic spirit and the Germanic word
and that Germany alone can utter that word. He finds it absurd even to
suppose that there is anything in the world, even if only in embryo, that
could contain something that Germany, ordained to lead the world, could
not contain. Yet it would certainly not be superfluous to note, though
in parentheses, that through all the nineteen centuries of her existence,
Germany has done nothing more than to protest; she herself has never
uttered her *new word* but has only lived the whole time by rejection and
protest against her enemy so that, for example, it is very possible indeed
that something as odd as this could happen: when Germany does achieve
her final victory and destroys that against which she has been protesting
for nineteen centuries, she herself will suddenly have to die spiritually,
in the wake of her enemy, for she will have nothing to live for; *she will
have nothing to protest against.* This may still be only my chimera, but
Luther's Protestantism is already a fact: this faith is one of protest and
of mere *denial,* and as soon as Catholicism disappears from the world,
Protestantism will also disappear right after it because it will have nothing
to protest against; it will be transformed into straight atheism and thus
will it end. But that, let's say, is still only my chimera. The German
despises the Slavic idea as much as he does the Catholic one, the only
difference being that he has always respected the latter as a strong and
powerful enemy, whereas he not only had no respect whatever for the
Slavic idea, he did not even acknowledge it until very recent times. But
lately he has begun to cast a very suspicious eye at the Slavs. Although
even now he finds it absurd to suppose that they also could have a goal
of some sort and an idea, that there could be some hope there of also
"saying something to the world," still, since the defeat of France his
unhealthy suspicions have increased, and the events of the past year and
of the present can scarcely do much to alleviate his mistrust. Germany's

position is now a rather worrisome one: in any case, she has to finish her mission in the West before she can entertain any Eastern ideas. Who can deny that France, still not beaten into submission, does not and did not trouble the German through all these five years after her defeat for the very reason that he had not beaten her into submission? In 1875 that unease reached an extraordinary level in Berlin, and Germany would certainly have rushed to render a final blow to her age-old enemy while there was still time, but certain very powerful circumstances prevented her from doing so. Now, however—this year—there is no doubt that France, which grows ever more powerful materially every year, terrifies Germany even more than she did two years ago. Germany knows that her enemy will not die without a struggle; she knows, moreover, that when that enemy feels he has recovered completely, he himself will begin the battle, so that three or five years hence may be too late for Germany. And so, in view of the fact that the east of Europe has been so completely permeated with its own idea that sprang up suddenly there and that it has too many of its own affairs to look after—in view of that, it may very well happen that Germany, feeling her own hands untied for the moment, will make a final assault on the western enemy, on that terrible nightmare that torments her; and all this may even happen in the very nearest of the near future. On the whole, one can say that though the situation in the east is tense and difficult, Germany herself is perhaps in an even less enviable position. And she may well have even more fears and various anxieties to face, despite her excessively haughty tone. And this, at least, we ought to keep particularly in mind.

And meanwhile, in the East, the third world idea—the Slavic idea, a new idea that is coming into being—has truly caught ablaze and has begun to cast a light that has never before been seen; it is, perhaps, the third future possibility for settling the destinies of Europe and of humanity. It is clear to everyone now that with the solution to the Eastern Question, a new element, a new phenomenon will enter into humanity, one that until now has lain passive and inert and that, in any case and at the very least, cannot but exert an extraordinarily powerful and decisive influence on the fate of the world. What sort of idea is this? What will the union of the Slavs bring? This is all too indefinite at the moment, but that something truly will be contributed and something new will be uttered—that scarcely anyone doubts. And all these three enormous world ideas have come together to be resolved almost at the same time. Of course, this is not simply some idle wish; nor is it a war arising over some legacy or argument between two highly placed ladies, as happened in the last century. This is a matter of universal significance and of ultimate importance; and although it will certainly not resolve *all* human destinies, there is no doubt that it brings with it the beginning of the end of all the previous histories of European humanity, the beginning of the resolution of their eventual destinies, which are in the hands of God and which humans can scarcely foresee, even though they may have forebodings.

And now, the question that cannot help but present itself to every thinking person: can such events be stopped in their course? Can ideas of such dimensions be subordinated to petty, Yiddifying, third-rate considerations? Can anyone postpone their resolution? Is this a useful thing to do? Wisdom, no doubt, must preserve and protect the nations and serve philanthropy and humanity, but there are some ideas that have their own immutable, powerful and all-engulfing force. You cannot hold back with one hand the summit of a cliff that has crumbled away and is falling. Of course, we Russians have two awesome powers that are worth all the others in the world—the intactness and spiritual indivisibility of the millions of our People and their most intimate link with their monarch. The latter, of course, is beyond dispute; but our "pondering Peters" not only do not understand the People's idea, they do not even want to understand it.

from CHAPTER TWO

Article 4, extract. Russian Satire. *Virgin Soil.*
Last Songs. Old Reminiscences.

[. . .] I read Nekrasov's *Last Songs* in the January number of *Notes of the Fatherland.* Passionate songs and words that do not say quite everything, as is always the case with Nekrasov; but what painful groans of a sick man! Our poet is very sick and—he told me himself—sees his own situation clearly. But I find that difficult to believe. . . . His is a hardy and percipient organism. He suffers terribly (he has some sort of intestinal ulcer, an ailment which is difficult even to diagnose), but I cannot believe that he will not last until spring; and if he spends the spring at a health resort abroad, in another climate, he will quickly recover, I am certain of it. Strange things happen to people; we rarely saw one another, and there were misunderstandings between us as well, but there was one event in our lives that I can never forget. This was the time we first met. And imagine, not long ago I called on Nekrasov and he, ill and suffering, began at once to tell me that he remembered those days. At that time (that was thirty years ago!) something happened so characteristic of youth, and so fresh and fine—one of those things that remains forever in the hearts of those involved. We were then in our early twenties. I was living in St. Petersburg and had resigned from the Corps of Engineers a year before, not knowing myself why, and with only the foggiest and most uncertain goals. It was May of 1845. At the beginning of the winter, having written nothing previously, I had suddenly begun my first tale, *Poor People.* When I had finished, I didn't know what to do with it and where I should try to have it published. I had no contacts in literature at all, save for D. V. Grigorovich, but he himself had not written anything then except for one little article, "The Organ Grinders of Petersburg," which had appeared in an anthology. As I recall, at the time he was preparing to spend the summer on his country estate and was living for the time being in Nekrasov's apartment. When he stopped by to see me he said, "Bring me your manuscript" (he himself had not read it); "Nekrasov wants to publish an anthology next year, and I'll show it to him." I brought the manuscript, saw Nekrasov for a minute, and we shook hands. I was embarrassed at the thought that I had come with my work and left quickly, having said scarcely a word to Nekrasov. I had few thoughts of success and was apprehensive of that "*Fatherland Notes* party," as people then used to call it. I had been reading Belinsky with great interest for some years, but he seemed to me to be someone awesome and terrible; "He'll make fun of my *Poor People*" was the thought that sometimes came to me. But only sometimes. I wrote the work with passion, almost with tears: "Can it be that all this, all those moments I lived through with pen in hand while writing this story—can it be that all this is a lie, a mirage, counterfeit emotion?" But such thoughts, of course, came only in moments, and my sense of apprehension would quickly return. On the evening of the same day I had handed over the manuscript, I went off to visit an old friend who lived some distance away; we spent the whole night talking about *Dead Souls* and reading the work—I can't remember how many times we had read it before. This is what young people did in those days; two or three would get together: "Why don't we read Gogol, gentlemen!" And they would sit down and read, perhaps all through the night. Many, many of the young people of the day seemed to be filled with a spirit of some sort and seemed to be awaiting something. When I came home it was already four o'clock on a Petersburg "white night," as bright as day. The weather was fine and warm, and when I came into my apartment I did not go to bed but opened the window and sat by it. Suddenly the bell rang, giving me a great start, and then Grigorovich and Nekrasov, in utter rapture and both almost in tears, burst in to embrace me. They had come home early the evening before, taken up my manuscript, and begun to read it to see what it was like: "We'll be able to tell from the first ten pages." But when they had read ten pages they decided to read ten more; and then, without putting it down, they sat up the whole night reading aloud, taking turns as one grew tired. "When he was reading about the death of the student," Grigorovich told me later when we were alone, "I suddenly noticed that at the point where the father was running after the coffin, Nekrasov's voice broke; it happened once, and again, and suddenly he couldn't restrain himself; he slapped the manuscript and exclaimed, 'Ah, the so-and-so!' He meant you, of course. And so we kept on all night." When they had finished (there were 112 pages in all!) the two of them agreed they must come to see me at once: "What does it matter if he's asleep! We'll wake him; *this* matters more than sleep!" Later, when I had a better grasp of Nekrasov's character, I often marveled at that moment: his is a reticent, almost suspicious, cautious, and uncommunicative nature. Such, at least, he always seemed to me; so that this moment of our first meeting was truly a display of the deepest feeling. They spent about a half-hour with me then, and in that half-hour we discussed God knows how many things, one catching the other's meaning before he had finished a word, speaking hastily and with exclamations; we spoke of poetry and of truth and of the "current situation," and of Gogol too, of course, quoting from *The Inspector-General* and *Dead Souls;* but mainly we spoke of Belinsky. "I'll bring him your story this very day, and you'll see; what a man he is, after all, what a man! You'll meet him and you'll see: what a splendid soul he is!" Nekrasov said with delight, both his hands gripping my shoulders and shaking them. "Now, go to bed, we're leaving; you'll come see us in the morning!" As if I could have slept after their visit! What delight, what success, and I clearly remember the main thing: it was the feeling I cherished. "Others have success; people praise them, come to greet them, congratulate them; but these two came running here in tears, at four o'clock in the morning, to wake me up because this matters more than sleep. . . . Ah, how fine!" That is what I was thinking; how could I sleep!

Nekrasov took the manuscript to Belinsky that same day. He revered Belinsky and, I think, loved him more than anyone else he ever knew. At the time, Nekrasov had still not written anything on the scale which he did shortly thereafter, a year later. Nekrasov turned up in Petersburg, as far as I know, at the age of sixteen and completely alone. He also began writing virtually at the age of sixteen. I know little about his acquaintance with Belinsky, but Belinsky perceived his talent from the very beginning and, perhaps, had a powerful influence on the attitudes of his poetry. Despite Nekrasov's youth at the time and the difference in their ages, there certainly must have been some moments between them and some words spoken that had a permanent influence and bound them indissolubly. "A new Gogol has appeared!" cried Nekrasov as he came to Belinsky with *Poor People.* "You find Gogols springing up like mushrooms," Belinsky remarked sternly, but he took the manuscript. When Nekrasov visited him again, in the evening, Belinsky greeted him "plainly excited": "Bring him here, bring him as soon as you can!"

And so (this, then, being on the third day), they took me to Belinsky. I recall that at first glance I was much struck by his appearance, his nose, his forehead; somehow I had imagined him quite differently—"this awesome, this terrible critic." He greeted me with great solemnity and restraint. "Well, I suppose that is as it should be," I thought; but I think not more than a minute passed before everything changed: the solemnity was not that of a great personage, not that of a great critic meeting a twenty-two-year-old novice writer; it came, so to say, from respect for those sentiments which he wished to instill in me as quickly as possible, a respect for those important words which he so hastened to say to me. He spoke ardently, with burning eyes: "Do you, you yourself, realize what it is you have written?" he repeated several times, raising his voice to a shriek, as was his habit. He would always shriek when speaking in the grip of strong emotion. "You, as an artist, could have written this only guided by your God-given instinct; but have you yourself comprehended all the terrible truth that you have shown us? It cannot be that you, with your twenty years, have understood that. This wretched clerk of yours—why, he has been mired in the civil service for so long and has brought himself to the point where his humility will not even allow him to acknowledge his own wretchedness; he considers even his slightest complaint to be a virtual act of freethinking; he does not dare claim even the right to his own unhappiness. And when a good man, his general, gives him those hundred rubles, he is shattered, destroyed from the amazement that 'His Excellency' could take pity on such a one as he. And the button that fell off, and the moment when he kissed the general's hand—why, here it's not a matter of compassion for the poor fellow, it's horror, real horror! The horror is in the fact that he's grateful! It's a tragedy! You've touched the very essence of the matter; straightaway you've shown the most significant thing. We critics and journalists only talk about such things; we try to explain them in words, but you, an artist, immediately and with one stroke, reveal the very essence in an image that is tangible, so that the most unthinking reader suddenly understands everything! That is the secret of art; that is truth in art! That is how the artist serves the truth! To you, an artist, the truth has been revealed and proclaimed; it has come to you as a gift. So cherish your gift, remain faithful to it, and be a great writer! . . ."

He said all that to me then. He said all that about me later, and to many others who are still alive and could attest to it. When I left him I was in ecstasy. I stopped at the corner of his house, looked at the sky, at the luminous day, at the people passing by, and with my entire being I sensed that there had occurred in my life a solemn moment, an irrevocable turning point, that something quite new had begun, but something I had not anticipated even in my wildest dreams. (And I was a terrible dreamer in those days.) "And can I, in truth, be so great?" I thought diffidently, in a kind of timid rapture. Oh, don't laugh; later on I never thought that I was great, but then—how could I resist it! "Oh, I shall be worthy of that praise. And what people there are! This is where the real people are! I shall earn their praise; I shall strive to become as fine as they are; I shall remain 'faithful'! Oh, but how frivolous I am, and if Belinsky only knew what rotten, shameful things there are within me! And everyone says that these literary men are proud and haughty. But people like him one finds only in Russia; they are alone, but they alone have the truth; and truth, goodness, and authenticity always win and triumph over vice and evil; we will win. Oh, to join them, to be one of their number!"

All these things I thought; I recall the moment with the most complete clarity. And never could I forget it thereafter. It was the most delightful moment of my entire life. Recalling it while in prison used to strengthen my spirit. Even now, I recall it each time with delight. And so, thirty years later, sitting by Nekrasov's sickbed not long ago, I recalled the moment and seemed to relive it once more. I did not remind him of all the details, but only that we had had such moments then; and I could see that he himself was recalling them. I knew that he remembered them. When I returned from prison he showed me one of the poems in his book: "It was you I was writing about then," he told me. And we spent our whole lives apart. On his sickbed he now recalls friends who are no longer:

> Those who, in the flower of their days,
> Fell victim to foul perfidy and hate;
> Whose songs of prophecy remain unsung;
> Whose portraits now *reproach* me with sad gaze. . . .

It's a painful word, this "reproach." Did we remain "faithful"? Did we? Let every one decide this for himself, by his own conscience. But read these suffering songs yourself, and may our beloved and passionate poet be restored! A poet with a passion for suffering! . . .

Article 5. The Boy Celebrating His Saint's Day

Do you remember Count Tolstoy's *Childhood and Youth*? It has a young boy in it, the hero of the whole poem. But he is not just a boy like the other children and like his brother Volodia. He's only about twelve, and his head and heart are already visited by thoughts and feelings unlike those of other children his age. He passionately abandons himself to his dreams and feelings, already aware that it is better to keep them to himself. His shy disposition to purity and his lofty pride prevent him from revealing them. He envies his brother and considers him incomparably higher than he, especially as regards adroitness and good looks; and yet he secretly senses that his brother is far beneath him in all respects; but he drives away this thought, which he considers mean. Too often he regards himself in the mirror and decides that he is repulsively ugly. Through his mind flashes the notion that no one loves him, that people despise him. ... In short, he is a rather unusual boy, and yet he belongs to that type of upper-middle landowning family that found its poet and historian, fully and completely—and in accordance with Pushkin's behest—in Count Leo Tolstoy. And so some guests arrive at their house—a large, Moscow, family house; it is the saint's day of the boy's sister. Along with the adults arrive children—both boys and girls. Games and dancing begin. Our hero is awkward; he is the poorest dancer of all; he wants to show off his wit, but he fails—and in front of so many pretty girls; he has his perennial notion, his perennial suspicion that he is inferior to all of them. In despair he resolves to do something rash so as to impress them all. In front of all the girls and all those haughty older boys who take no account of him, he, like one possessed, with the feeling of one who hurls himself into a chasm that has suddenly opened before him, sticks his tongue out at his tutor and strikes him with all his might! "Now everyone knows what sort of fellow he is! Now he's made a mark!" He is removed in disgrace and shut up in a storeroom. Feeling that he is ruined forever, the boy begins to dream: now he's run away from home; he's joined the army, and in battle he kills a host of Turks and falls from his wounds. "Victory! Where is our savior?" everyone cries, as they embrace and kiss him. And now he's in Moscow, walking along Tverskoi Boulevard with a bandaged arm; he meets the Emperor. ... And suddenly the thought that the door will open and his tutor will come in with a bundle of switches makes these dreams fly away like so much dust. New dreams begin. Suddenly he thinks up a reason why "everyone so dislikes him": very likely he is a foundling, and they've never told him. . . . His thoughts grow into a whirlwind: now he's dying; they come into the storeroom and find his body: "The poor boy!" says everyone, pitying him. "He was a good boy! You're the one who ruined his life," says his father to the tutor . . . and now the dreamer is choked with tears. . . . This whole episode ends with the boy falling ill with fever and delirium. It is a remarkably important psychological study of the soul of a child, beautifully written.

I had a reason for bringing up this study in such detail. I had a letter from K——v that described the death of a child, also a twelve-year-old boy; and it is quite possible that there was something similar here. However, I shall quote portions of the letter without changing a single word. The *topic* is interesting.

> On the 8th of November, after dinner, the news went round the city that there had been a *suicide: a twelve- or thirteen-year-old lad,* a student in a junior high school, had hanged himself. It happened this way. The teacher, whose lesson the victim had not studied that day, punished him by making him stay after school until five o'clock. The boy kept pacing the floor of the room; he happened to see the cord on a pulley; he untied it, fastened it to a nail on which the honor roll usually hung and which, for some reason, had not been put up that day, and he hanged himself. The janitor, who was washing floors in the other classrooms, spotted the unfortunate boy and ran to get the inspector. The inspector rushed in and pulled the boy from the noose, but they were unable to revive him. . . . What is the reason for this suicide? The boy had never been rowdy and had shown no signs of vicious behavior; on the whole, he had been a good student, but in the period before the suicide he had received a few unsatisfactory marks from his teacher, for which he had been punished. . . . People say that both the boy's father, who was very strict, and the boy were celebrating that day their common saint's day. Perhaps the young lad was dreaming with childish delight of how his mother, father, and little brothers and sisters would greet him at home. . . . But here he is, having to sit all alone and hungry in an empty building thinking about his father's terrible wrath that

he will have to face, and about the shame, humiliation and, perhaps, also the punishment he will have to bear. He knew of suicide as an alternative (and in our day what child does not?). One feels terrible pity for the deceased lad, and pity for the inspector, an excellent person and pedagogue who is adored by his pupils; one fears for the school that sees such things happen within its walls. What were the feelings of the classmates of the deceased when they learned of what had happened? And what of the other children who study there, some of whom are only tiny little things in the preparatory classes? Is such training not too stringent? Is there not too much significance given to grades—to "Ds" and "Fs" and to honor rolls from whose nails pupils hang themselves? Is there not too much formalism and arid lack of feeling when we deal with education?

Of course, one feels terribly sorry for the poor young lad who was celebrating his saint's day; but I shall not enter into a detailed commentary on the probable causes for this heartbreaking *incident,* and particularly not on the topic of "grades, 'Ds,' excessive severity," and so on. All those things existed formerly, without suicides, and so evidently the reason does not lie here. I chose the episode from Tolstoy's *Boyhood* because of the similarity between both cases, but there is also an enormous difference. There is no doubt that the young lad, Misha, who was celebrating his saint's day, killed himself not from anger and fear alone. Both these feelings—anger and morbid dread—are too simple and would most likely have been *a result in themselves.* However, the fear of punishment could also really have had an influence, especially given a state of morbid anxiety. But still, even with that, the feeling must have been much more complex, and again, it is very possible that what occurred was something akin to what Count Tolstoy described: that is, suppressed and still unconscious childish questions, a powerful sense of some oppressive injustice, an anguished, precocious and tormenting sense of one's own insignificance, a morbidly intensified question: "Why do they *all* dislike me so?" There is the passionate longing to compel people to pity, which is the same as a passionate longing for love *from them all*—there are these things, and a great host of other complications and subtleties. The fact is that some or other of these subtleties certainly were involved; but there are also features of a new sort of reality quite different from that of the placid, middle-stratum Moscow landowning family whose way of life had long been solidly established and whose *historian* is our Count Leo Tolstoy, who, it seems, appeared just at the time when the former structure of the Russian nobility, established on the basis of old landowners' ways, had arrived at some new, still unknown but radical crisis, or at least at a point when it was to be totally recast into new, not yet manifest, almost entirely unknown forms. In the incident here, of the boy whose saint's day it was, one particular feature comes entirely from our time. Count Tolstoy's boy could dream, with bitter tears of enervated emotion in his heart, of how *they* would come in, find his dead body, and begin to love and pity him and blame themselves. He could even dream of killing himself, but only *dream:* the strict order of the historically configured noble family would have made its mark even in a twelve-year-old child and would not have allowed his *dream* to become *actuality;* the other child *dreamed it, and then he did it.* In pointing this out, however, I have in mind not only the current epidemic of suicides. One senses that something is not right here, that an enormous part of the Russian order of life has remained entirely without any observer and without any *historian.* At least it is clear that the life of the upper-middle level of our nobility, so vividly described by our writers, is already an insignificant and "dissociated" corner of Russian life generally. Who, then, will be the *historian* of the other corners, of which, it seems, there are so awfully many? And if, within this chaos that has gone on for so long and that is particularly prevalent in the life of our society now—a life in which, perhaps, even an artist of Shakespearean proportions cannot find a normative law and a guiding thread—who, then, will illuminate even a little part of this chaos, never mind dreaming of some guiding thread? The main thing is that it seems no one is capable of doing this; it is as if it were still too early even for our greatest artists. One cannot deny that a way of life in Russia is disintegrating; consequently, family life disintegrates as well. But certainly there is also a life that is being formed anew, on new principles. Who will pick these out and show them to us? Who can, even in small measure, define and express the laws of this disintegration and this new formation? Or is it still too early? But have we even taken complete note of what is old and past?

February

from CHAPTER ONE

Article 2, extract. Home-grown Giants and a Humiliated Son of a Mountain Village. An Anecdote about Skin Flayed from the Back. The Higher Interests of Civilization, and "May They Be Damned If They Must Be Purchased at Such a Price!"

[. . .] Among these Slavic children who have been brought to Moscow (this same friend who has come back from Moscow was telling me), there is one girl of eight or nine who has frequent fainting spells, for which she is being given special care. She faints because of her recollections: last summer, with her own eyes, she watched a group of Circassians flay the skin from her father, and do it completely. The memory of this never leaves her and, most likely, will remain with her forever; as years pass it may grow less terrible, although I don't know if one can speak of something less terrible in a case like this. Oh, civilization! Oh, Europe, whose interests would suffer so were she actually to forbid the Turks to flay the skin from fathers while their children watch! These higher interests of European civilization are, of course, trade, maritime navigation, markets, factories: what can be higher than these things in Europe's eyes? Interests like these cannot be touched, not only by fingers but even by thought, but—but "may they be damned, these interests of European civilization!" These are not my words, these are the words of *The Moscow News,* and I consider it an honor to add my voice to this exclamation: indeed, may they be damned, these interests of civilization; and may civilization itself be damned if its preservation demands the stripping of skin from living people. Yet this is a fact: preserving it demands the stripping of skin from human beings!

Article 3. On Flaying of Skins Generally and Various Aberrations in Particular. Hatred of Authority with Toadyism of Thought.

"From human beings? What human beings? From only a tiny number of human beings living in some obscure corner. From some Turkish subjects whom we'd never have known about if the Russians hadn't shouted it far and wide. On the other hand, the rest of the organism—the huge part of it—is alive and well; it flourishes, trades, and manufactures!"

That story of the little Bulgarian girl who kept fainting I heard in the morning; later that same day I happened to be walking along Nevsky Prospect. Between three and four o'clock, mothers and nursemaids were walking their children there. Suddenly an involuntary thought fell heavily on me: "Civilization!" I thought, "who dares to say a word against civilization? No, civilization truly does mean something: at least these children of ours who are peacefully strolling here on Nevsky Prospect will not see the skin flayed from their fathers, and their mothers will not have to watch these children being tossed into the air and caught on bayonets, as happened in Bulgaria. That bit of progress, at least, can be credited to civilization! And what if it does exist only in Europe, i.e., in one little corner of the globe, and in a corner which is rather small in comparison with the surface of the planet (a terrible thought!); but still, it is there, and though it may be only in some little corner, it exists; although the price we pay for it—flaying the skin from our own brothers who live somewhere off on the edge of civilization—is a high one, it exists among us, at least. Just think that in times past, and not that long ago, there was nothing of this sort in solid form even in Europe; and if it now does exist in Europe, then it is for the first time in the history of the planet. No, still, this is an accomplishment and, perhaps, one that will never be reversed; and that is a remarkably important consideration which enters one's soul involuntarily; it is certainly not some small thing unworthy of attention, the more so that the world is still a mystery as before, despite civilization and its gains. God knows what things the world can still engender and what may subsequently happen, even in the very near future."

And so, the moment I felt like exclaiming rapturously to myself: "Long live civilization!" I was suddenly overcome by doubt: "Have we, in fact, achieved even this much, even for these children of Nevsky Prospect? Isn't this, perhaps, entirely a mirage, even here, and aren't we merely deceiving ourselves?"

You know, gentlemen, I ended by thinking that it was a mirage, or, to put it less harshly, virtually a mirage; and if fathers are not skinned alive here on the Nevsky while their children watch, then it is only a matter of chance, so to say, a matter of "circumstances beyond the public's control," and also, of course, because of the policemen standing here. Oh, let me clarify my thought at once: I'm certainly not trying to make up some allegory; I'm not hinting at the sufferings of some proletariat in our present age, nor at some parent who tells his seven-year-old son: "Here is my testament to you: if you steal five rubles, I will curse you; if you steal a hundred thousand, I will bless you." Oh, no; I mean my words to be taken literally. I mean the literal flaying of skin, the same as happened in Bulgaria in the summer and in which, it appears, the victorious Turks are so fond of indulging. And it is that flaying of skin I have in mind when I state: if it does not happen on the Nevsky, then it is only "by chance, through circumstances beyond our control," and, most important, because for the moment it is still against the law; but were it to depend on us, perhaps, nothing would stop us despite all our civilization.

In my view, if one is to be absolutely frank, people are simply intimidated by some sort of habit, some rule taken on faith, almost a prejudice. But if some "expert" were to come up with even the most meager "proof" that there are occasions when flaying the skin from the back of some other person can even be of benefit to the common cause and, though it may be repulsive, still "the end justifies the means"; and if some expert were to say things of this sort using the appropriate style and under the appropriate circumstances, then, believe me, immediately there would be people willing to carry out the idea—very jolly people, even. Oh, let this just be my quite absurd paradox! I'll be the first to set my name to such a description of it and will do so with both hands; nevertheless, I assure you that this is exactly what would happen. Civilization exists; its laws exist; belief in those laws even exists. But all that's needed is for some new fad to appear and hordes of people would instantly be transformed. Not every one, of course, but only such a small handful would be left that even you and I, dear reader, would be astonished; and even we do not know where we would find ourselves: among the flayed or among the flayers? Naturally, people will shout right in my face that this is all a lot of rubbish and that there could never be such a fad and that this, at least, is something civilization did achieve. Gentlemen, how gullible you are! You're laughing? Well, what about France in 1793 (so as not to look into things much more recent)? Did they not affirm that very fad of flaying, and did they not do so even under the guise of civilization's most sacred principles? And this after Rousseau and Voltaire! You may object that this is not what happened at all, and that it was long ago; but note that I resort to history only, perhaps, so as not to speak of the present day. Believe me, the most complete aberration in human hearts and minds is always possible; and in Russia, and specifically in our time, it is not only possible but even inevitable, judging by the course of events. Just look: are there many among us who can agree on what is good and what is bad? And I'm not talking about some "eternal verities" but about the very first question that comes up. And how quickly changes and volte-faces occur among us! What are these "Jack of Hearts" bands in Moscow? It seems to me that they are only a part of that portion of the Russian nobility that was unable to tolerate the peasant reform. They may not be landowners themselves, but they are the children of landowners. The peasant reform left them beggared and down at the heels. Of course, it was not the reform alone that caused this; they simply were unable to cope with "new ideas": "If all the things we were taught were a lot of prejudices, then there's no point in abiding by them. If there is *nothing*, then we can do *anything*—there's an idea!" Note, please: this is an idea that is unbelievably widespread; nine-tenths of those who follow new ideas profess this one; in other words, nine-tenths of our progressives can't even understand new ideas in any other way. Darwin, for instance, is quickly transformed into a pickpocket in Russia: that's what the "Jack of Hearts" means. Oh, of course, over centuries of experience humanity has accumulated a huge number of rules of humane behavior, some of which are now considered unshakable. But I want only to say that despite all these rules, principles, religions, and civilizations, it is always only the most imperceptible, tiny group of people that is saved by them; true, this is the group that emerges victorious, but only in the final analysis; while in the day-to-day and current course of history, people remain much the same as they were, i.e., in huge majority lacking even any moderately solid concept of duty or sense of honor; and the moment some new fad appears, they immediately go running after it, quite naked and with great pleasure. There are rules, but it is people who are not at all ready to observe them. Some will say that there is no need to be ready; we need only to discover what the rules are! But is that so? And are these rules, whatever they may be, likely to last for long when people are so eager to go running about naked?

This is my view: one can, correctly and immediately, comprehend and feel something deeply; but one cannot, immediately, become a person;

one must be formed into a person. It is a discipline. This same relentless discipline over oneself is precisely what our thinkers of today reject:
"There's been too much despotism already; we need some freedom." But
this freedom leads the huge majority of people only toward toadyism to
someone else's ideas, for people are terribly in love with all things they
are given ready-made. Moreover, thinkers proclaim general laws, meaning
rules that will suddenly make everyone happy, without any need for them
to be shaped and formed: it's simply a matter of letting these rules come
into force. But even if this ideal were attainable, no rules, not even the
most obvious ones, could be implemented with people who *have not been
re-formed.* It is through this relentless discipline and unceasing work on
himself that our citizen might be born. It is with such a noble process of
work on ourselves that we must begin, so as subsequently to turn up our
"Virgin Soil"; otherwise there will be no point in turning it up.

Is that not so? But what is good and what is bad—why this, above all,
is what we do not know. We have lost all our sense for determining this.
All the old authorities have been smashed to bits and new ones have been
set up; but anyone who is a bit cleverer than the rest has no faith in the
new authorities, while he who is bolder in spirit is transformed from a
citizen into a Jack of Hearts. Moreover, he'll start flaying the skin from
someone's back, honest to God, he will; and he'll even proclaim that this
advances the common cause and so is a sacred act. How, then, and in
what sense, can you set to working to refashion yourself when you don't
know what is good and what is bad?

Article 4. Metternichs and Don Quixotes

But so as not to speak in abstractions, let's turn to the topic at hand. Now,
really, we don't strip the skin from people; moreover, we don't even like
that sort of thing (but God alone knows, people who do like that sort of
thing often hide themselves; they remain obscure and, for the time being,
are embarrassed—"afraid of prejudice"). But if we don't like that sort of
thing to go on here and *never do it,* then, really, we should abhor it in
others as well. Abhorring it, in fact, is not enough: we should simply not
allow anyone to do it; we must simply not allow it. And yet, is that what
actually happens? The most indignant people among us are not nearly

as indignant as they ought to be. I am not talking even about the Slavs alone. If we are truly so compassionate, then we ought to act by the full measure of our compassion, not by the measure of a ten-ruble donation. You may say that one can't donate all one has, after all. I agree, although I'm not sure why I agree. Why couldn't one give away everything? That's precisely the point here: one has absolutely no understanding even of one's own nature. And all of a sudden the question of "*the interests of civilization*" comes up with enormous authority!

The question is put directly, clearly, clinically, and with cynical frankness. "The interests of civilization"—these are the production, the wealth, the tranquillity required by capital. What is needed is immense, continuous and growing production at reduced prices, in view of the terrible increase in the numbers of the proletariat. In providing the proletarian with earnings, we are also providing him with consumer goods at lower prices. The more tranquil things are in Europe, the lower the prices will be. Accordingly, what is most necessary is a tranquil situation in Europe. The noise of war frightens away production. Capital is cowardly; it will take fright at war and hide itself. If the right of the Turks to flay the skin from the backs of their Christian subjects is to be limited, then a war must be begun; and if a war is begun, Russia will at once step forward; and this might cause complications that could involve the whole world in the war. In that case, say good-bye to production; and the proletarian would be out on the street. And the proletarian is dangerous out on the street. Speeches in various parliaments already declare directly, openly, for the whole world to hear, that the proletarian is dangerous, that he is restless, that he is hearkening to socialism. "No, better let them skin people alive way off there in the wilds. The inviolability of Turkish rights must remain unquestioned. The Eastern Question must be put down; let them skin people. What do these skins matter in any case? Is the tranquillity of Europe worth the hides of some two or three people—or of twenty or thirty thousand people—what's the difference? If we choose to, we won't hear a thing; we'll just plug our ears. . . ."

That's what Europe thinks (perhaps that's what she's decided to do); such are *the interests of civilization*—and, again, may they be damned! And damned all the more in that we are faced with the aberration of minds (and Russian minds above all). The question is plainly put: which is better—for many tens of millions of workers to be thrown onto the street or for a few millions of Christians to suffer at the hands of their Turkish rulers? The numbers are set forth; the figures are used to frighten people. As well as that, the politicians and pundits make their statements: there exists, they say, a rule, a doctrine, an axiom that says that the moral principles of one person—a citizen, an individual—are one thing, and the moral principles of the state are another. Accordingly, what can be considered wickedness on the part of a single individual may, when related to the state, take on the appearance of the greatest wisdom!

This is an ancient and very widespread doctrine, but let it be damned as well! The main thing is that we should not be frightened by figures. Let them do as they like over there in Europe, but let us do things differently. It is better to believe that happiness cannot be purchased with evil deeds than it is to feel happy knowing that you have allowed evil to happen. Russia has never known how to produce her own real Metternichs and Beaconsfields; to the contrary, through the entire period of European life she has lived not for herself but for others, and specifically for "the common interests of humanity." And, in truth, there were occasions during these two hundred years when, perhaps, she did try to copy Europe somehow and acquired a few Metternichs of her own; but somehow it always turned out in the end that the Russian Metternich suddenly proved to be a Don Quixote, something which amazed Europe. Of course, they laughed at the Don Quixote; but now, it seems, the time is at hand, and Don Quixote has begun no longer to amuse people but to frighten them. The fact is that he has certainly comprehended his position in Europe and no longer goes off to tilt at windmills. But yet he has remained a faithful knight, and this is what they find most terrible of all. Indeed, people in Europe shout about "Russian seizure of territory and Russian cunning," but this is only done to strike fear into their own mobs when they need to, while those who do the shouting don't believe it themselves and never did believe it. On the contrary, what troubles and frightens them now in the image Russia presents is rather something upright, something too unselfish and honorable, something that loathes profit and ill-gotten gain. They sense that she cannot be bribed or enticed into a mercenary or violent act by any political advantage. It might be done by deceit; but even though Don Quixote is a great knight, he is sometimes terribly sly, so that he will not allow himself to be deceived. England, France, Austria—is there even one nation there with which we could not have an alliance, at an opportune moment, for political gain and with mercenary, violent intent? We need only not let slip the moment at which the bribed nation can sell herself for the highest price. Russia alone cannot be seduced into an unjust alliance, not at any price. And since Russia at the same time is awfully powerful, and she is obviously growing and maturing at an amazing rate—something that people in Europe see and thoroughly understand (even though they sometimes shout that the colossus has feet of clay)—then why shouldn't they be afraid?

Incidentally, this view on the incorruptibility of Russia's foreign policy and her continual service to the common interests of humanity, even to her own detriment, is borne out by historical fact; and this is something to which we ought to pay attention. This is what makes us distinct from all of Europe. Moreover, this view on the nature of Russia is so little known that even among us there are few who believe it. Of course, Russia should not be held to account for the *errors* in her policy, because the point now is only the spirit and moral character of our policy, not its successes of the recent or distant past. In regard to the latter, there truly were some windmills in times of yore; but, I repeat, I think that their time has passed completely.

But seriously, what is the point of that prosperity purchased at the price of injustice and flaying of people's skin? Let that which is truth for the individual person remain truth for the entire nation as well. Yes, of course, there may be some temporary setback, some short-term loss of income, a loss of markets, a drop in production, and a rise in prices. But in exchange, let the organism of the nation remain morally healthy— and the nation will certainly gain more, even in a material sense. We note that Europe has indisputably reached the point where she places supreme value on her current advantage, on the advantage of the present moment, no matter what the price, because over there they live only from day to day and only for the present moment, not knowing themselves what will become of them tomorrow; we in Russia, however, still believe in something solid which is being created among us, and as a result we seek advantages which are constant and substantive. And therefore we, as a political organism as well, have always believed in an enduring moral system, not in a relative one valid only for a few days. Believe me, Don Quixote also knows where his advantages lie and is capable of calculation: he knows that he will gain in dignity and in awareness of that dignity if he continues to remain a knight; moreover, he is convinced that in following this path he will not forfeit any sincerity in his striving for goodness and truth and that such an awareness will strengthen him in his further pursuits. He is certain, finally, that such a policy is also the best school for the nation. It is essential that no "Jack of Hearts" dare to say to my face: "Everything with you is relative, after all; it's all based on your own self-interest." It is essential that the youthful enthusiast should conceive a love for his own nation and not go off to seek truth and an ideal apart from it and outside society. And he will end by coming to love his nation, once we have passed through this hard, terribly hard, school. Truth is like the sun: it cannot be hidden away; Russia's mission will at last become clear to even the most venal minds, both here at home and in Europe. Why are such intellectual aberrations possible among us now as they are nowhere else? Because under the system that lasted for a century and a half our entire intelligentsia did nothing but become a stranger to Russia; it ended by ceasing to know her altogether and had its dealings with her only via the bureaucrat's office. A new age began with the reforms of the present reign. The work has begun and it cannot be stopped.

And Europe read this fall's manifesto from the Russian emperor and has it fixed in her mind—fixed in her mind not for the present moment alone but for years to come and for future "current moments." We will draw our sword, if need be, in the name of the oppressed and unfortunate, even though it may be to the detriment of our own current advantage. But at the same time, may our faith grow ever firmer that this is precisely where Russia's real mission, strength, and truth lie, and that self-sacrifice, in the name of the interests of civilization, for the oppressed who have been forsaken by everyone in Europe, is real service to the real and true interests of civilization.

No, it is essential that political organisms acknowledge the same truth, the very truth of Christ, that is acknowledged by every believer. That truth must be preserved somewhere, at least; at least one of the nations must cast forth its light. Otherwise, what will happen? Everything will grow dark and confused and will drown in cynicism. Otherwise, you will not be able to keep in check the moral standards of individual citizens, and in that case, how will the whole organism of the state be able to live? Authority is necessary, the sun is necessary so that it can cast forth its light. The sun has appeared in the East, and a new day for humanity is beginning from the East. When the sun shines forth in all its radiance, people will understand what the real "interests of civilization" are. Otherwise, they will only raise the banner carrying the inscription *Après nous le déluge!* Can it be that such a glorious "civilization" will lead the people of Europe to a motto like this and then be done with them? That is what it is coming down to.

from CHAPTER TWO

Article 1. One of Today's Most Important Questions

My readers perhaps have already noted that I, who have been publishing my *Writer's Diary* for over a year now, try to say as little as possible about current things in Russian literature; and if I do permit myself a few words on this topic now and again, then they are expressed exclusively in a rapturously laudatory tone. And yet, what injustice there is in this voluntary abstention of mine! I am a writer, and I put out a *Writer's Diary;* and indeed, I, more than anyone else perhaps, took an interest through the course of this year in the things that appeared in literature: so how, then, can I conceal what may be my most powerful impressions? "You're a writer yourself," I say, "and so every opinion you have about literature, aside from out-and-out accolades, is regarded as showing partiality; unless, of course, you speak of things from the distant past." It was that consideration which kept me from expressing myself.

And yet I will now take the risk of violating this consideration. True, I will not be speaking about anything in a purely literary or critical sense, but will say something "apropos" if the need arises. Such an occasion has arisen now. The fact is that a month ago I happened on a work of current literature which is so serious and so characteristic that I read it in amazement, because it's been a long time since I thought I would find anything of this sort and on this scale in literature. I read a few pages of the work of this writer—an artist in the highest degree and preeminently a writer of fiction—pages that are truly on the topic of the day—all the most important things in our current Russian political and social issues and concentrated in a single point, as it were. And most important, this topic is treated with all the most characteristic nuances of our present moment, precisely in the way in which we now pose the question—pose it and leave it unresolved. I am speaking about a few pages in Count Leo Tolstoy's *Anna Karenina,* which appeared in the January issue of *The Russian Messenger.*

About the novel as a whole I shall say only a few words, and those merely in the form of a most necessary preface. I began reading it, as we all did, very long ago. At first it made a very good impression on me; later, although details of the novel continued to produce this good impression, so that I was unable to put the book down, it appealed to me rather less, on the whole. I kept thinking that I had read this somewhere before, namely in *Childhood and Youth,* by the same Count Tolstoy, as well as in his *War and Peace;* and in these works it was even fresher. Here we have the same story of a noble landowning family, although, of course, the plot is different. Figures such as Vronsky (one of the novel's heroes), who can only speak to one another on the topic of horses and who, indeed, are even incapable of finding any other topic of conversation, were interesting in that one learns about such a type; but they are all the same and represent but one small class. It seemed, for instance, that the love affair of this "stallion in uniform," as a friend of mine called him, could be portrayed only ironically. But when the author began, seriously and without irony, to allow me entry into the inner world of his hero, I found it even rather boring. Then, suddenly, all my prejudices were shattered. There came the scene of the heroine's death (later she completely recovered), and I understood all the essential part of the author's intent. At the very center of this petty and shameless life there appeared a great, everlasting, vital truth, and at once it illuminated everything. These petty, insignificant, and dishonest creatures suddenly became genuine and truthful, worthy of the name of human beings—solely through the power of natural law, the law of human mortality. Their outer shells dropped away and their truth alone was left. The least among them were transformed into the first, while the first (Vronsky) suddenly became the least; they lost their halos and were humbled; but being humbled, they became immeasurably better, worthier, and more genuine than when they had been the first and the eminent. Hatred and lies began to speak in words of forgiveness and love. In place of vapid social conceptions there appeared only a love of humanity. Each one forgave and supported the other. Narrow, exclusive feelings of class suddenly vanished and became unthinkable, and these cardboard figures began to resemble genuine humans! No one was found guilty: each admitted his own guilt without reservation, and in so doing he was at once acquitted. The reader sensed the existence of the truth of life, entirely real and inescapable, a truth which must be believed; he sensed that all our lives and all our problems—both the pettiest and most shameful, as well as the ones we often consider most serious—are for the most part merely the petty, fantastic scramble of life that falls away and vanishes without a struggle before the moment of life's truth. The most important thing here was showing that such a moment truly exists, even though it rarely appears in all its revealing fullness; and in some lives, indeed, it never appears. The poet sought this moment out and revealed it to us in all its awful truth. The poet proved that this truth exists in actual fact, not only as a matter of faith, not only as an ideal, but inescapably, unavoidably, and in plain view. I think that this is precisely what the poet wanted to prove to us when he began his poem. The Russian reader certainly had to be reminded of this everlasting truth: many among us have begun to lose sight of it. The author has done a good deed in reminding us of this, to say nothing of the fact that he has done it as an artist of exceptional power.

Thereafter the novel continued its progress; and then, somewhat to my surprise, I encountered in its part six a scene that reflected the actual topic of the day; most importantly, the scene developed not in any deliberate, tendentious way but sprang from the very artistic essence of the novel. Nevertheless, I repeat that I did not expect this and was somewhat surprised by it: I still did not anticipate such reference to the burning issue of the day. Somehow I did not think that the author would resolve to allow his characters to develop as far as these "Pillars of Hercules." It is true that the entire significance of our lives today lies in these "pillars" and in the drastic conclusions that are drawn; without them the novel would have had an indeterminate air that would be far from corresponding either to immediate or substantive Russian interests: a certain little corner of life would have been portrayed, with deliberate disregard for what is most important and most disturbing in it. However, it seems that I am entering specifically into literary criticism, and that is not my concern. I wanted only to point out this one scene. It is only a matter of two characters depicted from the very aspect that now makes them most characteristic for us; and in doing that, the author has shown us, in a most interesting way, the present social significance of the category of person to which these two characters belong.

They are both hereditary noblemen and dyed-in-the-wool landowners; the scene in which they are depicted occurs after the peasant reform. They have both been serf landowners, and now the question is: what will remain of those noblemen—in the sense of their status as noblemen—after the peasant reform? Since the type represented by these two landowners is very common and widespread, the question, in part, is answered by the author. One of them is Stiva Oblonsky, an egotist, an urbane Epicurean, an inhabitant of Moscow, and a member of the English Club. Such people are usually regarded as innocent and genial good fellows, affable egotists who do no one any harm, witty, and enjoying their pleasures to the full. Such people often have large families as well; they are kind to their wives and children but give them little thought. They are very fond of easy women, but of the respectable sort, of course. They have scant education, but love refinement and art and love to converse on all subjects. After the peasant reform this type of nobleman at once realized what was happening: he considered and calculated that he would still have something left and, consequently, there was no point in changing his life, and—*après moi le déluge.* He doesn't trouble himself with thinking about the fate of his wife and children. Through connections and the remnants of his estate, he is spared the fate of the "Jack of Hearts"; but should his estate evaporate and were he to find it impossible to receive a salary for doing nothing, he might well become one of this band, though naturally exerting all the powers of his mind (which are at times very sharp) to become as respectable and as well-bred a "Jack" as possible. In the old days, of course, he had to send off some of his serfs to the army in order to provide for his gambling debts or his mistress; but such memories never troubled him, and he has forgotten them altogether. Although he is an aristocrat, he never put much stock in his pedigree; and with the abolition of serfdom such notions disappeared for him forever: the only *people* that mattered for him were *the man whose favor he might win,* the bureaucrat of certain rank, and the rich man. The railway magnate and the banker became forces in society, and he quickly undertook to establish relations and friendship with them. And so the conversation begins with Levin reproaching him—Levin being his relative and another landowner (but one of a completely opposite type who lives on his estate). Levin chides him for visiting railway magnates and attending their dinners and festivities, such people being dubious and harmful in Levin's view. Oblonsky rejects Levin's reproach sarcastically. And, on the whole, once they became related by marriage, their relations rather soured. In our day, in any case, the scoundrel who takes issue with the honest man always has the upper hand because he has the appearance of merit deriving from common sense, while the honest man, trying to be an idealist, looks like a fool. Their conversation takes place on a summer night, while out hunting. The hunters are spending the night in a peasant barn, lying on the hay. Oblonsky is trying to prove that it makes no sense to be contemptuous of railway magnates, their scheming, their quick profits, their wheedling of railway concessions, and their speculation; he claims that they are people like everyone else, working and using their heads, and thus are agents of progress.

"But any acquisition that doesn't correspond to the work put into it is dishonest," says Levin.

"So who will determine the proper proportion?" Oblonsky continues. "You haven't defined the line between honest and dishonest work. The fact that I receive a higher salary than my chief clerk, even though he knows the job better than I—is that dishonest?"

"I don't know."

"Well, I'll tell you: the fact that your work on the estate brings you, let's say, an extra five thousand, while this peasant, no matter how hard he works, won't get more than fifty rubles is just as dishonest as my earning more than my chief clerk. . . ."

"But wait," Levin continues, "You say that it's unjust for me to get five thousand rubles while the peasant gets fifty: that's true. It's unjust, and I feel it, but. . . ."

"Yes, you feel it, but you won't give him your estate," said Stepan Arkadievich, as if deliberately trying to provoke Levin. . . .

"I won't give away my estate because no one is demanding that I do; and even if I wanted to give it away, I couldn't . . . and there's no one to give it to."

"Give it to this peasant; he won't turn it down."

"Very well, but how should I give it to him? Should I go off with him to execute a deed of purchase?"

"I don't know, but if you're convinced that you don't have the right to. . . ."

"I'm not convinced at all. I feel, rather, that I don't have the right to give it away, that I have obligations to the land and to my family."

"But wait: if you think that this inequality is unjust, then why don't you act accordingly. . . ."

"I do act, only in a negative sense, in the sense that I am not going to try to increase the difference in the situation that exists between me and him."

"No, please, excuse me: this is a paradox. . . ."

"That's how it is, my friend. You must choose one or the other: either regard the present order of society as just, and insist on your rights; or admit that you are enjoying privileges that are unjust, *as I do, and take real pleasure in them.*"

"No, if it were unjust you couldn't take real pleasure in these benefits; *at least I couldn't; for me, what is most important is to feel that I am not to blame.*"

Article 2. The Issue of the Day

Such was their conversation. And you have to agree that here we have the issue of the day, in fact, we have everything that constitutes the heart of our issue of the day. And how many characteristic, purely Russian traits we see here! In the first place, some forty years ago all these ideas were barely beginning even in Europe; even there, only a few people knew anything about Saint-Simon and Fourier, the original "idealistic" exponents of such ideas, while here—here scarcely fifty people in the whole country knew of this new movement that had begun in western Europe. And now, suddenly, a couple of landowners out hunting, spending the night in a peasant's barn, begin talking of these "questions," and talking in a most characteristic and knowledgeable fashion, so that at least the negative aspect of the question is already resolved, signed, and sealed by them. It's true that these are landowners from the best society; they have conversations at the English Club, they read newspapers, they follow legal trials from newspaper accounts and other sources; nevertheless, the fact alone that such highly idealistic poppycock is recognized as the most urgent topic of conversation by people who are certainly not professors or specialists but simply society people—Oblonskys and Levins—this fact, I say, is one of the most characteristic peculiarities of the present Russian state of mind. The second very characteristic trait in this conversation conveyed by the author-artist is that the man who is deciding the question of the justice of these new ideas is one who doesn't give a hang for the happiness of the proletariat and the poor; on the contrary, given the opportunity, he would strip them like bark from a linden tree. But with a light heart, and with the pleasure of someone making a pun, he at once affirms the bankruptcy of the entire history of humanity and declares the existing order to be the height of absurdity. "I agree fully with this," he says in effect. Note that it's these very same Stivas who are always the first to agree with such things. With a single stroke he has condemned the entire Christian order, the individual, the family; oh, this costs him nothing. Note also that we in Russia have no science, but these gentlemen—who acknowledge with complete lack of shame that they have no science and that they have begun speaking about this only yesterday, using someone else's ideas to do so—still resolve questions of such magnitude without the slightest hesitation. But here is the third very characteristic feature: this gentleman states frankly: "It must be one or the other: either admit that the present order of society is just and then insist on your rights, *or admit that we are enjoying unjust privileges, as I do, and take full pleasure in them.*" In other words, having in essence signed the sentence on the whole of Russia and condemned her, as he has his own family and the future of his children, he declares frankly that this is of no concern to him: "I admit that I am a scoundrel, but I shall remain a scoundrel for my own pleasure. *Après moi le déluge.*" The reason he is so calm is that he still has some capital; but should he lose it—why shouldn't he become a "Jack of Hearts"? That would be the most logical step. And so here we have this citizen, this family man, this Russian person—what a very characteristic, purely Russian trait! You may say that he is still an exception. But what kind of exception can he be? Just recall how much cynicism we've seen over these last twenty years, how easily people have made deviations and turnabouts, how lacking they have been in deep-seated convictions, how quick they have been to adopt the first convictions to come along, with the aim, naturally, of selling them for a few pennies tomorrow. There is no moral reserve except *après moi le déluge.*

But most curious of all is that along with this numerous and prevalent type is another—another type of Russian nobleman and landowner who is his direct opposite, his opposite in every way. This is Levin; but there

are multitudes of Levins in Russia, almost as many as there are Oblonskys.
I am not talking about his personality, the character the artist created for
him in the novel; I am talking only about one trait of his essence, but it
is the most basic trait; and I maintain that this trait is so terribly widespread among us that it is amazing—I mean given our cynicism and our
primitive attitude toward our common task. For some time now this trait
has been constantly evident; people with this trait are frantically, almost
pathologically striving to find answers to their questions; they are stead-
fastly hoping and passionately believing, even though they are still able
to resolve scarcely anything. This trait is completely expressed in Levin's
answer to Stiva: "No, if it were unjust you couldn't take real pleasure in
these benefits; *at least I couldn't; for me, what is most important is to feel
that I am not to blame."*

And in fact he will not be at peace until he decides whether he is or
is not to blame. And do you know how difficult it will be for him to find
peace? He will go to the very Pillars of Hercules, and if it is necessary, if
it truly is necessary and he proves it to himself, then, in contrast to Stiva,
who says: "I may be a scoundrel, but I will go on living for my own pleasure," Levin will turn into a "Vlas," into Nekrasov's Vlas, whose heart
melted in a fit of great awe and who gave away his money.

> And, gathering alms, the world he roamed;
> To build God's temple here, he sought.

And if he does not go off to gather alms for building a church, then
he will do something on the same scale and with the same zeal. Note this
trait, I hasten to repeat once more: there is a multitude, a huge multitude
of these new people today, of this new root of Russian people who *must
have the truth,* the truth alone, without the lies we unthinkingly accept;
these are people who, in order to find this truth, are prepared to give
away absolutely everything they have. These people have also made
their presence known in the last twenty years, and they are becoming
more and more visible, although earlier, even before Peter the Great, it
was always possible to anticipate their presence. This is the developing
future Russia of honorable people who need only the truth. Oh, there's a
lot of intolerance in them as well: through lack of experience they reject

every sort of convention and even every attempt at interpretation. But I want only to declare as strongly as I can that they are moved by genuine feeling. Something else very characteristic about them is that they are a terribly long way from coming to terms with one another and still belong to the broadest range of categories and subscribe to the broadest range of convictions: here we have aristocrats and proletarians, men of the cloth and unbelievers, rich men and poor, scholars and the uneducated, old men and young girls, Slavophiles and Westerners. There are immense differences among their convictions, but their striving for honesty and truth is steadfast and constant; and for a word of truth each one of them will give up his life and all his privileges; as I say, he will become a Vlas. People may object that this is a wild fantasy, that such integrity and such a *quest for integrity* does not exist among us. I proclaim that it does exist, side by side with terrible corruption; that I see and sense these people of tomorrow, to whom the future of Russia will belong; that they cannot be seen now; and that the artist who, setting this obsolete cynic Stiva side by side with his new man Levin, juxtaposed this hopeless, corrupt, multitudinous Russian society—which has already ended its life through its own verdict on itself, however—with the society of the new truth, a society that cannot live with the conviction that it is to blame and that will give up everything in order to cleanse its heart of its guilt. Also remarkable here is the fact that our society really is divided almost only into these two categories—so broad are they and so completely do they embrace Russian life—naturally, after one has eliminated the mass of completely lazy, untalented, and indifferent people. But the most characteristic, the most Russian trait of this "issue of the day" to which the author has drawn our attention is that his new man, his Levin, *does not know how* to resolve the question that is troubling him. I mean to say, he has already *almost* resolved it in his heart, and not in his own favor, when he *suspects* that he is *to blame;* but something solid, direct, and real arises from his whole being and still holds him back from pronouncing the final verdict. On the other hand, Stiva, who does not care whether he is to blame or not, can decide without the least hesitation; this is even to his advantage: "If everything is absurd and there is nothing sacred, then one can do anything he likes; I still have some time ahead of me; judgment day isn't tomorrow, after all." It is also interesting that it is precisely the easiest part of the question that has troubled Levin and led him to an impasse; and this is something purely Russian that the author has quite correctly noted: the whole point is that all these ideas and questions among us in Russia are only a matter of theory; they have all come to us from an alien order of things, from Europe, where they have long had their own historical and practical aspects. So what is to be done? Both our noblemen are Europeans, and it is not easy for them to free themselves from European authority; even here they must give Europe its due. And so Levin, the Russian heart, confuses the purely Russian and only possible answer to the question with the European approach to the question. He confuses the Christian solution with historical "right." For the sake of clarity, let us visualize the following little scene:

Levin stands deep in thought after his conversation when hunting with Stiva that night; and, as an honest soul, he has an agonizing longing to solve the question that is troubling him now and that must have been troubling him for a long time previously.

"Yes," he thinks, halfway to a decision. "If one really looks at the matter, then why do we—as Veslovsky was saying the other day—'eat, drink, hunt and do nothing, while the poor man has a life of everlasting toil'? Yes, Stiva is right, I *must* share my estate with the poor and go off to work for them."

Next to Levin stands "the poor man," and he says, "That's truly what you must do; it's your duty to give your estate to us, the poor, and to go and work for us." Levin emerges as completely right, and the "poor man" as completely wrong, at least when they decide the matter in what might be called its higher sense. But this is just where the whole difference in approach to the question lies. For the moral solution must not be confused with the historical one; otherwise there will be hopeless confusion, which is happening even now, particularly in the heads of Russian theoreticians as well as in the heads of the scoundrel Stivas and in the heads of the pure-in-heart Levins. In Europe, life and practice have already posed the question—though absurdly in terms of its ideal solution, but still realistically in terms of its current development, and without confusing the two different views—the moral and the historical—at least insofar as it is possible not to confuse them. Let me continue to explain my idea, though briefly.

Article 3. The Issue of the Day in Europe

Europe had its feudalism and its knights. But over the course of more than a thousand years the bourgeoisie gathered its strength and finally joined battle everywhere; it defeated the knights, drove them out, and then—it set itself up in their place. The truth of the saying "Ote-toi de là que je m'y mette" ("Get out of the way so I can take your place") was demonstrated in practice. But having taken the place of their former masters and taken over their property, the bourgeoisie totally bypassed the people, the proletarian; refusing to accept him as a brother, they transformed him, in exchange for a piece of bread, into a work force for their own well-being. Our Russian Stiva decides privately that he is in the wrong but deliberately chooses to go on being a scoundrel because he has a fine, soft life; the foreign Stiva does not agree with our Russian one and sees himself as being entirely in the right, and of course in his own terms he is more logical, for in his view there is no *right* here at all, there is only *history*, the historical course of events. He has taken the place of the knight because he conquered the knight by force, and he understands very well that the proletarian, who was still insignificant and weak during the struggle of the bourgeois with the knight, may very well gather his strength; indeed, he is gathering it with every day that passes. He can foresee quite clearly that when the proletarian is strong enough, he will push him aside, as the bourgeois once did the knight, and will say the very same words to him: "Get out of the way so I can take your place." There is no question of right here, there is only history. Oh, he would be ready for a compromise, for coming to terms somehow with his enemy; he's even made an attempt at it. But since he has very clearly deduced— and also knows from experience—that his enemy is not at all disposed to make peace, that he does not want to share but wants *everything;* since he knows, moreover, that if he makes any concession, he will only weaken himself—he has decided to yield nothing and is preparing to do battle. His situation may be hopeless, but it is human nature to strengthen one's spirits before battle; he does not despair but, on the contrary, girds up his loins for the fight, using all means at his disposal and exerting all his efforts so long as he has strength; he is weakening his opponent and, for the moment, that is all he is doing.

And so that's the point at which the matter now stands in Europe. It is true that formerly, and not that long ago, there was a *moral* approach to the question over in Europe as well; there were Fourierists and Cabetists, there were questionings, arguments, and debates about various most subtle issues. But now the leaders of the proletariat have put these things aside until the right time comes. They plainly want to do battle; they are organizing an army and marshaling it in their associations; they are raising funds, and they are confident of victory: "And then, after our victory, everything will take shape of itself in a practical fashion, although it's quite possible that this will happen only after rivers of blood have been shed." The bourgeois realizes that the leaders of the proletariat are enticing their followers simply with the prospect of plunder, and that, accordingly, there is no point in raising the moral aspect of the matter. However, even among the vanguard of the proletariat today there are a few ringleaders who also propound the moral rights of the poor. Those who head the movement tolerate these ringleaders specifically for show, so as to enhance their cause and give it an appearance of higher justice. Among these "moral" ringleaders are many schemers, but there are also many ardent believers. They state plainly that they want nothing for themselves but are working only for humanity; that they want to establish a new order of things for the good of humanity. But here the bourgeois can meet them on rather firm ground and point out that they want to compel him to become a brother to the proletarian and to share his property under threat of club and blood. Although this is rather close to the truth, the ringleaders answer that they in no way consider the bourgeoisie capable of becoming brothers to the people and that is why they are simply marching against them in force; they entirely exclude the bourgeoisie from their brotherhood: "Brotherhood will develop later, among the proletarians, but you—you are the hundred million heads condemned to extermination, and nothing more. You must pass from the scene, for the good of humanity." Other ringleaders plainly say that they need no brotherhood at all, that Christianity is nothing more than rubbish, and that the future of humanity will be built on scientific foundations. None of this, of course, can move or convince the bourgeois. He understands and replies that this society on scientific foundations is pure fantasy; that they have an image of humanity that is utterly different from the one nature has created; that it is difficult and impossible for a person to renounce his unconditional right to private property, the family, and freedom; that they demand too many sacrifices from their man of the future, as an individual; that it is possible to fashion such a human being only by means of terrible violence, after subjecting him to a terrible system of spying and continuous control by a most despotic power. In conclusion, the bourgeois challenges them to show him the power that could unite the man of the future into a society based on accord and not on force. In reply, the ringleaders cite utility and necessity, recognized by humans themselves, and the fact that, in order to save themselves from destruction and death, humans will consent voluntarily to make all the concessions demanded of them. The objections made to this point are that utility and self-preservation alone are never enough to engender complete and voluntary unity; that there is no utility that can replace self-will and the rights of the individual; that these forces and motives are too weak, and that all this, accordingly, remains a matter of conjecture as before. Were the leaders' actions to stem only from the moral aspect of the matter, the proletariat would pay no attention to them; and if they do follow them now and organize themselves to do battle, then it is only because they have been enticed by the promise of plunder and stirred up by the prospect of destruction and battle. In the final analysis, therefore, the moral aspect of the question should be entirely discarded because it will not withstand the slightest criticism; they should simply prepare to fight.

That is how the Europeans approach the matter. Both sides are terribly wrong, and both sides will perish in their sins. I repeat, what is most difficult for us Russians is that even our Levins are pondering these very same questions when the only possible solution to the question, the Russian one—which holds true not only for the Russians but for all of humanity—is the moral, i.e., the Christian approach. Such an approach is unthinkable in Europe, although even there, sooner or later, after rivers of blood and a hundred million heads, it will have to be acknowledged, for only in it is there a way out.

Article 4. The Russian Solution to the Problem

If you have felt it a hard thing only "to eat, drink, do nothing, and go hunting," and if you have really felt this, and if you really feel sorry for "the poor," of whom there are so many, then give them your property; if you wish, donate it to the common good; go and work for all and "you will find your reward in heaven, where they neither hoard nor covet." Go, like Vlas, with

> All the might of his great soul
> Devoted to his Godly cause.

And if you do not want to collect money for God's temple, as Vlas did, then take some concern for the enlightenment of the soul of this poor man; improve him, teach him. And if, indeed, everyone did as you and gave his property to the poor, then all the wealth of the wealthy of the world, divided among all, would be no more than a drop in the sea. And therefore we must take more concern for enlightenment, for education, and for the strengthening of love. Then wealth will grow in actual fact; and it will be genuine wealth, because wealth is not found in golden raiment but in the joy of common unity and in the steadfast hope of each for the help of all others in time of need, to him and to his children. And do not say that you are only a single, weak person and that if you are the only one to give away your property and go off to serve humanity, you will thereby accomplish nothing and make nothing better. On the contrary, if there be but a few such as you, the cause will be advanced. And, really, there is not *necessarily* any need even to give away your property, for any kind of *necessity* here, where love is the issue, will have the air of conformity, regulations, and literal-mindedness. The conviction that one has fulfilled the letter of the law leads only to pride, formalism, and indolence. One must do only that which the heart commands: if it commands you to give away your property, then give it away; if it commands you to go and work for the benefit of all, then go and do so. But even here, do not follow the example of some idealists who at once take up a wheelbarrow and say: "I'm not a nobleman; I want to work like a peasant." The wheelbarrow is only another expression of conformity.

No, it's quite the contrary: if you feel that you will be useful to all as a scholar, then go to university and keep sufficient means to finance your studies. It is not the giving away of your property and the donning of a peasant coat that is obligatory: all that is only literal-mindedness and formalism; what is obligatory and important is merely *your determination to do all for the sake of active love,* all that you possibly can, all that you yourself sincerely believe is possible for you to do. All these efforts to "simplify" one's life are merely the assuming of a disguise, disrespectful to the People and demeaning to you. You are too "complex" to simplify yourself and, in any case, your education will not let you become a peasant. You would do better to elevate the peasant to your level of "complexity." You must only be sincere and open-hearted; this is better than any sort of "simplification." But above all, do not let yourself be frightened; do not quote our proverb: "One man on the field is not a warrior," and so on. Every one who has conceived a sincere desire to find the truth is already awfully powerful. Likewise, do not ape certain phrase-mongers who continually repeat for all to hear: "They won't allow us to do anything; they tie our hands; they fill our hearts with despair and disillusionment!" and so on. All these are only phrase-mongers and characters from some second-rate poem, idlers who are showing off. He who wishes to be useful can, even with hands literally tied, accomplish a mass of good deeds. A real worker who sets out to do something will at once see so many tasks before him that he will not start to complain that he isn't allowed to do anything; he will surely find something and manage to do it. All genuine workers know this. The study of Russia alone will take up so much of our time, because it is only the rarest person among us who knows our Russia. Complaints about disillusionment are utterly stupid: joy at the edifice which is being erected should soothe any soul and assuage any thirst, even though your own contribution to the edifice may have been merely a few grains of sand. Your sole reward is love, should you merit it. Let's suppose you need no reward; still, you are working in the cause of love, and so you cannot help but encourage love. But let no one tell you that you should have done all this even without love, for your own benefit, as it were, and that if you hadn't you would have been forced to do so. No, we in Russia must implant other convictions, and particularly in regard to conceptions of freedom, equality, and brotherhood. The way the world conceives freedom today is as license, whereas real freedom lies only in overcoming the self and the will so as ultimately to achieve a moral condition in which one at each moment is the real master of himself. But giving license to your desires only leads to your enslavement. That is why almost the whole of today's world supposes that freedom lies in financial security and in laws guaranteeing that financial security: "I have money and so I can do whatever I like; I have money and so I will not perish and will not have to ask help from anyone; not having to ask for anyone's help is the highest freedom." Yet in essence this is not freedom but slavery once again, a slavery that comes from money. On the contrary, the very highest form of freedom is not laying up money and seeking security in it, but "dividing up all that you have and going off to serve everyone." If a person is capable of that, if he is capable of overcoming himself to that extent—is he then not free? This is the highest manifestation of the will! And then, what does equality mean in today's civilized world? A jealous watching of one another, conceit, and envy: "He's clever; he's a Shakespeare who takes pride in his talent; he must be humbled, destroyed." Meanwhile, genuine equality says: "What do I care if you are more talented than I, more clever, more handsome? I'm glad of it, rather, because I love you. But though I may be less important than you, I respect myself as a person; and you know this and respect me yourself, and I am happy with your respect. If you, through your abilities, can bring me and everyone else a hundredfold more benefit than I can bring you, then I bless you for it; I marvel at you and thank you, and in no way do I hold my awe for you as something shameful; on the contrary, I am happy that I am grateful to you, and if I work for you and for all in so far as my feeble abilities allow, then it is certainly not to try to balance my account with you, but because I love you all."

If all people speak in this way, then, of course, they will also become brothers, and not merely because of economic benefit but because of the fullness of the joy of life, because of the fullness of love.

Some may say that this is a fantasy, that this "Russian solution to the problem" is the "Kingdom of Heaven" and is possible only in the Kingdom of Heaven. Yes, the Stivas would get very angry if the Kingdom of Heaven were to arrive. But one must take into consideration the fact alone that there is much less fantasy and much more plausibility in this "Russian solution to the problem" than in the European solution. Such people—the "Vlases," I mean—we have already seen and continue to see among all our social classes; we even see them quite often; Europe's "man of the future" we have never yet seen anywhere, and he himself has vowed to come only after wading through rivers of blood. You may say that individuals, and tens of individuals, are of no help and that we must strive for well-known, universal principles and forms of organization. But even if there existed such principles and forms as could organize society without

345

a flaw, and even if it were possible to acquire such principles and forms without trying them in practice—just so, a priori, from heartfelt dreams and "scientific" statistics which, besides, derive from the former social order—then, given people who have not been prepared and fashioned for this new order, no rules could hold up or be put into practice; on the contrary, they would only be a burden. I have unbounded faith in our people of the future and in those who are already beginning now; I was just speaking of them, above, and saying that they had not yet managed to reach any accord, that they seemed very much broken into small groups and camps according to their convictions; yet all of them were seeking the truth before all else and, were they only to learn where that truth could be found, they would be ready to sacrifice all, even their lives, in order to attain it. Believe me, if they set forth on the true path and find this truth at last, they will draw everyone else after them, and not by force but freely. That is what single individuals can do to begin with. And that is the plow with which we can turn over our "Virgin Soil." Rather than go preaching to people about what they ought to be, show them through your own example. Carry it out yourselves in practice, and everyone will follow you. What is utopian, what is impossible here I do not understand! It's true that we are very corrupt, very fainthearted, and therefore we do not believe and we scoff. But the ones who matter now are scarcely we, they are the people of the future. The People are pure in heart, but they need to be educated. But the pure in heart are rising up in our milieu as well, and that is what truly matters! This is what we must believe above all, and this is what we must learn to discern. And for the pure in heart I have one piece of advice: self-control and self-mastery before taking any first step. Carry it out yourselves before compelling anyone else—herein lies the entire secret of the first step.

March

CHAPTER TWO

Article 1. "The Jewish Question"

Oh, don't think that I'm really planning to raise "the Jewish question"! I wrote the title as a joke. Raising a question of such magnitude as the position of the Jew in Russia, and the position of Russia, who numbers three million Jews among her sons, is too much for me. This question is beyond my limits. But I still can have some opinion of my own, and it turns out that some Jews have suddenly begun to take an interest in my opinion. I have been getting letters from them for some time now; they reproach me severely and bitterly for "attacking" them and for "hating the Yids," hating them not for their flaws, "not as an exploiter," but specifically as a race, supposedly because "Judas betrayed Christ." Such things are written by "educated" Jews, i.e., by those who (I have noted this, but I am in no way making a generalization—this I wish to point out in advance) always seem to try to let you know that they, with their education, have long ceased to share the "prejudices" of their nation; that they no longer carry out their religious rites as do other petty Jews; that they consider this beneath the level of their enlightenment; that, moreover, they do not even believe in God. I note, apropos of this and in parentheses, that all these gentlemen from the "higher Jews" who defend their nation in this way find it too great a sin to ignore their forty-centuries-old Jehovah and to renounce him. And it is a sin, not only because of feelings of nationality, by any means; there are also other reasons of very great importance. It's an odd thing, indeed: a Jew without God is somehow unthinkable; one can't even imagine a Jew without God. But this is one of those immense topics, and we will drop it for the moment. What surprises me most is how and why I could be placed among the haters of the Jews as a people, as a nation. Even these gentlemen themselves permit me, to some extent, to condemn the Jew for some of his flaws and for being an exploiter, but—but this is only in words: when it comes to deeds, it is difficult to find anything more irritable and punctilious than an educated Jew and more ready than he to take offense—as a Jew. But once again: when and how did I declare my hatred for the Jews as a people? Since there was

never any such hatred in my heart—and those Jews who are acquainted
with me and who have had dealings with me know this—I, from the very
outset and before saying anything else, reject this accusation once and for
all so as not to make special mention of it later. Might they not be accusing
me of "hatred" because I sometimes call the Jew a "Yid"? But in the first
place, I never thought this was so offensive, and in the second place, as far
as I can recall, I always used the word "Yid" to denote a well-known idea:
"Yid, Yid-ism, the Kingdom of the Yids," etc. These designated a well-
known concept, a tendency, a characteristic of the age. One can argue
with that idea, one can disagree with it, but one should not take offense at
a word. I shall quote one portion of a letter from one highly educated Jew
who wrote me a long and, in many respects, a beautiful letter that aroused
great interest in me. It is one of the most characteristic accusations of me
of hating the Jews as a people. It goes without saying that the gentleman
who wrote me this letter will remain strictly anonymous.

> . . . but I intend to touch upon one subject which I truly cannot
> explain to myself. This is your hatred of the "Yid," which reveals
> itself in virtually every issue of your *Diary*.
>
> I would like to know why you rise up against the Yid and not
> against the exploiter in general; I can tolerate the prejudices of my
> nation no less than you—I have suffered from them in no small
> measure—but I will never agree that shameless exploitation lives in
> the blood of this nation.
>
> Can it be that *you* are incapable of rising to the basic law of all
> social life: that *all* citizens of a state, without exception, so long as
> they bear all the obligations essential for the existence of the state,
> must enjoy *all* the rights and privileges of its existence, and that
> those who do not abide by the law, the noxious elements of society,
> must be subject to one and the same measure of penalty, common
> to all? . . . Why, then, must the rights of all Jews be limited and why
> must there be special punitive laws for them? In what way is foreign
> exploitation (Jews, after all, are Russian subjects)—by Germans,
> Englishmen, and Greeks, of whom there are such numbers in
> Russia—better than exploitation by Yids? In what way is the
> Russian Orthodox kulak, the peasant exploiter, the tavern keeper,
> the one who preys on the peasant and sucks his blood and who has

so proliferated over *the whole of* Russia—in what way is he better
than those Yids who, still, operate within a limited sphere? In what
way is the one better than the other? . . .

(At this point my worthy correspondent compares several well-known
Russian kulaks with European ones to show that the Russians do not take
second place. But what does this prove? We don't boast about our kulaks,
after all; we don't display them as models to be emulated; on the contrary,
we agree completely that both types are bad.)

I could pose thousands of such questions to you.

Meanwhile, when you speak of the "Yid," you include in
this concept the entire, terribly impoverished mass of the three
million Jewish population of Russia of which 2,900,000, at least,
are waging a desperate struggle for a wretched existence, who are
morally purer not only than other nationalities but even purer than
the Russian People whom you deify. In this term you also include
the honorable numbers of Jews who have received higher education, who have distinguished themselves in all fields of the life of the
state; take, for example . . .

(Here again there are several names which, apart from Goldstein's, I
do not consider myself entitled to publish because some of them, perhaps,
might be displeased to read that they are of Jewish descent.)

. . . Goldstein (who died heroically in Serbia for the Slavic idea) and
who worked for the benefit of society and humanity? Your hatred
for the "Yid" extends even to Disraeli . . . who, probably, did not
know himself that his forebears were once Spanish Jews and who,
of course, does not regulate English Conservative policy from the
point of view of a "Yid" (?) . . .

No, unfortunately, you know neither the Jewish *people,* nor
their life, nor their spirit, nor, finally, their forty centuries of history.
Unfortunately—because you, in any case, are a sincere and absolutely honorable person; but you are unconsciously doing damage
to an enormous mass of impoverished people, while the powerful
"Yids" who receive in their salons the powerful people of this world

are, of course, afraid neither of the press nor even of the impotent
rage of the exploited. But enough of this subject! I will scarcely be
able to persuade you to my view, but I would very much like you to
convince me.

   That's the excerpt. Before I make any reply (for I do not want to accept
so serious an accusation), I will note the intemperance of the attack and
the degree of touchiness. During the entire year of publishing my *Diary*
there positively was no article of such dimensions against the "Yid" as
could justify an attack of such vehemence. In the second place, one cannot
help but note that the honorable correspondent, when he touches on the
Russian People in these few lines, could not restrain himself and could not
resist treating this poor Russian People with rather excessive contempt.
It's true that in Russia even the Russians themselves haven't left a single
spot unspat upon (as Shchedrin expressed it), so it's all the more excusable
for a Jew. But in any case, this bitterness clearly testifies to the way the Jews
themselves regard the Russians. This was written, indeed, by an educated
and talented person (only I think he is not without prejudices); so, after
that, what can we expect from the uneducated Jew, of whom there are so
many? What feelings must they have toward the Russians? I say this not in
accusation: this is all natural; I want only to point out that when it comes to
motives for our alienation from the Jew, it is, perhaps, not only the Russian
People who are at fault and that these motives have accumulated, naturally,
on both sides, and that one still does not know which side has more of
them. Having noted that, I will say a few words in my defense and, generally, on how I regard the matter. And even though, I repeat, this question is
too large for me to cope with, I still can express a thing or two about it.

Article 2. Pro and Contra

Granted, it is very difficult to learn the forty centuries of history of a
people such as the Jews; but one initial thing I do know is that certainly
no other people in the whole world have complained so much about their
fate, complained constantly, at their every step and every word, about
their oppression, their suffering, their martyrdom. One would think that
it is not they who rule in Europe, not they who at least control the stock

exchanges there and, accordingly, the policy, the internal affairs, and the morality of the states. The noble Goldstein may die for the Slavic idea. But still, were the Jewish idea not so powerful in the world, that same "Slavic" question (last year's question) might well have been solved long ago in favor of the Slavs, not the Turks. I am prepared to believe that Lord Beaconsfield himself, perhaps, has forgotten about his descent, some time ago, from Spanish Yids (however he certainly hasn't forgotten); but that he "regulated English Conservative policy" over the last year *in part* from the viewpoint of a Yid—in this, I think, there can be no doubt. That this happened "in part" is impossible not to admit.

But let all this be my idle talk that proves nothing, merely my casual tone and casual words. I grant that. Yet I am still unable to believe completely the cries of the Jews that they are so downtrodden, tormented, and oppressed. In my view, the Russian peasant, and the Russian commoner generally, bears burdens that are almost greater than the Jews'. My correspondent writes me, in another letter:

> First of all it is *essential* to grant them (the Jews) all the civil rights (just think that they are still deprived of the most basic right: that of free choice of place of residence, which results in a host of terrible restrictions for the whole mass of the Jews) that are enjoyed by all other non-Russian nationalities in Russia, and only then demand from them that they fulfill their obligations to the state and to the native population.

But you, Mr. Correspondent—you who tell me in this same letter, on the next page, that you "have a lot more love and pity for the toiling masses of the Russian People than for the Jews" (which, for a Jew, is surely too strongly stated)—you must keep in mind that while the Jew "was enduring the consequences of his lack of free choice of place of residence," at the same time twenty-three million of the "Russian toiling masses" were enduring serfdom, which, of course, was a bit more painful than "choice of place of residence." And so, did the Jews take pity on them then? I don't think so; people on the western frontier of Russia and in the south will give you a detailed answer to that. No, even then they were crying in just the same way about rights that the Russian People themselves did not have, crying and complaining that they were downtrodden and martyrs and that once they were given more rights, "then demand from us the fulfillment of obligations to the state and to the native population." And so the liberator came and liberated the native People; and who do you think were the first to fall upon them as on a victim? Who was foremost in taking advantage of their weaknesses? Who, in their eternal pursuit of gold, set about swindling them? Who at once took the place, wherever they could manage it, of the former landowners—with the difference that though the landowners may have thoroughly exploited people, they still tried not to ruin their peasants, out of self-interest, perhaps, so as not to wear out the labor force, whereas the Jew doesn't care about wearing out Russian labor; he takes what he can and he's gone. I know that when they read this the Jews will at once cry out that it's untrue, that it's a slander, that I am lying, that I believe all these stupid remarks, that I "do not know the forty centuries of history" of these immaculate angels who are incomparably "morally purer not only than other nationalities but even purer than the Russian People whom I deify" (according to my correspondent—see above). But I'll grant that; let them be morally purer than all the other peoples of the world, and purer than the Russians, naturally; yet I have only just read in the March issue of the *European Messenger* the news that the Jews in America, in the Southern states, have already thrown themselves en masse on the many millions of liberated Negroes and have already got them in their clutches in their usual style via the well-known and eternal "pursuit of gold" and by taking advantage of the inexperience and weaknesses of the exploited people. Imagine that when I read this I at once recalled that five years ago the very same thing had occurred to me—namely, that now the Negroes have been liberated from their slavery, they still won't come off unscathed because the Jews, who are so numerous in the world, will at once fling themselves on this fresh little victim. That is what I thought and, I assure you, several times thereafter in those days it occurred to me: "Why is it that we hear nothing of the Jews over there? Why don't the papers write about it? Why, these Negroes are a treasure trove for the Jews; surely they won't pass that up?" And so I waited, and the papers did write about it; I read it. And some ten days ago I read in *New Times* (no. 371) a report from Kovno, a most characteristic one, that says "the Jews have made such an onslaught on the local Lithuanian population that they have almost destroyed all of them with vodka, and it was only their Catholic priests who managed to save the poor drunkards by threatening them with the torments of hell and organizing temperance societies among them." The enlightened correspondent, it's true, blushes with embarrassment for his compatriots, who still believe in priests and the torments of hell, but he adds here that some enlightened local economists have risen up in the wake of the priests and have begun to organize rural banks, specifically to save the people from the money-lending Jew, as well as rural markets so that "the poor toiling mass" can acquire the necessities of life at proper prices, not the ones set by a Jew. Well, I've read all that and I know that at once people will begin shouting at me that none of this proves anything; that it happens because the Jews themselves are oppressed and poor; that all this is merely the "struggle for survival"; that only an idiot would be unable to figure that out; and that if the Jews themselves were not so poor but, rather, could enrich themselves, then they would at once show their humane side so that the whole world would be astonished. But, of course, all these Negroes and Lithuanians are even poorer than the Jews who are squeezing them dry, and yet the former (just read the news item) disdain the sort of trade for which the Jew is so avid. In the second place, it's not hard to be humane and moral when you're happy and rolling in money, but once it's a question of "struggle for survival"; then you'd best keep your distance. As far as I'm concerned, that's not such an angelic quality; and in the third place, I'm not, after all, setting forth these two stories from *The European Messenger* and *New Times* as absolutely fundamental facts that explain everything once and for all. If one begins to write the history of this worldwide tribe, one can at once find a hundred thousand such facts, and ones even more significant than these, so that one or two extra facts will not add anything in particular; yet there's something curious here: it's curious that just as soon as you need some information about the Jew and his dealings—whether it be for an argument or simply in a moment of your own ponderings—you needn't go to a public library; you needn't go rummaging in any old books or in your own old notes; you needn't make an effort, you needn't search, you needn't strain yourself; you needn't move, you needn't even get up from your chair: just reach over to the first newspaper that happens to be lying next to you and take a look at the second or third page: you'll certainly find something about the Jews and certainly something that interests you; certainly it will be something most characteristic and certainly it will be

the same old thing—the same old exploits, I mean! And so you have to
agree that this really does mean something; it does indicate something; it
does reveal something to you, even though you may be a total ignoramus
about the forty centuries of history of this tribe. Naturally, people will tell
me that everyone is obsessed with hatred and so everyone lies. Of course,
it could well be that everyone, to the last man, is lying, but in that case a
new question arises: if everyone, to the last man, is lying and is obsessed
with such hatred, then this hatred must have stemmed from something;
this universal hatred must mean something, after all; "the word *everyone*
means something, after all!" as Belinsky once exclaimed.

   "Free choice of place of residence!" But is the "native" Russian person
really so absolutely free in his choice of place of residence? Do not the
former restrictions on completely free choice in the place of residence—
restrictions that are undesirable survivals from the time of serfdom and
have long been an object of the government's attention—continue to exist
for the Russian commoner as well, right up to the present day? But as far as
the Jews are concerned, it's obvious to everyone that their rights in choice
of place of residence have broadened immensely over the last twenty years.
At least they have appeared in Russia in places where they were never
seen formerly. But the Jews keep on complaining about hatred and restrictions. I may not have the most thorough knowledge of Jewish life, but
there is one thing I do know for certain and am prepared to argue about
with anyone: namely, that among our common People there is no preconceived, a priori, obtuse, religious hatred of the Jew, supposedly based on
the notion that "Judas betrayed Christ." If one does hear this from some
little urchins or drunkards, still the whole of our People regard the Jew, I
repeat, without any preconceived hatred. I have seen this over the course
of fifty years. I even happened to live among the People, among a mass of
them, in the same barracks, and sleep on the same bunks as they. There
were several Jews there, and no one *hated* them, no one excluded them or
persecuted them. When they prayed (and the Jews pray with loud exclamations, wearing a special garment), no one found this strange or hindered
them or laughed at them, something, however, which was just what one
would expect from such a coarse (as we see it) People as the Russians; on
the contrary, when they looked at them they would say: "That's the sort of
faith they have; that's how they pray"—and they would pass by peacefully
and almost approvingly. And yet these same Jews shunned the Russians

in many respects: they did not want to eat with them; they regarded them almost haughtily (and this, of all places, in prison!); and, in general, they showed loathing and aversion toward the Russians, these "native" People. Exactly the same things happen in soldiers' barracks, over the whole of Russia: just pay a visit and ask whether a Jew in the barracks is abused as a Jew, as a *Yid*, because of his customs and his faith. Nowhere is he abused, and this is the case among the People everywhere. On the contrary, I assure you that in the barracks and everywhere else the Russian common person sees and understands all too well (and, indeed, the Jews themselves don't hide it) that the Jew does not want to eat with him, turns up his nose at him, avoids him, and does his best to build a wall between them; and yet, instead of taking offense at this, the Russian common person calmly and clearly says, "That's the sort of faith they have; it's because of his faith that he won't eat with us and keeps to himself" (not because he is hostile, that is), and having understood this great reason, he forgives the Jew with all his heart. Yet at times, a wild notion would come into my head: what if it weren't the Jews who numbered three million in Russia but the Russians; and what if there were eighty million Jews? Now how would they trans- form the Russians, and how would they treat them? Would they allow them to become their equals in rights? Would they allow them to pray freely in their midst? Would they not turn them directly into slaves? Even worse: would they not strip them utterly bare? Would they not massacre them altogether, exterminate them completely, as they did more than once with alien peoples in times of old in their ancient history? No, ladies and gentlemen, I assure you that there is no preconceived hatred of the Jew in the Russian People, although there is, perhaps, an antipathy, in certain areas particularly, and even a very strong antipathy, perhaps. Oh, this can't be avoided; it exists, but it certainly does not arise from the fact that he is a Jew; it is due neither to racial nor religious hatred of any sort but comes from other motives, for which it is not the native people but the Jew himself who is responsible.

Article 3. *Status in Statu.* Forty Centuries of Existence.

Hatred, and hatred caused by prejudice—that is the accusation the Jews make against the native population. But since we've begun on the topic of prejudices, then what do you think: does the Jew harbor fewer prejudices toward the Russian than the Russian toward the Jew? Doesn't he have a few more of them? I just gave you some examples of how the Russian common person regards the Jew; but I have before me letters from Jews, not common people but educated Jews, and how much hatred these letters express toward the "native population"! What's most important is that they don't notice the hatred contained in what they write.

You see, in order to exist on the earth for forty centuries, i.e., for almost the entire historical period of humanity, and to exist in such a close and indissoluble unity; in order to lose so many times their territory, their political independence, their laws, almost even their religion—to lose these things and each time to unite once more, to be reborn once more *in their old idea,* even though in another form, and to create themselves, their laws, and almost their religion once more—no, a people of such vitality, a people so unusually strong and energetic, a people so unprecedented in the world cannot exist without *status in statu,* something they have maintained always and everywhere during their most awful, thousand-year-long Diaspora and persecution. When I speak of *status in statu* I am certainly not making any accusation. But still, what is the meaning of this *status in statu;* what is its centuries-old, unchanging idea, and where does the essence of this idea lie?

To expound this would take a long time and, indeed, would be impossible in a short little article; it would also be impossible because, despite the forty centuries that have elapsed, *all the times and the seasons* have not yet arrived, and the final word of humanity about this great tribe still remains to be said. But without entering into the essence and the depth of this subject, one can outline at least some of the characteristics of this *status in statu,* even if only superficially. These characteristics are: alienation and estrangement on the level of religious dogma; no intermingling; a belief that there exists but one national individuality in the world—the Jew, and though there may be some others, one still has to think of them as nonexistent, as it were. "Go forth from the other nations, form thine own entity and know that henceforth thou art *the only one before God;* destroy the others or enslave them or exploit them. Have faith in thy victory over the whole world; have faith that all will submit to thee. Shun everyone resolutely, and have no communion with any in thy daily life. And even when thou art deprived of thy land, thy political individuality, even when thou are scattered over the face of the earth and among all the other peoples—pay no heed; have faith in all these things that have been promised unto thee; believe, once and for all, that all this will come to pass; and meanwhile thou must live, shun, cling together, exploit and— wait, wait. . . ." That is the essential idea of this *status in statu;* and then, of course, there are the internal and, perhaps, mysterious laws that preserve this idea.

Gentlemen—you educated Jews and opponents—you say that this is all nonsense and that "if there really is a *status in statu* (i.e., that there was, but now, supposedly, there remain only the weakest traces of it), then it is only because the persecutions have led to it; persecutions have given birth to it, religious persecutions from the Middle Ages and earlier; and this *status in statu* has arisen exclusively from a sense of self-preservation. If it does continue, particularly in Russia, then it is because the Jew still does not have rights equal to those of the native population." But this is how it seems to me: even if the Jew really did have equal rights, he would still never give up his *status in statu.* Moreover, to attribute the *status in statu* only to persecutions and a sense of self-preservation is insufficient. Indeed, the tenacity in self-preservation would not have lasted forty centuries; the Jews would have grown tired of trying to preserve themselves over such a period. Even the mightiest of the world's civilizations never lasted half of forty centuries and lost their political force and their tribal characteristics. It is not self-preservation alone that is the main reason here, it is a certain idea that has a motive power and an attraction; it is a certain something, universal and profound, on which, perhaps, humanity is still incapable of pronouncing its last word, as I said above. That we have something here which has a predominantly religious character—that is beyond doubt. That their Providence, under the former, original name of Jehovah, with his ideal and his covenant, continues to lead his people to a fixed goal—that is certainly beyond doubt. Besides, it's impossible, I repeat, even to imagine a Jew without God; moreover, I don't believe that there are godless people among educated Jews either: they are all of the same essence, and Lord only knows what the world can expect from these educated Jews! Even in childhood I read and heard the legend about the Jews that told how they were all faithfully awaiting the Messiah, every one of them, from the very lowest Yid to the very highest and most learned among them, the philosopher and cabalist-rabbi; that

they all believe the Messiah will gather them together in Jerusalem once
more and will use his sword to bring down all the other peoples to sit
at their feet; that for some reason the Jews, at least the overwhelming
majority of them, prefer but one profession—the trade in gold or, at least,
the working of that metal; and they do this, supposedly, so that when the
Messiah appears they will not have a new fatherland and not be attached
to an alien land, which they would own, but will possess everything only
in the form of gold and jewels that will be easier to take away when

> The ray of dawn casts forth its glow:
> The cymbal, flute, and tambourine,
> The silver, gold, and holy shrine,
> We shall bring to our ancient home,
> Our much beloved Palestine.

I heard all this, I repeat, as a legend, but I believe that the essence of the
thing exists without a doubt, particularly among the great mass of Jews,
in the form of an instinctive and irresistible predilection. But in order for
such an essence to be preserved, it's essential, of course, that the strictest
status in statu be preserved as well. It is being preserved. And so it is not
only persecution that was and is the motive here, but another *idea*. . . .

If the Jews truly do have such a special, strict, internal makeup that
binds them into something integral and particular, then one might almost
give some thought to the question of granting them *rights* that are equal
in all respects to the rights of the native population. Naturally, everything
required by humaneness and justice, everything required by compassion
and Christian law—all this must be done for the Jews. But if they, fully
equipped with their particularity and their own special makeup, their
racial and religious segregation; if they, armed with laws and principles
entirely opposed to the idea by which the entire European world has
developed until now, at least—if they should demand complete equality
of *all possible* rights with those of the native population, then will they
not receive something more, something extra, something beyond that of
even the most native of native populations? Here, of course, the Jews will
point to other alien peoples: "These people, now, have been given equal
or almost equal rights, while the Jews have fewer rights than any aliens;

and that's because they're afraid of us, the Jews, because we're supposedly more harmful than other aliens. Yet how is the Jew harmful? If,
indeed, the Jewish people have some bad qualities, then it's only because
the Russians themselves encourage these through their own Russian
ignorance, through their own lack of development, through their own
incapacity for independence, through their own economic backwardness. The Russians themselves ask for an intermediary, a leader, someone
to look after their economic affairs, a creditor; they themselves call for
this and they themselves submit to him. On the other hand, just look at
Europe: the peoples there are strong and independent of spirit; they have
a strong sense of nationality; they have long been used to working and
know how to work; and so over there they aren't afraid of giving all rights
to the Jew! Have you ever heard anything in France about the harm from
the *status in statu* of their Jews?"

On the surface, this is a powerful argument; first of all, though, one
envisions, in parentheses, one observation—namely, "It follows, then, that
Jewry thrives in places where the people are still ignorant or not free or
economically backward—that's just where they're in clover!" And instead
of using their influence to raise the level of development, to encourage
knowledge, to give rise to economic competence among the native population—instead of this, the Jew, wherever he has settled, has humbled and
corrupted the people even more; humaneness in such places declined
even further; the level of education fell still lower; hopeless, inhuman
poverty spread even more abominably, and with it, despair. Ask the native
population in our border areas: what is it that drives the Jew and what
is it that has driven him for so many centuries? You will always get the
same answer: *mercilessness;* "They've been driven for so many centuries
by their mercilessness to us, solely by their thirst for our sweat and our
blood." And, in truth, the entire activity of the Jews in these border areas
of ours has consisted only in making the native population as hopelessly
dependent on them as possible by *taking advantage of the local laws.* Oh,
in this case they have always found the possibility of taking advantage of
rights and laws. They have always known how to maintain friendship with
those on whom the people depended, and it was certainly not for them to
grumble, at least in this regard, about *their limited rights in comparison
with the native population.* They've received from us quite enough of

these rights over the native population. The history of our border regions bears witness to the fate of the Russian People, over decades and centuries, in areas where the Jews have settled. And what do we see? Just point out any other tribe among Russia's aliens that could compete in this sense with the terrible influence of the Jew. You will not find any; in this sense the Jew preserves all of his distinctiveness compared with Russia's other aliens, and the reason for it, of course, is his *status in statu*, whose spirit is imbued precisely with this merciless attitude toward everyone who is not a Jew, this disrespect for every tribe and nation and for every human creature who is not a Jew. And how can that be justified by saying that in the west of Europe the peoples have not allowed themselves to be overcome and so, accordingly, the Russian People themselves are to blame? Because the Russian People in Russia's borderlands proved to be weaker than the European peoples (and solely as a result of their harsh, centuries-long political circumstances), must they, for that reason alone, be utterly crushed by exploitation and not be helped?

And if people are going to point to Europe—to France, for example— then it is hardly the case that the *status in statu* has been harmless there either. Of course, Christianity and its idea have declined and continue to decline there not through fault of the Jew but of the Europeans; yet there, too, one cannot fail to note the effective triumph of Jewry which has replaced many of the old ideas with its own. Oh, of course human beings always and at all times idolized materialism and tended to see and understand freedom only as safeguarding one's self with wealth accumulated with one's every effort and hoarded by every possible means. But never before have these strivings been elevated so openly and held up as a higher principle as in our nineteenth century. "Every man for himself and only for himself; all communion among people only for oneself"—such is the moral principle of the majority of today's people,* and not even of the bad people but, on the contrary, of those who labor and who do not rob and murder. But mercilessness to the lower masses, the decline of brotherhood, the exploitation of the poor by the rich—oh, of course, all these things existed before as well, and they always did,

*The basic idea of the bourgeoisie which, at the end of the last century, replaced the former world order and became the main idea of the entire present century throughout the entire European world. [Dostoevsky's note]

but—but they were not elevated to the level of higher truth and science; they were condemned by Christianity, while now, on the contrary, they are elevated to a virtue. And so it is not without significance that the Jews reign over all the stock exchanges there; it is not without significance that they control the credit, and not without significance, I repeat, that they are the ones who control the whole of international politics as well; and what will happen hereafter is, of course, known to the Jews themselves: their reign, their complete reign, is drawing nigh! Coming soon is the complete triumph of ideas before which feelings of love for humanity, the longing for truth, Christian feelings, the feelings of nationhood and even of national pride of Europe's peoples must give way. What lies ahead, on the contrary, is materialism, a blind, carnivorous lust for *personal* material security, a lust for personal accumulation of money by any means—it is this, and not the Christian idea of salvation only through the closest moral and brotherly unity of people, that is acknowledged as a higher goal, as something rational, as representing freedom. People will laugh and say that this is certainly not caused by the Jews over there. Of course, it is not only because of the Jews, but if the Jews have had their complete triumph and have flourished in Europe precisely when these new principles have triumphed there, even to the point of being elevated to a moral principle, then one cannot help but conclude that the Jews have also exerted their influence. Our opponents will point out that the Jews, on the contrary, are impoverished, impoverished everywhere, even, and in Russia particularly; that only the very top level of the Jews are wealthy—the bankers and the kings of the stock market—while almost nine-tenths of the rest of the Jews are, literally, beggars who rush about looking for a crust of bread, offering their services as middlemen, looking for a place to pick up a kopeck for bread. Yes, that's true, it seems, but what does it signify? Does this not mean precisely that in the very work of the Jews (I mean in the work of the overwhelming majority of them, at least), in their very exploitation, there is something wrong, abnormal, something unnatural that bears its own punishment within it? The Jew offers his services as intermediary and trades in the labor of another. Capital is accumulated labor; the Jew loves to trade in the labor of another! But none of this changes anything for the moment; yet the top level of Jews gains a stronger and surer hold over humanity and strives to mold the world to its image and its essence. The Jews keep shouting that there are good people among them as well.

Oh, heavens! Is this really the point? We aren't even talking about *good* or *bad* people now. And surely there are good people among them. Wasn't the late James Rothschild of Paris a good man? We are talking about the whole and its idea; we are talking about *Yidism* and about the *idea of the Yids,* which is creeping over the whole world in place of "unsuccessful" Christianity. . . . .

Article 4. But Long Live Brotherhood!

But what am I talking about, and why? Or am I, too, an enemy of the Jews? Can it be true, as one Jewish girl who is—of this I have no doubt— most honorable and educated (that's quite evident from her letter and from the sincere, ardent feeling expressed in it)—can it be true that I, too, am (in her words) an enemy of this "unfortunate" race which I "seem to attack so cruelly at every opportune moment"? "Your scorn for the race of Yids which 'thinks of nothing but itself,' etc., etc., is obvious." No, I will speak up against this "obviousness" and deny even the fact itself. On the contrary, I say and write specifically that "everything required by humaneness and justice, everything required by compassion and Christian law—all this must be done for the Jews." I wrote these words above, but now I will add that, despite all the considerations I have already set forth, in the end I still stand for the full extension of rights to the Jews in formal legislation and, if such is possible, also for the fullest equality of rights with the native population (N.B.: although in some instances, perhaps, they already now have more rights or, to put it better, more *possibility to exercise them,* than the native population itself). Of course, a fanciful picture like the following occurs to me: what if, for some reason, our rural commune, which defends our poor, native peasant from so many evils, should collapse? What if the Jews should descend like a horde upon that liberated peasant who has so little experience, who is so little able to restrain himself from temptation and who, until now, has been watched over by the entire commune? Why, that would be the end of him at once: all his possessions, all his strength would tomorrow pass into the hands of the Jew, and an era would begin that could not be compared with serfdom, or even with the Tatar yoke.

But despite all the "fanciful pictures" and despite everything that I wrote above, I still stand for complete and conclusive equality of rights—because this is Christ's law, because this is a Christian principle. But if that is so, then why on earth did I fill so many pages with writing, and what point did I want to make if I *contradicted myself* in such a fashion? Precisely this: that I am not contradicting myself and that from the standpoint of the Russians—the native population—I can see no obstacles to broadening Jewish rights; yet I do contend that there are many more of these obstacles on the Jewish side than on the Russian, and that if this thing so wholeheartedly desired has still not come to pass, then the Russian is much, much less to blame for it than the Jew himself. What I indicated about the common Jew—who did not want to associate and eat with the Russians, while they not only did not get angry at him and reply in kind but, rather, immediately understood the situation and forgave him, saying, "That's because of his religion"—in just the same way as in this common Jew we very often see the same boundless and arrogant anti-Russian prejudice in the educated one as well. Oh, they shout that they love the Russian People; one of them even wrote to me along those lines, saying that he was grieved that the Russian People were without a religion and understood nothing of their own Christianity. This is too strongly said for a Jew and only gives rise to the question as to whether this highly educated Jew himself understands anything about Christianity. But self-importance and arrogance are traits of the Jewish character that are very painful for us Russians. Which of us, the Russian or the Jew, is less able to understand the other? I avow that I would rather vindicate the Russian: the Russian, at least, has no (absolutely no) religious hatred for the Jew. And who has more of the other prejudices, and on which side are they? Now we hear the Jews shouting that they have been oppressed and persecuted for so many years, that they are oppressed and persecuted even now, and that the Russian must at least take this into account when he makes judgments on the Jewish character. Very well, we do take that into account and can prove it: among the educated classes of the Russian people voices have been raised in favor of the Jews on more than one occasion. Now what about the Jews: have they ever, and do they now, when they complain and make accusations against the Russians, take into account the many centuries of oppression and persecution the Russian

People themselves have endured? Can one really claim that the Russian
People have endured fewer misfortunes and evils "in their history" than
the Jews, in any place you care to mention? And can one really claim
that it was not the Jew who, so very often, joined with the oppressors
of the Russians, who indentured the Russian People and became their
oppressor himself? All this happened, after all; such things went on; this
is history, historical fact, but we've never heard anywhere that the Jewish
people have repented for it, yet they still accuse the Russian People of
having little love for them.

But still: "Let it come to pass! Let it come to pass!" May there be a
complete and a spiritual union of the tribes and no disparity in their rights!
And to this end I first implore my opponents and Jewish correspondents
to be, on the contrary, a bit more indulgent and fair to us Russians. If their
arrogance, if the perennial "resentful affliction" of the Jews toward the
tribe of Russians is only a prejudice, a "historical tumor," *and is not buried
among some far deeper mysteries of their law and their makeup*, then may
all this disappear as quickly as possible and may we all join together in a
single spirit, in complete brotherhood, for mutual help and for the great
cause of service to our land, our state, and our fatherland! May the mutual
accusations be softened; may the perennial intensification of these accusations, which stands in the way of a clear understanding of things, vanish
away. But one can vouch for the Russian People: oh, they will accept the
Jew in complete brotherhood, despite the difference in religion, and with
complete respect for the historical fact of this difference; nevertheless,
for brotherhood, for complete brotherhood, *brotherhood is needed on
both sides.* Let the Jew himself show the Russian even a little brotherly
feeling so as to encourage him. I know that among the Jewish people even
now one can find enough individuals who seek and long for the misunderstanding to be dispelled; these are humane people as well, and I will
not be the one to ignore that fact and hide the truth. It is specifically in
order that these useful and humane people should not grow despondent
and lose courage, that their prejudices might be weakened in some small
measure and that they might thus find it easier to begin to act—it is for
these reasons I would like to see the complete broadening of the rights
of the Jewish race, as far as is possible, at least, precisely in so far as the
Jewish people themselves demonstrate their capacity to accept and to use
these rights without damaging the interests of the native population. It

might even be possible to make some concessions in advance, to take still more steps forward on the Russian side. . . . The only question remains: will the new, good people among the Jews manage to do this, and to what extent are they themselves capable of serving the new and beautiful cause of *genuine* brotherly unity with people who are alien to them by religion and by blood?

from CHAPTER THREE

Article 1. The Funeral of "The Universal Man"

There are a lot of things I wanted to talk about in this March issue of my *Diary*. And here again it somehow happened that the thing I wanted to say only a few words about took up all the space. And there are so many topics I've been planning to discuss for a whole year, yet I just don't manage to get to them. There are certain things, particularly, about which a lot needs to be said, but since it very often happens that it's impossible to say a lot, one just doesn't take up the topic.

Apart from all these "significant" topics, I also wanted to say a few words this time about art, if only in passing. I saw Rossi in *Hamlet* and came to the conclusion that instead of Hamlet I had seen Mr. Rossi. But I'd better not begin that topic if I don't intend to say everything. I would like to say something (just a little) about Semiradsky's painting, but most of all I'd like to put in even a few words about idealism and realism in art, about Repin and about Mr. Raphael—but, obviously, all that will have to be put off to a more convenient moment.

And then I wanted to write, and at somewhat greater length, about a few of the letters I have received during the whole time I have been publishing my *Diary*, and about the anonymous letters in particular. Generally, I'm not able to answer all the letters I receive, and naturally not the anonymous ones, yet in the course of these nearly eighteen months these letters (on topics that concern all of us) have led me to make a few observations that are, perhaps, interesting—in my view, at least. At least one can make a few special remarks, based on experience, regarding today's intellectual mood in Russia; on the things that interest our active minds and the direction in which these minds are moving; on just who our active minds are; and in this regard, some very interesting traits emerge regarding age, sex, social class, and even one or another locality in Russia. I think that I might set aside a few places in some future issue of the *Diary* to take up at least a few of these anonymous letters and look at their characteristics, and I don't think that it would be all that boring, because there's a great range of views here. Of course, one can't talk about everything and convey it all—not even, perhaps, the most interesting things. And therefore I'm afraid to undertake it, not knowing whether I'll be able to manage the topic.

However, I do want to cite one letter now, and not an anonymous one; it is from a Miss L., a very young girl, a Jew, whom I know very well and whom I met in Petersburg and who now writes to me from the city of M——. I scarcely ever spoke to the respected Miss L. about "the Jewish question," although it seems that she is one of the strict and serious Jews. I can see that, oddly enough, this letter fits with the whole chapter on the Jews that I have just written. It would be too much to keep going on about the same topic. But the letter is on a different topic; and if it does, in part, concern the Jewish question, then it shows, as it were, an entirely different and quite opposite side of the question, and even something that might hint at its solution. I hope that Miss L. will graciously forgive me for my permitting myself to quote her words from that whole part of her letter on the funeral of Dr. Hindenburg in the city of M——; it was under the immediate impression of this funeral that she wrote these lines, so sincere and touching in their truth. I also did not want to conceal the fact that this was written by a Jew and that these feelings are the feelings of a Jew. . . .

> I am writing this under the fresh impression of a funeral march. Dr. *Hindenburg* was buried at the age of eighty-four. He was a Protestant, so his body was first taken to the church and only then to the cemetery. Never before at a funeral had I seen such sympathy, such ardent tears, or heard such words that came straight from the heart. . . . He died in such poverty that he lacked the means to pay for his burial.
>
> He had been practicing in M—— for fifty-eight years, and what an amount of good he did during that time. If only you knew what sort of man he was, Fedor Mikhailovich! He was a doctor and an obstetrician; his name will be preserved for posterity here; legends have already grown up around him; all the common people called him "father," and loved him, adored him; and only with his death did they realize what they had lost in this man. While he still lay in his coffin (in the church), there was not a single person, I think, who failed to go and shed tears over him and kiss his feet; and, in

particular, the poor Jewish women whom he helped so much, wept and prayed for him to go straight to heaven. Our former cook, an awfully poor woman, came to us today and said that when she gave birth to her last child, he saw that she had no food at home and gave her thirty kopecks to make herself some soup; after that he used to come every day and leave her twenty kopecks; and seeing that she was making her recovery he sent her a pair of partridges. In the same way, when he was called to one terribly poor woman who was about to give birth (these were the kind of women who would call him), he saw that she had nothing with which to clothe the child and took off his outer shirt and handkerchief (he wore a handkerchief tied round his head), tore them up and gave them to the woman.

He also cured one poor Jew, a wood-cutter; then the man's wife fell ill, and then his children; twice every single day the doctor would call on them, and when he had set them all on their feet again he asked the Jew: "How are you going to pay me?" The Jew replied that he had nothing at all except for a goat that he would sell that same day. And so he did; he sold the goat for four rubles and brought the money to the doctor; and then the doctor gave his servant twelve rubles in addition to the four and sent him off to buy a cow, and told the wood-cutter to go home. An hour later the servant brought the cow to the wood-cutter and said that the doctor believed that goat's milk was not good for them.

And so he lived all his life. There were cases when he left thirty or forty rubles with poor people; he would also give money to poor peasant women in the villages.

And in return they buried him like a saint. All the poor people closed up their shops and ran after the coffin. Among the Jews it is the custom to have boys who sing psalms at funerals, but it is forbidden to sing such psalms at the funeral of a non-Jew. This time the boys marched in the procession, ahead of the coffin, and sang these psalms. Prayers were said for his soul in all the synagogues, and the bells of *all* the churches were rung all during the procession. There was a military band, and Jewish musicians as well called on the son of the deceased to request, as an honor, permission to play during the procession. All the poor people donated something—five kopecks or ten—while the wealthy Jews gave a great deal and provided a magnificent, enormous wreath of fresh flowers with black and white ribbons at its sides on which, in gold letters, his major public services were listed—for instance, setting up a hospital, and so on—I couldn't make out what else was there; in any case, is it really possible to list all the good things he did?

A pastor and a Jewish rabbi spoke at his graveside, and both wept; but he just lay there in his old, worn uniform coat with an old handkerchief tied around his head—that dear head; and it seemed that he was sleeping, so fresh was the color of his face. . . .

Article 2. An Isolated Case

An isolated case, you may tell me. Well, gentlemen, what can I say? Once more I'm guilty: once more I see in an isolated case almost the beginning of the solution to the whole question . . . well, at least to that same "Jewish question" I used as title for my second chapter of this *Diary*. By the way, why did I call this old doctor "the universal man"? He was not a universal man but, rather, a common man. This city of M—— is a large provincial town in our western region and many Jews live there; there are Germans, Russians, of course, Poles, and Lithuanians—and all of them, all these nationalities recognized the righteous old man as one of their own. He himself was a Protestant and a German, very much a German: his way of buying a cow and sending it to that poor Jew was an example of purely German *Witz*. First he confounded him: "How are you going to pay me?" And, of course, when the poor fellow sold his last goat to pay his "benefactor," he didn't grumble in the least but, rather, was deeply pained because the goat was worth only four rubles, while "this poor old man who's working for all us poor folks has to live, too, and what's four rubles for all the fine things he's done for the family?" And the old fellow's a sly one: he chuckles, but his heart is full: "Now I'll show that poor down-and-out some of our German *Witz*!" How he must have laughed to himself when the cow was brought to the Jew; how his spirits must have been strengthened; and perhaps he spent all of that night in some wretched hovel fussing over a poor Jewish woman who was giving birth. And an eighty-year-old man would be happy to get a bit of sleep at night and give some rest to his tired old bones. If I were a painter I would paint just such a "genre" picture, that night at the bedside of the new Jewish mother. I'm awfully fond of realism in art, but some of our contemporary realists have *no moral center* in their paintings, as one mighty poet and refined artist expressed it the other day when he was speaking to me of Semiradsky's painting. Here, in this subject I propose for a "genre," there would be such a center, I think. And it's a lavish subject for an artist. In the first place, there's the absolute, incredible, stinking misery of a poor Jewish hut. One could even show a lot of humor here, and it would be awfully apropos: humor, after all, is the wit of deep feeling, and that definition appeals to me very much. Using refined feeling and intelligence, an artist can do a lot simply by reassigning the roles of all these wretched objects and household articles in the poor hut, and with this *amusing* reassignment he can touch your heart deeply at once. Even the lighting could be made interesting: a guttering tallow candle is burning out on a crooked table, while through the single, tiny window, covered with ice and hoarfrost, there glimmers the light of a new day, a new day of toil for the poor people. Women who have difficulty in giving birth often do so at dawn: they suffer the whole night through and give birth toward morning. And here's the tired old man, who's left the mother for a moment, looking after the child. There's nothing to wrap it in, there are no swaddling clothes, there's not even a rag (such poverty exists, gentlemen, I swear it does; this is realism of the purest sort, a realism that approaches the fantastic, so to say), and so the righteous old man has taken off his own wretched, worn uniform coat, has taken off his own shirt and is tearing it up to make swaddling clothes. His face has a severe, concentrated expression. The poor, newborn little Jewish baby is squirming on the bed before him; the Christian takes the little Jew in his arms and wraps him with the shirt taken from his own back. The solution to the Jewish question, gentlemen! The eighty-year-old torso of the doctor, naked and shivering from the morning damp, could take up a prominent place in the painting, as well as the face of the old man and the face of the worn-out, young mother who is looking at her newborn and at what the doctor is doing with it. Christ sees all this from on high, and the doctor knows it: "This poor little Yid will grow up and, perhaps, he himself may take the shirt from his back and give it to a Christian when he recalls the story of his own birth," thinks the old man to himself with

naive and noble faith. Will this come to pass? Most likely it will not, yet
it could come to pass; and on earth one can do nothing finer than believe
that this *can* and *will* come to pass. And the doctor has a right to believe
it, because in him it already has come to pass: "I did it, and another will
as well; am I any better than another?"—he reassures himself with such
a line of reasoning. A tired, ragged old Jewish woman, the mother of the
one who gave birth, is busy fussing at the stove. A Jew who has gone out
for a bundle of kindling opens the door of the hut and a cloud of frozen
vapor bursts into the room for a moment. Two little boys are asleep on
the floor on a felt blanket. In short, the background details could be very
effective. Even thirty copper kopecks on the table, which the doctor had
laid there for soup for the mother, could provide another touch: a copper
stack of three-kopeck pieces, methodically piled up and not just thrown
down. There could even be some mother-of-pearl, as in Semiradsky's
painting, where a piece of mother-of-pearl is amazingly rendered: doctors
are sometimes given such pretty little things, after all (so as not to pay
much in cash); and so the doctor's little mother-of-pearl cigar case is lying
here next to the stack of kopecks. Yes, indeed, the little picture would
come off with a "moral center." I invite someone to paint it.

An isolated case! A couple of years ago, from somewhere in the south
of Russia (I've forgotten where) there came news of some doctor who,
on the morning of a hot day, had just emerged from his bathing cabin,
refreshed, invigorated, and in a hurry to get home to have his coffee and
therefore unwilling, despite the urgings of a crowd, to help a drowned
man who had only just been pulled from the water at that same spot. I
think he was taken to court for this. And yet he was, perhaps, an educated
man with new ideas, a progressive, but one who "rationally" demanded
new, common laws and rights for all and who paid no heed to isolated
cases. He may well have supposed, rather, that isolated cases damage the
cause by postponing general solutions to the question, and so as far as
isolated cases are concerned, "the worse, the better." But without isolated
cases, common rights cannot be put into effect. This common man of
ours, though he may have been an isolated case, brought the whole city
together around his grave. Together those Russian peasant women and
poor Jewish women kissed his feet in his coffin; together they crowded
around him; together they wept. Fifty-eight years of service to humanity
in this city, fifty-eight years of ceaseless love united them all, if only

once, over his coffin in a common rapture and common tears. All the
town comes out for his funeral; the bells of *all* the churches peal; prayers
are sung in all the languages. The pastor, in tears, gives his speech over
the open grave. The rabbi stands off to one side, waiting, and when the
pastor has finished he takes his place and gives his speech and sheds the
same tears. Why, at that moment this very "Jewish question" had almost
been solved! The pastor and the rabbi were united in common love; why,
they almost embraced over this grave in the presence of Christians and
Jews. What does it matter that, when the crowd dispersed, each one took
up his old prejudices? Drops of water wear away even the stone, as the
proverb says, and these "common people" conquer the world by uniting
it; prejudices will pale with every isolated case, and finally they will disappear altogether. Legends will grow up around the old man, writes Miss
L., who is also a Jew and who also wept over the "dear head" of this lover
of humanity. And legends—they are the first step toward action, they are
a living recollection and a ceaseless reminder of these "conquerors of the
world," to whom the earth belongs. And once you believe that these really
are conquerors and that such people truly will "inherit the earth," you
have already almost become united in everything. All this is very simple;
only one thing seems complicated: just to become convinced that without
these same isolated instances you will never arrive at a total; everything
may be about to fall apart, but it is these people who can bring it together.
They are the ones who inspire ideas; they are the ones who give us faith;
they provide a living example, and so a proof as well. And there's certainly
no need to wait until everyone, or at least very many people, are as good
as they are: we need very few such people in order to save the world, so
powerful are they. And if such is the case, then how can we not hope?

April

from CHAPTER ONE

Article 1, extract. War. We Are Stronger Than the Others.

"It's war! War has been declared!" Such were the shouts we heard two weeks ago. "Is it to be war?" asked others when they heard. "It's true, it's been declared!" was the reply. "It may have been declared, but will it happen?" the others kept asking....

And, truly, questions such as these were asked; perhaps they are being asked even now. And it's not only the drawn-out diplomatic dawdling that has made people so skeptical; it's something else, an instinct. Everyone senses that something decisive has begun, that there is somehow going to be a resolution of an issue from the past—a long, drawn-out issue from the past—and that a step is being taken toward something quite new, toward something that means a sharp break with the past, that will renew and resurrect the things of the past for a new life and . . . that it is Russia who is taking this step! This is just the thing that makes our "wise" people so skeptical. There is an instinctive premonition, yet the skepticism continues: "Russia! But how can she? How does she dare? Is she ready? Is she ready inwardly and morally, never mind materially? That's Europe over there, and Europe is no small matter! While Russia . . . well, what is Russia? And to take such a step?" [. . .]

Article 2, extract. War Is Not Always a Scourge; Sometimes It Is Salvation

[. . .] Oh, let today's "universal men" and those full of contempt for their own People laugh at these "fantastic" words, but we cannot be blamed if we believe these things, that is, if we go hand in hand with our People who believe precisely these things. Ask the People; ask the soldier; why do they rise up, why do they go to war, what do they expect from the war that has just begun? They will tell you, as one man, that they are going to serve Christ and to liberate their oppressed brethren, and not a single one of them is thinking about seizing territory. Indeed, it is precisely here, in this present war, that we shall demonstrate our whole idea about Russia's future mission in Europe and demonstrate it precisely by the fact that when we do liberate the Slavic lands, we shall not acquire a single inch of them for ourselves (as Austria now has visions of doing); we shall, rather, watch to see that they live in mutual harmony and shall defend their freedom and independence, from the whole of Europe if need be. And if such is the case, then our idea is sacred, and our war is not at all "the age-old and bestial instinct of improperly developed nations," but is precisely the first step toward attaining that eternal peace in which we are fortunate enough to believe, toward attaining international unity *in truth,* and a humane state of well-being *in truth!* And so, one need not always preach only peace, and it is not in peace alone, despite everything, that salvation is to be found; sometimes it is also in war.

Article 3, extract. Does Shed Blood Save Us?

[...] Indeed, one can say generally that if society is unhealthy and infected, then even such a fine thing as a prolonged peace can, instead of benefiting society, be harmful to it. One can even apply this to all of Europe generally. It is not without reason that no generation has passed in the history of Europe, as far as we can remember it, without a war. And so, evidently, even war is essential for something; it is healing; it relieves humanity. This is shocking if one thinks in abstract terms, but in practice it turns out that way, it seems, and precisely because in an infected organism even such a fine thing as peace is transformed into something harmful. But still, the only useful war is one undertaken for a grand idea, for a higher and noble principle and not for material interests, not for greedy seizure of territory, not for contemptuous violence. Wars of that sort have only led nations along wrong paths and have always destroyed them. If not we, then our children, will see how England ends. Now, for everyone in the world, "the time is at hand." And about time, too.

from CHAPTER TWO

The Dream of a Ridiculous Man: A Fantastic Story

1

I'm a ridiculous man. Now they call me a madman. It would have been a promotion if I hadn't remained just as ridiculous in their eyes as before. But now it doesn't bother me; now they're all dear to me, and even when they laugh at me—even then there are things that make them especially dear. I'd laugh along with them—not at myself, but loving them—if I didn't feel so sad when I look at them. I feel sad, because they don't know the truth, while I know the truth. Ah, what a hard thing it is to be the only one who knows the truth! But they won't understand that. No, they won't understand.

But in times past I used to worry a good deal because I seemed a ridiculous man. Not seemed: I was. I was always a ridiculous man, and I've known it, I suppose, ever since I was born. Perhaps I knew it already at the age of seven. Then I went to school, and then to university, and what do you think? The more I studied, the more I came to realize that I was a ridiculous man. So far as I was concerned, the more deeply I became involved in my university studies, the more its ultimate purpose seemed only to prove and make clear to me that I was a ridiculous man. My life followed the same pattern as my studies. With every year the same awareness—that I looked like a ridiculous man in every respect—grew and strengthened within me. Everyone always laughed at me. But not one of them knew or suspected that if there was one person on earth who knew better than anyone that I was a ridiculous man, then that person was I myself; and this was just the thing that was most painful to me—that they didn't know it. But that was my own fault: I was always so proud that I could never have admitted this to anyone. This pride grew inside me over the years, and if there had ever come a time when I permitted myself to admit to someone that I was a ridiculous man, then I think that at once, that very same evening, I would have blown my head off with a revolver. Oh, the pains I suffered in my adolescence, thinking that I might give in and suddenly somehow confess to my comrades. But as I grew to manhood, for some reason I became calmer, even though with every year I became more and more aware of my awful quality. I say "for some reason" because even now I can't explain why. Perhaps it was because in my soul there kept growing a terrible ache caused by one thing that was infinitely beyond anything in my own self—namely, the conviction that everywhere on earth *nothing mattered.* I had sensed this long before, but the complete conviction somehow suddenly struck me in the last year. I suddenly sensed that, as far as I was concerned, *it wouldn't matter* whether the world existed or whether there were nothing anywhere. I began to sense and feel with all my being that *nothing existed around me.* At first I kept thinking that a good many things used to exist in the past; then I concluded that even in the past there had not been anything, but that for some reason it had only seemed as if there had been something. Little by little I became convinced that there would never be anything in the future either. At that point I suddenly stopped being angry at people and almost ceased to notice them. It's true that this showed itself even in the most trivial things: for instance, I'd be bumping into people as I was walking along the street. And this wasn't because I was deep in thought: what did I have to think about? At that point I'd stopped thinking altogether; it didn't matter to me. It would have been very well if I'd answered my questions; oh, but I hadn't answered a single one, and yet how many of them were there! But I began to feel that *nothing mattered,* and all the questions vanished.

And so, just after that, I discovered the truth. I discovered the truth last November, on the third of November to be precise, and I can recall every moment of my life since then. It happened on a gloomy evening, the gloomiest evening there could ever be. Some time after ten o'clock I was going back home, and I recall thinking specifically that there could be no gloomier time than this. Even in a physical sense. Rain had been pouring down all day, and it was the coldest and gloomiest rain, even a sort of menacing rain, I recall, with an open hostility toward people; and then, suddenly, towards eleven o'clock it stopped and a horrible dampness set in—damper and colder than when the rain was falling, and a kind of vapor rose from everything, from every stone on the pavement and from every side street, if you peered down to its farthest recesses. I suddenly imagined that if they were to shut off the gas everywhere it would be more cheerful, but one's heart was heavier with the lights on, because they illuminated everything. I had scarcely had any dinner that day and had spent the whole evening visiting an engineer, who had two of his friends there as well. I never opened my mouth the whole time and, I imagine, must have got on their nerves. They were discussing some controversial topic and suddenly even grew excited. But I could see that it really didn't matter to them and that they were excited just for form's sake. And suddenly I told them so: "Gentlemen," I said, "this really doesn't matter to you, does it?" They didn't take offense, and they all laughed at me. That was because I said what I did with no reproach and simply because it didn't matter to me. They saw very well that it didn't matter to me and were amused.

When the thought about the gaslight occurred to me out on the street, I looked up at the sky. The sky was awfully dark, but you could clearly make out some tattered clouds and bottomless black depths among them. Suddenly I noticed a tiny star in one of these depths and began looking at it intently. That was because this tiny star had given me an idea: I resolved that night to kill myself. I had made such a firm resolution even two months before, and despite my poverty I had bought a beautiful revolver and had loaded it that same day. Two months had passed, and it was still lying in my drawer; but so little did it matter to me that I wanted, at last, to catch a moment when it might matter, even just a little—for what reason, I don't know. And so it was that every night for these two months I came home thinking I would shoot myself. I kept waiting for the right moment. And now this tiny star had given me the idea, and I resolved that it would *definitely* happen on this very night. Why the tiny star gave me that idea I don't know.

And so, just as I was looking up at the sky, this little girl suddenly seized me by the elbow. The street was already deserted and there was scarcely a soul about. Off in the distance a cabbie was dozing in his droshky. The girl was about eight, wearing a kerchief and only a wretched little dress, and was soaked to the skin; but I particularly noticed her tattered boots, and remember them even now. The boots struck me particularly. She suddenly began tugging at my elbow and calling me. She wasn't weeping, but kept jerkily crying out some words that she couldn't pronounce clearly because she was all atremble from the cold. She was terrified of something and kept crying out desperately, "Mamma! Mamma!" I considered turning to face her, but said not a word and went

on my way; but she ran after me and plucked at my sleeve, and I could
hear in her voice the note that in very frightened children means despair.
I know that sound. Although she didn't say so in words, I understood
that her mother lay dying somewhere, or something had happened to
them there and she had run out to call someone or find something to help
her mother. But I didn't follow her and, on the contrary, suddenly got the
notion to drive her away. First I told her that she should find a policeman.
But she suddenly folded her tiny hands and, sobbing and choking, kept
running alongside me and would not leave. At that point I stamped my
foot and shouted at her. She only cried out, "Sir, oh sir! . . ." But suddenly
she left me and rushed across the street: some passerby had appeared
there, and she rushed over to him.

I went up to my fifth floor. I rent a place in a rooming house. My
room is wretched and small, with a semicircular garret window. I have
an oilcloth sofa, a table with some books on it, two chairs and a comfort-
able armchair, a very ancient thing but a "Voltaire one," for all that. I sat
down, lit a candle, and fell to thinking. In the room next door, behind the
partition, the row was still going on. They'd been at it for three days now.
A retired captain lived there, and he had visitors—six or more good-for-
nothings who were drinking vodka and playing faro with some old cards.
Last night there had been a brawl, and I know that two of them spent a
long time tearing at each other's hair. The landlady wanted to complain,
but she's awfully afraid of the captain. The only other lodgers in our place
are a short, skinny lady—an army officer's wife from out of town—with
three small children who have already fallen ill since coming to live here.
She and the children are deathly afraid of the captain and spend their
nights trembling and crossing themselves; the smallest child was so afraid
he had a fit of some kind. I know for certain that this captain sometimes
stops passersby on the Nevsky and begs money from them. They won't
take him into the civil service, yet the strange thing is (and this is why
I'm telling you this), the whole month the captain has been living here he
hasn't caused me the least bit of annoyance. From the very beginning, of
course, I shied away from any acquaintance with him, and in fact he was
bored with me from our first meeting; but no matter how much shouting
went on behind the partition and no matter how many of them there
were, it didn't matter to me. I sit up all night long and, truly, I don't hear
them—that's how well I'm able to ignore them. I never get to sleep until

dawn, you see, and it's been that way for a year now. I sit by the table in my armchair all night long and do nothing. Books I read only during the day. I sit, not thinking about anything in particular, just like that; vague thoughts wander through my mind, and I let them flow as they please. A whole candle burns up during the night. I sat down quietly by the table, took out the revolver and put it down in front of me. I recall asking myself as I put it down, "Is this how it is to be?" And I answered myself absolutely affirmatively, "Yes, it is." That's to say, I'll shoot myself. I knew that I would certainly shoot myself that night, but how much longer I would go on sitting by the table—that I didn't know. And of course I would have shot myself had it not been for that little girl.

2

You see, even though it didn't matter to me, I could still feel pain, for instance. If someone were to strike me, I would feel pain. It was just the same way in a moral sense: if something very sad were to happen, I would feel pity, just as before, when things in life still did matter to me. I had felt pity earlier that evening: I would certainly have helped out a child. So why didn't I help the little girl? It was because of a thought that came to me then: when she was tugging at my sleeve and calling me a question suddenly arose in my mind, and I wasn't able to answer it. It was an idle question, but it made me angry. I got angry because if I had already decided that I would kill myself that same night, then nothing on earth ought to matter to me, now more than ever. Why was it, then, that I suddenly felt that I was not indifferent to everything and pitied the little girl? I recall that I felt a great deal of pity for her, to the point even of a strange pain, even an improbable pain, given my situation. Truly, I don't know how better to convey that fleeting sensation I had then, but the sensation continued at home as well, when I had taken my seat by the table, and I was very irritated, as I hadn't been for a long time. One train of thought followed another. It seemed clear that if I were a human being and not yet a nonentity—and until such time as I became a nonentity—I was living, and accordingly could suffer, get angry, and feel shame for my actions. Granted. But if I were going to kill myself in two hours, say, then what should I care about this girl and about shame and about anything on earth? I was going to be transformed into a nonentity, an absolute nonentity. Could it be that the awareness of the fact that shortly I would *absolutely* cease to exist and that, accordingly, nothing else would exist—could that not have had the least influence either on the feeling of pity for the little girl or on the feeling of shame after the vile thing I had done? After all, that was the reason I had stamped my foot and shouted in a savage voice at the unfortunate child—that I could think "not only do I feel no pity but I can permit myself to commit some inhuman, vile deed because in two hours everything will be extinguished." Can you believe that this was why I shouted? Now I'm almost convinced of it. It seemed clear that from this point life and the world were dependent on me, as it were. I can even say that now the world had been created for me alone, as it were: I'll shoot myself and the world will exist no longer, at least as far as I'm concerned. To say nothing of the possibility that, perhaps, nothing really would exist for anyone else after me and that as soon as my consciousness was extinguished, the whole world would be extinguished with it, like a mirage, like a product of my own consciousness alone; and it would be done away with because this entire world and all these people were, perhaps, nothing more than myself. I recall that as I sat there thinking this out, I gave all these new questions that were crowding into my mind one after the other an entirely different twist and conceived something quite new. For example, I suddenly had the following strange notion: suppose I had formerly lived on the moon or on Mars and had committed there the most disgraceful and dishonorable act one can imagine for which I had been defamed and dishonored to an extent one can imagine only in some dream or nightmare; and, if I had later found myself on earth, still with the awareness of what I had done on the other planet, and knew, as well, that I would never ever return there, then would I, as I looked from the earth to the moon, feel as if *it didn't matter*? Would I have felt shame for my act or not? These were idle, unnecessary questions, since the revolver was lying on the table before me, and I knew with all my being that *it* would certainly happen; yet they excited me and worked me into a frenzy. It seemed I could not die now without having first resolved something. In short, that little girl saved me because the questions led me to put off shooting myself. Meanwhile, everything began to quiet down in the captain's room: they finished their card game and were settling down to sleep, still grumbling and lazily abusing one another. And at this point I suddenly dropped off to sleep in my chair by the table, something that had never happened to me before. I didn't notice falling asleep at all.

Dreams, as we know, are extraordinarily strange things: you'll have one that has an awful clarity, with all its details presented with lapidary precision, while in another you don't even notice how you swoop through time and space. Dreams, I think, are governed not by reason but desire, not by the head but the heart; and yet what crafty tricks my reason sometimes plays on me in dreams! Furthermore, some quite incomprehensible things happen to my reason in sleep. My brother, for instance, died five years ago. I sometimes dream of him: he takes part in my affairs; we are deeply involved with one another, yet throughout the dream I know and remember full well that my brother is dead and buried. How is it that I'm not amazed at the fact that even though he's dead, he's still right here beside me, concerning himself with my affairs? Why does my reason accept all this so completely? But enough. I'll get back to my dream. Yes, this is the dream I had then, my dream of the third of November. They tease me about it now, saying that it was only a dream, after all. But surely it doesn't matter whether it was a dream or not since this dream revealed the Truth to me. If once you've recognized the truth and have seen it, then you surely know that it is the truth and that there is not and cannot be any other, whether you are asleep or awake. Well, it was a dream—let it be so; yet I was going to put an end to this life which you make so much of, but my dream—oh, my dream revealed to me a new life, renewed, intense, and majestic!

Listen.

3

I said that I drifted off to sleep without noticing it and even went on mulling over those same matters, as it were. Suddenly I dreamed that I took up the revolver and, still sitting in my chair, was aiming it right at my heart—at my heart and not my head; earlier I had decided that I would definitely shoot myself in the head, in the right temple, to be specific. With the revolver pointed at my chest I hesitated for a second or two, and suddenly my candle, the table, and the wall before me began to move and sway. Quickly I fired.

In dreams you sometimes fall from a great height or are being stabbed or beaten, but you never feel any pain unless you somehow bump yourself against the bedpost; then you feel pain and almost always wake up. So it was in my dream: I felt no pain, but it seemed that after my shot everything within me was shaken, and suddenly everything went blank and there was an awful blackness all around me. I seemed to be blind and mute and was lying on my back, stretched out full-length on something hard, seeing nothing, and unable to make the least movement. All around me people were walking and shouting; the captain rumbled and the land-lady screeched—and suddenly there was another quiet interval, and now I was being carried in a closed coffin. And I could feel the coffin swaying and was thinking about that; and suddenly for the first time I was struck by the thought that I was dead, quite dead, and knew it without a doubt; I could not see and could not move, yet I could feel and think. But I quickly become resigned to that and, as usual in a dream, accepted the facts with no argument.

And so they were burying me. Everyone went away, and I was alone, completely alone. I made no move. Formerly, whenever I used to imagine what it would be like to be buried, the only sensation I would associate with the grave was cold and damp. And so it was now: I felt very cold, especially the tips of my toes; but I felt nothing more than that.

I lay there and, strangely enough, expected nothing, accepting without demur that a dead man had nothing to expect. But it was damp. I don't know how much time passed—an hour or a few days or many days. But suddenly a drop of water that had seeped through the lid of the coffin fell on my left eye, which was closed; a minute later there was another one, and a third a minute later; and so it continued, a drop every minute. Deep indignation suddenly welled up in my heart, and suddenly I felt a physical pain there: "That's my wound," I thought, "it's the shot, there's a bullet there. . . ." and the drops kept falling every minute, directly on my closed eyelid. And suddenly I called out—not with my voice, for I could not move, but with my whole being—to the One who governed all that was happening to me: "Whoever Thou may be, but if Thou art and if there does exist anything more rational than what is now coming to pass, then grant that it happen here as well. But if Thou art taking vengeance upon me for my unwise suicide, through the ugliness and absurdity of life after death, then know that no torment that might ever befall me could compare with the contempt that I shall always feel in silence, though it be through millions of years of martyrdom! . . ."

I cried out and fell silent. A profound silence continued for almost a whole minute, and one more drop of water even fell; but I knew, I knew and believed infinitely and unshakably that now everything must certainly change. And then suddenly my grave opened wide. I mean to say, I don't know whether all the earth had actually been dug away, but I was taken up by some dark and unfamiliar creature and we found ourselves in open space. I suddenly recovered my sight: it was the depths of night, and never ever had there been such darkness! We were flying through space, and the earth was already far behind us. I did not ask anything of the one who bore me; I waited, proud. I assured myself that I was not afraid and was dizzy with delight at the thought that I was not afraid. I don't recall how long we flew and can't even imagine it: everything happened as it always does in dreams, when one leaps through space and time and over the laws of existence, stopping only where one's heart longs to stop. I recall that I suddenly caught sight of one tiny star in the darkness. "Is that Sirius?" I asked, suddenly unable to hold back, for I had decided not to ask about anything. "No," answered the creature who bore me, "it is that same star you saw among the clouds when you were coming home." I knew that the face of the creature was in the likeness of a human. But, strangely enough, I did not like that creature and even felt a deep aversion toward it. I had been expecting complete nonexistence, and with that in mind had shot myself in the heart. And now I was in the hands of a creature which was not human, of course, but which *was,* which existed. "And so there is a life beyond the grave!" I thought, with the bizarre frivolity of dreams, but the real essence of my heart remained unchanged: "And if I must *be* once more," I thought, "and live again by someone else's intractable will, then I will not be vanquished and humiliated!"

"You know that I am afraid of you, and therefore you despise me," I said suddenly to my companion, unable to resist a humiliating question that held an admission and sensing the humiliation in my heart like a pinprick. He did not answer my question, but I suddenly sensed that I was not despised and that I was not being laughed at, that I was even being pitied, and that our journey had a goal, unknown and mysterious and concerning only me. Fear welled up in my heart. Something was passing from my silent companion to me, mutely but agonizingly, and it seemed to pierce to the core of my being. We were rushing through dark and unknown regions of space. I had long lost sight of the constellations familar to me. I knew that there are such stars in the vastness of the heavens whose rays reach the earth only after thousands and millions of years.

Perhaps we were already flying through these spaces. I was expecting something, in a terrible agony that gripped my heart. And suddenly I was shaken by a familiar and most nostalgic feeling: I suddenly caught sight of our sun! I knew that it could not be *our* sun that had given birth to *our* earth and that we were an infinite distance from our sun, but somehow I realized, with all my being, that this was just the same kind of sun as our own, its duplicate and twin. A sweet, welcoming feeling roused an ecstasy in my soul: the old, familiar power of the light, the same light that had given me life, made my heart respond and restored it, and I sensed life, the former life, for the first time since my burial.

"But if this is the sun, if this is exactly the same sun as ours," I cried, "then where is the earth?" And my companion pointed to a little star that glittered in the darkness with an emerald light. We were rushing directly toward it.

"And are such duplicates really possible in the universe? Is there really such a law of nature? . . . And if that is the earth over there, then is it really the same kind of earth as our own . . . just the same—unhappy, wretched, yet dear and eternally beloved, one that engenders as painful a love in its most ungrateful children as does our own?" I cried, trembling with irresistible, rapturous love for that once native earth I had abandoned. The image of the wretched little girl whom I had offended flitted before me.

"You shall see it all," answered my companion, and there was a kind of sorrow in his words.

But we were quickly drawing near the planet. I could see it seeming to grow in size; I could already make out the ocean, the outlines of Europe; and suddenly a strange feeling of some tremendous and sacred journey began to burn in my heart: "How can there be such a duplication, and why? I love—I can love only the earth I have left behind, which I have spattered with my blood when I, ungrateful wretch, extinguished my life with a bullet in my heart. But never, never did I cease to love that earth, and even on the night I parted with it I loved it, perhaps, more agonizingly than ever. Does suffering exist on this new earth? On our earth we can truly love only with suffering and only through suffering! We know not how to love in any other way, and know no other love. I want to suffer in order to love. This very instant I want, I long, to kiss and to water with my tears the one and only earth I have abandoned, and I do not want and do not accept life on any other! . . ."

But my companion had already left me. Suddenly, without really knowing how it happened, I was standing on this other earth in the sunny brightness of a day as lovely as paradise. I think I was on one of those islands that on our earth form part of the Greek archipelago, or somewhere on the mainland coast adjacent to that archipelago. Oh, it was all just the same as it is on our earth, but everything seemed to have a festive glow, as if some glorious and holy triumph had at last been achieved. The friendly emerald-green sea lapped quietly against the shore and kissed it with a love that was unmistakable, visible, almost conscious. Tall, beautiful trees stood in full splendor, and their countless little leaves— I'm convinced of it—welcomed me with their gentle, calming rustle and seemed to be whispering words of love. The meadow was ablaze with bright, fragrant flowers. Flocks of little birds wheeled through the air and landed unafraid on my shoulders and hands, beating joyfully at me with their dear little fluttering wings. And at last I met and came to know the people of this happy land. They came to me themselves, gathered around me, and kissed me. Children of the sun, children of their sun—and oh, how beautiful they were! Never on our earth have I seen such beauty in people. Perhaps only in our children of tenderest age could you find a distant, though pale reflection of this beauty. The eyes of these happy people shone with a clear light. Their faces radiated wisdom and a consciousness that had attained serenity, but their faces were happy: the voices and words of these people rang with childlike joy. Oh, at once, the moment I looked at these faces, I understood everything, everything! This was an earth that had not been defiled by sin; on it lived people who had not sinned, who lived in just such a paradise in which our fallen ancestors had once lived, according to the traditions of all of humanity, the only difference being that the entire earth here was one and the same paradise. These people, laughing joyously, crowded around and caressed me; they took me to their dwellings, and each one of them was anxious to comfort me. Oh, they did not question me about anything but seemed to know everything already and wanted quickly to banish suffering from my face.

4

Now, I'll say it once more: what would it matter if it had been only a dream! Still, the feeling of the love of these innocent and beautiful people has remained ever within me, and I feel that their love comes pouring down on me even now. I saw them myself, came to know them, and became convinced; I loved them and I suffered for them afterward. Oh, even then I realized at once that there were many things about them I would never understand; for instance, I, a modern Russian progressive and wretched inhabitant of Petersburg, found it inexplicable that they, who knew so much, had none of our science. But I soon realized that their knowledge was supplied and nourished by insights different from those on our earth and that their aspirations were also quite different. They had no desires and were content; they did not strive for knowledge of life as we strive to comprehend it, because their lives were complete. But their knowledge was more profound and more elevated than our science; for our science seeks to explain what life is and itself strives to comprehend it so as to teach others how to live, while they knew how to live even without science; I realized that, but could not understand their knowledge. They showed me their trees, and I could not understand the intensity of love with which they regarded these trees: it was just as though they were speaking to creatures like themselves. And, you know, I may not be wrong in saying that they spoke with them! Yes, they had found their language, and I am convinced that the trees understood them. They regarded the whole of nature in the same way—the animals, which lived peaceably with them and did not attack them, conquered by their love. They showed me the stars and told me something about them that I was unable to grasp, but I am convinced that they were able somehow to make contact with these heavenly stars, not only through thought but in some living way. Oh, these people did not strive to make me understand them, they loved me without that; and yet I knew that they would never understand me either, and therefore I scarcely ever spoke to them of our earth. I merely kissed the earth on which they lived, in their presence, and adored them wordlessly; and they saw this and let me adore them, unashamed that I was doing it because they themselves deeply loved me. They felt no pain for me when I, in tears, would kiss their feet, for in their hearts they joyously knew the strength of love with which they would return my feeling. At times I would ask myself in amazement how they managed never to offend a person like me and never to make me feel any jealousy or envy. Many times I asked myself how I, a braggart and liar, could refrain from speaking of the things I knew, things of which they, naturally, hadn't the least conception. How could I not want

to astonish them with my knowledge, even if only out of love for them?
They were as full of life and joy as children. They wandered through
their magnificent groves and forests; they sang their beautiful songs; they
ate but lightly, of the fruits of their trees, the honey of their forests, and
the milk of their devoted animals. Acquiring food and clothing cost them
little and easy toil. They loved and begot children, but never did I see
in them the outbursts of *cruel* sensuality that befall almost everyone on
our earth—each and every one—and serve as the single source of almost
all the sins of our human race. They rejoiced in their newborn children
as new participants in their bliss. There were no quarrels and jealousy
among them, and they did not even understand what these things meant.
Their children were the children of all because they all were part of
one family. They had scarcely illnesses, although there was death; but
their old people died peacefully, as if sinking into slumber, surrounded
by people who had come to bid them farewell, blessing them, smiling
at them, and departing life accompanied by the radiant smiles of others.
I saw no grief or tears on these occasions, only a love that seemed to
multiply to the point of rapture, but a rapture that was calm, contem-
plative, and complete. There was reason to think that they were able to
keep in touch with their dead even after death and that the earthly union
among them was not broken by death. They could scarcely understand
me when I asked them about eternal life, but apparently they were so
utterly convinced of it that it was not even a question for them. They had
no temples, but they did have a kind of essential, living, and continuous
union with the Totality of the universe; they had no religion; instead they
had a certain knowledge that when their earthly joy had fulfilled itself to
its limits there would ensue—both for the living and for the dead—an
even broader contact with the Totality of the universe. They awaited this
moment joyfully but unhurriedly, not with painful longing but as if their
hearts held a presentiment of it that they communicated to one another.
Before going to sleep in the evenings they loved to sing in harmonious
and melodious chorus. In these songs they expressed all the feelings the
passing day had brought them; they sang praise to the day and bade it
farewell. They sang praises to nature, the earth, the sea, the forests. They
loved to compose songs to one another and heaped praises on each other
like children; these were the simplest of songs, but they came from the
heart and moved the heart. And not only their songs but, it seemed, their

whole lives were devoted only to admiring one another. It was a kind of complete, all-encompassing devotion to one another. Yet some of their songs were solemn and ecstatic, and I could scarcely understand them at all. While understanding the words, I could never comprehend their full meaning. That remained inaccessible to my mind, as it were, yet my heart seemed more and more to grasp instinctively its essence. I often told them that I had had a presentiment of all this long ago, that all this joy and glory had affected me while still on our earth by evoking a longing that at times reached unbearable sorrow; that the dreams of my heart and the fancies of my mind had given me a presentiment of all of them and their glory; that on our earth I often could not look upon the setting sun without tears. . . . That my hatred for the people of our earth was always touched with anguish: why could I not hate them without loving them? why could I not help but forgive them? And in my love for them there was anguish: why could I not love them without hating them? They listened, and I saw that they could not comprehend what I was telling them; but I did not regret telling them of this: I knew that they understood the full force of my anguish over those I had left behind. And, indeed, when they looked at me with their tender gaze so filled with love, when I sensed that in their presence my heart as well was becoming as innocent and as honest as theirs, then I was not sorry I could not understand them. The sensation of the fullness of life almost took my breath away, and I could only worship them in silence.

Oh, how everyone laughs in my face and tells me that it's impossible to dream all of these details I'm telling you here; they say that in my dream I saw or felt only some sensation that my own heart engendered in a fit of delirium, while I invented all the details after I woke up. And when I admitted that, perhaps, this is really how it was—Lord, how they laughed in my face and what entertainment I provided them! Oh, yes, of course, I was overcome only by the sensation of that dream, and it alone survived in my wounded and bleeding heart; yet the actual images and forms of my dream—I mean those things I actually saw during the very time of my dreaming—were so filled with harmony, were so filled with charm and beauty, and were so filled with truth, that when I awakened I was naturally unable to embody them in our feeble words, so they were bound to become blurred in my mind; and so I may very well have been unconsciously forced to invent some of the details afterward and, of course, I distorted them, especially in my passionate longing to express them in some way or other as quickly as possible. And yet, how can I not believe that all this happened? That it happened, perhaps, a thousand times better, more brightly and joyously than I am telling it? Let it be a dream, but all of this had to have happened. You know, I'll tell you a secret: this whole thing, perhaps, wasn't a dream at all! For at this point something happened, something so awfully true that it could not have been the product of a dream. Let's suppose that my heart did give birth to my dream; but could my heart alone have been able to give birth to that awful truth that befell me then? How could I alone have invented it? How could it have been a product of my heart's fancy? As if my petty heart and my frivolous, trivial mind could have risen to such a revelation of the truth! Oh, judge for yourselves: I've kept this from you until now, but now I shall tell you this truth as well. The fact is that I . . . I corrupted them all!

5

Yes, yes, it ended in my corrupting them all! How it could have happened I don't know, I don't remember clearly. The dream encompassed thousands of years and left me merely with a sense of the whole. I know only that the cause of their fall into sin was I. Like some filthy trichina, like some atom of the plague that infects entire countries, so I infected that whole happy earth which had been sinless until my coming. They learned to lie, they came to love falsehood and to know the beauty of the lie. Oh, it may well have begun *innocently*, with a joke, with a bit of flirtation or amorous play, or it may really have been from an atom, but this atom of falsehood penetrated their hearts and pleased them. And then it was not long before sensuality was born; sensuality gave birth to jealousy, jealousy to cruelty. . . . Oh, I don't know, I can't remember, but soon—very soon— the first blood was shed: they were astonished and horrified and began to separate from one another and lose their unity. Alliances were formed, but now they were against one another. Recriminations and reproaches began. They came to know shame and elevated shame as a virtue. The concept of honor was born, and its banner was raised in each of the alliances. They began to abuse the animals, and the animals fled from them into the forests and became their enemies. There began a struggle for separation, for dissociation, for individuality, for "mine" and "thine." They began to speak in different languages. They tasted of sorrow and came to love it; they longed for suffering and said that Truth was attained only through suffering. At that point science made its appearance among them. When they had become wicked, they began to speak of brotherhood and humaneness and understood the meaning of these ideas. When they had become criminal, they invented justice and prescribed entire codes of law in order to maintain it; and to enforce these codes they set up a guillotine. They could scarcely remember what they had lost, and did not even want to believe that they had once been innocent and happy. They even laughed at the thought that they had once been happy and called it an idle fancy. They could not even imagine it in specific forms and images, yet the strange and marvelous thing was that though they had lost all faith in their former happiness and called it a fairy tale, they wanted so much to be innocent and happy again that, like children, they succumbed to the desires of their hearts and deified those desires, built temples and began to worship this idea of theirs, these "desires" of theirs, even while believing fully that these desires would never be fulfilled or achieved; still, they worshiped them in tears and bowed down to them. And yet, had it become possible for them to return to the innocent and happy state that they had lost, and should someone have suddenly shown it to them again and asked whether they wanted to return to it, they would certainly have refused. They told me: "We may be deceitful, wicked, and unjust; we *know* this and we lament it and torment ourselves over it; we inflict more punishment and torture on ourselves, perhaps, than will that merciful Judge who will weigh our sins and whose name we know not. But we have science, and with its help we shall again find the truth, but now we shall accept it consciously. Knowledge is higher than feelings, consciousness of life is higher than life. Science will give us true wisdom, wisdom will reveal the laws, and a knowledge of the laws of happiness is higher than happiness." That is what they said, and after saying it each one began to love himself more than he loved the others; and, indeed, they could not do otherwise. Each one became so jealous of his own individuality that he tried with all his might only to humiliate and belittle the individuality of others; and therein he saw the very purpose of his life. Slavery appeared, even voluntary slavery: the weak eagerly submitted to the strong merely so that the strong could help them crush those who were still weaker than they. Righteous men appeared, and they came to these people in tears and spoke to them of their arrogance, of their loss

of measure and harmony, of their loss of shame. But the righteous men
were mocked or stoned. Sacred blood was spilled on the porches of the
temples. Then there appeared people who began trying to find some
manner in which all might be united once again so that each, without
ceasing to love himself more than everyone else, might at the same time
not interfere with anyone else, so that they all might live in a harmonious
society. Entire wars were waged for the sake of this idea. At the same time,
all the warring parties believed that science, true wisdom, and a sense
of self-preservation would at last compel humanity to unite in a harmonious and rational society; and so in the meantime, to speed the matter,
the "wise" attempted as quickly as possible to annihilate all the "unwise"
who did not understand their idea, so that the latter should not stand in
the way of its triumph. But the sense of self-preservation began quickly to
weaken; proud men and sensualists appeared who flatly demanded, "All
or nothing." To achieve everything they wanted they resorted to crime
and, if that failed, to suicide. Religions appeared with a cult of nonexistence and self-destruction for the sake of eternal peace in nothingness. At
last, these people tired of their senseless labor and suffering appeared on
their faces; and they proclaimed that suffering was beauty, for in suffering
alone was there thought. Their songs were hymns to suffering. I walked
among them wringing my hands, and I wept over them, yet I loved them
even more, perhaps, than I had before, when suffering had not yet been
written on their faces, when they were innocent and so beautiful. I came
to love the earth they had defiled even more than when it had been a
paradise, solely because grief had made its appearance on it. Alas, I have
always loved grief and sorrow, but only for myself, only for myself, while
I wept over them in pity. I stretched out my arms to them, accusing,
cursing, and despising myself in despair. I told them that I had done all
this, I alone, and that it was I who had brought them corruption, contami-
nation, and falsehood! I implored them to crucify me; I taught them how
to make a cross. I could not, I did not have the strength to kill myself,
but I wanted to suffer at their hands; I longed for suffering, I longed for
my blood to be spilled to the last drop in these sufferings. But they only
laughed at me and at last began to consider me a holy fool. They tried to
defend me, saying that they had taken only that which they themselves
desired and that everything that now was happening could not have been
otherwise. At last they declared that I was becoming a danger to them and

that they would put me into a madhouse if I did not keep silent. Then sorrow entered my soul with such force that my heart contracted and I felt that I would die, and then . . . well, and then I woke up.

It was already morning; I mean, it wasn't daylight, but it was about six o'clock. I awoke in my same armchair, my candle had already burned itself out; everyone in the captain's room was asleep, and all around there was a silence that is rare in our house. I at once jumped to my feet in extreme amazement; nothing like this had ever happened to me before, even so far as the little details were concerned: I had never fallen asleep this way in my armchair, for instance. Then suddenly, while I was standing there coming to my senses, I caught sight of my revolver lying in front of me, loaded and ready—but in an instant I pushed it away! Oh, now I wanted life, and more life! I raised my arms and called out to eternal Truth; or rather, I did not call out but wept; rapture, infinite rapture elevated my entire being. Yes, life and—preaching! I decided on preaching at that very moment and, of course, to go on preaching for my whole life! I am going off to preach; I want to preach, but what? The Truth, for I have beheld it, beheld it with my own eyes, beheld all its glory!

And since then I have been preaching! What's more, I love all those who laugh at me, love them more than all the others. Why that is so I do not know and cannot explain, but so be it. People say that even now I'm confused, and that if I'm so confused now, what will happen in the future? It's absolutely true: I am confused, and perhaps in the future it will be even worse. And of course I shall get confused a few times before I find out how to preach—I mean to say, which words to use, and which deeds, because this is a very difficult thing to do. Why, even now I see it all as clear as day, but listen: who doesn't get confused? And yet we're all moving toward the same thing, at least we're all striving toward one and the same thing, from the wise man to the meanest bandit, only we're traveling by different roads. It's an old truth, but here's what's new: even I can't be all that confused, you know. Because I've seen the truth, I've seen it and know that people can be beautiful and happy without losing their capacity to live on the earth. I don't want to believe, and can't believe, that evil is man's normal state. And yet they all just laugh about that belief of mine. But how can I not believe it: I have seen the truth—it was not some invention of the mind; I saw it, I truly saw it, and its *living image* has filled my soul forever. I saw it in such consummate wholeness that I cannot believe it could not exist among people. And so, how will I get confused? I'll stray from the path, of course, and do so more than once, and I may even speak with someone else's words, although not for long: the living image of what I saw will always be with me and will always correct and guide me. Oh, I am of good cheer and full of strength, and I am on my way, though the trip may take a thousand years. Do you know, at first I even wanted to hide the fact that I had corrupted them all, but that was a mistake—my first mistake already! But truth whispered to me that I was *lying* and preserved and guided me. But how we are to build paradise I do not know, because I do not have the words to express it. I lost the words after my dream. At least all the main words, the most essential ones. But never mind: I shall go off and shall keep talking tirelessly, for I have indeed seen it with my own eyes even though I do not know how to tell of what I saw. But this is just what the scoffers do not understand: "He had a dream," they say. "It's just ravings and hallucinations." Well! How wise is that? And they're so proud of themselves! A dream? What's a dream? Is our very life not a dream? I'll say even more: suppose this never comes to pass, suppose paradise never is realized (that much I do understand, after all)—well, I shall still go on preaching. And yet it could happen so easily: in a single day, *in a single hour*—everything could be established at once! The main thing is that you must love others as you love yourself; that's the main thing, and that's everything, and absolutely nothing more than that is needed: you'll at once find a way to build paradise. And yet this is only an old truth that has been read and repeated a billion times, but it has still not managed to take root! "Consciousness of life is higher than life, knowledge of the laws of happiness is higher than happiness"—that's what we need to fight against! And I shall. If only we all want it, everything will be arranged at once.

And I've found that little girl. . . . And I shall go on! Yes, I shall go on!

The Defendant Kornilova Is Freed

On April 22 of this year the defendant Kornilova was tried a second time in the local circuit court by new judges and jurors. The former verdict, pronounced last year, was quashed by the Senate on the grounds that the medical evidence produced was insufficient. Most of my readers, perhaps, remember this case well. A young stepmother (who at the time had still not reached the legal age of maturity), pregnant, angry at her husband who kept citing the example of his first wife to reproach her, and after a bitter quarrel with him, threw her six-year-old stepdaughter (her husband's daughter by his former wife) from a fourth-floor window, nearly forty feet above the ground; a near-miracle occurred: the girl was not dashed to pieces, she sustained no fractures or other injuries, and quickly regained consciousness; she is now alive and well. The young woman's bestial act took place within the context of her other actions, so senseless and myste- rious that one could not help but wonder whether she was acting in her right mind. Was she not, at least, in a state of temporary derangement caused by her pregnancy? When she woke up in the morning, after her husband had gone off to work, she let the child sleep; then she dressed the little girl and gave her some coffee. Then she opened the window and threw the girl out of it. Without even bothering to look down to see what had happened to the child, she closed the window, got dressed, and set off for the police station. There she stated what had happened and answered questions rudely and strangely. When she was told, several hours later, that the child had survived, she displayed neither joy nor chagrin and remarked, quite indifferently and cold-bloodedly, as if deep in thought, "She's got the lives of a cat." For nearly a month and a half thereafter, in the two prisons where she happened to be confined, she continued to be sullen, rude, and uncommunicative. And suddenly all these traits disappeared at once: through all the four months that remained until her delivery, and through all her trial and after it, the wardress of the women's section of the prison could not say enough in her praise: her disposition became stable, calm, kind, and serene. However, I have described all this before. In short, the former verdict was quashed, and then on April 22 a new verdict was rendered by which Kornilova was acquitted.

I was in the courtroom and took away many impressions. It is a pity, though, that I'm quite unable to pass them on to you and am literally compelled to limit myself merely to a very few words. Besides, I am discussing this case only because I wrote a good deal about it earlier and so I feel that it is not superfluous to inform the readers about its outcome. The trial went on twice as long as the former one. The composition of the jury was particularly noteworthy. A new witness was called—the wardress of the women's section of the prison. Her testimony about Kornilova's character weighed heavily in the defendant's favor. The testimony of Kornilova's husband was also quite remarkable: he spoke with extraordinary frankness and hid nothing—neither the quarrels nor the things he had done to abuse her; he spoke from the heart—directly and openly. He is still only a peasant, though it's true he's dressed in European style, reads books, and has a monthly salary of thirty rubles. Then came the assortment of expert witnesses, which was also remarkable. Six people were called, all of them well-known luminaries of medical science; five of them gave testimony: three of them declared unequivocally that the pathological condition peculiar to a pregnant woman certainly *could have* had an influence on the crime that had been committed in this instance. Only Dr. Florinsky was not in agreement with this opinion, but fortunately he is not a psychiatrist and his opinion was not given any particular weight. The last to testify was our well-known psychiatrist, Diukov. He spoke for almost an hour, answering questions from the prosecutor and the presiding judge. It's hard to imagine a more subtle understanding of the human soul and its pathological states. The wealth and variety of his extraordinarily interesting observations, culled over many years, was also striking. As for me, I listened to parts of the testimony of this expert with real admiration. The opinion of this expert witness was entirely in favor of the defendant; he stated *positively* and *conclusively* that, in his opinion, when the defendant had committed the crime she was in pathological mental state.

The result was that the prosecutor himself, despite his formidable speech, withdrew the charge of premeditation, i.e., the most serious aspect of the indictment. Lustig, the defense attorney, also very skillfully countered several accusations; one of the most damaging ones—the stepmother's alleged long-standing hatred for her stepdaughter—he discredited entirely by clearly showing it was no more than backstairs gossip. Then, after a lengthy speech by the presiding judge, the jury retired and in less than a quarter-hour brought back an acquittal, which produced near delight among the large crowd of spectators. Many crossed themselves, some congratulated each other and shook hands. The husband of the acquitted took her home that same evening, after ten o'clock; the happy woman entered her own home again after nearly a year's absence, with the impression of the enormous lesson she had learned, a lesson that would last for her whole life, and an impression of the clear intervention of the hand of God in this case—beginning with the miraculous sparing of the child, to take but one example.

May and June

from CHAPTER ONE

Article 1, extract. From the Book of Predictions of Johann Lichtenberger, 1528

[. . .] What is most miraculous are very often the things that happen in the reality around us. We see reality almost always in the way we *want* to see it, as we ourselves, *in a preconceived manner*, wish to interpret it to ourselves. If once in a while we suddenly analyze it and see in the visible not the things we wished to see but the things that exist *in actual fact*, then we at once take what we have seen as a miracle; and this happens not rarely, and once in a while, I swear, we would sooner believe in a miracle and an impossibility than in reality, than in the truth *we did not wish to see*. And so it always happens on earth; in this is the whole history of humanity.

Article 3. A Plan for a Satirical Novel of Contemporary Life

I still haven't finished with the anonymous abuser, though. The fact is, such a person can become a very significant literary type for a novel or tale. The main thing is that one can and must approach the thing from a different point of view, a broad, humane viewpoint, harmonizing it with the Russian character generally and with the contemporary factors that now cause this type in particular to appear among us. In fact, no sooner do you begin to elaborate such a character than you immediately realize that we simply cannot help but have such people or, to put it more properly, that in this age of ours such people are the very ones that we should expect above all, and that if there are comparatively few of them as yet, it is due specifically to the particular grace of God. In fact, these are all people who have been raised in the unstable families we have had of late, with discontented, skeptical fathers, who have passed on to their children nothing but indifference to everything most vital and little more than a kind of vague apprehension over some future which is terribly fanciful but in which even these so-called *ready-made* realists and cold-blooded enemies of our present put their faith. And beyond that, such fathers passed on to their children their skeptical, impotent mockery, scarcely conscious but always utterly complacent. Were there only a few children who grew up in the last twenty or twenty-five years among such vile, envious people who had run through the last of their redemption money and who bequeathed their children poverty and a precept of baseness— were there only a few such families?

And so, let's suppose a young person takes up a job. He doesn't cut a fine figure; he "lacks wit"; he has no connections at all. He has his native-born intelligence, however, everyone else has that too; but since that intelligence was developed predominantly through the aimless sneering that we have taken as liberalism for twenty-five years now, our hero naturally and immediately takes his intelligence for genius. For heaven's sake, when a person has grown up without the least moral support, could you expect anything other than boundless egoism? At first he puts on a terrific show, but since he does have some intelligence, after all (and I prefer my type to be somewhat more intelligent than average rather than have him more stupid, for it is only in these two variants that such a type can appear), he soon figures out that his sneering is only something negative and certainly cannot lead him to anything positive. And if sneering was enough for his daddy, then it was because daddy was just an old duffer, though a liberal fellow, while he, the young lad, is a genius, after all, and has only been having some temporary problems proving his talents. Oh, of course in his soul he's ready to commit any of the meanest acts, "for why shouldn't one resort to meanness to get something done? And anyway, in times like these, who can prove that meanness is meanness?" etc., etc. In short, he's been raised with a stock of these ready-made questions. But he soon realizes that these days even resorting to some mean trick to get something done means a long wait in line, and besides, even a person like him may see that it's a long way from the moral readiness to employ a mean trick to the deed itself, and that first he must take some practical measures to get himself into the line. Well, of course if he were a bit less clever he'd arrange things in a moment: "To hell with these feeble impulses toward higher things; I'll just change myself to suit Mr. A. or Mr. B. and follow in his wake, settle submissively and confidently into the daily grind, and sooner or later I'll make a career for myself." But his egoism, this conviction of his own genius, still stands in his way: even in

his own mind he cannot merge the glorious fate he had conjured up for
himself with the fate of Mr. A. or Mr. B. "No, sir, we're still in opposition,
and if they want me, let them come to me on their knees." And so he keeps
waiting for someone to come to him on his knees, waiting full of malice and
spite; and meanwhile, right beside him, some other fellow has managed
to get a step ahead of him; another one has settled in nicely, while a third
has already become his boss—this third being the very fellow for whom
he had invented a nickname when they studied together in their "higher
school" and about whom he'd written an epigram for the school magazine
when he edited it and was thought to be a genius. "No, sir, that's an insult!
Why was it he and not I? And wherever you look the places are taken!
No," he thinks, "my career isn't here. What's the point of working in the
civil service? Only numskulls serve. My career is literature." And so he
begins sending his works around to various editors, at first incognito and
then giving his full name. He gets no reply, of course; impatient, he sets
to haunting the thresholds of editors' offices. On the occasions a manuscript is returned to him, he even permits himself to make jokes about
it and sneer biliously, giving vent to his rage, as it were; but none of this
helps. "No, it's obvious that all the places are taken here, too," he thinks
with a bitter smile. The main thing is that he is continually tormented
by the fatal need to seek out, always and everywhere, as many people
he can find who are worse than he. Oh, he could never understand how
anyone could rejoice in the fact that there are people better than he! And
it's at this point that he first hits upon the notion of sending some nasty
little unsigned letter to an editor, and to an editor who had insulted him
most deeply. He writes it, sends it, and then he does it again—it pleases
him. Still, it brings no results; everything around him is deaf, dumb, and
blind as before. "No, this is no kind of career," he decides, once and for
all, and decides to "settle in" at last. He selects a *personage*—his boss,
the director, to be precise; here, perhaps, a bit of luck and a few minor
connections help him out. Gogol's Poprishchin, after all, began by distin-
guishing himself in sharpening pens and was summoned for that purpose
to the apartment of His Excellency, where he saw the director's daughter
and sharpened two pens for her. But Poprishchin's time has passed, and
anyway, these days pens don't need sharpening; besides, our hero can't
change his nature: it's not pens that are on his mind but the most daring
thoughts. Briefly, then, in the shortest time he becomes convinced that he

has captivated the director's daughter and that she is pining for him. "Well now, here's a career," he thinks, "and in any case, what good are women if a clever man can't use them to make a career; that, in essence, is the whole woman question, if one judges it realistically. And the main thing is that it's not shameful: more than a few careers have been launched by women." But—but at this point, just as with Poprishchin, a new assistant turns up! Poprishchin reacted characteristically: he went out of his mind over his notion that he was the king of Spain. And how natural that was! What else was left for the mortified Poprishchin, with no connections, no career, no fortitude, and no initiative whatsoever, particularly during the Petersburg period; how could he help but plunge into the most desperate fantasies and believe in them? But our Poprishchin, our contemporary Poprishchin, is utterly incapable of believing that he's the very same as the original Poprishchin, only duplicated thirty years later. His soul is full of regular fireworks, contempt, and sarcasm and—and so he also plunges into fantasy, but of a different sort. He recalls that there are such things on earth as anonymous letters and that he has already resorted to them once; and so he risks writing his little missive, but this time not to an editor; this one is something finer, if you please: he feels that he is entering a new, practical phase. Oh, how he shuts himself up in his little room, away from his landlady; how he trembles lest someone look in on him; but he scribbles line after line, changing his handwriting, and composes four pages of slander and abuse; he reads it over with relish; and, having sat up the whole night, in the morning he seals up the letter and addresses it to the fiancé, the assistant. He's changed his handwriting, so he's not afraid. And now he counts the hours; and now the letter ought to be arriving— it's to the fiancé about his intended; and the fiancé, naturally, will turn her down; he'll take fright; why, it's not a letter, it's a masterpiece! And our young friend knows full well that he's mean little wretch, but that only pleases him: "These are the days of bipartite thinking, a breadth of approach; these days a straightline approach gets you nowhere."

Of course the letter had no effect and the wedding took place; but a beginning had been made, and our hero seemed to have hit upon his career. He was seized by a kind of illusion, just as Poprishchin was. He plunges feverishly into this new activity of writing anonymous letters. He dredges up information about the general, his boss; he calculates, he pours out all the things that have accumulated inside him over whole

years of unsatisfying service, wounded vanity, bile, and envy. He criticizes
the general's every action, he ridicules him in the most merciless fashion,
and he does so in a number of letters, a whole series of them. And how
pleasing this is at first! The actions of the general, his wife, his mistress,
and the stupidity of their whole department—he's depicted every bit of
it in his letters. Little by little he even ventures into matters of state; he
composes a letter to the minister in which he proposes to reform Russia
in quite unceremonious fashion. "No, the minister cannot help but be
impressed; the genius of the thing will impress him, and the letter may be
passed on to ... passed on to such a personage who. ... In short, *courage,
mon enfant;* and when they start to look for the author, I'll declare myself,
so to say, with no more shyness." In short, he revels in his compositions
and continually imagines his letters being opened and the effect they
then produce on the faces of those people. ... In such a frame of mind
he sometimes even permits himself a bit of mischief: as a joke he writes
even to some quite ridiculous people, not overlooking even some Egor
Egorovich, his old head clerk, whom he nearly drives out of his mind
by anonymously telling him that his wife has become involved in a love
affair with the local police officer (the most important thing is that half of
it could be true).

And so, some time passes, but ... but suddenly a strange idea dawns on
him: that he, in fact, is Poprishchin, nothing more than Poprishchin, that
very same Poprishchin, only a million times more base, and all these libels
from around the corner, all this anonymous might of his is essentially only
a mirage and nothing more, and the vilest kind of a mirage besides, the
nastiest and most disgraceful, worse, even, than the dream of the Spanish
throne. And at this very point something serious happens—not something disgraceful. "What's disgrace? Disgrace is nonsense. Nowadays
only pharmacists are afraid of disgrace." But this is something really and
truly terrible. The fact is that although he had a clear head, he still was
unable to restrain himself, and during his period of rapture over his new
career—specifically, after his little missive to the minister—he let something slip about his letters, and to whom?—to his German landlady. Of
course he didn't tell her everything; she wouldn't have understood everything, of course; just a bit, just in passing, because his heart was so full;
but imagine his astonishment when, a month later, the meek little clerk
from another department, who rented a tiny room in an out-of-the-way

corner of this same landlady's establishment, a spiteful and uncommunicative little fellow who, when he suddenly got angry over something,
suggested as he passed by our hero in the corridor that he—this same
meek little fellow, that is—was "a man of morals and did not write anonymous letters in the manner of certain gentlemen." Imagine! At first he did
not get so frightened; moreover, after questioning the clerk—for which
he deliberately and even humiliatingly had to make up with him—he was
convinced that the fellow knew scarcely anything. But . . . well, what if
he does know? Besides, the rumor had begun in the department a long
time ago that someone was sending abusive letters to the superiors via
the local mail and that this must certainly be someone who worked there.
Our unhappy hero sets to thinking and can't even sleep at night. In
short, one could show his inner torment with particular vividness—his
morbid doubts, his mistakes. At last, he is all but convinced that everyone
knows everything, that they're just holding off telling him; and as far as
his dismissal from the service is concerned, that's already been decided,
though it won't only be dismissal, of course—in short, he almost loses
his mind. And so, one day he's sitting in the department and his heart
is seized with an almost boundless indignation toward everything and
everyone: "Oh, you wicked, damned people," he thinks, "how can you
put on such a show of pretense! They know very well that *it's I*, every last
one of them knows it; they whisper about it to each other when I pass by;
they even know about the document that's been drawn up about me in
the office there and . . . and they're all pretending! They all hide it from
me! They want to enjoy it, they want to see me being dragged off. . . .
But it won't happen! It won't happen!" And so an hour later he chances
to deliver some document to His Excellency's office. He enters, places
the document respectfully on the desk; the general is busy and pays no
attention; our hero turns to leave silently, grasps the door knob, and—
suddenly, as if falling into an abyss—he flings himself at His Excellency's
feet, though a second earlier he hadn't even suspected he would do so:
"All the same, I'm finished; it's better I confess on my own!" "Just be
calm, Your Excellency; let's please be quiet, Your Excellency! I'll tell you
everything, absolutely everything, but I don't want anyone else to hear!"
So, like a madman, he implores the bewildered excellency, clasping his
hands foolishly in front of him. And so, in broken, incoherent phrases,
all atremble, he stupidly confesses everything, to the utter amazement of

His Excellency, who never suspected any of it. But yet, even here our hero fully lives up to his character, for why does he fling himself at the general's feet? Of course, it's his illness, his morbid doubts, but *mainly* it is because he, frightened, humiliated, blaming himself for everything, still dreams as before, like a little fool intoxicated by his own conceit, that His Excellency, having heard him out but nonetheless struck by his genius, so to say, may stretch out his hands, with which he signs so many papers for the benefit of his fatherland, and take him into his embrace: "Oh, you unfortunate but gifted young man, have you really been driven to such lengths! Oh, it is I, I who am to blame for everything; I have overlooked you! I take the entire blame on myself. My God, the things our talented young people are compelled to do by fault of our antiquated procedures and prejudices! But come, come to my bosom and share my post with me, and we . . . we shall revolutionize the department!"

But it did not happen that way, and later—much later, in disgrace and humiliation, recalling the kick from the tip of the general's boot that he happened to receive full in the face, he almost sincerely put the blame on fate and other people: "For once in my life I opened myself fully to people, and what did I get in return?" One could invent some very natural and contemporary finale for him; for example, now kicked out of the service, he is hired for a hundred rubles to take part in a fictitious marriage; after the ceremony, he goes one way and she another, to her flour dealer. "Sweet and noble," as Shchedrin's policeman expresses it in a similar instance.

In short, I think that the type of an anonymous abuser is not at all a bad subject for a short novel. And it's a significant subject. We'd need a Gogol here, of course, but. . . . I'm glad at least that I happened to come upon this idea. Perhaps I may actually try to include it in a novel.

from CHAPTER TWO

Article 2, two extracts. Diplomacy Facing World Problems

[. . .] This is what is curious and what really stands out: the Eastern
Question flared up among us, for example; at the same time, and
even earlier, it flared up all over Europe, and it's very easy to understand why: everyone, even the nondiplomats (and even particularly
the nondiplomats)—everyone has known for a long, long time that the
Eastern Question is, one might say, one of the world questions, one of
the principal *divisions* of the worldwide and imminent resolution of
the fates of humanity, their new and approaching phase. We know that
this matter concerns not only the East of Europe, not only the Slavs, the
Russians, and the Turks, or, specifically, some Bulgarians over there, but
that it concerns also the whole of the West of Europe, and not only in
relation to the seas and the straits, access and egress, by any means; it is
much deeper, more fundamental, more elemental, more necessary, more
essential, more primary. And therefore one can understand that Europe
is alarmed and that diplomacy has so much business. But really, what is
the business of diplomacy?—that's my question! What is it doing (now,
primarily) on the Eastern Question? The business of diplomacy (and
otherwise it would not be diplomacy)—its business now is to lay hold
of the Eastern Question in all respects and to assure everyone, involved
and uninvolved, as quickly as possible, that no question whatever has
come up, that these things are nothing more than some little excursions
and maneuvers and even—if at all possible—to assure everyone that not
only has the Eastern Question not come up but that there never was
such a thing at all, that it never existed but is only a fog that was spread a
hundred years ago for certain reasons (diplomatic ones as well), and that
this unexplained fog persists to this day. Frankly speaking, even this could
be believed were it not for one riddle, no longer a diplomatic one (that's
the problem!), for diplomacy never ever tackles such riddles; moreover,
it turns scornfully away from them, for it considers them mere fantasies
unworthy of superior intellects. One might formulate the riddle in this
way: why does it always happen, and particularly lately—I mean from the

middle of the nineteenth century, and the more recently, the more obviously and tangibly—that the moment some issue in the world touches on something general and universal, *all the other* world problems at once rise parallel to it? For instance, in Europe it's now not enough to have just one world problem, the Eastern Question; no—in France, Europe suddenly and unexpectedly raises another question of world importance—the Catholic one. [...]

[...] Why does one question impinge upon the other? Why does one evoke the other when, it would seem, there is no link between them? And, indeed, it's not only these two questions that were raised at the same time: along with the Eastern Question came still others, and more and more of them will be raised if the Eastern Question develops properly. In short, all the most important questions of Europe and humanity generally in our age are always raised simultaneously. And this very simultaneity is striking. The condition whereby all these questions appear simultaneously is what constitutes the riddle! But why am I saying all this? It's precisely because diplomacy regards such questions scornfully. [...]

from CHAPTER THREE

Article 3, extract. Both Angry and Strong

[. . .] It's worth noting that Prince Bismarck hates socialism no less than papacy and that the German government, particularly in most recent times, has begun somehow to be excessively fearful of socialist propaganda. Without a doubt, this is because socialism depersonalizes the national principle and eats away at the very root of nationality, whereas the principle of nationality is the fundamental, leading idea of the whole German unification and of all that has taken place in Germany in recent years. But it is very possible that Prince Bismarck is looking even more deeply into the matter, i.e.: that socialism is the force of the future for the whole of western Europe, and if papacy should someday be abandoned and cast aside by the governments of this world, then it really and truly could be thrown into the embrace of socialism and merge completely with it. The pope, on foot and barefoot, will go forth to all the poor and will say that everything the socialists teach and all they desire has long been found in the Gospels; that hitherto the time had not yet come for them to learn about this, but that it has now come and that he, the pope, will turn Christ over to them and that he believes in the ant heap. Roman Catholicism (and this is all too clear) needs not Christ but universal dominion: "What you need is unity in the face of the enemy," it will say. "So join together under my power, for I alone among all the powers and sovereigns of the world am *universal;* let us go together." Prince Bismarck probably can foresee this picture, for he alone among all the diplomats was keen-sighted enough to foresee the tenacious vitality of the Roman idea and all the energy it is prepared to use to defend itself, whatever the means. It has an infernal desire to live, and it is as hard to kill as a serpent! That is what Prince Bismarck alone, the chief enemy of papacy and the Roman idea, understands with every fiber of his being!

But the little old men trying to be young, the French republicans, were incapable of understanding this. [. . .]

July and August

from CHAPTER ONE

Article 3, extract. The Case of the Dzhunkovsky Parents and Their Children

[. . .] As I said earlier, the defendants were acquitted. And why not? What's remarkable is not that they were acquitted but that they were charged and brought to trial. Who—what court—could have found them guilty, and of what? Oh, of course there is a court that could find them guilty and show clearly of what, but it is not a criminal court with jurors who judge by written law. And nowhere in written law is there any article that makes a father's laziness, incompetence, and heartlessless in raising his children a criminal offense. If so, we would have to condemn half of Russia—a lot more than half, in fact. And what do we mean by heartlessness? Now if there had been cruel torture, something terrible, inhuman. But I recall how the defense attorney in the trial of Kroneberg, who was accused of cruel treatment of his young child, opened the code of laws and read the article on cruel treatment, brutality, and so on, having in mind to prove that his client did not fall under any one of those articles in which it is clearly and exactly set out what must be considered as cruelty and brutality. And, I recall, these definitions of cruelty were themselves so cruel that they positively resembled the bashibazouks' torture of the Bulgarians; and if there were no impalings on a stake or cutting of strips of flesh from the back, then there were broken ribs, hands, legs, and I don't know what else, so that a lash of some sort, and a small one to boot, as Miss Shishova testified, positively cannot enter into the article of the code of laws and form grounds for indictment. "They were beaten with birch rods," they said. Well, who doesn't beat children with birch rods? Nine-tenths of Russia does. There's just no way you can make this subject to criminal law. "The children were beaten for no special reason," they said, "for a potato." "No, sir, not for a potato," Mr. Dzhunkovsky would reply, "it was for everything taken together—for their vices, for the fact that they, the little brutes, beat my deceased daughter Ekaterina on the face." "The children were locked up in a toilet," they said. "Yes, but it was a heated toilet, so what more do you want? A jail is always a jail." "But why did you

415

feed them servants' food and send them to sleep in a virtual pigsty, on a mat of some kind with one ragged blanket?" "This is also for punishment, you see; and what does it matter if the blanket was ragged? Even so, I'm spending beyond my means for my children's education; the law has no business looking in my pockets to count my money." "Why, then," we say, "did you show no affection to your children?" "But come now, show me an article in the code of laws that would force me, under threat of punishment by criminal court, to show affection to my children, and especially to naughty, heartless, wretched little thieves and brutes. . . ." "Why, at last, did you choose the wrong system for raising your children?" "Well, what system of child-rearing does criminal law prescribe, under threat of punishment? This certainly isn't any concern of the law. . . ."

In short, I want to say that it was impossible to drag this Dzhunkovsky case into criminal court. And so it happened: they were acquitted; nothing came of the charge. And yet the reader feels that this case could give rise to, and perhaps there already has given rise to, a whole tragedy. Oh, this is a matter for another court, but which one?

Which one? Well, let's take Miss Shishova, the teacher, for instance; she gives her testimony and already pronounces the sentence in it. Let's note that although this Miss Shishova herself had lashed the children with a belt ("but it was only a little one"), it seems that she is still a very intelligent woman. One can't give any more exact and intelligent assessment of the character of the Dzhunkovskys than she does. Mrs. Dzhunkovsky is *an egotist,* she says. The Dzhunkovsky house is *disorderly . . . due to the indifference of the defendants toward everything and even toward themselves.* Their affairs are in a constant state of confusion and they live with constant problems; they have no ability to manage their household; they worry, yet more than anything they seek peace and quiet: Mrs. Dzhunkovsky, who continually *tried to ensure that nothing should trouble her,* even gave her husband the responsibility of punishing the children. . . . In short, Miss Shishova received from the Dzhunkovsky household the impression that these people were heartless egotists and, above all, indolent egotists. It all stems from indolence, and their hearts are indolent. It was indolence, of course, that caused the eternal disorder in the house, disorder in their affairs, and yet there is nothing they want more than peace and quiet: "Ah, to hell with you; just let me get on with my life!" What the cause of their indolence and apathy was, God only

knows! Did they find it difficult to live amid the chaos of today's world in
which it's so difficult to understand anything? Or did today's life provide
so few answers to their spiritual needs, to their wishes and questions? Or
was it, at last, because they could not understand what was happening all
around them, so that their own conceptions of life fell apart and could
not be put together again and they became disillusioned? I don't know,
I really don't know; but evidently these are people with some education who once, perhaps—and maybe even now—cherished the beautiful
and the sublime. The business we saw of massaging the feet wouldn't
contradict that. Massaging the feet is just something in the nature of lazy,
apathetic disillusionment, a lazy self-indulgence, a longing for seclusion,
peace, warmth. It's a matter of nerves—and not so much laziness as this
longing for peace and seclusion, for cutting oneself off from all duties
and obligations. Yes, of course there's egotism here, and egotists are irre-
sponsible and cowardly when it comes to duty: they have a permanent,
cowardly aversion to saddling themselves with any duties. Note that this
permanent and ardent wish to free oneself from all duties almost always
gives rise to and develops in the egotist the conviction, conversely, that
everyone he encounters is obligated to him in some way, is, as it were,
charged with some duty to him, must pay him tribute, owes him something. However ridiculous this fantasy may seem, it finally takes root and
is transformed into an irritable dissatisfaction with the whole world and a
harsh, often embittered attitude toward everything and everyone. When
these imagined debts are not fulfilled, the heart of the egotist often takes
it as an insult, so that sometimes you can spend your whole life unable to
imagine why such a person is always angry and spiteful toward you. This
embittered feeling often extends even to their own children—oh, to the
children most of all. Children are precisely the preordained victims of
this capricious egotism, and besides, they are the nearest to hand; worst
of all, there is no constraint here: "They're my children, my own and no
one else's!" Don't be astonished that this odious feeling, this permanently
irritating reminder of the children's unfulfilled obligations, the irritating,
constant presence underfoot of these new little individuals who demand
everything from you and who brazenly (alas, not brazenly, just childishly!)
refuse to understand that you need peace and quiet and who put no value
at all on that peace and quiet—don't be astonished, I say, that this odious
feeling even toward one's own children can at last be transformed into a

real feeling of vengeance and, encouraged and incited by the absence of any punishment, even into brutality. Indolence, indeed, always gives rise to brutality; it ends in brutality. And this brutality comes not from cruelty but precisely from laziness. These hearts are not cruel, they are just lazy.

And so this lady who was so fond of peace and quiet, who loved it so much she needed to have her feet massaged, who at last became embittered because only she, *she alone,* never had any peace and quiet because everything around her was in a muddle and demanded her constant presence and attention—this lady at last jumps up from her bed, picks up a branch, and beats her own child, beats him insatiably, voraciously, maliciously, so that "it was terrible to watch," as the servant testifies; and why, for what? Because the boy brought his hungry little sister (who suffered from epilepsy) a few potatoes from the kitchen; in other words, she beats him for a kindly feeling, for the fact that the child's heart has not yet become hardened and depraved. "It doesn't matter," she says. "I forbade it, but you did it. So I'll show you: you mustn't do your kindly deed, you must do my wicked deed." No, sir, this is a case of hysterics. The children sleep in filth, "worse than a pigsty," with one ragged blanket for the three of them. "Let them stay there, that's just what they need," thinks their own mother. "They never give me any peace and quiet!" And she thinks that, not because her heart is cruel; no, her heart, perhaps, is naturally very kind and good, but they just won't give her any peace and quiet; never in her life has she been able to find any peace, and as each day passes it gets worse; and here these children ("Why are they here? Why did they have to come along?") are growing up, playing pranks, and demanding more and more effort and attention as each day passes! No, if this is a case of hysterics it has been accumulating for years on end. At the side of this unhealthy (she's been reduced to a state of ill health) mother, the father, Mr. Dzhunkovsky, stands before the court. Well, perhaps he may even be a very good man; he seems an educated fellow, by no means without ideals; on the contrary, he is aware of his fatherly duty, aware of it to the point of being grieved at heart. Here he is in court, complaining almost in tears about his young children; he stretches out his hands: "I've done everything for them, everything; I've hired tutors and governesses; I've spent more on them than my means allow, but they're brutes; they've taken to stealing; they beat their deceased sister across the face!" In short, he considers himself completely in the right. The children stand there beside him; it's remarkable that they gave testimony that was "calm, guarded"; that's to say, they made few complaints and only barely tried to defend themselves, and I think that this was not only out of fear of their parents, to whom they will still have to return. On the contrary, it would seem that the fact their father is already being tried for abusing them would have made them bolder. They simply felt awkward at being involved in the trial of their father, at standing next to him and testifying against him; whereas he, with no regard for the future and for the kind of feelings this day will leave in the hearts of these children, not even suspecting what they will take with them into their future from this day—he accuses them and reveals all that was bad in them, all their shameful acts; he complains to the court, to the spectators, to society. But he believes that he is right, and Mrs. Dzhunkovsky even believes in the future as well, and believes in it totally! She declares to the court that *everything* has been caused by bad tutors and governesses, that she has become disillusioned with them and that now, when her husband himself undertakes to teach and rear the children, the children will be "completely rehabilitated" (Certainly! Certainly!). May God help them, however. [. . .]

from CHAPTER TWO

Article 1. Dissociation Again. Part Eight of *Anna Karenina*

Many educated Russians these days have taken to saying: "What People? I am one of the People myself!" In part eight of *Anna Karenina*, Levin, beloved hero of the novel's author, says that *he is one of the People*. Speaking of *Anna Karenina* once some time ago, I called Levin "pure in heart." While I continue to believe as before in the purity of his heart, I do not believe that he is "one of the People"; on the contrary: I see now that he is aiming, with love, to dissociate himself. I became convinced of it when I finished that same part eight of *Anna Karenina* that I mentioned at the beginning of this July and August portion of my diary. The Levin we speak of is not a real person, of course, but merely the invention of a novelist. Nevertheless, this novelist—an enormous talent, a remarkable mind, and a man highly respected by educated Russia—this novelist depicts in part in this ideal, i.e., invented, character his own view of our contemporary Russian reality, something that is clear to anyone who reads this remarkable work. Thus, when we discuss the non-existent Levin, we shall also be discussing the actual view of one of our most remarkable contemporary Russians on current Russian reality. And this is already a serious topic for discussion, even amid the many rumblings of our age, filled as it is with enormous, shattering, and quickly changing events of real life. This view of so remarkable a Russian writer, and on a matter holding such interest to all Russians as does the general national movement of all Russian people over the last two years regarding the Eastern Question, is expressed precisely and decisively in this same eighth and final part of his work, the part rejected by the editors of *The Russian Messenger* because the author's convictions did not coincide with their own and that appeared only recently as a separate booklet. The essence of this view, as I understand it, consists mainly in the following: first, that the People by no means share the aims of this so-called national movement and do not even understand it; second, that it has all been deliberately fabricated, first by certain well-known people who were subsequently supported by journalists aiming to profit from it by increasing their readership; third, that all the volunteers were either desperate and drunken people or simply fools; fourth, that this whole so-called upsurge of Russian national feeling for the Slavs was not only fabricated by well-known people and supported by hired journalists but had been fabricated contrary to our most fundamental principles, so to speak. . . . And finally, fifth, that all the barbarities and unprecedented torture inflicted on the Slavs cannot arouse in us Russians any direct feeling of compassion and that "such direct feeling for the oppression of the Slavs *does not and cannot exist.*" The last point is expressed finally and categorically.

So it is that the "pure-in-heart" Levin has set off to dissociate himself and has split away from the overwhelming majority of Russians. His view, however, is by no means new or original. It would have been all too useful and would have suited the taste of many (people who are by no means at the bottom of the social ladder) who were thinking almost the same thing here in Petersburg last winter; and so it's a pity that this little book appeared a bit too late. What caused Levin, in such gloom, to dissociate himself and "secede" in so morose a fashion I can't determine. It's true enough that he's an ardent, "restless" person who is given to analyzing everything and who, if you look closely, has nothing within him in which he can believe. But still, this man is "pure in heart," and I maintain this even though it is difficult to imagine by what mysterious and sometimes even ridiculous ways the most unnatural, most artificial, and most ugly things can enter into what is otherwise a heart of great sincerity and purity. However, I will also note that even though many insist—and even I can see clearly (as I said above)—that the author uses Levin to express many of his own views and convictions, putting them into Levin's mouth almost by force and even sometimes clearly sacrificing his artistry by doing so, I still refuse to confuse the author himself with the figure of Levin as his creator depicted him. As I say this I find myself in a certain painful quandary, because even though very much of what the author expresses through Levin evidently concerns only Levin himself as an artistically depicted character, I still did not expect this from such an author!

Article 3, two extracts. *Anna Karenina* as a Fact of Special Importance

And so, at that very time—one evening last spring, that is—I happened to meet one of my favorite writers on the street. We meet rarely, once every few months, and somehow always by chance on the street. He is one of the most prominent among those five or six writers who are usually called the "Pleiade," for some reason. The critics, at least, have followed the readers and have set them apart and placed them above all the other writers; this has been the case for some time now—still the same group of five, and the Pleiade's membership does not increase. I enjoy meeting this dear novelist of whom I am so fond; I enjoy showing him, among other things, that I think he is quite wrong in saying that he has become old-fashioned and will write nothing more. I always bring away some subtle and perceptive insight from our brief conversations. We had much to talk about this time, for the war had already begun. But he at once began speaking directly about *Anna Karenina.* I had also just finished reading part seven, with which the novel had concluded in *The Russian Messenger.* My interlocutor does not look like a man of strong enthusiasms. On this occasion, however, I was struck by the firmness and passionate insistence of his views on *Anna Karenina.*

"It's something unprecedented, a first. Are there any of our writers who could rival it? Could anyone imagine anything like it in Europe? Is there any work in all their literatures over the past years, and even much earlier, that could stand next to it?"

What struck me most in this verdict, which I myself shared completely, was that the mention of Europe was so relevant to those very questions and problems that were arising of their own accord in the minds of so many. The book at once took on, in my eyes, the dimensions of a fact that could give Europe an answer on our behalf, that long-sought-after fact we could show to Europe. Of course, people will howl and scoff that this is only a work of literature, some sort of novel, and that it's absurd to exaggerate this way and go off to Europe carrying only a novel. I know that people will howl and scoff, but don't worry: I'm not exaggerating and am looking at the matter soberly: I know very well that this is still only a novel and that it's but a tiny drop of what we need; but the main thing for me here is that this drop already exists, it is given, it really and truly does exist; and so, if we already have it, if the Russian genius could give birth to this *fact,* then it is not doomed to impotence and can create; it can provide something *of its own,* it can begin *its own* word and finish uttering it when the times and seasons come to pass. [...]

[...] Nevertheless, *Anna Karenina* is perfection as a work of art that appeared at just the right moment and as a work to which nothing in the European literatures of this era can compare; and, in the second place, the novel's idea also contains something of ours, something truly *our own,* namely that very thing which constitutes our distinctness from the European world, the thing which constitutes our "new word," or at least its beginnings—just the kind of word one cannot hear in Europe, yet one that Europe still so badly needs, despite all her pride.

I cannot embark upon literary criticism here and will say only a few things. *Anna Karenina* expresses a view of human guilt and transgression. People are shown living under abnormal conditions. Evil existed before they did. Caught up in a whirl of falsities, people transgress and are doomed to destruction. As you can see, it is one of the oldest and most popular of European themes. But how is such a problem solved in Europe? Generally in Europe there are two ways of solving it. Solution number one: the law has been given, recorded, formulated, and put together through the course of millennia. Good and evil have been defined and weighed, their extent and degree have been determined historically by humanity's wise men, by unceasing work on the human soul, and by working out, in a very scientific manner, the extent of the forces that unite people in a society. One is commanded to follow this elaborated code of laws blindly. He who does not follow it, he who transgresses, pays with his freedom, his property, or his life; he pays literally and cruelly. "I know," says their civilization, "that this is blind and cruel and impossible, since we are not able to work out the ultimate formula for humanity while we are still at the midpoint of its journey; but since we have no other solution, it follows that we must hold to that which is written, and hold to it literally and cruelly. Without it, things would be even worse. At the same time, despite all the abnormality and absurdity of the structure we call our great European civilization, let the forces of the human spirit remain healthy and intact; let society not be shaken in its faith that it is moving toward perfection; let no one dare think that the idea of the beautiful and sublime has been obscured, that the concepts of good and evil are being distorted and twisted, that convention is constantly taking the place of the healthy norm, that simplicity and naturalness are perishing as they are crushed by a constant accumulation of lies!"

The second solution is the reverse: "Since society is arranged in an abnormal manner, one cannot demand that human entities be responsible for the consequences of their actions. Therefore, the criminal is not responsible, and crime at present does not exist. In order to put an end to crime and human guilt we must put an end to the abnormality of society and its structure. Since curing the ills in the existing order of things is a long and hopeless process, and the medicines needed have not even been found, it follows that the whole society must be destroyed and the old order swept away with a broom, as it were. Then we can begin it all anew, on different principles as yet unknown but which, nevertheless, can be no worse than those of the present order; on the contrary, they offer many chances of success. Our main hope is in science." And so this is the second solution: they wait for the future ant heap and in the meantime will wet the earth with blood. The world of western Europe offers no other solutions for guilt and human transgression.

The Russian author's view of guilt and transgression recognizes that no ant heap, no triumph of the "fourth estate," no abolition of poverty, no organization of labor will save humanity from abnormality and, consequently, from guilt and transgression. This is expressed in a monumental psychological elaboration of the human soul, with awesome depth and force and with a realism of artistic portrayal unprecedented among us. It is clear and intelligible to the point of obviousness that evil lies deeper in human beings than our socialist-physicians suppose; that no social structure will eliminate evil; that the human soul will remain as it always has been; that abnormality and sin arise from that soul itself; and, finally, that the laws of the human soul are still so little known, so obscure to science, so undefined, and so mysterious, that there are not and cannot be either physicians or *final* judges; but there is He who says: "Vengeance is mine, I will repay." He alone knows *all* the mystery of this world and the final destiny of man. Humans themselves still cannot venture to decide anything with pride in infallibility; the times and the seasons for that have not yet arrived. The human judge himself ought to know that he is not the final judge; that he himself is a sinner; that the measure and the scales in his hands will be an absurdity *if* he, holding that measure and scales, does not himself submit to the law of the yet unsolved mystery and turn to the only solution—to Mercy and Love. And so that man might not perish in despair and ignorance of his path and destiny, of his conviction of evil's mysterious and fateful inevitability, he has been shown a way out. This the poet has brilliantly shown in a masterful scene in the novel's penultimate part, in the scene of the heroine's mortal illness, when the transgressors and enemies are suddenly transformed into higher beings, into brothers who have forgiven one another everything, into beings who, through mutual forgiveness, have cast off lies, guilt, and crime and thereby at once have absolved themselves with full awareness of their right to absolution. But later, at the end of the novel, we have a gloomy and terrible picture of the full degeneration of a human spirit; this we follow step by step through the depiction of that compelling state in which evil, having taken possession of a human being, trammels his every movement and paralyzes every effort toward resistance, every thought, every wish to struggle with the darkness that falls upon the soul; deliberately, eagerly, with a passion for vengeance, the soul accepts the darkness instead of the light. In this picture there is such a profound lesson for the human judge, for the one who holds the measure and the scales, that he will naturally exclaim in fear and perplexity, "No, vengeance is not always mine, and it is not always for me to repay." And the human judge will not cruelly charge the grievously fallen criminal with having scorned the light of the age-old solution and with having *deliberately* rejected it. He will not, at least, cling to the letter of the law. . . .

If we have literary works of such power of thought and execution, then why can we not *eventually* have *our own* science as well, and our own economic and social solutions? Why does Europe refuse us our independence, *our own* word? These are questions that cannot help but be asked. It would be absurd to suppose that nature has endowed us only with literary talents. All the other things are a matter of history, circumstances, and the conditions of the time. Our own homegrown Europeans, at least, ought to be thinking this way while they await the judgment of the European Europeans. . . .

Article 4. A Landowner Who Gets Faith in God from a Peasant

Now that I have expressed my feelings, people may understand how I was affected by the defection of such an author, by his secession from the great Russian and general cause, and by the paradoxical untruth he tells about the People in the unfortunate eighth part of his novel, which he published separately. He simply takes away from the People all their most precious things and deprives them of what means most in their lives. He would have found it far more gratifying had our People's hearts not risen up everywhere for the sake of their brethren who suffer for their faith. In that sense alone, he denies this phenomenon, despite its obviousness. Of course, he does all this only through the fictional characters of his novel; but, I repeat, it's only too plain that the author himself shares their views. True enough, this little book is sincere, and the author speaks from his heart. Even the touchiest of things (and there are some *touchy* things there) have been fitted in as if quite casually, so that despite all their touchiness, you accept them quite literally and never admit the possibility of any underhandedness at all. Nevertheless, I still think this little book is not so innocent as all that. Now, of course, it does not and cannot have any influence, except maybe to give another nod of assent to some little group that has cut itself off from everyone else. But the fact that such an author can write this way is very sad. It's sad for the future. But I'd best get down to business: I'd like to voice my objections and point out the things that struck me particularly.

First, however, let me say something about Levin—obviously the main character of the novel: in him the positive side is expressed, as if in contrast to those abnormalities that have brought suffering and ruination to the other characters of the novel; Levin, apparently, was specifically destined by the author to be the expression of all these things. And yet Levin is still not complete; he still lacks something, and this should have been taken up and solved so that there would be no more doubts and questions about what Levin represents. The reader will eventually understand the reason why I am dwelling on this and not moving directly to the main thing.

Levin is happy; the novel ends with his glorification, but his inner, spiritual world is still lacking something. He is tormented by the age-old questions of humanity: God, eternal life, good and evil, and so on. He is tormented by the fact that he is not a believer and that he cannot peacefully settle into the things that everyone else settles peacefully into, i.e., self-interest, worship of one's own self or one's own idols, vanity, and so on. That's a sign of a noble spirit, is it not? But one couldn't have expected less of Levin. It appears, by the way, that Levin has read a great deal: he's familiar with the works of philosophers and positivists and ordinary natural scientists. Yet none of this satisfies him; rather, it confuses him even more, so that in moments of freedom from his work on the estate he runs off into the woods and groves, gets angry, and even appreciates Kitty much less than she merits. And so, once, he suddenly meets a peasant who, in talking about two other peasants, Mitiukha and Fokanych, whose moral qualities are very different, expresses himself as follows:

". . . Mitiukha, now, he'll be sure to get his due! He'll lean on a person till he gets what's owing. He's got no pity for a fellow Christian; but take old Fokanych—do you think he'd try to strip a man's hide from his back? He'll give a fellow credit, and sometimes he'll just forget about it. And there's times when he won't ask for all of it back—he's a human being, you see."

"But why would he let people off?"

"Well, you see, folks are all different: one fellow lives only for his needs; take Mitiukha, here—all he thinks about is stuffing his belly. But Fokanych is a righteous old man. He lives for his soul and remembers God."

"What do you mean, 'remembers God'? How does he live for his soul?" Levin almost shouted.

"Why, that's plain enough: he lives rightly, in God's way. Folks are all different, you see. Take you, now, you wouldn't harm a fellow either."

"Yes, yes! Good-bye, then!" said Levin, choking with emotion; and turning away he took up his stick and set off quickly for home.

However, he ran off to the forest once again, lay down under some aspen trees, and began thinking, almost in a kind of ecstasy. The word had been found, all the age-old riddles had been solved, and this through a few simple words from a peasant: "To live for one's soul, to remember God." The peasant, of course, had told him nothing new; he himself had known all that for a long time; but the peasant still suggested the idea and prompted him to a solution at the most critical moment. Thereafter follows a series of Levin's thoughts, very fitting and aptly expressed. Levin's idea is as follows: why should one seek with one's mind for something that has already been *given* by life itself, something with which every person is born and which (even involuntarily) every person should observe and does observe. Every person is born with a conscience, with a conception of good and evil, and so every person is also born with a direct aim in life: to live for good and not to love evil. Both peasant and master are born with this, as are the Frenchman, the Russian, and the Turk—they all cherish good (N.B.: Although many of them do so in a way that's very much their own). But, says Levin, I was trying to comprehend all this through mathematics, science, reason, or was expecting some miracle, whereas this was given to me as a gift; it was born along with me. And that it is given as a gift can be proven directly: everyone on earth understands or can understand that we must *love our neighbor as ourselves.* That knowledge, in essence, contains the entire *law* of humanity, as was also declared to us by Christ Himself. Yet this knowledge is innate, and so it has been sent as a gift, for reason could never ever have provided such knowledge. Why? Because "loving one's neighbor," when you look at it rationally, is something irrational.

> "Where did I get this?" [asks Levin]. "Was it reason that proved I must love my neighbor and not strangle him? I was told that as a child, and I *believed it gladly,* because they told me something that was already in my soul. But who discovered this? Not reason. Reason discovered the struggle for survival and the law that demands I strangle everyone who stands in the way of my satisfying my desires. That's what reason deduces. But loving one's neighbor is something reason could never discover, because it's unreasonable."

Then Levin thought back to a recent scene with his children. The children had started cooking raspberries in a cup over a candle and squirting streams of milk into their mouths. When their mother caught them at their antics she began scolding them, saying that if they ruined the dishes and wasted the milk they would be left with neither dishes nor milk. But the children obviously didn't believe her because they could not imagine "the full scope of all the things they enjoyed, and so they could not imagine that what they were destroying was the very same thing by which they lived."

"This all happens by itself," they thought. "And there's nothing interesting or important about it because it's always been so and always will be. And it's always just the same. There's no point in our worrying about it, it's all done for us; but we want to think up something of our own, something new. And so we got the idea of putting some raspberries in a cup and cooking them over a candle, and squirting streams of milk into each other's mouths. That's fun, and it's new, and it's not a bit worse than drinking out of cups."

"Don't we do just the same thing, and didn't I do it in trying to use reason to discover the meaning of the forces of nature and the purpose of human life?" Levin continued thinking.

"And don't all the philosophical theories do the same thing, trying by an approach of thought that is odd and unnatural to humans to lead them to the knowledge of something they have known for a long time, and known so surely that they could not live without it? Isn't it clearly obvious in the development of the theory of every philosopher that he knows beforehand, and knows as certainly as the peasant Fedor and not a bit more clearly than he, the most important things about the meaning of life and is only trying through some dubious intellectual process to come back to something that everyone knows?

"Well, then, suppose we let the children fend for themselves, make their own dishes, milk the cows, and so on. Would they get up to such antics? They'd die of hunger. Well, then, suppose we were left to our own passions and thoughts, without any concept of the one God and Creator! Or without any concept of what is good, without any explanation of moral evil!

"Well, then, just try to construct anything without these conceptions!

"We only destroy, because we have had our fill spiritually. Just like the children!"

In short, his doubts are ended and Levin comes to believe—in what? He still has not strictly defined this, but he already believes. But is this a faith? He gladly poses this question to himself: "Can this be faith?" One must suppose that it is not yet faith. Moreover, it's hardly likely that people like Levin can have a conclusive faith. Levin likes to call himself "one of the People," but he's the son of a nobleman, the son of a Moscow nobleman of the upper-middle level whose foremost historian was Count L. Tolstoy. Although the peasant never told Levin anything new, he still nudged him toward the idea, and with this idea began a faith. In that very thing alone Levin should have seen that he is certainly not "one of the People" and that he cannot say, "I myself am one of the People." But I'll talk about that later. I only want to say that men like Levin, no matter how long they live with the People or near the People, will still never fully transform themselves into the People; moreover, there are many things about the People that they will never understand at all. It's not enough simply to think oneself one of the People or to try to become so through an act of will, and a very eccentric will at that. He may be a landowner, a landowner who works his land and who knows peasant work; he may go out mowing himself and know how to harness a horse and know that honey in the comb is served with fresh cucumbers. Still, no matter how he tries, his soul will still show the effects of what I think can be called *idling*—that same idling, physical and spiritual, which, no matter how much he tries to resist it, is still part of his inheritance and which, of course, the People see in every nobleman since they do not see with our eyes. However, I'll talk about that later as well. And he will destroy his faith again, destroy it himself; it will not last long: there will be some new hitch and everything will collapse at once. Kitty set off in life and she stumbled; so why did she stumble? If she stumbled, then she could not help but stumble; it's only too clear that she stumbled for this reason or for that reason. It's clear that everything here depended on laws that can be strictly defined. And if that's so, then science is everywhere. Where is Providence, then? What role does it play here? Where is human responsibility? And if there is no Providence, then how can I believe in God? And so on, and so on. Take a straight line and project it into infinity. In short, this honest soul is a most idly chaotic soul, otherwise he would not be a contemporary Russian educated nobleman, and one from the upper-middle level besides.

He proves this brilliantly only an hour or so after the acquisition of his faith; he is trying to prove that the Russian People have no feeling at all for the things that people in general feel; he destroys the soul of the People in a most autocratic manner; moreover, he declares that he himself feels no pity at all for human suffering. He declares that "there is not and cannot be any immediate feeling of compassion for the oppression of the Slavs"—i.e., not only in him but in the Russians as a whole: "I myself am one of the People," he says. They put much too cheap a value on the Russian People. But they've been appraising them that way for a long time. Not more than an hour had passed since the acquisition of faith, and again raspberries started being cooked over a candle.

from Chapter Three

Article 1. The Irritability of Vanity

The children came running and told Levin that guests had arrived: "One of them waves his arms around just like this." The guests, it turns out, are from Moscow. Levin seats them under the trees in the garden, serves them honey in the comb and fresh cucumbers, and the guests at once start in on the honey and the Eastern Question. All this happens last year, you see; you can remember: Cherniaev, the volunteers, collecting donations. A heated conversation quickly develops because everyone has an irrepressible urge to get to the major topic of the day. Those involved, apart from the ladies, are, first, some little professor from Moscow, a dear man but not awfully bright. Next is a man of enormous intellect and erudition (he's brought in for just this reason), Sergei Ivanovich Koznyshev, Levin's half-brother. This character is skillfully drawn in the novel, and eventually we understand him (he's a man of the 1840s). Sergei Ivanovich has only just plunged, completely and passionately, into work for the Slavs, and the Committee has given him so many responsibilities that it's difficult even to imagine, when you recall last summer, how he could drop everything and come to the country for two whole weeks. It's true that if he hadn't come there wouldn't have been any conversation by the apiary about the People's movement and, accordingly, no eighth part of the novel, which was written for this conversation alone. You see, this Sergei Ivanovich had published in Moscow a month or two before some scholarly book about Russia, a book he had been working on for a long time and for which he had high hopes; but the book was an unexpected failure, and not just a failure but a fiasco; no one made any comment about it and it passed without notice. And so at that point Sergei Ivanovich plunged into work for the Slavic cause, and with a passion one never expected from him. It appears, therefore, that this was an unnatural thing to do; all his passion for the Slavs is *ambition rentrée* and no more, and you sense clearly that Levin cannot help but emerge victorious over such a person. Sergei Ivanovich was very skillfully drawn in a comic light in the earlier parts as well; in part eight, however, it becomes completely clear that he was conceived only so that at the end of the novel he could serve as a pedestal for Levin's greatness. But he is a very successful character. Among the most unsuccessful characters, however, is the old prince. He's also sitting there discussing the Eastern Question. He is unsuccessful throughout the whole novel, not just in regard to the Eastern Question. He is one of the positive figures in the novel, intended as an expression of positive beauty—though not without some sinning against realism, of course: he does have his weaknesses and almost has a touch of absurdity about him; yet he is ever so respectable. He's also the novel's kindhearted character, as well as a fountain of common sense, but not some Mr. Goodsense of the Fonvizin kind who, once he takes to something, just keeps on like a trained donkey: common sense and nothing more. No, he has humor and, in general, truly human traits. The amusing thing is that this old man was designed to illustrate wittiness. Having passed through the school of life, the father of many children (who are well established in life, however), he gazes at everything around him in his old age with the quiet smile of a wise man; his smile is far from being meek and inoffensive, though. He'll give you advice, but watch out for the play of his wit: it'll tell you what for. And so, suddenly, there's a mishap here: Mr. Goodsense, designed to illustrate wittiness, appears—God knows why—as not witty in the least; in fact he's even rather common. It's true that he makes a real effort, just as he does all through the novel, to say something witty, but all we see is the effort and nothing more. Out of consideration for him the reader is prepared at last to give him credit for trying and to accept these vain attempts at wit for real wit; but what's far worse is that this same character, in the eighth part of the novel that was published separately, is intended to express things that, granted, are again not witty (in this respect the old prince remains thoroughly in character), but which are cynical and slanderous toward a part of our society and our People. Instead of a Mr. Goodheart we have some sort of clubman who rejects both the Russian People and all that is good in them. One senses a clubman's irritability, an old man's bile. However, the political theory of the old prince is not new at all. It's the same thing, repeated for the hundred-thousandth time, that we're constantly hearing even without him:

> "My view as well," said the prince. "I was living abroad, reading
> the newspapers and, I confess, even before the Bulgarian atrocities

I simply couldn't understand why all Russians developed such a sudden affection for their Slavic brethren, while I didn't feel any love for them at all. I was very grieved indeed and thought I must be a monster [he's being witty here, you see: just imagine, he thinks he must be a monster!] or that the waters of Karlsbad were having that effect on me [a particularly good quip]. But since I've come home I've stopped worrying [I should think so!]; I see that there are others besides me who are interested only in Russia, and not their Slavic brethren. . . ."

Now here we see real profundity! We must take an interest *only* in Russia. So that aid and comfort to the Slavs is flatly regarded as none of Russia's business; had he regarded it as Russia's business he would not have said that we must take an interest *only* in Russia, since taking an interest in the Slavs would then mean an interest in Russia herself and in her mission. The nature of the prince's views is, accordingly, a narrow conception of Russian interests. Of course we've heard that; we've heard it a thousand times, and there are some circles in which you hear nothing else. But here's something far more malignant, however; this is a conversation that took place a few minutes earlier. The old prince asks Sergei Ivanovich:

". . . for heaven's sake, Sergei Ivanovich, explain to me where all these volunteers are going and whom they're going to fight?"

"Why, the Turks," answered Sergei Ivanovich, with a calm smile. . . .

"But who has declared war on the Turks? Ivan Ivanovich Ragozov and Countess Lidia Ivanovna along with Mme. Stahl?"

Now here he's let the cat out of the bag. You understand that this was what he was getting at, and perhaps it was why he hurried back from Karlsbad. But this is a question of another sort, and the fact that the prince raised it seems not such a good thing. Of course, even this idea isn't new; but why, then, is it repeated once more? Last winter there were quite a number of people who, for their own reasons, kept saying that someone in Russia had declared war on the Turks. This idea was set forth; but this little idea made the rounds and came back to those who had invented it. Because absolutely no one in Russia last year declared war on the Turks; and to make such a claim is, at very least, an *exaggeration*. True, Sergei Ivanovich later dismisses it with a joke, but the naive and honest Levin, like a genuine enfant terrible, plainly expresses the thing that is on the prince's mind:

> "No one has declared war; but people sympathize with the sufferings of those close to them and want to help them," said Sergei Ivanovich.
>
> "But the prince isn't talking about help," said Levin, interceding for his father-in-law. "He's talking about war. The prince means that private individuals cannot take part in a war without permission of the government."

Now do you see what Levin is worrying about? The matter is put quite plainly; beyond that, it is clarified by Katavasov's silly remark. This is what Levin goes on to say:

> "Well, this is my theory: on the one hand, war is such a bestial, cruel, and terrible thing that no one—to say nothing of a Christian—can himself personally assume the responsibility of starting a war; this can only be done by a government, instituted to do such things when they are inevitable. On the other hand, both science and common sense tell us that in matters of state, and in matters of war in particular, citizens have to renounce their personal will."
>
> Sergei Ivanovich and Katavasov, with ready objections, both began to speak at once.
>
> "But my dear fellow, the point is that there may be instances when the government is not expressing the will of the citizens, and then society expresses its will," said Katavasov.
>
> But Sergei Ivanovich evidently did not approve of this argument....

In short, they advance and support the view that someone in Russia, behind the back of the government, really did declare war on the Turks last year. Given his intellect, Levin should be able to figure out that Katavasov is a fool, that Katavasovs are to be found everywhere, that last year's movement was precisely opposed to the ideas of the Katavasovs because it was something Russian, national, and genuinely ours, and not the game of some opposition. But Levin insists on his own view; he takes his accusation to its conclusion; what matters to him is not truth but the thing he has invented. Here are the arguments with which he concludes his ideas on this topic:

> ...He [Levin] was speaking in the same spirit as Mikhailych and the People who expressed their idea in the legend of the summoning of the Varangians: 'Be our princes and rule over us. We gladly swear our complete submission. All the toil, all the humiliations, all the sacrifices we shall take on ourselves; but we do not wish to judge and make decisions.' And now, Sergei Ivanovich claimed, the People *had renounced this right they had purchased so dearly.*
>
> He wanted also to ask that if public opinion were such an infallible judge, then why were the revolution and the commune not as legitimate as the movement on behalf of the Slavs? ...

Do you hear that? And no considerations can lead these gentlemen astray, and no facts, no matter how evident they are. I have already said that it would have been better had the prince and Levin never made such accusations; but who can't see that one of them suffers from injured vanity and the other is a paradoxicalist. However, perhaps Levin also suffers from injured vanity, because one never knows what may suddenly injure a man's vanity! And yet the issue is clear, the accusation is nonsensical; and besides, there can be no such accusation because it simply cannot exist. The facts were altogether different.

Article 4, two extracts. Levin's Agitation. A Question: Does Distance Have an Influence on Love for Humanity? Can One Agree with the Opinion of One Turkish Prisoner on the Humaneness of Some of Our Ladies? So What, Then, Are Our Teachers Teaching Us?

But his agitation goes still further: Levin flatly and exasperatingly proclaims that there can be no compassion toward the torments of the

Slavs, that *"there is no immediate feeling for the oppression of the Slavs, and there cannot be any."* Sergei Ivanovich says:

". . . There is no declaration of war here, only an expression of humane, Christian feeling. Our brothers, of our blood and our faith, are being killed. Now suppose they were not our brothers and not of our faith but simply women, children, and old people; feeling is aroused and Russians run off to help put an end to these horrors. Just imagine if you were walking along the street and saw some drunken men beating a woman or a child; I think you wouldn't stop to ask whether or not a war had been declared on those men; you would simply rush at them and defend the victim."

"But I wouldn't kill them," said Levin.

"But you might."

"I don't know. If I should see such a thing, I might yield to my immediate feeling; *but I can't say that beforehand.* But there is no such immediate feeling for the oppression of the Slavs, and there cannot be any."

"Perhaps there isn't any for you. But it exists for others," said Sergei Ivanovich, frowning with displeasure. "Among the People there still survive the legends of Orthodox Christians suffering under the yoke of the 'godless Agarians.' The People have heard of the sufferings of their brethren and they have spoken."

"That may be," said Levin evasively, "but I don't see it; *I'm one of the People myself,* and I don't feel it."

Again we have "I'm one of the People myself." I repeat once more: it's only been two hours since this Levin got his faith from a peasant—or at least the peasant gave him the idea of how to believe. I am not praising the peasant or disparaging Levin and, indeed, won't now undertake to decide which of them had the better faith and whose soul was in the higher and more developed state, etc., etc. But you have to agree, I repeat, that this very fact alone should have led Levin to realize that there is a certain *fundamental* difference between him and the People. And then he says: "I'm one of the People myself." But why is he so certain that he's one of the People himself? Because he knows how to harness a horse to a cart and knows that cucumbers with honey make tasty eating. Such people! And what vanity, what pride, what arrogance!

Yet this isn't the most important thing. Levin insists that *there is not and cannot be* any immediate feeling for the oppression of the Slavs. Sergei Ivanovich objects that "the People have heard of the sufferings of their brethren and they have spoken"; Levin replies: "That may be, but I don't see it; I'm one of the People myself, *and I don't feel it.*"

Does he mean he doesn't feel compassion? Note that Levin's argument with Sergei Ivanovich about compassion and immediate feeling for the oppression of the Slavs is developed with a bias, as if it were intended to end with Levin's victory. For instance, Sergei Ivanovich does his best to argue that, were Levin to be walking along and see some drunken men beating a woman, he would rush to save her. "But I wouldn't kill them!" Levin objects. "But you might," insists Sergei Ivanovich and, of course, he's talking nonsense, because would anyone helping out a woman being beaten by drunkards have to kill those drunkards? She could be rescued without any killing. But the main thing is that this certainly isn't a matter of some street brawl; the comparison is false and without basis. They are talking about the Slavs, about the torments, tortures, and massacres they suffer, and Levin knows full well they are talking about the Slavs. Accordingly, when he says that he doesn't know whether he would help, that he doesn't see anything and *doesn't feel anything,* etc., etc., he is stating plainly that he feels no compassion for the torments of the Slavs (and not for the torments of a woman beaten up by drunken men) and he insists that there is not, and cannot be, any immediate feeling for the sufferings of the Slavs. In fact that is literally what he says.

There is a rather interesting psychological fact here. The book came out only two and a half months ago, and two and a half months ago it was already very well known that all the countless stories of the countless torments and tortures of the Slavs were the absolute truth—a truth to which thousands of informants and eyewitnesses of all nations can now attest. What we have learned over the last year and a half about the tortures suffered by the Slavs goes beyond the fantasies of even the sickest and most frenzied imagination. We know, first, that these massacres are not incidental but systematic, instigated deliberately, and encouraged in every way. People are being exterminated by the thousands and tens of thousands. Tortures have been refined to such a degree as we have not read or heard of before. The skin is stripped from living people while their children watch; children are tossed in the air and caught on the point of a bayonet while their mothers watch; women are raped, and during the act the woman is stabbed with a dagger; worst of all, infants are tortured and abused. Levin says that he feels *nothing* and recklessly affirms that there is no immediate feeling for the oppression of the Slavs and there cannot be any. But I venture to assure Mr. Levin that there can be such a feeling and that I myself have witnessed it on more than one occasion. For instance, I saw one gentleman who does not like talking about his feelings but who, when he heard how one two-year-old boy had his eyes pierced with a needle while his sister watched and was then impaled on a stake so that he did not die quickly but screamed for a long time—when he heard that, this gentleman almost fell ill, did not sleep that night, and for two days thereafter was so depressed and worn-out that he could not work. In this regard, I venture to assure Mr. Levin that this gentleman is an honest person and is certainly a respectable one; he is certainly not "idle trash" and is far from being a member of Pugachev's gang. I wanted only to state that immediate feeling for the torments of the Slavs can exist, feeling of even the strongest kind, and even in all classes of society. But Levin insists that *there cannot even be* any feeling and that he himself feels *nothing*. For me, that is an enigma. Of course, there are people who are simply unfeeling, coarse, and perverted. But Levin, it seems, is not such a person; he is depicted as altogether a sensitive man. Is it simply the distance that influences the matter? In fact, does this *psychological* peculiarity exist in some characters: "I can't see it myself," they say; "it's happening far away, and so I don't feel a thing." Jokes aside, just imagine that there are people living on the planet Mars and that they are piercing the eyes of some infants there. Do you think we'd feel any pity here on earth, any great amount of pity, at least? The same thing happens on earth, perhaps, when very great distances are involved: "Ah, it's happening in another hemisphere, not right here!" I mean to say, he may not state that frankly but that's how he feels—he feels *nothing*, in other words. In that case, if distance really does have such an influence on humaneness, then a new question arises of itself: at what distance does love of humanity end? And Levin really does pose a great enigma in terms of love of humanity. He states flatly that *he does not know* whether he would kill: "If I should see such a thing, I might yield to my immediate feeling; but I can't say that beforehand."

So he doesn't know what he would do! And yet, he's a sensitive man, and so, as a sensitive man, he's afraid to kill . . . a Turk. Imagine such a scene: Levin is standing right there, with rifle and fixed bayonet, and two paces away a Turk is voluptuously holding a needle, ready to pierce the eyes of the child already in his arms. The boy's seven-year-old sister screams and rushes madly to tear him away from the Turk. And here stands Levin, thinking and hesitating: "I don't know what I'll do. I don't feel anything. I'm one of the People myself. There isn't any immediate feeling for the oppression of the Slavs and there cannot be any."

But, seriously, what would he have done after all the things he's told us? How could he not save the child? Would he really let the child be tortured? Would he really not snatch him from the hands of the villainous Turk?

"Well, yes, I'd snatch him away, but suppose I had to give the Turk a good hard push?"

"Then push him!"

"Push him, you say! And if he doesn't want to let the child go and draws his saber? Why, suppose I had to kill the Turk?"

"Well then, kill him!"

"But how can I kill him! No, I mustn't kill the Turk. No, it's better to let him pierce the child's eyes and torture him; I'll go home to Kitty."

That's what Levin would do; it emerges directly from his convictions and from all that he says. He says frankly that he *does not know* whether he would help the woman or the child if he had to kill a Turk to do so. And he's awfully sorry for the Turks.

> "Twenty years ago we would have kept silent" [says Sergei Ivanovich], but now we hear the voice of the Russian People, ready to rise up as one man, ready to sacrifice themselves for their oppressed brethren; that's a great step forward and a token of strength."
>
> "It's not only a matter of sacrificing themselves, though, but of killing Turks," Levin said meekly. "The People make their donations and are prepared to make more for the sake of their souls, but not for the sake of murder. . . ."

In other words: "Here you are, little girl, we donate this money for the sake of our souls; your little brother will just have to have his eyes pierced. We can't kill a Turk. . . ."

And then, later on, the author himself says of Levin: "He could not agree that a dozen people, including his brother, should have the right to say, on the basis of what they had been told by a couple of hundred volunteer rabble rousers who were swarming into the cities, that they and the newspapers were expressing the will and the ideas of the People, especially when it was an idea *that expressed itself through vengeance and murder*."

[. . .] Turks are being killed in war, in honorable battle, not for *vengeance* but only *because* there is no other way to wrest their dishonorable weapons from their hands. That was so last year as well. And if we do not take away their weapons and—so as to avoid killing them—simply go away, then they will at once begin again to cut off women's breasts and poke out children's eyes. What's to be done? To let them poke out eyes, just so we can avoid somehow killing a Turk? But that's surely a distorted understanding of things; that's the most obtuse and gross sentimentalizing; that's fanatical single-mindedness; that's utter and total perversion of nature. Furthermore, the soldier who is compelled to kill a Turk is himself bearing his own life in sacrifice and, besides, endures suffering and tribulation. Was it to seek vengeance, was it only to commit murders that the Russian People rose up? And when was it that helping whole provinces of those being massacred and exterminated, helping women and children who are being violated and who have no one else on earth to stand up for them—when was it that this was considered a crude, ridiculous, almost immoral action, a thirst for vengeance and blood? And what a lack of feeling, side by side with sentimentalism! Why, Levin himself has a child, a little boy; surely he loves him; and when this child is given a bath, why it's a regular event in the household; so why doesn't his heart bleed when he hears and reads about mass killings, about children with crushed heads crawling after their raped mothers, about murdered women with breasts cut off? This happened in one Bulgarian church, where two hundred such corpses were found after the city had been plundered. Levin reads all this and stands thinking: "Kitty is in fine spirits and had a good appetite today; we've given the boy a bath and he's begun to recognize me; what do I care what goes on over there in another hemisphere? *There is no immediate feeling for the oppression of the Slavs and there cannot be any,* because I don't feel *anything.*"

Is this how Levin ends his epic? Is he the one the author wants to set forth as an example of a righteous and honorable man? People like the author of *Anna Karenina* are the teachers of society, our teachers, while we are merely their pupils. So what is it, then, that they are teaching us?

September

from CHAPTER ONE

Article 5, two extracts. Who's Knocking at the Door? Who Will Come In? Inescapable Fate.

When I was beginning this chapter the facts and reports that are suddenly filling the entire European press had not yet appeared, so that everything I wrote here as speculation has now been borne out almost word for word. My *Diary* will come out next month, on October 7, while today is only September 29 and the "soothsayings," if I may call them that, on which I rather riskily embarked in this chapter will look somewhat dated, like established facts from which I merely copied my "soothsayings." But I will be so bold as to remind readers of the *Diary* of this summer's May and June issue. Almost everything I wrote in it about Europe's immediate future has already been confirmed or *is beginning to be confirmed.* And yet, at the time I heard views expressed about the article (the views of nonspecialists, it's true) that called it "frenzied raving" and preposterous exaggeration. [...] But for the record, I shall try, in conclusion, once more to indicate the points and the signposts along the road that is already beginning to appear before us all, and on which, like it or not, it seems we are all destined to set forth. I do this for the record so that it may later be verified. However, this is only a simple and concluding summary of this chapter.

1. The road begins in Rome, in the Vatican, where a dying old man, the head of the crowd of Jesuits surrounding him, has traced it long ago. When the Eastern Question flared up, the Jesuits realized that the most opportune moment had come. They burst into France, following the road that had been indicated, created a coup d'état there, and placed the country in such a position that a war with Germany in the near future was almost inevitable, even if France did not want to begin it. Prince Bismarck had foreseen and realized all this long before. It seems, at least, that he alone—and perhaps even several years before the present moment—was able to make out and comprehend who his principal enemy was, as well as the immense world significance of this last battle for survival that *papal Catholicism in its ultimate death throes* will certainly offer to the whole world in the very near future.

2. This fateful struggle is already assuming its ultimate shape at the present moment, and the final battle is drawing near with awesome speed. France was selected and designated as the terrible battleground, and there will be a battle. The battle is inevitable, that is certain. However, there is still a slight chance that it will be postponed, but merely for a very short time. In any case, it is *inevitable and near at hand.*

3. As soon as the battle begins, it will at once be transformed into an all-European one. The Eastern Question and the Eastern war, by the force of destiny, will also merge with this all-European war. One of the most remarkable episodes of this battle will be Austria's final decision: to which side will she lend her sword? But the most essential and important part of this final and fateful struggle will consist, on the one hand, in the fact that it will resolve the thousand-year question of Roman Catholicism and, on the other hand, that by the will of Providence a reborn Eastern Christianity will take its place. In such manner our Russian Eastern Question will expand into a worldwide, universal question with an extraordinary, preordained significance, even though this preordination may occur before eyes that are blind and do not recognize it, eyes that are incapable until the last minute of seeing the obvious and of comprehending the meaning of what has been preordained. Finally—

4. (And you may call this the most hypothetical and fantastic of all my predictions—I'll admit that beforehand.) I am certain that the battle will end in favor of the East, of the Eastern alliance; that Russia has nothing to fear if the Eastern war merges with the all-European one, and that it would even be better if the matter should broaden in this way. Oh, there's no denying that it will be a terrible thing if so much precious human blood is shed! But there is at least consolation in the thought that the blood that has been shed will certainly spare Europe from ten times more bloodshed should the matter be postponed and drawn out even further. The more so that the great struggle will certainly end quickly. And, in return, so many problems will finally be solved (the Roman Catholic problem, along with the fate of France, the German, Eastern, and Mohammedan problems); so many matters that were utterly insolvable, given the former course of events, will now be settled; the face of Europe will be so altered; so many new and progressive things will begin in human relationships that, perhaps, there is no cause for spiritual anguish and excessive fear

over this last convulsion of old Europe on the eve of its great and certain renewal. . . .

Finally, I'll add one more consideration: if you make it a rule to judge all world events, even those that the most superficial view can see as being of the greatest importance, according to the principle "Today as yesterday, and tomorrow as today"—then isn't it clear that this rule goes utterly contrary to the history of nations and of humanity? Meanwhile, this is just what is prescribed by so-called realistic and sober common sense, so that ridicule and scorn are heaped upon almost anyone who ventures to think that tomorrow everyone may see some matter in quite a different aspect from the one in which they saw it yesterday. Even now, for instance, when the facts are already at hand, does it not seem even to very many people that the clerical movement is a most insignificant little thing; that Gambetta will give a speech and everything will be restored to the way it was yesterday; that our war with Turkey, very, very possibly, will end by winter and thereupon the stock-exchange gambling and railroad business will resume, the ruble will rise, we'll happily go traveling to Europe, and so on? The inconceivability of continuing the old order of things was an evident truth for all the leading minds in Europe on the eve of the first European revolution that began in France at the end of the last century. Meanwhile, was there anyone in the whole world, even on the eve of the summoning of the Estates-General, who could have foreseen and foretold the form this event would assume virtually the day after it began? . . . And once it had assumed its form, who could have predicted the rise of Napoleon I, for instance, the one who, in essence, was virtually preordained to complete the first historical phase of this same event that began in 1789? Moreover, in the time of Napoleon I, perhaps, everyone in Europe thought that his rise was, without a doubt, an entirely external matter of chance in no way linked with that same universal law by which the former face of this world had been destined, at the end of the last century, to change its whole appearance. . . .

Yes, indeed; and now again someone is knocking; someone, a new man, with a new word, wants to open the door and come in. . . . But who will come in? That's the question. Will it be an entirely new man, or will it once more be someone like all of us, the old homunculi?

from CHAPTER TWO

Article 1. A Lie Is Saved by a Lie

Once upon a time Don Quixote—that very well-known knight of the doleful countenance, the noblest of all the knights the world has ever seen, the simplest in soul and one of the greatest in heart—while wandering with his faithful attendant, Sancho, in search of adventure, was suddenly struck by a puzzle that gave him cause to think for a long while. The fact is that often the knights of old, beginning with Amadis da Gaula, whose stories have come down to us in the absolutely truthful books known as the romances of chivalry (for acquisition of which Don Quixote did not regret selling several of the best acres of his little estate)—often these knights, during their glorious peregrinations that were so beneficial to the whole world, would suddenly and unexpectedly encounter entire armies of even a hundred thousand warriors sent forth against them by some evil power, by evil sorcerers who envied them and prevented them in all sorts of ways from achieving their great goal and being united at last with their fair ladies. It usually happened that when a knight encountered such a monstrous and evil army he would draw his sword, invoke the name of his fair lady for spiritual succor, and then hack his way into the very midst of his enemies, whom he would annihilate to the last man. This would seem to be quite a simple matter, but Don Quixote suddenly fell to thinking, and on this problem: he suddenly found it impossible to believe that a single knight, no matter how strong he might be and no matter if he were to go on wielding his armipotent sword for a whole day without getting tired, could at once lay low a hundred thousand enemies, and this in only one battle. Killing each man would still take some time; killing a hundred thousand men would take a great deal of time; and no matter how he wielded his sword, a single person could not do this at once, in a few hours or so. And yet these trustworthy books told of such deeds being done in just a single battle. How could it happen?

"I have solved this puzzle, Sancho, my friend," Don Quixote said at last. "Inasmuch as all these giants, all these wicked sorcerers, were the evil spirit, their armies likewise possessed the same magical and evil nature.

I presume that these armies were composed of men quite unlike you and me, for instance. These men were no more than an illusion, the product of magic, and in all probability their bodies were unlike our own but were more akin to those of slugs, worms, and spiders, for example. And thus in his powerful hand the knight's steadfast and sharp sword would, when it fell upon these bodies, pass through them in an instant, almost without resistance, as if through air. And if that is so, then truly with a single blow he could cut through three or four bodies, and even through ten if they were standing close together. Hence one can understand that the thing would be greatly expedited and a knight really could annihilate whole armies of such evil blackamoors and other monsters. . . ."

Here the great poet and seer of the human heart perceived one of the most profound and most mysterious aspects of the human spirit. Oh, this is a great book, not the sort that are written now; only one such book is sent to humanity in several hundred years. And such perceptions of the profoundest aspects of human nature you will find on every page of this book. Take only the fact that this Sancho, the personification of common sense, prudence, cunning, the golden mean, has chanced to become a friend and traveling companion to the maddest person on earth—he precisely, and no other! He deceives him the whole time, he cheats him like a child, and yet he has complete faith in his great intellect, is enchanted to the point of tenderness by the greatness of his heart, believes completely in all the preposterous dreams of the great knight, and the whole time he never once doubts that the Don will at last conquer the island for him! What a fine thing it would be if our young people were to become thoroughly steeped in these great works of world literature. I don't know what is now being taught in courses of literature, but a knowledge of this most splendid and sad of all books created by human genius would certainly elevate the soul of a young person with a great idea, give rise to profound questions in his heart, and work toward diverting his mind from worship of the eternal and foolish idol of mediocrity, self-satisfied conceit, and cheap prudence. Man will not forget to take this *saddest* of all books with him to God's last judgment. He will point to the most profound and fateful mystery of humans and humankind that the book conveys. He will point to the fact that humanity's most sublime beauty, its most sublime purity, chastity, forthrightness, gentleness, courage, and, finally, its most sublime intellect—all these often (alas, all too often) come to naught, pass without benefit to humanity, and even become an object of humanity's derision simply because all these most noble and precious gifts with which a person is often endowed lack but the very last gift—that of *genius* to put all this power to work and to direct it along a path of action that is truthful, not fantastic and insane, so as to work for the benefit of humanity! But genius, alas, is given out to the tribes and the peoples in such small quantities and so rarely that the spectacle of the malicious irony of fate that so often dooms the efforts of some of the noblest of people and the most ardent friends of humanity to scorn and laughter and to the casting of stones solely because these people, at the fateful moment, were unable to discern the true sense of things and so discover their *new word*—this spectacle of the needless ruination of such great and noble forces actually may reduce a friend of humanity to despair, evoke not laughter but bitter tears and sour his heart, hitherto pure and believing, with doubt. . . .

However, I wanted only to point out this most interesting feature which, along with hundreds of other such profound perceptions, Cervantes revealed in the human heart. The most preposterous of people, with a crackpot belief in the most preposterous fantasy anyone can conceive, suddenly falls into doubt and perplexity that almost shake his entire faith. What's curious is the thing that was able to shake it: not the absurdity of the crackpot notion itself, not the absurdity of wandering knights who exist for the benefit of humanity, not the absurdity of those magical wonders told of in those "absolutely truthful books"—no, on the contrary, it was something external and secondary, an altogether particular thing. The preposterous man suddenly *began yearning for realism!* It wasn't the appearance of sorcerers' armies that bothered him: oh, that's beyond any doubt; and how else could these great and splendid knights display all their valor if they were not visited by all these trials, if there were no envious giants and wicked sorcerers? The ideal of the wandering knight is so great, so beautiful and useful, and had so captivated the heart of the noble Don Quixote that it became utterly impossible for him to renounce his faith in it; that would have been the equivalent of betraying his ideal, his duty, his love for Dulcinea and for humanity. (When he did renounce his ideal, when he was cured of his madness and grew *wiser*, after returning from his second campaign in which he was defeated by the wise and commonsensical barber Carrasco, the skeptic and debunker, he promptly passed away, quietly, with a sad smile, consoling the weeping Sancho, loving the whole world with the mighty force of love contained in his sacred heart, and yet realizing that there was nothing more for him to do in this world.) No, it was not that; what troubled him was merely the very real, mathematical consideration that no matter how the knight might wield his sword and no matter how strong he might be, he still could not overcome an army of a hundred thousand in the course of a few hours, or even in a day, having killed all of them to the last man. And yet such things were written in these trustworthy books. Therefore, they must have lied. And if there is one lie, then it is all a lie. How, then, can *truth* be saved? And so, to save the truth he invents another fantasy; but this one is twice, thrice as fantastic as the first one, cruder and more absurd; he invents hundreds of thousands of imaginary men having the bodies of slugs, which the knight's keen blade can pass through ten times more easily and quickly than it can an ordinary human body. And thus *realism* is satisfied, *truth* is saved, and it's possible to believe in the first and most important dream with no more doubts—and all this, again, is solely thanks to the second, even more absurd fantasy, invented only to salvage the *realism* of the first one.

Ask yourselves: hasn't the same thing happened to you, perhaps, a hundred times in the course of your life? Say you've come to cherish a certain dream, an idea, a theory, a conviction, or some external fact that struck you, or, at last, a woman who has enchanted you. You rush off in pursuit of the object of your love with all the intensity your soul can muster. It's true that no matter how blinded you may be, no matter how well your heart bribes you, still, if in the object of your love there is a lie, a *delusion*, something that you yourself have exaggerated and distorted because of your passion and your initial rush of feeling—solely so that you can make it your idol and bow down to it—then, of course, you're aware of it in the depths of your being; doubt weighs upon your mind and teases it, ranges through your soul and prevents you from living peaceably with your beloved dream. Now, don't you remember, won't you admit even to yourself what it was that suddenly set your mind at rest? Didn't you invent a new dream, a new lie, even a terribly crude one, perhaps, but one that you were quick to embrace lovingly only because it resolved your initial doubt?

Article 3, extract. An Intimation of the Future Educated Russian Man. The Certain Lot of the Future Russian Woman.

[. . .] But the most important and most beneficial role in the regeneration of Russian society will certainly fall to the Russian woman. After the present war, in which our Russian woman has displayed such lofty, radiant, and sacred qualities, it's impossible to doubt the lofty role that certainly awaits her among us. At last the age-old prejudices will fall away, and "barbaric" Russia will reveal the place she will give to the "little mother" and "little sister" of the Russian soldier, the self-renouncer and martyr for the Russian man. Can we really continue to deny her, that woman who has so graphically displayed her valor, full equality of rights with men in education, employment, and official positions, when it is upon her that all our hopes now rest, after her glorious feat in the spiritual regeneration and moral elevation of our society! That would be shameful and unreasonable, the more so that this will now not depend entirely on us, because the Russian woman herself has assumed her proper place, has herself climbed above those rungs that hitherto had been considered her limit. She has shown the heights she can attain and what she can achieve. In saying that, however, I am speaking about the *Russian woman* and not about those sentimental ladies who gave candies to the Turks. There's no harm in showing kindness to the Turks, of course, but still, this isn't what *those women* accomplished over there; and so *the former* are only *old* Russian ladies, while *the latter* are the *new* Russian women. But I am not talking only about the women who pursue God's cause and serve humanity; their appearance has shown us only that in the Russian land there are many women who are great of heart and who are prepared to work for the common good and to sacrifice themselves because, once again, where did they come from if not from here? [. . .]

October

from CHAPTER THREE

Article 1, extract. Roman Clericals Here in Russia

Not long ago *The Moscow News*, No. 262, made the following observation in its editorial:

> A few days ago we drew attention to a certain party in Russia that is acting in accord with Russia's enemies and that is prepared to assist the Turks in their conflict with us—a party of Anglo-Magyars that hates every manifestation of our national spirit and every action of our government made in this spirit; it is a party that places Russian patriotism on the same level as nihilism and revolution, a party that feeds the foreign press, hostile to us, with the most disgusting information. Our article had scarcely been sent to press when a telegram from our Petersburg correspondent supplied us with the essence of the communiqué, made public in *The Government Messenger,* which provided ample evidence of new machinations of this party. At the same time our army was winning brilliant victories between Plevna and Orhanie, the conspirators, in an attempt to demoralize the public, spread rumors of the defeat these same victorious troops supposedly suffered; the efforts of the conspirators are so intense that the government considered it necessary to alert the public against such malicious rumors.

The very next day, *New Times* remarked in this connection—only in passing, however—that *The Moscow News* had overstated the matter somewhat and that *The Government Messenger* had in mind, perhaps, simply some idle talk among the public which had no such significance. (I am setting forth the idea of *New Times* in my own words, from memory.)

It's very possible that this is so and that *The Government Messenger* really was speaking only of some "idle talk." Nevertheless, the hypothesis of *The Moscow News* does have real foundation. Only who are these Anglo-Magyars *The Moscow News* refers to? In Russia, in the border areas as well as the interior, we do have our own Roman clericals. It's no longer May, however; now everyone knows and writes about the worldwide clerical conspiracy, and even the most liberal of our newspapers have agreed that this conspiracy does exert its influence. But it would be a strange thing if a Vatican conspiracy overlooked our Roman clericals and failed to use them in its cause. Disturbances in the rear of the Russian army would be extremely useful to the Vatican, especially at the present moment. [...]

Article 2. Old Poland's Summer Attempt at Reconciliation

At the beginning of the summer these clerical-agitators tried to make their presence felt among us even via Russian periodicals. The wolves dressed themselves in sheep's clothing and began speaking as if they represented the entire Polish "emigration" abroad. They began proposing a reconciliation: "Accept us," they said. "We can also see that Slavic brotherhood certainly exists and we don't wish to be left out." They spoke with extraordinary tenderness and set forth their reasons:

> "We have engineers, chemists, technologists, tradesmen, bookkeepers, agronomists and so on," they say. There are many such people among the emigrés. Let them in! A resident of Lithuania, writing in *The St. Petersburg News*, No. 172, said: "Is there no work among you for people of the class that once produced a Tengoborski for Russia and a Wolowski for France? And in art, which does so much to refine manners and ennoble character, Brotzki the sculptor and Matejko the painter are now known all over the world as representatives of Polish society. Do you not need such people? And what do you say about the whole assembly of literary men, journalists, entrepreneurs, manufacturers, and every other kind of active person? Do you not need these people either?"
>
> (*New Times*, from Kostomarov's article)

Mr. Kostomarov gave a superb answer, in *New Times*, to all this currying of favor. I regret that I do not have space to include excerpts from this excellent article. Mr. Kostomarov proves, in clear and precise arguments, that all this is merely a trap laid for us, that they would send us traitors like Konrad Wallenrod; that the Pole of Old Poland instinctively, blindly hates Russia and the Russians. Mr. Kostomarov admits, however, that there are some very fine Polish people who can live even in friendship with a Russian, save him in times of misfortune, and lend him money. That's true, of course; but the moment this Russian, even after twenty years of friendship, expressed to this very fine Pole any truly Russian political convictions about Poland, this same Pole would at once become, openly or in secret, the enemy of his Russian friend, for the rest of his life, to the end—the implacable and perpetual enemy. Mr. Kostomarov forgot to add that point.

This whole summer attempt at "reconciliation," which found both Russian supporters and an opponent as powerful as Mr. Kostomarov, is unquestionably a covert act of the clericals in Europe, an offshoot of the all-European clerical conspiracy. Oh, these Poles of Old Poland assure us that they certainly aren't clericals or papists or Romans and that we should have realized this long ago. But can you really suppose that Old Poland, this Polish emigration, does not cling to the pope in the Jesuitical sense and is far from the wild imaginings of the clericals—oh, what an absurd notion! Aren't they the very ones who would cling to the Vatican when they are so fully aware of its strength and have always been aware of it? The Vatican never ever betrayed Old Poland, after all; on the contrary, the Vatican gave full support to Old Poland's every wild notion when other states would not even listen. No, they won't betray the Vatican, and the Vatican won't betray them. The summer foray to seek reconciliation was made precisely at the time the entire emigration came out against the Russians, when Polish legions were being formed, when the aristocrats of the emigration appeared in Constantinople with huge sums of money (not their own, of course). This whole attempt at reconciliation was no more than an act of perfidy, as Mr. Kostomarov defined it. By the way: they are offering us their scientists, technologists, and artists, and they tell us, "Take them; don't you need them?" One might add here that they probably regard us as a savage people and do not know that we have all the things they are offering us, perhaps even better ones than theirs. But there's no point in taking offense; the main thing is: why don't they come? We did have several Poles who showed their talents, and Russia honored them, respected them, gave them a place of distinction, and in no way treated them differently from the Russians. So why all these arrangements? Come! Be reconciled and accept the situation, but know that Old Poland will never exist again. There is New Poland, a Poland liberated by the tsar, a Poland that is being reborn and certainly may expect to have, in time to come, a fate equal to those of the other Slavic tribes when Slavdom is liberated and resurrected in Europe. But Old Poland will never exist again because she could never get along with Russia. Her ideal is to assume Russia's place in the Slavic world. Her motto, in regard to Russia, is: "*ôte-toi de là, que je m'y mette*" ("get out of the way so I can take your place"). It's curious that this Polish advance skirmisher speaks only of scientists and artists. Well, what of the leaders of the emigration, the aristocrats? Just picture the result were Russia to give in to these flattering words and declare that she wants to make peace; and there they would sit, asking haughtily: "What are your terms?"

Because if you suggest that we allow the emigrés back into Russia, and they don't come on their own, *it means they are waiting for terms.* And so, imagine that Russia suddenly acknowledges that they amount to something, accepts them as a belligerent party, and begins these talks! Then they would make their way back to Russia; the magnates would at once start to find fault and demand high positions and honors; and then they would at once shout to the whole of Europe that they had been deceived; and then they would begin a Polish rebellion. . . . And Russia would be drawn into such a catastrophe and would make such a stupid mistake! Of course, the Poles themselves could not have believed that such a crude trick would deceive Russia. But they were counting on their Russian partisans who are so pure in heart. That this is the work of the clericals, a clerical move into Russia—of this there can be no doubt. People will ask what the purpose of this move was. But don't the clericals need to put out some feelers, to sow confusion, to conceal their real intentions, to acquire some Russian pens, to arouse Russian Poland, and so on, and so on? There's many another such notion they could have had!

November

CHAPTER THREE

Article 1, extract. Rumors of Peace. "Constantinople Must Be Ours"—Is That Possible? Various Opinions.

And suddenly everyone's begun talking about the end of the war, not only in Europe but here as well. Everyone's started to argue over possible peace terms. It's pleasing to see that even the majority of our political newspapers now have a more or less proper appreciation of Russia's sacrifices of labor, blood, and effort and are suggesting peace terms that are as appropriate as possible to the scale of these efforts. It is particularly comforting to see the majority of those considering the question also beginning to acknowledge Russia's independence in the face of the certain, imminent European intervention once peace is concluded, and her right to conclude a separate, individual peace without calling in Europe and even without paying much attention to her, if this is possible. The lot of the Slavs is also being taken into account. There is talk of reparation and heated demands for the iron-clad Turkish monitors. Many have expressed their full support for our right to annex Kars and Erzerum.

There are people, however, who are still offended by the suggestion that we might make so bold as to annex something like Kars. On the other hand, there are those who talk even of Constantinople—never mind Kars—and who say that Constantinople must be ours. Such talk and discussions of peace and the terms of peace will come up continually, after every one of our major military actions. I'd like only to observe that among all (or almost all) these current opinions of our press there seems to lurk something that is not exactly a blunder but an oversight. It is that everyone considers Europe as . . . as Europe; that's to say, as the same Europe that has existed, with certain variations, throughout the century: there is an acceptance of almost the same great powers, the same political balance, and so on. Meanwhile, Europe hour by hour is now becoming something different from what she was even six months ago; and this has even reached the point where one can't now guarantee anything three months in advance—such is the degree to which her former aspect may change even by next spring. Colossal and fateful facts of the present time, which will likely need to be formulated and settled very soon, are still not being considered in the true dimensions in which the world must regard them. It is difficult to envisage correctly even the kind of Europe there will be to intervene, perhaps, in our affairs at the conclusion of peace. Therefore, to talk of peace terms on the basis of only the former facts— without fully appreciating that all these former facts have now shifted of themselves, are moving, slipping away, and awaiting new definition— seems to me also to be a mistake. [. . .]

Article 2, two extracts. Once More, for the Last Time, Some "Soothsayings"

You keep saying that "the majority of European powers" will not permit it. But what is meant by "the majority of European powers" nowadays? Can that even be defined at the present moment? I repeat what I said earlier: hour by hour Europe is becoming different from what she was in earlier times, different, perhaps, from what she was only six months ago, so that at present one cannot guarantee that she will remain as she is even three months in the future. The fact is, we are certainly on the eve of the greatest and most stupendous changes and revolutions in Europe herself, and I say that *without the least exaggeration*. At the given moment, now, in November, this "majority of European powers" that could issue us an intimidating *veto* on anything once peace is concluded, amounts merely to England and, perhaps, Austria, although England will draw her into an alliance whatever the cost and even has hopes for an alliance with France. But we shall not be alone (that is already obvious). In Europe there is Germany, and she is on our side.

Indeed, Europe is awaiting enormous upheavals, of a sort that the human mind refuses to believe them, thinking that such things must be utterly preposterous. Meanwhile, many things that even this summer were regarded as preposterous, impossible, and exaggerated came to pass quite literally in Europe as the year was ending; and the view of the power of the worldwide Catholic conspiracy, for instance—a view that in the summer *everyone* was inclined to ridicule, or at least ignore—is now shared by *everyone* and has been borne out by facts. I bring this up only so that the readers may have some faith in my current "soothsaying" and not regard it as a preposterous and exaggerated picture, as many no doubt regarded my summer predictions of last May, June, July, and August—things which came to pass with literal exactitude. [...]

And so it's most likely that Prince Bismarck has already predetermined the fate of France. The fate of Poland awaits France, and she will not live politically; either that, or Germany will cease to exist. Having achieved this, Bismarck will then force militant Roman Catholicism (whose militancy will continue to the end of the world) to enter a new phase of existence and struggle for existence—a phase of underground, reptilian, and conspiratorial war. And he is awaiting this new phase of Catholicism. The sooner it arrives, the better, since for him it means the alliance of both enemies of Germany and of humanity; thus he is hoping to crush them both more easily, at once....

Article 3. The Moment Must Be Seized

The alliance of both enemies will certainly take place just as soon as France collapses politically. Both these enemies have always had an organic connection with France. Catholicism, until almost recently, was her unifying and fundamental idea. Socialism was also engendered within it. Having deprived France of a political life, Prince Bismarck plans to deal a blow to socialism as well. Socialism as the legacy of Catholicism and France are the things most hateful to a true German, and one can excuse Germany's leaders for thinking they can deal with socialism so easily, by the mere political destruction of France, its source and its cradle. But this is what will happen, in all likelihood, should France collapse politically: Catholicism will lose its sword and will turn for the first time to the people, whom it has scorned for so many centuries while paying court to the kings and emperors of the world. But now it will turn to the people, for it has nowhere else to go; it will turn specifically to the leaders of the most volatile and restive element among the people—the socialists. It will tell the people that everything the socialists are preaching to them has also been preached by Christ. It will distort Christ and sell Him to them once more, as it sold Him so many times before for the sake of earthly dominion, upholding the rights of the Inquisition, torturing people for freedom of conscience in the name of a loving Christ—a Christ who

valued only those disciples who came freely to him, not those who had
been bribed or frightened. It has sold Christ, giving its blessing to the
Jesuits and justifying "any means for the cause of Christ." From time
immemorial it has transformed the cause of Christ into mere concern for
its earthly possessions and its future political domination of the whole
world. When the Catholic peoples turned away from the monstrous
image in which Christ was finally presented to them, after several centuries of protests, reformations, and so on, there at last appeared, at the
beginning of the present century, some attempts to arrange life without
God and without Christ. Lacking the instincts of the bee or the ant,
which flawlessly and accurately construct their hives and anthills, people
sought to construct something in the nature of a flawless human anthill.
They rejected the single formula for their salvation that came from God
and was proclaimed through revelation to humanity, "Thou shalt love thy
neighbor as thyself," and replaced it with practical conclusions such as,
"*Chacun pour soi et Dieu pour tous*" (Every man for himself and God for
all), or scientific slogans such as "the struggle for survival." Lacking the
instincts by which animals live and flawlessly arrange their lives, people
proudly placed their hopes in science, having forgotten that, in regard
to matters such as constructing a society, science is still in its swaddling
clothes. Wonderful visions appeared. The future tower of Babel became
the ideal and, at the same time, the dread of all humanity. But in the wake
of the visionaries there soon came other doctrines, simple and comprehensible to all, such as: "Rob the rich, pour blood over the earth, and
then *somehow everything will come to right by itself.*" Finally, things went
even beyond what these teachers were saying: the doctrine of anarchy
appeared, after which, should it be realized, would certainly ensue a new
period of cannibalism, and people would be compelled to begin everything from the beginning, as they did some ten thousand years ago.

Catholicism realizes all this very well and will manage to seduce the
leaders of an underground war. It will tell them: "You have no center, no
orderly way of managing your work; you are a force that is fragmented
all over the world; and now, with the collapse of France, you are also
oppressed. I shall provide your unity and shall also bring you all who
still believe in me." One way or another, the alliance will come into being.
Catholicism does not want to die; a social revolution and a new, social
period in Europe is also certain: two forces, doubtlessly, must come to

an accord, two currents must merge. Naturally, Catholicism will find slaughter, blood, pillage, and perhaps even cannibalism to be advantageous. It is just in such circumstances—in troubled waters—that it can hope to hook its fish once more, sensing the moment when at last a humanity worn out by chaos and lawlessness will rush into its embrace; and it will once more find itself, now totally, exclusively, and in reality, "sovereign of the earth and authority in this world," sharing its power with none; and thus will it achieve its ultimate goal. This picture, alas, is no fantasy. I avow positively that many, many people in the West can already foresee this. And no doubt the lords of Germany also foresee it. But the leaders of the German people are wrong in one thing: the ease with which these two fearsome and already united enemies can be conquered and crushed. They rely on the might of a renewed Germany, on her Protestant spirit protesting against the ancient and the new Rome, its principles and its *consequences*. But they will not stop the monster: it will be stopped and vanquished by a reunited East and the new Word it will utter to humanity. . . .

In any case, one thing seems clear: Germany *needs* us even more than we think. And she needs us not for a temporary political alliance, *but forever*. The idea of a reunited Germany is a broad, majestic one with roots in ages gone by. What can Germany share with us? Her object is the whole of Western humanity. She has assigned herself the Western world of Europe, to instill there her principles in place of the Roman and Romanic ones and eventually to become its leader, leaving the East to Russia. Two great peoples, thus, have been destined to change the face of this world. These are not some fanciful inventions of the mind or of ambition: this is the way the world is composing itself. There are new and strange facts and they are appearing every day. While we in Russia, scarcely more than a few days ago, were considering it preposterous to speak and dream of Constantinople, many people in the German newspapers spoke of our occupation of Constantinople as of a most ordinary thing. This is almost strange when compared with Germany's former attitudes toward us. One has to think that the friendship of Russia and Germany is not hypocritical but solid and will become more solid as time passes, that it will spread and gradually take root in the consciousness of the peoples of both nations; and so, perhaps, there was never a moment more favorable than now for Russia for the ultimate solution of the Eastern Question. People in Germany, perhaps, await the end of our war even more impatiently than we do. Meanwhile, now one really cannot guarantee what will transpire even three months hence. Shall we end this war before the final and fateful cataclysms begin in Europe? This we do not know. But whether or not we manage it in time to help Germany, Germany still is relying on us not as *temporary* allies but as *eternal* ones. As far as the present moment is concerned, once again the whole key to the thing is in France and in the election of the pope. Here we can expect a collision between France and Germany; this is already assured, the more so that there are people trying to provoke it. England will make special efforts in this regard, and then, perhaps, Austria will move as well. But we spoke about all these things not long ago. Nothing has changed since then to alter our former opinions; on the contrary, they have been strengthened. . . .

In any case, Russia must seize the moment. But will this favorable European moment of ours last for long? So long as Germany's current great leaders are acting, this moment is *most surely* guaranteed for us. . . .

December

from CHAPTER ONE

Article 1, extract. The Concluding Explanation of an Old Fact

As I conclude the two-year publication of my *Diary* with this final, December issue, I find it necessary once more to say a few words about a matter I have spoken about at very great length already. I had decided to say something about it as long ago as May, but for particular reasons I had to postpone it until this final issue. Once more, it concerns that stepmother Kornilova who, in a fit of anger at her husband, threw her six-year-old stepdaughter out of a window; the girl, who fell from a height of nearly forty feet, survived. As we know, the perpetrator was tried and found guilty; then the sentence was appealed; and finally she was acquitted at a second trial on April 22 of this year. (See *A Writer's Diary*, October 1876 and April 1877.)

I happened to play a certain role in this case. The president of the court, and subsequently the prosecutor as well, declared publicly in the court room that the initial guilty verdict on Kornilova was quashed precisely as a result of the idea set forth in the *Diary* that "the pregnant condition of the perpetrator may have had an influence on her act." I set forth and developed this idea as a result of the extraordinary and strange psychic peculiarities that were so compellingly obvious and that arrested one's attention on reading the details of the crime. My readers know all this already, however. They may also know that after a most rigorous investigation and the most stubborn and insistent arguments by the prosecutor, the jury still deliberated for no more than ten minutes before acquitting Kornilova, and the spectators left the court with wholehearted approval of the acquittal. Yet even so, at the time and on that same day, it occurred to me that in a case as important as this, involving the very highest questions of civic and spiritual life, it is useful for everything to be explained as thoroughly as possible so that no doubts, hesitations, or regrets remain, either in society or in the hearts of the jurors who acquitted Kornilova, that a woman who had undoubtedly committed a crime had been let off unpunished. Children are involved here, the fate of a child (often a terrible thing, especially among the poor) is involved, as is the whole question of children—and now one who would have murdered a child is acquitted, and with the approval of the public! And here I myself was partly responsible for it (according to the statement of the court itself)! I was acting out of conviction, yet after the verdict was brought in I suddenly began to be tormented by doubt: had the public not been left dissatisfied, puzzled, mistrustful of the court, even angry? Our press said little about Kornilova's acquittal—people had other things to think about at the time; they sensed the coming of war. But in *The Northern Messenger,* a newly opened newspaper at that time, I did read an article full of indignation over the acquittal and even of anger at me for my part in the case. This article was written in an unworthy tone; and indeed, I was not the only one to suffer the indignation of *The Northern Messenger:* Leo Tolstoy also suffered it for *Anna Karenina* and was subjected to malicious and unworthy mockery. I would not have responded personally to the author, but in this article I saw the very thing I had dreaded seeing in a certain part of our society, i.e., a confused impression, puzzlement, indignation at the verdict. And so I decided to wait a whole eight months so as to convince myself in that time, as best and as thoroughly as possible, that the verdict had had no ill effect on the accused; that, rather, the mercy of the court had fallen like a good seed on fertile soil; that the accused *truly had been worthy* of compassion and mercy; that the fits of incomprehensible and almost fantastic fury, in one of which she had committed her evil deed, had not returned and *could not* ever return to her again; that she really was a kind and meek soul and not a ravager and murderess (of which I was convinced all through the trial); and that the crime of this unfortunate woman truly had to be explained by some special, accidental circumstance, pathological condition, or "affect"—by just those pathological fits which occur rather often among pregnant women (given a whole range of other adverse conditions and circumstances, of course) during a particular period of their pregnancy; and that, at last, it followed that neither the jurors, nor society, nor the people present in the court who greeted the verdict with wholehearted approval had any more reason to doubt the appropriateness of the verdict and regret their mercy.

And so now, after these eight months, I am able to report something and say more about this case of which, perhaps, everyone may have already grown weary. I shall address my reply to society, as it were—I mean, to that portion of society which, I suppose, may not agree with the verdict rendered, has doubts about it, and is indignant over it—at least if there has been such a portion of the dissatisfied within our society. And since, of all these dissatisfied people, I know (not personally, however) only the one "Observer" who wrote the intimidating article in *The Northern Messenger,* I shall direct my answer to this Observer. It's most likely that my conclusions will in no way change his mind, but perhaps my readers will understand me. [...]

Article 3, extract. Distortions and Manipulation of the Evidence—These Cost Us Nothing

[...] It is not for you but for my readers that I shall attempt to delineate both these characters, the quarreling husband and wife, as I understood them even before the verdict and as they revealed themselves to me even more, under my most careful observation, after the verdict. In discussing these two people I am committing no great indiscretion; a good deal more was said about them in court. In any case, I am doing this specifically to vindicate them. And so the point is this. The husband, first and foremost, is a steady, frank, utterly honest and kind man (there is even some nobility about him, as he later showed); but he is rather too puritanical, too naive, and given strictly to following a view and conviction he has accepted once and for all. There is also a certain difference in age between him and his wife, he being a good deal older than she and a widower besides. He works all day, and though he wears European ("German") clothes and looks as if he were an "educated" person, he has never had any particular education. I might also note that his overall appearance conveys his real sense of his own dignity. I can add that he is not very talkative, not very cheerful or humorous; his disposition is perhaps rather gloomy. He married Kornilova while she was still very young. She was an honest girl, a seamstress by trade, who earns a decent wage through her work.

I don't know how they met. She married him by choice, "out of love." But disagreements quickly began, and though they did not go to extremes for a long time, misunderstanding, estrangement, and, at last, even malice grew on both sides—slowly, yet steadily and surely. The fact is—and it may be the whole reason—that both, despite their growing malice, loved one another even too passionately and continued to do so to the very end. It was love that hardened the demands on both sides, strengthened them, further aggravated them. And at this point her character came into play. Hers is a character rather reserved and somewhat proud. Among both men and women there are such characters who, though they may cherish even the most ardent feelings in their hearts, are always somehow ashamed to display them; they show little affection, have few affectionate words, few embraces, and little open display of emotion. If they are called heartless and unfeeling because of this, then they become even more aloof. If accused of something, they rarely try to explain the matter themselves; rather, they leave this task to the accuser: "Figure it out yourself; if you love me, you ought to know that I'm right." And if he does not understand and grows more and more aggravated, her response is to become more and more aggravated as well. And so, from the very beginning this husband began severely (although by no means cruelly) reproaching her, admonishing her, teaching her, holding up the example of his first wife, something she found particularly painful. Things did not go that badly, however; yet it happened that when he reproached and accused her, she would begin quarreling and making spiteful remarks instead of seeking to clear things up and end the misunderstanding by offering some final explanation or indication of its cause. At last, even this was abandoned. It ended with morose disillusionment, not love, filling her heart (it happened first to her, not her husband). And all these things developed rather unconsciously: this is the life of working people, a hard life in which there's not a lot of time to think about feelings. He leaves for work, she is busy with the housework, the cooking, and even washing the floors. On each side of the long corridor in the government building where they live are tiny rooms, one for each married worker employed by that government establishment. It happened that she had gone, with her husband's permission, to a name-day party at the family of the tradesman with whom she had learned to sew in her childhood and youth and with whom she and her husband had kept up an acquaintance. The husband, busy with his work, stayed at home this time. The party turned out to be a very happy one; there were many guests, refreshments, and people started dancing. The celebration went on until morning. The young woman was accustomed to a rather dull life at home with her husband, living in one cramped room and always toiling; evidently, she recalled the years of her youth and went on enjoying herself "at the ball" so long that she forgot

the curfew her husband had imposed on her. At last, she was persuaded
to spend the night at her hosts', since she was a long way from home. It
was at this point that the husband, who for the first time had spent a night
apart from his wife, grew angry. He grew very angry: the next day, not
going to work, he set off to fetch her; he found her and, right there in the
presence of the guests, he *punished* her. They returned home in silence
and for two days and nights thereafter did not speak to one another and
did not eat together. I learned all this in bits and pieces; despite my questions, she herself revealed little to me about her state of mind at that time.
"I can't recall what I was thinking about then, over those two days, but
I just kept on thinking. *I didn't even look at her* (meaning the little girl)
at all. I remember everything about how it happened, but just how I did
it I can't explain." And so, on the morning of the third day, the husband
left for work early and the girl was still asleep. The stepmother is busy at
the stove. Finally, the girl wakes up; the stepmother mechanically washes
and dresses her as usual, puts on her shoes and seats her at the table to
have breakfast . . . "and I wasn't thinking about her at all." The child sits
there, sipping from her cup and eating—"and all of a sudden I looked at
her. . . ."

Article 5. One Incident That Explains a Good Deal, in My View

Now let me tell you about one incident that, in my view, can provide a
final explanation for certain things in this case and that can directly serve
the purpose for which I undertook this article. On the morning of the
third day after the acquittal of the defendant Kornilova (April 22, 1877),
the husband and the wife came to see me. The previous day they had
been at the children's home where the victim, the little girl who had been
thrown out of the window, had been placed; now, the next day, they were
going there once more. Incidentally, the fate of the child has now been
assured and there is no need to exclaim, "Woe to the child, now! . . ." and
so on. When his wife was taken to prison, the father himself placed the
child in this children's home because he had no possibility of looking after
her himself, being away at work from morning till night. And after his wife
returned they decided to leave her at the home because she was being so
well looked after there. But on holidays they often take her home with

them. She had spent Christmas with them. Despite her own work, which lasts from morning till night, and despite another nursing infant (the one born in prison) on her hands, the stepmother even now sometimes finds time to tear herself away and run off to see the little girl at the children's home, to bring her some little treat, and so on. When she was still in prison, recalling the sin she had committed against the child, she often dreamed of finding some way to see her and of doing something to make the little girl forget what had happened. These fantasies seemed strange somehow, coming from a woman as reserved and as wary as Kornilova was during her trial. But her fantasies were destined to become real. About a month ago, just before Christmas, not having seen the Kornilovs for some six months, I dropped in at their apartment; Kornilova's first words to me were that the little girl "comes running joyously to her and hugs her each time she visits her in the children's home." And as I was leaving Kornilova suddenly told me, "She'll forget. . . ."

And so they came to see me that morning, the third day after her acquittal. . . . But I keep getting off the topic and will do so once more, just for a minute. In his article "The Observer" makes some malicious jokes about these visits of mine to Kornilova when she was in prison. "He truly has captured that state of mind" (meaning the state of mind of a pregnant woman), he says about me; "he has visited the lady in question in prison, been struck by her humility, and over several issues of his *Diary* has come out as her ardent defender." In the first place, what is the point of the word *lady* here? What is the point of this nasty tone? "The Observer" knows very well that she is not a lady but a simple peasant woman, one who toils from morning till night; she cooks, scrubs floors, and sells her sewing, if she can find time to do any. I visited her in prison precisely once a month, spent no more than ten or at most fifteen minutes with her each time, for the most part in a cell she shared with other women awaiting trial and who had nursing infants. If I did examine this woman with curiosity and tried to comprehend her character, then what was the harm in that? Did it deserve mockery and humor? But let's return to my story.

And so they came to visit me; they sat there, both in a thoughtful, serious mood. Until then I had known the husband only slightly. And suddenly he said to me, "The other day, when we came back home"— (this was after her acquittal and so was after eleven o'clock, and he gets up at five)—"we sat right down at the table, and I took out the Gospel and began reading to her." I confess, when he told me this it suddenly occurred to me as I looked at him: "Yes, he couldn't have done anything else; he's a type, a thoroughly consistent type; I could have guessed it." In short, he's a puritan, a most honest and serious fellow, kind and noble, to be sure, but one who will never make any compromises and never surrender any of his convictions. This husband, with total faith, regards marriage as a sacrament. He is one of those husbands we still can find in Holy Russia, who, following old Russian tradition and custom, on returning from the wedding and retiring to the bedroom with his new bride, would first cast himself down on his knees before the icon and pray for a long time, asking God's blessing on his future. In this case he acted in a similar fashion: bringing his wife into his house once more and renewing the marriage that had been sundered by her terrible crime, he first opened the Gospel and began to read it to her, his manly and serious resolve not restrained in the least even by the consideration that this woman was almost ready to collapse from exhaustion, that she had been under terrible strain even while preparing for the trial, while on this last crucial day of her judgment she had endured so many overwhelming impressions, both moral and physical, that it would naturally now be no sin even for such a strict puritan as he to let her have just a moment to rest and collect herself first, something that would have been even more in keeping with the aim he had when he opened the Gospel in front of her. And so this act of his struck me as almost clumsy—too single-minded, meaning that this very thing might cause him to fail to achieve his aim. A very guilty soul—and particularly one such as hers, all too aware of its own guilt and already having endured much torment because of it, should not be too plainly and *hastily* reproached for its guilt, for the result may be just the opposite, particularly when the soul is already repentant. Here is the man on whom she depends, raising himself above her, wearing the halo of a judge; she sees something merciless in him; he autocratically intrudes into her soul and sternly casts aside her repentance and the good feelings that have been born within her: "One such as you needs no rest, or food, or drink; just sit and listen to how you must live." As they were leaving, I managed to remark in passing that he should undertake *this business* again with somewhat less severity or, to put it better, that he should not be in such a hurry, not forge ahead so directly, and that such an approach might prove better. I spoke briefly and clearly, yet I thought that he still might not understand. And suddenly he said in reply, "But right then, as soon as we came into the house and started to read, she told me everything—how on your last visit you taught her the right way to behave if they exiled her to Siberia, and gave her some advice about getting on there. . . ."

And this is what had happened: I had, in fact, gone to visit her in prison on the very eve of the trial. No one, neither I nor her lawyer, had any firm hopes for an acquittal. Nor did she. I found her looking rather resolute; she was sitting sewing something; her baby was fretful. It wasn't that she was downcast, yet she seemed somehow oppressed. Several gloomy thoughts about her kept running through my mind, and I had dropped in specifically to give her some friendly advice. We had firm hopes that she would be exiled only to a settlement, and so a woman barely the age of maturity would set off to Siberia with a baby in her arms. The marriage would be annulled; I was thinking that out there, alone, defenseless, pretty as well, and so young—how could she resist the temptations she would face? Fate was truly pushing her into debauchery, for I know Siberia: there are a good many people there eager to corrupt a young woman; very many unmarried men—some in service, some after easy money—go there from Russia. It is easy to fall, but the Siberians—both the simple peasants and the townsfolk—are utterly merciless toward a fallen woman. No one would think to stand in her way, but once a woman has tarnished her reputation she can never restore it: she will face endless scorn, words of criticism and reproach, mockery; and so it will remain until her old age, to her very grave. They will give her a special nickname. And her child (a girl) will at once be *compelled* to follow her mother's career: coming from a bad home, she will not find a good and honest husband. But it's another thing if the exiled mother conducts herself honorably and strictly in Siberia: a young woman who leads a chaste life enjoys enormous respect. Everyone defends her, everyone wants to do her favors, everyone takes his hat off to her. She will certainly be able to set her daughter on the right path in life. With time, once people have managed to come to know her and trust her, even she herself may enter into an honorable marriage and an honorable family. (In Siberia, neither in the prisons nor in any place of exile, no one asks about one's past, meaning the reason for one's exile, nor do they show any curiosity about it. That may be because virtually everyone in Siberia, over the course of these three centuries, is descended from exiles, and the country has been populated by them.) And so this was what I had in mind to tell this young woman, barely the age of maturity. I even deliberately chose to tell her this precisely on this last day before her trial: it would remain more graphic in her mind and be stamped more surely on her soul, I thought. After listening to me tell her how to get on in Siberia should she be exiled, she thanked me, gloomily and seriously, scarcely raising her eyes. And so, tired, worn-out, shaken by this whole terrible impression of the many hours of her trial, and then at home, where her husband sternly made her sit and listen to the Gospel, she did not think to herself, "He could at least have had some pity on me; he could at least have put it off until tomorrow, and given me something to eat and let me rest now." Neither was she offended by the fact that *he so elevated himself above her.* (N.B.: The most dreadful criminal, fully aware of his own crime, and even the most repentant one, can still feel offended that others *elevate themselves above him.*) But on the contrary: she could find nothing better to say to her husband than *promptly* to tell him that in prison people had also taught her the right way to behave, that they had taught her something about living in an alien land, honorably and chastely. And clearly she did this because she knew the story would please her husband, would fit in with his tone and cheer him: "So, she is truly repenting, she does truly want to live rightly," he would think. And that is just what he did think; and as to my advice not to frighten her by too much hasty severity, he told me plainly and, of course, with joy in his heart, "There's no need to fear for her and be suspicious; she herself is glad to be honest. . . ."

I'm not sure, but it seems to me that all this is clear. The readers will understand why I am revealing all this. At least one may now hope that the court's great mercy did not spoil the guilty woman even more; rather, it is very possible that this mercy fell on good soil. After all, even before, and while she was in prison, and even now she considered and considers herself clearly guilty and attributes her acquittal only to the great mercy of the court. She herself does not understand this "affect of pregnancy." And, truly, she certainly is guilty; she was fully aware while committing the crime, she remembers every moment and every detail of it; the only thing she does not know and even now cannot explain to herself is: "*How could she have done such a thing then; how could she have brought herself to it?*" Yes, Mr. Observer, the court has pardoned an actual criminal, despite the now indubitable and fateful "affect of pregnancy" which you so ridicule, sir, and of which I am now deeply and surely convinced. Now then, decide for yourself: had the marriage been dissolved; had she been torn away from a man whom she certainly loved and still loves, and who represents her entire family; had she, alone, twenty years old, with a baby in her arms, been exiled, helpless, to Siberia to shame and corruption (she would certainly have fallen in Siberia)—tell me, what sense would there be in her ruination, in reducing her life to ashes, a life which now, it seems, has been regenerated, returned to the truth through a severe process of purging and repentance, and with a heart that has been renewed? Is it not better to reform, to find, and to restore a human being than simply to cut off his head? Cutting off heads is easy if one follows the letter of the law, but it is always much more difficult to settle a matter in accordance with the truth, in a humane and paternal fashion. Finally, you surely knew that along with this young, twenty-year-old mother—an inexperienced woman who certainly would become a victim of want and debauchery—her infant child was also being exiled. . . . But permit me to say a few words to you about infant children in particular.

Article 6, two extracts. Am I an Enemy of Children? On What the Word "Happy" Sometimes Means.

Your entire article, Mr. Observer, is a protest "against condoning the abuse of children." The fact that you stand up for children does you credit, of course, but you behave much too haughtily toward me. You say about me:

> One must have all the power of imagination in which, as we know, Mr. Dostoevsky so excels in order to capture fully the state of mind of the woman and reach an awareness of all the compelling affects of pregnancy. . . . But Mr. Dostoevsky is too impressionable, and besides "the pathological manifestations of the will" are right in his line as author of *The Devils, The Idiot,* etc., so he may be excused for having a weakness for such things. I take a simpler view of the matter and maintain that after such instances exonerating the physical abuse of children—and they happen not infrequently in Russia, as they do in England—we are left without even a shadow of a deterrent to such crimes.

And so on, and so on. In the first place, as far as my "weakness for the pathological manifestations of the will" is concerned, I will say merely that it seems I actually did sometimes manage, in my novels and tales, to *reveal* certain people who considered themselves healthy and to prove to them that they were ill. Do you know that there are very many people whose illness is precisely their good health; that's to say, their excessive confidence in their own normalcy infects them with a terrible conceit, a shameless narcissism that sometimes reaches the point of a virtual conviction of their own infallibility? [...]

And so I am condoning physical abuse of children—a terrible accusation! In that case, then, permit me to defend myself. I shall not point to my past thirty years of literary work to settle the question of whether I am a great enemy of children and a proponent of abusing them; but I will merely recall the two last years of my writing, i.e., the publication of *A Writer's Diary*. When Kroneberg's trial was going on, despite my penchant for "the pathological manifestations of the will," I happened to stand up for the child, the victim, and not for the torturer. And so, even I *sometimes* take the side of common sense, Mr. Observer. Now I even regret that you did not then also step forward to defend the child, Mr. Observer; surely you would have written a most passionate article. But somehow I can't seem to recall even a single passionate article on behalf of the child. And so it never occurred to you, then, to stand up for the child. Subsequently, and not long ago—last summer—I happened to stand up for the young children of the Dzhunkovskys, who had also been tortured in their parents' home. You did not write anything about the Dzhunkovskys either; however, no one wrote about them, and that's understandable: everyone was busy with such important political questions. Finally, I could point out not merely one but several instances when I, over these two years, have spoken up about children in my *Diary*—about their education, about their wretched fate in our families, about young delinquents in our correctional institutions; I even mentioned one little boy at Christ's Christmas party—not an actual occurrence, of course, but still, one that provides no direct evidence of indifference and heartlessness toward children. Let me tell you this, Mr. Observer: when I first read in the newspaper about Kornilova's crime, about the irrevocable verdict on her, and when I was involuntarily struck by the idea that, perhaps, this guilty woman was not nearly as guilty as it seemed (please note, Mr. Observer, that even then almost nothing was said about "the *stepmother's* beatings" in the newspaper accounts of the trial and that even then this charge was not pressed)—then I, having decided to write something on Kornilova's behalf, realized full well what I was taking on. I now frankly admit that to you. I knew very well that I was writing an article that would find little sympathy, that I was standing up for one who had inflicted suffering and on whom?—on a little child. I foresaw that *some people* would accuse me of being heartless, self-important, even diseased: "He's standing up for a stepmother who tried to murder her child!" I could clearly foresee such a "straight-and-narrow" accusation from certain arbiters—from you, for instance, Mr. Observer; and so I even hesitated for some time, but ended by deciding to do it just the same: "If I believe that I have a truth here, then is it worth serving a lie in order to court popularity?" That was what I came to in the final analysis. Besides, I was also encouraged by faith in my readers: "They will understand, at last, that I can't be accused of wishing to condone the abuse of children, and if I stand up for a murderess, setting forth my suspicion of her pathological and deranged state of mind while she was committing the crime, thereby I'm surely not supporting the crime itself and am not pleased at the fact that a child was beaten and nearly killed; on the contrary, I perhaps have the utmost compassion for the child, and no less than anyone else...."

You ridiculed me maliciously, Mr. Observer, for one sentence in my article about the acquittal of the defendant Kornilova. You say: " 'The husband of the acquitted woman,' writes Mr. Dostoevsky in his *Diary* that came out just recently, 'took her home that same evening sometime after ten o'clock and she came back to her own home again, happy.' How touching. But woe to the poor child," etc., etc.

I think I could not have written such stupid things. It's true that you quote my sentence accurately, but this is what you did: you have cut it in half and inserted a period where there was none. This gave it the particular sense that you wanted it to have. In my article there is no period there; the sentence continues to its second half; I think that, taken together with this other half which you threw out, the sentence is by no means as inane and "touching" as it seems. Here is my sentence, but the entire sentence with nothing left out: "The husband of the acquitted woman took her home that same evening sometime after ten o'clock and she came back into her own home again, happy, after a year's absence, *with the impression of an enormous lesson learned for the rest of her life and a clear sense of the hand*

of God at work in this case—even if only beginning with the miraculous
survival of the child. . . ."

You see, Mr. Observer, I am even prepared to qualify my remarks here
and apologize for reproaching you just now for cutting my sentence in
half. In fact, I can now see that this sentence may certainly not have come
out as clearly as I had hoped and that one might interpret it incorrectly.
It needs a little clarification, and that I shall now make. The whole point
here is in my understanding of the word "happy." I saw the happiness
of the acquitted woman not only in the fact that she had been freed, but
in the fact that "she came back into her own home with the impression
of an enormous lesson learned *for the rest of her life* and a clear sense of
the hand of God stretched over her." There is no greater happiness, after
all, than to be assured of people's mercy and love for one another. This
is faith, a whole faith, for an entire life! And what happiness is superior
to faith? Can this former transgressor now ever doubt people at all? Can
she doubt people or humanity as a whole, in their lofty, sensible, and
sacred substance? For one who was about to perish and be ruined, to
enter her own home bearing such a powerful impression of a great new
faith is the greatest happiness there could be. We know that some very
noble and superior minds have often suffered their whole lives from lack
of faith in the soundness of the lofty purpose of humanity, in its goodness
and ideals, in its godly origin; and they have died in bleak disillusionment. Of course, you will smile at what I am saying and tell me, perhaps,
that here too I am letting my imagination run wild; that the ignorant and
coarse Kornilova, who has emerged from the common rabble and has no
education, can experience neither any such disillusionment nor any such
tender feelings. Ah, but that's untrue! These "dark people" simply don't
know the names we would give to all these things and how to explain
them in our language; but they do feel, completely and utterly, just as
deeply as we "educated people" do; and they experience their feelings
with just the same happiness or just the same sorrow and pain as we do.

They become disillusioned with people and lose faith in them just
the same way as we do. Had Kornilova been exiled to Siberia and had
she fallen and perished there, do you really think she would not have felt,
at some bitter moment in her life, the full horror of her fall? And would
she not have carried in her heart, perhaps to her very grave, a malice that
was all the more bitter because it would have been aimless? For apart

from herself she would have no one to blame because, I repeat, she is completely convinced even now that she is *truly guilty* and merely does not know how it all happened to her at the time. But now, feeling that she is guilty and considering herself such, and suddenly having been forgiven by people, showered with mercy and blessings, how could she not feel restored and reborn into a new life, higher than her old one? It was not just one person who forgave her; *everyone*—the court, the jurors, and therefore society as a whole—showed mercy to her. After that, how could she not take with her a sense of the enormous debt that would last all her life—a debt to all who had shown mercy to her, meaning all people on the earth. Every *great* happiness bears a certain suffering within it, for it arouses in us a higher consciousness. Such a clarity of consciousness within is aroused more rarely by grief than by great happiness. Great— meaning sublime—happiness places an *obligation* on the soul. (I'll repeat: there is no greater happiness than to come to believe in the goodness of people and their love for one another.) When the woman taken in adultery and condemned to stoning was told, "Go, thou, and sin no more," do you really think that she returned home to commit more sins?

And so the whole question in the Kornilova case amounts merely to the kind of soil in which the seed fell. And that is why it seemed necessary for me to write this article now. After reading your attack on me seven months ago, Mr. Observer, I specifically decided to delay my reply to you so as to expand my knowledge of the case. And so, I think, on the basis of some of the particulars I have gathered, I would not err now in stating that the seed has fallen on good soil; that a person has been restored to life; that this has caused no wrong to anyone; that the soul of the guilty woman has been crushed both by repentance and by an eternal, beneficent impression of the boundless mercy of people; and that now, after experiencing such goodness and love, it would be difficult for her heart to go wrong again. She certainly does not think herself justified because of the incontestable "affect of pregnancy" that so troubles you, Mr. Observer. In short, it seemed to me not at all futile to pass on this information, not only to you, Mr. Observer, but to all my readers as well, and to all those merciful people who acquitted her. And as far as the little girl is concerned, Mr. Observer, you needn't worry about her or exclaim, "Woe to the child!" Her fate now has also been rather well settled, and "she will forget"—there is real hope of that.

from CHAPTER TWO

Article 5. To the Readers

The December and final issue of the *Diary* appears after such a delay for two reasons: because of my very poor health throughout the whole month of December and as a result of the unforeseen move to a different printer after the former one closed down his business. There were inevitable delays in this new, unfamiliar place. In any case, I assume the responsibility and beg the indulgence of my readers.

To the many questions of my subscribers and readers as to whether I might publish issues of the *Diary* from time to time in the next year, 1878, without restricting myself to monthly publication, I hasten to reply that I find this impossible for many reasons. Perhaps I shall venture to put out one issue and speak with my readers once more. I have been putting out my little periodical for myself as much as for others, after all, from a compelling need to express myself in our curious and most peculiar age. If I do put out one more issue, I shall make an announcement in the newspapers. I do not think I shall be writing for other publications. I might publish only a tale or a novel in some other publication. In this year of rest from the *deadlines* of publication I truly intend to devote all my time to a literary work that has imperceptibly and involuntarily been taking shape within me over these two years of publishing the *Diary*. But I have firm hopes of renewing the *Diary* a year from now. With my whole heart I thank all those who have so warmly declared their support. To those who wrote to tell me that I am abandoning my publication at a most exciting time, I would reply that a year from now there may ensue a time that may be even more exciting and more distinctive, and then we shall serve the good cause together once more.

I write *together,* because I plainly regard my many correspondents as my coworkers. Their letters, remarks, advice, and the sincerity with which they all treated me have helped me a good deal. How I regret that I was unable to reply to so many of them, owing to lack of time and poor health. I ask the kind, good-hearted indulgence of all those to whom I have still not replied. I feel particularly guilty toward the many who wrote to me in the last three months. To the person who wrote of "the anguish of poor young boys and that she does not know what to tell them" (the one who wrote that will probably recognize herself from those words)—I now take the final opportunity to say that I was profoundly and whole-heartedly interested in her letter. Had it only been possible, I would have printed my answer to her letter in the *Diary;* I had to give up this idea only because I found it impossible to print her whole letter. And yet it testifies so graphically to the ardent, noble frame of mind among the larger part of our young people, to their so sincere wish to serve every good cause for the common weal. I shall say but one thing to this correspondent: perhaps it is just the Russian woman who will save us all, our whole society, through the new energy she has generated and through the most noble urge *to serve the cause,* even to the point of sacrifice and heroic deed. She will cast shame on the inactivity of others and draw them after her, while those who have strayed she will return to the true path. But enough: I am replying to my most worthy correspondent here in the *Diary,* as I suspect that the former address she gave me may no longer be valid.

I was unable to answer the questions of many correspondents because such important and vital issues as now absorb them cannot be answered in letters. To do this one must write articles or even whole books, but not letters. A letter cannot help but leave out some things and lead to a certain confusion. There are some issues that are certainly not matters for correspondence.

To the person who asked me to announce in the *Diary* that I had received her letter about her brother who was killed in the current war, I hasten to say that I was sincerely touched and moved both by her grief over her lost friend and brother and, at the same time, by her joy that her brother had served an admirable cause. I hasten, with pleasure, to tell this person that I have met here one young man who knew her late brother personally and who confirms everything she wrote me about him.

I give a hearty handshake to the correspondent who wrote me a long letter (five pages) about the Red Cross; I thank him sincerely and ask him to continue to write to me in the future. I shall certainly send him what he requested.

To those several correspondents who recently asked questions *point by point,* I shall certainly reply individually, just as I shall to the one who asked "Who is a striutsky?" (I trust that the correspondent will recognize himself from these words.) I apologize particularly to the correspondents from Minsk and Vitebsk for my tardiness in answering them. Once I have had a rest, I shall set about my replies and will answer everyone as best I can. And so please do not complain, and please wait.

My address will remain as before, but I ask that you indicate the house number and the street and not address your letters to the office of *A Writer's Diary*.

Once more, my thanks to you all. I hope we may look forward to a happy meeting in the near future. We now live in a glorious but difficult and critical time. How much now hangs by a thread at this very moment, and somehow we shall manage to speak about it all a year from now!

P.S. The publisher of a new book that has just appeared—*The Eastern Question in Its Past and Present. A Defense of Russia,* by Sir T. Sinclair, Baronet, member of the English Parliament, translated from the English—has asked me to insert an advertisement about it in this issue of the *Diary.* But having looked at the book and learned something about it, I wanted to recommend it personally to the readers instead of placing the usual advertisement. It would be difficult to write a more popular, more interesting, and more judicious book than this. We are so much in need of such a book now, and we have so few people competent in the history of the Eastern Question. And yet *everyone* now must be informed on this question. This is absolutely essential. Sinclair is a defender of Russian interests. He has long been known in Europe as a writer on political matters. This compact little volume of 350 pages costs only one ruble (one ruble, twenty kopecks with postage); it is sold in all the bookstores.

1880

August

[SINGLE ISSUE FOR 1880]

CHAPTER TWO

Pushkin (A Sketch)
Delivered on June 8 at a Meeting of the Society of Lovers of Russian Literature

"Pushkin is an extraordinary and, perhaps, unique manifestation of the Russian spirit," said Gogol. I would add that he is a prophetic one as well. Indeed, for all us Russians there is something unquestionably prophetic in his appearing. Pushkin arrived just as we were beginning to be truly conscious of ourselves, a self-consciousness that had barely begun and that developed in our society after the whole century that followed the reforms of Peter the Great, and his appearance did so much to cast a guiding light along the shadowy path we traveled. It is in this sense that Pushkin is prophetic and revelatory. I divide the work of our great poet into three periods. I am speaking now not as a literary critic: in discussing Pushkin's creative work I wish merely to explain my idea of his prophetic significance for us and what I mean by those words. I might note in passing, however, that I see no firm boundaries between these periods of Pushkin's work. For example, it seems to me that the beginning of *Onegin* is still a part of the first period of the poet's work, but *Onegin* ends in the second period, when Pushkin had already found his ideals in his native land, had fully taken them into his loving and perceptive soul, and had come to cherish them. The accepted view is also that during the first period of his work Pushkin imitated the European poets—Parny, André Chenier and others, particularly Byron. Yes, there is no doubt that the poets of Europe had a great influence on the development of his genius and that they continued to exert an influence on him for the rest of his life. Nevertheless, even Pushkin's first narrative poems were no mere imitations, so that even they express the extraordinary independence of his genius. Imitations never contain the kind of personal suffering and depth of self-consciousness that Pushkin displayed, for example, in "The Gypsies"—a poem I place entirely within the first period of his creative work. And I am not taking into account the creative power and energy that would not have been so evident had he been

491

merely an imitator. In the character of Aleko, the hero of "The Gypsies," one already finds a powerful, profound, and completely Russian idea, subsequently expressed in such harmonious fullness in *Onegin*, where we see almost this same Aleko, no longer as an outlandish figure but as someone palpably real and comprehensible. In Aleko, Pushkin had already found and brilliantly rendered that unhappy wanderer in his native land, that historical, suffering Russian who appeared with such historical inevitability in our educated society after it had broken away from the People. Such a character Pushkin derived not only from Byron, of course. This is a genuine and flawlessly conceived character, a type that has long become a permanent fixture in our Russian land. These homeless Russian wanderers continue their wandering even now and, it seems, are unlikely to disappear for a long time yet. And if in our day they no longer frequent the camps of the gypsies to look for universal ideals in their wild and distinctive way of life and to seek in the bosom of nature some respite from our confused and ridiculous Russian life—the life of educated society—then, still, they go running off to socialism, which did not yet exist in Aleko's time; they take their new faith to a different field and work it zealously, believing, as did Aleko, that through their bizarre labors they will achieve their goals and find happiness not only for themselves but for the whole world. For what the Russian wanderer needs is the happiness of the whole world in order to find his own peace of mind: he will not settle for less—so long as matters are confined to theory, of course. This is still the same Russian, only belonging to a different era. This person, I repeat, came into being in our educated society, detached from the People and the People's strength, just at the beginning of the second century after the great Petrine reforms. Oh, the vast majority of educated Russians even then, in Pushkin's day just as in our own time, served and serve peacefully as functionaries, for the state, the railways, the banks, or simply made a living by other means; some even took up scholarly work, giving lectures, and they did all these things in a regular, leisurely, peaceful fashion, receiving their salaries and playing cards, with never the slightest notion of running off to the gypsy camps or whatever their equivalent might be in our time. At most they might flirt with liberalism "with a tinge of European socialism" but with a certain Russian softheartedness about it—but this is only a question of the age, after all. What does it matter that one fellow still hasn't begun to be troubled, while another has already managed to get as far as the locked door and painfully knocked his head against it? The same thing awaits them all in due time if they do not take the road to salvation through humble communion with the People. Granted, the same fate does not await every one of them; still, it is enough if it happens merely to "the chosen few," merely to a tenth of those who began to be troubled, since through them the remaining vast majority will be deprived of their peace of mind.

Of course, Aleko still does not know how to express his anguish properly: for him it is still all some kind of abstraction; he has merely a longing for nature, a grievance against fashionable society, universal aspirations, a lament for the truth which someone, somewhere, has lost and which he simply cannot find. There is a bit of Jean-Jacques Rousseau here. Of course, he himself cannot say what this truth is, where and in what it might appear, and just when it was lost, yet he is genuinely suffering. This bizarre and impatient character still seeks salvation from external things first of all, and so he must: "The truth," he imagines, "is somewhere outside him, perhaps in some other land, in Europe, for instance, with her stable historical order and well-established social and civic life." And he will never understand that the truth is to be found, first of all, within himself; indeed, how could he understand that? He is a stranger in his own land, after all; for a whole century he has been unaccustomed to work; he has no culture; he has grown up behind solid walls like a boarding-school miss; he has carried out some odd, unaccountable duties associated with one or another of the fourteen classes into which Russian educated society is divided. He is still no more than a blade of grass, torn from its stem and carried off by the wind. And he can sense that and suffer for it, and often suffer so painfully! So what does it matter if he, who perhaps belongs to the hereditary nobility and very likely owns serfs, took advantage of the freedoms of the nobility and indulged in a little fantasy to fall in with people who live "outside the law" and lead a trained bear in a gypsy camp? One can understand that a woman, a "wild woman" as one poet has called her, would be most likely to give him hope of relieving his anguish; and so, with frivolous yet passionate faith, he throws himself at Zemfira: "Here," he says, "is my way out; here I may find happiness, in the bosom of nature, far from society, here, among people who have no laws or civilization!" And what happens? In his first encounter with this wild nature he cannot restrain himself and reddens his hands with blood. The unhappy dreamer is not only unsuited to universal harmony, he is even unsuited to the gypsies, and they drive him away—without vengeance, without malice, in a dignified, simple-hearted fashion: "Depart from us, O haughty man; / Savages are we, not bound by law, / We neither punish nor chastise."

This is all rather farfetched, of course, but "the haughty man" is real, and Pushkin's perception here is apt. Pushkin was the first among us to perceive him, and we must remember that. The very moment Aleko finds something not to his liking, he angrily attacks his opponent and punishes him for the offense or—what he finds even handier—he remembers that he belongs to one of the fourteen classes and may appeal (for this also happened) to the law to attack and punish; and he will resort to the law, so long as his personal grievance can be redressed. No, this is not an imitation, this is a brilliant poem! Here we already find a suggestion of the Russian solution to the question, the "accursed question," in accordance with the People's faith and truth: "Humble thyself, O haughty man; first curb thy pride. Humble thyself, O idle man; first labor on thy native soil." That is the solution in accord with the People's truth and the People's wisdom. "The truth is not outside you but within; find yourself within yourself; submit yourself to yourself; master yourself, and you shall see the truth. This truth is not to be found in things; it is not outside you or somewhere beyond the sea but is to be found first in your own work to better yourself. Conquer yourself, humble yourself, and you shall be freer than ever you imagined; you will embark on a great task and make others free, and you will find happiness, for your life will be made complete and you will at last understand your People and their sacred truth. Universal harmony is not to be found among the gypsies or anywhere else so long as you yourself are still unworthy of it, if you are spiteful and proud and expect life as a gift, not even supposing that it must be paid for." This solution to the question is already strongly suggested in Pushkin's poem. It is still more clearly expressed in *Eugene Onegin,* a poem that is not farfetched but palpably realistic, a poem in which actual Russian life is embodied with a creative power and accomplishment such as had never been seen before Pushkin or, perhaps, after him.

Onegin arrives from Petersburg—it had to be from Petersburg; this was absolutely essential to the poem, and Pushkin could not have omitted such a major, realistic feature of his hero's biography. I repeat once more:

he is the same Aleko, particularly later in the poem, when he exclaims in anguish: "Oh, why, like some poor Tula assessor, / Am I not lying paralyzed?"

But at the beginning of the poem he is still half a dandy and socialite and has not yet lived enough to be completely disillusioned with life. But even he begins to be visited and troubled by "The noble demon of secret ennui."

Deep in the provinces, in the heartland of his native country, he naturally feels out of place and not at home. He does not know what to do and feels as if he were a guest in his own home. Subsequently, when he wanders in anguish through his native land and through foreign parts among strangers, he, as an undoubtedly intelligent and sincere man, feels even more a stranger to himself. It's true that he loves his native land, but he has no faith in it. Of course, he's also heard of the ideals of his native land, but he doesn't believe in them. He believes merely in the utter impossibility of any sort of labor on his native soil, while—then, as now—he regards those who do believe in this with sad mockery. He killed Lensky simply out of spleen; and who knows?—his spleen may have been caused by his longing for a universal ideal; this is very much in our style, this is very probable.

Tatiana is another matter: she is a strong character who stands solidly on her own native soil. She is deeper than Onegin and, of course, more intelligent than he. Her noble instinct alone tells her where and in what the truth is to be found, and this is expressed in the poem's ending. Pushkin might have done even better to name his poem after Tatiana rather than Onegin, for she is unquestionably its protagonist. She is a positive, not a negative character, a type of positive beauty; she is the apotheosis of Russian womanhood, and the poet has given her the task of expressing the poem's idea in the remarkable scene of her last meeting with Onegin. One might even say that a positive type of Russian woman of such beauty has almost never been repeated in our literature except, perhaps, in the character of Liza in Turgenev's *A Nest of Gentlefolk*. But Onegin's manner of looking down on people caused him to disregard Tatiana entirely when he met her the first time, in a provincial backwater and in the humble image of a pure, innocent girl who was so timid in his presence. He was unable to see the accomplishment and perfection in this poor girl and perhaps really did take her for a "moral embryo." She, an embryo, and this after her letter to Onegin! If there is anyone who is a moral embryo in the poem, then of course it is he, Onegin himself: there is no disputing that. Indeed, he was utterly incapable of recognizing her: what did he know of the human soul? He is a man of abstractions, he is a restless dreamer, and has been so all his life. He did not recognize her later either, as a grand lady in Petersburg, when, in the words of his letter to Tatiana, "his soul perceived all her perfections." But these are merely words: she has passed through his life unrecognized and unappreciated by him; herein lies the tragedy of their romance. Oh, had Childe Harold or, somehow, even Lord Byron himself come from England to Onegin's first meeting with her in the country, and had one of them noticed her shy, humble charm and pointed her out to him—oh, Onegin would at once have been amazed and astonished, for these people afflicted by Weltschmerz often have such servility of spirit! But this did not happen, and once the seeker after world harmony had given her a lecture and had, still, treated her honorably, he set off with his Weltschmerz, his hands stained with blood spilled in a foolish fit of anger, to wander over his native land without ever perceiving it, brimming with health and strength, exclaiming with curses: "I am young and full of life, But what awaits me? / Inner strife."

Tatiana understood this. In some of the novel's immortal stanzas the poet has shown her visiting the home of this man she finds so fascinating and mysterious. I need not speak of the artistry, the matchless beauty, and the profundity of these stanzas. We see her in his study, examining his books, his possessions, his trinkets, trying through them to comprehend his soul and solve her riddle; the "moral embryo" stops at last, deep in thought, with a strange smile on her face, sensing that she has solved the riddle; and she gently whispers, "Is he a parody, perchance?"

Yes, she had to whisper that; she has solved the riddle. Much later, when they meet again in Petersburg, she understands him completely. Incidentally, who said that society and court life had a pernicious effect on her soul and that it was precisely her standing as a society lady and her new ideas inspired by society that were part of her reason for refusing Onegin? No, that was not what happened. No, this is the same Tanya, the same country girl as before! She has not been corrupted; rather, she is depressed by this ostentatious Petersburg life; her heart aches and she suffers; she despises her position as a society lady, and anyone who sees her differently does not understand anything Pushkin was trying to say.

She tells Onegin firmly: "But now I am another's wife, / And will be true to him for life."

She said this specifically as a Russian woman; this is her apotheosis. She expresses the truth of the poem. Oh, I shall say not a word about her religious convictions, about her view of the sacrament of marriage—no, I shall not mention that. But still, why did she refuse to follow him even though she admitted she loved him? Was it because she, "as a Russian woman" (and not a southern woman or some Frenchwoman), was incapable of taking such a bold step, unable to break her shackles, unable to overcome her worship of honors, wealth, and social standing, to break with conventional virtue? No, the Russian woman is bold. The Russian woman will boldly follow one in whom she believes, and she has proved that. But she "is now another's wife, and will be true to him for life." To whom, then, and to what is she being true? To what obligations? To this old general, whom she cannot love because she loves Onegin, and whom she married only because "in tears her mother begged, implored," while in her aggrieved and lacerated soul there was only despair and no hope, no glimmer of light? Yes, she is faithful to this general, her husband, an honorable man who loves her, respects her, and is proud of her. Her mother may have "implored her," but still it was she and no one else who gave her consent; it was she, after all, who swore to be a faithful wife to him. She may have married him in despair, but now he is her husband, and betrayal would cast shame and disgrace upon him and would mean his death. And can one person found his happiness on the unhappiness of another? Happiness is found not only in the pleasures of love, but also in the higher harmony of the spirit. How can one's spirit be set at rest if in one's past there is a dishonorable, merciless, inhumane act? Is she to run off simply because the one who represents her happiness is here? But what kind of happiness can it be if it is founded on the unhappiness of another? Can you imagine that you are erecting the edifice of human destiny with the goal of making people happy in the end, of giving them peace and rest at last? And now imagine as well that to do this it is essential and unavoidable to torture to death just one human creature; moreover, let that creature be not an entirely worthy one, a person some may find even ridiculous—not some Shakespeare, but simply an honorable old man, the husband of a young wife whose love he blindly believes in; even though he knows nothing of her heart, he respects her, is proud of her, happy with her, and is at peace. And so you need only to disgrace, dishonor, and torment him and build your edifice on the tears of this dishonored old man! Will you consent on those terms to be the architect of such an edifice? That is the question. And can you admit, even for a moment, the idea that the people for whom you were building this edifice would themselves agree to accept such happiness from you if its foundations rested on the suffering of, say, even one insignificant creature, but one who had been mercilessly and unjustly tortured—and, having accepted this happiness, would they remain happy ever after? Tell me, could Tatiana, with her noble soul and her heart that had suffered so much, have settled the matter in any other way? No; this is how a pure Russian soul settles it: "Let it be that I alone have no happiness; let my unhappiness be immeasurably greater than the unhappiness of this old man; finally, let no one, not even this old man, ever learn of my sacrifice and appreciate it; but I do not want to be happy after having destroyed another!"

This is the tragedy: it unfolds, and the line cannot be crossed; it is already too late, and so Tatiana sends Onegin away. People will say that Onegin is also unhappy, after all; she has saved one and ruined another! That may well be, but that is another question, perhaps even the most important one in the poem. Incidentally, the question of why Tatiana did not go off with Onegin has, at least in our literature, a very characteristic history of its own, and so that is why I allowed myself to go on at such length about it. What is most characteristic is that for such a long time we cast doubt on the moral solution to this question. This is what I think: even if Tatiana had become free, if her old husband had died and she had become a widow, even then she would not have gone off with Onegin. One must understand the whole essence of this character! She can see what he is, after all: the eternal wanderer has suddenly seen a woman, whom he formerly spurned, in a new, dazzling, unattainable setting; and it is the setting, perhaps, that is the entire essence of the thing. This girl, whom he all but despised, is now the one to whom society pays homage—society,
. . .   authority for Onegin, despite all his universal strivings; and
                                  rhy he rushes blindly to her! "This is my ideal!" he exclaims,
                                  vation, this is the solution to my anguish; I overlooked it,
                                  was so possible, so near!'" And just as Aleko rushed to
                                  ushes off to Tatiana, seeking all his solutions in some odd

new fantasy. Does Tatiana really not see this? Has she not seen through him long ago? She knows very well that in essence he loves only his new fantasy and not her, the Tatiana who is as humble as before! She knows that he takes her for something other than what she is, that it is not even her he loves, that, perhaps, he does not love anyone and is incapable of loving anyone, despite the fact that he suffers such torment! He loves his fantasy; indeed, he himself is a fantasy. Should she follow him, he would grow disenchanted the very next day and look mockingly at his infatuation. He has no soil under his feet, this blade of grass borne by the wind. She is altogether different: in her despair and her agonized awareness that her life has been ruined, she still has something solid and unshakeable on which her soul can rely. These are her memories of childhood, her memories of her native home deep in the provinces where her humble, pure life began; it is the "cross and the shade of boughs o'er the grave of her poor nurse." Oh, these memories and images from her past are what she treasures most now; these images are all she has left, but it is they which save her soul from ultimate despair. And they are no small thing; no, they mean a great deal, because they provide a complete foundation, something unshakeable and indestructible. They represent contact with her native land, her native People and their sacred values. But what does he have, and who is he? She cannot follow him out of compassion, simply in order to console him, to use her infinite loving pity to provide him, at least temporarily, with an illusion of happiness, knowing full well that the very next day he would ridicule that happiness. No, there are profound and steadfast souls that cannot consciously give up their most sacred values to be defiled, even though it may be from infinite compassion. No, Tatiana could not have followed Onegin.

And so in *Onegin*, in this immortal and unsurpassable poem, Pushkin appeared as a great Popular writer, as no one before him ever had. At one stroke, in a most apt, perceptive manner, he identified the innermost essence of the upper levels of our society that stand above the People. Having identified the type of the Russian wanderer, who continues his wandering even in our days; having been the first to divine, through his brilliant instinct, that wanderer's historical fate and his enormous significance in our future destiny; having placed beside him the type of positive, indisputable beauty of the Russian woman, Pushkin, in his other works of this period (first among Russian writers once again, of course), showed

us a whole series of positively beautiful Russian types he found among
the Russian People. The beauty of these types lies above all in their truth,
an unquestionable and palpable truth that makes them impossible to
disavow; they stand before us as if carved in stone. Let me remind you
once more that I am not speaking as a literary critic and so I shall not try
to explain my idea through a detailed literary analysis of these brilliant
creations of our poet. One could write a whole book, for instance, about
the type of Russian chronicler-monk, pointing out all the importance and
significance there is for us in this majestic Russian image Pushkin found
in the Russian land, brought forth and sculpted, and whose indisputable, humble, and majestic spiritual beauty has now been placed before
us forever as testimony to the powerful spirit of Popular life capable
of producing images of such unquestioned beauty. The type has been
provided; it exists; it cannot be denied by saying it is a mere invention,
merely the poet's fantasy and idealization. Think well about it and you
must agree: yes, it does exist, and so, within the spirit of the People who
created it the vital force of this spirit also exists; and it is great and limitless. Everywhere in Pushkin we perceive a faith in the Russian character,
a faith in its spiritual power; and if there is faith, then there must be hope
as well, a great hope for the Russian: "With hopes for glory and for good,
/ I look ahead and have no fear," said the poet himself when speaking
of another subject; but these words of his can be applied directly to the
whole of his creative activity drawn from his nation. And never has any
Russian writer, before him or since, been so akin in spirit to his People as
was Pushkin. Oh, we have many experts on the People among our writers,
ones who write with such talent, so aptly and so lovingly about the People;
and yet if one compares them with Pushkin, they are, truly (with perhaps
two exceptions from his latest followers), merely "gentlemen" who write
about the People. The most talented of these, even these two exceptions
I just mentioned, will now and then suddenly show a haughty attitude,
something from another world and another way of life, something that
shows a wish to raise the People to their own level and make them happy
by doing so. In Pushkin there is precisely something that *truly* makes
him akin to the People, something that reaches almost the level of simple-
hearted tenderness. Take his "Tale of the Bear" and the peasant who
killed his "lady bear," or recall the verses "Brother Ivan, when you and I
start drinking," and you will see what I mean.

Our great poet left all these treasures of art and artistic vision as sign-posts for the artists who came after him and for those who would toil in the same fields as he. One can positively state that had Pushkin not existed neither would the talented people who came after him. At least they, despite their great gifts, would not have made their presence felt with such power and clarity of expression as they did later, in our time. But the point is not merely in poetry and not merely in creative work: had Pushkin not existed, it might well be that our faith in our Russian individuality, our now conscious hope in the strength of our People, and with it our faith in our future independent mission in the family of European peoples would not have been formulated with such unshakeable force (this did happen later, but was by no means universal and was felt by merely a few). This feat of Pushkin's becomes particularly evident if one studies what I call the third period of his creative work.

Once more, I repeat: these periods do not have such firm boundaries. Some of the works of even this third period could have appeared at the very beginning of our poet's career, because Pushkin was always a complete, integrated organism, so to say, an organism bearing all its beginnings within itself and not acquiring them from without. The outside world only aroused in him those things already stored in the depths of his soul. But this organism did develop, and the particular nature of each of the periods of this development actually can be shown and the gradual progression from one period to the next indicated. Thus, to the third period belongs the series of works in which universal ideas shine forth most brightly, which reflect the poetic images of other nations and which incarnate their genius. Some of these works appeared only posthumously. And in this period of his career our poet stands forth as an almost miraculous and unprecedented phenomenon, never before seen anywhere else. In fact, the European literatures had creative geniuses of immense magnitude—the Shakespeares, Cervanteses, and Schillers. But show me even one of these great geniuses who possessed the capacity to respond to the whole world that our Pushkin had. And it is this capacity, the principal capacity of our nationality, that he shares with our People; and it is this, above all, that makes him a national poet. The very greatest of these European poets could never exemplify as intensely as Pushkin the genius of another people—even a people that might be near at

hand—the spirit of that people, all the hidden depths of that spirit and all
its longing to fulfill its destiny. On the contrary, when the European poets
dealt with other nationalities they most often instilled in them their own
nationality and interpreted them from their own national standpoint.
Even Shakespeare's Italians, for instance, are almost to a man the same
as Englishmen. Pushkin alone, of all the poets of the world, possesses
the quality of embodying himself fully within another nationality. Take
his "Scenes from Faust," his "Covetous Knight," his ballad "Once There
Lived a Poor Knight." Read "Don Juan" once more, and were it not for
Pushkin's name on it you would never guess that it had not been written
by a Spaniard. What profound, fantastic images there are in the poem
"A Feast in Time of Plague!" But in these fantastic images you hear the
genius of England; this marvelous song sung by the poem's hero about
the plague, this song of Mary with the verses, "Once the noisy school
rang out, / With the voices of our children," these English songs, this
longing of the British genius, this lament, this agonizing presentiment of
the future. Just recall the strange verses: "Once, wandering 'midst a valley
wild. . . ."

This is almost a literal reworking of the first three pages of a strange,
mystical book written in prose by one ancient English religious
sectarian—but is it merely a reworking? In the melancholy and rapturous
music of these verses one senses the very soul of northern Protestantism,
of an English heresiarch whose mysticism knows no bounds, with his
dull, gloomy, and compelling strivings and with all the unchecked force
of mystical visions. Reading these strange verses, you seem to sense the
spirit of the age of the Reformation; you begin to understand this militant fire of incipient Protestantism; you begin to understand, finally, the
history itself, and understand it not only rationally but as though you had
been there yourself, had passed through the armed camp of sectarians,
sung hymns with them, wept with them in their mystical ecstasies, and
shared their beliefs. Incidentally, right next to this religious mysticism we
find other religious stanzas from the Koran, or "Imitations of the Koran":
do we not find a real Moslem here? Is this not the very spirit of the Koran
and its sword, the simple-hearted majesty of the faith and its awesome,
bloody power? And here, too, we find the ancient world—"The Egyptian
Nights"; here we see these earthly gods, who have been enthroned as
divinities over their people, who despise the very spirit of their people

and its aspirations, who no longer believe in it, who have become solitary gods in truth and who have gone mad in their isolation, who in their anguish and weariness while waiting to die seek diversion in outrageous brutalities, in insectlike voluptuousness, the voluptuousness of a female spider devouring her mate. No, I will say positively that there has not been a poet so able to respond to the whole world as Pushkin; and the point is not only in this ability to respond but in its astounding depth and in his ability to infuse his spirit into the spirit of other nations, something that was almost complete and so was marvelous as well, because nowhere in any other poet anywhere in the world has such a phenomenon been repeated. This we find only in Pushkin, and in this sense, I repeat, he is unprecedented and, in my view, prophetic, for . . . for it was just here that his national Russian strength was most fully expressed, that the national spirit of his poetry was expressed, the national spirit as it will develop in the future, the national spirit of our future, already concealed within our present and expressed prophetically. For what is the strength of the spirit of Russianness if not its ultimate aspirations toward universality and the universal brotherhood of peoples? Having become completely a national poet, Pushkin at once, as soon as he came in contact with the force of the People, at once senses the great future mission of this force. Here he is a visionary; here he is a prophet.

In fact, what did Peter's reform mean for us, not only in terms of the future but even in terms of what has already happened and already is evident to all? What was the significance of this reform for us? It meant not only our adopting European clothing, customs, inventions, and European science. Let us try to understand what happened and look into it more closely. Indeed, it is quite possible that Peter first began to carry out his reform in just this sense, that is to say, in an immediately utilitarian sense; but subsequently, in his further development of his idea, Peter undoubtedly followed a certain secret instinct that led him to work toward future goals that certainly were immensely broader than mere immediate utilitarianism. The Russian People as well accepted the reforms in just the same spirit—not merely one of utilitarianism but having certainly sensed almost at once some further and incomparably more elevated goal than immediate utilitarianism; I must repeat, of course, that they sensed that goal unconsciously, yet also directly and as something absolutely vital. It was then that we at once began to strive toward a truly vital reunification, toward the universal brotherhood of peoples! It was not with hostility (as should have been the case, it would seem) but with friendship and complete love that we accepted the genius of other nations into our soul, all of them together, making no discriminations by race, knowing instinctively almost from our very first step where the distinctions lay, knowing how to eliminate contradictions, to excuse and reconcile differences; and in so doing we revealed the quality that had only just been made manifest—our readiness and our inclination for the general reunification of all people of all the tribes of the great Aryan race. Indeed, the mission of the Russian is unquestionably pan-European and universal. To become a real Russian, to become completely Russian, perhaps, means just (in the final analysis—please bear that in mind) to become a brother to all people, a *panhuman,* if you like. Oh, all our Slavophilism and Westernizing is no more than one great misunderstanding between us, although it was historically necessary. To a real Russian, Europe and the lot of all the great Aryan tribe are just as dear as is Russia herself, as is the lot of our own native land, because our lot is universality, achieved not through the sword but through the strength of brotherhood and our brotherly aspirations toward the unity of people. If you care to look closely into our history after the Petrine reforms, you will already find traces and indications of this idea—this vision of mine, if you wish to call it that—in the way we dealt with the peoples of Europe, even in our official policy. For what was Russia doing in her policy over these whole two centuries if not serving Europe, far more, perhaps, than she was serving herself? I do not think that this happened merely through the ineptness of our politicians. Oh, the nations of Europe simply do not know how dear they are to us! And subsequently, I am certain, we (I mean not we, of course, but Russian people to come) will realize to the very last man that to become a genuine Russian will mean specifically: to strive to bring an ultimate reconciliation to Europe's contradictions, to indicate that the solution to Europe's anguish is to be found in the panhuman and all-unifying Russian soul, to enfold all our brethren within it with brotherly love, and at last, perhaps, to utter the ultimate word of great, general harmony, ultimate brotherly accord of all tribes through the law of Christ's Gospel!

I know, I know full well that my words may seem ecstatic, exaggerated, and fantastic. So be it: but I do not regret having said them. This had to be said, and particularly now, at the moment of our celebration, at the moment we pay honor to our great genius who embodied this very idea in his artistic power. And, indeed, this idea has been expressed more than once; I have said nothing new. What is most important is that all this might seem conceited: "Is it for us," some may say, "for our impoverished, crude land to have such a destiny? Can it be we who are ordained to utter a new word to humanity?" But, after all, am I speaking about economic prominence, about the glory of the sword or science? I am speaking merely of the brotherhood of people and of the fact that, perhaps, the Russian heart is most plainly destined, among all the peoples, for universally human and brotherly unity; I see traces of this in our history, in our gifted people, in the artistic genius of Pushkin. Our land may be impoverished, but this impoverished land "Christ Himself, in slavish garb, traversed and gave His blessing." Why can we not accommodate His ultimate word? Was He not born in a manger Himself? I repeat: at the very least we can now point to Pushkin and to the universality and panhumanness of his genius. He could accommodate the geniuses of other nations within his soul as if they were his own. In art, in his artistic work, at least, he showed beyond dispute this universal striving of the Russian spirit, and that in itself reveals something important. If my idea is a fantasy, then in Pushkin, at least, there is something on which this fantasy can be founded. Had he lived longer, perhaps, he would have shown us immortal and grand images of the Russian soul that could have been understood by our European brethren and might have attracted them to us much more and much more closely than now; he might have managed to explain to them the whole truth of our aspirations, and they would have understood us more clearly than they do now; they would have begun to divine our purpose; they would have ceased to regard us as mistrustfully and haughtily as they do now. Had Pushkin lived longer, perhaps there would be fewer misunderstandings and disputes among us than we see now. But God did not will it so. Pushkin died in the full flower of his creative development, and unquestionably he took some great secret with him to his grave. And so now we must puzzle out this secret without him.

CHAPTER THREE

*Taking Advantage of an Opportunity. Four Lectures
on Various Topics Apropos of One Lecture Given to Me by
Mr. A. Gradovsky. With an Address to Mr. Gradovsky.*

Article 1, extract. On One Most Basic Point

I was already about to conclude my *Diary,* having limited it to the speech
I gave in Moscow on June 8 and the foreword I wrote to it, foreseeing the
row that was, in fact, raised later in our press after my speech appeared
in *The Moscow News.* But after reading your criticism, Mr. Gradovsky, I
stopped the printing of the *Diary* so as to append to it a reply to your
attacks. Oh, my apprehensions came true; a fearsome row was raised.
I was full of pride, I was a coward, I was a Manilov, I was a poet, and
the police should have been summoned to restrain outbursts from the
public—the moral police, the liberal police, of course. But why not the
real police, after all? And nowadays our real police are liberal as well, no
less liberal than the liberals who raised the howl against me. In truth, the
latter haven't far to go to become the former! But let us leave this for the
moment; I shall proceed directly to reply to your points. I frankly admit
from the very beginning that I have no personal grounds for quarreling
with you or anything to discuss with you. You and I will never come to an
agreement; and so I have no intention whatsoever of trying to persuade
or dissuade you. When reading some of your articles in the past I have
naturally always been astonished at your train of thought. And so why do
I reply to you now? I do it solely having in mind some other people who
will settle our dispute, i.e., the readers. It is for these others that I write. I
hear, I sense, I even see the rise of new elements who are longing for a new
word, who have grown weary of the old liberal snickering over any word
of hope for Russia, who are tired of the former old toothless liberal skepticism, tired of the old corpses that people have forgotten to bury, and
who still see themselves as the young generation, tired of the old liberal,

the leader and savior of Russia who, for the entire twenty-five years he's been present among us, has at last shown himself to be "a fellow raising a senseless ruckus in the marketplace," as the People say. In short, I wanted to say *a great deal* beyond replying to your remarks, so that in replying now I am merely taking advantage of an opportunity. [. . .]

Article 2, extract. Aleko and Derzhimorda. Aleko's Sufferings for a Peasant Serf. Anecdotes.

[. . .] That's precisely the point: "the wanderers" hated serfdom "in their own way, in a European way"; that's the whole essence of the matter. The point is precisely that they hated serfdom not for the sake of the Russian peasant who worked for them and fed them and who, accordingly, was oppressed by them as well as by others. Who prevented them, if they were so overcome by civic sorrow that they had to run off to the Gypsies or the barricades in Paris—who prevented them from simply liberating at least their own peasants and giving them land, thus eliminating the cause of their civic sorrow, or at least the portion of it that was their own responsibility? But somehow we heard very little about such liberations, yet we heard a good deal of civic wailing. "Corrupted by his environment," was the verdict, "and besides, how could he give up his capital?" But why shouldn't he give it up when his sorrow for the peasants was so profound that he had to run off to the barricades? That's precisely the point: one still needs money to live in "gay Paree," even if one is busy on the barricades, and so the peasants still had to send off their quitrent. Some made it even easier: they mortgaged, sold, or exchanged (is there any difference?) their peasants and, taking the money thus raised, went off to Paris to support the publication of radical French newspapers and magazines for the salvation of the whole of humanity, not merely the Russian peasant. Are you trying to tell us that they all were consumed with sorrow over the peasant serf? Not so much for the peasant serf as a generalized, abstract sorrow over the slavery that existed in humanity: "This should not be; it's unenlightened; we must have *liberté, égalité et fraternité.*" As for the Russian peasant personally, perhaps these noble hearts were not so terribly oppressed by sorrow for him at all. I know and can recall many things said privately even by some of the most "enlightened" people of

the good old days gone by. "There's no doubt that slavery is a great evil,"
they would agree during intimate conversations among themselves. "But,
all things considered, are our People really a People? Are they at all like
the people of Paris in 1793? Why, they've grown used to slavery; their
faces, their demeanor are those of the slave; or take flogging, for instance:
of course it's a vile thing, generally speaking, but, good heavens, when
you're dealing with the Russian you can't do without flogging: 'Our dear
little peasant has got to be flogged; he'll start grieving if he isn't; that's
the sort of nation we have.'" I tell you that I did hear things like that in
days gone by, even from highly enlightened people. That's the "sober
truth," ladies and gentlemen. Perhaps Onegin did not flog his servants,
although, truly, it's hard to say that positively; but as to Aleko, I'm certain
that he did—and not out of any cruelty in his nature but almost even
from pity, almost for some good purpose: "Why, he needs it; he can't
get by without a little flogging; why, he'll come on his own and ask: 'Flog
me, master; make a man of me! I've gone altogether soft!' Now I ask you,
what can you do with a nature like that? So you grant his wish and have
him flogged!" I repeat, their feelings toward the peasant often reached
the point of loathing. And how many contemptuous anecdotes about
the Russian peasant made the rounds among them—contemptuous
and obscene anecdotes about his slavish soul, about his "idol worship,"
about his priest, about his wife; and such stories were told, with complete
insouciance at times, by those whose own family lives were frequently
reminiscent of houses of ill repute—oh, of course this was not always due
to some sort of wickedness but at times merely to the excessive passion
with which the latest European ideas were accepted, in the fashion of
Lucrezia Floriani, for instance, with all our Russian impetuous rush to
understand and take in. They were Russians in every respect! [...]

Article 3, extract. Two Halves

And now I shall turn to your views on "personal betterment in the
spirit of Christian love" and its complete inadequacy—supposedly—as
compared with "social ideals" and, above all, with "social institutions."
Oh, you yourself begin by saying that this is the most important point of
our disagreement. You write:

Now we have come to the most important point of my disagreement with Mr. Dostoevsky. In demanding humility before the truth of the People and their ideals, he accepts this "truth" and these ideals as something given, unshakeable, and eternal. We venture to tell him—no! The *social* ideals of our People are still in a process of *formation and development.* They still have a great deal of work to do on themselves before being worthy of the name of a great People.

In the first section of my article I already replied to you in part on the "truth" and the ideals of the People. You find this truth and these ideals of the People to be plainly inadequate to develop Russia's social ideals. Religion, you suggest, is one thing, while social matters are another. Your scholarly scalpel cuts a living, homogeneous organism into two separate halves, and you maintain that these two halves ought to be entirely independent of one another. Let's look a little more closely, analyze each of these halves separately, and perhaps we shall be able to come to some conclusion. Let's first analyze the half that deals with "personal betterment in the spirit of Christian love." You write:

Mr. Dostoevsky urges us to work on ourselves and humble ourselves. Personal betterment in the spirit of Christian love is, of course, the first prerequisite for any activity, large or small. But it does not follow that people *who have personally perfected themselves in a Christian sense* would necessarily form a perfect society [?!]. Let me give an example.

The Apostle Paul instructed masters and slaves about their mutual relationships. Both the former and the latter may have heeded and usually did heed the words of the apostle; *personally* they were good Christians, but because of this *slavery* became enshrined and remained as an immoral institution. In just the same way, Mr. Dostoevsky, along with every one of us, has known both landowners and peasants who were excellent Christians. Yet *serfdom* remained an abomination in the eyes of the Lord, and the Russian Tsar-Liberator came as one who expressed the demands of not only a *personal* but also a *social* morality, the latter being a thing of which there were no proper conceptions in times of old, despite the fact that there were no fewer "good people" then perhaps, than there are now.

Personal and social morality are not the same. From this it follows that no *social* betterment can be realized *only* through improvement of the personal qualities of the people who comprise that society. Let me cite another example. Let us suppose that beginning in the year 1800 a series of proponents of Christian love and humility had undertaken to improve the morals of the Korobochkas and Sobakeviches. Could one suppose that they would have managed to abolish serfdom, that this "phenomenon" could have been eliminated without *the tsar's* word? On the contrary: Korobochka would have begun to demonstrate that she was a genuine Christian and a real "mother" to her peasants, and she would have held to this conviction, despite all the efforts of the preachers to prove otherwise. . . .

The betterment of people in a *social* sense cannot be done only through work "on oneself" and through "humbling oneself." One can work on oneself and curb one's passions in a wilderness or on an uninhabited island. But as *social* creatures, people develop and improve in working *alongside one another, for one another, and with one another.* That is why people's social betterment depends in such a large measure on the betterment of *social institutions* that develop, if not their Christian, then their civic virtues.

Just look at how much I've quoted you! This is all terribly haughty, and "personal betterment in a spirit of Christian love" has certainly been raked over the coals: it's scarcely good for anything where civic matters are concerned, you suggest. Yet what a strange conception of Christianity you have! Imagine if Korobochka and Sobakevich were to become genuine Christians, already *perfect* (you yourself speak about perfection)—could they then be convinced to renounce serfdom? That's a sly question you're posing, and, naturally, you answer it: "No, one could not convince Korobochka to do that, even if she were a perfect Christian." But to that I shall answer directly: had Korobochka only become, or could she have become, a *genuine*, perfect Christian, then serfdom on her estate would have disappeared altogether, so that there would be nothing to worry about, despite the fact that all the deeds and bills of sale would have remained in her trunk as before. One more thing, if you please: was Korobochka not a Christian even before and was she not born such? Thus, when you speak of new proponents of Christianity, even though you speak of a Christianity that was in essence the same as before, do you mean a Christianity that has already attained its ideal, an intensified, *perfected* one, so to say? If that's the case, then for heaven's sake what slaves and masters could there be? You should at least have some basic acquaintance with Christianity! And what difference would it then make to Korobochka, a *perfect* Christian, whether her peasants were serfs or not? She would be a "mother" to them, a real mother, and the "mother" would at once have done away with the former "mistress." This would have happened of its own accord. The erstwhile mistress and erstwhile slave would have vanished like mist before the sun and entirely new people would have appeared, with entirely new and unprecedented relationships among them. Indeed, the thing itself would have been unprecedented: perfect Christians would have appeared *everywhere*, people who had formerly existed in such scant numbers that they were scarcely perceptible. You were the one who put forth such a fantastic proposition, Mr. Gradovsky; you yourself began this amazing fantasy, and once you've begun it, you must accept the consequences. I assure you, Mr. Gradovsky, that if this had been so, Korobochka's peasants would not have left her, for the simple reason that everyone looks for the place where he can be better off. Do you think they would have been better off with those institutions of yours than they would living with their own mother-landowner who loved them?

I also make so bold as to assure you that if slavery was maintained in the time of the Apostle Paul, it was simply because the churches that had arisen at the time were not yet *perfect* (something that is evident from Paul's Epistles). Those members of the churches who had attained personal perfection no longer owned and could not own slaves because the slaves had become brothers; and a brother, a true brother, cannot keep his brother as a slave. The way you describe it, it would appear that the preaching of Christianity had no effect at all. At least you do acknowledge that slavery was not enshrined by the apostle's preaching. Yet there are other scholars, European historians in particular, who have heaped many reproaches on Christianity for its alleged enshrinement of slavery. This is to misunderstand the essence of the matter. Can you imagine Mary of Egypt having peasant serfs and not wanting to set them free? What an absurdity! In Christianity, in genuine Christianity, there are and will be masters and servants, but a slave is inconceivable. I am speaking of genuine, perfect Christianity. Servants, though, are not slaves. The disciple Timothy served Paul when they traveled together, but read Paul's Epistles to Timothy: do you really think he is writing to a slave, or even to a servant? Indeed, he writes to his "son in the faith," his beloved son. Now those are just the kind of relations there would be between masters and servants should both become perfect Christians! There will be servants and masters, but the masters will no longer be masters, nor will the servants be slaves. Imagine that Kepler, Kant, and Shakespeare are living in the future society: they are carrying out a great labor for all, and everyone is aware of it and reveres them. But Shakespeare has no time to leave his work to tidy up, clean his room, and carry out the rubbish. And believe me, some other citizen will certainly come to work for him; he himself will want to do this, and he will come of his own free will and will carry out Shakespeare's rubbish. Will he be humiliated by this, or made a slave? Certainly not. He knows that Shakespeare is infinitely more useful than he: "Honor and glory be thine," he will tell him; "I am glad to serve thee; in so doing I contribute to the general good, though it be but a drop, for I shall save thee time for thy great work; but I am not a slave. By my conscious admission that thy genius, Shakespeare, makes thee superior to me, and by coming to serve thee, I have shown that I am in no way beneath thee in moral worth and that, *as a person,* I am equal to thee." In fact, he would not say such things for the sole reason that if this were to happen, such questions would never arise and, indeed, would be unthinkable. For, in truth, all would be new people, the children of Christ, and the former animal in man would be conquered. You will say, of course, that this is just another fantasy. But it was not I who first began to spin fantasies, after all, it was you: you were the one who tried to show Korobochka as a *perfect* Christian with "serf *children*" whom she did not want to set free; that's much more of a fantasy than mine.

At this point clever people will laugh and say: "So what's the point of advocating personal betterment in the spirit of Christian love when it seems that genuine Christianity doesn't exist on earth, or exists in such small measure that it's difficult to find? If it did exist (according to what

I said, that is), everything would be settled instantly—all forms of slavery would be abolished, the Korobochkas would be reborn as bright spirits, and there would be nothing left for people to do but sing hymns to God." Well, of course (I reply to the gentlemen who are scoffing), there are still terribly few genuine Christians (although they do exist). But how do you know precisely how many are needed to keep the ideal of Christianity alive among the People and, with it, their great hope? Apply this to social conceptions: how many genuine citizens are needed to keep the ideal of civic virtue alive in society? You can't supply an answer to that, either. There's a political economy of its own at work here, one of a special kind which we do not know and which even you do not know, Mr. Gradovsky. People will say, again, "If there are so few who profess this great idea, then what benefit does it bring?" But how do you know what benefit it will bring, when all is said and done? Until now, evidently, all that was needed was that the great idea should not die out. But now, when something new is transpiring all over the world, we have a different situation and we must be prepared. . . . And, indeed, the point here is not at all one of benefit but of truth. If I believe that the truth is here, in those very things in which I put my faith, then what does it matter to me if the whole world rejects my truth, mocks me, and travels a different road? Indeed, that is the strength of a great moral idea, and that is the way in which it joins people into the surest union: that it is not measured in terms of immediate benefit but is directed toward the future, toward eternal ends and absolute joy. How can you unite people to accomplish your civic goals if you have no basis in a fundamental, great, moral idea? And moral ideas are all alike: they are all based on the idea of absolute personal betterment in the future, on an ideal; for this idea contains all within it, all aspirations and all longings; accordingly, all your civic ideals emerge from it. Do you think you could unite people in some civic association with "saving one's neck" as the only goal? Nothing would be achieved, save for the moral motto *Chacun pour soi et Dieu pour tous.* No civic institution will last long with a motto like that, Mr. Gradovsky.

But let me go on; I intend to surprise you: please be aware, my learned professor, that there are no social, civic ideals as such, ones that are not linked organically with moral ideals but exist independently as separate halves sliced off from the whole by your scholarly scalpel; there are no such ideals that, at last, can be taken from outside and transplanted successfully into the spot of your choosing in the form of distinct "institutions"; such ideals, I say, do not exist, never did exist, and cannot exist! Besides, what is a social ideal? What do we mean by this term? Of course, its essence lies in people's strivings to find a formula for social organization, one that, if possible, would be without flaws and would satisfy everyone—isn't that so? But people do not know this formula; people have been looking for it for the whole six thousand years of their history, and they cannot find it. The ants know the formula for their ant heap; the bee knows the formula for his hive (they may not know it in human terms, but they know it in their own way, and that is enough); but humans do not know their formula. If that is so, then where is the source of the ideal of civic organization in human society? If you follow it historically you will see at once where the source is. You will see that it is solely and exclusively the product of the moral betterment of individuals; this is where it begins, and so it has been from time immemorial, and so it shall remain for all time to come. In the origin of every people and every nationality the moral idea always preceded the genesis of the nationality itself, *for the idea was the force that created the nationality.* This moral idea always arose from some mystical ideas, from convictions that humans were eternal, that they were not simply animals roaming the earth but were linked with other worlds and with eternity. Always and everywhere these convictions were formulated in religion, in the confession of some new idea; and always, as soon as a new religion came into being, a new nationality was at once created on the civic level. Look at the Jews and the Moslems: the idea of nationality among the Jews took shape only after the law of Moses, although its beginning goes back to the law of Abraham, while the Moslem nationalities appeared only after the Koran. In order to preserve the spiritual treasure they have received, people are at once drawn to one another; and only then, zealously and anxiously, "working *alongside one another, for one another and with one another*" (as you put it so expressively)—only then do people begin to seek out ways to organize themselves so as to preserve the treasure they have received and not lose anything from it, to find some *civic* formula for living in common, one that would help them advance throughout the world the full glory of that moral treasure they have received. And note that, with the passage of centuries and ages (because such a process also has a law of its own, one we do not know), as soon as the spiritual idea of any nationality began to be shaken and weakened, the nationality itself also began to decline, and with it all their civic precepts; and all the civic ideas they managed to establish within their nationality faded away. The forms a religion has assumed among a people determine the way in which their civic system took shape and expressed itself. Thus, civic ideals are always directly and organically linked with moral ideals; what is most important, the former are always derived exclusively from the latter. Civic ideals never come about *of their own accord,* for when they do appear their sole purpose is to satisfy the moral aspirations of a given nationality in the manner and degree in which those moral aspirations have taken shape within it. And thus, "personal betterment in a religious spirit" is the basis for everything in the lives of nations, for personal betterment in fact *is the confession of the acquired religion,* while "civic ideals" themselves, without this aspiration toward personal betterment, can never appear and, indeed, can never even be born.

You will say, perhaps, that you yourself have stated that "personal betterment is the basis of everything" and that you have not made any divisions with your scalpel. The point, however, is precisely that you did make such a division and cut a living organism into two halves. Personal betterment is not merely "the *beginning* of everything," it is also the continuation and the outcome of everything. It embraces, provides the foundation for, and preserves the organism of nationality; and only it can do this. The civic formula of the nation exists for the sake of personal betterment, for the nation was created only for the purpose of preserving it as the treasure originally acquired. When a nationality loses the urge for general individual self-betterment *in that spirit in which it originated,* then all "social institutions" begin to die out, for there is nothing more to preserve. Thus one simply cannot say what you have said in your last sentence: "That is why people's social betterment depends in such a large measure on the betterment of *social institutions* that develop, if not their Christian, then their civic virtues."

"If not their Christian, then their civic virtues!" Don't you see here the scholarly scalpel that tries to sever what cannot be severed, that cuts the homogeneous, living organism into two separate, lifeless halves—a moral one and a civic one? You say that the most sublime moral idea can be found both "in social institutions" and in the dignity of "a citizen," that a "civic idea" within nations that are already mature and developed always takes the place of the original religious idea, which degenerates into a civic idea and which it legitimately inherits. Yes, many people maintain such things, but we have never yet seen such a fantasy in real life. Whenever the moral-religious idea within a nationality has worn itself out, there has always ensued a panicky, cowardly urge to unite for the sole purpose of "saving one's neck"—there are no other goals for civic union in such cases. Take the French bourgeoisie now, which unites for this very purpose of "saving its neck" from the fourth estate that is trying to break down its door. But "saving one's neck" is the very weakest and last of all the ideas that unite humanity. This is already the beginning of the end, a presentiment of the end. They unite, but keep their eyes peeled so that at the first sign of danger they can break apart all the more quickly. And what, here, can an "institution" as such, taken on its own, save? If there were brothers, then there would be brotherhood. If there are no brothers, then you will not achieve brotherhood through any sort of "institution." What sense is there in setting up an institution and inscribing on it: *Liberté, égalité, fraternité?* You will achieve nothing at all worthwhile here through an "institution," so that it will be necessary—absolutely, inescapably necessary—to add to these three "institutional" words a fourth *ou la mort, fraternité ou la mort*—and brother will set forth to chop the head off brother so as to achieve brotherhood by means of this "civic institution." [. . .]

Article 4, extract. To One—"Humble Thyself"; To Another—"Exalt Thyself." A Tempest in a Teapot.

[. . .] At the very end of your article you ask me to excuse any remarks I might consider to be harsh. As I end my article, I do not ask you to excuse me for any harsh expressions, if there be such in my article, Mr. Gradovsky. My reply was directed not to A. D. Gradovsky personally but to the publicist A. Gradovsky. I haven't the slightest reason not to respect you personally. But if I do not respect your opinions and continue to hold to my own, then how could I moderate anything by asking your forgiveness? But I found it painful to see a very serious and portentous moment in the life of our society portrayed in a distorted way and interpreted wrongly. It was painful to see the idea I serve dragged through the streets. And you were the one who was dragging it.

I realize that people on every side will tell me that it was ridiculous and pointless to write such a long reply to your article, which was rather brief in comparison with mine. But, I repeat, your article served only as a pretext: I wanted to make a general statement about certain things. I intend to resume publishing *A Writer's Diary* beginning next year. And so this present issue of the *Diary* may serve as my *profession de foi* for the future, a "trial" issue, so to say.

People may also say that in my reply to you I invalidated the whole meaning of the speech I delivered in Moscow, where I myself called upon both Russian parties to join together and to be reconciled and acknowledged the legitimacy of each one. No, not at all: the meaning of the speech has not been invalidated; it has, rather, been reinforced even more, for I make the specific point in my reply to you that both parties, in their alienation from one another, in their mutual enmity, place themselves and their activity in an abnormal position, whereas in unity and accord with one another they might be able to lift up all our spirits, save everything, rouse limitless energies, and mobilize Russia for a new, healthy, grand life such as has not been seen before!

1881

January

from CHAPTER ONE

Article 1, extract. Finances. A Citizen as an Offended Thersites. Crowning from Below and the Musicians. A Refuge for Windbags and the Windbags.

Good Lord! Can it be that after three years of silence I now resume my *Diary* with an article on economics? What sort of economist and financial expert am I? I've never been either of those things. Despite the current epidemic, I have not been infected with the virus of economism, yet here I am, following all the others and coming out with an article on economics. That there is a regular epidemic of economism these days is beyond doubt. Everyone is an economist these days. Every new magazine looks as if it is specializing in economic issues and announces itself as such. Indeed, how can one not be an economist, and who can avoid it nowadays? The fall of the ruble! The deficit! [. . .]

Article 2, extract. Can We Expect European Finances in Russia?

"So what about finances? Where's your article on finances?" I'll be asked. But, again, what sort of economist am I? What kind of expert on financial matters? In fact, I don't think I even have the nerve to write about finances. So why, then, did I embark on such a venture and start writing such an article? I did so precisely because I'm sure that once I've begun to talk of finances I'll change the subject to something else entirely and the result will be an article not about finances but something altogether different. That's the only thing that encourages me. [. . .]

Article 3, extract. Forget Immediate Problems So That the Roots Can Be Restored. Through Lack of Ability I Enter into Something Spiritual.

My nature is such that I shall begin at the end and not at the beginning and set forth my whole idea at once. I've never had the knack of writing in measured fashion, of approaching a thing from the proper approaches and setting forth an idea only after doing all the preliminary ruminations and proving the point as best I can. I've never had the patience, my character stood in the way; and this, of course, harmed me, because some final conclusion, stated plainly, with no preparations and no preliminary supporting arguments, sometimes does nothing more than astonish and confuse people and maybe even make them laugh; but I have precisely the kind of conclusion—and I can sense it—that might at once cause the reader to burst out laughing if I haven't prepared him for it in advance. My idea, my formula, is as follows: "In order to establish sound finances in a state that has experienced certain upheavals, don't think too much about immediate needs, no matter how urgent they may seem; think only about restoring the roots, and you'll get sound finances." [. . .]

Article 4, extract. The First Root. Instead of an Authoritative Financial Tone I Lapse into Old Words. The Broad Ocean. The Longing for Truth and the Necessity for Serenity, So Useful in Financial Matters.

[. . .] I know that our educated people have laughed at me: they do not even want to admit the existence of "that idea" among the People, pointing to their sins, their abominations (for which they themselves, who oppressed the People for two centuries, are responsible); they point to their prejudices, to the People's supposed indifference to religion, and some of them even imagine that the Russian People are atheists, pure and simple. Their great error lies in the fact that they do not recognize the existence of the church among the Russian People. I am speaking now not about church buildings and not about sermons; I am speaking about our Russian "socialism" (and however strange it may seem, I am taking this word, which is quite the opposite of all that the church represents,

to explain my idea), whose purpose and final outcome is the establishment of the universal church on earth, insofar as the earth is capable of
containing it. I am speaking of the ceaseless longing, which has always
been inherent in the Russian People, for a great, general, universal union
of fellowship in the name of Christ. And if this union does not yet exist, if
the church has not yet been fully established—not merely in prayers alone,
but in fact—then the instinct for this church and the ceaseless longing for
it—sometimes even quite unconscious—is still certainly to be found in
the hearts of the millions of our People. It is not in communism, not in
mechanical forms that we find the socialism of the Russian People: they
believe that salvation is ultimately to be found only in *worldwide union
in the name of Christ*. That is our Russian socialism! So, you European
gentlemen, you are laughing at the presence of this higher, unifying,
"ecclesiastical" idea among the Russian People. [. . .]

Article 1. A Witty Bureaucrat. His Opinion of Our Liberals and Europeans.

But having finished my first chapter, I shall now break off my article on finance since I feel that what I'm writing is very dull. But I'm breaking off only for a time. I would still like to say something about the other roots and basic elements which, it seems to me, could be made healthy. I'm also ending my article because I couldn't manage to fit the whole thing into the thirty-two pages of my *Diary* and so, like it or not, would have to put off some of it to subsequent issues. . . .

"There's no point in that; you needn't bother to write any more, even in subsequent issues," some fussy voices interrupt (I knew I'd be hearing those voices). "None of this is about finances, it's just . . . self-indulgence. None of it is realistic" (although I don't see why it isn't); "it's all some sort of mysticism, and there's nothing essential in it, nothing that deals with immediate problems! Give us a story in your subsequent issues."

Strange voices these! You see, I am specifically arguing that we have to turn aside from many things we now see as essential and immediate and create for ourselves a different set of essential and immediate problems, ones even much more actual than those in which we've now become involved and are sticking—if you'll excuse the expression—like a fly in molasses. That was my whole idea. I mean specifically that we have to turn our heads and our eyes in another direction altogether—that's my idea. Those in power could start such a thing, and in that respect my fancies are not that fanciful at all, since if the authorities were to begin it, we could achieve a good deal even now. It is principles—some of our principles—that must be changed completely, the flies must be pulled out of the molasses and set free. This idea isn't a popular one, I suppose: we've long grown accustomed to our inability to move, and we've even begun to taste the sweetness of sitting in molasses.

It's true that I've gone off the topic again, and I might be reminded at this point that, despite all I've written so far, I still haven't managed to explain just what contemporary and immediate things I have in mind and just what immediate things I would prefer in the future. Now this is just what I want to devote my energies to explaining in future issues of my *Diary*. But to finish things now, let me tell you of one encounter I had with a rather witty bureaucrat who told me one rather interesting thing about some of those very principles relating to changes in our contemporary "immediate problems." In a certain gathering the talk turned to financial matters and the economy, but specifically to frugality in respect of our financial resources, building up those resources, and using them so that not a single kopeck should be lost or spent extravagantly. People are always talking about our economy in that respect now, and in fact the government as well is constantly occupied with the same thing. Controls have been set up, and every year there are reductions in the civil service. Lately there has also even been talk of cuts to the army; the newspapers have suggested specific figures, namely fifty thousand troops, while others have assured us our army could be cut by half: no harm would come of it, they said. That might be all very well, yet one can't help thinking: suppose we do cut the army by, say, fifty thousand in the first instance; still, the money saved would slip through our fingers once more, here and there—for the needs of the state, of course, but for needs which, perhaps, don't merit such a radical sacrifice. The fifty thousand troops cut will never be restored, or only with great effort, because once we have removed them they will be difficult to replace; but we really and truly need an army, especially now, when everyone's nursing a grudge against us. It's dangerous to set off on such a road, at least *now,* given the contemporary, immediate situation that gives rise to our expenditures. We could only be assured that this precious money was really being spent on a worthy cause if we were to embark, for instance, on an irrevocable, severe, gloomy policy of economizing such as Peter the Great might have instituted had he decided to cut expenditures. But are we capable of this, given the "crying" needs of the current reality in which we have become so enmeshed? I might note that were we to do this, or begin it, it would be one of the first steps toward turning away from our former, fantastic "immediate problems" toward something new, actual and appropriate. We quite often make cuts in the civil service, yet the result is that the number of government employees seems somehow to go on increasing. Are we capable of making the kind of cut that would at once reduce every forty functionaries to, say, four? That four functionaries can quite often accomplish the same as forty—that, of course, is beyond anyone's doubt, especially if official paperwork were to be cut down and present bureaucratic methods radically reformed. It was just such a topic that our group began discussing. Someone observed that this would mean a major shake-up. Others objected that we have had far more fundamental reforms than this one. Still others added that the new functionaries—meaning the four who had replaced the forty—could even have their salaries tripled, and that they would work very happily and not complain a bit. But if we were to triple their salaries and spend as much on those four as we now do for twelve, even so we would be reducing our expenditures by almost three-quarters.

At this point my bureaucrat interrupted me. I should note first that, to my great astonishment, even he made no objection whatever to the possibility of replacing forty functionaries by four, agreeing, apparently, that things would get done even with four people; and so he did not see this as an impossibility. But he did object to something else, namely to the principle, to the erroneousness and criminality of the principle that had been stated. I am not citing his objections word for word, and have even edited them extensively. I repeat: I am citing them specifically because his ideas seemed interesting in their fashion and even contained an almost piquant idea. Of course, he didn't consider it worthwhile replying to me in detail, since I'm not a specialist in such matters and "understand little" (something which, of course, I'm quick to admit); still, he hoped that I would understand the principle.

"Cutting the number of functionaries from forty to four," he began sternly and with feeling, "not only fails to help the cause but in essence is even harmful, despite the fact that state expenditures would be significantly reduced. A reduction of that scale is harmful and impossible, but so is one even from forty to thirty-eight, and this is why: because in so doing you would be making a vicious attack on a fundamental principle. For almost two hundred years now, since the time of Peter the Great himself, we, the bureaucrats, have constituted *everything* within the state; in essence, it is we who are the state and are *everything*—the rest is merely excess baggage. At least this was so until recent times, until the liberation of the peasants. All the former elective offices—the nobility's, for instance—automatically took on our spirit and sense simply by force of gravity, so to say. And we weren't the least troubled when we saw this because the principle set forth two hundred years ago was in no way violated. But after the peasant reform something new really began to be felt: self-government appeared, the zemstvo, and so on. . . . It's clear now that all these new things automatically and immediately began to take on our image, our body and soul, and to be embodied in our form. And it certainly wasn't our pressure that caused this (that's a mistaken notion)— it happened strictly of itself, since it's difficult to drop centuries-old habits and, perhaps, that's as it should be, particularly in such a great and fundamental national matter. You may not believe me, but if you're able truly to analyze the matter, you'll understand what I mean. For what are we? We are *everything, everything,* and to this day we continue to be everything; and, once again, it's happened without much effort on our part, without any particular strain; it's happened automatically, through the natural course of events. People have long complained that all we do is office work, nothing living, only dead paperwork, and that Russia has outgrown this sort of thing. Perhaps she has, but for the moment we are still the only ones who support her, build her up, and keep her from falling to pieces! For what you call bureaucratic deadweight—meaning we ourselves, as an institution, and all the things we do—is, to use a simile, the skeleton in a living organism. If the skeleton is taken apart, if the bones are scattered, the living body will perish as well. Our work may be done in a lifeless way, to be sure, yet it proceeds by a system, a principle, a great principle, if I may say so. The work may be done in tired, bureaucratic fashion; it may even be done badly and incompletely, yet in one way or another it is done; and the most important thing is that everything still stands and does not collapse—that's precisely the main point, that it still hasn't collapsed.

"I agree and am ready to concede to you that, perhaps, we aren't *every-thing,* in fact—oh, we're clever enough to realize that we don't constitute everything in Russia, these days in particular; and so I'll grant that we are not everything, yet we are still *something,* meaning something real and actually existing, although, of course, we may be partly lacking a body. Now, tell me, what do you have? What would you replace us with so that we could depart knowing that you could also provide *something* to keep it all from collapsing? You see, all those self-governments and zemstvos of yours are still nothing more than the proverbial birds in the bush: they might be beautiful, but you don't have one in your hand yet. And therefore, no matter how lovely they may be, they don't mean a thing; we, on the other hand, are not lovely; you're fed up with us, yet we are *something* and aren't meaningless. You keep blaming us for the birds in the bush: why is it, you say, that we still haven't caught one? You say that it's our fault, that we are supposedly trying to shape those beautiful birds to our image and spirit. Now, it would be a very fine thing if it really were only our fault, since we could thereby prove that we stand for a centuries-old, fundamental, and most noble principle and can transform a useless nonentity into a useful something. But believe me, it's not our fault at all, or at least it's only a very little fault of ours; the fact is that the beautiful birds themselves can't make up their minds and don't know what they'll finally be: will they be like us, or will they be something independent? They're hesitating; they have no faith in themselves and are almost at a loss. I assure you that they came to us of their own free will and not because of our pressure. It turns out that we are, so to say, like a natural magnet to which everything even now is still drawn and will be drawn for a long time to come.

"You're still not convinced? You're amused? Well, I'm willing to make a bet for whatever you'd like: just try unfolding the wings of your beautiful little birds, give them full scope to fly; send your zemstvo a proper decree, in stern language and with a file number: 'Henceforth you are independent and no longer a bureaucratic bird in the bush.' Believe me, all of them, every single bird that's there, will start begging even more to come to us, and they'll end by becoming full-blooded bureaucrats, taking on our spirit and image and copying everything from us. Even the peasant deputy would ask to be admitted; that would flatter him immensely. Not for nothing have tastes been cultivated for two centuries. And now you want us—something solid and standing on its own feet—to be exchanged for this riddle, this charade, your beautiful birds in the bush? No, I think it's better to hold on to the one modest little bird in our hand. Better that we ourselves sort things out somehow, tidy things up, introduce something new and more progressive, so to speak, in keeping with the spirit of the age; and then, why, we may even become more virtuous. But we're not going to exchange our actual, real *something* for a mirage, for some suddenly dreamt dream, since there is nothing and no one to replace us, that's for certain! It's through inertia, so to say, that we resist being abolished. This inertia of ours is something precious because, to tell the truth, these days it's the only thing holding everything together.

"And so cutting our staff even to thirty-eight from forty (never mind from forty to four) would be a most harmful and even immoral measure.

You'd save a few pennies and destroy a principle. So go ahead and abolish or change our formula, if your conscience permits you to make such a threatening move: but don't you see that this would be a betrayal of all our Russian Europeanism and enlightenment? It would be a denial of the fact that we are also a state, that we are also Europeans; it would be a betrayal of Peter the Great! And, you know, your liberals (and ours, too, for that matter), who in the newspapers so zealously support the zemstvos against the bureaucracy, are essentially contradicting themselves. After all, the zemstvos and, indeed, all these new things set up in the spirit of populism, are those very same 'principles of the People,' or at least the rudimentary expression of those 'principles,' that our 'Russian party' (you may have heard that it was given that name in Berlin), which is so hated in Europe, is shouting about; these are the same 'principles' that our Russian liberalism and Europeanism so furiously deny and ridicule; they refuse even to acknowledge that these principles exist! Oh, liberalism truly fears those principles: what if they actually do exist and come to be realized? Why, that would be a real surprise! That means that all your Europeans are actually on our side, and we on theirs, and they should have understood this long ago and committed it to memory. If you like, we are not only at one with them, we are entirely one and the same thing: those Europeans of yours have our spirit within them; they even bear our very image, and that's the truth!

"Let me add just this: Europe—meaning Russian Europe, Europe and Russia—consists exclusively of us, and us alone. It is we; we are the incarnation of the entire formula of Russian Europeanism, and we contain it all within ourselves. We alone are its interpreters. And I can't understand why they shouldn't be given proper medals for their Europeanism when we are so flawlessly merging with them. They would be pleased to wear them, and they might even find us more attractive thereby. But we don't know how to do such things. And they abuse us—truly a case of kith not recognizing kin! So as to put an end to all your zemstvos and all these other innovations, let me tell you once and for all: no, sir! This is a lengthy matter, not a brief one. It requires its own culture beforehand, its own history—perhaps one that is also two centuries' long. Well, let's say a century, or even half a century, since we now live in the age of telegraphs and railways and all relationships are speeded up and made easier. Yet this is still a matter for half a century, it can't happen at once. 'At once,' 'right now'—these are nasty little Russian phrases. Nothing comes into being 'right now,' except for people like us. And such will be the case for a long time."

At this point my bureaucrat fell silent, with a proud and dignified air, and, you know, I didn't even argue with him because there really did seem to be a "something" in his words, a kind of melancholy truth that actually exists. Of course, inwardly I didn't agree with him. Besides, it is only people who are on their way out who speak in such a tone. But still, there was "something" in his words. . . .

Article 3, two extracts. Geok-Tepe. What Does Asia Mean to Us?

Geok-Tepe has been taken; the Turkomans have been defeated, and although they have not yet been fully pacified, our victory is beyond doubt. Both society and the press have been jubilant. Yet it was not long ago that society, and the press as well, in part, were remarkably indifferent to this affair, particularly after General Lomakin's failure and at the beginning of the preparations for a second offensive. "Why do we have to go there? Why all this fuss about Asia? How much money it costs us, while we have famine, diphtheria, no schools, and so on." [. . .]

"For what, and for what future? What need is there for some future annexation of Asia? What are we going to do there?"

There is a need because Russia is not only in Europe but in Asia as well; because the Russian is not only a European but an Asian as well. Moreover, we have more hopes in Asia, perhaps, than in Europe. Moreover, it is Asia, perhaps, that provides the main outlet for our future destiny!

I can anticipate the indignation with which some people will read this reactionary proposition of mine (but for me it is axiomatic). Yes, if there is one most important root we must make healthy, then it is precisely our view of Asia. We must cast aside this servile fear that Europe will call us Asiatic barbarians and say that we are more Asian than European. This shame that Europe will consider us Asians has been hanging over us for almost two centuries now. But the shame has become particularly strong in us during the present nineteenth century and has almost reached the point of panic, almost the kind of fear that the new words "metal and brimstone" once aroused in Moscow merchants' wives. This mistaken shame of ours, this mistaken view of ourselves as exclusively Europeans and not Asians (and we have never ceased to be the latter)—this shame and this mistaken view has cost us dearly, very dearly, over these two centuries, and we have paid for it by the loss of our spiritual independence, by the failures of our European policies, and, at last, by money—by God knows how much money we have spent proving to Europe that we are only Europeans and not Asians. [. . .]

Article 4, two extracts. Questions and Answers

[. . .] "On the Eastern Question at the moment I would say the following: in political circles in Russia at the moment we could probably find not a single political mind that would consider it a sound proposition that Constantinople should be ours (except, perhaps, in some distant and still enigmatic future). And if that's so, then why should we wait any longer? The whole essence of the Eastern Question at this moment lies in the alliance of Germany and Austria and in the Austrian annexations of Turkish territory, which Prince Bismarck encourages. We can and will protest only in extreme cases, of course, but so long as these two nations are united, what can we do now without disrupting our lives enormously? [. . .]

"Well, what about England? You've forgotten England. When she sees our push into Asia, she'll panic immediately."

" 'If you're afraid of England, then don't leave your house.' That's my reply, to recast an old proverb in modern terms. She'll have nothing new to cause her panic in any case, since she's in panic over the same old things even now. On the contrary, it is now that we can keep her confused and ignorant about the future, and she's expecting only the worst from us. When she does realize the real nature of all our movements in Asia, then, perhaps, a lot of her fears will be alleviated. . . . However, I have to concede that her fears won't be alleviated; she has a long way to go before that happens. But, I repeat, if you're afraid of England, then don't leave your house! And so, once more, long live the victory at Geok-Tepe! Long live Skobelev and his good lads, and eternal memory to the heroes who were 'struck off the roll!' We shall inscribe their names in our roll."
[These are the concluding lines of *A Writer's Diary.*—Ed.]

NOTES

The following notes are intended to provide the English-speaking reader with at least minimal background information about references in the text. The most important source is provided by the voluminous and quite excellent annotations included in the USSR Academy of Sciences' thirty-volume edition of Dostoevsky's *Complete Works*, F. M. Dostoevsky, *Polnoe sobranie sochinenii v tridstati tomakh* (Leningrad: Nauka, 1972–88), abbreviated hereafter as *PSS*. However, these notes are based on a set of assumptions that are not always applicable to nonspecialist readers in the West: Soviet readers need not be told about Belinsky or Nekrasov, for example, whereas the Western reader might. Thus, I have not provided a complete translation of the notes in *PSS* but have used them, rather, as a guide. I have attempted to check independently each reference derived from this source, but this has not always been possible: many of the nineteenth-century Russian newspapers Dostoevsky read so avidly are not available in North America and are difficult to access even in the Soviet Union. Additional material was derived from specific works cited in the notes themselves, and from the works of individual writers whom Dostoevsky mentions in the *Diary*. The sources listed below were repeatedly consulted.

All dates mentioned in the notes are old style (o.s.), i.e., twelve days behind the Gregorian calendar, unless otherwise indicated.

Sources

Baedeker, Karl. *Russia, with Teheran, Port Arthur, and Peking: Handbook for Travellers*. Leipzig: Karl Baedeker, 1914.

Bol'shaia entsiklopediia [Great encyclopedia]. Ed. S. N. Iuzhakov. 22 vols. St. Petersburg: Prosveshchenie, 1896.

Bol'shaia sovetskaia entsiklopediia [Great Soviet encyclopedia]. Ed. O. Iu. Shmidt. 65 vols. Moscow: Sovetskaia entsiklopediia, 1926–47.

536 NOTES

Bol'shaia sovetskaia entsiklopediia [Great Soviet encyclopedia]. 3d ed. Ed. A. M. Prokorov. 30 vols. Moscow: Sovetskaia entsiklopediia, 1970–78.

Dostoevskaia, A. G. *Vospominaniia* [Memoirs]. Moscow: Khudozhestvennaia literatura, 1971.

Encyclopaedia Britannica. 11th ed. 29 vols. Cambridge: Cambridge University Press, 1910–11.

Encyclopaedia Britannica. 14th ed. 24 vols. Chicago, London, and Toronto: William Benton, 1958.

New Encyclopaedia Britannica. 15th ed. 32 vols. Chicago: Encyclopaedia Britannica, 1987.

Entsiklopedicheskii slovar' [Encyclopedic dictionary]. 82 vols. St. Petersburg: Brokgauz and Efron, 1890–1904.

Entsiklopedicheskii slovar' [Encyclopedic dictionary]. 58 vols. St. Petersburg and Moscow: Granat, 1910–40.

Frank, Joseph. *Dostoevsky: The Seeds of Revolt, 1821–1849.* Princeton, N.J.: Princeton University Press, 1976.

———. *Dostoevsky: The Years of Ordeal, 1850–1859.* Princeton, N.J.: Princeton University Press, 1983.

———. *Dostoevsky: The Stir of Liberation, 1860–1865.* Princeton, N.J.: Princeton University Press, 1986.

Der Grosse Brockhaus. 15 vols. Wiesbaden: F. A. Brockhaus, 1977–81.

Grossman, Leonid. *Seminarii po Dostoevskomu: Materialy, bibliografiia i kommentarii* [Seminars on Dostoevsky: Source materials, bibliography, commentaries]. Moscow and Petrograd: Gos. Izdatel'stvo, 1922.

———. *Zhizn' i trudy F. M. Dostoevskogo: biografiia v datakh i dokumentakh* [The life and works of F. M. Dostoevsky: A biography in dates and documents]. Moscow and Leningrad: Academia, 1935.

Guedalla, Philip. *The Second Empire.* London: Hodder and Stoughton, 1932.

Istoriia Moskvy [The history of Moscow]. 6 vols. Moscow: AN SSSR, 1952–59.

Istoriia russkoi literatury XIX veka [A history of Russian literature of the nineteenth century]. Ed. D. N. Ovsianiko-Kulikovsky. 5 vols. Moscow: Mir, 1908–10.

Kratkaia literaturnaia entsiklopediia [Short literary encyclopedia]. Ed. A. A. Surkov. 9 vols. Moscow: Sovetskaia entsiklopediia 1926–78.

Mochulsky, Konstantin. *Dostoevsky: His Life and Work.* Trans. and intro. by Michael Minihan. Princeton, N.J.: Princeton University Press, 1967.

Modern Encyclopedia of Russian and Soviet History. Ed. Joseph L. Wieczynski. Gulf Breeze, Fla.: Academic International Press, 1976–.

Modern Encyclopedia of Russian and Soviet Literature. Ed. Harry B. Weber. Gulf Breeze, Fla.: Academic International Press, 1977–.

Nechaeva, *V. S. Zhurnal M. M. i F. M. Dostoevskikh "Vremia," 1861–1863* [M. M. and F. M. Dostoevsky's journal "Time," 1861–1863]. Moscow: Nauka, 1972.

———. *Zhurnal M. M. i F. M. Dostoevskikh "Epokha," 1864–1865* [M. M. and F. M. Dostoevsky's journal "Epoch," 1864–1865]. Moscow: Nauka, 1975.

Ocherki istorii Leningrada [Outlines of the history of Leningrad]. Ed. M. P. Viatkin et al. 7 vols. Moscow and Leningrad: AN SSSR, 1955–89.

Petrovich, Michael Boro. *A History of Modem Serbia, 1804–1918.* 2 vols. New York: Harcourt, Brace, Jovanovich, 1976.

Abbreviations

BV	*Birzhevye vedomosti* [The Stock Exchange News]—liberal daily
D	*Delo* [The Cause]—radical monthly
DP	*Dnevnik pisatelia* [A Writer's Diary]
E	*Epokha* [The Epoch]—St. Petersburg monthly edited by Dostoevsky (1864–65)
G	*Golos* [The Voice]—St. Petersburg daily, moderately liberal
Gr	*Grazhdanin* [The Citizen]—conservative weekly edited by Dostoevsky (1873)
MV	*Moskovskie vedomosti* [Moscow News]—conservative daily
NV	*Novoe vremia* [New Times]—leading St. Petersburg daily
OZ	*Otechestvennye zapiski* [Notes of the Fatherland]—monthly, edited by N. N. Nekrasov and M. Saltykov-Shchedrin (1868–84)
PG	*Peterburgskaia gazeta* [The Petersburg Gazette]—popular daily
RM	*Russkii mir* [The Russian World]—conservative daily
RV	*Russkii vestnik* [The Russian Messenger]—conservative monthly; a leading literary journal of the nineteenth century
S	*Sovremennik* [The Contemporary]—radical monthly, edited by N. Chernyshevsky and N. Dobroliubov (1856–62)
SV	*Sankt-Peterburgskie vedomosti* [St. Petersburg News]—conservative daily
V	*Vremia* [Time]—monthly, edited by F. M. and M. M. Dostoevsky (1861–63)
VE	*Vestnik Evropy* [The European Messenger]—liberal monthly
Z	*Zaria* [Dawn]—neo-Slavophile monthly

1873.1: Introduction

The Citizen: Dostoevsky's appointment as editor of *Gr* was confirmed by the Main Administration of Press Affairs on December 20, 1872. His tenure as editor began on January 1, 1873.

Chinese emperor: *MV*, no. 315, December 13, 1872, carried an account of the elaborate ceremonies accompanying the wedding of the emperor of China, T"ung-Chi, which took place on October 16, 1872.

Meshchersky, Vladimir Petrovich, prince (1839–1914), publisher, political figure, and extreme conservative.

Bismarck: Meshchersky's novel *Odin iz nashikh Bismarkov* [One of our Bismarcks] was appearing in *Gr* in 1872–73.

Moscow News: *MV* was published by the conservative M. N. Katkov (1818–87), who frequently wrote its editorials.

The Voice: *G* was published by A. A. Kraevsky (1810–99) and frequently exchanged barbs with *Gr*.

From the Other Shore: Dostoevsky met Alexander Herzen (1812–70), writer, journalist, political thinker, and nineteenth-century Russia's most famous political emigré, in London in July 1862. Herzen's *S togo berega* [From the other shore] (1850) conveys his disillusionment after the failure of the European revolutions of 1848.

Pogodin, Mikhail Petrovich (1800–75), Russian historian, journalist, and panslavist. His article on Herzen appeared in *Z*, no. 2, 1870.

Belinsky, Vissarion (1811–48), nineteenth-century Russia's most famous literary critic. Herzen relates this story in *Byloe i dumy* [My past and thoughts], pt. 2, chap. 16. Belinsky's article, "Russkaia literatura v 1841 godu" [Russian literature in 1841] appeared in *OZ*, no. 1, 1842.

1873.3: Environment

new (just) courts: In 1864 occurred a major reform of the Russian judicial system, one of the main features of which was the institution of trial by jury.

I was in prison: Dostoevsky was sentenced to four years of hard labor, followed by a term of Siberian exile, on December 22, 1849; his period of hard labor ended on February 15, 1854.

Not long ago: Dostoevsky lived in Europe from April 1867 to July 1871.

The woman's story: The trial of the peasant N. A. Saiapin, accused of abusing his wife, occurred in the Tambov circuit court on September 30, 1872.

hang by the heels: The daughter's plight, as described by Dostoevsky, roused

a group of Moscow ladies to take steps to have her sent to a trade school in
Moscow.

1873.6: Bobok

my portrait: A portrait of Dostoevsky, by V. G. Perov, was exhibited in the
Academy of Arts in early 1873. A commentator in *G*, no. 14, 1873, noted:
"This is a portrait of a man exhausted by a serious ailment."

Collegiate Councilor: Rank of the 6th class, equivalent to the rank of colonel in
the army.

the smell, the smell!: Dostoevsky's narrator makes an untranslatable pun here: *dukh*
(spirit), which colloquially can mean "smell," and *dukhovnyi*, "ecclesiastic."

people trained as engineers: As in Dostoevsky's novel *The Devils* [Besy] (1871),
where Kirillov, an engineer, is involved in a political conspiracy and has
developed philosophical ideas.

Moscow Exhibition: In the summer of 1872 a polytechnical exhibition
commemorating the two hundredth anniversary of the birth of Peter I was
held in Moscow.

bread crumbs on the ground: M. M. Bakhtin's explanation: "bread may
be crumbled and left on the earth: this is a planting of the seed, an act of
fecundation. It must not be left on the floor, since that is infertile." (M. M.
Bakhtin, *Problemy poetiki Dostoevskogo*, 3d ed. (Moscow: Khudozhestvennaia
literatura, 1972), p. 238.

Suvorin's *Almanac*: A. S. Suvorin, *Russkii kalendar' na 1872 god* (St. Petersburg,
1872). A reference book and compilation of facts about Russia; the fourth
section dealt with popular customs and beliefs.

Your Excellency: An official in the civil service of the third and fourth ranks,
equivalent to a lieutenant- or major-general in the army, would be addressed
as "Your Excellency" [*vashe prevoskhoditel'stvo*] and, although not a military
man, would be called a general nonetheless, particularly by those attempting
to flatter him.

"Rest, beloved ashes . . .": *Pokoisia, milyi priakh, do radostnogo utra!* was the
epitaph on the grave of the Russian writer and historian N. M. Karamzin
(1766–1826), and was frequently reused.

Court Councilor: 7th rank, equivalent to lieutenant-colonel in the army.

forty-day memorial: Memorial prayers [*sorokoviny, sorochiny, sorokoust*] were
said forty days after a death. It was popularly believed that during these forty
days the soul of the deceased was in torment.

rice porridge: A porridge of rice or wheat with honey [*kut'ia*], a symbol of resurrection, was customarily eaten after the funeral.

Actual Privy Councilor: 2d rank, equivalent to general in the army.

The Vale of Jehoshaphat was considered the site at which the Last Judgment would take place (Joel 3:12).

Ekk, Vladimir Egorovich (1818–75), professor and well-known physician.

Botkin, Sergei Petrovich (1832–89), eminent physician and scholar, one of the finest diagnosticians of his day.

State Councilor: A rank of the 5th class, equivalent to the rank between that of colonel and major-general in the army.

Lebeziatnikov is also the name of an obsequious character in *Crime and Punishment*. The name suggests the verb *lebezit'*, "to fawn upon someone, ingratiate oneself."

Bobok means "bean."

1873.8: A Half-Letter from "A Certain Person"

"a certain person": The author here is therefore the same fictional character who narrated "Bobok" (1873.6). Later in the *Diary* another character, "the paradoxicalist," makes more than one appearance.

my supposed literary enemies: Prominent among Dostoevsky's literary "enemies" here are N. K. Mikhailovsky, who in *OZ*, no. 1, 1873, had taken issue with Dostoevsky's suggestion, made in 1873.2, that socialism was necessarily atheistic and revolutionary. Socialists, Mikhailovsky argues, have no uniform views on religious matters; "Socialism in Russia," he stated, "is conservative." Another "enemy," V. P. Burenin, had written a critical review of *The Devils* (*SV*, nos. 6 and 13, 1873). Throughout much of 1872, *OZ* and *SV* had also carried on a public quarrel between Mikhailovsky and Burenin. Burenin is one of the prime targets of "A Certain Person's" abuse, but his letter is also directed generally at the rancorous polemics and personal attacks that had been common among journals and journalists since the 1860s. A few excerpts from one of Burenin's attacks on Mikhailovsky show that "A Certain Person's" portrayal of this literary squabble is not unduly exaggerated: "Tell me, Mr. Mikhailovsky, are you feeling all right? Do you now think that you have crushed me like a bedbug? What's now being spattered, after your reading of this column—is it my 'bedbuggish blood' or tears of impotent fury squeezed from your tender soul . . . ? . . . From here I can see Mr. Mikhailovsky, his face now red, now pale, struck with fear and heartache as he casts his eye over these opening remarks. . . . In despair he pulls his hair, and a horrible thought runs through his mind: 'My God, this Z. [Burenin] wants to make me out a madman in front of my readers . . .'" (*SV*, no. 205, 1872).

Dear old Krylov: Krylov, Ivan Andreevich (1769?–1844), Russian fabulist; many of his fables are frequently quoted.

Palkin's: A tavern on the corner of Nevsky and Liteiny Prospects.

"I fear amidst war's strident clamor": The verse comes from Pushkin's "Iz Gafiza" [From Hafiz] (1829).

Berg's Theater in St. Petersburg staged mainly light entertainment.

Antropka appears at the end of Turgenev's story "Pevtsy" [Singers] (1850).

Dussault's: A fashionable restaurant on St. Petersburg's Bolshaia Morskaia Street.

the last day of Carnival: The last Sunday before Lent was traditionally the day upon which one sought forgiveness of one's acquaintances.

1873.9: Apropos of the Exhibition

the exhibition: Some hundred paintings and sculptures were exhibited in March 1873 at the Academy of Arts in St. Petersburg.

Hood, Thomas (1799–1845), English poet. His "Song of the Shirt" (1843) is a poem of social protest against the exploitation of women's work.

two latest poems by Nekrasov: The poems are "Kniaginia Trubetskaia" [Princess Trubetskaia], *OZ*, no. 4, 1872, and "Kniaginia M. N. Volkonskaia" [Princess M. N. Volkonskaia], *OZ*, no. 1, 1873, published under the common title *Russkie zhenshchiny* [Russian women]. They deal with the Decembrists' wives.

Repin, Ilia Efimovich (1844–1930). His *Burlaki na Volge* [Barge-haulers on the Volga] (1870–73) was the most discussed painting at the Exhibition. See O. A. Liaskovskaia, *Il'ia Efimovich Repin: zhizn i tvorchestvo* [Ilia Efimovich Repin: Life and work] (Moscow: Iskusstvo, 1982), p. 59.

stuffed with porridge: Dostoevsky may have taken this detail from Leskov's *Cathedral Folk*, which had appeared in *RV*, nos. 4–7, 1872.

Bronnikov, Fedor Andreevich (1827–1902). His painting *Gimn pifagoreitsev voskhodiashchemu solntsu* [The hymn of the Pythagoreans to the rising sun] (1869) was in the pseudoclassical academic style.

Ge, Nikolai Nikolaevich (1831–94). His painting *Petr I doprashivaet tsarevicha Alekseia Petrovicha v Petergofe* [Peter I interrogates the tsarevich Aleksei Petrovich at Peterhof] (1871) was among those exhibited (see *Nikolai Ivanovich Ge* [Moscow: Iskusstvo, 1978], plate 31). His earlier *Tainaia vecheria* [The Last Supper] (1863) was extremely controversial because of what many considered a mundane treatment of an event having profound religious significance. See V. Porudominskii, *Nikolai Ge* (Moscow: Iskusstvo, 1970), p. 32, plate 1.

1873.15: Something about Lying

Liebig, Justus von (1803–73), German chemist. His work on the chemistry of life processes was particularly influential in Russia.

1873.16: One of Today's Falsehoods

Nechaev, Sergei (1847–82), Russian revolutionary and conspirator. On November 26, 1869, Nechaev and four members of his group murdered a student of the Moscow Agricultural College and former member of the group, Ivanov. Nechaev himself escaped abroad, but many of his followers were arrested. Dostoevsky attended their trial in July 1871. In *The Devils*, the ruthless and cynical methods of Peter Verkhovensky are modeled on those of Nechaev. The article appeared in *RM*, no. 301, November 13, 1873.

one Nechaev: In part 2, chap. 8 of *The Devils* Dostoevsky's manipulative schemer, Pyotr Stepanovich, says this to Stavrogin as he explains the tactics he plans to use to seize political power.

Blanc (Jean Joseph Charles) Louis (1811–82), French politician and historian. His study *L'Organisation du travail* (1839) had argued for the equalization of wages. He became a member of the Provisional Government in 1848 and was instrumental in having the government guarantee that all workers could earn their livelihood. Such proposals held great appeal for workers but alarmed the middle classes. On May 15, 1848, a large crowd of workers invaded the National Assembly and disrupted its functioning; Blanc was accused of instigating the affair. His parliamentary immunity was lifted and he had to flee to England. His friend and colleague François Arago helped save him. Dominique François Jean Arago (1786–1853), French physicist and politician, director of the French Royal Observatory, minister of war and marine in the Provisional Government.

Considérant, Victor Prosper (1808–93), French Utopian socialist. His journals *Le Phalanstère* (1832–34) and *La Phalange* (1836–49) popularized the ideas of Fourier. Pierre Joseph Proudhon (1809–65), French socialist and political writer. His treatise *Qu'est-ce que la propriété?* concluded that "La propriété, c'est le vol [property is theft]."

Belinsky: See notes to 1873.1.

Karamzin: See notes to 1873.6.

Kel'siev, Vasilii Ivanovich (1835–72), Russian journalist and revolutionary. Writing in the journal *Zaria* [Dawn], no. 3, 1861, he tells the story of the former cavalry officer Burovin, who made his way on foot, penniless and without documents, from St. Petersburg to London.

In *My Past and Thoughts*, pt. 7, chap. 3, Herzen tells of a young Russian landowner, P. A. Bakhmetev, who in 1857 went to New Zealand to found a socialist colony.

inspection: In 1871–72 an educational reform, carried out by the very conservative minister of education D. A. Tolstoi (1823–89), limited access to universities and emphasized the teaching of Latin, Greek, and mathematics in secondary schools. Study of the natural sciences, which were seen as a source of inspiration for revolutionary ideas among students, was minimized.

[Announcement]

This announcement appeared in *G*, no. 352, December 21, 1875, and at the end of the January 1876 issue of *DP*.

January 1876, 1.1: In Place of a Foreword. On the Great and Small Bears, on Great Goethe's Prayer, and, Generally, on Bad Habits.

Khlestakov: Gogol's inspired liar in his play *Revizor* [The Inspector-General].

In Goethe's *The Sorrows of Young Werther*, a passage from the last letter Werther wrote before his suicide reads: "I walk over to the window, my dearest one, and look out. Through the storm clouds flying by, I can still see a few stars in the eternal sky. No, you will not fall. The Eternal One carries you in his heart, as he carries me. I can see the handle of the Big Dipper, my favorite of all the constellations. When I left you that night, as I walked out the gate, it stood in the sky facing me. In what a state of intoxication have I been often when I looked at it. Then I would lift my hand and make a sign of it, a sacred marker for my present bliss" (Johann Wolfgang von Goethe, *The Sorrows of Young Werther and Selected Writings*, trans. Catherine Hutter [New York: The New American Library/Signet Classic, 1962], p. 125).

"Mr. X" (*Neznakomets*) was the pseudonym of A. S. Suvorin (1834–1912), journalist and publisher. His column of January 4, 1876 (*NV*, no. 3), commented on the uniformly liberal tendency of Russian newspapers of the day, noting that Dostoevsky's *Diary* would provide a refreshing change.

"Je suis un homme heureux . . .": Dostoevsky's paraphrase of the townspeople's opinion of Jean Valjean as mayor of Montreuil-sur-Mer, in *Les Misérables* (pt. 1, bk. 5, chap. 3).

January 1876, 1.2: A Future Novel. Another "Accidental Family."

The Artists' Club: A favorite gathering spot for Petersburg artists and writers. *G,* no. 356, December 25, 1875, noted: "On Friday, December 26, a large children's festival—a Christmas tree—will take place in the Petersburg Assembly of Artists, with free gifts for all children, acrobats, magicians, two musical orchestras, toboggan slides, electrical illumination, and much more. The Christmas parties of the Petersburg Assembly of Artists have long been renowned for the beauty of their appointments."

Nekrasov: Dostoevsky published his *Raw Youth* in Nekrasov's *OZ* in 1875; his three previous novels had appeared in Katkov's *RV.*

Fathers and Sons: Dostoevsky had been thinking of a novel about fathers and children since the early 1870s. His *Raw Youth* realized at least part of his plan; relations between father and sons are also central to *The Brothers Karamazov.*

Perova, Avdotia Ivanovna, was murdered by her common-law husband on January 14, 1876.

"all the impressions of existence . . .": A paraphrase of lines from Pushkin's poem "Demon" [The demon] (1823).

January 1876.1.3: The Christmas Party at the Artists' Club. Children Who Think and Children Who Are Helped Along. A "Gluttonous Boy." "Oui" Girls. Jostling Raw Youths. A Moscow Captain in a Hurry.

"gluttonous boy": Pushkin, *Eugene Onegin* (1825–33), "The Travels of Onegin."

Noblemen's Club: *PG* of January 3, 1876, carried an item describing a fistfight between two merchants in the Noblemen's Club and a disturbance caused by a drunken army officer at a ball.

Skvoznik-Dmukhanovskys: Characters from Gogol's *The Inspector-General.* Skvoznik-Dmukhanovsky is mayor of the town, Derzhimorda is a policeman; both are portrayed as crude Russian types.

high-society balls: In act 3 of Gogol's *Dead Souls,* Khlestakov boasts that he has attended a society ball in Petersburg where a watermelon costing 700 rubles was served.

Hypocrisy: A maxim from François de la Rochefoucauld, *Réflexions ou sentences et maximes morales* (1665): "L'hypocrisie est un hommage que le vice rend à la vertu."

January 1876, 1.4: The Golden Age in Your Pocket

Piron, Alexis (1689-1773). French poet, renowned for his epigrams and witty ripostes.

January 1876, 2.1: The Boy with His Hand Out

"... and pitilessly": A paraphrase of lines from N. A. Nekrasov's poem "Detstvo" [Childhood] (1844), one portion of which describes a peasant boy being forced to drink vodka by his elders.

January 1876, 2.2: The Boy at Christ's Christmas Party

As noted by G. M. Fridlender ("Sviatochnyi rasskaz Dostoevskogo i ballada Riukkerta" [Dostoevsky's Christmas Story and F. Rückert's Ballad], in *Mezhdunarodnye sviazi russkoi literatury* [Russian literature's international links] [Moscow-Leningrad: AN SSSR, 1963], pp. 370-90), Dostoevsky borrowed the basis for this story from the ballad of the German poet Friedrich Rückert (1788-1866), "Des fremden Kindes heiliger Christs" (1816).

famine: A series of poor harvests in Samara Province between 1871 and 1873 led to a disastrous famine.

All the more: i.e., as Dostoevsky promised in his "Announcement," above.

January 1876, 2.3: A Colony of Young Offenders. Dark Individuals. The Transformation of Blemished Souls into Immaculate Ones. Measures Acknowledged as Most Expedient Thereto. Little and Bold Friends of Mankind.

Powder Works: Dostoevsky, accompanied by the lawyer and writer A. F. Koni, visited the colony on December 27, 1875.

P. A. R——sky: Rovinsky, Pavel Apollonovich (1831-1916), ethnographer, traveler, and journalist. His accounts of his travels in Mongolia and Serbia appeared in *VE* in the early 1870s.

The "Lithuanian Castle," located at the corner of the Moika and Nikolsky canals in St. Petersburg, housed a prison that held both adults and (until 1875) juveniles.

all our schools: The educational reforms of 1864 virtually abolished corporal punishment in schools.

Sevastopol Tales: L. N. Tolstoy, "Sevastopol v dekabre 1854"; "Sevastopol v mae 1855"; "Sevastopol v avguste 1855" [Sevastopol in December 1854; Sevastopol in May 1855; Sevastopol in August 1855] (1855-56); *Vechera na khutore bliz Dikanki* [Evenings on a farm near Dikanka] (1831), Nikolai Gogol's first collection of stories; M. Iu. Lermontov, *Pesnia pro tsaria Ivana Vasil'evicha, molodogo oprichnika i udalogo kuptsa Kalashnikova* [The tale of Kalashnikov] (1838). Aleksei Vasilevich Kolstov (1808–42), Russian poet who wrote verse in a folk style.

the duck: Dostoevsky refers to the visual method of education favored by some "progressive" teachers. The pupils were asked, for example, why a duck had feathers and were gradually led to deduce the reason.

"he who labors": A paraphrase of Matthew 10:10: "For the workman is worthy of his meat. . . ."

Potugin, a character from Turgenev's novel *Dym* [Smoke] (1867). In chapter 14, he argues forcefully that Russia has made no real contribution to world civilization and expresses views that are strongly Westernizing.

January 1876, 3.1: The Russian Society for the Protection of Animals. The Government Courier. Demon-Vodka. The Itch for Debauch and Vorobev. From the End or from the Beginning?

The Russian Society for the Protection of Animals was founded on October 4, 1865, in St. Petersburg; branches were later established in other centers. Its president through the first decade of its existence was Prince A. A. Suvorov-Ryminsky (1804–82). In 1871 the society's efforts helped pass a law levying a fine of up to ten rubles for cruel treatment of domestic animals.

Pushkin had died: Dostoevsky errs here: Pushkin died on January 29, 1837.

flogging: After 1861, specified civil and criminal offenses committed by peasants had been tried in rural district (*volostnoi*) courts, whose members were chosen from among the peasants themselves. Flogging was frequently chosen as a punishment in such courts.

railway disaster: On December 24, 1875, a train carrying army recruits on the line between Elisavetgrad (now Kirovgrad) and Odessa derailed, killing sixty-six and injuring fifty-four. The subsequent inquiry revealed widespread shortcomings in the administration of the railway line.

In July of 1873, A. S. Suvorin (see note to January 1876, 1.1), writing in *SV*, no. 199, reported that Golubev, manager of the Orel-Vitebsk railway, had expelled the passengers from a first-class compartment that he wanted for his own use. Golubev denied this accusation and eventually sued Suvorin for slander. The case was not heard until September 1874.

penknife: The incident, which took place on January 5, 1876, was widely reported in the press.

January 1876, 3.2: Spiritualism. Something about Devils. The
Extraordinary Cleverness of Devils, If Only These Are Devils.

The Decembrists were the group of young men, mostly army officers, who attempted a coup on December 14, 1825. Five were executed, many others exiled to Siberia for long terms.

Annenkov, Ivan Aleksandrovich (1802–78), Russian army officer, Decembrist, and memoirist. *Les Mémoires d'un maître d'armes* (1840), by Alexandre Dumas-père, was based very loosely on the experiences of a French fencing master, Grisier, who had given fencing lessons to Annenkov in the 1820s. Muravev-Apostol, Matvei Ivanovich (1793–1886), brother of S. I. Muravev-Apostol, one of the five Decembrists who were executed. Petr Nikolaevich Svistunov (1803–89). Mikhail Aleksandrovich Nazimov (1800–88), exiled 1825–56.

devils and spiritualism: Spiritualism was frequently discussed in the Russian press in the 1870s. Seances, with table-turning and attempts to communicate with spirits, were not an uncommon form of entertainment in some social circles; the emperor Alexander II himself had seances conducted in the Winter Palace. Among the leading proponents of spiritualism were A. N. Aksakov (1832–1903) and N. P. Vagner (1829–1907). The noted chemist D. I. Mendeleev was instrumental in organizing a Scholarly Commission, in which he participated, to study spiritualism. The commission attended a number of seances and exposed fraudulent practices by several mediums.

Eddy, Horatio, and Eddy, William, brothers who owned a small farm in the township of Chittenden, Vermont. Various psychic phenomena occurring at their homestead aroused considerable interest in the 1870s. Dostoevsky combines their name with Harriet Beecher Stowe's *Uncle Tom's Cabin,* a novel widely known in Russia. See Sir Arthur Conan Doyle, *The History of Spiritualism* (London: Cassell, 1926), 1:259ff.

Gogol: *G,* no. 6, January 6, 1876, reported that a respected Moscow intellectual (whom the newspaper did not identify) had become a medium and had claimed that Gogol had dictated to him portions of volume 2 of *Dead Souls* from the manuscript Gogol had burned. A number of people in Moscow had seen portions of the manuscript, and some of them agreed that its style did indeed resemble Gogol's.

"Who can be likened ... ?": Dostoevsky here combines two verses from the Book of
Revelations, chapter 13, verse 4: "... Who is like unto this beast?" and chapter
13, verse 13: "... and he doeth great wonders, so that he maketh fire to come
down from heaven on the earth in the sight of man." The same verses are quoted
by his Grand Inquisitor in *The Brothers Karamazov*, bk. 2, pt. 5, chap. 5.

the pope himself: Dostoevsky has in mind Bismarck's conflict with the Catholic
church during the 1870s, which was partly prompted by the declaration of
papal infallibility of 1870. His *Kulturkampf* aimed at limiting the power of
the Catholic church and making it subservient to the state. The Jesuits were
expelled from Germany, and a number of priests and bishops were imprisoned.
In his encyclical of February 5 (n.s.), 1875, Pope Pius IX excommunicated
German Catholics who opposed the notion of papal infallibility and accepted
teaching positions from the state.

Crookes and Olcott: Crookes, William (1832–1919), noted English chemist.
He became interested in making a scientific study of spiritualism and, after
seances with a medium, concluded that a certain "psychic force" actually
did exist. Henry Steel Olcott (1832–1907), American lawyer and journalist,
cofounder (with Mme. Blavatsky) of the Theosophical Society. In 1874 he
was sent by the New York *Daily Graphic* to write a series of articles about the
psychic powers of the brothers Eddy.

Ivan Filippovich: Dostoevsky here apparently combines the names of two figures
from the Flagellant sect, Ivan Timofeevich Suslov and Danila Fillipovich.
The name may also reflect the Moscow "prophet" Ivan Iakovlevich Koreisha
(1780–1861), whom Dostoevsky portrays as Semen Iakovlevich in his novel
The Devils.

The Tuileries Palace was burned on orders of the Paris Commune during fighting
in the Paris revolution of 1871.

Polonsky, Iakov Petrovich (1819–98), Russian poet. His poem "Starye i novye
dukhi" [Old spirits and new] appeared in December 1875 and contrasted the
"new spirits" that caused tables to turn with the old ones that had inspired
humanity for centuries.

January 1876, 3.3: A Word Apropos of My Biography

Mr. V. Z.: The author of the articles on Dostoevsky and his brother, Mikhail,
was Vladimir Rafailovich Zotov (1821–78), writer, journalist, and historian of
literature. Zotov's article is often very critical of Dostoevsky's writings.

1822: Dostoevsky himself errs here. He was born on October 30, 1821.

February 1876, 1.2: On Love of the People. An Essential Contract with the People.

Slavic Committees were founded in St. Petersburg in 1856 and in Moscow in 1858 with the aim of promoting education, culture, and religion in non-Russian Slavic countries. The committees subsequently took on a more political and panslavist role and helped to rally Russian support for the Serbs in their uprising against Turkish rule. K. S. Aksakov (1817–60), writer, memoirist, and one of the founders of the Slavophile school; he was an active member of the Moscow Slavic Committee during the first years of its existence. *Fraternal Aid* [Bratskaia pomoch' postradavshim semeistvam Bosnii i Gertsogoviny], an anthology published to raise funds to aid families displaced by the Slavic uprising against the Turks in Bosnia and Herzegovina, was put out by the St. Petersburg section of the committee in 1876. Aksakov's article, "O sovremennom cheloveke" [On contemporary man], argued that successful communal living demanded a high degree of education or development [*obrazovanie*] and that the Russian peasants had achieved this through years of participation in their peasant commune, the *mir*.

Sergei of Radonezh, Saint (c. 1321–92), founder of the Trinity Monastery (located near present-day Zagorsk). St. Sergei was also noted for his efforts in consolidating the power of the Duchy of Moscow and for promoting the unity of Russian duchies before the Tatar threat. Saint Theodosius of Pechersk (d. 1074), founder of the Kiev Crypt Monastery. Saint Tikhon of Zadonsk (1724–83), Bishop of Voronezh and Elets, and one of the prototypes for Zosima in *The Brothers Karamazov*.

Belkin: Pushkin's collection of five short stories, *Povesti Belkina* [The tales of Belkin] (1831) is narrated by Ivan Petrovich Belkin, an artless, good-natured character who had been held up by the critic Apollon Grigorev as a typically humble Russian type.

Oblomov (1859), novel by Ivan Goncharov. *A Nest of Gentlefolk* [*Dvorianskoe gnezdo*] (1859), novel by Ivan Turgenev.

February 1876, 1.3: The Peasant Marey

I'll tell you a story: According to the memoirs of Dostoevsky's younger brother, Andrei, Marey was an actual personage.

The Pole M——cki: The Polish revolutionary Aleksandr Mirecki was an exile in Omsk while Dostoevsky was serving his term of hard labor there. The conversation he describes probably took place in April 1851. He also figures

in Dostoevsky's *Notes from the House of the Dead.*
Gazin likewise appears in *Notes from the House of the Dead.*

March 1876, 1.2: A Hundred-Year-Old Woman

a lady told me: The lady was Dostoevsky's wife, Anna, as noted in Grossman, *Seminarii po Dostoevskomu,* p. 64.
One of the buildings on Nikolaevsky Street (now Marat Street) housed the facility where *DP* was printed.

March 1876, 1.3: Dissociation

"things I have seen . . .": Again, as promised in his "Announcement," which precedes January 1876.
Dobroliubov, Nikolai Aleksandrovich (1836–61), literary critic and, during his brief life, one of the leading figures among the radicals of the 1860s.
a certain manuscript: The manuscript was the work of Nikolai Pavlovich Peterson (1844–1919), a one-time revolutionary who became a disciple of the Russian philosopher Nikolai Fedorov. Peterson introduced Fedorov's ideas to Dostoevsky (and to Tolstoy). He had spent six months in prison for his revolutionary activities.

March 1876, 2.1: Don Carlos and Sir Watkin. More Signs of "The Beginning of the End."

Carlos, Don (Carlos Maria de los Dolores) (1848–1909), Prince of Bourbon, claimant, as Don Carlos VII, to the Spanish throne. After the defeat that ended the Second Carlist War, he fled to France. The French republican government refused to give him refuge, and, on March 4, 1876, he was received in England.
Kupernik, Lev Abramovich (1845–1905), lawyer and journalist. On February 5, 1876, he created an incident by threatening the manager of a coaching station and then firing several shots at a coachman to urge him to drive faster.
Chambord, Henri Charles Ferdinand Marie Dieudonne, Comte de (1820–83), claimant, as Henry V, to the French throne. One of his conditions for accepting the throne was the abandonment of the republican tricolor and the return of the white banner of the Bourbons as flag of France.
Heinrich Heine, in chapter 16 of his *Reisebilder,* describes this reaction to the passage. Near the end of *Don Quixote* (pt. 2, chap. 64), Don Quixote encounters the Knight of the White Moon (who in fact is the bachelor Sansón

Carrasco); Carrasco defeats Quixote in a duel and forces him to return to his [Quixote's] native village for a year. Heine (and Dostoevsky) apparently confuses this episode with an earlier one (pt. 1, chap. 46), in which the Don is bound while asleep and imprisoned in a cage after a brawl over the "helmet of Mambrino," a brass basin the Don had taken from an itinerant barber.

March 1876, 2.3: A Word or Two about the Report of the Scholarly Commission on Spiritualistic Phenomena

home of Mr. Aksakov: The report appeared in *G*, no. 85, March 25, 1876. For Aksakov see notes to January 1876, 3.2.

April 1876, 2.3: Just a Bit More about Spiritualism

Mendeleev's first lecture took place on April 24, 1876. (See also the notes to January 1876, 3.2.)

Solianoi Gorodok: The account appeared in *NV*, no. 56, April 26, 1876.

Mendeleev's second lecture took place on April 25, 1876. For Suvorin, see notes to January 1876, 1.1. Petr Dmitrievich Boborykin (1836–1921), Russian novelist. Both Suvorin and Boborykin had written newspaper articles on spiritualism.

May 1876, 1.1: From a Private Letter

The Kairova case: Vasilii Aleksandrovich Velikanov, manager of a theatrical company in Orenburg, had gone bankrupt in the spring of 1875. Leaving his wife, an actress in his company, in Orenburg, Velikanov traveled to St. Petersburg with his mistress, Anastasia Kairova, who was also an actress in his company; they hoped to find work in the theaters of the capital. Velikanov's wife arrived in St. Petersburg at the end of June and found her husband and his mistress at a suburban summer cottage. She announced that she intended to remain with her husband, and Kairova at first gave way and moved to the city. On the night of July 7/8, however, Kairova returned to the cottage and inflicted several razor cuts, which did not prove fatal, on Mrs. Velikanova's throat. The case came to trial on April 2, 1876; Kairova was acquitted. Russian newspapers commented extensively on the case; many of them regarded it as a test of the relatively new system of trial by jury.

May 1876, 1.3: The Court and Mrs. Kairova

Jack of Hearts: The name of a band of Moscow hooligans, many of whom were from gentry families. An investigation into crimes committed by the band was being conducted in 1876.

Utin, Evgenii Isakovich (1843–94), liberal lawyer and frequent contributor to *VE*.

May 1876, 1.5: The Defense Attorney and Velikanova

six-year-old stepdaughter: Dostoevsky writes of this case in detail in *DP*, October 1876, 1.1.

May 1876, 2.2: One Inappropriate Thought

New Times: The letter was published in *NV*, no. 85 (May 26, 1876).

paid her dues to progress: Midwifery was one of the few professions open to women at the time; radical young women in particular chose it as a career.

May 1876, 2.3: A Democratic Spirit, for Certain. Women.

Shchapov's wife: Olga Ivanovna Shchapova (née Zhemchuzhnikova) met Shchapov when he was gravely ill and about to be exiled. Against the wishes of her family, she married him and shared the hardships of his exile for ten years.

June 1876, 2.1: My Paradox

tussle with Europe: Russian newspapers wrote of the growing possibility of war between Turkey and her restive possessions, Serbia and Montenegro. Serbia in fact declared war on Turkey on June 30 (n.s.). Russian involvement in the Balkans, which in turn could lead to conflict with the other European powers, was raised as a possibility.

"kvasnik" and "zipunnik": The words derive from "kvas," a traditional Russian fermented drink, and "zipun," a peasant coat of rough homespun material; they imply crude and specifically Russian qualities.

June 1876, 2.4: The Utopian Conception of History

Diary: See February 1876, 1.2.

document concocted by Poles: Charles-Louis Lesur (1770–1849), French writer, publicist, and an official in Napoleon's Foreign Ministry, describes a secret "document" outlining Russian plans for expansion in Europe, which included the expulsion of the Turks from Europe and the seizure of

Constantinople. The document was his own invention and formed part of a campaign of anti-Russian propaganda. See his *Des progrès de la puissance russe depuis son origin jusqu'au commencement du XIX siècle* (Paris, 1812). The "testament" was subsequently republished a number of times.

Tsargrad: Here Dostoevsky uses the traditional Russian name (which is also akin to the name used in several other Slavic languages) for Constantinople—literally, "the tsar's city." He thereby suggests its significance in Russian history and, perhaps, even Russia's claim to it. Constantinople/Tsargrad was a holy city for medieval Russians and a common place of pilgrimage.

capital of Slavdom: The possibility of a Slavic federation whose capital would be Constantinople was raised a number of times in the nineteenth century but was set forth in detail by the Russian publicist and ideologist of panslavism, N. Ia. Danilevsky (1822–85), in his *Rossiia i Evropa* [Russia and Europe] (St. Petersburg, 1871). The Slavic peoples, Danilevsky argued, should turn away from Europeanism and pursue national goals, the first of which was to resolve the Eastern Question through seizure of Constantinople. War with Europe would ensue, and Russia would unite the Slavs under her leadership. The capital of this panslavic union would be Constantinople (Tsargrad), which Danilevsky envisaged as becoming the common property of all the Slavic peoples, belonging to no one of them. Dostoevsky read Danilevsky with great interest, but later (see *DP*, November 1877, 3.1) expressed his disagreement with him, arguing that Constantinople must belong to the Russians.

Ivan III (1440–1505), grand duke of Muscovy. His conquests consolidated Moscow's dominance over other Russian city-states and established a strong centralized power. After his marriage to Sofia Paleologa, niece of the last Byzantine emperor, he adopted the Byzantine double-headed eagle and many of the trappings of the Byzantine court. The notion of Russia as heir to Byzantium was strengthened during his reign.

June 1876, 2.5: About Women Again

a young girl: The girl was Sofia Efimovna Lure (1858–189?), identified by Anna Dostoevskaia as the daughter of a wealthy banker from Minsk (Grossman, *Seminarii po Dostoevskomu*, p. 65). Dostoevsky publishes a portion of a letter from her in *DP*, March 1877, 3.1. She in fact conceded to the wishes of her family and did not go to Serbia.

July-August 1876, 1.1: Going Abroad. Something
about Russians in Railway Carriages.

Ems: Dostoevsky left St. Petersburg on July 5, 1876, to spend the summer in
Bad-Ems, a fashionable German resort noted for its mineral springs.

July-August 1876, 4.1: What Effects the Cure When
Taking the Waters: The Water or the *Bon Ton*?

Doctor Hirschorn's: A. Iu. Girshgorn, *Ems i tselebnye ego istochniki. Deistvie ix
na zdorovyi i bol'noi organizm, primenenie v razlichnykh bolezniakh, pravila
upotrebleniia vod, i t.d.* [Ems and its healing springs. Their effect on the
sound and on the unhealthy organism, their applicability to various illnesses,
procedures for the use of the waters, etc.] (St. Petersburg, 1874).

Pechorin: "Kavkazskii plennik" [Captive of the Caucasus] (1822), poem by A.
S. Pushkin.

the verses: Matthew 6:28–30.

July-August 1876, 4.4: The Land and Children

Clovis (466–511), king of the Franks and founder of the Frankish monarchy.

Potugins: See note to January 1876, 2.3.

memoirs of a certain Russian landowner: The book in question was *Zapiski
Ivana Dmitrievicha Iakushkina* [Notes of Ivan Dmitrievich Iakushkin]
(London, 1862). Iakushkin, who was involved in the Decembrist movement,
offered his peasants their freedom, but without land, in 1819. He taught serf
children to read and write (not singing, as Dostoevsky states) so as to allow
them to be trained in trades.

October 1876, 1.1: A Case That Is Not as Simple as It Seems

survived in good health: See May 1876, 1.5. Dostoevsky discusses this case again
in December 1877, 1.

October 1876, 1.2: A Few Remarks about Simplicity and Simplification

Meshchansky Street: According to Dostoevsky's wife, the incident he describes
was an actual one (Grossman, *Seminarii po Dostoevskomu*, p. 65). The period
he refers to, 1862–63, marked a high point in the influence of radical and
utilitarian doctrines.

Pushkin: In the 1860s, the radical critics V. A. Zaitsev (1842–82) and D. I. Pisarev
(1840–68), basing their thesis on utilitarian principles, argued that a pair of

boots were of more value to humanity than the entire works of Shakespeare or Pushkin.

October 1876, 1.3: Two Suicides

one of our writers: The writer is Mikhail Evgrafovich Saltykov-Shchedrin (1826–89), then an editor of *OZ*, which wanted to publish something by Dostoevsky.

Molchalin, a character from Griboedov's play *Woe from Wit*. Saltykov-Shchedrin recast Molchalin in his satirical cycle *The Messrs. Molchalin* (1874).

daughter of one very well-known Russian emigré: The girl was Elizaveta Aleksandrovna Herzen, daughter of Alexander Herzen (see note to 1873.1), who committed suicide in Florence at the age of seventeen. The suicide note Dostoevsky quotes here is an abbreviated paraphrase of the original. The original also does not contain the phrase "Ce n'est pas chic!" This, apparently, was a comment made by Konstantin Pobedonostsev, who wrote to Dostoevsky about the suicide, and which the latter assumed to be part of Miss Herzen's note.

a suicide in the city: One such report was carried in *NV*, no. 215, October 3, 1876. The girl served as a prototype of the heroine of "The Meek One" (*DP*, November 1876).

October 1876, 1.4: The Sentence

suicide *out of boredom*: An acquaintance of Dostoevsky's, the writer L. Kh. Khokhriakova (1838–1900), stated that Dostoevsky admitted that this was not a genuine suicide note but his own creation (L. Simonova [L. Kh. Khokhriakova], "Iz vospominanii o Fedore Mikhailoviche Dostoevskom" [From my recollections of F. M. Dostoevsky], *Tserkovno-obshchestvennyi vestnik* [The Clerical and Social Messenger], no. 18, February 1881).

November 1876: Author's Foreword

his last moment of life: Victor Hugo's *Last Day of a Condemned Man* [*Le Dernière Jour d'un condamné*] is a first-person "confession" written by the hero. It ends with his description of the sound of the footsteps of those coming to take him to be executed. In his preface to the first edition of the story, Hugo also attempted to explain its origins: "There are two ways of accounting for the existence of the ensuing work. Either there really has been found a roll of papers on which were inscribed, exactly as they came, the last thoughts of a condemned prisoner; or else there has been an author, a dreamer, occupied in observing nature for the advantage of society, who, having been seized with those forcible ideas, could not rest until he had given them the tangible form of a volume."

November 1876, 1.1: Who Was I and Who Was She?
" 'I am a part of that whole . . .' ": A paraphrase of Mephistopheles's remark in Goethe's *Faust,* part 1, scene 2:

> . . . Ein Teil von jener Kraft,
> Die stets das Böse will, und stets das Gute Schafft.

November 1876, 1.3: The Noblest of Men, but I Don't Believe It Myself
" 'The first impressions of existence' ": An inaccurate quotation from Pushkin's poem "The Demon" [Demon] (1823).

November 1876, 1.4: Plans and More Plans
The Pursuit of Happiness [Pogonia za schast'em] (1876), a play by Petr Ilych Iurkevich; *The Singing Birds* [Ptitsy pevchie] (1868), an operetta by Jacques Offenbach, more commonly known as *La Périchole.*

John Stuart Mill noted: "If we consider the works of women in modern times, and compare them with those of men, either in the literary or the artistic department, such inferiority as may be observed resolves itself essentially into one thing: but that is a most material one: deficiency of originality" (*The Subjection of Women* [Cambridge, Mass.: MIT Press, 1970], p. 69).

November 1876, 1.5: The Meek One Rebels
the Viazemsky house: A notorious lodging in the slums of St. Petersburg whose horrors were thus described in *G*, no. 298, October 28, 1876: "One can say without exaggeration that this house is the breeding ground and receptacle of every form of vice of which a human, oppressed by poverty and ignorance, is capable."

November 1876, 2.3: I Understand All Too Well
Gil Blas: In book 7, chapter 4 of Alain René Le Sage's novel, *L'Histoire de Gil Blas de Santillane* (1715–35), the archbishop of Grenada asks Gil Blas for his honest opinion on a sermon the archbishop has delivered; when Gil Blas offers some very tactful criticism, the archbishop dismisses him.

November 1876, 2.4: I Was Only Five Minutes Late

"hero of the Russian epic": The narrator uses here the word *bogatyr'*, the exceptionally strong and courageous hero of the traditional Russian epic poems, the *byliny*.

is it not a corpse?: The image of the dead sun may derive from Revelations 6:12: "and lo, there was a great earthquake, and the sun became black as sackcloth of hair, and the moon became as blood." P. V. Bekedin, in "Povest' 'Krotkaia' (K istolkovaniiu obraza mertvogo solntsa)" [The tale "The Meek One": Toward an interpretation of the image of the dead sun], *Dostoevskii: materialy i issledovaniia* (Leningrad: Nauka, 1987), 7:102–24, suggests some other possible sources, including Shakespeare and Goethe.

December 1876, 1.1: More about a Case That Is Not as Simple as It Seems

one very fortunate circumstance: An official in the Ministry of Justice who had read Dostoevsky's October *Diary* urged Dostoevsky to convince Kornilova to submit an appeal for clemency and helped him arrange a meeting with her.

December 1876, 1.2: A Belated Moral

Several of my friends: Khokhriakova (see note to October 1876, 1.4) states that when she suggested that this note itself might prompt someone to suicide, Dostoevsky became quite alarmed and was anxious to correct any misunderstanding the note may have caused.

weekly *Recreation*: The article appeared in the humor magazine *Razvlechenie* [Recreation], no. 51, December 14, 1876.

December 1876, 1.5: On Suicide and Arrogance

"No man shall hate his flesh": Quotation from Ephesians 5:29: "For no man ever yet hated his own flesh...."

competent member: The lawyer and writer A. F. Koni (1844–1927) provided Dostoevsky with these suicide notes.

December 1876, 2.1: A Story from the Lives of Children

mother and her twelve-year-old daughter: As Dostoevsky's wife notes (in Grossman, *Seminarii po Dostoevskomu*, p. 66), the mother was L. Kh. Khokhriakova. (See also notes to October 1876, 1.4.)

Gostiny Dvor: A large block of shops in central St. Petersburg.

January 1877, 1.1: Three Ideas

Dostoevsky does not quote himself accurately here; notably, the word "almost" does not appear in the *Diary* of December 1876.

vote in the Assembly: Dostoevsky refers to the attacks made on religion in revolutionary France in 1793 and the concomitant attempt to institute the worship of reason. Robespierre, however, came to the conclusion that outright atheism was having a negative effect on the populace. Friedrich Schlosser, Dostoevsky's source here, notes: "On the 7th of May 1794, Robespierre delivered a tedious and pompous speech in the convention respecting the connexion of religion and morality with republican principles; which in his mouth was in the highest degree ridiculous . . . and proposed a decree which was accepted and passed by the convention, and was to the following effect: 'The national convention acknowledges the truth of the existence of God and the immortality of the soul'" (F C. Schlosser, *History of the Eighteenth Century and of the Nineteenth till the Overthrow of the French Empire* [London: Chapman & Hall, 1846], 6:510). Schlosser's work appeared in Russian translation in 1868.

Arminius: Latinized form of Hermann or Armin (17 B.C.–A.D. 21), German chieftain and national hero. In the year A.D. 9 he led a rebellion against Roman rule, inflicting a major defeat on a Roman army in the Teutoburger Wald.

January 1877, 2.4: Russian Satire. *Virgin Soil. Last Songs.* ### Old Reminiscences.

Nekrasov's *Last Songs:* A cycle of poems written during his final illness, in 1876–77; nine were published in *OZ*, no. 1, 1877.

difficult to diagnose: Nekrasov suffered from cancer of the bowel.

Grigorovich: His sketch, "Organ Grinders of Petersburg" [Peterburgskie sharmanshchiki], appeared in 1844 in an anthology, *The Physiology of Petersburg, Comprising Works of Russian Writers and Edited by N. Nekrasov* [Fiziologiia Peterburga, sostavlennaia iz trudov russkikh literatorov pod redaktsieiiu N. Nekrasova].

Fatherland Notes party: In the 1840s *OZ* was the leading journal of the Westernizers; Turgenev, Nekrasov, and Herzen published their writings in it. From 1839, Belinsky was the journal's principal literary critic.

completely alone: Nekrasov arrived in St. Petersburg in late July 1838.

The verse is from Nekrasov's "The Unfortunates" [Neshchastnye] (1856), an unfinished narrative poem centering on a revolutionary in exile; its hero is probably modeled on Belinsky.

January 1877, 2.5: The Boy Celebrating His Saint's Day

Tolstoy's *Childhood, Boyhood, Youth,* which is its full title, appeared in *S,* no. 9, 1852; no. 10, 1854; and no. 1, 1857.

a letter from K——v: The letter came from M. A. Iurkevich, deputy inspector of the Kishinev Seminary.

February 1877, 1.2: Home-grown Giants and a Humiliated Son of a Mountain Village. An Anecdote about Skin Flayed from the Back. The Higher Interests of Civilization, and "May They Be Damned If They Must Be Purchased at Such a Price!"

The Moscow News: Dostoevsky quotes an editorial from *MV,* no. 33, February 9, 1880, which condemned the Western powers for supporting Turkey and tolerating Turkish outrages against the Balkan Christians.

February 1877, 1.3: On Flaying of Skins Generally and Various Aberrations in Particular. Hatred of Authority with Toadyism of Thought.

"Jack of Hearts": Many of the members of the gang came from landowning families.

"Virgin Soil": Dostoevsky refers here to the peasantry as a whole, as is suggested by the title of Turgenev's novel, which was then appearing. The epigraph to the novel reads: "Virgin soil should be turned up not by a harrow skimming over the surface but by a plough biting deep into the earth."

February 1877, 1.4: Metternichs and Don Quixotes

manifesto from the Russian emperor: On October 18, 1876, Alexander II threatened to break off diplomatic relations with Turkey unless she agreed to a cease-fire against the insurgent Slavs.

February 1877, 2.I: One of Today's Most Important Questions

Anna Karenina: Chapters 1 to 12 of part 6 of the novel, describing Dolly's visit to Levin and Kitty in the country, appeared in *RV,* no. 1 (1877).

agents of progress: The conversation among Levin, Oblonsky, and Vasenka Veslovsky, excerpts of which Dostoevsky quotes, takes place in *Anna Karenina,* pt. 6, chap. 11.

February 1877, 2.3: The Issue of the Day in Europe

Fourier, François Marie Charles (1772–1837), French socialist writer whose theories sought ways to achieve social harmony and the free development of the individual; his ideas had considerable influence on a generation of Russian radicals. Cabet, Etienne (1788–1856), French utopian socialist.

hundred million heads: The motif of "a hundred million heads" as the revolutionaries' price for instituting a new order in Europe is also found in *The Devils*, pt. 2, chap. 7.

February 1877, 2.4: The Russian Solution to the Problem

"where they neither hoard nor covet": "You will receive . . . :" Mark 10:21: "Then Jesus . . . said unto him, One thing thou lackest; go thy way, sell whatsoever thou hast, and give to the poor, and thou shalt have treasure in heaven: and come, take up the cross, and follow me."

March 1877, 2.1: "The Jewish Question"

beautiful letter: The four articles in chapter 2 are largely a response to three letters Dostoevsky received from Arkady Grigorevich Kovner (1842–1909), in January and February 1877. Kovner, a journalist and writer, had been a fervent disciple of the radical Dmitry Pisarev in the 1860s. Although a Jew himself, Kovner had attacked traditional Judaism, seeing it as a barrier to the full integration of the Jews into Russian life. In the 1870s, however, he was alarmed by the upsurge of anti-Semitism and took Dostoevsky to task for his remarks about the Jews as exploiters. Kovner's letter to Dostoevsky of January 26, 1877, which Dostoevsky answers here, can be found in F. M. Dostoevsky, *Pis'ma* [Letters], ed. A. S. Dolinin (Moscow and Leningrad: Academia, 1934), pp. 377–82. See also David I. Goldstein, *Dostoevsky and the Jews* (Austin and London: University of Texas Press, 1981), pp. 106–16.

D. A. Goldstein, a teacher in a Moscow or Petersburg high school, had gone to Serbia as a volunteer and had been singled out by General Cherniaev as an example of courage and sangfroid in battle.

Disraeli, Benjamin (Earl of Beaconsfield) (1804–81), British statesman and man of letters, prime minister of Great Britain 1874–80.

Shchedrin: In chapter 1 of his *Contemporary Idyll* [Sovremennaia idilliia] (1877–78), the narrator says of a St. Petersburg restaurant: "And I had such a sudden urge to go there, into those low-ceilinged rooms in the back, into that stinking, raw atmosphere, to one of those cheap oilcloth sofas whose entire expanse, without a doubt, contains not a single spot that hasn't been spat upon."

March 1877, 2.2: Pro and Contra

Lord Beaconsfield: Benjamin Disraeli.

restrictions for the whole mass of the Jews: As a result of the three partitions of Poland (1772, 1793, 1795), over a million Jews became subjects of the Russian Empire. Catherine II imposed restrictions limiting Jewish settlement to an area of western Russia, which became known as the Pale of Settlement (Cherta osedlosti). The Pale was expanded over the years to include underpopulated areas around the Black Sea that had been annexed from Turkey. By the 1860s, the Pale included all of Russian Poland, Lithuania, Belorussia, most of the Ukraine, the Crimea, and Bessarabia. Some loosening of restrictions on Jewish rights of residence occurred over the nineteenth century, so that certain merchants and artisans, those with higher education and those having completed military service, were permitted to reside anywhere within the empire except Finland.

the *European Messenger*: The article, "Iuzhnye shtaty severoamerikanskoi respubliki i ikh nastoiashchee" [The southern states of the North American republic and their present condition], appeared in *VE*, no. 3, 1877, and was by Iu. A. Rossel.

New Times (no. 371): The report in fact appeared in *NV*, no. 375, March 15, 1877.

March 1877, 2.3: *Status in Statu*. Forty Centuries of Existence.

Status in statu: A state within a state (Latin). The ideas expressed in this chapter were taken in part from *Kniga Kagala. Materialy dlia izucheniia evreiskogo byta. Sobral i perevel Iakov Bravman* [The book of the kahal: Materials for the study of Jewish life. Collected and translated by Iakov Bravman] (Vilnius: Izd. Vilenskogo gubernskogo pravleniia, 1869). Dostoevsky's library contained three editions of this book. It is the work of a convert from Judaism and was used to help fuel the anti-Semitic movement in the later nineteenth century. Bravman maintained that the Jews recognized only Talmudic laws, not the laws of the Russian Empire; they thus formed "a state within a state" that exploited their non-Jewish neighbors. See David I. Goldstein, *Dostoevsky and the Jews* (Austin and London: University of Texas Press, 1981), pp. 96ff.

The verses are paraphrased from act 2, scene 2 of *Prince Daniel Vasilevich Kholmsky* [Kniaz' Daniil Vasil'evich Kholmskii] (1840), a play by Nestor Kukolnik (1809-68). The same play is probably the source of the "legend" Dostoevsky describes.

Rothschild, Jacob (James), baron (1792–1868). Banker and founder of the Rothschild family's business interests in France.

March 1877, 2.4: But Long Live Brotherhood!

The girl was Sofia Efimovna Lurye; Dostoevsky discusses an earlier meeting with her in June 1876, 2.5.

In *Crime and Punishment,* pt. 6, chap. 6, immediately before Svidrigailov shoots himself, he encounters a Jewish soldier. The narrator describes the soldier's face as wearing "the eternal expression of resentful affliction which is so sharply etched on every Jewish face, without exception."

March 1877, 3.1: The Funeral of "The Universal Man"

Rossi, Ernesto (1827–96), Italian writer, actor, translator, playwright, and critic. Rossi toured Russia in 1877 and played Hamlet in St. Petersburg in February of that year. Dostoevsky apparently found his performance somewhat overdone; *NV,* no. 350, February 18, 1877, gave Rossi a rather positive review, however.

Semiradsky, Genrikh Ippolitovich (1843–1902), Russian painter. Dostoevsky has in mind Semiradsky's massive painting *The Lamps of Christianity* (later renamed *The Lamps of Nero* [Svetochi Nerona]), which was shown at the Academy of Arts exhibition in March 1877 and aroused much comment.

Miss L.: Sofia Efimovna Lurye (see notes to March 1877, 2.4), who was living in Minsk at the time.

March 1877, 3.2: An Isolated Case

one mighty poet: Probably Apollon Nikolaevich Maikov (1821–97).

mother-of-pearl: One detail in Semiradsky's painting is the mother-of-pearl on Nero's sedan chair.

April 1877, 1.1: War. We Are Stronger Than the Others.

Alexander II declared war on Turkey on April 12, 1877. The immediate cause of the war was Turkey's refusal to implement the reforms for its Christian population that had been set forth by the Constantinople Conference of 1876, as well as Turkish atrocities committed against Bulgarian civilians in response to a Bulgarian uprising in May 1876. Pan-Slavist sentiments, Russian rivalry with Austro-Hungary in the Balkans, and Russia's desire for free and safe egress from the Black Sea were other causes.

April 1877, 1.3: Does Shed Blood Save Us?

"the time is at hand": Matthew 26:18: "And he said, Go into the city to such a man, and say unto him, The Master saith, My time is at hand; I will keep the passover at thy house with my disciples."

April 1877, 2: The Dream of a Ridiculous Man

"Voltaire" one: A low-seated, high-backed armchair.

April 1877, 2: The Defendant Kornilova Is Freed

new judges and jurors: Dostoevsky discusses Kornilova's case in October 1876, 1.1, December 1876, 1.1, and again in December 1877, 1.1, 1.3–1.6.

Florinsky, Vasily Markovich (1833–99), physician; in the late 1870s and 1880s, professor of obstetrics and gynecology at Kazan University; author of a number of books on obstetrics.

Diukov, Petr Andreevich (1834–99), psychiatrist and author of many articles on mental illness. Lustig, Vilgelm Iosifovich (1843–1915), prominent St. Petersburg lawyer.

May and June 1877, 1.3: A Plan for a Satirical Novel of Contemporary Life

redemption money: As part of the arrangements for the abolition of serfdom in 1862, the government advanced landowners interest-bearing bonds to the amount of 80 percent of the total value of the land they had deeded to their former serfs. Some landowners were thus provided with a substantial yearly income.

Poprishchin: Protagonist of Gogol's story, "Notes of a Madman" [Zapiski sumashedshego] (1835).

"only pharmacists are afraid of disgrace": An echo of Gogol's Poprishchin, who says: "Letters are even written by pharmacists. . . ."

as Shchedrin's policeman expresses it: In chapter 3 of Saltykov-Shchedrin's "Contemporary Idyll" [Sovremennaia idilliia], which appeared in April, 1877.

May and June 1877, 2.2: Diplomacy Facing World Problems

fog that was spread a hundred years ago: Dostoevsky probably has in mind the Treaty of Kuchuk Kainardji (1774), under which Turkey acknowledged Russia's interest in the fate of the Christian population of the Balkans and undertook to protect the Christian religion there.

July and August 1877, 1.3: The Case of the
Dzhunkovsky Parents and Their Children

massaging their feet: A traditional Russian means of relaxing and inducing
sleep.

July and August 1877, 2.1: Dissociation Again. Part Eight of *Anna Karenina*.

he is one of the People: Levin says this in *Anna Karenina,* part 8, chapter 15.

speaking of *Anna Karenina* once some time ago: See February 1877, 2.

"such direct feeling for the oppression of the Slavs *does not and cannot exist*":
Levin says this in part 8, chapter 15. The italics are Dostoevsky's.

July and August 1877, 2.3: *Anna Karenina* as a Fact of Special Importance

one of my favorite writers on the street: Probably I. S. Goncharov.

"Pleiade": Tolstoy, Goncharov, Turgenev, Nekrasov, and Ostrovsky. Lomonosov,
Mikhail Vasilevich (ca. 1711–65), Russian scientist, poet, grammarian,
founder of Moscow University; Russia's first great linguistic reformer.

"Vengeance is mine, I will repay": Deuteronomy 32:35, Romans 12:19—and, of
course, the epigraph to *Anna Karenina.*

penultimate part: Dostoevsky errs here. The scene in which Karenin and Vronsky
are reconciled at Anna's sickbed occurs, not in part 7, but in part 4, chapter
17.

darkness instead of the light: The scene leading up to and including Anna's
suicide, part 7, chapters 23 through 31.

July and August 1877, 2.4: A Landowner Who
Gets Faith in God from a Peasant

some *touchy* things there: Dostoevsky may have in mind Levin's doubts about
religion and the Orthodox church, expressed in part 8, chapters 12 and 13
of *Anna Karenina.*

expresses himself as follows: The sections quoted here, and following, are from
part 8, chapters 11 through 13. There are some omissions, and the italics are
Dostoevsky's.

July and August 1877, 3.1: The Irritability of Vanity

"waves his arms around just like this": In part 8, chapter 14, of *Anna Karenina,*
Dolly's children tell Levin: "Uncle Kostia! Mama's coming, and grandpapa,
and Sergei Ivanych, and another man. . . . An awfully dreadful man! And he
waves his arms just like this! . . ."

honey and the Eastern Question: The scene occurs in part 8, chapters 15 and 16.

Committee: The Slavic Committee. See notes to February 1876, 1.2.

passed without notice: Only one mention was made of Sergei Koznyshev's book, *An Outline of a Survey of the Principles and Forms of Government in Europe and Russia. The Northern Beetle* "suggested in a few contemptuous words that everyone had seen through it long ago and consigned it to general ridicule" (*Anna Karenina,* part 8, chapter 1).

in the earlier parts as well: Dostoevsky probably has in mind the scenes of Koznyshev's abortive courtship of Varenka (*Anna Karenina,* part 6, chapters 4 and 5).

the old prince: I.e., Prince Shcherbatsky, Kitty's father.

Fonvizin, Denis Ivanovich (1744–92), Russian dramatist. The characters in his plays are often "humors," whose names suggest the qualities or vices they personify—e.g., Prostakov (Mr. Simpleton), Pravdin (Mr. Truthful), Starodum (Mr. Oldsense).

even without him: The passage quoted here, as well as those that follow, are taken from part 8, chapters 15 and 16. There are minor omissions and errors, and the italics are Dostoevsky's.

Mikhailych: A peasant character, Levin's beekeeper.

summoning of the Varangians: The Russian *Primary Chronicle* [Povest' vremennykh let] (ca. 1040–1118) begins its account of the origin of the Russian state with the tale of the summoning of the Varangians, or Norsemen, who were invited to come and rule over the city of Novgorod and end the strife between tribes. Their leader, Rurik, founded a dynasty that ruled Russia until 1598.

July and August 1877, 3.4: Levin's Agitation. A Question: Does Distance Have an Influence on Love for Humanity? Can One Agree with the Opinion of One Turkish Prisoner on the Humaneness of Some of Our Ladies? So What, Then, Are Our Teachers Teaching Us?

two and a half months ago: Dostoevsky errs here; part 8 appeared in July 1877.

eyewitnesses of all nations can now attest: Among the first accounts of Turkish atrocities in the Balkans was William Gladstone's pamphlet "The Bulgarian Horrors and the Question of the East" (September 1876). A portion of this appeared in a supplement to *Gr* entitled *Russkii sbornik* [Russian anthology], vol. 1 (January 1877), together with accounts of Turkish atrocities witnessed by an English colonel, MacIver, who served as a volunteer with Serbian forces, and by the correspondent of the London *Daily News*, J. A. MacGachan (1844–78). MacGachan's vivid accounts of the Bulgarian massacres of 1876 did much to rouse public opinion in Europe and Russia against the Turks; Dostoevsky's evidence of Turkish atrocities derives mainly from this source.

screamed for a long time: Dostoevsky discusses this event in *DP*, May and June 1877, 4.2.

September 1877, 1.5: Who's Knocking at the Door? Who Will Come In? Inescapable Fate.

almost word for word: During the summer of 1877 the European press carried many items dealing with the political crisis in France and the growing possibility of war between France and Germany, matters which Dostoevsky had discussed in his May and June *Diary*. One of Dostoevsky's "speculations" that appeared to be borne out by reports in the Russian press was the influence of the Catholic church on French politics. *NV*, no. 565, September 24, 1877, called the French government of the day "a genuine *gouvernement des curés*."

the Estates-General: The representatives of the three estates in France (nobility, clergy, and bourgeoisie) were summoned on May 5 (n.s.), 1789—i.e., on the eve of the French Revolution.

September 1877, 2.1: A Lie Is Saved by a Lie

Amadis de Gaula: Romance of chivalry dating probably from the thirteenth century; Cervantes pronounced it "the best of all the books of this kind that have ever been written."

"Sancho, my friend": As first noted by the Spanish scholar M. de Guevara, no such episode occurs in *Don Quixote* (see V. E. Vagno, "Dostoevskii o 'Don-Kikhote' Servantesa" [Dostoevsky on Cervantes's *Don Quixote*], *Dostoevskii: materialy i issledovaniia* [Dostoevsky: Source materials and studies], [Leningrad: Nauka, 1978], 3:126–35). Vagno shows, however, that many of the elements of the scene Dostoevsky created were taken from Cervantes.

September 1877, 2.3: An Intimation of the Future Educated Russian Man. The Certain Lot of the Future Russian Woman.

the lofty role that certainly awaits her among us: The bravery and selfless behavior of the many women who served as nurses in field hospitals during the war was frequently mentioned in the Russian press (e.g., *MV*, no. 214, August 28, 1877; *NV*, no. 533, August 23, 1877; *NV*, no. 559, September 18, 1877).

sentimental ladies who gave candies to the Turks: See July and August 1877, 3.4.

October 1877, 3.1: Roman Clericals Here in Russia

in its editorial: The quotation comes from *MV*, no. 262, October 22, 1877.
New Times remarked in this connection: The article to which Dostoevsky refers in fact appeared in *NV* three days later, in no. 596, October 25, 1877. *NV* did dismiss the "conspiracy" as merely the product of rumors, inevitable in time of war. The original article, in *The Government Messenger* [Pravitel'stvennyi vestnik], merely noted the prevalence of false information about the war and cautioned its readers about accepting wild rumors as truth; certain reports appearing in foreign newspapers should likewise be viewed skeptically, the newspaper added.

this conspiracy does exert its influence: Dostoevsky refers to the May "coup d'état" in France; several Russian newspapers carried stories of the efforts of the Catholic church to influence the outcome of the French elections, which were imminent. As "the most liberal of our newspapers" Dostoevsky has in mind *G*.

October 1877, 3.2: Old Poland's Summer Attempt at Reconciliation

Old Poland: Dostoevsky has in mind the Polish aristocrats and intelligentsia who emigrated to France after the uprising of 1863 and who hoped for a restoration of an independent Poland.

via Russian periodicals: Over the summer of 1877 the Russian press carried several articles by Polish emigrés calling for reconciliation and economic cooperation between Russia and Poland (e.g., in *SPV*, no. 148, May 31, 1877).

Tengoborski, Liudvig Valerianovich (1793–1857), Russian-Polish economist and statistician, author of a number of works on trade and finance. He began his career in Poland and continued as an active participant in Russian financial and tariff negotiations with various European countries.

Wolowski, Louis-François-Michel-Raymond (1810–76), political economist, born in Warsaw, who emigrated to France in 1831 and spent the remainder of his life there. His economic views influenced Napoleon III.

Brotski: Wiktor Brodzki (1817–1904), sculptor, born in Volynia, he settled in Rome in 1855 but became a professor at the St. Petersburg Academy of Arts in 1868.

Matejko, Jan (1838–93), Polish artist. His paintings of subjects from Polish history were very popular in Europe in the 1870s.

from Kostomarov's article: Nikolai Ivanovich Kostomarov (1817–1885), noted Russian historian, writer, and ethnographer. Kostomarov's article, a response to a letter from "A Resident of Lithuania" (*SPV*, no. 172, June 24, 1877), appeared in *NV*, no. 478, June 29, 1877. The "quotation" cited here is actually a combination of Kostomarov's remarks and Dostoevsky's own commentary.

Konrad Wallenrod: Central character in the narrative poem of the same name, written by the Polish poet Adam Mickiewicz in 1828. In the poem, Wallenrod, a legendary character from fourteenth-century Lithuania, entered the Teutonic Order with the aim of undermining it in revenge for the Order's ravaging of his homeland.

(not their own, of course): *NV*, no. 487, July 8, 1877, carried a note about a Polish legion being assembled in Constantinople to fight against the Russians. *NV*, no. 573, October 2, 1877, reported that Count Wladyslaw Plater, one of the leaders of the Polish emigrés, had arrived in Constantinople with four million francs to support the legion.

November 1877, 3.1: Rumors of Peace. "Constantinople Must Be Ours"—Is That Possible? Various Opinions.

not only in Europe but here as well: As the war began to turn in Russia's favor, the European press began discussing possible terms of a peace treaty. Britain and Austro-Hungary, whose policies had been pro-Turkish, expressed some apprehension at the possibility of a Russian victory. A number of Russian writers, including Danilevsky (in his article "O nastoiashchei voine" [On the current war], *RM*, no. 207, August 2, 1877, and no. 279, October 13, 1877, which Dostoevsky discusses below), wrote of the "rewards" to be claimed by Russia for her efforts in liberating the Balkan Slavs.

demands for the iron-clad Turkish monitors: Danilevsky, in his August article noted above, stated: "As a compensation for her military expenditures Russia should be given the fleet of Turkish ironclads, which will become a useless burden for Turkey, as well as a part of Asia—at least Kars and Batumi."

annex Kars and Erzerum: *NV*, no. 613, November 23, 1877, and in subsequent issues, also demanded Turkish territory.

November 1877, 3.2: Once More, For the Last Time, Some "Soothsayings"

the power of the worldwide Catholic conspiracy: Dostoevsky discussed this in May and June 1877, September 1877, and October 1877.

November 1877, 3.3: The Moment Must Be Seized

everything the socialists are preaching to them has also been preached by Christ:
The ideas that follow are, of course, developed further in *The Brothers
Karamazov*, "The Legend of the Grand Inquisitor."

December 1877, 1.1: The Concluding Explanation of an Old Fact

stepmother Kornilova: Dostoevsky wrote of the Kornilova affair in October
1876, 1.1, and December 1876, 1.1.

malicious and unworthy mockery: *The Northern Messenger* [Severnyi vestnik],
no. 8, May 8, 1877, carried an article, "Beseda" [A conversation], signed by
"Nabliudatel" [An observer]. The reviewer maintained that Anna Karenina's
death occurred, not because Vronsky ceased to love her, but because readers
of the novel had grown bored with her.

December 1877, 1.5: One Incident That Explains a Good Deal, in My View

only to a settlement: Exile to Siberia could take the form of hard labor, settlement
in a penal colony, or simple exile for a specific term. The second category
was considerably less harsh than the first. See George Kennan, *Siberia and
the Exile System,* abridged ed. (Chicago: University of Chicago Press, 1958),
p. 26.

December 1877, 1.6: Am I an Enemy of Children? On What the Word "Happy" Sometimes Means.

Dzhunkovskys: See July and August 1877, 1.3.
Christ's Christmas party: See January 1876, 2.2.
woman taken in adultery: John 8:11.

December 1877, 2.5: To the Readers

a literary work: Dostoevsky refers to his plans for *The Brothers Karamazov*, a
work that was to engage him for most of the next three years.
Red Cross: The letter came from V. V. Mikhailov (1832–95), a writer and teacher.
Mikhailov's letter has not survived, but probably dealt with the activities of
the Russian Red Cross during the Russo-Turkish War.
Sinclair: The book is Sir John George Tollemache Sinclair, *A Defence of Russia
and the Christians of Turkey; including a sketch of the Eastern Question
from 1686 to September, 1877* (London, 1877). Sinclair's work appeared in
Russian in 1878.

1880, 2: Pushkin

said Gogol: The quotation is from Gogol's essay "Neskol'ko slov o Pushkine" [A few words about Pushkin], which appeared in his collection, *Arabesques* (1835).

Parny, André Chénier and others: Evariste-Désiré de Parny (1753-1814), French poet. Parny had profound influence on the verse of the young Pushkin. André de Chénier (1762-1794), French poet, the greatest French lyricist of the eighteenth century. Chenier influenced Pushkin in the 1820s, in his "Byronic" period.

"The Gypsies": [Tsygany] (1827), narrative poem by Pushkin. Its central figure, Aleko, is a weak but vicious character who, disgusted with civilization, flees the city to seek freedom among the "primitive" gypsies in southern Russia. He wants freedom only for himself, however; eventually he murders a gypsy girl and her lover and is banished from their community.

"Depart from us. . . .": At the end of the poem, an old man dismisses Aleko with these words.

"Oh, why. . . .": From *Eugene Onegin*, "The Travels of Onegin."

"Noble demon. . . .": From Nekrasov's poem "Otradno videt', chto nakhodit. . . ." [A joy to see. . . .] (1845).

"moral embryo": Belinsky, in his ninth article on Pushkin, thus describes Tatiana. V. G. Belinsky, *Sobranie sochinenii* [Collected works] (Moscow: Khudozhestvennaia literatura, 1981), 6:422.

"all her perfections": Paraphrase of Onegin's remarks in his letter to Tatiana, chap. 8, stanza 32.

exclaiming with curses: In chap. 8, stanzas 12 and 13, after Onegin has killed his friend Lensky and has been rejected by Tatiana, he travels aimlessly through Russia. The couplet quoted is from the uncompleted "Fragments from Onegin's Travels."

"a parody, perchance": From chap. 7, stanza 24.

reason for refusing Onegin: Belinsky, like Dostoevsky, regarded Tatiana as the essence of Russian womanhood, but he said: "Tatiana does not like society and for the sake of happiness would leave it forever to live in the country; but while she is in society, its opinion will always be her idol, and fear of its judgment will always be the basis of her morals." V. G. Belinsky, *Sobranie sochinenii* [Collected works] (Moscow: Khudozhestvennaia literatura, 1981), 6:423.

". . . true to him for life": Chap. 8, stanza 47.

old general: As N. O. Lerner has shown, Tatiana's husband is probably about thirty-five, hardly an old man. See "Muzh Tatiany" [Tatiana's husband], *Rasskazy o Pushkine* [Stories about Pushkin] (Leningrad: Priboi, 1929), p. 215.

"her mother begged, implored": Chap. 8, stanza 47.

peace and rest at last: The ideas that follow were developed by Ivan in *The Brothers Karamazov*, book 4 ("The Grand Inquisitor").

"'happiness was possible, so near'": Chap. 8, stanza 47.

"the grave of her poor nurse": Chap. 8, stanza 46.

"I look ahead and have no fear": The opening lines of Pushkin's "Stanzas" [Stansy] (1826).

"Scenes from Faust" [Stsena iz Fausta] (1825) involves characters from Goethe's *Faust,* although the remainder is Pushkin's own creation. "Once There Lived a Poor Young Knight" [Zhil na svete rytsar' bednyi] (1829), set in Europe during the Crusades, is in the form of a legend or ballad and describes a knight who dedicates himself utterly to an ideal of purity.

"Don Juan": Pushkin's "Stone Guest" [Kamennyi gost'] (1830), in which he treats the Don Juan legend.

"A Feast in Time of Plague" [Pir vo vremia chumy] (1830), one of Pushkin's "Little Tragedies"; it is an adaptation of a scene from John Wilson's *City of the Plague*; "Mary's Song," sung by one of the characters, laments the fact that the plague has emptied the once noisy village school.

"Once, wandering. . . .": From Pushkin's poem "The Pilgrim" [Strannik] (1835), a free adaptation, in verse, of motifs from chapter 1 of John Bunyan's *Pilgrim's Progress.*

"Imitations of the Koran": Pushkin's "Podrazhaniia Koranu" (1824), verses in the style of the Koran.

"Egyptian Nights": [Egipetskie nochi] (1837), a fragment of a proposed novel, it deals with Cleopatra.

"gave His blessing": From F. I. Tituchev's poem, "These Poor Villages. . . ." [Eti bednye seleniia] (1855).

1880, 3.1: On One Most Basic Point

The Moscow News: Dostoevsky's speech was first published in *MV*, no. 162, June 13, 1877. Liberal newspapers such as *Strana* and *Molva* were quick to challenge the ideas Dostoevsky expressed and argued that the speech's initial impact came more from the emotionally charged atmosphere surrounding it than from its content. *VE*, no. 7, 1880, dismissed it as a rehash of old Slavophile ideas.

Gradovsky, Aleksandr Dmitrievich (1841–89), professor, writer, historian of law. His article taking issue with Dostoevsky appeared in *G*, no. 174, June 25, 1880, and can also be found in his *Sobranie sochinenii* [Collected works] (St. Petersburg: M. M. Stasiulevich, 1901), 6:375–83.

a fearsome row was raised: The newspaper *Strana*, no. 64, August 17, 1880, for example, accused Dostoevsky of attacking liberalism without making his own position clear or fully expressing his own ideals. The newspaper's columnist A. Vvedensky accused Dostoevsky of fantasizing and of distorting the facts of Russian life.

Manilov: obsequious and shallowly sentimental character in Gogol's *Dead Souls*.

1880, 3.2: Aleko and Derzhimorda. Aleko's Sufferings for a Peasant Serf. Anecdotes.

Lucrezia Floriani: George Sand's novel of 1846.

1880, 3.3: Two Halves

mutual relationships: "Servants, be obedient to them that are your masters . . ." (Ephesians 6:5); "Exhort servants to be obedient unto their own masters . . ." (Titus 2:9).

Mary of Egypt: early saint who, after her conversion to Christianity, lived for forty-seven years in the desert praying for forgiveness of her sins.

1881, 1.1: Finances. A Citizen as an Offended Thersites. Crowning from Below and the Musicians. A Refuge for Windbags and the Windbags.

I now resume my *Diary* with an article on economics?: Dostoevsky's wife notes that at the beginning of 1881 "he decided to take up the publication of *A Writer's Diary* once more, since during the troubled years preceding he had gathered a good many disquieting ideas about Russia's political situation and he could only express them freely in his own magazine. In addition, the rousing success of the single issue of *A Writer's Diary* for 1880 led us to hope that the renewed publication would find a wide circle of readers, and Fedor Mikhailovich truly valued the opportunity to make his heartfelt ideas known. He planned to publish *A Writer's Diary* for two years and then hoped to write the second part of *The Brothers Karamazov* . . ." (A. G. Dostoevskaia, *Vospominaniia* [Memoirs] [Moscow: Khudozhestvennaia literatura, 1971], p.

370). Dostoevsky suffered a pulmonary hemorrhage on January 26, however, and died on January 28, the day the censor passed the final issue of the *Diary* for publication.

the current epidemic: Russian newspapers through the latter part of 1880 abounded in articles on economics offering a wide range of advice in dealing with the financial crisis in the country. A state budget, published on January 1, 1881, showed an anticipated deficit of over five hundred million rubles. A feuilleton in the newspaper *Novosti i birzhevaia gazeta* [The News and Stock-Exchange Gazette], no. 263, October 5, 1880, complained: "At today's rate of exchange, the value of the paper ruble is sixty-three silver kopecks, i.e., nearly half. . . . We complain of the terrible rise in prices of all consumer goods, from bread and meat to 'regal' drinks and ladies' fashionable garments; we blame the elements, we blame the producers and the retailers, we criticize the government; but at the same time we do not notice that in fact it is not the prices of goods that have risen so much as it is the value of our money that has fallen." Many of these financial problems were results of the expense of the 1877-78 war with Turkey.

1881, 2.1: A Witty Bureaucrat. His Opinion of Our Liberals and Europeans.

cut by half: *NV*, no. 1741, January 2, 1881, suggested that Russian finances might be repaired by cutting fifty thousand troops from the army and that reducing it even by half would weaken the country less than chronic budgetary deficits. Earlier, an editorial in the liberal newspaper *Strana,* no. 87, November 6, 1887, had stated: "We will state plainly that the best minister of finance for Russia will be the one who could manage energetically to restrain the growth of expenditures in the ministries of war and the navy."

given that name in Berlin: *Novosti i birzhevaia gazeta* [The News and Stock-Exchange Gazette], no. 309, November 20, 1880, quoted an article from the Berlin *National Zeitung* written by an anonymous German statesman who knew Russia well. The article stated: "The *greatest* event in Russian history to our day was the decision of Peter the Great to bring Russia into the life of Europe by *drawing in forces which were not present within the country itself.* All the *great* rulers of Russia, beginning from the sixteenth century, acted in this spirit. But at the beginning of each new reign there arose a Russo-Slavic reaction to such a movement. This reaction was regularly suppressed (the last time in 1855). Now the strongest process of rejection is taking shape, a rejection in principle. Meanwhile, practical experience and the facts that have always followed from it shows the necessity for *help from the Germans* if the Russians actually want to emerge from their present disorder and negligent attitude toward work."

1881, 2.3: Geok-Tepe. What Does Asia Mean to Us?

Geok-Tepe has been taken: Since 1879 Russian forces had been waging a war of conquest of the Akhal-Tekin oasis in Turkmenia. After an unsuccessful attempt by General N. P. Lomakin, in August 1879, to seize the Turkoman stronghold of Geok-Tepe, a second expedition, commanded by General M. D. Skobelev, took the town on January 12, 1881, after a three-week siege.

"metal and brimstone": In act 2, scene 2 of his comedy *Hard Times* [Tiazhelye dni] (1863), Ostrovsky ridicules the backwardness and fear of progress common among Moscow merchants. Two merchants' wives talk of the danger of reading modern, secular books and express their fear of unfamiliar (to them) words such as "metal" and "brimstone."

1881, 2.4: Questions and Answers

alliance of Germany and Austria: On October 7 (n.s.), 1879, Bismarck signed a defensive alliance with Austria under which each party agreed to come to the aid of the other in the event of an attack by Russia.

Turkish territory: Article 25 of the Treaty of Berlin, July 13 (n.s.), 1878, stated that Austria would occupy Bosnia and Herzegovina, formerly possessions of Turkey.

"don't leave your house": Dostoevsky's variation on the Russian proverb "If you're afraid of wolves, don't go into the forest."